NATIONAL
GEOGRAPHIC
TRAVELER

CALIFORNIA

CALIFORNIA

by Greg Critser
photography by Gilles Mingasson

National Geographic
Washington, D.C.

CONTENTS

Pages 2–3: The Pacific coast at sunset

Opposite: San Francisco's classic cable cars are one of the city's top attractions.

TRAVELING WITH EYES OPEN

Alert travelers go with a purpose and leave with a benefit. If you travel responsibly, you can help support wildlife conservation, historic preservation, and cultural enrichment in the places you visit. You can enrich your own travel experience as well.

To be a geo-savvy traveler:

- Recognize that your presence has an impact on the places you visit.

- Spend your time and money in ways that sustain local character. (Besides, it's more interesting that way.)

- Value the destination's natural and cultural heritage.

- Respect the local customs and traditions.

- Express appreciation to local people about things you find interesting and unique to the place: its nature and scenery, music and food, historic villages and buildings.

- Vote with your wallet: Support the people who support the place, patronizing businesses that make an effort to celebrate and protect what's special there. Seek out shops, local restaurants, inns, and tour operators who love their home—who love taking care of it and showing it off. Avoid businesses that detract from the character of the place.

- Enrich yourself, taking home memories and stories to tell, knowing that you have contributed to the preservation and enhancement of the destination.

That is the type of travel now called geotourism, defined as "tourism that sustains or enhances the geographical character of a place—its environment, culture, aesthetics, heritage, and the well-being of its residents." To learn more, visit National Geographic's Center for Sustainable Destinations at *www .nationalgeographic.com/travel/sustainable.*

CALIFORNIA

ABOUT THE AUTHORS & THE PHOTOGRAPHER

Greg Critser was born in Steubenville, Ohio, and raised in Whittier, California. He received his B.A. in history at Occidental College in Los Angeles and his M.A. from UCLA. His biographical research about the California author and social activist Carey McWilliams has appeared in the American Historical Association's *Pacific Historical Review* and the *UCLA Historical Journal.* Critser has worked as a senior editor at four magazines: *California Business, California* (formerly *New West*), *Buzz,* where he edited an award-winning stable of young Los Angeles writers, and *Worth,* where he was responsible for the magazine's first National Magazine Award nomination in public interest journalism. His own work has appeared in *Harper's,* the *Washington Post Magazine,* the *Wall Street Journal,* the *Los Angeles Times,* the *Washington Monthly,* the *New Yorker,* and *Worth.* Critser's acclaimed study of obesity, *Fat Land: How Americans Became the Fattest People in the World,* was published in 2003.

Gilles Mingasson grew up in Grenoble, France, and moved to Paris to pursue photojournalism. After arriving in the United States on an assignment, he traveled through Latin America before making Los Angeles his home base. In 2005, his work on Latinos in the United States won him an American Photography Award. His photography can be seen in the National Geographic *Traveler* guidebooks on Panama, the Dominican Republic, and France. Mingasson's website is *www.mingasson.com.*

California-based **Christopher P. Baker**—the Lowell Thomas Award 2008 "Travel Journalist of the Year"—wrote the updates and sidebars for this edition. He is the author of *National Geographic Traveler* guidebooks to Colombia, Costa Rica, Cuba, Dominican Republic, and Panama, and the update editor for the Arizona, Scotland, Walking London, and Walking Washington, D.C. guides, among others. He has written six other guidebooks about California.

CHARTING YOUR TRIP

Stretching nearly 800 miles (1,290 km) from north to south, California covers a massive expanse. Superimposed on the East Coast, it would extend from Philadelphia to Jacksonville, Florida—across *nine* states—with far more variety in climate and terrain than you find along the eastern seaboard. So think of your California trip as a journey not so much to a single state, but to a diverse collection of geographical areas with their own unique attributes and personalities.

Opportunities Abound

While it's certainly possible to hit the highlights in a single week, travelers with specific interests might want to focus on a particular area or theme. In Southern California, you could hit a brand new beach every day for a month and still not sample half the strands, let alone set aside time for the bounty of museums, theme parks, and historical attractions. Likewise, the state boasts enough ski and snowboard areas to keep you busy for an entire winter. California offers two types of desert—the sand dune—laden Colorado and the Joshua tree—studded Mojave—and experiences that range from Palm Springs posh to Death Valley solitude. The Sierra offer three of the country's oldest and largest national parks (Yosemite, Kings Canyon, and Sequoia), while the north coast throws up the planet's tallest trees and little-visited volcanic landscapes. With so much to see and do, California easily lends itself to multiple visits.

Getting Around

California created modern car culture—freeways, drive-in movies, and drive-time DJs—and cars are still the best means of exploring the state, especially given the scarcity of public transportation in many areas. Modern interstate freeways connect the big cities, but the most rewarding drives are off the beaten path—Calif. 1 along the Big Sur coast, Tioga Road over the crest of the Sierra, and the Redwood Highway—U.S. 101—through the big trees.

Still, the distances can be daunting. The fastest route between Los Angeles and San Francisco (Interstate 5) is still 380 miles (612 km) or roughly 6.5 hours of driving. Travelers who dislike long drives might want to consider flying between major destinations. Southwest Airlines (*www.southwest.com*) is a

JOHNNY DEPP

Find film stars of every era on the Hollywood Walk of Fame.

popular option. Prices can be high on popular commuter routes (San Diego–Los Angeles, San Francisco–Sacramento), but you can often find bargains on flights into smaller airports like San Jose, Oakland, Burbank, and Long Beach.

Amtrak California (see Travelwise p. 347; *tel 800-872-7245, www.amtrak.com/california-train-routes*) stops at more than 175 California towns and cities on three services: the Pacific Surfliner, which runs between San Diego and San Luis Obispo (via Orange County, Los Angeles, and Santa Barbara); the San Joaquins, which connects the Bay Area and Los Angeles (via the Central Valley, with connections to Yosemite); and the Capital Corridor, running between the Bay Area and Sacramento, plus Auburn in Gold Country.

Once you reach your destination, you might want to hold onto your rental car (see Travelwise p. 347). You can do without it in Yosemite Valley and San Francisco. But it's tough to get around much of California without your own wheels. Los Angeles is gradually expanding its bus, light rail, and subway network (see Travelwise p. 347; *www.metro.net*). Likewise, San Diego's red trolleys trundle along an ever-increasing track network *(www.sdmts.com).* But enough holes exist in both systems to make private vehicles the preferred choice, especially for those short on time.

NOT TO BE MISSED:

Los Angeles: From the beach to Beverly Hills   54–89

The glamour of Hollywood   82–85

Disneyland's magic   134–138

Driving the Big Sur coast along Calif. 1   176–177

The Golden Gate Bridge   212

Napa's sublime wines and pastoral ambience   256–260

The giant trees of Redwood National Park   278–279

The natural wonderland of Yosemite Valley   304–309

Visitor Information

The state tourism commission has created Visit California *(www.visit california.com)*, **a comprehensive and easy-to-use website with information on destinations, attractions, transportation, places to stay, road trips, and more.**

California Welcome Centers are dotted throughout the state, some of them strategically placed along transportation corridors like Interstate 80 from northern Nevada (Truckee), Interstate 5 from inland Oregon (Anderson), Interstate 15 from Las Vegas (Barstow), State Route 62 from Arizona (Yucca Valley), U.S. 101 along the Central Coast (Pismo Beach), and U.S. 395 in the Owens Valley (Mammoth Lakes).

If You Only Have a Week

If this is your first visit to California or if you've only got one week, it's possible to hit the highlights in seven days—but only if you are willing to rise early, hit the sack late, and cover plenty of ground each day. Our one-week travel plan requires your own vehicle. It can be done northbound or southbound, but our itinerary starts in San Francisco and ends in Los Angeles.

On **Day 1,** rent a car at San Francisco International Airport (see Travelwise p. 347) and drive 13 miles (21 km) into the city on the Bayshore Freeway (U.S. 101). Leave the car at the hotel because the rest of the day can be done on public transport. Hop a cable car up and over the hills to Fisherman's Wharf, where you can board a harbor cruise or ferry to Alcatraz Island. If time permits,

When to Visit

A state for all seasons, the best time to visit California depends on what you like to do and where you are likely to spend the bulk of your time. Owing to coastal overcast and fog in the spring and early summer, the best beach weather is generally July to early October. Triple-digit temperatures dominate the desert regions in summer, but desert winters are the stuff of snowbird dreams—clear skies and comfortably warm temperatures. The snow season stretches between Thanksgiving and Easter, but the best powder usually comes toward the end of that period.

peruse the tall ships at the San Francisco Maritime National Historic Park. Grab a quick seafood lunch along the wharf and head back downtown. Browse the chic boutiques around Union Square and the kitschy shops of Chinatown before tucking into an Asian dinner along Grant Avenue.

Begin **Day 2** with a short drive west to Haight-Ashbury and its lingering 1960s vibe. Then discover the treasures of nearby Golden Gate Park: the artistic de Young Museum, cutting-edge California Academy of Sciences, and Japanese Tea Garden. Plan for a picnic lunch in the park. Due north is the equally leafy Presidio, the historic former Army base with the best views of the Golden Gate Bridge. Then head to the South of Market area, with a stop at the San Francisco Museum of Modern Art.

Rise early on **Day 3,** and drive across the Golden Gate Bridge, 7 miles (11 km) from downtown. Stop for a quick breakfast along the Sausalito waterfront and continue north into Wine Country. Spend the rest of the day sipping vintages at Sonoma or Napa wineries, beginning 50 miles (80 km) north of San Francisco. Spend the night in Wine Country. Drive south on **Day 4,** making your way around the eastern side of San Francisco Bay via Interstates 80 and 880. If you've got time, detour into Berkeley or Oakland for a dose of counterculture. Continue south to Monterey, 151 miles (243 km) south of Napa Valley, stopping in Salinas for lunch and a visit to the National Steinbeck Center. In the afternoon, cruise Cannery Row and visit Monterey Bay Aquarium. Take the 17-Mile Drive around the peninsula and have dinner in charming Carmel-by-the-Sea.

On **Day 5,** make your way south on Calif. 1 down the Big Sur coast. Along the way, stroll a secluded surf-swept beach and visit hilltop Hearst Castle. Continue the southward drive along U.S. 101 to Santa Barbara, 240 miles (386 km) south of Carmel, leaving time to visit the city's mission and waterfront. Dine along trendy State Street.

On **Day 6,** drive south into Los Angeles via Calif. 1 through Malibu, a total of 115 miles (185 km) from Santa Barbara. Cruise Sunset Boulevard through Brentwood to

Gas Prices & Gas Station Locations

Given the amount of driving you are likely to do in California, it's a good idea to keep track of fluctuating fuel costs on websites like Gas Buddy *(www .californiagasprices.com),* **which offers a dedicated California page. Covering the entire state, the site offers the lowest gas prices at thousands of gas pumps over**

the last 36 hours, as well as maps showing you where those stations are located.

The U.S. Department of Energy *(www.fueleconomy.gov)* **offers a fuel savings calculator, car fuel consumption comparisons, and alternative fuels resources through its online energy efficiency portal.**

■ Guests enjoy lunch aboard a historic car on the popular Napa Valley Wine Train.

the Getty Center. Have lunch in Westwood next to the UCLA campus, and then continue along Sunset through Beverly Hills. In Hollywood, compare your hand and feet sizes to famous celebs' outside the Chinese Theater, take a studio tour, and view the city from the Griffith Park Observatory. After dark, see a show at the Hollywood Bowl.

End your trip on **Day 7** with a full-day visit to Disneyland and Disney California Adventure, 27 miles (43 km) south of L.A., using a dual-entry "Park Hopper" ticket.

If You Have More Time

If you have more time, you can venture beyond California's two urban meccas. Head to **San Diego,** 120 miles (193 km) south of L.A., and visit Balboa Park and the much ballyhooed zoo. Then go east into the desert, traveling north through **Anza-Borrego State Park** to **Palm Springs,** 123 miles (198 km) from San Diego. Continue across the desert to **Joshua Tree** and **Death Valley,** a further 287 miles (461 km) north. With time you could cruise up the **Owens Valley** and take Tioga Road across the top of **Yosemite National Park,** 244 miles (392 km) from Death Valley. Then head for **Gold Country** in the foothills between Yosemite and Sacramento. Spend a day and a night at **Lake Tahoe,** 134 miles (215 km) northeast of Yosemite, and end your trip with a riverside picnic in **Sacramento,** 114 miles (183 km) farther west. ■

Hotel & Campsite Reservations

To make hotel reservations, consult **Visit California** *(www. visitcalifornia.com).* If you want to make a reservation at one of the campsites in California's state parks and state beaches, contact the **California Department of Parks and Recreation** *(tel 800-444-7275, www.reserve california.com).* Campsite reservations for California's national parks, national forests, and other federal lands should be made through the federal government's outdoor recreation portal *(tel 877-444-6777, www.recreation.gov).*

HISTORY & CULTURE

Padre Junípero Serra rises above the church of Mission Dolores. Opposite: The Chandelier Tree, north of Eureka, a giant redwood that was carved in the 1930s to let cars drive through its trunk

CALIFORNIA TODAY

The third largest state (after Alaska and Texas) in the United States, but by far the most populous, California comprises a dizzying potpourri of superlative landscapes. This, and a famously carefree lifestyle, have attracted an outdoorsy, entrepreneurial, forever upbeat, multicultural people inspired by California's open and inviting horizons. It's all part of the enviable California mystique.

Purely from a standpoint of numbers, Californians are remarkable: There are now more than 39.8 million of them, representing one in every eight U.S. residents. So great is California's allure to migrants that the state's population is expected to reach 50 million by the year 2050 (see sidebar p. 17).

Joshua Tree National Park is a favorite destination for California's many plein air artists.

Ethnically, Californians comprise the nation's most diverse population. While blacks represent less than 7 percent of the population—only half that of the U.S. average—and 37 percent are Caucasians of northern European descent, fully 40 percent of the state's population identify themselves as Hispanic, a reflection of the state's geographic and historic intimacy with its neighbors to the south. More than one in eight Californians is Asian, ranging from Hmong villagers to Hindu software programmers to Chinese financiers. Fewer than half of Californians were born in the state, and fully one-quarter were born outside the U.S.

The result of this compressed ethnic migration, according to California novelist and social observer Donald Waldie, is a *mestizaje*, "the promiscuous amalgamation of Hispanic, African, Asian, and Native American peoples." It is really little wonder, then, that one California university recently renamed its old 1960s-inspired ethnic studies program as, simply, American studies.

So great is California's allure to migrants that the state's population is expected to reach 50 million by the year 2050.

Geographically, Californians are still largely a coastal people—more than one out of four reside in the five major metropolitan areas of Los Angeles, San Diego, San Francisco, San Jose, and Long Beach—all close to the sea. Many newer arrivals, together with a large number of second- and third-generation Californians, have been moving eastward to thriving inland suburban and new-town destinations with names like Rancho Bernardo and Santa Clarita. Meanwhile, new arrivals from abroad continue to coalesce where their native peers are established, resulting in high concentrations of specific ethnicities. Thus, for example, Vietnamese Americans constitute an astounding 40 and 30 percent, respectively, of the populations of Westminster and Garden Grove.

Californians are as diverse in lifestyle as in heritage and skin tone. The rusticity-seeking dwellers of the forested far north have more in common with the cowboys of Idaho than with California's urban sophisticates. And few commentators would argue with the observation that San Franciscans differ markedly from Angelenos. The state's multifaceted nature is epitomized by the differences (and rivalries) between the two urban centers. Progressive, heavily gay San Francisco (birthplace of anti–Vietnam War hippiedom) has always been open minded, even nonconformist, despite being the West Coast's bespoke-suited "Wall Street." Laid-back L.A. is more self-possessed and money oriented, as befits the world capital of Hollywood fame and glamour.

Money and boundless optimism wed to an entrepreneurial spirit and individuality drive Californians ever forward. In

■ **The annual Electronic Entertainment Expo in Los Angeles draws thousands of video game industry professionals, retailers, and journalists from around the globe.**

the past two decades they have reinvented their state's economy—the fifth largest in the world—weaning it from its onetime dependence on defense spending and redirecting it toward high technology and finance. Silicon Valley, centered around San Jose, is the birthplace and epicenter of the computing industry—Apple, Google, Yahoo, Hewlett Packard, and IBM are among the behemoths headquartered here—and the spawning ground not only of the technological future but also of overnight fortunes. L.A.'s economy and culture remain heavily dependent on the movie industry, and the fascination with youthful looks has spawned its own industry—cosmetic surgery. Meanwhile, California is the world's fifth largest producer of agricultural produce, although agriculture accounts for only 3 percent of the state's economy. Indeed, the vast San Joaquin/Sacramento Valley, colloquially known as the Central Valley, is the most productive and profitable agricultural center in the world, thanks to incredibly fertile soils and a constant stream of migrant labor.

While the very name "California" is synonymous with Hollywood, the cultural milieu runs broader and deeper than movies and TV sitcoms. Highbrow art looks back with pride to the plein air art movement, birthed here, while radiant works by British-born L.A. adoptee David Hockney have helped secure California's artistic place in the sun. In music, too, there's something to sing about. Los Angeles and San Francisco are bastions of classical music, as well as the spawning grounds for contemporary sounds, from the Beach Boys and Grateful Dead to the Black Eyed Peas and Green Day.

There is, of course, a cost to all of this growth and creativity, much of it borne by the environment. While it is true that much of the state remains pristine and unimaginably beautiful, it's also true that air and water quality in many urban areas has worsened. Even the Central Valley is now mired in smog as foul as anywhere else in the nation. But California, always at the forefront of national trends, is a trendsetter in efforts to legislate on behalf of a cleaner environment—a process accelerated under the tenure of governors Arnold Schwarzenegger and Jerry Brown. The state has spent much of its time in recent years responding to natural disasters. Fires, floods, and earthquakes have always been part of the bargain of being Californian, but fires, in particular, have grown more calamitous each year due to the impact of climate change.

Yet Californians cannot be bowed down. Like the common concept of California's Mediterranean climate, their vision is always sunny. It is hard not to be so, one assumes, when blessed with such an abundance of sunshine and natural beauty. The ability of southern Californians to ski in the morning and sunbathe the same afternoon is the envy of anyone who doesn't actually live there. As East Coasters shiver through midwinter blizzards, Palm Springs residents sunnily sip iced martinis poolside in finger-snapping Sinatra style. True, chilling fogs smother much of the Pacific shoreline: Famously, San Francisco's coldest months are actually August and September, much to the surprise of many ill-equipped tourists. Anyone believing that even California's winter clime is always sunny should read up on the fate of the Donner party (forced to resort to cannibalism to survive when trapped by snowstorms in 1846 while attempting to cross the Sierra Nevada). And only mad dogs and Englishmen venture into Death Valley in the killer heat of midsummer.

> ## By the Numbers
>
> **Population:** 39,780,000
> **Area:** 158,706 sq miles (411,046 sq km)
> **Coastline:** 1,100 miles (1,770 km)
> **GDP:** $3.2 trillion in 2019
> **Capital:** Sacramento
> **State animal:** Grizzly bear
> **State motto:** "Eureka!"
> **Average number of earthquakes per year:** 37,283
> California is home to the highest and lowest elevations in the lower 48 states—Mount Whitney, 14,495 feet (4,418 m) high, and Death Valley, 282 feet (86 m) below sea level. It also has the world's tallest (coastal redwood), largest (giant sequoia), and oldest (bristlecone pine) trees.

But therein lies a deeper beauty. The physical diversity of both climate and terrain is astounding. North America's iconic low point, Death Valley (282 feet/86 m below sea level), is within a few hours' drive of the Sierra Nevada, where 15 peaks soar more than 14,000 feet (4,265 m). California's scale is big enough to guarantee amazing variety yet small enough to permit visitors to switch in a single day between mountain, coastline, desert, and forest. No wonder Californians are passionate about outdoor recreation. Mountain biking first evolved in the 1970s on the steep, winding trails of Mount Tamalpais. Whitewater rafting was birthed on the sparkling rivers that spill from the Sierra like effervescent champagne. And weekends are given to the health-conscious hedonism of sailing, snowboarding, surfing, or sundry other activities.

All this and more awaits visitors keen to sample the individual elements that combine to define the uniquely Californian quality of life. ■

THE LAND

Not everyone who comes to California reacts to its climate the way traveler Charles Dudley Warner did when he exclaimed, "Here is our Mediterranean!" (*Our Italy*, 1891). But few who have driven the state's byways and taken in the smells of orange blossom, sage, and sea remain impartial to its natural charms. If there ever were an American Mediterranean, California would be it.

The climate, in part, proceeds from the land, and the land—158,706 square miles (411,046 sq km) of it—proceeded from a series of giant tectonic collisions that began some 250 million years ago, when the offshore Farallon plate began to slip underneath the North American continent. In the process it formed a mountain

■ Death Valley is the world's hottest places, and one of its driest, as its wind-shaped sand dunes attest.

range. Then: more collision, more mountains. And so, very gradually, the basic basin-and-range geography of the state was formed.

About 130 million years ago, these collisions heated up the underlying mantle of the Earth, liquefied it as lava, and, eventually, formed the Sierra Nevada. Once the North American plate overtook the Farallon, it bumped (this time laterally) into the Pacific plate. This formed what is known as a transform fault, the San Andreas, a network of terrestrial stresses and cracks that stretches northwest from the Gulf of California to Point Arena, above San Francisco Bay. The Pacific plate and the North American plate slide past each other along this fault, sometimes imperceptibly, at other times explosively in an earthquake.

Rim of Fire: Volcanism in California

California ia probably best known for its earthquakes. This tectonic shiftiness relates to the state's location within the Pacific Rim of Fire, as part of a section called the Cascade Volcanic Arc that also includes Washington, Oregon, and southern British Columbia. Sheer size and splendor make Mount Shasta (see pp. 284–287) the state's most famous volcano, although the snowcapped giant has been silent since 1786. Lassen Peak (see p. 288), another stratovolcano, last erupted in 1917 but remains a threat. The region's third rumbler is Medicine Lake, a massive shield volcano that last exploded about a thousand years ago.

The result of this upheaval is a land of extremes. At 14,495 feet (4,418 m), Mount Whitney, in Sequoia National Park, is the highest point in the coterminous United States. Badwater, in Death Valley, at 282 feet (86 m) below sea level, is the lowest. The consequential extremes in temperature and precipitation are aided and abetted by two major oceanic currents along the state's 1,100-mile (1,770 km) coastline. The deep, cool California Current sweeps south bringing frigid Arctic waters and is thus responsible for San Francisco's long, cool summers and legendary fogs. A secondary current, shallower and fragmented, flows along the eastward-veering southern California Bight, thereby accounting for the south of the region's remarkably balmy weather.

Not much fails to thrive here. Botanists estimate that, due to the abundance of singular habitats, more than one-third of California's 5,000 native flora may be unique to the state. In the foothills you can find the live oak, *Quercus agrifolia,* its tiny, hollylike leaves ingeniously suited to the high temperatures and low humidity of the region. *Sequoia sempervirens,* the coast redwood, thrives in the moist conditions near the coast. *Sequoia gigantea,* the giant sequoia, grows higher up in the Sierra Nevada. The pickleweed, *Salicornia,* has adapted so successfully to the harsh, salty waterline of inland estuaries that, from afar, it appears as swaths of russet-colored snow. And there are the imports— date, orange, and madrone. California has made them all its own.

Weather changes with the land, flora and fauna adapt to weather— and Californians to all three. Witness, if you travel here at the right time, the quintessential California rite of nature worship: the grunion

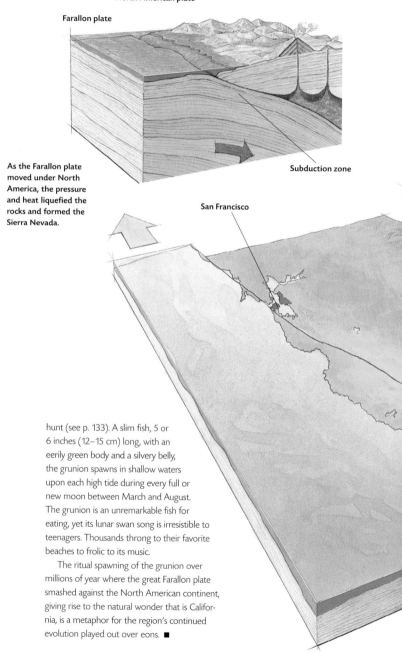

North American plate

Farallon plate

As the Farallon plate moved under North America, the pressure and heat liquefied the rocks and formed the Sierra Nevada.

Subduction zone

San Francisco

Pacific plate

hunt (see p. 133). A slim fish, 5 or 6 inches (12–15 cm) long, with an eerily green body and a silvery belly, the grunion spawns in shallow waters upon each high tide during every full or new moon between March and August. The grunion is an unremarkable fish for eating, yet its lunar swan song is irresistible to teenagers. Thousands throng to their favorite beaches to frolic to its music.

The ritual spawning of the grunion over millions of year where the great Farallon plate smashed against the North American continent, giving rise to the natural wonder that is California, is a metaphor for the region's continued evolution played out over eons. ∎

The North American plate and the Pacific plate slide past each other along the San Andreas Fault. Arising deep in the Earth's crust, earthquakes send primary waves (P-waves) pulsing through nearby rock; these set up slower, secondary waves whose shearing action can buckle the surface rocks and open up cracks and fissures along the fault line.

San Andreas Fault

San Andreas Fault

North American plate

Los Angeles

FOOD & WINE

For the past four decades, California has led the way in today's increasingly eclectic culinary world. The Golden State is the ultimate foodie mecca, offering gourmands a host of different cuisines. This diversity makes California cuisine hard to classify.

Sushi chef Tadashi Murakami prepares food at Hollywood's small, trendy Murakami.

Themes of California Cuisine

California cuisine embraces various **ethnic traditions.** The earliest sustained effort to create a California cuisine was made by *Sunset*, the "Magazine for Western Living." The publication was launched in 1898 by the Southern Pacific Railroad, whose aim was to exhort Easterners to "colonize the west and . . . travel in style to a new life of year-round sunshine and agricultural bounty." Almost immediately *Sunset*'s founders embraced the state's Mexican culinary past, launching an endless campaign to educate Golden Staters on everything about Mexican cuisine. Here was a way for a new Anglo migrant to invent a culinary history, a cuisine partly of memory and partly of psychological need.

Another theme—also one of *Sunset*'s editorial missions—was the notion that even middle-class Californians should have their own **kitchen gardens.** No issue of the magazine was (or, for that matter, is) complete without a gardening column and articles on topics like kiwi fruits or how to grow an Asian spice garden. Eating your own freshly grown food was not only pragmatic and thrifty; it could increase vigor, the key to fully appreciating all that California had to offer.

The third theme could be called the **"search for pure flavor,"** an activity born of the vast agricultural abundance and the belief among California chefs that theirs is a quest for absolute essence—whether it be of basil or orange or tomato or plum.

California Food Innovators

The first great modern synthesizer of these themes was Alice Waters, founder, in 1971, of the Berkeley restaurant **Chez Panisse** (see pp. 240–241). Having just returned from a trip to France, Waters applied the principles of Provençal cooking to California ingredients. As she later wrote, "My one unbreakable rule has always been to use only the freshest and finest ingredients; [my] quest led to Amador County for suckling pigs and peppery watercress; to Napa for Zinfandel made especially for our restaurant; to Gilroy for garlic; to Sonoma for locally made goat cheeses; to the ocean daily for oysters."

Inspired by Waters's injunction to "eat fresh from the garden," chefs from around the state literally reinvented all the classic cuisines—and a few nonclassic ones as well. In 1979 a young San Francisco Zen Buddhist named Annie Somerville, determined to make vegetarian cooking more, well, vegetarian, opened a new restaurant called, simply, **Greens** (www.greens restaurant.com). It was a refreshing contrast to the gloppy mess of overcooked grains and soy cheese that through the years had come to symbolize the genre.

In Los Angeles the innovators looked southward. The young chefs Susan Feniger and Mary Sue Milliken took up the old *Sunset* injunction about the importance of Mexico and started the **Border Grill** (www.bordergrill .com), where intense poblano chilies met the mesquite-grilled flavors of modern Santa Fe. In 1984, cooks Viana La Place and Evan Kleiman opened **Angeli Caffe**, which reinvigorated traditionally heavy Italian-American restaurant food by treating the tastes of the southern Italian kitchen "in a light, modern manner." Rather than following the convention of serving foods either hot or chilled, they served theirs at warm-to-room temperature because "we know that the true flavors of food can be best appreciated at these temperatures." And, of course, there was Wolfgang Puck's celebrated **Spago** (www.wolfgangpuck.com) in Los Angeles, where

EXPERIENCE: Bay Area Breweries

The global repute of California wine has long overshadowed the fact that some of America's best beer is also made in the Golden State. San Francisco's Anchor Steam and Chico-based Sierra Nevada are the best known, but the state's microbreweries are where beer snobs quaff their amber nectar. In fact, a recent ranking of the nation's top beermakers was dominated by small California breweries, including three of the top ten.

Beer aficionados visiting San Francisco should consider the three-hour afternoon **San Francisco Brew Tour** (*$$$$$*) offered by Vantigo (*tel 415-484-5240, www.*

vantigo.com). The tour includes round-trip transportation by vintage VW van to three breweries, with beer tastings, and a brewery tour. Or join a tour with **SF on Tap** (*tel 415-692-1644, www.sfontaptours. com, $$*). Customized itineraries are also available.

Bay Area Brewery Tours (*tel 415-999-4989, www.bayareabrewerytours.com, $$$$$*) visits three area breweries Fridays to Sundays. The price includes round-trip transportation, tastings, and a souvenir glass. Book online; tours begin in the morning and leave from the Caltrain Station (*700 4th St., San Francisco*).

California's entire ethnic archipelago fell onto a delicate pizza pie. No one would ever think of Beijing duck and goat cheese in the same way.

If the 1970s and '80s were about freshness and ethnic fusion, the 1990s were about the primacy of flavor, often in more traditional fare. At Napa Valley's **French Laundry** *(www.frenchlaundry.com)*, considered the "best restaurant in the United States" by Ruth Reichl of the *New York Times*, chef Thomas Keller draws from the surrounding countryside—and beyond from France and Italy—to create such startling dishes

■ Tex-Mex cuisine combines Mexican recipes with ingredients found in the southwestern U.S.

as white truffle custard, lobster in vanilla-saffron sabayon sauce, and pomegranate sorbet with champagne gelée. In San Francisco, Michelin 3-star chef Michael Tusk's **Quince** *(www.quincerestaurant.com)* in Jackson Square captures the essence of rustic Italian cooking wed to Alice Waters-inspired freshness.

In Oakland's thriving farmers market (see pp. 234–235) Hmong immigrants hawk fresh lemongrass and fiery Thai chilis, while African Americans offer bean pies and barbecue sauce. Nearby **Caffe 817** *(www.caffe817.com)* has pared its menu to the purest and freshest of what makes Italy Italy and California California. Over tiny Napa lettuce is drizzled only the freshest of local olive oils; over that, the most intense

cured Italian ham the founders of *Sunset* could ever have imagined. A sliver of Parmesan. A sprig of lemon basil. *Perfetto!*

Wine

With more than 3,500 wineries across the state, perhaps the only thing more surprising than the variety of California wines is their overall quality. As John Doerper writes in *Wine Country*, his influential book on the subject, "The quality of the *average* wines produced in Napa and Sonoma is now so high that the gap between them and premium wines has narrowed . . . Winemakers now feel they have to widen that gap—to keep distinctive wines truly distinct—by raising the quality of premium wines ever higher." For the aficionado of wines, whether experienced or amateur, the situation spells bonanza. Today more than ever, California is a wine-lover's heaven, unparalleled anywhere in the world, including by the ancient stands of France and Italy.

> **Today more than ever, California is a wine-lover's heaven, unparalleled anywhere in the world, including by the ancient stands of France and Italy.**

Modern California winemaking dates from as recently as 1966, when the Robert Mondavi Winery *(www.robertmondavi.com)* was founded in Oakville, near Napa, by Robert Mondavi and his elder son, Michael. Obsessed with elevating Napa Valley wines to world-class status, the Mondavis began experimenting with one of the mainstays of local viticulture, wines known as California sauternes. Soon they were applying contemporary European techniques learned during fact-finding expeditions across the Atlantic. The most important of their innovations involved sauvignon blanc grapes; like

■ Established in 1973, the Domaine Chandon winery in Napa Valley offers private wine samplings.

their friends in France, the Mondavis began to leave the skins on the grapes after the crush, and then ferment them in a stainless steel tank and transfer them to French oak barrels for aging. The result was one of the state's first blockbuster premiums—a new twist on an old favorite dubbed fumé blanc.

What followed was an explosion of vintners adapting similar classic techniques to California grape growing. Within ten years Mondavi's dream came true. At the Paris Wine Tasting of 1976, two California wines edged out French reds and whites for top place. *Sacré bleu!*

The story since then has at times bordered on the tragicomic: So many nouveau winemakers have set up shop in the Napa and Sonoma Valleys that, during the summer tourist peak, there may be more traffic jams there than in the cities. And there has been, predictably, a small but notable Disney effect, with some large wineries becoming so adept at marketing and branding that one might wonder which comes first, the wine or the label.

Such cynicism evaporates when one returns to first principles—making world-class wines. Perhaps the most important trend in recent years is the increasing value placed on a wine's appellation, the special geographic and climatic area from which it comes. California's 139 distinct American Viticulture Areas (AVAs)—some vast, some only a few hundred acres—are capable of producing wines of extra-high quality that have special taste characteristics.

A particularly popular appellation at present is the Carneros region of southern Napa, which runs westward into Sonoma County. Here, the cool breezes and fogs from nearby San Pablo Bay help produce some of the state's most spectacular pinot noirs, as well as several outstanding chardonnays. Farther north the nearly continuous cool weather of the Anderson Valley in Mendocino County has helped produce world-class gewürztraminers and rieslings. The warm Sierra Foothills AVAs are renowned for full-bodied zinfandels, and the compact Temecula AVA of southern California for equally robust syrahs.

HISTORY OF CALIFORNIA

"In contrast to history, the story of man in California would have different proportions, would take a longer view and recognize the Indians as the largest minority for a generation after 1849, heavily in the majority through the preceding 80 years, and the only residents for centuries and millennia prior to 1769."—John W. Caughey, California

Early Californians

If California's eccentric geography wrought a unique botany, its impact on human settlement was even stronger. Consider the archaeological record. Mainstream scholarship has long held that the first Californians probably arrived around 13,000

■ The ancient Chumash painted the caves of Chumash Pictograph State Historic Park.

to 15,000 years ago following the first migration of humans across the Bering Strait. By the time Europeans arrived in the 16th century, however, Native Americans numbering about 300,000 had fragmented into some 105 linguistic groups dispersed throughout the entire region.

These groups fell loosely into one of three linguistic families. The Penutian family resided largely in the north and included the Miwok and the Wintun, who may have been among those greeting the Spaniards in the late 18th century. Among the Hokan speakers, occupying the central coast, were the Chumash, perhaps the most technically sophisticated of the southern tribes. The Uto-Aztecan group in the south were distant descendants of Mexico's Aztec and the American Comanche; their numbers included the so-called Gabrieleños, one of the first fully Christianized, or missionized, Indians.

> **If California's eccentric geography wrought a unique botany, its impact on human settlement was even stronger.**

Details of daily life in pre-Columbian California remain scarce, but relatively new data suggest some compelling conjectures. Radiocarbon dating of inscribed animal bones found in the La Brea Tar Pits in Los Angeles, for example, indicates that the carvings were done on "green," or fresh, bones of now extinct animals, suggesting that early L.A. man led a life intricately tied to packs of wildly aggressive wolflike creatures. Reconstruction of the only complete human remains on the same site—those of a young woman—indicate that violence was not uncommon: Her skull had been bashed in with a blunt object. Close examination of the boats used by the Santa Barbara Chumash indicate that the tar pits were part of an important trade route. Modern-day Wilshire Boulevard in Los Angeles lies directly over the path they took to gather tar to waterproof their craft.

Still, the original Californians lagged significantly behind the Aztec, their brethren to the south, in several key areas. They had no organized system of agriculture, kept no domesticated animals (except for dogs), and were neither builders of roads nor creators of metallurgy. Their priesthood was relatively informal. Not surprisingly, these traits led the first European colonists to brand California's natives as rustics who lacked the self-sufficient backbone that Europeans considered a hallmark of civilization.

Yet there was little evidence that hunger was a problem for these people—at least until the Europeans came. This has led modern scholars to reconsider what, exactly, constitutes a "civilized" material culture. One item under their microscope is deer hunting as practiced by the Rumsen people of southern Monterey Bay. Far from being a simple, unplanned activity, Rumsen deer hunting not only involved high levels of skill, training, and knowledge but also demanded such religious and social preparations as praying, sexual abstinence, dietary restrictions, and even various mind-sharpening techniques. As scholar Malcolm Margolin points out, the hunter would usually give away part or all of his catch to elders and neighbors so that "hunting, in short, did not render a man 'self-sufficient,' but like other aspects of Indian life served to bind the hunter closer to others in a strand of reciprocity."

A fair question, then: Why did the Native Americans gravitate toward the mission system so easily and so freely (as was usually the case, despite assumptions to the contrary)? The answer must be found in what the Spaniards—with their legions of armored soldiers, exotic foods, elegant white horses, and sonorous-voiced padres—brought to the meeting when the two groups first encountered each other on a lonely beach in San Diego in 1769.

Spaniards & Mexicans

With few exceptions (among them the discovery of Point Reyes in 1579 by the English freebooter Sir Francis Drake), the pioneering of California was largely a Spanish undertaking. As such, its context was both medieval and colonial: medieval because it immediately followed the Spanish Inquisition and the expulsion of the Moors; colonial because it grew directly out of Cortés's 1521 conquest of the Aztec in Mexico.

Padre Junípero Serra founded 21 missions in California for Spain.

The new Pacific outpost derived its name from a 16th-century popular fantasy of chivalry, *The Exploits of Esplandian* (1510), by Garci Rodríguez de Montalvo. In it, the Christians of Constantinople must confront a great unknown: a force of Amazons led by a certain Queen Califia from the island of California, where everything was made of gold. Frustrated in his search for the fabled Seven Cities of Gold, Spanish explorer Francisco de Bolaños first applied the name to Baja in 1541—an allusion to a paradise, yet unfound.

Bolaños was followed by the better known Juan Rodriguez Cabrillo, who discovered San Diego Bay in 1542. Then came 125 years of benign neglect as Spain concentrated its resources on the silver and gold strikes in Mexico and the development of the Manila–Mexico spice trade. Only when incursions of British and Russian explorers threatened Spanish hegemony did Charles III of Spain finally make California a priority again: In 1768 he dispatched Gaspar de Portolà to secure the coast for Spain.

To do so, Portolà implemented the three most powerful elements of Spanish colonialism: the pueblo, the presidio, and the mission. The pueblo represented civil authority and was based on the medieval notion of a secure clustering of towns. The presidio, a fort, represented the military elite. The mission was the vehicle for the religious authorities charged with converting the Indians to Christianity.

Spain's most influential imperial cleric was the Franciscan Padre Junípero Serra, who founded the first mission, in San Diego, in 1769. A native of Majorca, Serra entered the

Must-Read Books on California

Numerous novels and nonfiction books dealing with aspects of California history have been published since the 1840s. The following, listed in chronological order according to when their stories are set, rank among the best:

• *Mark Twain's San Francisco* This stirring anthology includes articles, essays, poems, and other scribbles drawn from the bard's 1860s sojourn in California.

• *Ramona* A runaway best seller when first published in 1884, this novel by Helen Hunt Jackson exposed the mistreatment of Native Americans in late 19th-century California.

• *The Octopus: A Story of California* Frank Norton's classic 1901 novel doubles as a scorching social commentary on the greed of the railroad robber barons and the Gilded Age.

• *Ishi in Two Worlds* Theodora Kroeber's popular nonfiction book tells the story of Ishi, who walked out of the northern California woods in 1911 as the last surviving member of the Yahi tribe.

• *Oil!* Published in 1927, Upton Sinclair's epic novel about the early scramble for oil in southern California was made into the 2007 film *There Will Be Blood*.

• *The Grapes of Wrath* John Steinbeck's 1939 classic tells the tale of the dirt-poor Joad family migrating to California during the Great Depression.

• *L.A. Confidential* James Ellroy exposes the gritty underbelly of 1950s L.A. in this "nouvelle noir" crime thriller.

• *Tales of the City* This first of eight novels in a series by Armistead Maupin brings to life the rainbow coalition that made 1970s and '80s San Francisco such a vibrant place to live.

priesthood at 16, developed a reputation as an outstanding preacher, and was dispatched to the Americas in 1749. A stubborn, spirited, and often combative man, he was also a classic medievalist, believing, among other things, that pain and discomfort purified the soul. Serra's passion led him and his successors to establish 21 missions in California by 1821.

While few scholars doubt Serra's sincere religious motives, few also doubt that it was the mission system that led to the dramatic decline in the Indian population. This was tragedy laced with irony: The padres believed that they could only protect their neophytes from outsiders and often brutal Spanish soldiers by concentrating their wards together in large numbers. Yet by doing so, the padres also introduced the Indians to new European disease, while they were also physically brutalized and pressed into forced labor: The Missions became, in effect, charnel houses aimed at complete subjugation of California's native peoples. By the advent of the gold rush in 1848, Indian numbers had dropped from a pre-Columbian high of 300,000 to fewer than 35,000, and to fewer than 20,000 a decade later.

To this day, the destruction of the Indians in California is regarded as the original sin of the Golden State. Serra was eventually beatified by Pope John Paul II, but only after a 30-year, multimillion-dollar public relations campaign by some of California's richest and most influential Roman Catholics.

After Mexico won independence from Spain in 1821, California drifted under a succession of weak Mexican governors, who increasingly viewed the faraway colony as a drain on internal resources. To reward settlers and placate the ambitious, Mexico began granting large tracts of land to locals, or Californios. The result was the growth of an affluent rancho culture, with grizzly bear hunts and fiestas and rodeos. Eventually, these local land barons—the *gente de razón*—grew hostile to interference from Mexican authorities. In 1836, the Californio Juan Bautista Alvarado led a revolt against Mexican authorities and proclaimed California a free and sovereign state. Mexico soon regained sovereignty, but the stage was now set for independence—and eventual U.S. statehood.

Statehood of Gold

By 1846, two more potent elements had entered the amalgam of forces setting California on the path to independence and, eventually, statehood. Both of them resided among the 800 Anglo-Americans then living in Mexican-controlled Alta California (a huge region encompassing today's California, Nevada, Utah, and Arizona).

The first was mountain men, fur trappers, and reckless fortune seekers, who resented Mexico's control. The second was Yankee settlers and entrepreneurs looking for opportunity. Among them were William B. Ide, who led a large party over the Sierra to the Sacramento area; James Wilson Marshall, the eventual discoverer of California gold; Sam Brannan, a Mormon pioneer and real estate entrepreneur; and John Sutter, a Swiss American who founded a colony named New Helvetia that later became the state capital. These Americans of various stripes were united in their schemes to remake Mexican Catholic California into an American Protestant Yankee paradise.

Into this cauldron of ambition and prejudice rode a young Army commander, John C. Frémont, the leader of a secret 1845 government investigation into California's political affairs. President James K. Polk had provoked the Mexicans on the Texas border and needed to know how the Californios would react to a declaration of war. Under the guise of a scientific expedition (although he could not explain the presence of a howitzer in its midst), Frémont and his small band were staying in the then capital, Monterey. José Castro, the *gobernador* in Monterey, grew suspicious and threw out the protesting Frémont, who retreated to Hawk's Peak overlooking the town and hoisted an American flag before going on to Oregon.

Frémont's camp soon became a magnet for disaffected mountain men and entrepreneurs, many of whom had heard of the Hawk's Peak incident and feared eviction by Mexico. On June 14 a band of these men descended on the Sonoma quarters of Mariano Vallejo, the *commandante* of Alta California, to demand his surrender. Vallejo, a longtime supporter of independence, entertained the men generously with alcohol; he had been expecting them. Arriving later to find his comrades drunk, Ide, the leader of the insurgents, negotiated Vallejo's surrender and then raised a quickly improvised flag featuring a grizzly bear and blazoning the words "California Republic."

How Much Gold?

Given the random nature of gold prospecting and recordkeeping in the 19th century, it's almost impossible for historians to ascertain now the exact amount of gold that was discovered during the California gold rush of the late 1840s and early 1850s. The U.S. Geological Survey estimates that 12 million ounces was taken from Sierra foothill mines and streams during the first five years of the rush—an amount that is worth nearly $19 billion in today's dollars. By the turn of the 20th century, more than 40 million ounces of gold had been extracted, equivalent to about a third of the amount of gold that is currently stored at Fort Knox.

A few weeks later, Frémont rode in and declared the republic a "permanent territorial possession" of the U.S., under military rule. Commander John Sloat sailed into Monterey Bay and, without firing a shot, took formal possession from Castro. A year and a half later, upon victory in Mexico proper, the 1848 Treaty of Guadalupe Hidalgo formalized Frémont's coup, and California was part of the U.S.

Before clear heads could begin to reckon how to organize this new U.S. possession, California exploded in gold fever. The discovery by Marshall at Sutter Creek on January 24, 1848, represented the ultimate slap in the face to the Old World, which had begun its exploration for the Seven Cities of Gold more than 300 years before. In the first months of excavation at Yuba alone, five California argonauts took out more than $75,000 worth of ore every month. At Placerville, the average daily yield per man often topped five pounds (2.2 kg), while a group of seven men from Monterey, using 50 Indian laborers, took out 273 pounds (124 kg) of gold in just seven weeks.

> In 1849, a group of 48 men drew up a draft state constitution; one-quarter of them had come with the gold rush.

When the world beyond California heard of the strike, the young state's population began to soar. In San Francisco alone, more than 40,000 migrants arrived during the last weeks of 1848. The greatest and most lasting wealth was made by the businesspeople who rose to service this new population—from merchants providing the miners with over-priced pans, pick-axes, shovels, tents, and food (Levi Strauss was one such, although he didn't invent his riveted denim jeans until 1873) to hoteliers, bankers, and lawyers. Nonwhites played a substantial role in the gold rush. The number of black miners tripled to 2,000 during the first three years of the strike—literally a golden opportunity for men still not recognized as full U.S. citizens. Many so-called Free Negroes, for example, used their gold to buy freedom for other members of their families. And while racism was rampant throughout Gold Country, it was often tempered by the intimacy of side-by-side labor with whites, something quite new to many Free Negroes. As one freeman wrote to his wife from Cosumne Diggins mine, "This is the best place for black folk all over the globe. All a man has to do is work and he will make money."

The gold rush also ushered in official statehood. In 1849, a group of 48 men drew up a draft state constitution; one-quarter of them had come with the gold rush. Perhaps just as important was their youth: Only four of them were over 50, 30 were under 40, and nine were still in their 20s. The 31st state, admitted in 1850, would be run by some of the youngest old-timers in the country.

Boom Years

The 70-year period following California's admission into the Union witnessed a series of economic, demographic, and technological booms unparalleled in the nation's history. These booms were to shape the character and the image of the new state, which was perceived as a land of daring individualism and serendipitous success. California was where the young nation was able to act out its most youthful fantasies.

The story of the Central Pacific Railroad and the men who profited so mightily from it is a case in point. The line was originally the passionate vision of Theodore Judah, a young civil engineer who had successfully presided over the construction of the state's earliest line, the Sacramento Valley Railroad. As the gold rush towns rose around him, Judah connected California's economic dreams with the prevailing East Coast dream of a transcontinental railroad. He partnered with "The Big Four" Sacramento businessmen— Charles Crocker, Mark Hopkins, Collis Huntington, and Leland Stanford—and launched construction of the Central Pacific Railroad. Construction was aided by importation of 2,000 Cantonese emigrant laborers (by 1868 they constituted 80 percent of the entire work force; with later Chinese immigrants, they would reshape San Francisco as the largest such population outside China). On May 10, 1869, the "Golden spike" was hammered at the meeting of the western railroad with the Union Pacific Railroad (built mostly by Irish labor) at Promontory, Utah, hence creating the first transcontinental railroad in North America. An arduous months-long sea voyage, or by wagon-train, to reach California had been replaced by coast-to-coast train travel in eight days.

> **All these new ways of doing things seemed to congeal in the explosive growth of the early 20th century's ultimate boomtown: Los Angeles.**

Between 1880 and the onset of World War I, the number of miles of railroad in California increased from 2,195 (3,532 km) to more than 8,000 (12,875 km), creating new markets and fueling new industries. The boom in California agriculture—until then a small, regional affair—was led by the wheat growers, who planted such vast acreages that reapers would often have to camp at the end of a field, having completed but one pass during the day. Newly accessible markets led to all kinds of innovation. By the end of the 1880s, orange growers had figured out how to cool a railroad car sufficiently well to ship their goods to the East Coast; by 1892 they had succeeded in shipping their fruit to England.

The constant influx of immigrants from the rest of the U.S. and abroad also brought new ways of doing things. Where old-timers near Sacramento saw swampland, for example, the Japanese pioneer George Shima saw a veritable Eden for growing the potatoes he so loved in his homeland. Such was the road to success for the "Potato King." The expatriate Hungarian Count Agoston Haraszthy became the "father of California wine" when in 1857, reveling in the pleasant climate and rich soils of Sonoma Valley, he created the state's first winery, spurring on the labors of Charles Krug, Jacob Schram, and Paul Masson, who would make California wines world famous. Luther Burbank set up his horticultural laboratory in Santa Rosa, devoted to grafting and seed selection. The aggressive lending and collateral strategies of the Italian-American banker A. P. Giannini made his Bank of America the financial undergirding for generations of the state's farmers.

All these new ways of doing things seemed to congeal in the explosive growth of the early 20th century's ultimate boomtown: Los Angeles. The semidesert city used the latest engineering techniques to secure water from a faraway place called the Owens

Valley (which was left an environmental wreck). Advertising and the new motion picture industry lured residents to newly irrigated suburbs.

But how long would it look like that? Such growth might nurture the collective and the private pocket, but its price was the scarring of the landscape by mining and dumping and construction, the damming of great rivers, and the felling of great forests. A partial antidote was found in the activities of the Sierra Club and its rugged-mystic founder John Muir.

Muir, a Scot by birth, came to California in 1868. As a boy he had gone blind and, having regained his sight, had vowed to dedicate his life to the witnessing of nature. For decades he trekked the Yosemite Valley and other natural wonders, writing about them for various national newspapers and magazines. In 1892 he helped found the Sierra Club, was made its first president, and promptly went to war with the government over a plan to permit mining, lumbering, and grazing near Yosemite. During a three-night camping trip in Yosemite with President Theodore Roosevelt in 1903, Muir persuaded Roosevelt to protect it as a national park. It remains to this day an international symbol of a paradise rescued.

■ **This 4-4-0 American-type steam locomotive at the California State Railroad Museum was typical of the engines that plied California's railroads in the late 19th-century.**

Postwar Suburban Paradise

One would hardly have expected the good life to grow out of California's experiences in the Great Depression and World War II, yet that is precisely what happened. The Depression proved to Americans that California's much celebrated economic resilience was no fiction. The million new migrants who arrived during the 1930s experienced it for themselves. And what the Depression served to bolster, the war years cast in figurative and literal steel. Fueled by War Department contracts, California's total annual income almost tripled during the war. Thereafter, the Cold War kept California's defense economy, as the center of missile technology, buoyant throughout the 1950s, boosting the population to 15.8 million by 1960.

This growth and affluence, in proximity to the style-creating movie industry, helped give birth to the nation's first lifestyle culture. Here one could break with the past and, through personal consumer choices, become the person one wanted to be. A hypothetical composite of "California man" in 1960 might have read something like this: He works as a machinist or junior engineer at Douglas Aircraft, producing equipment for the U.S. Air Force or TWA. He holds a mortgage on a modern tract house in Lakewood, an "instant community" built from blueprint to landscape in two years. On weekends, dressed in a Hawaiian shirt and flip-flops, he attends a pool party in Palos Verdes. There, over barbecued steak and taco salad, he discusses contemporary politics—not conventional party politics, but specific ballot issues: a new tax to build the state university system into a world-class institution or maybe a measure to control handguns.

In the late 1960s and all through the 1970s, personal lifestyle culture broke new frontiers. California universities pioneered ethnic studies centers—one way for their students to regain the sense of personal history lost in the original race to become American. On the same campuses, the farmworker-rights leader César Chávez found some of his most dedicated organizers—youths who truly believed in the justice of *la causa*, but who could also use the involvement to rethink traditional laissez-faire notions about economics and poverty. San Francisco became the world's first gay metropolis, with gay power parades and the country's first openly gay political figure, Supervisor Harvey Milk.

The conventional middle class also asserted the primacy of individual rights, first with the passage of Proposition 13, which severely limited the growth of property taxes, then in their overwhelming support of antitax political conservatives, from President Ronald Reagan to Gov. George Deukmejian. Bold new ventures by and for the spiritually aware ranged from outdoor churches in drive-in theaters (one formed by the Rev. Robert Schuller later became the Crystal Cathedral) to Zen Buddhist centers. Outdoor enthusiasts demanded and got several new state and national parks.

Coast Road

One of the most ambitious road projects in American history, California's State Route 1 (Calif. 1) along the Big Sur coast was the route that many people thought would never be built. The geography was just too severe: deep ravines and cliffs rising to 1,200 feet (365 m), and frequent landslides. But the need became too acute. Construction of the highway began in 1922, with much of the labor provided by prisoners from San Quentin. The rugged terrain required construction of 32 bridges, including 716-foot-long (218 m), single-arch Bixby Bridge, the largest such structure in the western U.S. The highway was finished in 1934, when two crews working from opposite ends of the route finally came face-to-face.

Yet the most important contribution of the 1970s and '80s lay not in social or political developments, but in business. Heavy investment in education, combined with the stop-and-go nature of post-Vietnam defense spending, created a growing class of techno-whiz kids, concentrated around San Jose and the rest of the Bay Area. They included Steve Wozniak and Steve Jobs, who founded Apple; William Millard, an IBM dropout who started ComputerLand, the world's first computer retail chain; and Andrew Grove, a Hungarian immigrant who helped build Intel into the world's largest maker of microchips. Presiding over them all as father figure and mentor was David Packard, the founder of Hewlett-Packard. Silicon Valley was born!

Introduced in 1977, the Apple II was the first consumer computer sold by Apple Computers.

To the south, the boom in L.A. and San Diego owed much to the evolution of a more unstructured, fluid business establishment. Nonetheless, Southern California retained its dominance as the epicenter of the rapidly evolving aerospace industry, centered around Los Angeles, while San Diego's economy remained anchored as the base for the U.S. Pacific Fleet. Meanwhile, the Central Valley's fields and orchards accounted for almost half of the country's vegetables and fruits.

By the late 1980s, however, several new challenges confronted Californians. Although the state had already begun to wean itself from defense contracts, it was unprepared for the enormous cuts that followed the end of the Cold War. Nor was it primed for the social costs of unchecked immigration, regardless of the net gain these new Latin and Asian immigrants brought to the economic table. The population was still increasing, and constrained state spending (largely the legacy of the antitaxers, led by Ronald Reagan as governor, 1967–1975) exacerbated old inequities by beggaring poor school districts, libraries, and social welfare programs.

When the biggest race riot in the nation's history broke out in L.A. in April 1992, many Americans felt that Californians were finally getting their comeuppance. Referring to the faltering Golden State, social critic Michael Kinsley summed up the prevailing sentiment. "Ha ha!" he wrote in his nationally syndicated newspaper column. "Ha ha ha ha ha!"

Permanent Frontier

From 1989 through the first half of the 1990s, its economy adrift, California suffered a series of punishing environmental and social disasters. In October 1989 the Bay Area was struck by the most severe earthquake since 1906. A section of the Bay Bridge fell, and the Cypress Freeway collapsed, sandwiching traffic, while the Marina District crumbled, then burned. In October 1991 a wildfire hit the Oakland hills, destroying 3,000 homes.

Things were no better in Los Angeles. In 1991 a series of wildfires paralyzed the region from Malibu to Laguna. The 1992 riot erupted after an all-white jury acquitted four police officers accused of brutally beating Rodney King, an African American. The beating, captured on videotape and broadcast to a world audience, assumed epic proportions. When the acquittal was announced, the racially mixed south-central part of the city erupted. There followed four days of looting, burning, and shooting, leaving 58 dead and nearly 2,000 wounded. The National Guard was brought in to restore order. Measures taken to deal with race issues included changes in the police services and plans to build better schools in the inner city. In January 1994, the city was hit by a magnitude 6.7 earthquake originating in the San Fernando Valley. Some sections of freeway collapsed; neighborhoods of older tract housing crumbled. More National Guard troops and billions in federal aid were required.

> **The California Dream took on new meaning as tech-savvy youngsters became millionaires in the blink of an eye.**

And yet, by 1995 new migrants were again arriving in droves from all corners of the world as the state's economy began to sing again. Dwindling trade barriers and a soaring global economy had created huge new markets for California's products: wine, rice, computer chips, electronic games. Another critical component was Hollywood. While the 1930s and '40s are traditionally thought of as the film industry's Golden Age, the 1990s became its Platinum Age. Pushed by worldwide demand for "entertainment product" and the flourishing of cable and pay-per-view TV, new jobs created in the entertainment industry had, by 1997, replaced nearly all the jobs lost in defense cutbacks by the federal government.

California—and specifically San Francisco—was the hub of the Internet boom of the late 1990s, when the Bay Area grew giddy on the most spectacular growth since the 1849 gold rush. The California Dream took on new meaning as tech-savvy youngsters became millionaires in the blink of an eye. The multiplying economy fostered a massive new wave of migration from out of state, adding fuel to a concomitant real estate boom. Californians had good reason to celebrate the new millennium. By 2002, however, they were suffering an almighty headache following the collapse of the Internet and stock-market bubbles. Employee stock-option fortunes

■ **California Governor Gavin Newsom speaks during a campaign rally.**

evaporated overnight, along with jobs. With housing prices continuing to skyrocket, California witnessed a net exodus as residents headed out for greener pastures. In 2003, those that remained ousted the incumbent governor and voted in the Hollywood action-movie star Arnold Schwarzenegger on a "no new taxes" promise to resolve the state's overwhelming budget problems.

Schwarzenegger proved a popular governor at first due to his environmentally friendly agenda and his hands-on management of several devastating wildfires. However, his later years in office were plagued by a sexual scandal that led to separation from his wife, Maria Shriver, and by statewide economic malaise. In 2010, Californians reelected former governor Jerry Brown in a landslide. He successfully tackled the state's budget crises with austerity measures during his two-term tenure. However, the decade was marked by devastating floods, the hottest summer on record, California's most severe drought in over a millennium, and eight of the 10 largest wildfires ever recorded in the state.

Brown was succeeded in 2019 by former San Francisco mayor Gavin Newsom, with a promise of tackling climate change as a priority. He inherited a robust economy supported by more than half of all U.S. venture capital. Nonetheless, the state had become inordinately expensive, with sky-high housing costs—the highest in the nation—pricing many families out of the California Dream. As a result, during the past decade more people left California than moved in, slowing the growth rate of the nation's most populous state amid a Covid pandemic reshaping its future. ■

THE ARTS

When asked why so many of his fellow painters were drawn to California, 19th-century artist John Gutzen Borghum answered that "such pure and living color is found in but few parts of the world, and such variety of strange and 'paintable' matter does not exist elsewhere." Today, California's vibrant art scene continues to draw sustenance from the state's diverse landscape.

Painting

That nature should preoccupy generations of California artists is hardly surprising. The state covers more than 158,000 square miles (409,218 sq km), much of it still undisturbed. Yet scale and remoteness alone do not quite explain the appeal. California as a phenomenon does. The state was born in a critical period for the U.S., a time when conventional frontiers were perceived as settled and when new lands were deemed necessary for the reinvigoration of the Democratic Experiment. It was the impact of Americans on the land, and vice versa, that bolstered the self-confidence of the young nation. The name for this was manifest destiny.

The first art to trickle out of the gold rush consisted largely of genre paintings of everyday life, a preoccupation among American artists all over the country. Yet these early works veered from the period's aesthetic norms by consistently portraying everyday scenes from heroic daily life. "Miners in the Sierras," the 1851 work by Charles Nahl and Frederick Wenderoth, shows four miners shoveling dirt into a sluice box. The work is hard, the earth yielding only to mighty swings of the pickax. But the real point of the painting is what lies ahead of the miners—an enormous rocky valley, unsettled but for one ramshackle cabin in the distance. Only a hero could work on, undaunted.

> **That nature should preoccupy generations of California artists is hardly surprising.**

As the first impressions of California circulated—some of them accurate, many surely "stretchers," as Mark Twain would have it—more and more artists set out for the West. Although many of these first landscape painters were amateurs, not a few were professionals skilled in techniques of detail and illumination. Albert Bierstadt (1830–1902), a New Englander famed for his paintings of Yosemite Valley, was overwhelmed by his subject. "We are now here in the Garden of Eden," he wrote to one friend, "the most beautiful place I was ever in."

A sense of the mystic infuses Bierstadt's paintings. Trees seem ready to burst with colorful sap; the folds of great mountain faces appear still pliable, the Creator not yet finished with them. The High Sierra, explains scholar Ilene Susan Fort in the book *Paintings of California*, "epitomized the idea of divine immanence that had become central to the American concept of nature."

Younger artists soon transformed the genre. Impressionism's preoccupation with light combined with a growing sense of regional uniqueness. The underrated William Keith (1839–1911), for example, began his career using Bierstadtian detail in his 1869 "San Anselmo Valley Near San Rafael"; by 1880 his style had mutated into a more van Gogh–like evocation in "Sand Dunes and Fog, San Francisco." In the former, giant eucalyptus trees loom over plucky explorers. In the latter, the solitude of nature triumphs, the competing ecologies of sea grass, shrubs, and ocean quietly resolved. Urban versions of this trend were rendered by William Hahn (1829–1887) in "Market Scene, Sansome Street, San Francisco," and by Theodore Wores (1859–1939) in "New Year's Day in San Francisco Chinatown."

Albert Bierstadt's "Among the Sierra Nevada" (1868) celebrates California's wild beauty.

These two impulses—localism and impressionism—made up a variety of movements spanning the period from the late 1890s through the late 1930s. The first recognizable group, the tonalists, focused on the Monterey Peninsula. Inspired by George Inness's "California" (1894), these artists looked to somehow evoke the essence of a scene via the use of tone, or, as Fort writes, "a narrow range of muted colors that emphasized spareness of land, solitary nature."

Yet localism did not imply timidity; Inness's gold-toned scene of a small rural settlement dominated by two gnarled trees is, after all, titled simply "California," as if it were somehow the final word on the subject. A similar sense of authority resounds in "The Summer" (1932), by Gottardo Piazzoni, who once answered the question "What is your religion?" with the reply "I think it is California." By 1933, San Francisco painter Arthur F. Mathews had pushed the tonalist form to a point of precision. His "Monterey Cypress #3" has the authority of a five-color woodblock print—brown, gray, green, blue, and an unforgettable butter gold.

> **The well-documented works of the Bay Area's Society of Six show how profoundly European trends inspired California painters.**

The well-documented works of the Bay Area's Society of Six show how profoundly European trends inspired California painters. The group's "simple" use of brilliant hues and glowing palettes conspired to one end: to evoke the modern experience of nature. Yet, even in the works of one artist, the tactics of the typical Society of Six painter could be remarkably diverse. Was Selden Connor Gile (1877–1947), in his "Boat and Yellow Hills," a Post-impressionist? Or was he, as is suggested in his almost hallucinatory "The Soil" (1927), a modernist? How about a tonalist-modernist? The exercise in labeling may be silly, but it is irresistible, given the grandness of the works.

If the "modern experience of nature" was what enthralled the Society of Six, it was nature's pure "sensation" that preoccupied the southern California plein air scene. Painters such as Joseph Kleitsch and William Wendt seemed to proceed from the premise that the invariably perfect weather of southern California made for a perfectly invisible backdrop, allowing the subject of any painting there to vibrate with feeling. There is a wistful surrender to the everyday in Kleitsch's "Old Laguna" (1924), a surrender we would not trade for the world. In Wendt's "Where Nature's God Hath Wrought" (1925), a "typical" southern California hillock embodies the unknowable, the jagged geometry of purple rock rising forcefully from rolling green sage knolls—God's fist, raised in silent remembrance.

The onset of the Great Depression shook this Homeric idyll to its roots. The social and economic tumult of the nation was being played out on California's landscape, particularly upon its farms and orchards. Even before Steinbeck's groundbreaking *Grapes of Wrath* appeared in 1939, however, modern social realism flowed. Frances Brooks's "The Picnic" (circa 1930–1940) depicted the simple joys of the toiling class dancing in the evening shade after a long day in the fields. Painter Maynard Dixon's "Oakie Camp" and "No Place to Go" (both 1934) bear the indelible influence of his photojournalist wife, Dorothea Lange, known for her haunting photographs of the Depression dispossessed.

Watercolorist Millard Sheets (1907–1989) did some of his most memorable work in collaboration with Lange and fellow photographer Horace Bristol. Sheets's spare but charmingly forlorn "Miggs (Migrants), 1938" was used, in tandem with Lange and Bristol's works, by *Fortune* magazine in 1939 to illustrate the plight of migrant workers.

As in the rest of the country, the postwar period witnessed the rise of several modernist genres, from abstract expressionism to conceptual art. The content has been increasingly figurative, from the smudged impressionism of Elmer Bishoff (1916–1991) and Richard Diebenkorn (1922–1993). Landscape—the public landscape—has subsided.

Yet landscape—the private, personal landscape—remains at the core of the works of David Hockney (1937–), the preeminent figure of postwar California art. Using a self-described "playful" style of bold color and strong line, Hockney has consistently portrayed his, and by extension everyone's, private California. Intimate California. These are places that could only "feel" private in a state blessed with so much space and wealth: swimming pools ("A Bigger Splash," 1967), backyards ("A Lawn Being Sprinkled," 1967), even roads through deserts ("Pear Blossom Highway," 1986) and roads to Hollywood studios ("Mulholland Drive," 1980).

This last reveals how an artist's personal growth is often tied to the region itself. As Hockney tells it in his 1996 autobiography *That's the Way I See It,* "I'd moved to Los Angeles and was working on a painting of the view outside my studio on Santa Monica Boulevard. And it wasn't working. It was still stuffy, still asphyxiated by that sense of supposedly 'real' perspective. I gave up. I moved up to the Hollywood Hills and I began painting the drive down to the studio. The moment I moved up here into the hills, wiggly lines began appearing in my paintings. The only wiggly lines I'd had on my paintings before were those that were on water. I was painting ['Mulholland'] from memory—the memory of the drive down—[and it] was beginning to work. You see, it was all about movement and shifting views—although at the time I didn't yet fully understand the implications of such a moving focus."

EXPERIENCE: Listen to *la Música*

When it comes to live music festivals, California is perhaps best known for the alt- and modern-rock **Coachella Festival** (*www.coachella.com*) or the **Stagecoach Festival** (*www.stagecoachfestival.com*), the state's biggest country-and-western bash. In fact, the entire state hosts mariachi festivals! Chula Vista explodes with live music for the day-long **International Mariachi Festival** (*www.mariachifest.com*) each March. Mission San Juan Capistrano holds the annual **Battle of the Mariachis Festival** (*www.missionsjc.com*), in which mariachi groups from across Southern California and beyond compete for prizes. And **Mariachi USA** (*www.mariachiusa.com*) has been held in the Hollywood Bowl since its inception in 1990 as a celebration of Mexican traditional music and folkloric dancing. Ending with a legendary fireworks finale, Mariachi USA is a Californian cultural icon.

Literature

About 20 minutes north of Angels Camp in Gold Country, in a quiet stretch of live oak and chaparral, sits a forlorn wooden shack. Here, in 1865, the young Mark Twain (1835–1910) wrote his most famous short story, "The Celebrated Jumping Frog of Calaveras County." The story concerns Jim Smiley, a betting man who is "always ready and laying for a chance," particularly when it comes to animal races. One day Smiley decides to catch a frog and train it to jump for competition. After three months of dedicated training, the frog, Dan'l, becomes Smiley's prize, "whomping" all comers.

One day a stranger in camp, hearing Smiley bragging about his frog, says: "Well, I'm only a stranger here, and I ain't got no frog; but if I had a frog, I'd bet you." No problem, says Smiley, spying an easy mark. He hands Dan'l to the stranger and asks him to hold him while he fetches another frog. Smiley returns, and the race begins.

Kerouac, Ginsberg, and other Beatniks used to meet at San Francisco's famed City Lights bookstore.

"The new frog hopped off lively, but Dan'l give a heave, and hysted up his shoulders—so—like a Frenchman, but it warn't no use—he couldn't budge: he was planted solid as a church." Smiley pays the man then discovers that the "stranger" had filled Dan'l with shotgun pellets.

In fewer than three pages, Twain had sketched the elements of what would fascinate him and so many others writing about the Western experience: Here was a place where men made themselves up as they went; freed from the conventions of the East, they could reinvent themselves—and their language—as conditions changed. Environment trumped heredity. Indeed, environment made the man: Bret Harte (1836–1902; see sidebar p. 43), one of Twain's contemporaries, would even speak of a place called Roaring Camp, where "the strongest man had but three fingers on his right hand; the best shot had but one eye."

To Harte and Twain, these were minor men—characters—yet somehow universal men as well, creating new lives and new rules in a land they perceived as a blank slate. What could be more American? No wonder the author-raconteur Ambrose Bierce (1842–1914) is best known not for his poignantly beautiful short stories ("An Occurrence at Owl Creek Bridge") but for his bitter truths about life in San Francisco. As in: "A morning newspaper says three unclaimed gold watches are in the hands of the police, and that it is not definitely known who stole them. It is definitely known who *will* steal them."

If the first literary explorers of California were wits who discovered what California was doing to the forty-niners, the next generation rendered precise regional portraits of the new state, seeking the truth in life's detail. One of these, Scottish author Robert Louis Stevenson (1850–1894), arrived in Napa for a nine-week honeymoon during the summer of 1880. Having been ill, he was quickly revived by the mild weather of the countryside and soon took to long walks and carriage rides, meeting a host of idiosyncratic fellows who were, by turns, making wine, playing at silver mining, squatting for land, and, like Stevenson, recovering from various ailments. Stevenson had discovered a land of tonics. Standing in Jacob Schram's vineyard one day, he looked over the valley and mused, "In this wild spot, I did not feel the sacredness of ancient cultivation. It was still raw, it was no Marathon, and no Johannesburg; yet the stirring sunlight, and the growing vines, and the vats and bottles in the cavern, made a pleasant music for the mind."

Another self-described literary explorer, Helen Hunt Jackson (1830–1885), was also at work during this period. A writer, traveler, and activist for the much-abused California mission Indians, Jackson published her most influential work, the romantic novel *Ramona*, in 1883. By setting her story of a doomed love affair between Señorita Ramona and a mission Indian, Alessandro, against the deplorable conditions of the tribes, Jackson hoped to draw attention to the plight of Native Americans.

Instead, *Ramona* was extolled as a glowing evocation of the region's Spanish Catholic past, glorifying the treatment of the Indians under the Spanish and Mexican dons and padres and laying almost all of the blame for Indian woes upon the later Anglo immigrants. To this day, the popularity of the book, along with the pageants, tour guides, and plays that

California's Journalistic Giants

From John Steinbeck to William Saroyan, California boasts a wealth of famous fiction authors. But the state has also produced many celebrated journalists and newspaper icons. Having failed as a gold miner, **Mark Twain** (1835–1910) earned his first kudos as a writer in the 1860s working as a San Francisco–based journalist. Around the same time in the same city, **Bret Harte** (1836–1902) was honing a style that would make him one of the great correspondents of the Wild West

and an early champion of Native Americans. Following the Civil War, a young Union Army officer named **Ambrose Bierce** (1842–1914) was posted to San Francisco, where he discovered a passion for the written word. He would shine as a columnist and critic. Although not a writer, **William Randolph Hearst** (1863–1951) had an indelible effect on American journalism as the longtime publisher of the *San Francisco Examiner* and other newspapers.

it inspired, account for much of southern California's sweet-and-sour sense of itself—sweet for what once was (but really wasn't), sour for what is (but which may be better, if uglier).

By 1900, adventure writer Jack London (1876–1916), a former sailor, tramp, and gold miner, had settled down to write in the San Francisco Bay area. The hard-drinking London cut a wide swath. A self-educated socialist, he ran for mayor of Oakland and lost. He co-authored a book on sexual politics, then one about the underclass of London. Orating frequently on such subjects, he soon became America's best known socialist. Yet London seemed most at home on the Oakland waterfront. His short stories had a diverse cast of local characters: Mexican boxers, Portuguese wharf rats, Irish thieves, Chinese shrimp-catchers. Here were oyster-bed thieves with names like Porpoise, Centipede, and Barchi,

Robert Louis Stevenson wrote of Napa Valley as "a pleasant music for the mind."

who said things like, "You better slide outa this here or we'll fill you so full of holes you wouldn't float in molasses." So strong was London's writing—and so ambitious—that many critics believed he would become the West's first truly big author. By the eve of World War I, he had crafted some of the most compelling stories of his day, most famously *The Call of the Wild* and *White Fang.* In 1916, Jack London died of alcoholism. He was 40 years old.

Writers of the next generation tended—not always successfully—to seek a national stage for their California experience. Poet Robinson Jeffers (1887–1962) evoked such strong admiration for his passionate, violent etchings of mankind's follies that his self-built Tor House, in Carmel, became a place of pilgrimage for writers and critics from around the world. Short-story writer and playwright William Saroyan (1908–1981), from farm country in Fresno, won similar fame for *The Human Comedy* and *My Name Is Aram.* The characters in the works of John Fante, writing in L.A., were luminous enough to garner the praise of even the controversial and pungent cultural critic H. L. Mencken.

Yet in John Steinbeck (1902–1968) there would be a California Émile Zola, or at least a California William Faulkner. A native of the little farm town of Salinas, Steinbeck wrote about the ways of "the small man, the small woman." His characters were mainly ordinary people trying to make their way in an American Eden where all was not well. Some of his subjects were cannery workers *(Cannery Row),* others tramps *(Of Mice and Men),* and still others the wandering *paisanos* who harvested the state's agricultural bounty *(Tortilla Flat).* Their world was that of the Great Depression. Steinbeck was clearly taken with their plight, making it the basis, even in his most overwrought scenes, of something that was irreducibly brilliant, unforgettable , and for which he was awarded the 1962 Nobel Prize.

If Steinbeck was California's Faulkner, then Dashiell Hammett and Raymond Chandler would be its double-headed Balzac, peopling its landscape with cynical detectives, long-legged dames, and corrupt cops. Hammett's alter ego, Sam Spade, was the more hard-boiled of the two, although Humphrey Bogart's portrayal of him in *The Maltese Falcon* (1941) would forever leave Americans with the notion that he was somehow a good fellow beneath it all; apparently Hollywood did not believe the public could handle such amorality. The character of Philip Marlowe in Chandler's *The Big Sleep* (1939), however, *was* supposed to be a decent fellow, which the studios gladly accentuated. Yet the point of both characters is similar: What other reaction could an individual have to California? As critic Edmund Wilson later noted, bleak hard minimalism was the only logical reaction to a place where the only constant thing in life was the flat endless line in the sunset called the Pacific Ocean.

> **A native of the little farm town of Salinas, Steinbeck wrote about the ways of "the small man, the small woman."**

Much of California's postwar literature continued in this vein, often embracing the decadent, as with Charles Bukowski's "Meat School" of inebriate and direct, tough, masculine poetry. From the 1970s (although arguably traceable as far back as Christopher Isherwood's *A Single Man*, about gay life, in 1963), new and more optimistic themes began to reassert themselves, principally through ethnic writers. Authors such as Amy Tan, for example, began exploring their interior immigrant worlds, fusing Old Country inheritances with New World domestic drama.

But it is through nonfiction that the newest minorities have made their most noticeable mark. Mexican American Richard Rodriguez, often seen on public TV's *NewsHour*, specializes in the post-postmodern paradox: How does California transform the Old World, and how does the Old World change California and, in turn, the whole nation?

Style & Design

While California's literary impact on the world has been relatively minor, its influence in the world of style and design has been sizable. One reason is one of today's principal makers of "culture"—Hollywood, which is in the business of digesting large amounts of information about audiences and then feeding it back to them in just recognizable forms. This is why you might hear one of today's smart college kids describe a postmodern building in downtown Los Angeles or San Francisco as having "a *Blade Runner* look."

But California's impact on the look of our world does not begin and end with cinema. Henry and Charles Greene, architects of the late 19th-century Arts and Crafts movement, are a case in point. The British-born movement, which called for a return to simplicity and honesty in the arts, already had American proponents (such as the Prairie School of architecture under Frank Lloyd Wright). However, it fell to the Greene brothers to find a distinctively California version of the style, which became known as "American Craftsman."

Working in Pasadena from the early 1890s through 1915, the Greenes created a series of homes they dubbed "ultimate bungalows." The Gamble House (see pp. 112–113), designed for one of the country's biggest industrialists, may be the best of these efforts. Hallmarks of the style include Japanese-influenced overhanging eaves, the mission-influenced use of tile and stone, and a penchant for simple, handmade natural wooden furniture. The style was so resonant (and so widely imitated) that, to this day, the words "Craftsman" and "Greene and Greene" are often used interchangeably. However, the most famous of California Craftsman-era architects was Julia Morgan, who although best known for designing Hearst Castle (see pp. 174–175), imbued the San Francisco Bay Area with scores of prototypical buildings. The style is resurgent, reflected in Disney's Grand Californian Hotel, advertised as being in the "Greene and Greene craftsman style," as are hundreds of new tract homes now being built around the state.

In the U.S., architecture has often carried the extra burden of providing its own historical context; if a place has no past, the architect must evoke one. In California, this need for a past was exacerbated by the state's late entry into the Union and by its geographic remoteness. Thus architect Bernard Maybeck (1862–1957) imposed an imperial beaux arts style on his design for the 1915 Panama-Pacific Exposition, the better to signal to the world the grand ambitions of post–1906 earthquake San Francisco. Architect Bertram Grosvenor Goodhue (1869–1924) improvised a Spanish colonial revival style, replete with churriguresque ornamentation and tile domes, for San Diego's 1915 California Pacific Exposition. More recently, architect John Jerde has raised the profile of the genre, using larger-than-life signs and icons to create such faux landmarks as San Diego's Horton Plaza and the Universal Citywalk in Los Angeles.

Nevertheless, it may well have been the state's paucity of visual history that allowed internationalist Richard Neutra to create some of the world's best examples of modern architecture, particularly in the realm of private houses. An immigrant from Austria, Neutra had been trained in the modernist school of Bauhaus architecture, which advocated pragmatism, spare clean lines, and functionality. His 1933 V.D.L. House (see p. 108), in the Silverlake district of Los Angeles, represents the epitome of the style. The boxy, angular house is perhaps most distinctive for its use of large windows to blur the division between inside and outside. Copied by generations of architects, it is the DNA for many of the modernist homes and public buildings that in the 1950s and '60s would come to define Los Angeles' architectural vernacular style. The spare, sharp-lined designs of such architects as Neutra, Albert Frey, John Lautner, and E. Stewart Williams blossomed most fully amid the stark desert landscapes of Palm Springs—ground zero in the post-Millennium revival that has returned Modernism to a place in the sun.

California, by virtue of history and climate, permitted the ultimate experiments in the functional. Where else, after all, could one dress in what came to be called "leisure wear"? In the postwar period, the state produced such fashion and design innovators as Cole of California, known for loose-fitting yet elegant beachwear, which was often worn far from the shore. The popularity of the singing group the Beach Boys, and the growth of surfing, helped launch such firms as Ocean Pacific, which now sells surfwear and Hawaiian shirts from Topeka to Tokyo.

The focus on comfort and "the essentials" was also a driving force behind the Venice Beach–based designers Charles and Ray Eames, who in the 1950s produced the stripped-down

California's Greatest Living Architect

Born in Canada, **Frank Gehry (1929–)** ran away to California as a teenager and worked his way from driving trucks to being the state's preeminent architect. Along with Zaha Hadid and Rem Koolhaas, Gehry has emerged as a leading light of an edgy postmodern movement that emphasizes both form and function, sometimes to startling effect. Although the Guggenheim Museum Bilbao (Spain) is probably his most celebrated work, he has plenty of masterpieces in California, most notably the **Walt Disney Concert Hall** (see p. 103) in downtown Los Angeles and the **Gehry House** in Santa Monica.

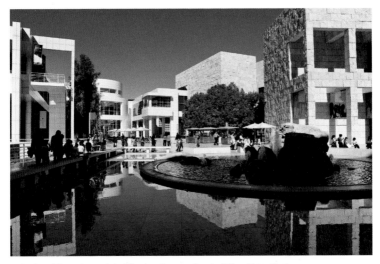

■ Pools and fountains cool the Museum Courtyard at the hilltop Getty Center.

"Potato Chip Chair," still much in evidence in offices around the world. And the need for easy mobility to cover routinely long distances in California soon elevated the automobile to icon status. No wonder that Detroit's most far-reaching innovations come from students at the Art Center College of Design in Pasadena. Or that Tesla, the groundbreaking electric vehicle and clean energy company, is headquartered in Palo Alto.

Three recent buildings point to California's role in determining the look of tomorrow. With its defiantly bold lines and chock-a-block appearance, Frank Gehry's (see sidebar opposite) Air & Space Building for the California Science Center (see pp. 106–107) shows how functionality and the need for historic reference can be married without the misleading romanticism of earlier practitioners. Conversely, Richard Meier's Getty Center (see pp. 60–66) in Los Angeles, with its endless (and blinding) travertine plazas, may establish a new coda for postmodernism: Because of height restrictions, half of the structure—an entire three stories—is below ground.

And what of Spanish architect Raphael Moneo's Cathedral of Our Lady of the Angels (see p. 103) in Los Angeles? It may well represent what, at least for California, is the ultimate aesthetic achievement: a monument that is more Mexico City than Madrid, and more Golden State than United States.

Cinema

Although Hollywood, and by extension California, has long been synonymous with the film industry, conventional wisdom now holds that physical location plays only a secondary role in determining what regions will profit most mightily from this economic powerhouse. Citing the rise of computer animation, special effects technology, and soundstages in places as far flung as Austin, Texas, and Raleigh, North Carolina, some pundits have even proclaimed that the old Hollywood—the place where dreams are made—has ceased to exist. Yet time and time again, after flights of fancy to other ports, the film industry has reinvested in California, betting its existence on the combination of talent, technique, and location that the state possesses in such abundance.

Although the first full-length film made in L.A. was produced in 1907, it was not until 1910 that one filmmaker would fully exploit southern California's climatic, geographic, and historic attributes. That man was David Wark Griffith (1880–1948). A Kentucky-born actor who desperately wanted to be a playwright, the tall and lanky Griffith had by 1910 become a dominant director of one-reelers in the budding New York film industry. Taking his acting troupe west on seasonal filming forays, Griffith found that he could save money and time by using the region's abundance of sunlight. In the first four months of 1910, Griffith produced 21 films with southern California locations as background. Location soon began to dictate content, as the historic missions prompted Griffith to make a version of Helen Hunt Jackson's *Ramona* (see pp. 43–44), among other California-themed films.

In the process of manipulating all that sunlight to dramatic effect, Griffith discovered film's fundamental storytelling techniques: the angle shot, the flashback, and the close-up. All of these he used to stunning effect in his 1915 *The Clansman* (later retitled *Birth of a Nation*), a racist saga of Civil War reconstruction that President Woodrow Wilson called "history written with lightning." The film was so popular that it established Hollywood as the center of moviedom. By the late 1920s, Hollywood accounted for approximately 90 percent of all films made around the world each year.

> **By the late 1920s, Hollywood accounted for approximately 90 percent of all films made around the world each year.**

Certainly no one needed to convince Louis B. Mayer—a Russian-born Jew and junk dealer turned Boston theater owner—that there was money to be made in Tinseltown. By the time Mayer moved to L.A. in 1918, he had already profited handsomely from movies. Among other wise moves, he had bought regional rights to such films as *Birth of a Nation*. More than money drew Mayer and a generation of Jewish emigré moguls to the West Coast: California, where everything was new and fluid, imposed none of the social constraints that Jews met in the East. Here, Mayer and his rivals Jack, Harry, Albert, and Sam Warner produced films that were more American than America. Optimistic and solidly midwestern, the Andy Hardy series, for example, starred Mickey Rooney as a rosy-cheeked teenager who loved sports, his wise "pop," and his nurturing "ma." At a time when the U.S. faced one of its greatest crises—its entry into World War II—Andy was unwavering in his belief that American values would always win out.

Mayer was also the creator of the studio system of film production, signing up young talent for years at a time and then driving them to make dozens of films, a kind of plantation system with champagne and silk scarves. His paternalism, combined with his studio's ownership of theaters, gave him formidable power over an actor's life. He famously behaved like an overprotective father to the point of obsession, managing actors' everyday lives (even arranging marriages). He also instituted a rule where actors were obliged by contract to be within 100-mile driving distance of the studio in the

▪ **Marilyn Monroe starred in John Huston's searing film noir drama** *The Asphalt Jungle* **(1950), in which she played the mistress of a crooked lawyer.**

event of re-shoots—the rule helped boost Palm Springs' fortunes as their preferred play-ground, and as a top filming locale.

Although elements of this restrictive studio system remained in place until the early 1960s, its decline began as early as 1939, when the Department of Justice began investigating fair-trade violations involving studio control of theaters. By the late 1950s, the moguls had been forced to divest themselves of most holdings, stripping them of a lucrative source of capital with which to support their burgeoning stables of winsome stars, cranky directors, and megalomaniac producers. The story of Hollywood of the next two decades was the story of brilliant individuals—from Robert Towne (*Chinatown*, 1974) to Francis Ford Coppola (*The Godfather*, 1972)—trying, and usually failing, to refashion certain elements of the old system.

Of all these attempts, DreamWorks proved the most ambitious and sucessful. At the core of DreamWorks, the first new studio in 50 years, were three men: mogul David Geffen (see sidebar p. 99), former Disney mastermind Jeffrey Katzenberg, and producer-director Steven Spielberg. The latter was the linchpin. An accomplished TV producer by his early 20s, Spielberg is the most commercially successful director in film history. Technology, in the form of special effects, has played a large role in making his work shimmer, as in *Jaws* (1975), *Raiders of the Lost Ark* (1981), *E.T.* (1982), *Jurassic Park* (1993), and *Shrek* (2003).

The decade since 2010 has shaken up Hollywood more than a magnitude 8 earthquake. Netflix, which was founded 1997 as a mail-order DVD company, launched its movie-streaming subscription service in 2010 and soon began filming original content, such as *The Irishman* (2019), starring Al Pacino and Robert DeNiro and directed by Martin Scorsese. In July 2020, Netflix overtook Disney to become the world's most valuable entertainment media company. Retail behemoth Amazon also began making original content in 2013, further threatening the traditional film-making and distribution structure.

Meanwhile, the blockbuster success of Marvel Studio's *Black Panther* (2018), with a majority black cast in front of and behind the camera, proved more than a celebration of the power and beauty of black women and traditional African society. It demonstrated that non-Caucasian talent could attract a mass global audience . . . and that Hollywood may never be the same.

TV in Hollywood

With so many early shows broadcast live on the East Coast, New York City dominated television production until the 1950s, when Hollywood entered the new medium. Among the first shows shot in Los Angeles were the iconic comedy *I Love Lucy* (1951–1957) and cop drama *Dragnet* (1951–1959). *Gunsmoke* (1955–1975) and *The Life and Legend of Wyatt Earp* (1955–1961) proved that TV could move outdoors. By the end of the decade, Hollywood was finally making more shows than New York. Many of them—like *Leave It to Beaver* (1957–1963) and *The Twilight Zone* (1959–1964)—remain small-screen classics.

Theater

The theater is one of the few enterprises in California to suffer from the presence of the film industry. The reasons are obvious, given some people's preference for wealth and fame. World-class playwrights such as Bertolt Brecht may sometimes take up residence but seldom stay under the palms for long enough to create the consistent audience demand that is required to sustain a distinct stage community.

Over the past few years, however, progress has been made. Director-provocateur Luis Valdez has pushed his Teatro Campesino to acclaimed performances of his Latino-themed plays, and San Diego's Old Globe theater (see p. 156) has won an international following for its presentations of modern and classical works. The brassy San Francisco Mime Troupe has refined the art of socially relevant drama. Another star of the California theater scene is the La Jolla Playhouse (see p. 146). Based on the campus of UC San Diego, the troupe was created in 1947 by Gregory Peck and other Hollywood actors craving a serious stage outlet closer to home. Starting in the 1980s, artistic director Des McAnuff crafted the playhouse into a national powerhouse of original plays, stunning revivals, and world premieres. Among its Tony Award–winning repertoire are *Dracula: The Musical, Jersey Boys, Memphis,* and *I Am My Own Wife.*

Under founding artistic director Gordon Davidson, L.A.'s Mark Taper Forum has also launched several Tony Award–winning plays. In 1993 the Forum took a gamble by throwing its weight behind the gay-themed *Angels in America* by Tony Kushner. The result was wide acclaim and the biggest compliment a California director can receive: a subsequent run on Broadway. ■

The nation's second biggest city, filled with art museums, beaches, and food and music scenes that have garnered vast acclaim

LOS ANGELES

The Chinese Theatre, host to many movie premieres

LOS ANGELES

It is, first and foremost, a flatland—a great desert plain. But it is a desert plain like no other. Irrigated with imported water, surrounded by glistening beaches and verdant foothills, and peopled by 18 million dreamers from the ends of the Earth, greater Los Angeles, North America's second largest metropolitan region, may well hold more surprises and delights than any other single destination in the world.

Certainly its short but action-packed history suggests so. Founded in 1781 by a group of Spaniards, Indians, and mestizos, the city was originally claimed for the king of Spain as el Pueblo de la Nuestra Señora la Reina de los Angeles—the City of Our Lady Queen of Angels. It quickly changed hands to Mexico in 1822, and then, reluctantly, to the United States in 1846. (The U.S. troops were initially so unpopular here that local *mujeres*—women—sent one stiff-necked U.S. Army

lieutenant packing, along with a poignant sign of their regard: ripe peaches wrapped in cactus needles.)

After a brief period of lawlessness, the region underwent a still continuing pattern of real estate boom and bust. L.A.'s resultant sprawl (now of 80 contiguous towns) would thus reflect the values of the city's predominantly midwestern founders, men and women who sought to re-create the village society they had left behind in places like Iowa and

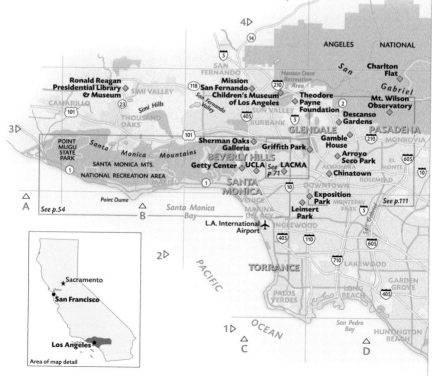

Indiana rather than become part of some looming cosmopolitan cluster.

Today these urban villages persist as identifiable, if constantly changing, regional cultures. The onetime beach resort town of Santa Monica is now a sophisticated, affluent city of achievers with one of the nation's most inclusive city governments, strong environmental laws, and a culture zone stretching from its historic pier to adjacent places like the Getty Center, which one critic has called the Athens of the West.

The Beverly Hills area offers world-class shopping (on Rodeo Drive), art (at the Los Angeles County Museum of Art), and people-watching (at the bustling Farmers Market). And, of course, Hollywood itself.

The late 19th-century "millionaires' retreat" of Pasadena, now a diverse community of Anglos, Asians, and Latinos, similarly thrives

NOT TO BE MISSED:

A stroll along the Santa Monica–Venice Beach boardwalk 54–56

Exploring 4,000 years of art at the Getty Center 60–66

Shopping on Rodeo Drive 72–74

Tinseltown's landmarks along Hollywood Boulevard 83–84

An evening performance at the Hollywood Bowl 84

Hiking in Griffith Park 86

Enjoying the ethnic neighborhoods of Little Tokyo, Chinatown, and Olvera Street 92–95, 99

The plush gardens and museums in and around Pasadena 110–117

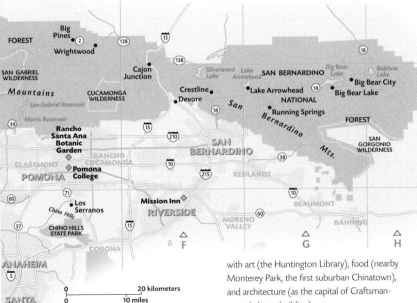

with art (the Huntington Library), food (nearby Monterey Park, the first suburban Chinatown), and architecture (as the capital of Craftsman-style homebuilding).

The traveler who settles into any one of these areas, all within 30 minutes' drive of each other, will be richly rewarded. ∎

FROM THE BEACH

With more than 30 miles (48 km) of sparkling beaches, Los Angeles is a sun lover's dream. Continentals flock to Santa Monica for upscale shopping, while water sports fans go north to surf at Malibu or windsurf at Will Rogers. Dog lovers can take their pooches to Leo Carrillo still farther north. Young lovers seek out quiet Marina del Rey to the south, while bohemians, oddballs, artists, and anyone in need of a laugh and a decent hot dog in-line skate over to Venice.

Venice & Marina del Rey

🅰️ 52 C2 & 55 G1

Visitor Information

✉️ Marina del Rey Visitors Center, 4701 Admiralty Way, Marina del Rey

☎️ 424-526-7900

www.visitthemarina .com

Just inland, pursuits turn to culture. The Getty Center has everything from van Gogh to Rembrandt in painting and out-standing decorative arts, as well as one of the most controversial public gardens in the country. UCLA, one of the state's most striking campuses, has more gardens (one of sculpture, one Japanese-style), as well as a stu-pendous museum devoted to cultural history.

Venice

Founded in 1904 as "the Venice of America" by enlightened tobacco tycoon Abbot Kinney, this part-bohemian, part-affluent jumble of wooden beach cottages, neo-Renaissance architecture, and idyllic canals is part of Marina del Rey.

Venice harkens back to L.A.'s original golden era, when beach-goers rode the Red Car line to Kinney's version of St. Mark's before jumping into a (now razed) saltwater plunge. "Old" Venice architecture can still be seen at **Windward Circle,** and enough remains to make the 3-mile (4.8 km) **boardwalk** one of the most frequented destina-tions for locals and tourists alike. At the southern end, near Venice

■ This lively skate park swirls alongside the Venice boardwalk, one of the best boardwalks in the U.S.

Boulevard, strollers will see the caged-in outdoor gym known worldwide as **Venice Weight Pen.** Muscle-bound exhibitionists, street artists, palm readers, musicians, religious preachers, and bikini-clad roller skaters add to the modern-day circus that defines Venice Beach. It was here that Arnold Schwarzenegger and a legion of Mr. Americas learned to pump iron.

The area around the last of the Venice canals *(near Dell Ave.)* is a placid, picturesque home to many of L.A.'s cultural elite, including Matt Groening, creator of *The Simpsons.* At the northern end stands the 30-foot-tall (9 m) public art piece **"Ballerina Clown"** *(corner of Main St. & Rose Ave.)* by Jonathan Borofsky.

Keep with the spirit of Venice by driving east to the **Museum**

Museum of Jurassic Technology

🗺 55 G2

✉ 9341 Venice Blvd., Culver City

☎ 310-836-6131

🕐 Closed a.m. & Mon.–Wed.

💲 Donation

www.mjt.org

The Palm Tree

Decades of "creative landscaping" have resulted in L.A.'s towering palm trees. Many strains came from Chile and the Canary Islands; only the fan palm (*Washingtonia filifera*) is native to the Southwest. At more than 50 feet (15 m), with fronds up to 5 feet (1.5 m) long, this transplant from the Southwest desert serves as unofficial icon to the region.

Sony Pictures Studios

🗺 55 G2

✉ 10202 W. Washington Blvd., Culver City

☎ 310-244-8687

🕐 Tours Mon.–Fri.

💲 $$$$$

www.sonypictures studios.com

Santa Monica

🗺 52 C3 & 55 F2

Visitor Information

✉ Santa Monica Travel & Tourism, 2427 Main St.

☎ 310-319-6263, 800-544-5319

www.santamonica .com

Santa Monica Pier

🗺 55 F1

☎ 310-458-8901

www.santamonica pier.org

of Jurassic Technology, which boasts an eclectic collection of strange phenomena (such as the deprong mori, or "piercing devil" bat) and weird human accomplishments (micro-sculptures of Snow White and the Seven Dwarfs built inside the eye of a needle). The museum's avant-garde program of evening speakers is one of L.A.'s best kept secrets.

A tour of **Sony Pictures Studios** leads you through sets where Spiderman swung from buildings and agents from *Men in Black* (1997) battled aliens. You can even sit in on a filming of *Jeopardy!* or *Wheel of Fortune*.

Santa Monica

Santa Monica is no longer the sleepy beachside town so aptly evoked as "Bay City" by the detective novelist Raymond Chandler. With a population of more than 92,000 and some of the best eating and shopping in L.A., Santa Monica now sports more of a European ambience— the Nice of California. The various musicians who perform at the four-times-weekly farmers markets are an indication of another facet of Santa Monica:

its prime position on the world music scene.

Fortunately for the seeker of old Santa Monica, there are still all the eternal beachside delights: salty air, tawny beaches, and magical sunsets. Perhaps the best place to take in the city's character is **Palisades Park.** Deeded to the city in 1875 by John Percival (J. P.) Jones, a city founder, this 26-acre (10.5 ha) strip of green lawn and Washington palm trees sits above Santa Monica Bay. The views sometimes include a glimpse of Catalina Island, some 22 miles (35 km) away.

A morning walk through Palisades Park could include several notable stops: The 110-year-old **Camera Obscura** *(1450 Ocean Ave.)* projects images through its rooftop lenses and prisms—a reminder of what passed for wonder before the age of Disney; the **statue of St. Monica** *(Ocean Ave. & Wilshire Blvd.)* by Eugene H. Monrahan is remarkable for its streamlined modern lines, as is the old **Shangri-La Hotel** *(1301 Ocean Ave., tel 310-394-2791, www .shangrila-hotel.com)* just across the street.

While the historic **Santa Monica Pier** now houses the reasonably priced **Pacific Park** *(tel 310-260-8744, www.pacpark .com)* amusement park, many come just to see the 1909 **Looff Hippodrome** and its refurbished carousel of hand-carved ponies.

On the south side of the pier is the original **Muscle Beach,** where the muscle-bound show off to the public. Underneath the pier is the **Santa Monica Pier Aquarium,** where three aquariums educate the public on marine science. Just north of the pier is the **Marion Davies Guest House** *(415 Hwy. 1),* built for the star in 1929 by noted architect Julia Morgan.

On Main Street, the **California Heritage Museum** is well worth a visit. Housed in the 1894 former home of city founder J. P. Jones, the museum offers a number of exhibits in displays that change regularly. Some of its past shows have featured the work of 1920s California tableware makers, the origins of the Hawaiian shirt, and artifacts of early surfing culture.

The **Edgemar Center for the Arts,** with art galleries and film-screening facilities, was originally designed as the Santa Monica Museum of Modern Art by architect Frank Gehry (see sidebar p. 46), whose work includes the Walt Disney Concert Hall in Los Angeles (see p. 103).

Architectural pilgrims can also see (from the outside only) Gehry's home at 1002 22nd Street.

Now settled in its new site on the north side of the Santa Monica airport, the **Museum of Flying** *(map p. 55 G2, 3100 Airport Ave., tel 310-398-2500, www .museumofflying.com)* is largely dedicated to honoring the legacy of the Douglas Aircraft Company, which, for more than 60 years, dominated the construction of both commercial and military aircraft. The museum displays functioning World War II planes along with dozens of more recent aircraft, plus a replica of the Wright brothers' "Wright Flyer."

People-watching and shopping at the **Third Street Promenade** *(map p. 55 F2, betw. Broadway & Wilshire Blvd., www.downtownsm.com)* can be a full-time pursuit. The best time is on Wednesday, when the famous **Santa Monica Farmers**
(continued on p. 60)

Santa Monica Pier Aquarium
- 55 F1
- 100 Ocean Front Walk, Santa Monica Pier, Santa Monica
- 310-393-6149
- Closed a.m.
- $, children free
- **www.healthebay.org**

California Heritage Museum
- 55 G1
- 2612 Main St., Santa Monica
- 310-392-8537
- Closed Mon.–Tues.
- $
- **www.california heritagemuseum.org**

Edgemar Center for the Arts
- 55 F2
- 2437 Main St., Santa Monica
- 310-399-3666
- **www.edgemarcenter. org**

EXPERIENCE: Malibu Creek Horseback Riding

A visit to Los Angeles doesn't have to be confined to the city. Nearly 30 years of environmental activism has resulted in cleaner beaches, better water, and new state parks dedicated to preserving the ecologies of western Los Angeles County.

The most scenic of these parks is **Malibu Creek State Park** *(map p. 54 D2, 1925 Las Virgenes Rd., Calabasas, tel 818-880-0367, www.malibucreekstatepark .org),* with reaches of rolling grasslands, sharp gorges, creeks, and towering old trees. One of the best ways to take in this

backcountry is on horseback. **Malibu Riders** *(tel 818-510-2245, www.malibu riders.com)* offers daily one-hour, 3-mile (4.8 km) round-trip loop rides *($$$)* from Paramount Ranch into Malibu Creek. You will ride through the former Ronald Reagan Ranch and beautiful forests to a breathtaking view of Malibu Lake. An optional one-hour, 3-mile (4.8 km) extension *($$$$)* takes you deeper into the Santa Monica Mountains to Century Lake and back. Riders must be 8 years or older. Price includes horse rental and a guide.

DRIVE: ALONG SUNSET BOULEVARD

Intrepid drivers can test their skills with a spin up scenic, winding Sunset Boulevard, memorably featured in one of moviedom's most stupidly terrifying chase scenes (*Against All Odds*, 1984). The sane motorist, however, begins the jaunt with a brunch at Gladstone's (*17300 W. Hwy. 1, Pacific Palisades, tel 310-454-3474, www.gladstones.com*), where French toast and coffee put you in the mood for an L.A. drive.

Heading east on Sunset Boulevard, the first stop is the **Self-Realization Fellowship Lake Shrine ❶** (*17190 Sunset Blvd., tel 310-454-4114, www.lakeshrine.org, closed Mon. & a.m. Sun.*). Founded in 1950 by the Paramahansa Yogananda, who preached that "there must be world brotherhood if we are to be able to practice the true art of living," the shrine underscores the highly ecumenical nature of Hinduism in Los Angeles. With its gardens of miniature roses and hydrangeas the size of basketballs, the shrine is a perfect place for an after-lunch nap. The gift store sells Indian curios, incense, and a range of self-improvement literature.

Still on Sunset, a left turn at Bienveneda Avenue will take you to the **Topanga Trailhead ❷**, the start of hikes into the mesquite-and-sage landscape of the Santa Monica Mountains. A nearby sign points to the easily negotiated **Phil Leacock Memorial Trail,** from which the view takes in Pacific Palisades as well as the ocean.

Continue up Sunset and past the famous **Gelson's Market ❸** (*15424 Sunset Blvd. & Via de la Paz, tel 310-459-4483, www.gelsons.com*), where you can stock up on picnic items. Beyond it, look out for the turnoff for **Will Rogers State Historic Park ❹** (*14253 Sunset Blvd., tel 310-230-2017, www.parks.ca.gov*). The beloved actor and humorist deeded his estate to California, which has maintained his home and polo field; a free audio tour of Rogers's living room and living quarters, with its charming cowboys-and-Indians decor, is a must. A hike up **Inspiration Trail** will put a flush of sun and wind on your face.

NOT TO BE MISSED:

Self-Realization Fellowship Lake Shrine • Will Rogers State Historic Park • Bel Air Estates

On Sunset again, you pass infamous **Rockingham Avenue ❺** (where noted non-killer O. J. Simpson's house has been razed). Stop for an espresso at Brentwood Village (*Barrington Ave., www.brentwoodvillage.org*) before passing

The 1.5-mile (2.4 km) portion of Sunset Boulevard known as the Sunset Strip is legendary for its nightlife.

I-405, the San Diego Freeway, and coming to **Bel Air Estates** ⑥, home of the rich and famous. Either of two ornate "gates" on the north side of Sunset admit the curious to a maze of small streets lined with some of L.A.'s priciest (if sometimes aesthetically troubling) estates. Note that the "star maps" hawked here are likely to be worthless. Content yourself with occasionally exclaiming, "That's gotta be Greta Garbo's house!" or "Isn't that where Don Johnson and Melanie Griffith got married?"

You can either end the drive here or continue to **UCLA** (see pp. 66–69) or to **Beverly Hills** (see pp. 70–89). Alternatively, turn right on Beverly Glen Boulevard to Santa Monica Boulevard and the **Century City shopping plaza** *(map p. 55 G2, 10250 Santa Monica Blvd., www.westfield.com/centurycity).*

🅰️ See also area map pp. 54–55
▶ Self-Realization Fellowship Lake Shrine
🕐 2 hours
↔ 12 miles (19.3 km)
▶ Bel Air Estates

Getty Villa

- 55 F2
- 17985 Hwy. 1, Pacific Palisades
- 310-440-7300, 310-440-7305 (hearing impaired)
- Closed Tues.
- $ (parking)

www.getty.edu

Market convenes at Third Street and Arizona Avenue. This is a "foodie" magnet, and a keen eye might spot celebrities and famous chefs scouting out the best organic mushrooms and brussels sprouts.

Getty Villa

The first home of oil billionaire J. Paul Getty's growing collection of antiquities and decorative

surprised critics by leaving a $700 million trust. Astute financial management increased the trust to $4 billion, enabling its trustees to commit $1 billion to the building of a new museum.

Their choice of architect was Pritzker Prize–winner Richard Meier. The key design issue was how to make a modernist structure that inspired a classical sense of permanence. Meier's answer

Plants favored by the ancients surround the Getty Villa's 220-foot-long (67 m) reflecting pool.

Getty Center

- 52 C3 & 55 F2
- 1200 Getty Center Dr., Getty Center exit from San Diego Freeway (I-405)
- 310-440-7300, 310-440-7305 (hearing impaired)
- Closed Mon.
- $ (parking)

www.getty.edu

arts was the recently restored Romanesque Getty Villa that Getty built in 1953 above Topanga Beach. The villa still houses his superb collection of more than 50,000 Greek and Roman antiquities. It also serves as an educational research center on ancient art and cultures.

Getty Center

An eccentric with a reputation for being a skinflint, Getty

was to use travertine, a form of limestone quarried in Italy. The result is a hulking complex of shifting hues of white, ranging from a retina-scarring *blanc majeur* in the morning to a pleasant, late-afternoon-in-Rome gold by dusk.

Perched on its 110-acre (44.5 ha) campus high above the drone of I-405, the Getty Center, which was completed in 1997, inspires conflicting emotions. The dazzling complex bespeaks all the ambitions of a great art institution. Yet the modernist campus also seems to be at once removed, reinforcing the old notion that in L.A. art has no organic connection with the community.

Nonetheless, since its opening, the Getty's actions have belied such concerns, and, through an outreach program, the center connects to the cultural life of the entire city. Key features are ongoing programs with local schools (guided and self-guided tours are offered, but must be reserved in advance) and educational programs covering photography, sculpture, and painting.

In addition, the Getty Center offers an eclectic range of events, from artist-at-work demonstrations and poetry readings to an annual Renaissance Family Festival, plus free "Friday Nights at the Getty" concerts featuring Afro-Latino, Cajun, folk, and blues music.

How to Visit: An electric tram shuttles visitors from the front entrance and parking to the **Arrival Plaza,** dominated by Martin Puryear's 45-foot (13.7 m) sculpture "That Profile." An orientation film is shown.

The Getty Center's five main buildings are arranged chronologically. All are connected, by either hallway or overpass, on both floors; at ground level, visitors can easily pass from 16th- to 18th-century works, then back to 17th-century, and so on. Free GettyGuide mobile audio guides are programmed to respond to inquiries about individual paintings, and can be downloaded online.

INSIDER TIP:

Regular films shown in the Getty auditorium include *Art Works: Behind the Scenes at the Getty* (30 mins.) and *Concert of Wills: Making the Getty Center* (90 mins.).

—GREG CRITSER
National Geographic author

North Pavilion: Paintings in the North Pavilion, which highlights art from before 1600, include the evocative "Mythological Scene," painted circa 1524 by the Italian Dosso Dossi *(room N205).* The work perfectly illustrates the Venetian penchant for dreamscape and allegory, but also gives the museum the opportunity to fulfill its aim of educating the public about the history of paintings. Fra Bartolommeo's "Flight Into Egypt" is a good example of the luminous quality of this early 16th-century Italian's work. A 1330 panel by Bernardo Daddi depicting the Virgin, St. Paul, and St. Thomas Aquinas has been particularly well preserved. According to author Letitia Burns O'Conner, "the conservator who examined it prior to its purchase in 1993 declared he had never seen a *trecento* picture so well preserved, its glazes still intact to modulate the bright colors of the drapery, its punched gold background glowing softly."

(continued on p. 64)

Getty Center

West Pavilion

Exhibition Pavilion

J. Paul Getty Museum

South Pavilion

Fran and Ray Stark Sculpture Terrace

Museum courtyard

East Pavilion

North Pavilion

Entrance hall

EAST BUILDING (Conservation Institute & Foundation/ changing exhibits)

NORTH BUILDING (Conservation Institute/ Foundation)

Restaurant

Café

Tram station

Harold M. Williams Auditorium

Central garden

Getty Research Institute
for the History of Art and the
Humanities/Exhibition Pavilion
(changing exhibits)/Lecture Hall

Upper Level

Plaza Level

Terrace Level

Paintings

Changing exhibits

Education

Sculpture

Decorative arts

Manuscripts

Drawings

Photographs

In 2003, the Getty acquired Titian's "Portrait of Alfonso d'Avalos, Marchese del Vasto," painted in 1533. Considered the Getty Center's most important portrait, this masterpiece—of an illustrious noble in his suit of armor—by the leading exponent of Venetian Renaissance painting, set the standard for court portraiture and the evolution of Western art.

East Pavilion: The East Pavilion covers art from the period between 1600 and 1800. While the emphasis here is largely on Dutch and Flemish works, two small 17th-century paintings, Italian and French respectively, show the collection's range: Domenichino's "The Way to Calvary" is done on copper; Valentin de Boulogne's "Christ and the Adultress" *(both in room E201)* is noted in a museum caption by the neoconceptualist L.A. artist John Baldessari as "a kind of film noir."

What follows is a blur of giants, including Rubens ("The Entombment," "The Murder of St. Francis," both in room E202) and Rembrandt ("The Abduction of Europa" in room E205). A memorable piece by a lesser known 17th-century Dutch artist is Hendrick Ter Brugghen's "Bacchante With an Ape" *(room E204).* Downstairs, the collection of sculptures and decorative arts includes Adreian de Vries' *Juggling Man* in bronze *(room E101).*

South Pavilion: The South Pavilion expands the scope of paintings and decorative arts from 1600 to 1800, the core of

■ **The Getty Center stands on a hill above Los Angeles with beautiful city views.**

Jewish History in a Boutique Setting

Set on a hilltop just north of the Getty Center, the Skirball Cultural Center represents one of the best developments to come out of the growing trend toward boutique museums. This is because the Skirball has refined its mission—"to present Jewish culture and experience as part of the living fabric of American life as a whole"—and presents only the best and most comprehensive shows on the subject. There is a depth and singularity of experience here, matched by few such museums in the country.

In recent years the 125,000-square-foot (11,612 sq m) center has refocused to be a broad-based exhibition center guided by the Jewish tradition of welcoming the stranger, and by the American democratic ideals of freedom and equality, to help shape a more just and tolerant society. Its temporary exhibitions reflect profound eclectic depth, from "Black is Beautiful: The Photography of Kwame Brathwaite" displaying iconic images portraying the cultural shift of the 1960s inspired by the writings of black nationalist Marcus Garvey, to "Star Trek: Exploring New Worlds," an immersive interactive exhibition guided by its famous opening line, "To boldly go where no one has gone before."

The center has a program of arts and cultural events, including plays, music (including blues legend John Hammond), and readings.

J. Paul Getty's personal collection. To do it justice, the museum brought in New York designer Thierry Despont to craft several period rooms, constituting a "museum within a museum." The effect is priceless, though some find it overwhelming. Despont's pale blue French-paneled room is a perfect medium for the ornate chairs, clocks, and furnishings. The enormous "Cabinet on Stand" (1675–1680) by André-Charles Boulle, in room S103, shows a craftsmanship unmatched by his contemporaries.

West Pavilion: Some visitors may prefer, with some justification, to make a separate trip to the Getty Center to see "Art after 1800," the exhibition in the West Pavilion. However, to do this would be to miss the effect of the dramatic buildup that the other pavilions provide.

While many have cynically criticized this collection as "Europe's greatest hits," it is hard to underplay the delight provoked by the works of Monet, Renoir, Cézanne, Manet, and van Gogh that are hung here. "Irises" by van Gogh (room W204) remains the biggest attraction. See it first thing in the morning before the crowds arrive. Lesser known paintings worth seeing here include Belgian painter James Ensor's huge 1888 work "Christ's Entry Into Brussels, 1889" (room W204).

Juxtapositions of "smaller" works—a specialty of the Getty Center—make this gallery sing. Put Cézanne's "The Eternal Feminine" next to his "Still Life With Apples," and see if you ever think of fruit in the same way again. The brilliantly arranged Center for Photographs on the Terrace Level makes a fitting coda.

Skirball Cultural Center

🅰 55 G3
✉ 2701 N. Sepulveda Blvd.
☎ 310-440-4500
🕐 Closed Mon. & a.m. Tues.–Fri.
💲 $$

www.skirball.org

Gorgeous Gardens

UCLA has two outstanding gardens, both open to the public. The **Mildred E. Mathias Botanic Garden** (*map p. 55 G2, 100 Stein Plaza Driveway, www.botgard.ucla.edu*) is a perfect place to read, write, or just sit and contemplate nature's wonder. The habitat diversity covers the spectrum from bamboo groves to streambeds and tropicals—some 4,000 plant species in all. The **Franklin D. Murphy Sculpture Garden**, in UCLA's northeast corner, is a testimony to the former chancellor's breadth of interests. The 5-acre (2 ha) sculpture garden is the largest on the West Coast. Some 70 pieces of sculpture stand in the shade of the jacaranda trees. Among the artists are Auguste Rodin, Isamu Noguchi, and Alexander Calder.

UCLA

52 C3 & 55 G2
405 Hilgard Ave.
310-825-4321

www.ucla.edu

Exhibitions Pavilion: No visit to the Getty Center would be complete without exploring the Exhibitions Pavilion, although its most famous and controversial piece, the Getty Kouros, is no longer here. It was one of several antiquities returned to Greece and Italy after they were proved to have been stolen or excavated illegally.

Sculpture Garden: In 2007, the Fran and Ray Stark Sculpture Garden opened to the south of the Exhibitions Pavilion to display the bulk of 28 contemporary outdoor sculptures that Hollywood producer Ray Stark and his wife donated to the museum.

Central Garden: While there are many places at the Getty to pause and ponder or relax, nothing conjures the sense of discovery quite like the 134,000-square-foot (12,449 sq m) Central Garden. Created by artist Robert Irwin, the garden is an example of "site-generated art." Irwin's notion is that a person's intimate experience of nature can be heightened by accentuating the configuration of foliage, sunlight, and shade.

The focal point of the garden is a maze of floating azaleas, surrounded by a terraced round ravine marked by geometrically arranged cacti. Irwin interrupts the sense of botanical order with a series of "specialty gardens"—a meadow, a stream garden, terraces of hydrangeas and nasturtiums and irises. Just how well the scheme furthers the museum's aesthetic ideals is up to the individual stroller, but a better place to rest and soak up the sun is nowhere in sight.

UCLA

Founded in 1919 as part of the University of California, the University of California at Los Angeles (UCLA) long languished in the shadow of its older sister, Berkeley (see pp. 238–239). Eventually, following a period of huge growth, the 400-acre (162 ha) campus began establishing a profile of its own (the turning point of which is said to have been former chancellor Franklin Murphy's command to answer the administration phones by saying "UCLA!" rather than "University of California"). Today UCLA ranks among the top ten research universities in the U.S., producing several recent Nobel Prize winners, and is fondly known as the "University of Caucasians, Latinos, and Asians," because of the diversity of its 25,000 undergraduates. South of Bel Air and north of Westwood Village, UCLA is at the heart of L.A.

Central Quad: Sitting on a low hilltop and overlooking surrounding valleys and mountain ranges, UCLA's Central Quad of four Romanesque-Renaissance-style buildings was built in 1929. Lush grounds and swaying old eucalyptus trees make it a perfect place for weekend strolls.

The university's **Powell Library** *(Quad, southwest corner)* is an architectural gem. Named for California bibliophile and longtime UCLA librarian Lawrence Clark Powell, the building has been restored to its 1929 grandeur. Soothing tile staircases lead to a reading room crowned by an ornate ceiling. The temporary structure used to house books during the remodeling, nicknamed "Towell," has won several architectural citations for its innovative use of materials.

Also restored is **Royce Hall** *(Quad, northwest corner),* another jewel. Named for California philosopher Josiah Royce, the Italianate auditorium is said to have been modeled on the Church of St. Ambrose in Milan.

The Museums: UCLA's main museum, the **UCLA Hammer Museum,** was founded by the late oil magnate Armand Hammer to house his then thin collection of old masters and Impressionist paintings.

Since then, the institution has matured. Among the works in the collection are "Summertime" by artist Mary Cassatt (1844–1926), whose work was exhibited with that of the Impressionists in Paris in the 1880s. Other highlights include Rembrandt's "Juno" (1662–65), van Gogh's "Hospital at Saint-Remy" (1889), and Gauguin's "Bonjour Monsieur Gauguin" (1889). There are also a number of works by prominent American artists, including George Bellows, John Singer Sargent, Gilbert Stuart, and Andrew Wyeth.

Several other collections warrant

attention. One is the largest U.S. collection of satirical drawings and watercolors by 19th-century French caricaturist Honoré Daumier. The other star, now also at the Hammer, is the **UCLA Grunwald Center for the Graphic Arts** *(tel 310-443-7078),* which features a wide range of paper works, from Dürer and Cruikshank to Picasso and Matisse. Because the Hammer is fond of traveling exhibitions—sometimes

INSIDER TIP:

Don't miss Richard Serra's "T.E.U.C.L.A." (Torqued Ellipse UCLA) in the sculpture garden: You can even walk through this beguiling plate of curved steel.

—KENNY LING
National Geographic contributor

UCLA Hammer Museum

▲ 55 G2

✉ 10899 Wilshire Blvd., Westwood Village

☎ 310-443-7000

🕐 Closed Mon.

$ $$, free Thurs.

www.hammer.ucla .edu

Fowler Museum at UCLA

✉ Fowler Hall, UCLA North Campus

☎ 310-825-4361

🕐 Closed a.m. & Mon.–Tues.

www.fowler.ucla.edu

at the expense of its permanent collection—it is best to call before visiting for current information.

The Hammer's new initiative to amass a collection of contemporary works created since the 1960s focuses on drawing and photographs, with an emphasis on pieces since the millennium, and especially of Los Angeles–based artists, while its **Billy Wilder Theater** hosts provocative public programs and provides a cinematheque for the UCLA Film & Television

Archive's vast documentary and movie collection.

The **Fowler Museum at UCLA** explores global arts with an emphasis on the indigenous and traditional cultures of Africa, the Americas, Asia, and the Pacific. With its strong emphasis on anthropology, the Fowler has staged acclaimed shows on subjects ranging from voodoo to the little-known Mochas people of pre-Columbian Peru.

Athletics: Sports fans should check out the **UCLA Athletics Hall of Fame** in the J. D. Morgan Center. With more than a hundred NCAA championships under their belt, the Bruins have won more college championships than any other school. Among its athletic alums are basketball players Kareem Abdul-Jabbar and Bill Walton, baseball legend Jackie Robinson, Super Bowl quarterback Troy Aikman, and Olympic track star Jackie Joyner-Kersee.

Performing Arts: The **Center for the Art of Performance at UCLA** *(B100 Royce Hall, tel 310-825-4401, www.cap.ucla.edu)* is one of the city's premier cultural institutions, presenting world-class, cutting-edge works in dance, music, spoken word, and experimental theater. Inaugurated in 2001 by pop music icon Elvis Costello, the center spans the globe with its wildly eclectic and often experimental performances offered year-round. The center's programs are hosted at venues around UCLA's campus and beyond, including the Freud

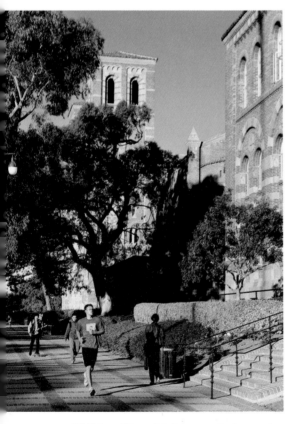

■ UCLA's Royce Hall: a study in Romanesque-Renaissance majesty

Playhouse, with its large proscenium stage, and Royce Hall (see p. 67), known for its state-of-the-art acoustics.

Westwood Village: An infusion of funds from mogul-philanthropist David Geffen (see sidebar p. 99) and topflight Hollywood talent has made the **Geffen Playhouse,** in Westwood Village, a major L.A. theater venue.

Just south of the main campus, Westwood Village serves as the proverbial (but pricey) "college town." Breakfast at **Primo's Donuts** (10948 Weyburn Ave., tel 310-208-8660)—formerly the iconic Stan's Corner Donut Shop—is de rigueur, if only to experience the best-rated donuts in town. The Modernist **Los Angeles California Temple** (10777 Santa Monica Blvd., tel 310-474-5569), operated by The Church of Jesus Christ of Latter-Day Saints, is topped by a 15-foot (4.6 m) statue of Angel Moroni. The grounds are open to the public and have a visitor center.

Around UCLA: The Bel Air Hills and Holmby Hills rise immediately north and east of UCLA, respectively. Together with Beverly Hills, they make up LA's "Platinum Triangle" of über-expensive homes of the rich and famous. Most notable is the French chateau–style **Spelling Manor** (594 S. Mapleton Dr.), with 123 rooms the largest home in the U.S. and also the most valuable—in 2019 it sold for a record $119.7 million, the highest residential real estate in California history.

Cemetery to the Stars

The unofficial cemetery to the stars, **Westwood Village Memorial Park** (1218 Glendon Ave., Los Angeles) is the last resting place of Marilyn Monroe and numerous other luminaries of the big and small screens. Baseball legend Joe DiMaggio chose the tiny graveyard for his ex-wife after her controversial 1962 death because her mother was already buried there. Monroe's simple tomb lies in the wall near the northeast corner. Among the many others buried at Westwood are actors Natalie Wood, Jack Lemmon, George C. Scott, Walter Matthau, and Burt Lancaster, musicians Roy Orbison and Dean Martin, comedians Rodney Dangerfield and Don Knotts, writer Truman Capote, and director Billy Wilder. Visiting hours are daily 8 a.m. to dusk.

Nearby is the **Playboy Mansion** (499 S. Mapleton Rd.), home of party-hearty publisher Hugh Hefner (1926–2017).

Driving east for ten minutes on Olympic Boulevard will take you to the **Museum of Tolerance,** a "teaching museum" dedicated to educating the public about racism and ethnic genocide. The focus is the Nazi Holocaust. The 90-minute guided tour of its interactive displays is unforgettable—and emotionally devastating. "Finding Our Families, Finding Ourselves" showcases the diversity and achievements of noted Americans of all faiths and ethnicities. The museum's Tolerancenter includes a high-tech "time machine," which details human rights abuses around the world in different ages, and a re-created 1950s diner that "serves" a menu of controversial topics on video jukeboxes. ∎

Geffen Playhouse

✉ 10886 Le Conte Ave., Los Angeles

☎ 310-208-5454

www.geffenplay house.com

Museum of Tolerance

🗺 55 G2 & 71 A1

✉ 9786 W. Pico Blvd., Los Angeles

☎ 310-772-2505

🕐 Closed Sat. & public and Jewish holidays

💲 $$$

www.museumof tolerance.com

FROM BEVERLY HILLS

The great urbanist Reyner Banham once referred to L.A.'s flat basin topography as "the plains of id." Here, life was so calm that anyone who lived in it for long would soon confront—or embrace—all their long-banished desires. If there is a "plain of id" in downtown and another at the beach, certainly there is a distinct one operating in and around the greater Beverly Hills area. This is the plain of money, both refined and crude—of money made and money spent.

The Beverly Hills Hotel remains a classic celebrity hangout.

Beverly Hills

52 C3 & 71 A1

Visitor Information

Conference & Visitors Bureau, 9400 S. Santa Monica Blvd.

310-248-1015

www.lovebeverlyhills .com

It has always been that way in Beverly Hills. Founded in 1906 by real estate developer Burton Green, the city grew slowly until the 1920s. In 1920, movie star Douglas Fairbanks purchased a prominent hilltop in the area for $35,000. There he built the legendary Pickfair mansion for "America's sweetheart," actress Mary Pickford. Pickfair attracted all who aspired to be a Fairbanks or a Pickford, and the real estate market boomed.

Be warned: You will probably spend more on accommodations, food, and shopping in Beverly Hills than in other parts of the city. But this is a perfect place from which to explore several adjacent areas.

Just south, the Wilshire Corridor leads eastward to the Los Angeles County Museum of Art, perhaps the West Coast's single best art destination. Along the northern boundary of Beverly Hills runs Sunset Boulevard (see pp. 58–59), which also leads eastward, first to West Hollywood, a strip of famous restaurants and gay life, then on to old Hollywood, where so much of the money to sustain Beverly Hills was made in the first place.

INSIDER TIP:

To see *Homo hollywoodis* in action, have lunch at the legendary Polo Lounge in the Beverly Hills Hotel. Order the tortilla soup and fresh crab plate, and then sit back and watch the scene.

—GREG CRITSER
National Geographic author

From there the old Hollywood Freeway (U.S. 101) leads over to the San Fernando Valley, land of the quintessential shopping mall, offering yet more opportunities to part with your money.

Beverly Hills Hotel

There was a time when many people believed that the Beverly Hills Hotel—the old "Pink Palace"—had permanently lost its glow, its lovely yet outdated accommodations overshadowed by the gleaming new Peninsula Hotel down the way. No more. Ever since its purchase by the Sultan of Brunei in 1989, the hotel has mounted a strong comeback, investing heavily in a complete makeover. The result is a glamorous retreat, with all the modern conveniences, that evokes the best of Hollywood's Golden Age.

Have lunch under the old pepper tree in the **Polo Lounge,** then wander down to the **Fountain Coffee Room,** where you will

Beverly Hills Hotel

🅰 71 A2
✉ 9641 Sunset Blvd.
☎ 310-276-2251

www.beverlyhills hotel.com

Cruise Through Hollywood's Past

For a trip into Hollywood history, drive **Mulholland Drive** along the crest of the Santa Monica Mountains. One of the most storied streets in the City of the Angels, Mulholland meanders 14.4 miles (23.1 km) from east to west, starting in the Cahuenga Pass above the Hollywood Bowl and twisting all the way to San Vincente Mountain Park, with its historic Nike missile launch pad. West of San Vincente Park, Mulholland continues as an unpaved hiking trail.

In addition to offering jaw-dropping views of Los Angeles and the San Fernando Valley, Mulholland Drive has also been home to myriad celebrities, including Jack Nicholson, Wilt Chamberlain, Britney Spears, Warren Beatty, John Lennon, Madonna, Marlon Brando, and Faye Dunaway.

Rodeo Drive

🅰 71 A1

Visitor Information

www.rodeodrive-bh.com

Beverly Wilshire

✉ 9500 Wilshire Blvd.

☎ 800-819-5053

www.fourseasons.com

often see younger stars preening, eating fatty no-no's, or irritably dealing with their equally irritated agents. Next, stroll the grounds and take in the architecture. If the mission-style exterior looks familiar, it may be because it was designed in 1912 by Elmer Grey, who with his partner Myron Hunt also did the Huntington Library (see p. 119–121). Paul Revere Williams was the architect for the newer Crescent Wing, built in 1949.

As the afternoon wears on and the heat rises, the hotel pool will look appealing. At poolside, cocktails are served 9 a.m. to 6 p.m.—or just jump in. After all, Katharine Hepburn did once—and she had all her clothes on. At night, celebs cluster at **Bar Nineteen 12,** the hotel's hip watering hole.

Rodeo Drive

The three blocks of Rodeo Drive north of Wilshire Boulevard rank among the most famous (and most expensive) shopping districts in the world, comparable to the Champs-Élysées in Paris or Florence's Ponte Vecchio. The one big difference is style; along Europe's great boulevards, one would never think of wearing a sweatshirt and jeans to go shopping for a $1,000 silk blouse. In Beverly Hills, a man in a tracksuit may well drop $15,000 in one afternoon, shopping at, say, House of Bijan. This does not mean you should not dress well to shop here—but if you choose to go casual, whip up a good dose of attitude to go with it.

Begin at the **Beverly Wilshire**, facing the southern end of Rodeo Drive on Wilshire Boulevard. You may recognize this legendary and stately hotel as a key setting for the movie *Pretty Woman*.

North on Rodeo, the first area to your right is known as **Two Rodeo** (www.2rodeo.com), a retail "alley" created in 1990 to house new outlets for Tiffany's and Ferre, along with several tasteful shops specializing in home decor. Real estate developer Douglas Stitzel spared no expense with the imported Italian cobblestones to create a European-style piazza with old street lamps. In the central median at the north end of Two Rodeo, the 14-foot-tall (4.3 m) aluminum nude female torso—**Torso** *(Rodeo Drive & Dayton Way)*—by Robert Graham marks the start of the Rodeo Drive Walk of Style: Bronze plaques honoring fashion legends are inset in the sidewalk. People-watching reaches its peak in the next two blocks where the palm-shaded sidewalks are flanked by posh fashion boutiques like Dolce & Gabbana, Yves Saint Laurent, Christian Dior, and Gucci, plus Cartier, the jewelers. Watch for Anderton Court, on the east mid-way between Dayton and Brighton Way; it was designed by Frank Lloyd Wright in 1952. Look for the yellow parking meter reserved for a yellow Aston Martin, and Bugatti and Rolls Royce cars outside Bijan *(443 N. Rodeo Drive)*, the bespoke men's store. You can take a free trolley *(tel 310-285-2442, Tue.–Sat., hourly 11 a.m.–4 p.m., $)* from Rodeo Drive and Dayton Way to the landmark **Civic Center**, built in 1932 in Spanish Renaissance style.

Once relieved of your excess cash, drive over to the **Witch's House** *(516 Walden Drive)*, with its pointy lopsided roof and crooked chimneys and windows. Built as a movie set for *Hansel and Gretel* (1921), it was moved here in 1934 as a private residence, set amid bizarrely twisted tree roots and moat-like pond. It's now the most visited non-celebrity house in Los Angeles, although it can only be viewed from the road. Next drive into the hills to visit the **Greystone Park & Mansion.** The 46,000-square-foot English Gothic Revival mansion was built in 1928 by oil baron Edward Doheny. Today a registered historic landmark, it is owned by the city of Beverly Hills, and the

Greystone Park & Mansion

🗺 71 A2
✉ 905 Loma Vista Dr.
☎ 310-285-6830
💲 Tour: $$$

www.greystone mansion.org

■ Home to the toniest boutiques in Beverly Hills, Rodeo Drive beckons shoppers of all kinds.

Los Angeles County Museum of Art (LACMA)

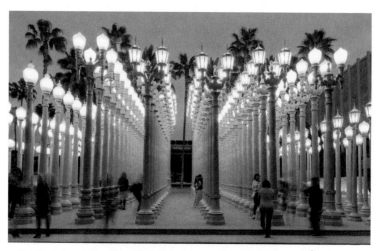

🅐 52 C3, 55 H2, & 71 B1

✉ 5905 Wilshire Blvd.

☎ 323-857-6000

🕐 Closed Wed.

💲 $$$ (free 2nd Tues. of month)

www.lacma.org

public enjoys its 18 acres (7.2 ha) of terraced gardens for picnics. Rangers lead guided tours of the mansion and grounds on Saturdays.

Los Angeles County Museum of Art

"Oh! I just can't believe it. There is so much great art at that place, I mean great, that sometimes it's overwhelming for the rest of us. You're so lucky to be from a city with that much great art." This

three decades of its existence, the museum has gathered together the greatest collection of art in the western United States: 42,000 works, most of them of singular taste and quality. One reason for this is curatorial continuity. The American, modern, and Southeast Asian collections were each largely built under the regime of former curator Pratapaditya Pal; this makes for a cohesiveness rare in most large mainstream museums.

Launched in 1961, LACMA's

■ **Chris Burden's roadside public art piece, "Urban Light," is a signature highlight of LACMA.**

telling recommendation comes not from the public relations crew at the Los Angeles County Museum of Art (LACMA), but from a public relations person at one of San Francisco's leading art institutions. Anyone familiar with the intense rivalry between the two cities knows that such remarks are rare.

But rare is perhaps the best word to describe LACMA. In the

Wilshire Boulevard campus opened to the public in 1965, with the Ahmanson Building housing the permanent collection, the Hammer Building for special exhibitions, and the 600-seat Bing Theater for public programs. It has since expanded considerably, with the addition of monumental public artworks and several new buildings including, in 2010, the **Lynda and Stewart Resnick**

Pavilion, the world's largest purpose-built, naturally lit, open-plan museum space. It houses the museum's temporary exhibitions.

In 2020, ground was broken on an ambitious four-year reconstruction that will replace the four aging buildings on the east side with a vast new structure—the David Geffen Galleries—for the permanent collection. The amoeba-shaped building by Pritzker Prize–winning architect Peter Zumthor will span Wilshire Boulevard and feature an elevated, organically-shaped main exhibition level with a floor-to-ceiling glass facade supported atop seven semi-transparent concrete-and-glass pavilions. Additionally, Pritzker Prize–winning architect Renzo Piano was hired to redesign the adjoining landmark 1938 art deco May Company department store building as the home of the Academy Museum of Motion Pictures, slated to open by 2022.

Visitors enter the boldly imagined campus through the **BP Grand Entrance,** an open-air pavilion featuring landscaped piazzas dominated by artist Chris Burden's "Urban Light," comprising 202 restored antique cast-iron street lamps from Los Angeles neighborhoods. To the west is the **Broad Contemporary Art Museum.** The latter's 60,000 square feet (5,574 sq m) of exhibition space include "Band," one of two monumental Richard Serra sculptures of contoured weathered steel. In keeping with the eclectic nature of modern art, the new collection runs a broad gamut from the whimsical "Michael Jackson and Bubbles" and "Balloon Dog

(Blue)" by Jeff Koons to iconic Roy Lichtenstein posters, Jean-Michel Basquiat graffiti art, and Cindy Sherman's offbeat portrait photography. Part of the fun is scaling the lipstick-red external staircase to the building's third floor.

Levitated Mass: The most monumental of LACMA's outdoor artworks is this 150-million-year-

How to Visit LACMA

The best time to visit LACMA is on a Friday evening, when the museum is open late and a free jazz concert thrums. The museum also hosts Latin Sounds on Saturday evenings and a classical concert series on Sunday evenings. During blockbuster exhibitions, the museum can become quite congested; if you want to see one of these shows, be sure to make a reservation.

The bulk of the collection will be housed in the David Geffen Galleries, with a new theater on the south side of Wilshire Boulevard providing an auditorium with an ambitious calendar. Its weekend film series (tel 323-857-6010) is the place for film buffs. There are also two new cafeterias, plus a research center, restaurant, and library (by appt. only).

old, 340-ton (308 tonne) granite megalith suspended above a 456-foot-long (139 m) concrete slot in a vast sand-covered space reminiscent of the desert, to the north of the Lynda and Stewart Resnick Exhibition Pavilion. Installed in 2012, "Levitated Mass" was originally conceived by conceptual artist Michael Heizer in 1969, but stymied by the sheer difficulties of transporting such a massive boulder. A 206-wheel,

294-foot-long (89.6 m) trailer had to be built, powered by six trucks pushing and pulling simultaneously to haul the boulder on its 105-mile (169 km) Homeric journey to LACMA! Visitors walk down the slot, which descends beneath the boulder and ascends the other side, forcing you into a sublime encounter as you stand under one of the largest megaliths to be moved since ancient times.

David Geffen Galleries: In late 2020, demolition began of the outdated Ahmanson, Hammer, Art of the Americas buildings and Bing Center. The four buildings will

---

INSIDER TIP:
Visiting LACMA with kids? Head to the Boone Children's Gallery, and check out the Family Art Class schedule on the LACMA website.

—CHRISTOPHER P. BAKER
National Geographic author

---

be replaced by the David Geffen Galleries, expected to open in early 2024 (LACMA will remain open during construction, showcasing its works in BCAM and the Resnick Pavilion; see *www.buildinglacma.org* for updates). Named for philanthropist David Geffen, who pledged $150 million toward construction, the 26 elevated, single-level galleries will have a floor-to-ceiling glass perimeter and be supported by seven semi-transparent pedestal structures housing cafés, a restaurant, a wine bar, and a theater.

With its amorphous horizontal layout and no back or front, the new galleries give every culture equal accessibility and focus. LACMA is known for its extraordinary wealth of Far Eastern, European, African, and American art, but it is the collection of Indian and Southeast Asian art that best reflects LACMA's curatorial brilliance. Its remarkable collection of Korean art is said to be the best in the world outside of Korea itself. Plus, the world-renowned Madina Collection of Islamic Art spanning works from the 7th through 19th centuries is one of the world's preeminent Islamic holdings, and includes a number of rare masterpieces. The ancient world is also well represented, including an outstanding pre-Columbian collection from ancient Mexico. LACMA is also a trove of ancient Near Eastern art: Among its treasures are silver vessels, large Assyrian stone reliefs, and prehistoric Iranian pottery.

To appreciate just how far artists have journeyed from their aesthetic forebears, take a look at the majestic collection of European painting and sculpture. Look for Rosso Fiorentino's "Allegory of Salvation" (1521), portraying the young St. John, who has fallen faint at his mother's side after learning of her terrible prophecy of what will befall the Christ Child. An ever still spot is in front of Rembrandt's stunning "Raising of Lazarus" (1630). So much is captured in the moment the picture portrays, and the artist has rendered it so skillfully, that gazing in silence seems the only appropriate reaction to such mastery.

The importance of some of the work in LACMA's Art of the Americas collection has been open to question: Exhibits range from Alison Saar's indulgent "Sledge Hammer Mamma" to moments of brilliance, such as Ed Kienholz's "Back Seat Dodge '38" (deemed lurid in the 1960s, when museum trustees voted to ban it, today it seems, well, *quaintly* lurid). The pantheon of contemporary notables represented includes Picasso and David Hockney, whose works here include "Mulholland Drive." Other key works include Winslow Homer's "The Cotton Pickers," painted in 1876, just before the artist retired to New England. Homer's experience as a correspondent-illustrator during the Civil War for *Harper's Weekly* propelled his rendering of rural America beyond the romantic pictures that were so preponderant at the time. A joyful American send-up of Michelangelo and Rubens is all over Paul Cadmus's "Coney Island" (1934). The work succeeds because it is fleshy, resolutely hoi polloi, and yet humane about it all. Also displayed are Arts and Crafts furniture and examples of work by Tiffany and others in the American decorative arts sections.

LACMA's ongoing effort to collect and display the Mexican modernists is represented by fine works by Rivera, Orozco, and Siquieros (see sidebar p. 93). Look for Rufino Tamayo's "Study for America" (1955) or Rivera's "Women Washing" (1925).

▪ "Band" (2006), by Richard Serra, dominates LACMA's Broad Contemporary gallery.

The Petersen Automotive Museum, one of the largest automotive collections in the world

LACMA's radical redesign also replaces the Cantor Sculpture Plaza & Garden, renowned for numerous bronze sculptures by Auguste Rodin (1840–1917), including "Jean d'Aire," "Jean de Fiennes," and the colossal Monument to Honoré de Balzac. The new David Greffen Galleries open up two-and-a-half acres (1 ha) of outdoor space that will feature new sculpture gardens to display such outdoor sculptures as Alexander Calder's "Three Quintains" and Tony Smith's massive 14,300-pound (6,486 kg) "Smoke."

Pavilion for Japanese Art:
At the eastern end of the complex is the Pavilion for Japanese Art, an eccentric and kitschy but perfect building for, among other things, the Shinenkan Collection of Edo-period screen art. Donated by philanthropists Joe and Etsuko Price, these scenes of nature—cranes flying, tigers prowling, roosters and hens foraging—have such a strong emotional impact that one leading Japanese art scholar confessed to having wept when he first saw them. That LACMA and the Prices agreed to build a pavilion with only natural lighting is a testimony to their good taste and sense of adventure. Particularly worth seeking out is Suzuki Kiitsu's "Seashells and Plums," painted, like almost all Edo art, without any preliminary sketching. As Price once explained, "He simply had to have the whole painting in his head before he executed one stroke."

Photography: LACMA's photography department puts on exhibitions drawn from its permanent collection of approximately 6,000 works, from the medium's invention in 1839 to the present, with works from the greats—Henri Cartier-Bresson, Walker Evans, Ansel Adams—to emerging artists. It also administers the Ralph M. Parsons Lectures on Photography series.

Around LACMA

LACMA merges easts into the **La Brea Tar Pits,** where natural hot tar still bubbles up from underground at the world's only active, urban Ice Age excavation site. Visitors can stroll the park grounds and watch excavations in process at a number of pits. The **Page Museum at La Brea Tar Pits** displays some of the million fossils recovered from the pits. These Pleistocene remains are between 10,000 and 40,000 years old. The displays chronicle the animal life of L.A. in the Ice Age. There are skeletons of the saber-toothed tiger, an imperial mammoth with 12-foot (3.6 m) tusks, and a Harlan's giant ground sloth, which once stood more than 6 feet tall (1.8 m) and weighed about 3,500 pounds (1,587 kg). Don't miss La Brea Woman, more than 9,000 years old. The Paleontology Lab is a must for parents who help on their children's science projects, and don't miss the eerily bubbling tar lake in front of the museum.

To LACMA's west side, the **Academy Museum of Motion Pictures** opened to the public in late 2021 in the historic May

Company Building on the corner of Wilshire and Fairfax. Reconfigured as a 300,000-square-foot (27,870 sq m) museum, it's dedicated entirely to the art, craft, business, history, and science of film, and the cultural and creative contributions that Hollywood and the film industry have made around the world. The Acad-

emy of Motion Picture Arts and Sciences' collection includes more than 12 million photographs, 61,000 posters, and 100,000 pieces of production art, with much of it on display here. A highlight is "Bruce," a replica of the great white shark in *Jaws* (1975), hovering menacingly above the main escalator. Architect Renzo Piano also designed The Sphere—a stunning, state-of-the-art 1,000-seat David Geffen Theater in the form of a globe.

Page Museum at La Brea Tar Pits

✉ 71 B1

✉ 5801 Wilshire Blvd.

☎ 213-763-3499

$ $$$ (free 1st Tues. of month)

www.tarpits.org

Academy Museum of Motion Pictures

✉ 71 B1

✉ 6067 Wilshire Blvd.

☎ 323-930-3000

$ $$

www.academymuseum. org

Reliving Hollywood's Earliest Days

Grab a bag of popcorn and sink into Hollywood history at American Cinematheque at the Egyptian Theatre (6712 Hollywood Blvd., tel 323-461-2020, www.american cinematheque.com). **The only local cinema that screens silent movies and early nitrate films, albeit on an irregular schedule, the theater is located in the heart of downtown Hollywood and is one of only four theaters in the U.S. that can project nitrate film. Recent screenings have included Alfred Hitchcock's** Rebecca, **which in 1940 earned Best Picture. The gorgeously restored Hollywood Legion Theater** (2035 N. Highland Ave., tel 323-792-7625, www.hollywoodlegion-theater.com), **just south of the Hollywood Bowl, hosts special film noir screenings of 35mm and 70mm movie classics, such as Fred Zinnemann's** Act of Violence **(1948).**

Petersen Automotive Museum

⊠ 71 B1

⊠ 6060 Wilshire Blvd.

☎ 323-964-6331

🕐 Closed Mon.

💲 $$

www.petersen.org

Farmers Market

⛰ 71 B1

⊠ 6333 W. 3rd St.

☎ 323-933-9211

www.farmers marketla.com

The last of the museums on Los Angeles' "Miracle Mile," the **Petersen Automotive Museum** is considered the world's premiere automotive museum. Totally transformed in 2015, it's as striking for its corrugated and illuminated red exterior encased by sculptural stainless-steel ribbons—perhaps the most stunning building exterior in all Los Angeles—as for its more than 250 vehicles from around the world. Twenty-five rotating exhibitions of curated cars on three floors trace the entire history of the automobile and range from "Hollywood Dream Machines" and "Supercars: A Century of Spectacle and Speed" to "Building an Electric Future." The basement Vault (*$$$$*), taking up an entire city block, holds the majority of vehicles, from a 1903 Cadillac and FDR's 1939 Lincoln Zephyr

(the first armor-plated U.S. presidential car) to Pope John Paul II's "popemobile" and a 24-carat gold anodized DeLorean. For car buffs this museum is a must, but even car cynics will come away extolling these wonders.

Farmers Market

About 15 blocks away from Museum Row (a pleasant walk when the weather is cool) is a place just brimming with the simple pleasures of life. Here, at the junction of Third Street and Fairfax Avenue, is a celebration of the pure sensual enjoyment of eating old-fashioned meals in a festive environment. The original Farmers Market is a complex of more than a hundred shops catering to your every gustatory whim. A 1930s counterpart to downtown's Olvera Street (see p. 93), it is themed, but in a charming way.

Originated by oil tycoon E. B. Gilmore in the 1930s, the market serves as a kind of village green. The phrase "Meet me at Third and Fairfax" is still synonymous with meals of ham and eggs, gumbo, fried chicken, fresh fish and oysters, Belgian waffles, gallons of "Joe," tacos and beans, giant peanut butter cookies, submarine sandwiches, Armenian grilled meats, pots of pasta in red sauce—you get the picture. The Farmers Market is what they call a "great good place" to be alone with other people. Some of those others may well be from the film industry. Director Tim Burton (*Beetlejuice, Batman*) is sometimes seen near the waffle bar, Clint Eastwood at Phil's Deli, and a group

The Ultimate Schmooze

If you are still hungry after the Farmers Market, a similar scene is repeated, around the clock, just across the street at **Canter's Deli** (*419 N. Fairfax Ave., tel 323-651-2030, www.cantersdeli.com, open 24/7*).

Located in the middle of Los Angeles' thriving Fairfax District, a hub of the Jewish community, Canter's serves up quintessential deli fare: bagels loaded with red onion, smoked salmon, and cream cheese; potato latkes; cheese blintzes; calf brains and eggs; *matzo brei* (a matzo-meal and egg pancake); brisket of beef; corned beef on rye; giant sour pickles; cream soda; and matzo-ball soup. The bakery counter sells outstanding fresh breads and pastries, but most clients prefer to dine in and be entertained by the waitresses' banter— a long-standing Canter's tradition.

Melrose Avenue offers an eclectic mix of restaurants, tattoo parlors, and funky boutiques.

of regulars led by director Paul Mazursky near Bob's Coffee and Donuts, near the east end. Stop by and give them a copy of your script. Bob's, by the way, makes about a thousand donuts a day.

Melrose Avenue

North of the Fairfax District, running east–west between La Brea Avenue and Robertson Boulevard, is a strip of ultimate urban grooviness. Melrose Avenue is responsible, among other things, for the resuscitation of Heather Locklear's career (via the hit TV show *Melrose Place*), for the popularity of Harley-Davidson motorcycles among film stars (via its Johnny Rockets burger hangout), and for $3,000 lingerie (via aptly-named Agent Provocateur, a specialist in sexy clothing "designed to intensify life's pleasures"). It's just so swell—where should one start?

One of the gourmet treats at the avenue's eastern end is **Blu Jam** *(7371 Melrose Ave., tel 323-951-9191, www.blujamcafe.com)*, which transforms from a casual café by day into a swanky bistro at night. For those getting a late start, breakfast is served until 5 p.m., and Sunday brunch is the way to refuel between bouts of shopping. The eclectic dinner menu is built around California cuisine dishes meant to share.

Farther west are clothing boutiques, specialty stores, and folk-art shops that sell affordable and interesting Mexican Day of the Dead works and painted tin *retabla* art. Despite its somewhat morbid name, **Necromance** *(7222 Melrose Ave., tel 323-934-8684)* is actually a curiosity shop filled with natural and historical curios, including skulls and skeletons, old cameras, beetles and butterflies, beads, and vintage medical instruments.

Nearby is the **Pacific Design Center,** a collection of 130

Melrose Avenue
🏔 71 B2

Visitor Information
✉ West Hollywood Travel & Tourism Board, 1017 N. La Cienaga Blvd.
☎ 310-289-2525, 800-368-6020

www.visitwest hollywood.com

Pacific Design Center
🏔 71 B2
✉ 7222 Melrose Ave.
☎ 310-657-0800

www.pacificdesign center.com

Beverly Center

🏛 71 B2

✉ 3rd St. &
La Cienega Blvd.

☎ 310-854-0070

**www.beverlycenter
.com**

showrooms offering furnishings by some of the best known designers in the world. The Center is more remarkable, however, for its three stunning, sharp-angled, dynamic, entirely glass-shrouded buildings—one red, one green, one blue—by Argentinian architect César Pelli. The behemoth also houses a branch of the Museum of Contemporary Art (see pp. 99–103). Back on Melrose, walk toward Robertson Boulevard for some outstanding tile, lighting, and furniture outlets.

longer concentrated in old Hollywood, but spread about—some in the Valley, some in Burbank, others in Culver City and other unsexy destinations. Hollywood itself, that stretch of boulevard so often photographed, has for years looked quite down at heel, the remnants of its glamour dulled by the reality of a gritty street culture. Although there have been, and continue to be, several worthwhile redevelopment projects designed to "bring Hollywood back to Hollywood," the

EXPERIENCE: Life on Screen

Paramount, the longest continuously running film studio in Hollywood, still holds some of the old magic. Two-hour guided tours of the **Studios at Paramount** *(map p. 71 C2, 5555 Melrose Ave., tel 323-956-1777, www.paramountstudiotour.com, $$$)* grant an exciting behind-the-scenes look at the movie business. You can also make reservations to watch the taping of a sitcom episode, and even visit the studio grounds on a VIP Studio Tour *($$$$$)*.

Audiences Unlimited *(tel 818-260-0041, www.tvtickets.com)* offers free tickets for a number of sitcoms, game shows, and talk shows, including *The Dr. Phil Show* (Paramount Studios), *One Day at a Time* (Sony Pictures Studio, in Culver City), and Disney's *Raven's Home* (Hollywood Center Studios). Tickets for some popular shows are available only from the show's website. To see *Jimmy Kimmel Live,* or *The Late Late Show with James Corden,* consult **1iota** *(www.1iota.com).*

Hollywood

🏛 71 C2

Visitor Information

✉ Chamber of
Commerce,
6855 Sunset
Blvd., Ste. 150

☎ 323-469-8311

**www.explore
hollywood.com**

From here, choose where to go next: north to West Hollywood, deemed the "Castro District of L.A."; south to the **Beverly Center,** the sine qua non of all galleria shopping experiences; or on to Hollywood itself.

Hollywood

For a city that is rightly considered the veritable engine of the world entertainment industry, Los Angeles is something of a letdown in this regard for most tourists. The reason is that the studios are no

results are often disappointing, thinly veiled attempts to unload second-class tourist souvenirs.

So, these pages offer a selective iconic tour of Hollywood, covering few of the oft-cited theme museums and restaurants but, instead, a few choice destinations, real places that function now as they did in the old days. Those seeking the quintessential "studio tour" with plenty of fanfare and special effects will be more than satisfied by a day at Universal Studios (see p. 89).

To get a good sense of "working on the lot," as studio life is called, the best place to begin is the **Studios at Paramount** (see sidebar this page). From Melrose, you can pause for a photo of the famous Bronson Gates entrance, with its palm trees nodding in the wind and fountains gurgling in the background; these are the portals through which the limousine drove in *Sunset Boulevard* (1950). This is also where Fred Astaire and Ginger Rogers danced and where Lucille Ball and Desi Arnaz literally invented the modern television production company.

For a relaxing, elegant lunch, drive north on Vine Street to the **Musso & Frank Grill** (*6667 Hollywood Blvd., tel 323-467-7788, www.mussoandfrank.com, closed Sun.–Mon.*), a Hollywood landmark where hip Angelenos take their out-of-town relatives who want to eat "flannel cakes" à la Philip Marlowe detective movies.

Sated, make your way along Hollywood Boulevard to the **Dolby Theatre** (formerly the Kodak Theatre), home to the annual Academy Awards ceremony; tours include the collection of photos of past Academy Award ceremony. Next door is the **Hollywood & Highland Center** (*www.hollywoodandhighland. com*), a glitzy eating and shopping complex with architecture that must have been inspired by Cecil B. DeMille's epic films.

Just down the block is a much older Hollywood landmark, the **Chinese Theatre.** Built in 1927 by Sid Grauman, this may well be the most famous movie theater in the world. While many of the old

Dolby Theatre
- 71 C2
- 6801 Hollywood Blvd.
- 323-308-6300
- $$$$ (tours daily)

www.dolbytheatre .com

Chinese Theatre
- 71 B2
- 6925 Hollywood Blvd.
- 323-461-3331

www.tclchinese theatres.com

Costumed characters interact with tourists for tips near the Hollywood & Highland Center.

Hollywood Wax Museum

🏔 71 C2

✉ 6767 Hollywood Blvd.

☎ 323-462-5991

💲 $$$

www.hollywoodwax
museum.com

Hollywood Museum

✉ 1660 N. Highland Ave.

☎ 323-464-7776

🕐 Closed Mon.–Tues.

www.thehollywood
museum.com

Hollywood Forever Park Cemetery

🏔 71 C2

✉ 6000 Santa Monica Blvd. (map available at office)

☎ 323-438-3833

www.hollywood
forever.com

Hollywood Bowl

🏔 71 B2

✉ 2301 N. Highland Ave.

☎ 323-850-2000, 323-850-2058 (museum)

🕐 Museum closed Mon.

www.hollywood
bowl.com

landmarks are gone, the theater's extensive patio will certainly take you back a few years, containing as it does the hand- and footprints of many legendary movie stars. Even Roy Rogers's horse, Trigger, is honored here.

The **Hollywood Wax Museum** lets you feel part of a red carpet event with its exhibits of movie stars like Halle Berry and Angelina Jolie shown arriving for the Academy Awards. It also has a horror exhibit, plus re-creations of scenes from movies like *Men in Black* (1997), *The Matrix* (1999), and *Star Wars* (1977).

No visit to Hollywood is truly complete without stepping on the sidewalk of five-pointed coral-pink terrazzo and brass-lined stars known as the **Hollywood Walk of Fame** *(www.walkoffame.com).* Orange signs mark the looped route, with more than 2,700 stars honoring luminaries in motion pictures, live theater, radio, recording, and television. The stars are inset along 17 blocks of Hollywood Boulevard (between Gower and La Brea), plus three blocks of Vine Street (between Sunset and Yucca). The Hollywood Chamber of Commerce provides a map, and its website has a directory.

More fulfilling is the **Hollywood Museum,** in the Max Factor Building, which has been restored to its original 1935 splendor. The museum is chock-full of mementos regaling fascinating lore of the Hollywood region and movie industry. The world-famous **Mel's Drive-In** *(tel 323-465-3111, www.melsdrive-in.com)* all-American diner is next door.

Late afternoon might suggest

a few quintessentially Hollywood outings. One is a visit to **Hollywood Forever Park Cemetery,** where Rudolph Valentino, Cecil B. DeMille, and other big names in movie history are buried.

When evening approaches, head to the **Hollywood Roosevelt Hotel** *(map p. 71 B2, 7000 Hollywood Blvd., tel 323-856-1970, www.thehollywoodroosevelt.com),* where the first Academy Awards were held, a location chosen perhaps because its investors were Charlie Chaplin, Mary Pickford, and Douglas Fairbanks. The Roosevelt has been revived in recent years, and its Cinegrill is a nice place for a martini and live music.

The perfect end to a day in

INSIDER TIP:

Don't miss the iconic swimming pool at the Hollywood Roosevelt Hotel. It was painted by David Hockney in the mid-1980s.

—MARY STEPHANOS
National Geographic contributor

Hollywood would be a concert at the **Hollywood Bowl.** Founded in 1922, the Bowl is the summer home of the L.A. Philharmonic, which offers an affordable evening concert series ranging from the classics to show tunes to star vocalist combinations. The season is also peppered with several world-class special events, such as the International Mariachi Competition and the Playboy Jazz Festival.

Visitors take in the view of the sprawling city from the balcony of the Griffith Park Observatory.

Just as important—some would say more so—is the scene at the Bowl. On July 4, for example, long-time box seat holders turn out for the "1812 Overture" and a fireworks display. Among them will be dozens of movie and TV stars and, often, the very cream of old L.A. society, men in white pants and bow ties, ladies in pastel linens and cashmere wraps, for the cool night air.

Bring a picnic dinner, or you will end up quite ravenous. Arrive at least an hour early to see the **Hollywood Bowl Museum,** where you can watch famous Bowl performances on film, from the Beatles to Judy Garland.

Griffith Park

The best kept secret in Los Angeles, far from being small or tucked away, is right under everyone's nose. Griffith Park, whose more than 4,200 acres (1,618 ha) make it the largest urban park in the United States, is five times the size of New York's Central Park. That the park remains undiscovered by many would hardly surprise its founder, Col. Griffith J. Griffith. For years, he attempted to persuade the city fathers to turn his 1896 bequest of land, once part of Rancho los Feliz, into the hub of a city-wide park system. (Of course, Griffith's circumstances at the time may not have helped his cause: The hard-drinking Welshman had just returned from a two-year term in San Quentin prison for trying to kill his wife.)

While previous Angelenos periodically embraced the park, only recently has it become a pre-ferred spot for weekend outings,

Griffith Park
🅰 52 D3, 71 C3, & 111 A2

Visitor Information

✉ Visitor's Center, 4730 Crystal Springs Dr.
☎ 323--644-2050
www.laparks.org

Griffith Park Observatory

🗺 71 C3

✉ 2800 E. Observatory Rd.

☎ 213-473-0800

🕐 Closed Mon., & a.m. Tues.–Fri. Laserium shows: call for times

💲 $ for Laserium

www.griffithobs.org

Autry Museum of the American West

🗺 71 C3

✉ 4700 Western Heritage Way

☎ 323-667-2000

🕐 Closed Mon.

💲 $$

www.theautry.org

with an estimated 10 million visitors each year. There are children's museums, a zoo, a museum for adults, a merry-go-round, and a place from which to gaze at the stars above and the city below.

Griffith Park Observatory: The renowned Griffith Park Observatory, is located at the top of Observatory Road, at 1,134 feet (346 m) elevation. As recounted by local historian Letitia Burns O'Conner, the colonel had been so stunned by looking through the Mount Wilson telescope that he proclaimed, "If all men could look through that telescope, it would revolutionize the world!" Griffith was long

gone before his dream finally came true here, in 1935. Since then, the observatory and its grounds have attained iconic status. Its exterior and the bronze statues of Galileo and company formed the backdrop to the famous switchblade fight in the James Dean movie *Rebel Without a Cause* (1955).

The observatory occupies a classic 1935 building and boasts 60 exhibits plus a state-of-the-art theater and even a Wolfgang Puck café. The museum on two levels is burgeoning with sensational exhibits on astronomic sciences and includes an enormous rotating globe in the main rotunda. The east dome holds the **Hall of the Eye Exhibits,** displaying a camera obscura; the **Hall of the Sky Exhibits,** in the west dome, focuses on the sun and moon and holds solar telescopes. The central dome forms the **Samuel Oschin Planetarium,** known for outstanding laser-light and music shows, as well as more standard planetary projections. The lower levels feature exhibits relating to deep space, and the **Leonard Nimoy Event Horizon** theater, with hourly shows.

Later, as the sun dips into the Pacific, the denizens of the City of Angels stroll onto the observatory's terrace to watch the horizon boil with pinks and reds and purples before it finally falls dark, winking with a million lights below and billions above.

"The Autry": The great surprise of Griffith Park's more recent additions is the Autry

---

EXPERIENCE:
Hiking Griffith Park

The best way to discover Griffith Park is by hiking all or part of its 53-mile (85 km) trail network. The 1-mile (1.6 km) **West Observatory Trail,** between Fern Dell and the iconic observatory, is popular. There is lots of shade along the way, and the elevation gain is gentle. Those with stouter legs and lungs should try the **Charlie Turner Trail** to the top of Mount Hollywood. The 3-mile (4.8 km) hike entails 650 feet (198 m) of elevation gain, but the view from the summit is worth it. More spectacular views await at the top of the **Mt. Lee Trail,** which begins at the upper end of Beachwood Drive on the western side of the park. The 1.6-mile (2.5 km) path peaks right above the Hollywood sign. Hikers should watch out for coyotes and rattlesnakes, among other wildlife. Information on trail closures and restrictions are available at the Ranger Station *(323-644-6661).*

Museum of the American West, formed in 2003 by the merger of the Southwest Museum, the Women of the West Museum, and the Museum of the American West. The center today comprises a first-class educational institution plus two outstanding museums featuring permanent collections and special exhibitions dedicated to exploring the life and times of American cowboys and Native Americans. Don't miss it.

The Museum of the American West was founded in 1988 with a $54 million gift from late cowboy film star Gene Autry (a bronze statue of "the singing cowboy" greets you at the entrance), and today has more than 500,000 artworks and artifacts from the American frontier. Totally reconfigured and updated in 2020, the galleries cover two levels.

On the ground floor, the **Art of the West** gallery showcases an eclectic realm of expression, and even includes a 1948 Indian Chief Roadmaster motorcycle. It abounds with paintings by masters from Frederic Remington and Charles Russell to Georgia O'Keeffe. Contemporary works include James Doolin's *Bridges* (1989), showing a graffiti strewn Los Angeles freeway overpass.

The **Ted and Marian Craver Imagination Gallery** explores how the West has been portrayed in movies, television, and the arts. Movie memorabilia include ricochet guns, faux-glass bottles that shatter but don't cut, and pistols used by Steve McQueen. A highlight is a miniature Old West town hand-carved by artist Gene Hoback. Also

here is the **Cowboy Gallery,** which examines the evolution of the cowboy, from the Mexican *vaquero* to Texas trail drives. Highlights include an extensive saddle display, plus buckskin jackets, cowboy hats, and paintings by Maynard Dixon and Newell Convers Wyeth.

On the top floor, the **George Gamble Firearms Gallery** displays an unrivaled wealth of Remington, Colt, Smith & Wesson, and Winchester firearms. The "Western Frontiers: Stories of Fact and Fiction" exhibition explores the role guns have played in the history of

---

INSIDER TIP:

To access the Autry's vast library and archives, visit its new Resources Center of the Autry, a state-of-the-art collections care, research, and educational facility in nearby Burbank.

—CHRISTOPHER P. BAKER
National Geographic author

---

the American West. Annie Oakley's gold-plated handgun with pearl grips is here, along with Teddy Roosevelt's 1876 Winchester and Gettysburg hero General George Meade's Remington revolver. The **Greg Martin Colt Gallery** hosts "The Colt Revolver in the American West" exhibit, with an entire section devoted to "the handgun that won the West"—the Colt 45 Single Action Army Model Revolver.

The **Journeys Gallery** explores the people and events that changed

Animals From Around the Globe

The **Los Angeles Zoo** at the northeast corner of Griffith Park, has been busily bringing its facilities up to international par in recent years. Its collection of more than 1,100 mammals, birds, amphibians, and reptiles now attracts increasing numbers of tourists. The zoo has experimented with evolving novel habitats. Chimpanzees of Mahale Mountains presents chimpanzees frolicking on an acre (0.4 ha) of grass and streams. Sea Life Cliffs, a saltwater habitat with underwater viewing of harbor seals, the Elephants of Asia enclosure, and Campo Gorilla Reserve are other popular attractions.

The zoo also specializes in rare and unusual animals like the Komodo dragon, golden lion tamarin, South American maned wolf, okapi, and indigenous Channel Island fox, although its hottest stars are several Sumatran tigers, including several cubs born here since 2005.

Los Angeles Zoo
- 71 C3 & 111 A2
- 5333 Zoo Dr.
- 323-644-4200
- $$$$

www.lazoo.org

Travel Town Museum
- 71 C3
- 5200 Zoo Dr.
- 323-662-5874

www.laparks.org

Live Steamers Railroad Museum
- 5202 Zoo Dr.
- 323-661-8958

www.lalsrm.org

San Fernando Valley
- 52 C3–C4

Universal CityWalk
- 100 Universal City Plaza, Universal City
- 800-864-8377

www.citywalk hollywood.com

the West in the late nineteenth century, including the changes wrought on Native cultures. Exhibits range from an 1850s California Stage Company stagecoach to Tlingit wooden bowls. Plus, the **Human Nature** exhibition investigates the interface of culture and ecology, and focuses on four California concerns—desert, fire, plants, and salmon.

The **Southwest Museum of the American Indian** *(234 Museum Dr, tel 323-221-2164)* draws from a collection considered second only to the Smithsonian Institution's National Museum of the American Indian. Spanning indigenous cultures from Alaska to Central America, it includes the world's largest collection of Native American baskets, plus some 10,000 ceramic items, 6,300 textiles and weavings, and more than 1,100 pieces of jewelry.

Travel Town Museum: For railroad buffs small and large, the park's Travel Town Museum is a must-see. Travel Town is home to 11 steam locomotives, a number of specialty cars (as in the Union Pacific's luxurious "Little Nugget"), and two operating diesel locomotives. A miniature train takes visitors around the grounds, and in addition to the museum's own historical exhibits and fire engines, there is a huge N-gauge model train track maintained by a local group of rail enthusiasts. It is up and running on weekends.

A different free train ride can be had by going to the nearby **Live Steamers Railroad Museum,** whose enthusiasts operate an elevated 2-mile (3.2 km) line on which 7-inch-gauge model trains run on Sundays.

San Fernando Valley

Earthquakes such as the 1994 one centered in Northridge have brought a certain notoriety to the San Fernando Valley, between Hollywood and San Fernando. This, the essential valley, is home to almost one-third of L.A.'s population and to one of the city's most popular attractions, Universal Studios.

The huge success of the themed **Universal CityWalk** has been something of a shock to L.A.'s self-proclaimed arbiters of cool. After all, the two-block-long congeries of neon and pop architecture is the kind of urban confection that most deep thinkers love to hate. The CityWalk entertainment and retail complex has become one of the leading destinations in the area precisely because it entertains people so well. The entertainment lies in three activities: eating, shopping, and people-watching. There are also street performers, including fire-jugglers, musicians, puppet masters, and all manner of eccentrics. CityWalk is eclectically hip enough to hold the attention of child, parent, and even the most jaded of eyeball-rolling teens.

Next door, Hollywood meets Disneyland at **Universal Studios Hollywood,** whose thrilling, action-packed movie-themed rides and attractions are visitor favorites. The Backlot Tram tour is the way to see the huge site and its dozens of movie and TV locations. A visit to Universal is an all-day affair, and not complete without spellbinding hours spent exploring the magical mysteries of Hogwarts Castle and Hogsmeade in "The Wizarding World of Harry Potter."

Mulholland Drive (see sidebar p. 72), which cuts between the valley and L.A. proper, is accessible from several of the north–south thoroughfares including I-405 and Sepulveda Boulevard. It gives breathtaking views of mansions, mountains, and the ocean, including downtown Los Angeles and the **Hollywood Sign** (www.hollywoodsign.org), erected in 1978 (replacing the original 1923 sign) and one of Los Angeles' most iconic landmarks. You can hike to the sign from the Griffith Park Observatory (see p. 86).

Burbank is home to a number of movie and television studios, including Walt Disney and Dream-Works. One of the oldest and largest in Hollywood is **Warner Bros. Studio** (3400 W. Riverside Dr., Burbank, tel 818-977-8687, www .wbstudiotour.com, closed Sun., $$$$$), where Casablanca (1942), The Maltese Falcon (1941), My Fair Lady (1964), Ghostbusters (1984), and Jurassic Park (1993) were filmed. Behind-the-scenes VIP tours take visitors through the studio's backlot streets, sound stages, film sets, and craft shops. ■

Universal Studios Hollywood

🄰 71 B3

✉ Universal City Dr. (off U.S. 101)

☎ 800-864-8377

💲 $$$$$

www.universal studioshollywood .com

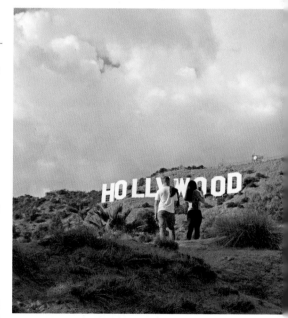

The iconic Hollywood Sign, seen from the trail

FROM DOWNTOWN

Almost every pundit worth his or her salt has cadged a cheap laugh over downtown Los Angeles. "An enormous village" is how author Louis Adamic saw it in the 1920s. A "harlot city," said author Carey McWilliams, viewing its "mob mad" yokelry intoxicated on cheap religion and bad movies. "It is as if one tilted the nation on its side and let all the loose nuts roll down into one corner," proclaimed Frank Lloyd Wright.

Downtown Los Angeles' glass-paneled skyscrapers reflect the city's glitz and glamour.

Much of this hostility derives from the fact that Los Angeles has little of a traditional downtown social scene. Yet even early on, L.A. did have an identifiable core, still present today, bounded by the Old Pueblo district to the north, the Santa Monica Freeway to the south, Central Avenue to the east, and the Pasadena Freeway to the west. So why all the jokes?

One answer may be that downtown L.A., either then or now, cannot be considered an American city at all, but rather a city of distinctly Mexican heritage. The early Spanish *pueblo* became Mexico's capital of Alta California after 1821 independence. It was, and is, a Latin American phenomenon. None has caught its essence as well as Mexican Nobel Laureate Octavio Paz.

"When I first arrived in the United States I lived for a while in Los Angeles, a city inhabited by over one million persons of

Mexican origin," Paz wrote in his 1961 masterpiece, *The Labyrinth of Solitude*. "At first sight, the visitor is surprised not only by the purity of the sky and the ugliness of the dispersed and ostentatious buildings, but also by the city's vaguely Mexican atmosphere, which cannot be captured in words or concepts. This Mexicanism—delight in decorations, carelessness and pomp, negligence, passion and reserve—floats in the air. I say 'floats' because it never mixes or unites with the other world, the North American world based on precision and efficiency.

Union Station

One might start a tour of Paz's floating world in the north by parking in the blacktop lot surrounding Union Station *(map below, Alameda St. at Cesar Chavez Ave.)*. Erected in 1939 (by some accounts on the site of an ancient Indian village), this was the last great train station to be built in the United States. A walk about its interior reveals many elements unchanged since then, from the massive wooden waiting benches to the muted earth tones of the designs modeled on Native American patterns.

Visitors might recognize the glistening travertine and marble interior from scenes in such movies as *Pearl Harbor* (2001), *Star Trek: First Contact* (1996), and *Blade Runner* (1982). From the station's rear, equally spiffy and super-efficient subway cars offer an air-cooled ride to Long Beach (see pp. 132–133) or MacArthur Park. Intended to revolutionize travel in the city, the new

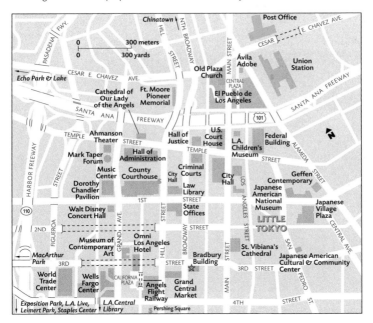

El Pueblo de Los Ángeles

🅰 91

Visitor Information

✉ Visitor Center, 622 N. Main St.

☎ 213-628-1274 or 213-485-6855

🕐 Closed Sun.

http://elpueblo .lacity.org

Metrorail system is estimated to have cost L.A. taxpayers a billion dollars a mile. Make use of it!

Outside the station, take a moment to look at the cityscape, the palms waving in the breeze, the old pueblo church beckoning, the cars zooming by on Alameda. This was the scene that millions of new Angelenos laid eyes on when they first arrived. To get a better idea of what they saw, take a historical tour offered by the Los Angeles Conservancy (*523 6th St., Ste. 826, tel 213-623-2489, www.laconservancy.org, $*).

El Pueblo de Los Ángeles

This 44-acre (18 ha) historic monument contains what might best be thought of as the sociological DNA of Los Angeles. In it are not only the remains of the historic pueblo but also several sites documenting the early presence of Italians, Chinese, Spaniards, and, of course, Native Americans. For these reasons, it hangs heavy with symbolism for so many in L.A., yet El Pueblo is nevertheless a place increasingly concerned with the present and the future. Its historic Roman Catholic church welcomes a new generation of Angelenos, learning the language and ways of a strange but promising land. Pretty high school girls practice folk dances on the Plaza Pavilion, calling home to mama on their cell phones. Toddlers squeal with delight under the blooming jacarandas, tearing apart giant pink clouds of sticky cotton candy proffered by street vendors.

Crossing Alameda Street from Union Station, you'll pass (on the north side) **Placita Dolores**—with its statue of Mexican actor, singer, and equestrian Antonio Aguilar—to arrive at the **Central**

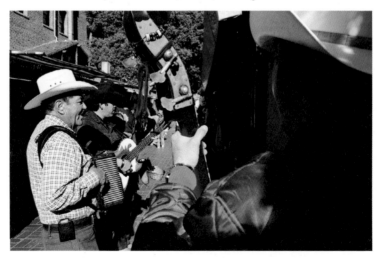

■ Enjoy lunch on Olvera Street and you just might be serenaded by a mariachi band.

"American Tropical"

Between the Hammel Building on Olvera Street and the Italian Hall in El Pueblo, you will find a remarkable mural painting by Mexican artist David Alfaro Siqueiros (1896–1974). Entitled "American Tropical," the work was almost immediately covered up after Siqueiros, an ardent trade unionist and onetime revolutionary (he fought to overthrow Porfirio Días in 1910–1911), was expelled from the U.S. in 1932.

Siqueiros went on to found the Center for Realist Art in Mexico City, eventually becoming one of the leading artists of 20th-century Mexico. "American Tropical" has in recent years been uncovered and "stabilized" by the progressive Getty Conservation Institute.

A guide to both old and new public art around downtown can be found by searching the Public Art in Los Angeles website (www.culturela.org).

Plaza, built in 1825–1830. The statue in front of you is of Felipe de Neve, the stoic *gobernador* who led the original settlers to the site in 1781; the one behind you is of his employer, King Juan Carlos III of Spain. To the northeast is the **Biscailuz Building,** which now houses the Museum of Social Justice (www.museumofsocialjustice.org).

Don't miss the outdoor shops along **Olvera Street** (www.olvera-street.com), named for Agustin Olvera, who fought against Frémont during the war of American conquest (see pp. 30–31). Closed to through traffic since 1930, Olvera Street today is a kind of pre-Disney ethnic theme park, complete with roving mariachi bands and guys who sell shaved-ice confections from rickety carts. What makes it so jolly today is its lack of slickness; it is a genuine anachronism. The food at the jam-packed street stalls tends to be pretty average, but the range of Mexican folk art (see sidebar above) and leather *huarache* sandals on sale here is hard to beat. Buy some before visiting the **Ávila Adobe** (map p. 91, 10 E. Olvera St.), built in 1818 by one of the first ruling families of Los Angeles, the Ávilas. (Francesco Ávila was an early Mexican *alcalde,* or mayor.) Many of its beams were made from cottonwood trees that once grew along the Los Angeles River.

Across from the Ávila Adobe is **Sepulveda House** (66 Main St.), where the visitor center on the first floor shows a free, short film on early L.A. history. The house, built by Señora Eloisa Martinez de Sepulveda in 1887, is in the Eastlake Victorian style—an early sign of the region's troubling aesthetic malleability. The center offers free morning tours, Tuesday through Saturday.

Leaving Sepulveda House on Main Street and walking westward, one can visit the **Old Plaza Church** (map p. 91), taking care to respect worship hours. Built in 1818 and restored and rebuilt several times since, it is worth walking through simply to witness how the church continues to be the principal portal into the existing society for new Americans To its southwests, the redbrick Brunswick

LA Plaza de Cultura y Artes

- ✉ 502 N. Main St.
- ☎ 213-542-6200
- 🕐 Closed Tue. & Mon., Wed.–Fri. a.m.

www.lapca.org

Chinese American Museum

- ✉ 425 N. Los Angeles St.
- ☎ 213-485-8567
- 🕐 Closed Mon.
- 💲 $

www.camla.org

Building houses the **LA Plaza de Cultura y Artes,** which celebrates the evolution and contribution of Mexican culture to the city.

On the south side of the park, the restored 19th-century Garnier Building (said to be the last surviving structure from the city's original Chinatown) today houses the **Chinese American Museum,** which is dedicated to fostering an understanding of Chinese-American heritage. The twin-level museum displays artifacts, photographs, period clothing, jewelry

sandwiched between Hill and Broadway just south of Chavez Ravine. The answer is simple: Chinatown has experienced a modern-day renaissance since celebrity chef Roy Choi relocated his first brick-and-mortar to the **Far East Plaza** (727 N. Broadway) in 2013. Since then, this unassuming shopping plaza, and Chinatown in general, have evolved as a pioneering ethnic culinary Nirvana among L.A.'s foodie crowd, with the tastiest dim sum west of the San Gabriel Valley (despite Choi's

Shifting perspectives: Los Angeles's new Chinatown was originally the site of the city's Little Italy.

Chinatown

- 🅰 52 D3 & 91

Visitor Information

- ✉ 943 N. Broadway, Ste. 208
- ☎ 213-680-0243

www.chinatownla .com

boxes, decorations, musical instruments, and ornamentation from years past to the present day.

Chinatown

Because the epicenter of Asian cuisine in L.A. has shifted farther east, to the San Gabriel Valley, many have taken to asking why they should even bother with the "old" Chinatown,

Chego! moving back to Westside in 2019).

Just down Hill Street is neon-drenched **Chinatown Central Plaza,** marked by the wildly gay **Gate of Filial Piety.** Both were built in the late 1930s. Inside is a statue, erected in 1966, of Sun Yat-Sen, the father of independent China, whose daughters later invested heavily in California banking and real estate.

On the Broadway side of the plaza is the **Phoenix Bakery** (*969 N. Broadway, tel 213-628-4642, www.phoenixbakeryinc.com*), packed at night with families from all over town buying almond cookies, gooey Rice Krispy bars, and, of course, fortune cookies. Across Hill Street, the drab Hollywood backlot appearance of Chung King Road belies its hip, under-the-radar art galleries tucked behind the facades.

If the north end of Chinatown still evokes the era of Suzy Wong and *Flower Drum Song* (1961), the south end feels more like something out of a John Woo film, with plenty of modern multistory mini shopping malls and ginseng parlors on every corner. In their midst, the **Thien Hau Temple** (*756 Yale St., www.thienhautemple.com*) stands out with its quintessential hip-and-gable roof. The Taoist temple is dedicated to Mazu, the ocean goddess.

Little Tokyo

If L.A.'s Chinatown feels a bit like an empty stage, Little Tokyo, the heart of the nation's largest Japanese-American community, feels like the third act in a Busby Berkeley musical. Once threatened by the tragic aftereffects of World War II internment of Japanese Americans, it now hums with a revived community spirit, not to mention millions in real estate investments.

The eastern anchors of Little Tokyo consist of two thriving arts complexes, the Geffen Contemporary at MOCA (see pp. 101–102) and the **Japanese American National Museum.** This thoughtfully curated institution occupies a magnificent modern pavilion by acclaimed architect Gyo Obata. Its dedicated to sharing 140 years of Japanese American history, from the first Issei pioneers of the 1880s to the World War II relocation camps and modern day culture.

Two blocks south and one block west, the **Japanese American Cultural & Community Center** has exhibits on aspects of Japanese culture such as bonsai and ikebana and is considered one of the best such centers in the United States. A must, if time permits, is one of the performances sponsored by the center, which often include world-class acts such as the Grand Kabuki of Japan.

(continued on p. 99)

Little Tokyo
▲ Map p. 91

Japanese American National Museum
▲ 91
✉ 100 N. Central Ave.
☎ 213-625-0414
🕐 Closed Mon.
💲 $$$$
www.janm.org

Japanese American Cultural & Community Center
▲ 91
✉ 244 S. San Pedro St.
☎ 213-628-2725
www.jaccc.org

EXPERIENCE:
Japanese Rituals

Get in touch with your inner Zen via Asian-style treatments and rituals in and around Little Tokyo. Combine shiatsu and reike treatments at **EZ Shiatsu & Massage** (*400 E. Second St., tel 213-680-4970, www.ezshiatsula.com*), then head for sushi in one of the Japanese restaurants in the adjoining Honda Plaza. **Yoga Circle Downtown** (*400 S. Main St., tel 213-620-1040, www.yogacircledowntown.com, $$–$$$*), on the western edge of Little Tokyo, offers a variety of daily yoga, alignment, and pilates classes. Visitors are welcome at the weekly Sunday morning services at the **Higashi Honganji Buddhist Temple** (*505 E. 3rd St., tel 213-626-4200, www.hhbt-la.org*).

BROADWAY WALK

Nowhere is the floating world of Octavio Paz's Los Angeles better illustrated than in the greater Broadway area, the undisputed capital of Latin L.A. You can best appreciate this part of the city by taking a walk through its heart. In the 1930s, this was the closest thing the city had to a "traditional" American city center, complete with big law firms, expensive restaurants, and opulent movie theaters. But the theater and other historic buildings are being reborn, much thanks to a long-term $1 billion revitalization plan that will eventually make Broadway traffic-free between First and Twelfth Streets, except for reintroduced streetcars.

The Grand Central Market offers fresh food and small eateries in an informal, authentic setting.

Having parked at Third Street and Broadway, start at the **Bradbury Building** ❶ *(304 S. Broadway, www.laconservancy.org)*, the extraordinary 1893 structure now best known for its appearance in the movie *Blade Runner* (1982). Behind its Romanesque exterior, the light-filled, soaring five-story atrium is a breathtaking Victorian architectural glory of glorious glazed brick, filigreed windows, marble stairs, ornate iron railings, and open-cage elevators.

NOT TO BE MISSED:

Bradbury Building • Grand Central Market • Angels Flight Railway • Museum of Contemporary Art

Across Broadway, the **Million Dollar Theater** ❷ *(307 S. Broadway, tel 213-617-3600)* was built by Sid Grauman in 1918 —one of the earliest movie palaces in the country—with a Hollywood baroque fantasy terra-cotta facade in elaborate Churrigueresque style, and featuring bison heads and naked maidens strumming lyres. It now screens a wide range of classic and popular films.

Walk south on Broadway to reach the back entrance to the **Grand Central Market** ❸ *(317 S. Broadway, www.grandcentralmarket. com)*, where all manner of foodstuffs, both raw and cooked, are for sale. Try the tasty El Salvadoran *pupusas* (stuffed tortillas) at Sarita's Pupuseria, or stand in line at the old-fashioned China Café, where you can get a plate of traditional fried rice. On the second floor, past the bargain spices at Del Rey Productos Latinos, is the Tropical Zone, where you can buy any of a hundred different combinations of fresh juices. Sitting in the Grand Central Market watching everybody eat reaffirms what writer Carey McWilliams

observed about Los Angeles in 1932: The city "is a nation of munchers. In L.A., no one misses a meal."

Cross Hill Street from the market to the **Angels Flight Railway** ❹ *(www.angelsflight .com)*, a beautifully restored 1901 funicular, which will whisk you up historic **Bunker Hill** to **California Plaza** on Grand Avenue. To the north, next to the **Omni Los Angeles** hotel, is the **Museum of Contemporary Art** ❺ (see pp. 99–101), and in the distance is the Walt Disney Concert Hall and Music Center (see p. 103), home

See also area map p. 91
➤ Bradbury Building
🕐 1 hour
↔ 1 mile (1.6 km)
➤ L.A. Central Library

Angels Flight Railway, which has two cars, began operation on a different site in 1901.

to the renowned L.A. Philharmonic and the L.A. Opera.

Circular steps lead to the sun-filled **Watercourt at California Plaza,** a lunch spot with entertainment provided by syncopated water spouts and fountains. Across Grand is the **Wells Fargo Center** *(333 S. Grand)* ❻, with its sharp-angled twin towers clad in rust-colored granite, and where several large pieces of public art include works by Louise Nevelson, Robert Graham, and Jean Dubuffet. Notable are Graham's bronze nudes adorning a network of pools and fountains. The **Wells Fargo History Museum** *(333 S. Grand Ave., tel 213-253-7166, www.wellsfargohistory.com)* houses a perfectly preserved 19th-century stagecoach.

Go down the escalator to Hope Street, past the "Four Arches" sculpture, and south one block on Hope Street to the **Bunker Hill Steps** ❼, L.A.'s version of the Spanish Steps in Rome. At the top is the highly symbolic sculpture by Robert Graham entitled "Source Figure" (1992). Down the steps and

through the lush landscaping is the pride of modern downtowners, the restored **L.A. Public Library** ❽ *(630 W. 5th St., tel 213-228-7000, www.lapl.org)*. Designed by Bertram Goodhue, who also worked on Caltech and Balboa Park, the building displays many elements that might be called neo-Byzantine, neo-Spanish, or neo-Egyptian. Inside the second-floor rotunda is a chandelier representing the solar system, and a 1933 mural by Dean Cornwell depicting the romance of L.A.'s past.

Outside, the art deco sculptures of Homer, St. John, Shakespeare, and others are by Lee Lawrie, best known for his sculpted main entrance to the RCA building in New York's Rockefeller Center. The **Maguire Gardens** to the west have been restored to Goodhue's basic design, embellished by modern elements, including the Grotto Fountain.

The L.A. Conservancy *(523 W. 6th St., tel 213-623-2489, www.laconservancy.org)* offers many reasonably priced walking tours.

Return to First Street to find **Fugetsu-do** *(315 E. 1st St., tel 213-625-8595, www.fugetsu-do.com),* a traditional Japanese candy store that still uses antique wooden forms to press sweets into delicate patterns. In **Japanese Village Plaza** *(map p. 91, www.japanesevillageplaza. net),* near the intersection of First Street and Central Avenue, you can experience several Japanese culinary pleasures. Ramen Maruya *(www.ramenmaruyala.com)* is a traditional noodle house specializing in authentic ramen. After dinner, pop into the nearby Mikawaya Mochi for traditional Japanese ice cream and *wagashi* pastries.

Museum of Contemporary Art

It has often been observed that when young artists want to make a name for themselves, they go to Manhattan. When they want to make art, however, they go to L.A., where the lack of a clear arts hierarchy and a less corporate culture has always made dreaming a respected art form in itself. But it was not until 1984, when MOCA opened, that L.A. had the clout, the will, and the money from younger patrons that are all necessary to make a modern art museum successful. Fueled by generous contributions from Hollywood's younger moguls, MOCA has quickly established itself as an institution with which to be reckoned, amassing in just a few years the most prestigious collection of postwar art in the western United States.

The works are displayed in the Geffen Contemporary at MOCA

(see pp. 101–102) and the main MOCA campus itself, two red sandstone pavilions on Grand Avenue, north of California Plaza (the MOCA Gallery at the Pacific Design Center closed in 2019). While it pays to phone for an exhibition schedule, the cavernous Geffen ensures that some of the museum's permanent collection remains on display for at least part of the year.

The best strategy for seeing the two main facilities (one ticket admits you to both) is to start in Little Tokyo at the Geffen, where

Museum of Contemporary Art (MOCA)

🄰 91

✉ MOCA Grand Avenue, 250 S. Grand Ave.

☎ 213-626-6222

🕐 Closed Tues. & Wed.

💲 $$$ (ticket valid for all venues). Free Thurs. 5 p.m.–8 p.m.

www.moca.org

Arts Sponsor

Movie mogul, record producer, and philanthropist, **David Geffen** (1943–) is one of the most powerful people in show business and one of the greatest art collectors in the world (see pp. 101–102). Along with Steven Spielberg and Jeffrey Katzenberg, Geffen formed DreamWorks in 1994. But he was already famous as the money behind *Cats, Dreamgirls, Little Shop of Horrors,* and many other Broadway hits, as well as the producer of such music icons as Bob Dylan, Janis Joplin, the Eagles, and John Lennon. He has channeled much of his billion-dollar-plus fortune into modern American art, a private collection that runs the gamut from Jackson Pollack and Jasper Johns to Willem de Kooning and Robert Rauschenberg.

---

you can buy your ticket and enjoy the capacious, light-filled building before eating lunch at one of the affordable restaurants over on First Street. Then walk or drive over to MOCA *(parking available in the garage under California Plaza).* If you are more interested in the MOCA building, designed by Japanese architect Arata Isozaki, reverse the order. But you may then regret that you spent too much time in MOCA's ill-lit exhibition space when you could have lingered at the Geffen.

MOCA's core collection was procured by the museum trustees in 1984 from Giuseppe and Giovanna Panza; by most

Neon!

Gas and glass come together at the Museum of Neon Art *(tel 213-489-9918, 216 S. Brand Blvd., www.neonmona.org),* **in Glendale's Culture Arts District. MONA offers popular workshops and nighttime neon walks, plus cruises of Hollywood and downtown in an old double-decker London bus, as well as the Lumens Project to restore and relight historic neon signs across the metropolis.**

critical measures, the acquisition is considered a coup. Among the 80 pieces in the Panza collection are works by Robert Rauschenberg, Mark Rothko, Roy Lichtenstein, and Claes Oldenberg. The latter's installation piece "The Store" (1961–62) grounds the collection in the 1960s, in this case underscoring the era's emergent genres of pop art and "happening" art. Lichtenstein's "Man With Folded Arms" (1962) shows the fullness of the Panzas' taste, opting for a subdued, almost

woodblock-print illustration rather than one of the artist's more over-the-top, comic-book-style works.

The museum has aggressively entered the fray over photographic art, scooping up 2,000 prints in 1995 alone. This makes for one of its best standing displays—the works of Larry Clark, known most recently for his disturbing film *Kids* (1995). In a series of 50 black-and-white photos taken in 1980, Clark, in pieces such as "Tulsa," documented the world of young white Texas outcasts: among them drug addicts, boozers, and gun freaks. MOCA's willingness to provoke is also typified by its 2019 purchase of Zoe Leonard's "Wax Anatomical Model" gelatin print.

In 1989, MOCA received perhaps its single most discerning collection, 18 works of sculpture, painting, and drawing from Rita and Taft Schreiber. Two bronze figures by Alberto Giacometti, "Tall Figure II" and "Tall Figure III" (1960), are at its heart; redolent of the Etruscan-era *Uomo sull'Ambras* found in Italy's oldest towns, the delicate forms cast one of mankind's oldest fears—that of evaporating in sunlight—and render it permanent. Some of the other pieces from the Schreibers are by Alexander Calder, Arshile Gorky, Joan Miró, Piet Mondrian, and Jackson Pollock.

The **Scott D. F. Spiegel Collection** is more problematic, perhaps reflecting the fact that some members of this group of "emerging artists" are still alive. The works by Jean-Michel Basquiat, with their icons of urban tribalism, are still vexing: Were they the work of a genius whose life was cut tragically

INSIDER TIP:

Use the Advanced
Parking System lot on
First Street and Central
Avenue, which is cheap
and open 24/7. But
remember, the Geffen
is closed on Tuesdays
and Wednesdays.

—DANIELLE FISHER
National Geographic contributor

short, or was it simply Basquiat's
mentor Andy Warhol's longest-
running joke? Robert Longo's series
of falling men surely provokes ("It
makes me want to choke him,"
was one recent comment), as does
Susan Rothenberg's "The Hulk."

To its credit, MOCA has made a
strong commitment to site-specific
artworks, something requiring
an enormous effort in audience

education. This has created a
platform for the works of Robert
Irwin.

Irwin is principally concerned with
the manipulation of light and
space, as his seminal garden at the
Getty illustrates (see p. 66).

**Geffen Contemporary at
MOCA:** Unlike its brother on
the hill, the Geffen Contemporary is free from the obligations
of being an institutional show-
place. Named for its mogul-
contributor David Geffen (see
sidebar p. 99), this is a more
flexible venue, its size and light
allowing for the accommoda-
tion of large-scale works. Initially
dubbed the "Temporary Contemporary," the giant old warehouse, just up the street from
the Japanese American National
Museum, has taken on a life of
its own in recent years, often
outperforming MOCA itself.

**Geffen Contem-
porary
at MOCA**

🏛 91

✉ 152 N. Central
Ave.

☎ 213-626-6222

▪ **MOCA is L.A.'s only museum devoted entirely to modern art.**

One major exhibition featured the works of sculptor Richard Serra. A Californian who worked in Paris and Florence before settling in New York, Serra works primarily with sheet steel, which he uses to produce large-scale minimalist works—giant cubes of steel plates leaning against each other and acres of sheet metal winding around city blocks. Usually encountered outdoors as public art, Serra's works take on a strangely fragile quality at the Geffen.

Similarly, L.A. performance artist Chris Burden, known for shooting himself and hammering nails through his hands—and recording the whole affair—has a rare permanent exhibit here, a whimsical piece entitled "Exposing the Foundations of the Museum," which he did with pick and shovel.

The Geffen has also expanded MOCA's ability to present architectural subjects, as in its successful "Blueprints for Modern Living: The History and Legacy of the Case Study Houses," which highlighted an important theoretical architectural movement with L.A. roots.

In 2019, MOCA received a $5 million gift from trustees Wonmi and Kihong Kwon to transform part of the Geffen Contemporary space into the **WAREHOUSE,** a multi-use anchor for a new performance-driven series titled "Wonmi's WAREHOUSE Programs." This includes large-scale sculptural works and experiential installations such as Los Angeles–based artist Barbara Kruger's untitled monumental wall mural (2018) on the north facade. Asking nine questions including "Who is beyond the law?", "Who is bought and sold?", and "Who is free to choose?", it is considered one of the museum's curatorial highlights. The programs also include concerts, screenings, dance, readings, and a wide

The First Electronic Evangelist

Sitting in the northwest corner of Echo Park, just beyond the quacking ducks, is the historic **Angelus Temple** (*1100 Glendale Blvd., www.angelustemple.org*), founded in 1923 by the Foursquare Gospel preacher Aimee Semple McPherson. One part actress, one part evangelist, and one part entrepreneur, "Sister Aimee" attracted thousands to her church by using highly theatrical techniques to engage their imaginations.

The Works Progress Administration guide to California gives this description of the temple in its heyday: "The ceiling of the huge unsupported dome is sky-blue behind fleecy clouds, and light enters through tall stained glass windows. The temple has four robed choirs, several orchestras, bands, and smaller musical organizations, an expensive costume wardrobe, a vast amount of stage scenery, and a 5,300-glass communion set. Also in the structure are the technical room and studio of Radio Station KFSG—the 'Glory Station of the Pacific Coast'—the Choir Studio and the Prayer Tower, where alternating shifts of men and women have prayed in continuous session night and day since the Temple opened in 1923. A display of X-ray photographs and discarded crutches is offered as testimony to the 'healing power of prayer.'"

spectrum of other "community oriented activities." Here you also find a bookstore, café, and reading and workspaces with free WiFi.

The Music Center

The Music Center is the West's preeminent performing arts venue, offering a critically acclaimed, year-round program of music and theater. The center itself is worth visiting during a trip downtown; its public art includes sculptures by Robert Graham and Jacques Lipchitz, the latter perched inside an inviting water sculpture. Free tours of the Music Center and, separately, the Disney Concert Hall are offered.

The 7-acre (2.8 ha) complex has four separate halls. The **Dorothy Chandler Pavilion** is home to the L.A. Opera and the L.A. Master Chorale. The **Ahmanson Theater** presents large-scale theatrical blockbusters, and the **Mark Taper Forum** is a more intimate house for innovative drama. The jewel in the crown is the **Walt Disney Concert Hall** *(map p. 91, 111 S. Grand Ave., tel 323-850-2000, tours: 213-972-4399, www.laphil. com)*, designed by Frank Gehry (see sidebar p. 46) and home of the L.A. Philharmonic. Recalling the Guggenheim in Bilbao, this bold statement in stainless steel is one of the most acoustically sophisticated concert halls in the world. Completing the complex is the cubist-inspired **Cathedral of Our Lady of the Angels** *(map p. 91, 555 W. Temple St., tel 213-680-5200, www. olacathedral.org)*, by architect José Rafael Moneo. Replacing the old

■ The Walt Disney Concert Hall boasts some of the world's best acoustics.

cathedral damaged beyond repair by a 1994 earthquake, it has an adjoining plaza and gardens with a **Native American Memorial.**

Echo Park & Lake

A drive west along Sunset Boulevard to Echo Park Avenue will take the adventurous to a delightful, if often overlooked, section of old Los Angeles: Echo Park and Lake. Here it is possible to get an idea of what early Angeleno civic planners hoped would be the heart of the city, a kind of West Coast Central Park under the palms. Today the park is a center of the thriving Central American community. Strollers can buy colorful shaved ices, roasted corn, and mango sticks sprinkled with chili powder and

The Music Center
- 🅰 91
- ✉ 135 N. Grand Ave.
- ☎ 213-972-7211, 213-972-4399 (tours)

www.musiccenter .org

Echo Park & Lake
- 🅰 91 & 111 A1
- ☎ 323-860-8874
- 💲 $ donation for walking tours

www.historicecho park.org

Exposition Park

🅰 52 D2 & 111 A1
✉ 700 Exposition Park Dr.
☎ 213-744-2294

www.expositionpark.ca.gov

Natural History Museum of Los Angeles County

✉ 900 Exposition Blvd.
☎ 213-763-3466
💲 $$

www.nhm.org

lime juice. Pedal boats can be rented for an invigorating turn about the lake.

The 21-acre (8.5 ha) park hosts two yearly events, the Lotus Festival in July, and the Echo Park Rising music festival (www.epr.la) in August.

Just to the park's east is **Carroll Avenue,** one of the city's earliest Victorian neighborhoods. You can arrange a tour of the area through the L.A. Conservancy (523 W. 6th St., tel 213-623-2489, www.laconservancy.org).

A bit farther to the west, down Sunset Boulevard, are numerous panaderias, Latino bakeries.

Exposition Park

Just west of I-110 and south of the University of Southern California (see p. 107) stands a cluster of buildings and greens known as Exposition Park. Founded in 1872 as a place for agricultural fairs, it became a public park at the turn of the 20th century. At its center is the 15-acre (6 ha) sunken **Rose Garden,** planted in 1913. The park's two main attractions can be found on its northern edge.

Natural History Museum of Los Angeles County:

With more than 35 million specimens, the Natural History Museum of Los Angeles County is the second largest museum of its kind in the United States, outranked only by the Smithsonian. Faced with the prospect of seeing such a huge collection, you would be well advised to do some advance planning. The

museum's website is extremely useful, outlining upcoming exhibitions and talks and detailing much of the permanent collection. The museum has a wealth of child-centered exhibits, as well as reading areas.

Of all the museum's permanent exhibits, none brings visitors back as often as its hallmark "Dueling Dinosaurs," in the foyer behind the main entrance, the complete, full-scale skeletons of a *Tyrannosaurus rex* and a triceratops posed in deadly battle. This memorable exhibit had its roots in a decision by museum trustees more than 30 years ago to fund a series of expeditions to Hell Creek in Montana. By 1969 the venture had reaped a treasure trove of dinosaur remains.

INSIDER TIP:

During the week, visit the Natural History Museum in the afternoon, when field trips and school groups taper off and the galleries are quiet.

—CHRIS MAES
National Geographic Television production manager

Unveiled in 2011, the cutting-edge **Dinosaur Hall** revolves around a young adult *rex* nicknamed "Thomas" (one of the world's best preserved *T. rex* skeletons), a massive mamenchisaurus, bigger than a bus, and an armored triceratops created from bones discovered at four different digs. Thomas is part of the world's only *T. rex* growth series, a unique exhibit that also includes baby and juvenile skeletons. The hall is fitted with interactive screens and touch stations where visitors can handle genuine dinosaur bones. Innovative displays and mounting techniques bring paleontology to life, revealing never-before-seen details like skin textures, internal organs, and even stomach contents.

Another major component is **"Becoming Los Angeles,"** a 14,000-square-foot (1,300 sq m) exhibit that traces the city's human history from ancient Native American times through the Spanish mission era, the Mexican hacienda period, the early American decades, and L.A.'s emergence into a global city in the 20th century. The exhibit embraces an eclectic array of original artifacts, from Spanish colonial religious objects and weapons to Walt Disney's first animation workshop, built in his uncle's garage in 1923.

The museum's **Gem and Mineral Hall** displays more than 2,000 precious stones and nuggets, including one of the world's largest gold exhibits. The **Schreiber Hall of Birds** has avian specimens from around the world, including more than 400 species found in southern California.

Fresh from a recent remake, the museum now features the **African and North American Diorama Halls,** with realistic scenes of wildlife in their natural settings; **Age of Mammals,** profiling 65 million years of mammalian evolution; and **P-22**

(popular with children), the tale of a mountain lion that recently took up residence in Griffith Park. Finally, the recently renovated **Parsons Discovery Center** takes the current fad for interactive museum displays to a wonderful and unusual extreme. The 6,000-square-foot (557 sq m)

pavilion not only lets visitors touch dinosaur bones, mammal fur, and fish scales but also features a new exhibit—**Bugtopia**—that includes a live insect zoo stocked with tarantulas, scorpions, Madagascan hissing cockroaches, and dung beetles. It has many fascinating interactive exhibits relating to the world's most numerous creatures.

L.A. LIVE

Downtown Los Angeles is expanding southward on the coattails of massive projects like the $2.5 billion **L.A. Live** *(map p. 91, 800 W. Olympic Blvd., tel 213-763-5483 or 866-548-3452, www.lalive.com)* entertainment complex, near the L.A. Convention Center. Set around an outdoor plaza that hosts the annual X Games and pro wrestling events, the complex includes the 7,100-seat **Microsoft Theatre** *(www.microsofttheater. com)*, where the *American Idol* finals and other live music events take place, as well as the ESPN broadcast studio. Its other anchor is the **Grammy Museum** *(tel 213-765-6800, www.grammymuseum.org, $$)*, an interactive multimedia collection dedicated to the artists who have captured America's top music award since it was established in 1959. Across the street from L.A. Live is the **Staples Center** *(map p. 91, 1111 S. Figueroa St., tel 213-742-7340, www.staplescenter .com)*, an arena that seats up to 21,000 for various sporting events.

The California Science Center is one of southern California's most popular museums.

California Science Center

✉ 700 Exposition Park Dr.

☎ 323-724-3623, 213-744-7400 (IMAX)

💲 $$ (IMAX)

www.california sciencecenter.org

California Science Center:

In the northeast section of Exposition Park is the California Science Center (CSC), which teaches scientific and technological literacy in interactive ways. Encompassing almost 500,000 square feet (46,450 sq m), its many marvelous exhibits include the **Air and Space Gallery,** dedicated to explaining the principles of air, space, and flight and how humans design aircraft and spacecraft. Housed in a 1984 Frank Gehry structure with an F-104 Starfighter bolted to its facade, the gallery displays stunning exhibits, including a full-scale model of the 1894 Lilienthal glider that inspired the Wright brothers' flight, the Bell X-1 (the world's first supersonic aircraft), a Gemini capsule, and a titanium A-12 Blackbird spyplane. The **Humans in Space** and **Mission to the Planets** rooms profile past and present space

exploration efforts, from the Mercury and Gemini programs to the Viking 1 Mars landing. Visitors can also explore the *Endeavour* space shuttle in the **Endeavour Experience** gallery. The orbiter flew 25 space missions (1992–2011) before being donated by NASA to the California Science Center in 2012. The Science Center is planning to house all the galleries in a new state-of-the-art Samuel Oschin Air and Space Center, with the *Endeavour* and its external tanks to be exhibited vertically in its launch position.

The recently reconfigured and updated Science Center's second central exhibit is **Ecosystems** (in Edgerton Court). Divided into several mini pavilions that separately profile a kelp forest, extreme environments (from the poles and deserts to the ocean depths), plus island and river zones, and the Los Angeles environment, this is a high-touch, high-tech exploration of how living things function and survive. The exhibits dramatize how organisms defend themselves, reproduce, make energy, and control interaction with their environments. A highlight is a 188,000-gallon (711,657-litres) tank with leopard sharks, moray eels, lobsters, and other marine environment denizens that live among the kelp forest.

The **L.A. Zone** gallery looks at the ways in which human endeavor has shaped—and will shape—the local environment. Visitors can become urban ecologists and tackle such themes as how wild animals get by in urban settings and what to do with all our garbage.

In the **IMAX Theater,** a variety of science films are projected both three-dimensionally and at several times their normal size.

California African American Museum: Set at the eastern edge of Culver City, home to much of Los Angeles's African-American community, Exposition Park is also home to the California African American Museum, with changing exhibitions honoring the contribution of blacks to American settlement and culture, with a particularly strong focus on art.

University of Southern California

Just to the north of Exposition Park is the campus of the University of Southern California, where the architecturally inclined can enjoy an educational—and free—90-minute walking tour past several graceful Gothic- and Renaissance-style buildings. ■

California African American Museum

- ✉ 600 State Dr.
- ☎ 213-744-2084
- 🕓 Closed Mon.
- 💲 $$ (parking)

www.caamuseum.org

University of Southern California

- ✉ Exposition Blvd. & Pardee Way
- ☎ 213-740-2311 (walking tours)

www.usc.edu

EXPERIENCE: African-American Culture

About 2 miles (3.2 km) west of Exposition Park (see pp. 104–107), you'll find a trove of African-American culture at Leimert (la-MERT) Park. One of Los Angeles's first planned communities, Leimert takes its 1920s design from the two sons of architect Frederick Law Olmsted, who designed New York's Central Park. Although its property deeds originally prohibited minorities from moving in, a mid-20th-century black migration and a Supreme Court strike-down of the restrictive deeds flip-flopped the racial ratio. Today Leimert is a gallimaufry of African-American culture, with an evolved diversity of jazz, hip-hop, poetry, gallery art, shopping, political activism, and authentic African cuisine.

Try Soul food at **Dulan's On Crenshaw** (4859 Crenshaw Blvd., tel 323-296-3034, www.dulans-crenshaw.com), maybe ox-tail over rice, or baked chicken with black-eyed peas, candied yams, and cornbread muffins. **Eso Won Books** (4327 Degnan Blvd., tel 323-290-1048, www.esowonbookstore.com) hosts readings; President Obama, Maya Angelou, and Misty Copeland have spoken here. In summer, catch celebrity readings, book signings, and music at the **Book Fair** (www.leimertparkbookfair.com). The recently restored 1931 **Vision Theatre**—an art deco gem—is also now a leading performing arts venue for local talent.

To check for festivals during your trip, visit www.leimertparkbeat.com. If nothing is scheduled, a single-digit donation will buy you—novice or pro—a spot in a jazz or drum workshop at the **World Stage** (4344 Degnan Blvd., tel 323-293-2451, www.theworldstage. org), which also has ticketed performances. Or visit the park plaza, where you might stumble upon a jam session; it hosts a renowned drum circle on Sundays.

ARCHITECTURE DRIVE

Between 1920 and 1950, perhaps no single region in the United States produced as much first-rate modern architecture as did the Los Feliz–Silver Lake area of Los Angeles. Why this is so is still the subject of debate. Whatever the reason, few areas of the world seemed to grasp with such intensity the words of the leading Bauhaus architect Walter Gropius, who in 1926 declaimed: "Modern man, who no longer dresses in historical garments but wears modern clothes, also needs a modern home."

This drive takes in a selection of these buildings, still architecturally stunning, though it is perhaps harder now to grasp just how innovative they were when first built. (Remember that they are private residences, so look at them from your car or from the sidewalk.)

Travel north from downtown on I-110 to the Los Feliz Boulevard exit, then head west to Commonwealth Avenue. Turn right to find Raphael Soriano's **Schrage House ❶** *(2648 N. Commonwealth Ave.),* built in 1951. Mentored by Richard Neutra, Soriano was a modernist known for his experimentation with steel and aluminum framing.

Return to eastbound Los Feliz. Make a quick right on Rowena Avenue and a quick left on Lowry Road to see two houses by Frank Lloyd Wright, Jr., the son of Frank Lloyd Wright: the **Carr House ❷** at 3450 Rowena, and the **Farrell House ❸** at 3209 Lowry. While Wright's son was building these fine small private houses in 1925–26, his father had just finished four of his enormously weighty "cast-block" houses.

Continue south on Rowena, past Hyperion Avenue, to Glendale Boulevard and turn left, then right on Waverly to Nos. 2717–2721. Here, R. M. Schindler's **McAlmon House ❹** of 1935 reflects the architect's search for a style that could be judged "not by the eyes, but by living."

Return to Glendale and proceed south to Silver Lake Boulevard. Here, turn right, follow the boulevard to the left to a cluster of houses by Richard Neutra, who began developing the area into a modernist housing colony in the late 1940s. (Nos. 2250, 2242, 2238, and

> **NOT TO BE MISSED:**
>
> Schrage House • V.D.L. House • Daniels House • Alexander House • Hollyhock House

2232 East Silver Lake Boulevard are just four of the houses he built between 1948 and 1961.) The architect's own home, the **V.D.L. House ❺** at 2300 Silver Lake, was originally built in 1933 with funds from a client named Van der Leeuw. Tours can be arranged by appointment *(www.neutra.org).* The house has an interesting history; after a fire, it was completely rebuilt by Neutra's son, Dion, who added some questionable elements, such as the reflecting pools, while trying to outdo his father.

The easiest route (albeit longer) to the next stop is simply to proceed south on East Silver Lake to Sunset Boulevard, turning right to Micheltorena Street, where you will see two outstanding examples of houses designed in 1939 by Gregory Ain: the **Daniels House ❻** *(1856 Micheltorena St.)* and the **Tierman House** *(2323 Micheltorena St.).* Ain used space, particularly small spaces, in a particularly masterful way, "framing" a home's volume to accentuate capacities, both functional and emotional.

Also on Micheltorena are two houses designed by John Lautner, a Wright apprentice who attempted to create highly individualized modern houses. He often integrated water features and a garden into the plan, as with the **Lautner House** ❼ (*2007 Micheltorena St.*), built in 1939, and the **Silvertop House** (*2138 Micheltorena St.*), built in 1957. At 2265 Micheltorena is the **Alexander House.** Built in 1940 by Harwell Harris, it reflects Harris's unique blending of Craftsman concern for natural materials with the modular configurations of Neutra, who was his mentor in the early 1930s.

Return to Sunset and follow it westward past Santa Monica Boulevard and Hillhurst onto Hollywood Boulevard. Go past Vermont

Avenue and on the left you will see the sign for Barnsdall Park. Here is the last and most famous stop, Frank Lloyd Wright's **Hollyhock House** ❽ (*4800 Hollywood Blvd., tel 323-913-4030, www.barnsdall.org/hollyhockhouse, tour: $$*), a spectacular concrete block residence built for an oil heiress in 1917–1920. The wonderfully light and airy interior is still complete with its original Wright furniture. Tours of the house are offered daily.

The Los Angeles Tourism & Convention Board (*www.discoverlosangeles.com*) has a "Discover the Landmark Houses of Los Angeles" webpage.

FROM THE FOOTHILLS

Along the foothills of the San Gabriel Mountains lies a swath of montane forests, unique architecture, tremendous museums, top scientific institutions, and a lively cultural life. No wonder that famous people from all walks of life—from Albert Einstein to Jon Bon Jovi—have chosen to call it home.

Dotted with sage and live oak, the foothills of the San Gabriel Mountains form one of the primordial historic landscapes of California, redolent of old Spanish *dons* on horseback, padres nodding in siesta after Mass, *señoritas* with the local Matalija poppy behind one ear. With that as a backdrop, today's foothill culture, located mostly on the borders of the Angeles National Forest, can be thought of as a hybrid: part Midwestern migrant, part Latin, and part Asian.

Pasadena

At the center of the region is Pasadena, "Crown of the Valley." Founded in the late 19th century by high-minded folk from Indiana who wanted "to get where life is easier," Pasadena evolved as one of southern California's wealthiest communities, complete with a Millionaires' Row (south on Orange Grove from Colorado), a Valley Hunt Club (still private), and more debutantes than there are flowers on a Rose Parade float.

Although conservative, the city of Pasadena could be politically tolerant, putting up with radicals such as writer Upton Sinclair in the 1930s. World War II made Pasadena a more representative town, open to light industry and affordable housing.

Inaugurated in 2003, the Gold Line *(tel 626-471-9050 or 800-266-6883, www.foothillgoldline.*

The west entrance of Pasadena's City Hall, completed in 1927, culminates in a grand dome.

org), a light-rail system, now links Old Pasadena with Union Station (see pp. 91–92) in downtown Los Angeles and with other foothill cities as far east as Montclair.

The city has experienced a renaissance in recent years as a hub of commerce, education, and the arts. Much of the impetus has come from neighborhood groups and architectural preservationists known as "bungalow huggers" for their defense of the small Crafts- man houses that are a hallmark of Pasadena architecture. As a result, the city's **Old Town** (Fair Oaks Ave. & Colorado Blvd.) is one of the best examples of downtown renewal in the state.

To the east, you'll find the new **Plaza Las Fuentes** (N. Los Robles Ave. & N. Euclid St.), with a land- scaped watercourse at its heart. The plaza successfully merges with the historic 16th-century Italianate revivalist architecture of Pasadena's **City Hall** (100 N. Garfield Ave., www.cityofpasadena.net) and the Mediterranean-style **Pasadena Public Library** (285 E. Walnut Ave., www.cityofpasadena.net).

The ornate tile-and-plaster **Pasadena Playhouse** (39 S. El Molino Ave., tel 626-356-7529, www. pasadenaplayhouse.org) is one of the top stages in the area.

Gamble House: Built in 1908

Pasadena

⚏ 111 B2 & 52 D3

Visitor Information

✉ Convention Center, 300 E. Green St.

☎ 626-795-9311, 800-307-7979

www.visitpasadena. com

The Rose Bowl Parade in Pasadena is an annual parade held on New Year's Day.

Gamble House

- 📍 111 B2
- ✉️ 4 Westmoreland Pl. (off Orange Grove Blvd.), Pasadena
- ☎️ 626-793-3334
- 🕐 Closed a.m. & Mon.–Wed. Soft-sole shoes required (coverings provided otherwise)
- 💲 $$$

http://gamble house.org

by the architect brothers Charles Sumner Greene and Henry Mather Greene for wealthy industrialist David Gamble, the Gamble House represents the epitome of the American Arts and Crafts movement. One can imagine the satisfaction the Greenes might now experience were they to rematerialize some sunny weekend afternoon and surreptitiously take one of the meticulous and informative afternoon guided tours of their "ultimate bungalow."

With all the hype surrounding the Craftsman aesthetic (fueled in no small part by singer and actress Barbra Streisand's $250,000 purchase of a Stickley side cabinet), it is easy to forget that the original

impulse of the bungalow movement was rather mundane. It was, above all, an attempt to create an affordable, regionally appropriate architecture. In southern California, this means three things: a patio, a covered porch, and large rooms with no dark hallways. It is a form that peppers the landscape in countless stucco houses in and around Pasadena.

In the Gamble House, however, the architects were given the resources to explore the outer limits of naturalism, emphasizing simplicity of construction, honesty of materials, and a deference to the designs of Mother Nature. "In a sense," California historian Kevin Starr has eloquently written, "the craftsman bungalows were themselves planted on the landscape as arboreal forms."

With its Japanese-inspired overhanging eaves and wooden shingles, the exterior of the Gamble House certainly suggests a radical departure from the fussy Victorianism that prevailed in late 19th-century Pasadena homebuilding. Gone are the tiny, lace-puddled windows, the faux English gardens, the gingerbread crenellations above lintel and column. In their place are wide windows, spare lighting fixtures, and Japanese koi ponds amid river stones and creeping mint. One can almost hear John Ruskin and William Morris cheering in the background.

The Gamble's interior, however, may be the greater masterpiece. One highlight is the **Tiffany doorway and entry room.** The rear of the hall is the best place from which to admire the cumulative effects of sunlight beamed through stained glass onto an endless variety of wood and glass surfaces. The interlocking wood casements and panels become structure and decoration, harmonizing organically with the light fixtures that were inspired by Japanese lanterns.

The spare **master bedroom** on the second floor carries the Japanese nature theme forward. Finished in rare Port Orford cedar, the room gets indirect lighting via wooden light fixtures dangling on leather straps and embedded with abalone shells. The fireplace is done in an earthy brown—a stone cedar, in effect. The furniture is linked together by a repeating oval shape inspired by the hand-guard on a Japanese sword known as a *tsuba.* A door leads to three open-air sleeping porches.

The **butler's pantry** and its tile wall and wooden cabinets represent the pinnacle of careful hand craftsmanship, everything fitting as if it had grown together.

No tour of the Gamble is complete without a brief tour of its **grounds.** The old garage now serves as a gift store, well stocked with books on California homebuilding and reproduction Arts and Crafts tiles, lamps, clocks, and bric-a-brac. You can also buy a map of the surrounding neighborhood that shows the location of dozens of Greene brothers

(continued on p. 115)

The Rose Bowl

One of the world's most celebrated stadiums, the Rose Bowl *(Arroyo Seco Park, Pasadena, tel 626-577-3100, www.rosebowl stadium.com)* was built in 1922 to host the annual showdown between the best college football teams from the Midwest and Pacific coast. The 90-year-old behemoth is now a national historic monument and host to a number of special events each year. The Rose Bowl game between the winners of the Pac-12 and Big-10 conferences takes place on New Year's Day but the stadium is also the home field of UCLA Bruins football, scene of a grand Independence Day fireworks spectacular, and venue for a huge monthly flea market (the largest in California), with more than 2,500 vendors. The annual Rose Bowl game is preceded in the morning by the **Tournament of Roses Parade** *(www.tourna mentofroses.com),* held along Colorado Boulevard and featuring flower-covered floats, marching bands, and equestrian units.

ARROYO CULTURE

Stand in the middle of the sweeping Arroyo Seco Bridge and, instead of looking toward the mountains, look southward. There flows the old arroyo, down a cement flood-control culvert and on into the ocean some 20 miles (32.1 km) away. It was this landscape, wilder than it is now and certainly without the cement, that inspired L.A.'s unique turn-of-the-20th-century culture, the "arroyo movement."

Like their upscale brethren up on Millionaires' Row, the rustic bohemians who lived along the arroyo were transplants from the East, men and women who had come here, first tentatively, then with enthusiasm. But if the Valley Hunt Club types on Orange Grove sought to replicate eastern institutions, the rustics of the arroyo sought roots in the region's past, with its innocent natives and Spanish dons, its life lived close to the wild.

The acme of the "Arroyo type" was Charles Fletcher Lummis, an itinerant newsman who, in 1885, walked to L.A. from Ohio, sending missives along the way to the *Los Angeles Times*, where he was later to become city editor. Lummis used boulders taken from the arroyo (see sidebar right) to build his home, **El Alisal** *(200 East Ave., tel 323-222-0546, www.californiahistoricallandmarks. com, closed a.m. & Mon.–Thurs.),* now home of the Historical Society of Southern California. The floor plan was one of rustic simplicity, with a patio and every manner of native basket and blanket. By 1907, he had founded the **Southwest Museum** *(234 Museum Dr., Avenue 43 exit off I-110)* for the preservation and study of Indian folk art, and now part of the Autry Museum of the American West (see p. 88).

His friends were of like mind. Bookseller John Vroman, whose Vroman's Bookstore *(695 E. Colorado Blvd., tel 626-449-5320, www.vromans bookstore.com)* is still central to Pasadena literary life, photographed local Native Americans. The period's leading plein air painters took up residence just upriver from Lummis, rendering the canyon rock and sumac in faded yellow and pale sage. Painter Maynard Dixon designed Lummis's enormous hand-carved doors. His friend,

EXPERIENCE:
Reclaiming the Arroyo

The most recent resurgence of California's early 20th-century "arroyo movement" is found in **Arroyo Seco Park** *(map p. 111 B2),* where, through the efforts of city government and business, the old riverside habitats are being revived. Exotic plants have been weeded out and replaced with native coffeeberry, elderberry, and willows, and parts of the concrete arroyo have been redirected to natural streams and ponds. Hawks, killdeers, and mallards have returned. Contact the **Arroyo Seco Foundation** *(tel 323-405-7326, www.arroyoseco.org)* for volunteer opportunities that include planting trees, ridding streams of trash, and clearing trails for horses and hikers.

university dean William Lees Judson, whose stained-glass studios became a center of the local Arts and Crafts movement, even emulated Lummis's homebuilding techniques.

By the 1920s, however, Lummis's star had fallen. Los Angeles had entered the 20th century with a great surge of urbanity; the simple precepts of Arroyo culture could certainly no longer contain it.

Yet everywhere in southern California are remnants of Lummis's rustic bohemianism. It is found in the patio outside even the tiniest apartment or condominium, in the inexpensive Tijuana serape hanging on a restaurant wall, and in the "mission" roof tiles atop the cheesiest strip mall in the San Fernando Valley or Chinatown.

houses within walking distance of the Gamble and identifies several ultimate bungalows in other parts of Pasadena—well worth the drive. Please remember that they are private houses, to be viewed only from the sidewalk.

One nearby house, behind a shrub-lined fence at 645 Prospect Crescent, is **La Miniatura,** Frank Lloyd Wright's first adobe-block house. The famous architect once described it as a "genuine expression of California in terms of modern industry and American life." Unfortunately it is not open to the public.

Also in the area, on Grand Avenue, is the restored **Arroyo Hotel** *(125 S. Grand Ave.),* in its heyday a gathering place for wintering millionaires. Converted, it now hosts the U.S. Ninth Circuit Court of Appeals. Nearby is the **Colorado Street Bridge,** which sweeps over the Arroyo Seco riverbed and park. Once known as "suicide bridge" for the convenient height it afforded despairing financiers of the 1930s, the bridge is a focal point for preservationists.

Norton Simon Museum:

Though Pasadena had long nurtured its own art museum, it was not until 1974, when the brilliant industrialist Norton Simon entered the picture, that the city's museum scene finally came to the fore. It was Simon who agreed to acquire the foundering Pasadena Art Museum and infuse it with talent, funds, and, most importantly, his own collection of art.

Called "picture for picture,

Norton Simon Museum

🏛 111 B2

✉ 411 W. Colorado Blvd., Pasadena

☎ 626-449-6840

🕐 Closed a.m. & Tues.

💲 $$$

www.nortonsimon .org

▪ **The expansive sculpture garden at the Norton Simon Museum impresses in every season.**

the greatest painting collection in town—indeed the Western United States" by the discerning *L.A. Times* critic Christopher Knight, the selections demonstrate Simon's affinity for what might be called the "primary example." That aesthetic informs the entire museum, from its stunning choice of old masters to the bronze gods and goddesses in the South Asian section. Simon's dedication has been carried forward by his widow,

and breadth of the collection is greatest in the baroque period, with works from Spain, Italy, France, Holland, and Belgium. Francisco de Zurbarán's "Still Life With Lemons, Oranges and a Rose" (1633) is an outstanding example of the period, its sensuous rendering of oversize fruits approaching realism. The rococo is represented by 18th-century French and Venetian works by Fragonard, Chardin, and Canaletto.

Asian Art, New & Old

Housed in a 1924 building that was built in Chinese imperial style, the **Pacific Asia Museum** *(map p. 111 B2, 46 N. Los Robles Ave., Pasadena, tel 626-449-2742, www. pacificasiamuseum.usc.edu, closed Mon.– Tues., $$)*, a long-standing Pasadena institution, takes a rare pan-Asian approach to its exhibitions. Its displays have included Burmese, Nepalese, Chinese, Thai, and Japanese art complemented by

nontraditional showings of art from New Guinea and "Oriental" woodblock prints by Western artists such as Paul Jacoulet and Lillian Miller.

Visit the serene Chinese garden in the inner courtyard and the bookstore, and take a look at the small permanent collection, all well worth the time. Walk up the street to Plaza Los Flores for lunch or a drink afterward.

actress Jennifer Jones, who presided over the museum's redesign by Frank Gehry in 1996–1999.

The fine art collection commences with works from the 14th century. The choice of "Saints Benedict and Apollonia" by Filippino Lippi (1483) is indicative of Simon's eye for color, texture, hue, and tone. Robes enfold all but the essentials—only the strong hands and purposeful gaze of the saints are revealed. The museum likes to mix media, standing four gold panels by Giovanni di Paolo and Pietro Lorenzetti near the oil paintings of Raphael, Bassano, Cranach, and Memling. The depth

One can nearly smell the baby powder in Giovanni Battista Tiepolo's glorious "Triumph of Virtue and Nobility Over Ignorance" (1740–1750).

The museum's holdings from the modern period remain the envy of the American curatorial world. Paul Cézanne's "Tulips in a Vase" (circa 1890–92) is a wistful, light-filled evocation of a humble glazed vase and imperfect flowers, the biomorphic agitation of the leaves a reminder of the obviously hasty arrangement of the flowers. Monet, Renoir, and van Gogh follow.

The 20th-century exhibit also

holds all the touchstones—Picasso, Klee, Braque, Kandinsky. The bohemian woman in Matisse's "Odalisque With Tambourine (Harmony in Blue)" (1926) is at once bawdy and delicate. Picasso's "Woman With a Hairnet" documents the artist's fascination with the female form. Rodin's painted bronze *Little Dancer: Aged Fourteen* is a sculptural highlight.

Later in his life, Simon took an interest in Southeast and South Asian art. Fortunately, he was living in L.A. where the great curator Pratapaditya Pal was monomaniacally amassing the Los Angeles County Museum of Art's (see pp. 74–79) collection from that part of the world. In an age when so many Asian antiquities were flooding into American institutions, Pal was brave enough to play the role of dour editor, throwing out showier, second-rate items and investing in high-quality essentials. That attitude simply reinforced Simon's own picky tendencies. The result is a splendid group of sculptures, primarily from Nepal, Thailand, Cambodia, and India. The 14th-century Nepalese bronze gilt "Tara" is a favorite.

The **Garden Café** in the sculpture garden (closed during rains), part of a 79,000-square-foot (7,339 sq m) garden planted in 1870, is a delightful place of repose. The museum also offers a film series and lectures *(tel 626-449-6840 ext. 6906)*.

Descanso Gardens

Founded in 1939 by Los Angeles publisher Manchester Boddy, the 160-acre (65 ha) Descanso Gardens sits in a natural bowl at the foot of the San Rafael Hills, once prime food-gathering territory for the Gabrieleño Indians, who used the nut of the live oak as a dietary staple. Its unique location in a cool spot amidst hot foothills has afforded Descanso

■ **Descanso Gardens is an urban retreat of year-round natural beauty.**

Descanso Gardens

🅰 111 A3

✉ 1418 Descanso Dr., La Cañada-Flintridge

☎ 818-949-4200

💲 $$$

www.descanso
gardens.org

Gardens a remarkable range of plantings, from its internationally recognized camellia garden to its native plant garden. This results in a succession of year-round colors.

Begin your tour in the **Camellia Forest,** the pride of Descanso. Situated under the canopy of a 25-acre (10 ha) live oak forest (some of the trees are more than 300 years old), the camellia collection is the largest in North America, with more than 700 varieties. Filtered light and fertile soil collaborate to produce some truly remarkable specimens. Several varieties of the red Chinese camellia are the result of founder Boddy's tenacious negotiations with the Chinese for propagation rights.

The **Japanese Garden,** next, contains authentic Japanese structures and its own Japanese teahouse, garden bridge, and ponds. Not far away is the **Lilac Garden,** featuring some 400 of the fragrant shrubs, among them Sierra Blue and Mountain Haze, developed for the mild southern California climate. From the Lilac Garden, walk to the 5-acre (2 ha) **International Rosarium,** where

---

INSIDER TIP:

In the zen calm of the Descanso's Japanese Garden, take time for contemplation and a cool drink at the Full Moon Tea House.

—LARRY PORGES
National Geographic Travel Books editor

---

much of the work of the famous hybridizer Walter E. Lammert remains in such classic cultivars as Sunny June, High Noon, and Chrysler Imperial. The **Iris Garden** is a seasonal delight, as is the **Spring Show,** with acres of tulips and other spring bulb plantings.

The 8 acres (3.2 ha) of **California Native Plants,** developed with naturalist Theodore Payne, are well worth the walk. In the **Lake and Bird Sanctuary,** grebes and mallards are commonly spotted from a bird observation station.

The gardens provide a number of guided tours, both on foot and by tram, as well as plant sales and lectures. A delightful children's railroad takes families to the home of founder Boddy aboard a one-eighth-scale diesel train.

Other Botanical Wonders

The **Los Angeles County Arboretum & Botanical Garden** *(301 N. Baldwin Rd., Arcadia, tel 626-821-3222, www.arboretum .org)* has impressive stretches of Australian and African plants, tropical greenhouses, and herb gardens.

Farther out of the city, off I-210, you will find a sizable display of desert flowers at the **California Botanic Garden** *(1500 N. College Ave., Claremont, tel 909-625-8767, www.calbg.org),* with 86 acres dedicated solely to plants native to California.

Closer to Pasadena are the **Huntington Botanical Gardens** (see p. 122) and **Arlington Garden** *(275 Arlington Dr., tel 626-578-5434, www.arlingtongarden pasadena.com).*

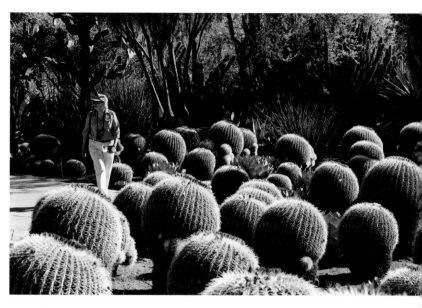

■ The Huntington's stunning Cactus Garden is one of the largest and oldest of its kind in the world.

The Huntington

Like its modern equivalent the Getty Center (see pp. 60–66), the Huntington represents nothing if not huge ambitions. And, like the Getty, these ambitions—research library, art collection, and garden—are realized with elegance, taste, and, for the most part, depth.

What makes the Huntington something the Getty Center should strive for can be described in one word: consistency. For more than 80 years, this brainchild of Henry E. Huntington, nephew of railroad baron Collis P. Huntington, has single-mindedly pursued excellence of the caliber found only in some of Europe's best-edited collections (the Musée d'Orsay in Paris comes to mind as one).

Huntington was a great booster of early 20th-century L.A.; his mark, in fact, is everywhere discernible in the routes of the modern freeway system, which still often follow the tracks of his Red Car line, a once popular trolley car system. (Urban legend—revived in the 1988 movie *Who Framed Roger Rabbit?*—has long blamed its demise on an evil oil company–car company lobby, but scrutiny reveals that, ultimately, Angelenos simply preferred cars to rail trams.) The Huntington was one of Henry's later passions, coming after his divorce from his first wife and his marriage to Annabelle Huntington, his aunt, in 1914.

The Huntington complex is set on 207 acres (83 ha) of breathtaking gardens. Its three art galleries and library preserve

The Huntington

🅰 111 B2

✉ 1151 Oxford Rd., San Marino

☎ 626-405-2100

🕐 Closed a.m. Mon.–Fri. & all day Tues.

💲 $$$$$

www.huntington.org

and show such masterpieces as a Gutenberg Bible, Rogier van der Weyden's "Madonna and Child," Gainsborough's "Blue Boy," Mary Cassatt's "Breakfast in Bed," and Edward Hopper's "The Long Leg." The botanical gardens range from an extensive collection of old roses to tropical plants and desert landscapes (look for the creeping devil cacti in the Baja California desert bed).

Each individual attraction is covered by an outstanding free brochure. Smart travelers will allocate an entire leisurely day to take in all the Huntington's sights, lunching at the restaurant near the Shakespeare Garden and having late afternoon tea as a relaxing finale. Bring a hat or umbrella in the summer—even with all that greenery, the Huntington can be hot, hot, hot.

The Bard's Blooms

The Huntington makes it possible for visitors to escape the noise and confusion of Los Angeles and commune with the Bard. Its **Shakespeare Garden**—which is located between the Art Gallery and the Scott Gallery—creates the illusion of a traditional English garden surrounded by forest. Poppies, marigolds, carnations, irises, pansies, and other beautiful blooms blanket a boggy dell that is at once pastoral retreat and literary lesson. This English-style perennial garden pays tribute to the Library's collection of rare editions of Shakespeare. Originally designed in 1959, the Shakespeare Garden aims to show the relationship between plants and the playwright's works. Watch out for the less obvious Shakespearean flora in the garden including woodbine, myrtle, lemon balm, and crab apple.

INSIDER TIP:

Take the primrose path in the Huntington's Shakespeare Garden and watch for plants and flowers mentioned in his plays. Small plaques quote the relevant lines.

—JUSTIN KAVANAGH
National Geographic International Editions editor

Passing through the **Entrance Pavilion** on Allen Avenue, bear right past the Palm Garden and into the **Library Exhibition Hall.** The high ceilings and large galleries in this building are a perfect place to cool off while taking in the remarkable Ellesmere manuscript, from 1410, of the *Canterbury Tales*. These pages, with their colorful border ornaments and renderings of the Wife of Bath, remind how far away is the world that first moved Geoffrey Chaucer to pen the great mythical yarns. Their foreignness is a reminder that the stories may well have origins not in Western civilization at all, but in the great Hindu tales of the *Pancatantra*, written about A.D. 200. Rarely does mere type prove so moving.

After looking at the Gutenberg Bible and admiring Audubon's exquisite illustrations in *Birds of America*, move on to the beaux arts **Huntington Gallery,** the onetime residence designed, with nods to the Mediterranean, by Elmer Grey and Myron Hunt. By

2006, the mansion, completed in 1911, had deteriorated markedly. Hence, the Huntington Gallery closed in 2006 and reopened in May 2008 after extensive restoration. This huge gallery contains the country's largest collections of British and French painting from the 18th and 19th centuries. But recognize Gilbert Stuart's "George Washington" (1797), the stern visage forever emblazoned on the memory of American schoolchildren everywhere.

Adjoining the Scott Gallery, the **Erburu Gallery** opened in 2005 as a showcase for the institution's growing collection of

Visitors admire Thomas Gainsborough's "Blue Boy" and other paintings in the Huntington Library.

don't spend too long in front of Gainsborough's "Blue Boy" or Lawrence's "Pinkie." The gallery has so many treasures, and with a few inquiries to the hovering guards, you might see some of William Blake's watercolors, which the museum owns in quantity.

The **Shakespeare Garden** (see sidebar p. 120) leads to the **Scott Galleries,** which trace the history of American art over three centuries. Here you may

American art, while nearby, Henry Huntington's garage has been transformed into the **Boone Gallery,** a world-class art venue for changing exhibitions.

On the way out, pass through the rose and herb gardens and linger for a while in the **Japanese Garden.** It has four main features: a formal garden, a Zen rock garden, a 19th-century Japanese teahouse, and an ikebana pavilion. Don't miss the view from the Zen

Getting in Touch With Nature

California the way it used to be is the theme of **Eaton Canyon Park** *(map p. 111 B3)* in northeastern Pasadena, an oasis of wildlife and natural vegetation on the outer edge of the vast metropolis. Cutting through the foothills of the San Gabriel Mountains, the canyon falls under the purview of both the L.A. County Department of Parks & Recreation and the U.S. Forest Service. So great was its repute in pioneer times that John Muir came to have a look at both the canyon and its eponymous **waterfall,** which the great naturalist described as "a charming little thing, with a low, sweet voice, singing like a bird." The park's other landmark is the old **Mount Wilson Toll Road,** constructed in the 1890s and now a strenuous hiking route that leads deep into the mountains. The fulcrum of the modern park is the **Eaton Canyon Nature Center** *(1750 N. Altadena Dr., tel 626-398-5420, www.ecnca.org),* which showcases the native flora and fauna of the San Gabriel Valley. Rangers and docents lead a variety of guided hikes.

**California
Institute of
Technology**

🄰 111 B2

✉ 1200 E.
California Blvd.,
Pasadena

☎ 626-395-6811

www.caltech.edu

garden to the house, where the zigzag bridge affords a rare Western insight into the spare, asymmetrical aesthetic of Japan.

Another must, particularly in spring when it is in flower, is the peach tree and stone pagoda in the canyon of the Japanese Garden proper. Intrepid strollers will also delight in the **Australian Jungle and Desert Gardens,** as well as the **Chinese Garden,** opened in February 2008 with 12 acres (4.8 ha)—the largest such garden outside of China—and a lake.

Caltech

Long synonymous with technological prowess, the California Institute of Technology produced some of the 20th century's biggest scientific breakthroughs. This was where, in the 1930s (while a fuzzy-haired fellow named Einstein rode around the campus on an old bicycle), Theodore Von Karmen pioneered the mathematical principles of aeronautics and where the Richter system for measuring earthquakes was developed. More recently, the subatomic particle dubbed the quark was discovered here. That the grounds should be such a marvelous repository of architectural finds makes them all the more worth a visit, perhaps on a Saturday afternoon between visits to the Gamble House and Pasadena's Old Town (see pp. 111–113).

Caltech originated as a vocational school in the late 19th century. It evolved along a master plan by the great architect Bertram Grosvenor Goodhue, who went on to do such memorable projects as the L.A. Public Library (see p. 98) and San Diego's Balboa Park (see pp. 152–156). Goodhue envisioned a dual-axis campus with portals, cypresses, and a central pool—something of the effect of the one leading to the Taj Mahal in India. Certainly Goodhue was into Spanish Renaissance, as indicated by his floral volutes and sculptured shells around the entry to the **Parsons-Gates Hall of**

Administration. Two remaining structures by Goodhue are the **Norman Bridge Laboratory of Physics** and the High Voltage Research Laboratory (now called the **Sloan Laboratory**). Both of these structures have been modified, but close inspection reveals many of the signature Goodhue touches: vaulted ceilings, water fountains, large expanses of plain exterior wall punctuated by regular patterns of windows. In fact, architectural detail plays a huge role in maintaining the campus's muted religious bearing, as in the old Alexander Calder sculptures preserved in the current facade of the **Beckman Laboratory of Chemical Synthesis.**

Campus social life centers on the **Athenaeum,** built in 1930 by British architect Gordon Kaufman. Again, a kind of eclectic Mediterranean style reigns. The **Beckman Institute** maintains the small **Caltech Science Museum** *(tel 626-395-2704, open by appt. only)* devoted to Caltech alumnus Arnold O. Beckman, a pioneer of scientific instrumentation, including a re-creation of the chemistry lab when he was a student. The college offers talks by visiting scholars, plus regular musical and cultural events *(tel 626-395-4652).*

Mission San Gabriel Arcángel

Founded by Spanish Franciscans in 1771 as the fourth in a chain of 21 California missions, Mission San Gabriel Arcángel has a rich heritage. It was from here that Gobernador Felipe

(continued on p. 126)

Mission San Gabriel Arcángel

🗺 111 B2

✉ 428 S. Mission Dr., San Gabriel

☎ 626-457-3048

www.missions california.com

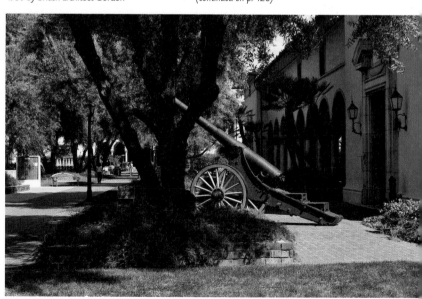

■ **Following World War II, Caltech's expanding campus became a microcosm of architectural styles.**

MONTEREY PARK

For travelers who consider food a destination in itself, the four-city area of Monterey Park, Alhambra, San Gabriel, and Rosemead may well be heaven. This part of the San Gabriel Valley, known as Monterey Park, is home to L.A.'s burgeoning Asian populations, many of whom come from Taiwan, Hong Kong, mainland China, and Vietnam. The result, as the august *Atlantic Monthly* pronounced, is that the "best Chinese food in the world is now being served in Los Angeles's new Sino-suburbs."

Even the most contemporary of Chinese restaurants in Monterey Park play up the ethnic decor.

It was not always thus. Until the mid-1970s, Monterey Park was just another of southern California's largely Anglo middle-class suburbs, where adventurous eating began and ended at the local taco house. Beginning in the early 1970s, however, a few Chinese immigrants began promoting the area's real estate in overseas Chinese newspapers. Loosened immigration laws made sales easier, and Hong Kong's imminent return to the People's Republic of China increased the heat on the middle class to move. By the mid-1980s, Monterey Park was 60 percent Asian, a booming Chinese-American suburbia with its own supermarkets, banks, and restaurants.

Travelers take note: This is not the Chinese food of your youth. While elements of the old "sweet-and-sour pork" menu remain, by and large this is the cooking of modern China, highly regional and very fresh. This means you must remain open-minded and willing to ask questions. While their employees may occasionally struggle with the vexing English language, most shops will have someone fluent enough to answer basic questions. But the watchword is *experiment*, rather than ordering as though you were taking a legal deposition. Unless you are into bird's-nest soup and platypus beaks, the food here is inexpensive, so try several different dishes.

Ready? To get the full range of the experience, start at **San Gabriel Square,** once a drive-in theater and now lined with restaurants and dubbed the Great Mall of China. A good introduction to Taiwanese cuisine can be found here at **Happy Family** *(140 W. Valley Blvd., tel 626-282-8986),* where L.A. food guru Jonathan Gold recommends the pan-fried string beans and the home-style tofu. The less adventurous can try any of the fish and seafood entrées, and the spicy eggplant is memorable.

A few blocks west on Valley Boulevard, is the **Hawaii Supermarket** *(120 E Valley Blvd., San Gabriel, tel 626-307-0062),* a family-owned grocery superstore specializing in exotic Asian groceries and other ethnic foodstuffs. If you're up to preparing your own dishes at home, the exotic stock runs a broad gamut from seaweed and sake to bok choy, pork feet, mung beans, and dried udon noodles.

Five blocks east, stop in at the **Saigon Sandwich & Bakery** *(718 E. Valley Blvd., San Gabriel, tel 636-288-6475),* one of colonial France's few contributions to the culinary world. This is the place to buy perfect, fresh-baked baguettes (crunchy exteriors and cloud-soft innards) and Vietnamese *bahn mi* sandwiches with fresh veggies and jalapeños, and the flan is delicious. Buy three sandwiches and get a free baguette.

Another divine option is **Alice's Kitchen** *(580 E. Garvey Ave., Monterey Park, tel 626-898-1828, www.aliceskitchen626.com, closed Tue.),* which opened in 2019 when soft-spoken Hong Kong native William Kwan sold his immensely popular Delicious Food Corner chain. Kwan now focuses all his energy on serving delicious Hong Kong–style breakfasts and dinners from a long-as-your-arm menu. First-timers might stick to the rice rolls dressed with a nutty sesame sauce, the fried noodles with toppings, or the clay pots (available only for dinner).

Three blocks east, the **Beijing Pie House** *(846 E Garvey Ave #3a. tel 626-288-3818, www.beijingpiehouse.com)* caused Jonathan Gold to wax lyrical about the meat- and vegetable-filled pies everyone comes for: "As promised, xian bing are finger-scorchingly hot, like a potato snatched straight from the embers, and the texture, although you sense a faint crackliness, is thin, warm and pliable, like skin. The menu warns you that it's hot, and the waitress warns you that it's hot, and the woman at the next table warns you, too, but there is probably nothing that can prepare you for the act of biting into a too-hot xian bing, when a jet of pressurized soup, as volatile as the steam from Old Faithful, arcs over your shoulder and drips harmlessly down the plate glass behind you."

EXPERIENCE: Chinatown Summer Nights

Visit L.A.'s Chinatown June through August when the area bursts into life during **Chinatown Summer Nights** *(Central & West Plazas, 943–951 N. Broadway, Los Angeles, tel 310-450-5183).* You'll experience three lively evenings of food, live music, and art. This free outdoor celebration lets you enjoy cooking competitions, live music performed by local bands, art displays, and video projections. Kids will enjoy the colorful Chinese cultural activities on offer. Kick up your heels on the large outdoor dance floor to music spun by local DJs, or relax in the craft beer garden. Just be sure to bring a good appetite; local food trucks and Chinatown's excellent restaurants provide an exotic array of choices.

Events take place from 5 p.m. to midnight. If you're taking the Los Angeles Metro, take the Gold Line and exit at the Chinatown station.

Angeles National Forest

🏞 111 B3–C3
&52 D4–53 E4

Visitor Information

✉ Big Pines Information Center, Angeles Crest Hwy. (Hwy. 2), Wrightwood

☎ 626-574-1613, or 760-249-3504

🕐 Closed Tues.–Thurs.

www.fs.usda.gov/angeles

de Neve led a party of soldiers and settlers in 1781 to establish El Pueblo de Nuestra Señora la Reina de los Angeles. It was from this mission (once dubbed San Gabriel de los Tremblores for the area's earthquakes) that the padres ruled more than 1.5 million acres (607,000 ha) of farmland, making them a formidable economic power.

Like all the other missions, secularization in 1833, and subsequent Americanization, led to San Gabriel's decline. For the past century, it has been subject to restoration efforts, the latest in 1996. The lovingly restored **church**

EXPERIENCE:
Mountain High Thrills

Perched at 6,000 feet in the San Gabriel Mountains, Wrightwood *(map p. 53 E4)* **is the most popular ski and snowboard resort in southern California. Located just west of town, Mountain High Resort** *(tel 888-754-7878, www.mthigh.com)* **comprises three distinct snow zones, with beginner, intermediate, and advanced pistes and terrain served by 14 lifts. The snow season generally runs early November to late April, with night skiing five times a week. Mountain High also offers ski and snowboard classes for children, adults, and seniors. During summer, hiking, mountain biking, and adventure zip lines take over the Wrightwood slopes.**

---

was badly damaged by fire in July 2020. Although the roof collapsed, the **altar** of Spanish design survived, as did the historic paintings, Stations of the Cross, and colorful **sculptures** of various

saints (one donated by Queen Maria in 1773), which had fortuitously been removed for restoration. The church's beautiful facade, with its six bells cast in Mexico in 1795, was also undamaged.

As with many of the missions, the **museum**—housed in an adobe built in 1812—and surrounding grounds and cemetery, with its Columbarium, provide ample opportunity to ponder the mixed legacy of Spanish colonization. Underneath are said to be the remains of some 5,000 Gabrieleño Indians.

Around the Foothills

Looming above the foothills and stretching from the San Fernando Valley east to San Bernardino is **Angeles National Forest.** This 650,000-acre (263,045 ha) area features hiking trails, picnic sites, and ski areas. Devastating fires often blaze through the forests, as in 2009.

At the old **Mount Wilson Observatory** *(map p. 111 C3, tel 562-413-2950, www.mtwilson.edu, open April–Nov.),* you can see the telescope used by generations of Caltech scientists to probe the mysteries of space or watch the hang gliders jump off the cliff and sail home to Altadena below. The **Charlton Flat** picnic area, farther up, is a prime spot for bird-watching. Still farther on, at **Jarvi Memorial Vista,** watch for bighorn sheep.

Back down the mountain, a worthwhile side trip to the west is to **Mission San Fernando** *(map p. 52 C3, 15151 San Fernando Mission Blvd., Mission Hills, tel*

818-361-0186, www.missions california.com). Founded by Padre Fermín Lasuén in 1797, this mission served early L.A. in much the same way as its counterpart in San Gabriel, by providing the new pueblo with food, clothing, and fuel. Lasuén was a masterful inculcator of the faith, and by 1819 San Fernando had a neophyte population of more than a thousand.

The fully restored chapel is worth viewing for its Indian and Spanish colors and ornamentation. The wide, tiled walkways under the mission loggia are a pleasure to stroll, particularly on a hot, dry summer day when the stillness encourages contemplation.

On the way back from the mission, everyone interested in the flora of the Southwest should visit the **Theodore Payne Foundation,** a shrine to native California botany that is a must for those wishing to buy Californian plants. In spring, the 23 acres (9.3 ha) are ablaze with wildflowers.

Driving back into Pasadena on I-210, you will pass the exit for the **Jet Propulsion Laboratory** *(map p. 111 B3, 4800 Oak Grove Dr., tel 818-354-4321 or 818-354-9314, www.jpl.nasa.gov).* You need to make reservations at least a month in advance in order to visit this wonderland of real space pioneering. It was from here that NASA explored the solar system with missions ranging from the first *Explorer* to the *Perseverance* Mars lander.

The road farther eastward (I-210) is dotted with small, down-home towns full of yesteryear

Theodore Payne Foundation

- 🗺 52 C3
- ✉ 10459 Tuxford St., Sun Valley
- ☎ 818-768-1802
- 🕐 Closed Sun.–Mon. mid-Oct.–June & Sun.–Wed. July–mid-Oct.

www.theodore payne.org

■ **Mount Wilson Observatory's Dome contains the 1917 Hooker 100-inch (2.45 m) telescope.**

The sun rises over Big Bear Lake, 25 miles (40 km) northeast of San Bernardino.

charm. A stop in the town of **Monrovia** (Myrtle exit; *www.cityof monrovia.org*) finds clusters of inexpensive antique stores. The quaint college town of **Claremont** *(map p. 53 E3, www.discoverclaremont. com)*, a 20-minute drive farther east, has a New England feel and several artistic and architectural places of pilgrimage, from Myron Hunt's Bridges Hall of Music at **Pomona College** *(map p. 53 E3, N. College Way, tel 909-621-8000, www.pomona.edu)* to the first mural painted in the U.S. by José Orozco, at the school's Frary Hall.

It is an hour-long drive to the city of **Riverside** *(map p. 53 F2, www.riversidecvb.com)*, where the astounding **Mission Inn** *(3649 Mission Inn Ave., tel 951-784-0300, www.missioninn.com)* is a prime example of blended Mexican and Spanish architectural styles, with ornate loggias and fountains.

The **San Bernardino**

National Forest *(map p. 53 G3, tel 909-382-2682, www.fs.usda.gov/ sbnf)* is an everlastingly popular vacation destination. In the 1920s, such stars as Charlie Chaplin made **Lake Arrowhead** the resort destination of preference. Now it is home to numerous mountain water-sports outfits in the summer and skiing in the winter.

The particularly scenic **Bluff Meadow,** at the end of **Champion Lodgepole Pine Trail,** can be found south of neighboring **Big Bear Lake** *(tel 800-424-4232, www.bigbearinfo.com)*, where you can see bald eagles during the winter months.

Good for biking and hiking in summer, Big Bear wears a snowy shawl for much of winter, drawing skiers and snowboarders to **Big Bear Mountain Resorts** *(tel 844-462-2327, www.bigbearmountain resort.com)*, offering southern California's premier ski runs. ■

Balmy evening breezes and azure blue skies, plus San Diego's Balboa Park and the fine architecture and good food of Santa Barbara

SOUTHERN CALIFORNIA

■ Palm trees in Heisler Park, Laguna Beach

SOUTHERN CALIFORNIA

While Los Angeles is the pulsating heart of the greater "Southern California" region, the moniker encompasses a vast coastal zone wrapped by mountains unfolding south from the Tehachapi Mountains to the Mexican border.

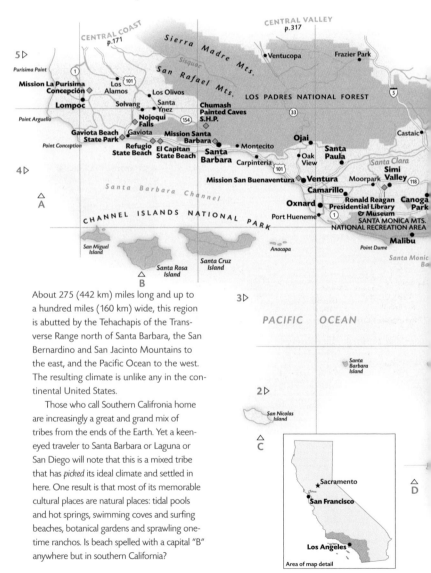

About 275 (442 km) miles long and up to a hundred miles (160 km) wide, this region is abutted by the Tehachapis of the Transverse Range north of Santa Barbara, the San Bernardino and San Jacinto Mountains to the east, and the Pacific Ocean to the west. The resulting climate is unlike any in the continental United States.

Those who call Southern Califronia home are increasingly a great and grand mix of tribes from the ends of the Earth. Yet a keen-eyed traveler to Santa Barbara or Laguna or San Diego will note that this is a mixed tribe that has *picked* its ideal climate and settled in here. One result is that most of its memorable cultural places are natural places: tidal pools and hot springs, swimming coves and surfing beaches, botanical gardens and sprawling one-time ranchos. Is beach spelled with a capital "B" anywhere but in southern California?

The beaches to the south, from Long Beach to San Diego, are nirvana to sun worshippers the world over; inland are theme parks galore (Disneyland, Knott's Berry Farm), a wine country (Temecula), and several great art and culture palaces. The beaches to the north, from Santa Barbara on, are cooler, more urbane places to stroll and explore. If you can tear yourself away from these beaches, inland you will discover still another wine country, lots of horses, and a bucolic little gem of a place called Ojai, where the intrepid might find the roots of the region's vaunted new spirituality. ■

NOT TO BE MISSED:

The original Magic Kingdom and the revamped Disney California Adventure 134–138

Posh seaside living in Laguna and Newport Beaches 140–143

Balboa Park's eclectic museums and world-famous zoo 152–158

San Diego's historic waterfront and Cabrillo National Monument 158–160

Shamu, sharks, and sea lions at SeaWorld 160–161

Santa Barbara's Spanish mission and charming city center 163–166

The wide open spaces of Channel Islands National Park 170

LONG BEACH & AROUND

Situated on the 8-mile (13 km) coastline of San Pedro Bay, Long Beach has always been in the shadow of Los Angeles, its more glamorous sister to the north. In recent years, however, Long Beach has resuscitated itself. It now claims one of the best ports in the world, a high quality of life, and several worthwhile attractions for visitors. At its hub is the multibillion-dollar Pike at Rainbow Harbor project, the largest seaside development in California history.

Feeding time at the Aquarium of the Pacific

Long Beach
🗺 131 E3

Visitor Information
✉ Long Beach
Convention &
Entertainment
Center, 301
E. Ocean Blvd.,
#1900,
Long Beach
☎ 562-436-3645,
800-452-7829

**www.visitlongbeach
.com**

The outstanding **Aquarium of the Pacific** *(100 Aquarium Way, tel 562-590-3100, www. aquariumofpacific.org, $$$$$),* one of the country's largest, displays 11,000 marine creatures in 19 major habitats. The vast **Shark Lagoon** and the **Penguin Habitat** are worth the visit alone. Other exhibits include Tropical Pacific, Northern Pacific, and Southern California galleries, and even a tour inside the **Molina Animal Care Center.** The **Honda Pacific Visions Theater,** new in 2019, features a state-of-the-art wraparound screen for an 8-minute experience that

immerses visitors in the underwater realm. And the **Ocean Science Center** uses high-tech "Science on a Sphere" technology to teach about pressing issues that affect the ocean.

From the aquarium entrance, catch the AquaBus to Long Beach's other big attraction, the **Queen Mary** *(1126 Queens Hwy., tel 562-435-3510, www.queenmary.com, $$$$).* This imperious ocean liner, launched in 1936, has been restored to its art deco glory. Admission includes a themed guided tour, from the boiler room "Steam & Steel Tour" to "Haunted Encounters."

For shopping or dining, return downtown to **Pine Avenue,** where Melrose meets the Pacific. Or visit the **Long Beach Museum of Art** (2300 E. Ocean Blvd., tel 562-439-2119, www.lbma.org, closed Mon.–Wed., $$, free Thurs. p.m. & Fri.). This little jewel, located in a historic Craftsman house overlooking the ocean, presents exquisitely curated shows on Western artists.

Also in Long Beach is the **Museum of Latin American Art** (628 Alamitos Ave., tel 562-437-1689, www.molaa.org, closed Mon.–Tues., $$), which focuses on local Latino artists. Many of them draw inspiration from David Siquieros (see sidebar p. 93), who painted in the Los Angeles area in the 1930s, and his contemporary José Orozco.

San Pedro

Once the hub of maritime culture in the Los Angeles area, San Pedro is now filled with quaint shops and seafood cafés. Worth a visit is the **Cabrillo Marine Aquarium,** focusing on local marine life. During nighttime high tides between March and August, the museum leads guided viewings of the grunion runs, when millions of small fish land on local beaches, burrow into the sand to mate, and then retreat to die in local waters.

Catalina Island

Situated 22 miles (35 km) offshore, and once favored by famous figures like gum magnate William Wrigley, this rugged island is lapped by pristine waters abounding in marine life. Ashore, explore the 42,000-acre (16,996 ha) **Catalina Island Conservancy** (tel 310-510-2595, www.catalinaconservancy.org), home to fox, buffalo, and bald eagles, as well as a botanical garden. The art deco Casino Building houses the **Catalina Island Museum** (tel 310-510-2414, www.catalinamuseum.org), which has an outstanding archaeological collection. ■

San Pedro

▲ 131 E3

Visitor Information

✉ San Pedro Convention & Visitor Bureau, 479 W. 6th St., San Pedro

☎ 424-364-6865

www.spcvb.com

Cabrillo Marine Aquarium

✉ 3720 Stephen White Dr., San Pedro

☎ 310-548-7562

🕐 Closed Mon. & Tues.–Fri. a.m.

💲 $$ ($ suggested donation)

www.cabrilloaq.org

Catalina Island

▲ 131 E2

Visitor Information

✉ Visitors Bureau, #1 Green Pleasure Pier, Avalon

☎ 800-626-1496

EXPERIENCE: The Crossing to Catalina

Getting to Catalina Island from the mainland is usually half the fun, especially on one of those crystal-clear southern California days when you have the snow-capped mountains on one side and the endless Pacific on the other. Dolphins are frequent companions, and it's not uncommon for travelers to spot gray, humpback, or finback whales during the hour-plus crossing.

Ferries depart from four different ports along the Los Angeles/Orange County coast. **Catalina Express** (tel 800-613-1212, www.catalinaexpress.com, $$$$$) runs boats from downtown Long Beach, San Pedro, and Dana Point to Avalon town and Two Harbors village at the north end of Catalina, with daily departures from each port. **Catalina Flyer** (tel 949-673-5245, www.catalinainfo.com, $$$$$) uses high-speed catamarans from Newport Beach, with one departure daily in each direction. Short on time? Opt for a helicopter crossing from Long Beach (or other destinations on demand) with **IEX Helicopters** (tel 800-228-2566, www.iexhelicopters.com, $$$$$), which will whisk you there in 15 minutes.

DISNEYLAND RESORT

For many travelers the principal destination in southern California, Disneyland has been the subject of so many interpretive essays in recent years that one might think that the Happiest Place on Earth, founded in 1955, had lost its happy sense of innocence and wonder. Nothing could be further from the truth. People keep coming in record numbers, spending tons of cash, and feeling happy, happy, happy!

Mickey Mouse has been welcoming guests to Disneyland since 1955.

Disneyland Resort

🗺 131 F3

✉ 1313 Harbor Blvd., Anaheim

☎ 714-781-4636 (tickets only)

💲 $$$$ (children under 3 free)

www.disneyland.com

Disneyland Resort is a 500-acre (202 ha) park comprising Disneyland Park and Disney California Adventure.

Disneyland Park

Disneyland Park is organized into nine themed "lands."

Main Street, U.S.A.: This section of the park is organized as a typical American burg of around 1890. Favorite attractions here are the various coin-operated games and **Great Moments with Mr. Lincoln,** in which an Audio-Animatronic Abe delivers his greatest oratory. The experience proves moving, even to Nintendo-jaded teens. While you are on Main Street, be certain to take in one of the park's many elaborate parades; at night, they end with a memorable fireworks show.

The Battle Plan

There are ways to maximize your enjoyment and minimize your discomfort during a visit to Disneyland Resort. First, the night before you go, get an idea of what your family absolutely must see in the park. The company's website is quite helpful, with maps, hotel and food information, and a list of rides scheduled to "go dark" for service and cleaning.

It's a good idea to download the Disneyland app to your mobile phone; you can even skip the ticket lines!

Then think about what you want to eat—you can't bring food in with you, so consider a hearty breakfast at one of Anaheim's local eateries before entering the park, preferably as early as possible. Food in Disneyland is not bad, but not great either.

Another strategy is to take in the park's live attractions, shopping, and dining during the day, saving the more popular rides for the cooler nights, when they are generally less crowded.

Lastly, there are now a number of specialized guidebooks to the park for families with small children.

Adventureland: This was once considered one of the park's quieter sections, dominated by such low-tech attractions as the **Enchanted Tiki Room** and the **Jungle Cruise.** But Adventureland's character was revved up with the addition of the ultrafast **Indiana Jones Adventure,** which has some of the most consistently long lines in the park.

Fantasyland: This section of the park enchants with **Sleeping Beauty Castle, Peter Pan's Flights,** and **Snow White's Scary Adventures,** while **Mr. Toad's Wild Ride** is well attended by teenagers and even young adults. For young children, **Dumbo the Flying Elephant** is a must-ride. More ambitious is the fast and wet **Matterhorn Bobsleds.** A word of warning: Don't ride too soon after eating.

Tomorrowland: Walt Disney's idea of the future, Tomorrowland combines action and education. **Innoventions,** for example, has interactive exhibits themed to transportation, health and sports, home, work and school, and entertainment. **Autopia** puts youngsters behind the wheel for a scenic ride in a "supercharged" coupe.

Finding Nemo Submarine Voyage is an underwater adventure. Hop aboard to experience a sub-shaking volcanic eruption and explore coral reefs while Nemo and his fishy friends go along for the ride thanks to futuristic projection technology. A recent addition, **Buzz Lightyear Astro Blasters** has you zapping the Evil Emperor Zurg with a laser cannon as a Space Ranger. Also new, *Star Wars:* **Launch Bay,** offers a behind-the-scenes documentary on the making of the Star Wars movies; while *Star Wars:* **The Adventure Continues** uses a flight simulator, digital 3D video, and "in-cockpit" special effects to take you on a hyperspeed 3D space flight.

Critter Country: Critter Country has a slower pace and gentler entertainments that make it perfect for tots and burned-out parents. The **Many Adventures of Winnie the Pooh** fun ride for honey is one highlight here. Another is the more action-oriented **Splash Mountain,** a highly recommended ride in the form of a superslick log flume. You can get wet on this ride.

Frontierland: Frontierland is one of the more traditional sections of the park, with attractions like the **Mark Twain Riverboat,** the **Pirate's Lair on Tom Sawyer Island,** and the **Frontierland Shootin' Exposition** show.

If you become bored by such fare, wake yourself up with a ride on the **Big Thunder Mountain Railroad.** At night, **Fantasmic!** turns the Rivers of America setting into a dazzling live-show spectacular for old and new Disney characters, directed by Mickey Mouse.

New Orleans Square: Perhaps the most memorable ride in the park is **Pirates of the Caribbean,** found in lively New Orleans Square. "Pirate" guests ride on a "floating" boat that, after two hair-raising plunges, lands them in a pirate- and damsel-filled land of Audio-Animatronic boozers, wenches, and assorted ne'er-do-wells. The line moves quickly, but waits of an hour are not uncommon. Spooky fun awaits, too, in the **Haunted Mansion** on a slow-moving ride full of spectral surprises.

Mickey's Toontown: A three-dimensional cartoon world, Mickey's Toontown benefits from new technologies and a younger, more aesthetically sophisticated group of

Downtown Disney District

Between the entrances to Disneyland Park and Disney California Adventure lies the Downtown Disney District, a lively promenade lined with shops, restaurants, and open-air cafés. In addition to a megaplex theater, entertainment possibilities include live music performances at the **Splitsville Kingpin Stage,** jazz shows at **Flambeaux's Jazz Club,** and the **Royal Theatre at Fantasy Faire,** which offers live big-band music on Saturday nights. Professional musicians help stoke the party atmosphere outside with live performances of everything from classical to blues.

The district charges no entry fee and you can also take the Disneyland Monorail (see sidebar p. 138) or drive. Parking is free for the first three hours, or up to five hours with validation. The parking lot is located on Disneyland Drive, between the Mickey & Friends Parking Structure and the Disneyland Hotel.

And if you need a place to rest your head after all this excitement, consider the **Grand Californian Hotel & Spa,** a 751-room deluxe hotel built in the Arts and Crafts style.

Star Wars: Galaxy's Edge lets Disneyland visitors live their adventure in a galaxy far, far away.

designers and architects. **Roger Rabbit's Car Toon Spin** is an old-fashioned pod ride in the tradition of Mr. Toad; guests can spin their vehicles as they career through various cartoon worlds. Other attractions here include **Goofy's Play House, Donald Duck's Boat,** the **Chip 'n' Dale Treehouse,** and **Gadget's Go Coaster.**

Stars Wars: Galaxy's Edge:

Added in 2019, Disneyland's thrilling new *Star Wars*-themed section especially appeals to Gen-Xers who grew up with the original trilogy. Expect to bump into Chewbacca, Kylo Ren, Stormtroopers, and even a fully mobile R2-D2 going about their business as visitors to planet Batuu. Take control of the fastest spaceship in the galaxy at the ***Millennium Falcon:* Smugglers' Run** ride as you

face danger at every exhilarating turn on a thrilling interactive smuggling mission. Then join the Resistance in a climactic battle against the First Order at **Star Wars: Rise of the Resistance,** a massive attraction with multiple rides and legions of stormtroopers: After being captured, visitors are given a fighting chance to escape and for the Resistance to rise in Disney's most epic attraction to date.

Disney California Adventure Park

Visitors to Disneyland Resort can also choose Disney California Adventure Park. According to Barry Braverman, its producer, the idea behind this attraction is to "immerse guests in compelling stories, evocative places, and fantastic adventures that will bring the California dream to life." This it does through a series of elaborately themed California districts—from beach to deserts to mountains—that capture northern, central, and southern California on 55 acres (22 ha).

Soarin' Over California allows guests to virtually "soar" on hang gliders over a re-creation of Yosemite National Park. **Grizzly River Run** plunges you through the Sierra Nevada on a thrilling white-water rafting ride. At **The Little Mermaid—Ariel's Undersea Adventure,** giant clamshells take visitors on a journey beneath the sea. And the **Twilight Zone Tower of Terror,** will make your hair stand up. The setting is the once-glamorous Hollywood Tower Hotel, now vacant and full of "ghastly ghostly guests." Adrenalin junkies experience a fright night as lightning strikes and you are plunged 13 stories down an abandoned elevator shaft into the "most thrilling recesses of the Twilight Zone."

California Adventure also pays homage to the state's fixation with car culture in **Cars Land,** with rides like **Radiator Springs Racers** and **Mater's Junkyard Jamboree** based on the animated movie series.

New in 2018, **Pixar Pier** boardwalk features the **Incredicoaster** roller-coaster, the **Pixar Pal-a-Round** Ferris wheel, plus **Jessie's Critter Carousel** and other attractions all populated by characters from Pixar movies. Linger for the after-dark **World of Color** multimedia spectacular. ■

INSIDER TIP:

If visiting Disneyland around the holidays, check out the candy cane making at Candy Palace. It's very popular—be sure to get tickets ahead of time.

—MARCELLA PLEGGE
National Geographic contributor

EXPERIENCE:
Photograph Disneyland by Monorail

To capture the feel of the "old" park, take your camera with you on the Disneyland Monorail. The first of its kind in the U.S. when it opened in 1959, the environmentally friendly train runs on electricity and does not emit exhaust or other pollutants. Riding the monorail is free, but Disneyland admission is required. Board the train at the Tomorrowland station or in the Downtown Disney District (see sidebar p. 136). The ride circles the park in about 15 minutes, passing over the main entrance and affording wonderful aerial views of Fantasyland (see p. 135) and Tomorrowland (see pp. 135–136). Set your camera to pan focus or landscape mode, and be sure to get your hand stamped for reentry.

AROUND ORANGE COUNTY

If you haven't run out of energy and money by the time you have finished with the Magic Kingdom, you may want to explore some of Orange County's other attractions.

With a mission to preserve, study, and exhibit the fine arts of the Americas, Africa, and the Pacific Rim, the **Bowers Museum** (2002 N. Main St., Santa Ana, tel 714-567-3600, www.bowers.org, closed Mon., $$$, free 1st Sun. of month) turns a fine curatorial eye on everything from late 18th-century Mexican copper brandy stills to funerary ritual objects from New Guinea.

If you need some non-Disney inspiration, head to the remarkable **Christ Cathedral** (13280 Chapman Ave., Garden Grove, tel 714-971-2141, www.christcathedral california.org, closed Sun. except services), formerly the Crystal Cathedral built for Rev. Robert Schuller in 1980 as the largest glass building in the world. If you need a dose of reality, however, the fascinating **Richard Nixon Presidential Library & Birthplace** (18001 Yorba Linda Blvd., Yorba Linda, tel 714-983-9120, www.nixonlibrary.gov, $$) has galleries on Nixon's life, world leaders, and the Berlin Wall, as well as Pat Nixon's rose garden with the tiny house where the President was born.

In downtown Anaheim, **The Muzeo** (241 S. Anaheim Blvd., tel 714-765-6450 www.muzeo.org, $$$) cultural center, art gallery, and museum hosts world-class traveling exhibitions, plus a gallery on local history.

The Christ Cathedral gleams with 10,000 panes of glass.

Angel Stadium in Anaheim is home field to the Los Angeles Angels, one of the top Major League Baseball teams; stadium tours are offered. Across the freeway is the **Honda Center** (www.hondacenter.com), which hosts the Anaheim Ducks of the National Hockey League. ■

Angel Stadium

✉ 2000 Gene Autry Way, Anaheim

☎ 714-940-2230

$ $$$ (tours)

www.mlb.com/angels/ballpark

Knott's Berry Farm

Disneyland (see pp. 134–138) may get most of the publicity, but Orange County's first theme park was **Knott's Berry Farm** (8039 Beach Blvd., Buena Park, tel 714-220-5200, www.knotts.com, $$$$$). The kernel for today's modern park took root in the 1920s when Walter and Cornelia Knott began adding onto their berry farm, starting with a fried chicken restaurant and Wild West ghost town with stagecoach rides and gunslinger shows. These original attractions remain, but Knotts is better known today for its thrill rides, plus a **Soak City** (www.knotts.com/soak-city) water park that's open only in summer.

LAGUNA BEACH

Homesteaded by Mormons in the 1870s and developed as an artists' retreat and resort town in the early 1900s, Laguna Beach has long proven irresistible to both visitors and natives seeking respite from inland heat and noise. All crisp sea air and primal canyonland, its geography holds a clue to why.

The town of Laguna Beach is fronted by a series of stunning coves with waters sometimes shimmering a light blue and sometimes brooding, nearly purple. Rising from the coves are a series of sculpted cliffs, which give way to a small basin flat enough for what many have called "a permanent village." Looming behind that are the *cañons de los lagunas*, or canyons of the lakes.

Water, sand, canyon. Such are the features that attracted California's plein air painters, many of whom set up here in the early 1900s. Although the Hollywood crowd soon followed, Laguna Beach has always retained a strong identification with the arts, as represented by its **Pageant of the Masters** *(tel 800-487-3378, www.foapom.com),* a live staging of masterpieces from Tiepolo to Toulouse-Lautrec.

The modern visitor might begin an exploration of the coves at any number of Laguna's beaches. **Main Beach,** situated at the foot of Laguna Canyon Road, is the epicenter of the city's beach culture, with a thriving volleyball and skateboarding scene. Its waters are often calm enough for a pleasant swim. Main Beach is also within walking distance of downtown Laguna Beach, fine for strolling and shopping in the summer months.

A more tranquil beach experience can be had by driving about a mile (1.6 km) north of Main Beach to **Crescent Bay.** This

Laguna Beach offers Orange County residents a thriving beach and arts culture.

aptly named stretch of sand is known for its great body-surfing waves and ample sunning areas. The tidal pools to its north are easily explored (take some old tennis shoes), and on a good day visitors may see the rare red sea anemone, sometimes bigger than a baseball glove. The more aquatically skilled can rent snorkeling or scuba equipment and swim out to **Seal Rock,** a protected sanctuary for the honking, boisterous California sea lion. The beds of giant sea kelp around the rock are particularly mesmerizing when viewed through a diving mask.

INSIDER TIP:

The annual Sawdust Art & Craft Festival (www. sawdustartfestival.org), where you can see and buy the work of more than 200 Laguna Beach artists, is a summer must.

—MARY STEPHANOS
National Geographic contributor

The unique ecology of Laguna's cliffs is the focus of the **Crystal Cove State Park,** to the north off the Pacific Coast Highway. Situated on onetime cattle-grazing land, with 3.2 miles (5.1 km) of beach, the park has undergone extensive rewilding with native plants. An extended boardwalk takes guests through the park and onto the beach below, and it serves as an educational nature trail extending into the backcountry up Moro Canyon. You may spot red-tailed hawks and northern harriers swirling above. Down on the beach, explore **Reef Point** for more tide-pooling adventures.

One benefit of a disastrous 1992 fire that ravaged Laguna's canyons was the creation of the 7,000-acre (2,832 ha) **Laguna Coast Wilderness Park.** Two walks justify taking the trouble to make a reservation. The first is the 3.5-mile (5.6 km) **Laurel Canyon Nature Trail,** its air perfumed with wild sage and sycamore, its undulating rockscape as dramatic today as it was in the early 20th century, when such painters as Guy Rose and Norman St. Clair depicted the area in their plein air canvases.

Farther up Laguna Canyon Road, past groves of old eucalyptus trees, is the **James Dilley Greenbelt Preserve.** Visitors follow a trail around a landscape of bulrushes, prickly pear, hemlock, and sycamores. Egrets and ospreys are common in the main lake (Lake Number One), to the north.

Just north of the Inn at Laguna Beach (the preferred vacation residence) is **Gallery Row,** on North Coast Highway. The work of many local painters, some doing a form of neo-plein air painting, is worth a look; prices are reasonable for good living room art. Some of the originals that inspired this work can be seen at the **Laguna Art Museum.** The delight of seeing William Wendt's original of "Spring in the Canyon" is just one thing that makes a visit here worthwhile. ∎

Laguna Beach
🗺 131 F2

Visitor Information
✉ Laguna Beach Visitors Center, 381 Forest Ave. Laguna Beach
☎ 949-497-9229

www.visitlaguna
beach.com

Crystal Cove State Park
🗺 131 F3
✉ N. of Laguna Beach off Pacific Coast Hwy. (Calif. 1)
☎ 949-494-3539, 949-497-7647 (interpretive walks)
💲 $$$

www.crystalcove
statepark.org

Laguna Coast Wilderness Park
✉ 18751 Laguna Canyon Rd. (near El Toro Rd.)
☎ 949-923-2235
💲 $

www.ocparks.com/
lagunacoast

Laguna Art Museum
✉ 307 Cliff Dr.
☎ 949-494-8971
💲 $$$

www.lagunaart
museum.org

BEACH CITIES

North and south of Laguna Beach, a string of beach cities edges the coast and offers the casual visitor an extreme close-up of the southern California surfing scene. On virtually any morning, the earlier the better, you can watch the practice sessions of some of the world's most skilled wave riders. Later in the day, check out the surfwear shops, health food cafés, and seafood restaurants.

 Surfers are rewarded with great waves near the pier, Huntington Beach.

Huntington State Beach

🏔 131 E3

Visitor Information

✉ Headquarters, 17851 Pacific Coast Hwy., Huntington Beach

☎ 714-536-1454

www.parks.ca.gov

North of Laguna Beach
Huntington State Beach: South of central L.A., the wide, clean stretches of Huntington State Beach beckon sunseekers. Those interested in marine life can drive the few miles to **Bolsa Chica Ecological Reserve** (3842 Warner Ave., tel 714-846-1114, www.bolsachica.org). Here a 1.5-mile (2.4 km) trail leads around a tidal lagoon, where stingrays and least terns are among the wildlife. Overlooks provide vistas of the restored wetlands.

Newport Beach: Farther south is fast-paced, glamorous Newport Beach. The principal social activity here is boating, which takes place in the "largest small craft harbor in the world." Even for those who can't afford the $200 deck shoes (let alone the boat), **Newport Harbor** provides ample sun-filled entertainments, from the historic **Balboa Pavilion** (www.balboapavilion.com) to the **Discovery Cube's Ocean Quest** (600 E. Bay Ave., Newport Beach, tel 949-675-8915, www.

oceanquestoc.org, $), which examines the past, present, and future of maritime exploration.

For shopping, **Fashion Island** (Jamboree Rd., off E. Pacific Coast Hwy., www.fashionisland.com) offers ultra-exclusive shops that rival those of Rodeo Drive (see pp. 72–73).

Inland, head for the **Upper Newport Bay Nature Preserve** (2301 University Dr., Newport Beach, tel 949-923-2290, www.ocparks.com), a lush 750-acre (303 ha) salt marsh that is home to thousands of birds, including such endangered species as the light-footed clapper rail.

Farther inland, in Santa Ana, the permanent collection of post-war California art at the **Orange County Museum of Art** (1661 W. Sunflower Ave., Santa Ana, tel 714-780-2130, www.ocma.art, closed Mon.–Wed., $$$, free 2nd Sun. of month) is known for some remarkable exhibitions.

Other Beaches: Back south on the Pacific Coast Highway (Calif. 1), you'll find two remarkable beaches. **The Wedge** is known mainly for its huge, bone-crunching waves. **Corona del Mar State Beach** (tel 949-718-1859, www.parks.ca.gov) is the epitome of the southern California bathing beach: swimmable waters, pristine sands, and a backdrop of palms, seagulls, and even the occasional pelican.

South of Laguna Beach

The picturesque coves and rugged cliffs of Laguna continue southward well beyond the city's limits. There is public access to all of these beaches, and they are

well worth the effort to escape the summer crowds. The pier and marina are the main attractions at **Dana Point** (Pacific Coast Hwy. & Street of the Golden Lantern), and a walk to the lookout yields memorable views.

Inland, off I-5, is **Mission San Juan Capistrano,** perhaps the most picture-perfect California mission. The Moorish-style architecture and burnished bells and arcades lend a romantic hue, while the gardens make a pleasant stroll. Migratory swallows return here every spring and are welcomed with a festival on March 19.

Returning to the Pacific Coast Highway, three contiguous beaches give you a choice for a fun-filled day of sunning and swimming: **Doheny State Beach, Capistrano Beach,** and **San Clemente Beach.** ∎

EXPERIENCE:
The Ocean Institute

If you're maritime minded, don't miss the experience of diving into marine lab activities, watching octopus and jellyfish feedings, piloting a remotely operated underwater vehicle, and cruising offshore on the *Sea Explorer* research vessel or the *Spirit of Dana Point* schooner. Tucked down at the southern end of Orange County, the Ocean Institute at Dana Point (24200 Dana Point Harbor Dr., tel 949-496-2274, www.ocean-institute.org) is a nonprofit, educational facility specializing in marine and environmental science and maritime history. Weekday programs are reserved for schools and members, but on weekends the institute's exhibits and aquariums are open to all. Guided tide pool hikes, native plant tours, plus kayak harbor tours are offered, along with ocean craft workshops.

Newport Beach
⛰ 131 F3

Visitor Information
✉ 401 Newport Center Dr., Suite 120, Newport Beach
☎ 949-719-6100

www.visitnewport beach.com

Corona del Mar State Beach
⛰ 131 F3

Mission San Juan Capistrano
⛰ 131 F2
✉ 26801 Ortega Hwy., San Juan Capistrano
☎ 949-234-1300

www.missionsjc.com

NORTH COASTAL SAN DIEGO

North of San Diego (see pp. 150–161) stretches an expansive coastal region noted for its exquisite beaches, protected wild places, and miles of open space. From Carlsbad south to La Jolla, just north of San Diego, you'll find a landscape dotted with picturesque small towns and unbeatable oceanside vistas. Whether you are after art and antiques or sunning and swimming, the area north of San Diego is bound to delight.

 The rugged coastline north of San Diego has attractive small towns and a laid-back atmosphere.

Carlsbad

131 F2

Visitor Information

✉ Visitor Center, 400 Carlsbad Village Dr., Carlsbad

☎ 760-434-6093

http://visitcarlsbad.com

Carlsbad

Located south of Laguna Beach (see pp. 140–141), Carlsbad is known for its flower farms and the interactive **Museum of Making Music** (*5790 Armada Dr., tel 760-438-5996, www .museumofmakingmusic.org, closed Mon., $$*). Its biggest attraction, however, is **Legoland California Resort** (*1 Legoland Dr., tel 760-918-5346, www.legoland.com/ california, $$$$$*), a high-tech American version of the celebrated Danish theme park.

The 128-acre (51 ha) park offers innovative rides, shows, and attractions, including the popular Pharaoh's Revenge laser game and Pirate Reef water-based rides. At the heart of the park are diminutive versions of Manhattan, Washington, D.C., Las Vegas, and others rendered in Lego bricks. Another popular attractions is the interactive Sea Life aquarium, specially designed to introduce children to the wonders of the sea. The Legoland Water Park opens during warmer months.

From Carlsbad, I-5 continues into **Encinitas,** hub of southern California surfer culture, followed by Solana Beach and Del Mar (see sidebar below).

Torrey Pines State Natural Reserve

Of all southern California's parks, the 1,750-acre (708 ha) Torrey Pines State Natural Reserve, an area of seaside cliffs and lagoons south of Del Mar, may well be the most sensuous. The scents of wild fennel, sage, and pine combine with sand, sun, and spray to make a heady mixture. Alas, only 9,000 of the drought-tolerant trees that give the reserve its name, *Pinus torreyana,* remain in all America.

Start with a short hike (about two-thirds of a mile/1 km) around the **Guy Fleming Trail** (leaflets from the visitor center). The eerily eroded cliffs and twisted pines are a joy, particularly from February through May when native California flowers blossom in hues of red, orange, purple, and green. Omnipresent is the "sticky" monkey flower, with its tiny orange trumpets; here also are the yellow mariposa lily, the lemonade berry, and the purple coast cholla.

Near the bottom of the **Broken Hill Trail** is the overlook for **Flat Rock,** dramatic in its simplicity. From January through March, you may spot a California gray whale on its annual migration. Seals, cormorants, and gulls add to the spectacle. Red-throated loons and great blue herons are found year-round.

On the park's north edge is **Los Peñasquitos Marsh,** once a Native American encampment and now an extensive mudflat, home to fiddler crabs and jackknife clams. Access is controlled; check with the ranger station for tours.

Torrey Pines State Natural Reserve

🗺 131 G1

✉ Visitor Center, 12500 N. Torrey Pines Rd. (exit off I-5)

☎ 858-755-2063

www.parks.ca.gov

Del Mar & Solana Beach

The seaside resort of **Del Mar** (see map p. 131 G1; visitor information, Del Mar Visitors Association, 1442 Camino del Mar, tel 858-735-3650, www.visitdelmarvillage.com closed Sat.–Sun.) lies at the mouth of the Dieguito River north of Torrey Pines. The city has long been famous for its horse-racing track, run by the **Del Mar Thoroughbred Club** (tel 858-792-4242, www.dmtc.com). Balmy summer evenings are pleasant here even when Lady Luck isn't going your way.

North of Del Mar is the laidback city of **Solana Beach,** with its **Cedros Avenue Design District** (www.cedrosavenue.com), two and a half vibrant blocks of interior design shops, funky bistros and cafés, art galleries, hip fashion boutiques, and bustling young architecture firms. A farmers market operates Sunday afternoons.

La Jolla

131 G1

Visitor Information

✉ 7590 Fay Ave.,
404

☎ 858-230-2725

**www.lajollaby
thesea.com**

Museum of Contemporary Art San Diego at La Jolla

✉ 700 Prospect St.,
La Jolla

☎ 858-454-3541

🕐 Closed Wed.

💲 $$$

www.mcasd.org

Birch Aquarium at Scripps

✉ 2300 Expedition
Way, La Jolla

☎ 858-534-3474

💲 $$

**www.aquarium.ucsd
.edu**

La Jolla Playhouse

✉ 2910 La Jolla
Village Dr.,
La Jolla

☎ 858-550-1010

**www.lajollaplay
house.org**

La Jolla

Founded in the early 20th century, the exclusive suburb of La Jolla shimmers with the essence of the Good Life. Its shopping arcades along sunny Prospect Street are vaguely European, and its homes, a fusion of modernism and recherché mission style, seem perfectly matched to the always changing ocean sky.

Many travelers head for the famed **La Jolla Caves** and **La Jolla Cove** (along Coast Walk). The former is a group of seven natural sea caves ripe for exploration; the latter is one of the most picturesque, albeit tiny, beaches on the coast, its deep blue waters attracting many snorkelers.

Back up on Prospect, the **Museum of Contemporary Art San Diego at La Jolla** offers a constantly changing palette of postwar art. It reopened in 2021 after a total revamp and expansion, with two levels of light-filled galleries and walls of glass that take advantage of its prime oceanfront setting. The museum's vast collection includes Andy Warhol and Robert Irwin. Don't miss the Nancy Rubins kayak-canoe-surfboard sculpture "Pleasure Point" (2006) above the entrance.

Those with a certain literary inclination should take time to walk over to **Windansea Beach** (Neptune Pl. & Bonair St.), immortalized in journalist Tom Wolfe's essay "The Pump House Gang."

"Spectacular" sums up the **Birch Aquarium at Scripps** (Non Torrey Pines Rd. to Expedition Way), the interpretive center for the Scripps Institute of Oceanography. In the **Hall of Fishes,** state-of-the-art tanks display Pacific marine life. Of hypnotic interest here is the giant kelp forest, located inside a sunlit 55,000-gallon (208,197 L) tank equipped with a wavemaking machine. Its new **Research**

INSIDER TIP:

Before taking in a play at the La Jolla Playhouse, enjoy cocktails at La Valencia (1132 Prospect St., tel 855-476-6870, www.lavalencia. com).

—GREG CRITSER
National Geographic author

---

in Action: 100 Year Challenge features an Indo-Pacific coral reef habitat and serves as a laboratory to study how reefs adapt to climate change.

One of the aquarium's most popular exhibits, **There's Something About Seahorses** features more than a dozen seahorse species. And at the outdoor **Shark Shores** exhibit, you can see eye-to-eye with La Jolla's Leopard sharks, which in summer gather en masse in the waters off Shore Beach.

The aquarium's activities schedule includes snorkeling with sharks and "Tidepooling for Tots." A visit to the **Tide Pool Plaza,** with its panoramic view of the La Jolla shoreline, is a stunning coda to the visit and perfect preparation for tide pool explorations (see pp. 148–149). ∎

GOING ON SAFARI

Sprawling across 1,800 acres (728 ha) of landscaped gardens and native chaparral terrain, the San Diego Zoo Safari Park offers visitors the chance to see more than 3,500 animals from around 400 species, many of them rare or endangered.

Located about 35 miles (56 km) north of San Diego (see pp. 150–161), the **San Diego Zoo Safari Park** (*15500 San Pasqual Valley Rd., Escondido, tel 629-231-1515, www.sdzsafaripark.org, $$$$$*) is country cousin to the San Diego Zoo (see pp. 156–158) and a major center for the captive breeding of rare and endangered species.

Much of the park's space is taken up by huge, open-air exhibits of African and Asian wildlife. It is home to the world's largest veterinary hospital and also boasts the **Institute for Conservation Research (ICR),** which contains a "frozen zoo" with the embryos of hundreds of endangered animals from around the globe. The efforts of the ICR have helped save several species from extinction, including the California condor, white rhino, and Arabian oryx.

Centered around a lake with flamingos and other waterfowl, the **Nairobi Village** area contains restaurants, shops, and exhibits for smaller animals, as well as the **Gorilla Forest** habitat and an amphitheater where a popular bird show takes the stage several times each day.

You can explore everything by following the trails that meander through the park, but the best way to explore the park is by "going on safari."

No reservations are needed for the **Africa Tram Safari** (*$$$, included in park admission*), a 25-minute open-air expedition on one of the park's colorful vehicles. Sit back and relax as your expert guide explains the behaviors and personalities of the African animals in the park. Children 11 and younger must be accompanied by an adult.

For something that's a little closer to an actual African motor safari experience, try the **Wildlife Safari** (*$$$$$*). You have three options to choose from: daytime, twilight, and night. All of them offer the opportunity to ride in the back of an open-top truck and to feed giraffes and rhinos.

The popular **Roar & Snore** adventure (*$$$$$*) includes overnight accommodation in a private safari tent, dinner and breakfast on a bluff overlooking the African grasslands, campfire programs, kid's crafts, guided walks, and an after-hours glimpse of the wildlife.

In addition to the many African species, from lions and cheetahs to okapis and warthogs, the park has other regional sections, including **Condor Ridge,** offering a chance to see the endangered California condor. Sumatran tigers roam the jungly **Tiger Trail.** Asian rhino are the highlight of the **Asian Savanna,** which also counts Arabian oryx, camels, and even Przewalski's horse among its denizens. And kangaroos and wallabies hop around the **Walkabout Australia** exhibit.

See giraffes up close in the San Diego Zoo Safari Park.

IN THE TIDE POOLS

The typical southern California tide pool consists of five zones, each with its own ecology. The topmost is the spray zone; then come, in descending order, the high, medium, and low intertidal zones, where most of the action is. The last is the subtidal, where many of these creatures live when not looking for food in the intertidal.

With its warm waters and accessible cliffside pools, La Jolla (see p. 146) provides some excellent opportunities for tide pooling. Linda E. Tway, author of *Tidepools of Southern California*, is a local expert. Her advice is to prepare by checking the local tide tables (in the newspaper daily). Remember that removing any marine life from the pools is against the law.

Although there are several outstanding tide-pooling sites in La Jolla, the location known as **Big Rock** *(enter from Camino de la Costa between Cortez Place & Via del Norte)* offers the opportunity of seeing some rare and colorful species. Come at low tide—but watch for strong surf surges.

The most continually exposed of the zones, the spray zone, is a treasure trove of thriving marine life. Outstanding examples of creatures that are numerous at Big Rock include the periwinkle, a snail-like mollusk about five-eighths of an inch (1.7 cm) long and spherical in shape, and the striped shore crab, a crustacean normally two inches (5 cm) long with green stripes.

Inhabitants of the **high intertidal zone** must be able to tolerate a good deal of sun and air; one response is for them to close up or seal themselves within a shell, preventing dehydration. The masters of this, found in abundance at Big Rock, are the California mussel and the leaf barnacle. The mussel grows to six inches (15 cm) in length and is brown to purple-black. It attaches itself to a rock with a single foot. The barnacle, up to five inches (12.7 cm) long, white, and more or less leaf-shaped, clings with grayish brown stalks in large numbers, often one on top of another. Also watch for the giant keyhole limpet, a shell-covered conical oval, gray to brown, clamped to the rock with a single yellow-orange foot.

As exposure to air decreases in the **medium intertidal zone,** coralline algae transform the

gray-green sandstone into a wonderland of pinks and purples. Into this surface burrows the troglodyte chiton, brown and one-and-a-half inches (3.8 cm) long. These remnants from dinosaur days spend their 20-year lives scraping into the sandstone. The result is the pock-marked surface of Big Rock.

Because the **low intertidal zone** is mostly submerged, more permanent "homes" are built. One of the most remarkable is that of the sandcastle worm. Two inches (5 cm) long, cream colored with a black tip and lavender tentacles, *Phragmatopoma californica* builds honeycomb-like clusters of delicate sand tubes (watch your step). Another star of this zone is the giant green anemone. A member of the same class of invertebrates as corals, anemones use their tentacles to catch passing prey. The green anemone can grow as large as seven inches (17.7 cm) wide. Also look for the giant acorn barnacle, which resembles a tiny volcanic crater.

The **subtidal zone** is where you will see fishes and the larger seaweeds of the area.

KEY TO DIAGRAM

1 rough limpet
2 sea lettuce
3 striped shore crab
4 giant owl limpet
5 striped sea slug
6 California mussels
7 pink encrusting coralline algae
8 volcano barnacles
9 velvety red sponge
10 Spanish shawl nudibranch
11 leaf barnacles
12 common surfgrass
13 sandcastle worms
14 rockweed
15 giant green anemone
16 Hopkins' rose
17 California sea hare
18 bat star
19 Panama brittle star
20 ochre star
21 warty sea cucumber
22 sea urchin
23 rock crab
24 spiny lobster
25 black abalone
26 sargasso weed
27 coralline red algae
28 giant keyhole limpet
29 chestnut cowry
30 chitons

SAN DIEGO

If its neighbor to the north, La Jolla (see p. 146), represents the ultimate California Good Life, then San Diego conjures the ultimate California Outdoor Life. With its huge range of water-sports facilities, its giant municipal culture parks, and the largest zoo in the United States, it is a giant adult playground. The fact that it is surrounded by frontierland—desert to the east, the Mexican border to the south, and the Pacific to the west—only underscores the city's relatively late development. Though it sprawls, it has yet to break out into megasprawl.

San Diego, America's eighth largest city, is surrounded by 70 miles (112 km) of beaches.

San Diego

131 G1

Visitor Information

San Diego
Visitor
Information
Center,
996-B Harbor
Dr., San Diego

619-737-2999

www.sandiego.org

From its birth in 1769 as the first Spanish settlement in Alta (Upper) California, San Diego has followed much the same pattern of development as other great Californian cities. The initial spurt of missionizing was so aggressive that, in 1775, the neophytes at Mission San Diego openly revolted and slew Padre Luis Jayme, making him the first martyr of Alta California. A period of Mexican neglect and wildcat Anglo fur trading was followed by a spate of Yankee entrepreneurialism, much of it focused on the area's climate and natural harbor.

In 1870, Alonzo Horton, considered the founder of modern San Diego, began touting the city as a mecca of tourism and health; eventually he built one of the most celebrated hotels of his time (see sidebar p. 158), launching San Diego to fame. Nowadays Horton is honored in the popular Horton Plaza outdoor mall.

By 1915 the city of San Diego was confident enough to enter the "world exposition" game, hiring gifted architect Bertram Grosvenor Goodhue, who was responsible for Caltech (see pp. 122–123) and L.A.'s Public Library (see p. 98), to design Balboa Park (see pp. 152–156), where the city fathers promoted the 1915 Panama-California International Exposition.

John D. and Adolph B. Spreckels, sons of a sugar magnate, caught the alfresco bug as well, building in 1915 the world's largest outdoor organ. To this day, on any warm Sunday afternoon, numerous San Diegans and visitors can be found in Balboa Park's open-air Spreckels Organ Pavilion (see p. 155), the music and sun washing over them as they sit like seals on a sandy beach.

During the mid-20th century, San Diego boomed. A heavy dose of federal government largesse, largely coming through the burgeoning naval complex, allowed the city to avoid some of the planning mistakes made by its northern neighbors, cities that often sabotaged their own zoning laws in order to attract new corporate residents. In San Diego, debate over growth has traditionally been framed by the phrase "Smokestacks versus Geraniums." Even the conservative former governor of California Pete Wilson, who was the mayor of San Diego in the late 1970s, is remembered as a proponent of restrained growth in the city.

More recently, huge population gains and economic shifts (the naval presence has been replaced in part by high-tech industries) have made planned growth more difficult. San Diego is now the eighth largest

EXPERIENCE: Wine Tasting in the Wild West

Fewer than 60 miles (96 km) north of San Diego along I-15 you'll discover **Temecula** *(map p. 131 G2; visitor information, Convention and Visitors Bureau, 28690 Mercedes St., Ste. A, tel 888-363-2852, www.visittemeculavalley.com),* an old Wild West town that has boomed again on a bounty of wine. Here about 50 wineries produce a variety of reds, whites, and grape-based drinks.

If you're a sparkling wine aficionado, then **Wilson Creek** *(35960 Rancho California Rd., tel 951-699-9463, www.wilsoncreekwinery.com)* is your first stop. Try the almond-flavored champagne and peach bellini. Next head to breezy, hilltop **Falkner Winery** *(40620 Calle Contento, tel 951-676-8231, www .falknerwinery.com),* where you can picnic

on the lawn and sip the exquisite syrah. For a killer white port and pinot gris, try **Wiens Family Cellars** *(35055 Via del Ponte, tel 951-694-9892, www.wienscellars.com).* Mechanically-minded wine lovers should stop at the Argentine-owned **Doffo Winery** *(36083 Summitville Rd., tel 951-676-6989, www.doffowines.com),* where an exotic motorbike museum can be enjoyed with a fine malbec.

The **Temecula Valley Winegrowers Association** *(34567 Rancho California Rd., tel 951-699-3626 or 800-801-9463, www.temeculawines.org)* offers maps and itineraries. Be sure to check out the association's various events like the annual **World of Wine** gourmet food, the wine weekend in March, and the **Harvest Celebration** in November.

Balboa Park

 131 G1

Visitor Information

✉ Visitors Center,
1549 El Prado,
San Diego

☎ 619-239-0512

**www.balboapark
.org**

city in the United States. Urban sprawl, as in the area around the old mission, to the northeast, is becoming more common.

Yet any discerning visitor would be hard pressed to come away from San Diego unhappy. The old California Tower in Balboa Park shines in the sun *and* in evening spotlights. Old San Diego is joined with new Tijuana in Mexico via an efficient, low-cost trolley car system and Bridge of the Americas. There are plays and concerts under the stars every

home to unquestionably the best preserved and most culturally vibrant relic of that era: 1,100-acre (445 ha) Balboa Park (see sidebar p. 153). In the park are 18 distinct museums and art institutes, three theaters, 19 formal and informal gardens, the nation's largest zoo, and more Spanish colonial architecture than anywhere else in the state.

The park is arranged in a series of plazas along the main road, El Prado, with the landmark tower at the east end. It was

Buildings for the Panama-California Exposition were centered around the Plaza del Prado.

night. Out on Mission Bay (see pp. 160–161), water-skiers skip over lacy wave crests like dolphins leaping. Don't forget the suntan lotion.

Balboa Park

Of the two major "exposition cities" built in 1915 to commemorate the opening of the Panama Canal (San Francisco and San Diego), San Diego is

designed with two purposes, one pragmatic, one aesthetic. By building a giant Pacific "Dream City," the park's founders hoped to establish San Diego as the preferred port of call for ships arriving through the new Panama Canal. By bringing in architect Bertram Grosvenor Goodhue, known for his flashy Mediterranean style, the city fathers also sought to communicate San

Diego's vision of itself as a merging of garden and city.

If Balboa Park's official purpose was, as its founders said in one 1930s pamphlet, "to illustrate the progress and possibility of the human race," the unofficial one was not unlike that of today's sophisticated relocation ads used to lure new companies to new cities. This effort was redoubled in 1935, when the city held another world exposition, adding Moorish and Italianate elements to the original Mediterranean aspects. As state librarian Kevin Starr notes, this was architecture as "romantic text." Yet it was the continuing enlistment of the city's mercantile elite that saved Balboa Park and preserved it for what it is today: one of the best kept secrets in American tourism.

How to Visit: To take full advantage of all that Balboa Park has to offer, set aside at least two days. The Explorer Pass is available for individuals and families and grants admission to all museums for an entire year; the latter pass is good for two adults and up to four children.

Park near the zoo and walk in, take the tram, or stroll across **Cabrillo Bridge,** which links the Prado area with the historic Banker's Hill district in the west. Ask your hotel concierge to make reservations at one of the evening theater performances in the park.

The San Diego Museum of Art: Although all of them are worth a visit, three Balboa Park museums warrant particular

The Look of Balboa

Balboa Park as we know it today is largely the result of two world's fairs: the 1915 Panama-California Exposition and the 1935 California Pacific International Exposition. Inspired by the recent opening of the Panama Canal, the 1915 event produced many of the park's Spanish Renaissance Revival landmarks, including the California Tower, Cabrillo Bridge, and Organ Pavilion, as well as the San Diego Zoo (see pp. 156–158). Aimed at boosting the local economy during the Great Depression, the 1935 fair brought a far different style to Balboa—the distinctive art deco buildings that now house the aerospace, automotive, and sports museums, but also the beloved Old Globe theater.

note. The largest of the city's museums, the San Diego Museum of Art has a significant collection of Renaissance and post-Renaissance works by Spanish artists. The best known work is "Quince, Cabbage, Melon, and Cucumber," painted in 1602 by Juan Sánchez Cotán. One wonders how a man could produce such a realistic depiction of fertility and then the following year, as Cotán did, renounce the world and become a monk. An outstanding work is Diego Rivera's "The Hands of Dr. Moore" (1940), with an anthropomorphic tree that represents both the natural world and the female anatomy. Although born in Greece, El Greco did his best work in Toledo, Spain, and belongs here among the Spaniards. "The Penitent St. Peter," painted in 1600, startles with its use of light, reminiscent

San Diego Museum of Art

- 1450 El Prado, Balboa Park
- 619-232-7931
- Closed Sun a.m. & Mon.
- $$$

www.sdmart.org

**Timken Museum
of Art–Putnam
Collection**

✉ 1500 El Prado,
   Balboa Park

☎ 619-239-5548

🕐 Closed Sun. a.m.
   & Mon.

**www.timken
museum.org**

of Rembrandt's "Raising of
Lazarus."

The museum also has a notable grouping of American painters,
chief among them Thomas Eakins.
His "Elizabeth Crowell With a
Dog," painted in 1871, will strike a
chord with any animal lover.

EXPERIENCE:
Balboa in December

Although Balboa Park is great at any time
of year, nothing beats **December Nights**
(www.balboapark.org/december-nights) during the yuletide season. Normally held on
the first weekend in December, the event
draws as many as 300,000 people to the
park for holiday foods, drinks, crafts, and
entertainment. All of the park's museums
are open for free from 5 p.m. to 9 p.m., and
a number of local arts groups stage free
dance, drama, and music performances.
Other highlights include international holiday foods at the House of Pacific Relations
cottages, the **Santa Lucia Procession,** the
Spanish Village arts fair, and **carnival
rides** in the Pan American Plaza.

**Mingei Interna-
tional Museum**

✉ 1439 El Prado,
   Balboa Park

☎ 619-239-0003

🕐 Closed Mon.

www.mingei.org

**Timken Museum of Art
–Putnam Collection:** Just
east, the **Timken Museum
of Art–Putnam Collection** is
housed in the only nonrevivalist
building in Balboa Park, a cool
modern temple of marble and
glass. This eccentric grouping
of European and American
masterworks is marked by its
even more eccentric juxtaposi-
tion with a world-class collection
of Russian iconography. From
late 16th-century Russia, the
wood panel "St. Basil the Great
and Scenes From His Life" is

full of quiet power; religious
icons were, after all, conceived
as a medium for meditation
upon God's kingdom. From
1838 comes a painting by Jean-
Baptiste-Camille Corot. Entitled
"View of Volterra," the work is a
masterful evocation of the long
approach from Siena to the old
Etruscan town of Volterra, which
Corot first sketched on a summer visit to Italy in 1834. The
sensuous realism of late 19th-
century American painters is
found in "The Magnolia Flower,"
painted in 1888 by Martin Johnson Heade.

Mingei International
Museum: Scholars and folk
art buffs flock to see the most
dynamic of the park's museums, the **Mingei International
Museum,** which is dedicated to
world folk art, both contemporary and historical. Titles of past
exhibitions hint at the diversity:
"American Expressions of Lib-
erty"; "India: Village, Tribal, Ritual
Arts"; "Folk Toys of the World";
and "¡Viva los Artisanos!" In
2020, the museum embarked
on a major transformation to
include a gorgeous new theater,
an education center for hands-
on learning, and a new grand
staircase lit by the Museum's
signature "Enlightenment" chandelier by Dale Chihuly.

Other Museums: Other
museums in the park include
the **Museum of Photo-graphic
Arts,** which offers an extensive
collection of the 20th century's
leading practitioners. The **San**

Diego History Center charts several hundred years of local history through temporary displays and a new permanent exhibit called "Place of Promise."

The Space Theater at the **Reuben H. Fleet Science Center** contains a planetarium and IMAX theater, while the **San Diego Air & Space Museum** has a superb collection of historic aircraft and exhibits on space exploration.

The collection at the **San Diego Automotive Museum** includes late 19th-century horseless carriages, muscle cars, and cars of the space age. The **Model Railroad Museum** *(Casa de Balboa, tel 619-696-0199, www.sdmrm. org, closed Mon.)* specializes in train scenes of San Diego and southern California.

The **Museum of Us** *(1350 El Prado, tel 619-239-2001, www. museumofus.org)* looks at humankind's evolution from cultural and physical perspectives. The **San Diego Natural History Museum** *(1788 El Prado, tel 619-232-3821, www.sdnhm.org)* specializes in exhibits explaining broad habitats and in the geology of gems and minerals.

Lastly, the **Comic-Con Museum** *(2131 Pan American Plaza, tel 619-414-1020, www.comic-con.org/museum)*, dedicated to an appreciation of comics, will occupy the former Hall of Champions.

Gardens & Organ Pavilion:
The **Spreckels Organ Pavilion** *(just S of the Plaza de Panama on El Prado)* also harks back to a simpler time, when, in 1915, civic leaders John D. and Adolph B. Spreckels spent the then huge sum of $100,000 on building the world's largest outdoor organ. On Sunday afternoons, young musicians try out this old classic. Free **Twilight in the Park** concerts are held on midweek evenings in summer.

East of the organ pavilion, the **Japanese Friendship Garden** is one of the more recent additions to the park. Its 11-acre (4.4 ha) site features winding paths, stone lanterns, and Zen rock gardens.

Built with more than 12 miles (19 km) of redwood lath, the **Botanical Building & Lily Pond** *(betw. Casa del Prado & the San Diego Museum of Art)* houses a wide variety of exotic plants. The enormous lily pond has proven highly adaptable over the years. During World War II, when many park buildings were used as troop hospitals, it served as a rehabilitation pool. In the blistering summer of 1945, the pond became a swimming pool for 22,000 local children.

Theaters:
Some of the best theater on the West Coast takes place at Balboa Park's three-venue complex. Built for the 1935 California Pacific International Exposition, the **Old Globe**

Museum of Photographic Arts
- ✉ 1649 El Prado, Balboa Park
- ☎ 619-238-7559
- 🕐 Closed Mon.

www.mopa.org

San Diego History Center
- ✉ 1649 El Prado, Balboa Park
- ☎ 619-232-6203
- 🕐 Closed Mon.
- 💲 $

www.sandiego history.org

Reuben H. Fleet Science Center
- ✉ 1875 El Prado, Balboa Park
- ☎ 619-238-1233
- 💲 $$

www.fleetscience.org

San Diego Air & Space Museum
- ✉ 2001 Pan American Plaza, Balboa Park
- ☎ 619-234-8291
- 💲 $$$

www.sandiegoairand space.org

San Diego Automotive Museum
- ✉ 2080 Pan American Plaza, Balboa Park
- ☎ 619-231-2886
- 💲 $$$

www.sdauto museum.org

EXPERIENCE: Behind the Scenes at the Zoo

As well as regular admission, the San Diego Zoo offers visitors special behind-the-scenes experiences for an additional price.

The zoo's popular **Inside Look Tours** (*$$$$$*), for example, afford visitors a rare opportunity for two-hour private guided adventures focused on how the zoo cares for its wildlife. Each tour focuses on either giraffes, polar bears, flamingos, or baboons. Insider Look Tours are suitable for everyone 5 years old and older. Children 15 and younger must be accompanied by an adult.

To see animals not usually displayed to the public, take an **Animals in Action Experience** (*$$$$$*), in which the zoo's wildlife behavior specialists introduce you to some ambassador species and educate you about the zoo's ongoing conservation efforts around the world.

Or maybe you want to see the zoo's world-famous cheetahs frolicking before the zoo opens by taking the private two-hour **Early Morning Cheetah Experience** (*$$$$$*), which also takes you to other African animal habitats. The staff will even customize a private visit to your interests on the popular five-hour **Exclusive VIP Experience** (*$$$$$*), which includes a sit-down lunch. Reservations must be made at least 72 hours in advance.

Children's programs include **Kid's Wild Night Out** (*$$$$*). Offered on select Saturdays in summer, it lets youngsters spend a fun evening at the zoo with Dr. Zoolittle and some animal friends.

The Old Globe

✉ 1363 Old Globe Way, Balboa Park

☎ 619-234-5623

www.theoldglobe. org

San Diego Zoo

✉ 2920 Zoo Dr., Balboa Park

☎ 619-231-1515

$ $$$$$

www.sandiegozoo .org

theater was dedicated to abbreviated performances of Shakespeare. After a series of fires, the Old Globe was incorporated into today's triplex to make this San Diego's largest arts institution. In 1984, it received a Tony award for Outstanding Regional Theater, and since then the complex has launched several new works.

Two other theaters operate alongside the Old Globe. They are the **Sheryl and Harvey White Theatre** and the **Lowell Davies Festival Theater,** each with its own unusual seating configuration—the former in the round, the latter open air.

San Diego Zoo: Founded in 1916 by the enterprising Dr. Harry Wegeforth, the San Diego Zoo has grown far beyond even its founder's grandest dreams. Resting on a hundred acres (40 ha) of northern Balboa Park, this state-of-the-art animal park now displays and cares for 3,700 animals representing more than 800 species. Its botanical credentials (more than 6,500 plant species) startle as well; with only a little imagination, one can, within one park, experience jungle, tundra, and rain forest. Many come to San Diego to see this attraction alone.

The zoo is divided into nine animal zones representing different continents or geographical areas. Right behind the flamingos at the entrance is the vast **Lost Forest,** a lush tropical habitat with streams, waterfalls, and meandering paths. Hidden among the trees is the **gorilla exhibit**—one of the zoo's top attractions—2.5 acres (1 ha) of simulated African rain forest within an 8,000-square-foot (745 sq m) enclosure that is home to a troop of western lowland gorillas. Inside the same zone is the **Scripps Aviary,** with more than 130 African birds in free flight.

In the canyon west of the great apes is the stunning **Tiger Trail,** where visitors walk down a misty forest path before coming to ten enclosures housing more than a hundred animals (including Burmese pythons, narrow-snouted crocodiles, and Malaysian tapirs). The tigers prowl about on a grassy hillside, their appearance made all the more dramatic by the rain forest environs.

At the bottom of the canyon is **Hippo Beach,** where you can view these 4,000-pounders (180 kg) both aboveground and underwater, through a two-inch-thick (5 cm) window of laminated glass.

If the weather is hot, the **Northern Frontier,** located at the park's outer boundary, provides a soothing scene. Conjuring two acres (.8 ha) of Arctic tundra, complete with Siberian reindeer and arctic foxes, the plunge features a group of playful polar bears busily cavorting in a 130,000-gallon (492,103 L) tank. Their underwater antics are visible through a large acrylic window. Many swim right up to the glass, curious about the odd creatures on the other side.

If you backtrack, the **Panda Canyon** is next. The zoo keeps adding to its population of these endangered creatures: Bai Yun, who arrived from China in 1996, has since given birth to several cubs, most recently in 2010. The exhibit area includes the **Giant Panda Research Station.** Because pandas and their offspring are only loaned by China, the last of San

The gorilla exhibit is always a crowd-pleaser. A visit to the zoo late in the day is most rewarding, as the crowds have thinned and animals become more active.

Julian

🗺 131 H2

Visitor Information

✉ Chamber of Commerce, 2129 Main St., Julian

☎ 760-765-1857

www.julianca.com

Diego's panda's returned to China in 2019.

The zoo's highly creative **Elephant Odyssey** on the east mesa, revolves around extinct animals that lived in southern California 12,000 years ago and their living relatives. The Pleistocene creatures come alive in full-scale models and a replica tar pit filled with fossils. The living animals—lions and jaguars, tapirs and capybaras, elephants and pronghorn antelope—roam large habitats in between.

Last, you come to the zoo's three latest additions. **Africa Rocks** and **Urban Jungle** are home to baboons, rhinos, giraffes, and penguins; **Outback** displays the requisite kangaroos and koalas.

To your left upon entering is the outstanding **Discovery Outpost,** complete with reptile house and a display of increasingly rare Galápagos tortoises. A **Nighttime Zoo** is open in summer.

INSIDER TIP:

In October, head north and east of San Diego to the old gold-mining town of Julian, known nowadays for its art galleries and annual Apple Festival.

—JOE YOGERST
National Geographic author

Historic San Diego

As the oldest Spanish settlement in California, San Diego and its environs are full of historic places, some major, some minor. The City of San Diego has made visiting several nearby sites both easy and comfortable. A trolley system offers an outstanding two-hour narrated tour, with the advantage that you can debark and reboard the trolley all day.

California's Iconic Hotel

The centerpiece of the 4,100-acre (1,659 ha) Silver Strand Peninsula that separates San Diego's harbor from the Pacific Ocean is the fanciful Victorian **Hotel del Coronado** *(1500 Orange Ave., tel 800-468-3533, www.hoteldel.com).* Built in 1888 by Elisha Babcock, Jr. , and H. L. Story, the hotel has been an enduring attraction ever since.

A favorite getaway of blue bloods and Hollywood doyens, the gleaming white structure oozes dated opulence and has hosted the likes of the Duke and Duchess of Windsor, Henry James, and L. Frank Baum, who wrote the *Wizard of Oz* (1900) here and supposedly modeled his Emerald City on the view from his room. Most famously, Marilyn Monroe paraded the hallways in *Some Like It Hot* (1959).

While the hotel is still a fanciful place to visit, with historical tours available, the wise traveler will limit outings here to the off-season or midweek, when the tour buses dwindle in number.

Today's "Hotel Del," often busy and crowded, is a place to see but not one to linger in, even for a meal. Instead, enjoy a drink in the woodsy old lobby bar, then jump back on the San Diego-Coronado ferry *(tel 619-234-4111, www.flagshipsd.com)* and return across the water to see a play in Balboa Park (see pp. 155–156).

Among the attractions are the revived **Gaslamp Quarter** *(Broadway & 4th–6th Aves.)*, where Wyatt Earp ran such a bawdy operation that he caused his more uptight neighbors to move north. Since the 1980s, the quarter has become the place to shop and eat in historic San Diego.

Old Town State Park, protected as the site of the early settlement, also offers the splendid **Junípero Serra Museum,** which holds relics and pieces of art from the original mission. Nearby you can view the restored Victoriana of **Heritage Park** *(2460 Heritage Park Row, tel 858-565-3600, www. sdparks.org)*, while kids can romp amid interactive displays at the **New Children's Museum.**

Besides taking you to **Balboa Park** (see pp. 152–156) and the **Coronado Peninsula** (see sidebar p. 158), the trolley also travels along San Diego's seafront. There, maritime buffs can explore the **Maritime Museum,** where the spectacular exhibits include some landmark historic vessels, including the 1860s *Star of India* clipper plus U.S. and Soviet Cold War–era submarines. Also here is a replica of explorer Juan Rodríguez Cabrillo's *San Salvador*, and a re-creation of the 24-gun H.M.S. *Surprise* frigate. Nearby is the **USS Midway Museum** *(Navy Pier, tel 619-544-9600, www.midway.org)*, showcasing the aircraft carrier that berthed here permanently in 2004 after a 47-year career and today rewards visitors with a virtual-reality flight experience, plus military aircraft spanning five decades.

San Diego's historic Gaslamp Quarter fills more than 16 blocks.

An ongoing redevelopment of downtown San Diego is transforming the long-dormant area into a vibrant neighborhood anchored by the 42,000-seat **PETCO Park** *(www.mlb.com/padres)* baseball stadium. Also in the downtown area is the **Museum of Contemporary Art** *(1100 Kettner Blvd., tel 858-454-3541, www.mcasd. org, closed Wed., $$$)*, a counterpart to the one in La Jolla (see p. 146).

Farther Afield

From San Diego, take Calif. 209 to **Cabrillo National Monument** *(map p. 131 G1; 1800 Cabrillo Memorial Dr., tel 619-523-4285, www.nps.gov/cabr)*, at the tip of the Point Loma Peninsula. As the name suggests, this is where Juan Rodríguez Cabrillo, the great Portuguese explorer—in service to Spain—became the first European to set foot in California. More appealing than the monument and the **Cabrillo Museum** is the surrounding parkland, 144 acres (58 ha)

Junípero Serra Museum

✉ 2727 Presidio Dr., San Diego

☎ 619-297-3258

$ $

www.sandiego history.org/ serramuseum

New Children's Museum

✉ 200 W. Island Ave., San Diego

☎ 619-233-8792

$ $$

www.thinkplay create.org

Maritime Museum

✉ 1492 N. Harbor Dr., San Diego

☎ 619-234-9153

$ $$$$

www.sdmaritime.org

Ocean Beach

Visitor Information

✉ MainStreet Association, 1868 Bacon St., #A, San Diego

☎ 619-224-4906

www.oceanbeach sandiego.com

Belmont Park

✉ 3146 Mission Blvd., San Diego

☎ 858-488-1549

www.belmont park.com

offering spectacular views of city and bay, as well as extensive hiking trails. You may also visit the lower rooms of the 1855 **Old Point Loma Lighthouse,** a short walk from the monument.

On the northwestern edge of Point Loma is the funky seaside neighborhood of **Ocean Beach,** where antiques shops, coffee-houses, and counterculture out-lets line Newport Avenue. At the end of the avenue are the Ocean Beach pier and a broad, white-sand strand with a special area where dogs can frolic in the surf.

On the north side of the San Diego River estuary is **Mission Beach,** a tightly packed neighbor-hood that hugs a narrow isthmus between Mission Bay and the ocean. Walking and biking paths run along both shores.

But the area's main attrac-tion is **Belmont Park,** an

old-fashioned seaside amusement park founded in 1925. Among its iconic features are the Giant Dipper roller coaster (listed on the National Register of Historic Places) and a huge indoor swim-ming pool called the Plunge.

On the north side of the bay is **Pacific Beach,** where the historic Crystal Pier Hotel *(tel 800-748-5894, www.crystalpier.com)* offers the only over-water accommoda-tion along the California coast.

Mission Bay & SeaWorld

Jubilant **Mission Bay** is a 4,600-acre (1,861 ha) aquatic park that is dedicated to just about every water-based activity imaginable (see sidebar p. 161). It's also where San Diegans go to stay healthy and let rip.

Every April, the bay hosts the boisterous **San Diego Crew Clas-sic** *(http://crewclassic.org)*, which

■ At SeaWorld San Diego you can see eye-to-eye with orcas in an underwater viewing area.

EXPERIENCE: Ocean Life, Southern California Style

Mission Bay has 17 miles (27 km) of beaches, with eight swim-only areas. You'll find sandy beaches open to the public at **Leisure Lagoon** and **De Anza Cove,** along the eastern shore, and **Ventura Cove,** on the west side. **Sail Bay,** in the northwest part of the park, is reserved for sailing and paddle craft. **Fiesta Bay,** in the northeast, is the domain of powerboats and those who like to water-ski, wakeboard, or tube.

Mission Bay Sportscenter (1010 Santa Clara Pl., tel 858-488-1004, www .missionbaysportcenter.com) rents a wide variety of watercraft, including sailboats, powerboats, pontoon boats, kayaks, paddleboards, and surfboards. It also offers guided sunset cruises, Jet Ski tours, and summer evening rentals to watch the SeaWorld fireworks.

The nearby **Mission Bay Aquatic Center** (1001 Santa Clara Pl., tel 858-488-1000, www.mbaquaticcenter.com) offers year-round instruction in a variety of water sports, including wakeboarding, stand-up paddling, and windsurfing.

The bay is flanked by 14 miles (22.5 km) of bike paths. The most popular of these are the fishhook-shape route between the Bahia Resort and the tip of Crown Point, and the meandering path between De Anza Cove and the big Tecolote Shores playground. **Cheap Rentals** (3689 Mission Blvd., tel 858-488-9070, www.cheap-rentals.com) rents bikes, rollerblades, and other sports equipment.

---

attracts collegiate rowing teams from around the U.S. and Canada. In September comes **Bayfair** (http://sandiegobayfair.org), the World Series of powerboat racing.

Located on the bay's southern shore, **SeaWorld San Diego** has long been at the leading edge of animal marine entertainment, education, rescue, and research. The park's emblematic attraction is its orcas ("killer whales"), which swim in a huge tank with underwater viewing windows and giant LCD screens. In 2017, the theatrical shows in an outdoor stadium were replaced with more educational shows that focus on the whales' natural behaviors. Other popular shows include the **Blue Horizons dolphin theater** and the **Clyde and Seamore sea lion cabaret**.

Animal habitats include those for sea otters and sea turtles, and the popular **Shark Encounter,** with an underwater tunnel that lets you get within inches of the prehistoric predators.

The chilly **Penguin Encounter** features 300 of the cute, aquatic birds. Next door, **Wild Arctic** presents a unique combination of walruses and white beluga whales.

SeaWorld recently updated its other thrill rides, including, in 2021, the new plunging, writhing **Emperor**—the tallest, fastest dive-coaster in North America. The **Electric Eel** roller-coaster, added in 2018, guarantees an electrifying ride, especially at 62 miles (99.8 km) an hour through its inverted roll. And an imaginary voyage to the mythical lost city is the theme of **Journey to Atlantis,** which starts with a 60-foot (18 m) plunge into a lagoon. ∎

SeaWorld San Diego

- 131 G1
- 500 Sea World Dr., San Diego
- 619-222-4732
- $$$$$

www.seaworld.com/ san-diego

MEXICAN FOLK ART

The Mexican city of Tijuana is a 15-minute trolley car ride south from San Diego (see pp. 158–159). These days, many come to this once rough border town not for the illicit delights of drink, dames, and gambling—although those still abound—but for Mexican tribal art. However, U.S. visitors to this city, a battleground in Mexico's drug wars, should exercise caution and follow Department of State advisories (www.travel.state.gov).

■ Typical Mexican folk art includes traditional bead-ornament *huichol* figures.

The origins of the Mexican folk art industry lie in 18th-century Mexico, when village priests and lay artisans began crafting ornamentation for new churches. These pieces often combine colorful pre-Columbian nature worship and traditional Old World religious iconography. The result is rustic, hallucinatory, festive, and even provocative.

To get to Tijuana by car, take I-5 or Calif. 805 south past San Ysidro to the International Border Crossing. Park, cross the bridge on foot, and pick up a cab on the other side. (Ask the driver how much he charges for the trip downtown.) If you choose to drive across the border, one-day insurance is available at several sites. You can also get to San Ysidro by trolley, available at a number of sites around the city. For the closest, call **San Diego Trolley** (tel 619-233-3004, www.sdmts.com). The inexpensive journey takes just 45 minutes. U.S. citizens should carry proof of citizenship for reentry.

While folk art of varying quality, new and old, can be found throughout Tijuana, one of the better shops is **Tolán** (between Calles 7 & 8 on Ave. Revolución, tel 011 52 664-294-9500). Go there first to get an idea of top price and top quality, then explore alternatives along the various calles to make comparisons. The key is to have fun. Bargain, but don't take it seriously.

What to Buy

Among the most popular items are **retablos,** painted tin-and-wood plaques used as votives in tiny household shrines across Mexico. They often bear the likeness of the Virgin of Guadalupe. Some of the best come from the state of Oaxaca. Look, too, for **cerámicas festas,** brightly colored ceramics used to commemorate the Day of the Dead. These range in size from the tiny clay skulls made in Oaxaca to the fantastic candelabra and Nativity scenes made in Puebla. Renderings of various **mythical beasts** are usually made in Metepec, outside Mexico City. You will also find **santos** and **bultos** (saints and "figures") in tin, clay, wood, and ceramic, and **milagros,** tin representations of body parts, often pinned to statues of saints in hope of a healing miracle.

Woven goods, both everyday and precious, include the **sarapes** of northern Mexico, **rebozos,** and **huipils,** tunics made popular by the Mixtec peoples, who dye them with colors from insects and sea snails. The Zapoteca people are known for their copying abilities. Huipils and **quechquemitls,** or capes, made during the 1920s and '30s, often display such European influences as Escher and Miró.

SANTA BARBARA

North from Los Angeles, Santa Barbara benefits from a near-perfect climate of sunny skies, refreshing sea breezes, and pleasantly warm temperatures. Outdoor enthusiasts come here for horseback riding, surfing, camping, and bicycling. There are also botanical gardens to explore and interesting wine country. Downtown, the street scene thrives with a diverse crowd of students, couples on holiday, and old-timers who stay for the late afternoon breeze.

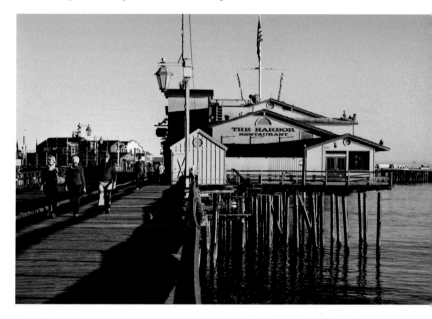

Stroll along Stearns Wharf for boutique shops, fishing opportunities, and on-the-water dining.

Santa Barbara, which has nurtured its Hispanic roots, revels in red-tiled roofs and mission revival architecture. But the atmosphere is not kitsch. The Chumash word *anacapa* ("pleasant illusion") seems to sum it all up.

Mission Santa Barbara

Founded in 1786 but not completed until 1820, Mission Santa Barbara *(2201 Laguna St. via Alameda Padre Serra,*

tel 805-682-4149, www.santa barbaramission.org, $) is one of California's most architecturally distinguished missions, its Ionic columns and Roman facade taking their cues from the drawings of Vetruvius Pollio, dating from 27 B.C. The Roman connection derives from St. Barbara, the mission's namesake, an early Christian martyr. Some of the leading hidalgos and Americanos of the era were educated in its mid-19th-century boys' school.

Santa Barbara

🗺 130 C4

Visitor Information

✉ Santa Barbara Conference & Visitors Bureau and Film Commission, 500 E. Montecito St.

☎ 805-966-9222

www.santabarbaraca .com

Arlington Theatre

✉ 1317 State St.

☎ 805-963-4408

**www.thearlington
theatre.com**

Casa de la Guerra Historic House Museum

✉ 15 E. de la
Guerra St.

☎ Tours: 805-965-
0093

🕐 Closed a.m. &
Mon.

💲 $

**www.sbthp.org/
casadelaguerra**

A big attraction is the mission's interior colors, which still glow. Be sure to see the **baptismal font.**

The grounds bear extensive Native American influence. The mission fathers still minister to the area's remaining Chumash, and the commemorative seal to "Juana Maria," a Chumash woman, is the only such plaque dedicated to a Native American in the entire mission system.

The City

The focal point of Santa Barbara's street scene is **State Street,** with its shops, restaurants, and mission revival landmarks like the

1931 **Arlington Theatre,** where concerts, lectures, and movies are part of an ever-changing entertainment menu.

Another relic of the same style and era is the nearby **El Paseo** *(812 State St.),* a shop-filled pedestrian zone created in the early 1920s. The shopping precinct incorporates a much older structure, the **Casa de la Guerra Historic House Museum,** built in 1819 by the Spanish commandante, José de la

Mission Santa Barbara

**A missionary bedroom
circa 1800**

Guerra. It was de la Guerra who, after Mexico won California from Spain, became the small pueblo's commercial leader. His wife was the daughter of Don Raimundo Carrillo, a veteran of the Sacred Expedition of 1869 that had founded the city. A look at the highbrow European furnishings so lovingly acquired by the Carrillo family brings to life the early days of the community here.

The immediate area is filled with other well-preserved remnants of Spanish days, including the **Hill-Carrillo Adobe** (1825–26) at 11–15 E. Carrillo Street, the **Lugo Adobe** (1830) at 114 E. de la Guerra Street, and the **Rochin Adobe** (1856) at 820 Santa Barbara Street. Five blocks east is the **Presidio Chapel** (1788), which contains the original fort's 18th-century decor. It offers a short slide show and a scale model of the Old Presidio.

To the north, the outstanding **Santa Barbara Museum of Art** has important holdings of works by O'Keeffe, Remington,

Santa Barbara Museum of Art

✉ 1130 State St.
☎ 805-963-4364
🕐 Closed Mon.
💲 $$

www.sbma.net

Cloister garden

Cloister

Mission church

Statues from the facade

Kitchen circa 1800

Santa Barbara County Courthouse

- ✉ 1100 Anacapa St.
- ☎ Tours: 805-962-6464
- 🕐 Guided tours 2 p.m. Mon.–Sat. & 10:30 a.m. Mon.–Tues. & Fri.

www.sbcourthouse.org

Santa Barbara Botanical Gardens

- ✉ 1212 Mission Canyon
- ☎ 805-682-4726
- 💲 $$$$

www.sbbg.org

Santa Barbara Zoo

- ✉ 500 Ninos Dr. (off Cabrillo)
- ☎ 805-962-5339
- 💲 $$

www.sbzoo.org

and Hopper. Two blocks east is the pièce de résistance of Spanish colonial revival, the **Santa Barbara County Courthouse** (1929), considered one of the most beautiful municipal gems in the U.S. Designed by architect William Moser, the courthouse offers daily guided tours. Don't miss it.

North of the mission district, the **Santa Barbara Botanical Gardens** are the most remarkable of Santa Barbara's public gardens. More than 5 miles (8 km) of trails wander through 78 acres (31.5 ha) of California native plants.

Directly east of the mission is 18-acre **Franceschi Park** (1501 Mission Ridge Rd.), named for Emmanuele Franceschi, who lived in Santa Barbara between 1893 and 1912. The panoramic views and old stone pathways through aloe gardens make this an intriguing botanical getaway.

Southeast, nearer the beach, are the **Santa Barbara Zoo,** a small zoo in a garden of an old estate, and, farther up Cabrillo, the 32-acre (13 ha) **Andree Clark Bird Refuge** (Los Patos Way, Cabrillo exit from U.S. 101), where you can bicycle through lush gardens squawking with waterbirds.

Many of the area's most scenic beaches are north of the city, but for plain seaside fun try **Leadbetter Beach** or **West Beach,** adjacent to historic **Stearns Wharf** (www.stearnswharf.org). The wharf itself is a major attraction, with several good seafood restaurants, a vintner's shop, and **Ty Warner Sea Center** (211 Stearns Wharf, tel 805-962-2526, www.sbnature.org/visit/seacenter, $). You could rent a bicycle and take in **Chase Palm Park,** also adjacent to Stearns.

EXPERIENCE: Riding Horses in Wine Country

Long before the advent of boutique wineries, the Santa Ynez Valley was known for its horse ranches. Spreads like **Barton Thoroughbreds** (4050 Casey Ave., Santa Ynez, tel 805-693-1777, www.bartonthoroughbreds.com) have produced a steady stream of thoroughbred champions over the years. Often seen riding the range, President Ronald Reagan transformed the Rancho del Cielo into the Western White House. Michael Jackson morphed another ranch into his Neverland nirvana.

Today, you can find equine adventures throughout the valley. In addition to scenic trail rides, **Little Big Riding School** (Rancho Olivos, 2035 Edison St., Santa Ynez, tel 805-886-2215, www.santaynez valleyhorsebackriding.com) hosts lessons and camps ($$$$–$$$$$) for adults and

children. As the name suggests, **Vino Vaqueros** (tel 805-944-0493, www.vino vaqueros.com, $$$$$) outside of Los Olivos combines horseback riding through scenic vineyards with a tasting at a local winery. **Alisal Guest Ranch** (1054 Alisal Rd., Solvang, tel 800-425-4725, www.alisal .com) offers rides to its overnight guests along 50 miles (80 km) of trails, as well as private lessons and a cattle round-up experience on Monday and Friday.

One of the valley's most unique establishments is **Return to Freedom** (tel 805-737-9246, www.returntofreedom.org), a wild horse sanctuary that provides a haven for more than 400 mustangs from around the West. Although not open to the public on a daily basis, the ranch hosts educational tours and hikes.

At sunrise and sunset, the glowing waves around Santa Barbara lure visitors to stunning Pacific vistas.

North of Santa Barbara

To get a sense of Santa Barbara's historic grandeur, drive northwest on U.S. 101, past three remarkable state beaches: **El Capitan, Refugio,** and **Gaviota.** The rangers can tell you where the old **hot springs** are located, just to the north off Vandenburg Road.

From here, the highway veers inland through some of the most beautiful oak and chaparral in the state. Stop at **Nojoqui Falls** *(off Alisal Rd.)* for a short hike up to the area's only major waterfall. Continuing north, take Calif. 246 to **Solvang** *(see map p. 130 B4; visitor information, Solvang Conference & Visitors Bureau, 1639 Copenhagen Dr., tel 805-688-6144, www.solvangusa.com),* a Danish village that is also home to **Mission Santa Inés.**

Drive through the Santa Ynez Valley before joining scenic Calif. 154. In tiny **Los Olivos** *(see map p. 130 B5; visitor information, www.losolivosca.com),* you can browse for antiques and visit the wine tasting rooms plus more than 30 wineries of this charming heart-of-wine-country town.

Return to Santa Barbara via Calif. 154, which parallels the old stagecoach route. Stop at **Chumash Painted Caves State Historical Park** to see the Native American cave art.

South of Santa Barbara

Go southwest on U.S. 101 to the exclusive enclave of Montecito where, by appointment, you can visit **Casa del Herrero,** a private, 11-acre (4.4 ha) estate known for its outstanding Spanish-Moorish-style garden. Then explore the antique shops in nearby **Carpinteria,** at the end of Calle Ocho Road and a grand lookout point.

Farther south on U.S. 101 is the harbor town of **Ventura,** known for its bargain antiques and the **Murphy Auto Museum** *(2230 Statham Blvd., tel 805-487-4333, www.murphyautomuseum.org, closed Mon.–Fri.),* displaying autos spanning the last hundred years. Little **Mission San Buenaventura** *(see map p. 130 C4, 211 E. Main St., Ventura, tel 805-643-4318, www.sanbuenaventuramission.org)* was rebuilt in 1809 after being destroyed by fire. ■

Mission Santa Inés

- 1760 Mission Dr., Solvang
- 805-688-4815

www.missionsantaines.org

Chumash Painted Caves State Historical Park

- 130 C4
- Painted Cave Rd.
- 805-733-3713

www.parks.ca.gov

Casa del Herrero

- 1387 E. Valley Rd., Montecito
- 805-565-5653
- Tours twice daily Wed. & Sat. Closed mid-Nov. to mid-Feb.
- $$$$

www.casadelherrero.com

Ventura

- 130 C4

Visitor Information

- 101 S. California St., Ventura
- 805-641-1400

www.visitventuraca.com

MISSION LA PURISIMA CONCEPCIÓN

There may be more beautiful missions than La Purisima Concepción, a humble grouping of adobe buildings, but no other mission better captures the essence of mission life in the early 19th century. Completely restored by the Civilian Conservation Corps in the 1930s, La Purisima—"the most pure"—is a perfect place to spend a meditative morning away from the crowds, wandering among the old mission buildings and delighting in the outstanding garden of herbs and native plants.

Mission La Purisima Concepción

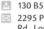 130 B5

✉ 2295 Purisima Rd., Lompoc (off Calif. 246, 3 miles NE of central Lompoc)

☎ 805-733-3713

 $

www.lapurisima mission.org

Completed in 1822 after its original structure was destroyed by the great earthquake of 1812, La Purisima is a repository of colonial history. And while much of its story underscores the tragedy wrought on the Chumash by newcomers to their lands, much also serves to dispel the stereotype of the Indian as a passive rustic.

Beyond the **visitor center,** which provides an introductory overview, is the **cemetery,** starting point for the mission's one-hour guided tours. Here you come face to face with the blunt fact that, between 1804 and 1807, more than 500 Chumash died at La Purisima from exposure to European smallpox and measles.

Next to the cemetery, the long, narrow **church** once accommodated up to a thousand worshippers for Sunday Mass. Its uneven floors and austere ornamentation reflect the rawness of mission life. The "river of life" pattern on the main doors suggests that the Chumash imbued their churches with their own art.

The nearby **soldiers' quarters, carpenter's shop,** and **weavery** tell of the entrepreneurial nature of the mission system. Each unit was expected to grow and prosper through its own labors. Grain was milled and tallow processed for soap on the back patio. Nearby stands the **dormitory** for unmarried women.

In 1824, the tension between the Chumash and soldiers grew so great at La Purisima that neophytes here joined a rebellion that had begun at nearby Mission Santa Inés (see p. 167). Surrounding La Purisima, a group of Chumash seized two cannon, built a wooden wall around the mission, and held their Spanish captives for a month before backup troops arrived to quash the action.

The last major building consists of the **padres' quarters,** a **convent,** and a small **chapel**. From here, Padre Mariano Payeras designed the mission's irrigation system and managed a shop that sold candles, wool, and goods made of leather.

The **herb and flower garden** outside the compound has been completely restored to its original glory. In what might these days be called "Mission Ayurvedic," Chumash and padres created the first bicultural apothecary. ∎

OJAI

Among the rites of passage for young Angelenos, a trip to Ojai is considered a spiritual journey and the ideal antidote to busy city life. Tucked in the valley of the Topatopa Mountains, this restorative holistic retreat is most renowned for its natural hot spring spas.

The venerable **Krotona Institute of Theosophy** *(46 Krotona Hill, tel 805-646-1139, closed Mon., www.krotonainstitute.org)* was founded by American followers of Annie Besant, a 19th-century proponent of Theosophy, a universalistic amalgam of Hindu and Christian thought. Regardless of one's religious orientation, a visit to Krotona will help explain the more complex spiritual landscape, which includes 100 acres of natural beauty.

The other culture in Ojai—that of rest and civilized sport—can best be found at the **Ojai Valley Inn & Spa** *(905 Country Club Rd., tel 855-697-8780, www.ojaivalleyinn. com)*. The renovated hotel, in the mission revival style, sits in spectacular country, which you can explore on a rented bicycle. For pure bliss afterward, try a treatment at **The Day Spa of Ojai** *(209 N. Montgomery Ave., tel 805-640-1100, www.thedayspa.com)*.

For real food in classic Ojai fashion, go to the **Ranch House** *(S. Lomita Ave. & Besant Rd., tel 805-646-2360, www.theranchhouse.com)*, where the roasted pork and pâté are out of this world.

Farther east, you can visit the **Ronald Reagan Presidential Library & Museum.** The Gallery of Presidents honors 200 years of the Presidency. The museum also hosts rotating exhibitions, and you can tour Air Force One. ∎

Ojai
- 130 C4

Visitor Information
- Visitors Bureau, 206 N. Signal St., Ojai
- 888-652-4669

www.ojaivisitors.com

Ronald Reagan Presidential Library & Museum
- 130 D4
- 40 Presidential Dr., Simi Valley
- 805-577-4066
- $$$$

www.reagan foundation.org

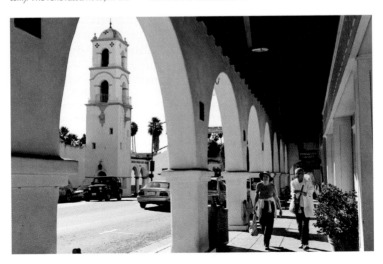

Spanish arches frame the colonial-revival-style post office in Ojai.

CHANNEL ISLANDS NATIONAL PARK

Surrounded by giant beds of gleaming green kelp, punctuated by deep blue coves and the mysterious remains of ships sunk long ago, the Channel Islands became a national park in 1980. From January through March, nature adds a further attraction: the gray whale migration. Visitors can spot the 40-foot (12 m) beasts swimming in schools, often with calves, their spouts shooting high in the air. Bald eagles soar overhead after recently being reintroduced.

Channel Islands National Park

🗺 130 B3–D2

✉ Headquarters, 1901 Spinnaker Dr., Ventura

☎ 805-658-5730

www.nps.gov/chis

HOW TO VISIT
To get a closer look, or simply to take in the adventures and scenery offered by these five islands, make a reservation with **Island Packers** *(tel 805-642-1393, www.islandpackers.com),* the official day boat concessionaire.

On **Anacapa,** itself composed of three islets, watch for whales, bottlenose dolphins, California sea lions, and northern elephant seals. Explore the tide pools at **Frenchys Cove,** and then go on to Anacapa, where, just offshore, you can see the remains of the *Winfield Scott,* which sank here in 1853.

Santa Cruz Island is the largest in the chain. The Chumash were its principal inhabitants for nearly 6,000 years, fishing and plying the waves in their sophisticated canoes. The island is an ecological miracle, home to 600 plant species, nine of which occur only here.

Santa Rosa Island is home to almost 200 bird species. Keep an eye out for dinosaur fossils; in 1994, explorers discovered the skeleton of a dwarf mammoth.

On **San Miguel Island,** explore the beaches and hike 3.5 miles (5.6 km) to the caliche forest to see mineral casts of old tree trunks and 10-foot-tall (3 m) specimens of the flowering plant *Coreopsis.*

Some 50 miles (80 km) to the southeast is **Santa Barbara Island.** Because it had no source of fresh water, the region's Native Americans did not reside on this island. Park authorities aim to restore the island's native flora, once overrun by foreign grasses. ∎

EXPERIENCE: Kayaking the Channel Islands

Channel Islands National Park offers ample attractions for experienced paddlers, from gliding alongside migrating gray whales to exploring cathedral-size sea caves. Cart your own kayak to the islands (20 miles/32 km offshore) on a private boat or with Island Packers (24 hours advance reservation required). Or join a guided excursion.

Channel Islands Adventure Company *(32 Haley St., Santa Barbara, tel 805-884-9283, www.islandkayaking.com, $$$$$)* offers three kayak trips (from 90 minutes to 5 hours) to sea caves around Santa Cruz island's Scorpion Anchorage. A "Snorkel & Kayak Trip" lets you slip under the surface to explore a kelp forest.

You can rent kayaks from **Channel Island Kayak Center** *(1691 Spinnaker Dr., Centura, tel 805-984-5995, http://cikayak. com),* which also offers guided sea cave excursions. It also has a "History & Wildlife Tour" by kayak in Ventura Harbor, although the educational focus is on the Channel Islands.

Before setting out, you should always check with park authorities for the latest information on weather, currents, and sensitive habitats that are off-limits. Because sea kayaking is a high-risk activity, and Channel Island sea conditions can be challenging, the park service recommends that only experienced kayakers attempt independent trips.

The pull of the Pacific revealed in Hearst's fabulous castle, Steinbeck's novels, cozy Carmel, rugged Salinas, and beyond

CENTRAL COAST

The beautiful Pacific Coast Highway (Calif. 1), lined with wildflowers, along the Central Coast

CENTRAL COAST

A single image conveys the essence of California's Central Coast. A Monterey cypress, alone and defiant, is cast against the bruised blue sky of the Pacific over Cypress Point in Pebble Beach. First photographed by Carleton Watkins in 1885, the Monterey cypress has become a kind of visual haiku, denoting a primal Eden by the sea. Certainly John Steinbeck, who hailed from here, thought so.

Bixby Creek Bridge in Big Sur, opened in 1932

The drama of the Central Coast grows directly from its geography, particularly its relationship with the sea. Between Santa Cruz and Morro Bay is the nation's largest marine sanctuary. Under the waves, Monterey Canyon–the size of the Grand Canyon–wells with the cold, nutrient-rich waters that start the food chain that reaches up to the sea otter, the elephant seal, and the blue whale. It also has one of the world's largest kelp beds.

Land and sea create drama where the Santa Lucia Range tumbles into the Pacific at Big Sur, or on Point Lobos, where oak-and-cypress-dotted cliffs finally relent to the turbulence below. It's little wonder that photographers Ansel Adams and Edward Weston created some of their most memorable images here.

Travelers in search of drama will be rewarded by many historic sites. Spanish troops and padres settled here in 1770, and five years later the king made Monterey the capital of Spanish California. Here, too, the "original sin" of California history was committed. In 1775, Padre Junípero Serra ordered the recapture of a band of Native American converts who had fled Mission Carmel. The forced return of indigenous peoples to a culture that eventually wiped them out haunted Serra's march toward sainthood (in 2015) ever since. The historical drama climaxed in Monterey in 1845–46, when Thomas Larkin, consul to Mexican California, began a series of intrigues that led to the state becoming a U.S. territory.

The Central Coast offers outdoor delights galore. Golfers can play at outstanding courses such as Pebble Beach. The offshore canyons of Monterey Bay yield spectacular scuba diving, while hikers can spend days exploring the trails of the Santa Lucia Range. Bird-watchers find their mecca north of Monterey on the Elkhorn

Pescadero

7▷ Big Basin
Redwoods
State Park
Pt. Año Nuevo
p.237
BAY AREA

Boulder
Creek
Felton
Morgan Hill

Santa Cruz
Natural Bridges
State Beach
Pacific
Migrations
Visitor Center
Soquel
Corralitos
Capitola
Rio
del Mar
Gilroy

6▷ Watsonville
Monterey Bay
Pajaro

Elkhorn Slough Reserve
Moss Landing
Castroville
San Juan
Bautista
Hollister

Marina
Fremont Peak
3171ft
Paicines

Pacific Grove
Monterey Bay
Aquarium
Monterey
Seaside
Carmel-by-the-Sea
17-Mile Drive
Salinas
Chualar

5▷ Point Lobos
State Reserve
Bixby Creek
Landing
Point Sur
Light Station
Andrew Molera
State Park
Pfeiffer Big
Sur State Park
Carmel
Valley
Gonzales

Jamesburg
Soledad
Mission Nuestra
Señora de
la Soledad
Big Sur
Tassajara
Hot Springs
Greenfield

Julia Pfeiffer Burns
State Park
Esalen Institute
LOS PADRES
NATIONAL FOREST
Lonoak
King City

4▷ Lucia
Mission
San Antonio
de Padua
San Lucas
Jolon
Lockwood

PACIFIC

OCEAN
Cape San Martin
Gorda

Bradley

CENTRAL VALLEY *p.317*

PINNACLES
NATIONAL
PARK

Coast Ranges

Santa Lucia Range

San Andreas Fault Zone

Arroyo Seco

San Antonio

Salinas

40 kilometers
20 miles

A

Hearst
Castle
Point Piedras Blancas
San Simeon
Lake
Nacimiento
San Miguel
Mission
San Miguel
Arcángel

3▷ Hearst
San Simeon
State Park
Cambria
Whitley
Gardens
Cholame

Harmony
Paso Robles
Templeton

Slough National
Estuarine Reserve.

More restful pursuits
include Hearst Castle,
a onetime cavorting
palace for Hollywood
stars. Romantics are also drawn to
Carmel, set among pines. Carmel
attracted poet Robinson Jeffers,
who wrote, "The human spirit can find its
peace by realizing its unimportance, and its
value by realizing the beauty of the outer
world." If any place in the world can inspire,
it is the Central Coast. ■

Cayucos
Atascadero

Morro Bay
Morro Bay State Park
Los Osos
Montaña de Oro
State Park
Santa Margarita

Sea Life Center
San Luis
Obispo
Pozo
LOS PADRES
NATIONAL
FOREST

2▷ Point San Luis
Pismo Beach
Grover Beach
Arroyo
Grande

La Panza Range

B
Guadalupe
Nipomo

Point Sal
Santa Maria

1▷ Orcutt
SOUTHERN CALIFORNIA
p.129

SOUTHERN CALIFORNIA

Sacramento
San Francisco
Los Angeles
Area of map detail

Lake
San Antonio

HEARST CASTLE

As a boy traveling in Europe, publisher-tycoon William Randolph Hearst had told his mother that he would one day occupy Windsor Castle and buy the Louvre. Hearst kept his grand aspirations, and in 1919 commissioned his own *castello grande*. "Would it not be better," he wrote to his architect Julia Morgan, "to do something a little different than other people are doing in California as long as we do not do anything incongruous?" The result was an eclectic fusion of Mediterraneanism, tempered by California botany and topography.

Neptune Pool at Hearst Castle, built at 1,600 feet (487 m), holds 345,000 gallons (1,305,967 L) of water.

Hearst Castle

🏔 173 B3

✉ 750 Hearst Castle Rd., San Simeon

☎ 800-444-4445 (ticket information; reservations recommended)

💲 $$$$$

www.hearstcastle .com

The Hearst-Morgan collaboration (as he saw it) produced **La Casa Grande,** the estate's centerpiece. Choosing acquired elements of European decoration, such as the Spanish and Italian choir stalls used as wainscoting, Morgan fashioned a stunning new aesthetic, a mix of traditional European creations and modern techniques.

La Casa Grande was Hearst's salon, where he and Marion Davies entertained celebrities. As one account has it, guests were free to do as they liked as

long as they followed four rules: congregate nightly in the ornate **Assembly Room** around the 16th-century French fireplace, take dinner in the adjoining **Refectory,** view the evening's motion picture in the **Theater,** and, most important, never utter the word "death" in the presence of their host.

The three guesthouses—**Casa del Mar** (often used by the Hearsts during construction of the main house), **Casa del Monte,** and **Casa del Sol**—were built in the Mediterranean style and are all mansions in their own right.

Around Hearst Castle

An easy side trip from Hearst Castle is to take Calif. 1 south to **Hearst San Simeon State Park,** where gorgeous scenery unfolds beneath rocky promontories and jagged cliffs. The park incorporates **Pa-Nu Cultural Preserve,** a significant archaeological site dating back almost 6,000 years. In winter, northern elephant seals gather at the state park beach up the coast from San Simeon Cove.

Farther south, at **Morro Bay State Park,** you may spot marine otters, peregrine falcons, and great blue herons.

At **Montaña de Oro State Park,** the Bluff Trail leads to interesting rock formations and tide pools. Inland is **San Luis Obispo** (map p. 173 C2; Visitor Center, 895 Monterey St., tel 805-541-8000, http://visitslo.com), a good base for exploring two exciting new wine regions, **Paso Robles** (map p. 173 C3; Visitor Center, 1225 Park St., tel 805-801-1650, www.travelpaso.com) and **Arroyo Grande** (map p. 173 C2; tel 805-489-1488, www.visitarroyogrande.org).

Pismo Beach (map p. 173 C2; Visitor Information Center, 581 Dolliver St. (tel 805-556-7397, experiencepismobeach. com) has huge sand dunes designated as a Special Vehicle Recreation Area. Nearby, the **Sea Life Center** (map p. 173 B2; 50 San Juan St., Avila Beach, tel 805-595-7280, www.centralcoastaquarium.com) has hands-on marine science exhibits.

Most people's best memory of Hearst Castle is the 104-foot-long (31 m) **Neptune Pool.** Tiled in deep blue and set in front of a Greco-Roman temple facade, it overlooks one of the estate's most spectacular vistas. The smaller indoor **Roman Pool** is lined with Venetian and gold-leaf tiles.

Hearst ordered that the estate be kept in year-round color. To do so, he built five **greenhouses** and hired a huge gardening staff to raise more than 500,000 annuals for rotational planting. Into these **gardens** he carefully positioned several gigantic coastal live oaks and California bay trees and built a 1.25-mile (2 km) pergola.

Like many gilded-age millionaires, Hearst acquired a collection of **European art** to decorate his home: antique ceilings, Greek vases, tapestries, and wall panels. Adriaen Ysenbrandt's 16th-century "Madonna and Child" adorns one wall in the main house. In the Gothic Suite sits "La Virgen de la Leche," a tiny statue carved in Spain some 500 years ago. Outside are four colossal stone lion-face goddesses carved in Egypt during the 13th century B.C.

How to Visit

Road access to the castle is restricted, so visitors must take a scheduled tour. One tour includes the ground floor of La Casa Grande, one of the guesthouses, both pools, and part of the gardens. Another tour visits the upper rooms of the main house. Three new daytime tour options include self-guided access to the grounds after the guided portion indoors. Evening tours in spring and fall are guided by docents in period costume. Special evening dinner events include an annual Christmas Holiday Feast. ∎

Hearst San Simeon State Park

🏞 173 B3

Visitor Information

✉ Park Office, Van Gordon Creek Rd. at San Simeon Creek Rd., Cambria

☎ 805-772-6101

www.parks.ca.gov

Morro Bay State Park

🏞 173 B2

✉ Morro Bay State Park Rd., Morro Bay

☎ 805-772-7434

www.parks.ca.gov

Montaña de Oro State Park

🏞 173 B2

Visitor Information

✉ Park Office, Pecho Rd.

☎ 805-772-6101

www.parks.ca.gov

DRIVE: CAMBRIA TO CARMEL

With its dramatically twisting roads and stunning scenic promontories, Calif. 1 between Cambria and Carmel is to many Californians a kind of modern pilgrimage, the object of reverence being the Big Sur River (crossed by the awe-inspiring Big Sur Bridge) and its beautiful forested hinterlands. It is often closed due to landslides.

Begin a trip north on Calif. 1 by first getting gas and a meal in **Cambria ❶** *(visitor information, Chamber of Commerce, 767 Main St., tel 805-927-3624, www.visitcambriaca.com);* the distances between the few towns are long, and the road is a workout in itself at times.

Beyond the small town of **Lucia** (the southernmost limit of the redwood tree) lie the three state parks of central Big Sur. First is **Julia Pfeiffer Burns State Park ❷** *(tel 831-667-1112, www.parks.ca.gov).* A trail leads to Saddle Rock, location of the only waterfall on the Pacific Coast that falls directly into the ocean. Behind it looms **Anderson Peak,** at 4,099 feet (1,249 m) the highest point of the Santa Lucia Range. A few miles farther north is the **Henry Miller Memorial Library ❸** *(48603 Calif. 1, Big Sur, tel 831-667-2574, closed Mon.–Wed., www.henrymiller. org),* in the place where the writer spent the postwar years with a coterie of fellow artists.

The star of the Big Sur coast is **Pfeiffer Big Sur State Park ❹** *(tel 831-667-2315, www.parks.ca.gov),* the largest of the three state parks, with a substantial stand of redwoods. A good swim in the Big Sur River before making a campsite is an old California tradition.

About 6 miles (9.6 km) north again is **Andrew Molera State Park ❺** *(tel 831-667-2315, www.parks.ca.gov),* where the scenic Big Sur River ends in a fine habitat for birds and wildlife. Look for mule deer, gray foxes, and raccoons. Much in the way of classic drama surrounds the location of **Point Sur Light Station** *(tel 831-625-4419, www.parks.ca.gov, walking tours: $$),* built in 1889 after two shipwrecks.

The Big Sur area has a series of interesting places to stay or eat. The cabins at **Deetjen's Big Sur Inn** *(48865 Calif. 1, Castro Canyon, Big*

> **NOT TO BE MISSED:**
>
> **Julia Pfeiffer Burns SP ● Point Lobos SNR ● Nacimiento Fergusson Road**

Sur, tel 831-667-2378, www.deetjens.com), which has a good Norwegian restaurant, are named for various literary figures. Not far away is the restaurant-bar **Nepenthe** *(48510 Calif. 1, Big Sur, tel 831-667-2345, www.nepenthe.com),* designed by a student of Frank Lloyd Wright. The deck overlooks the Pacific.

Long considered the ultimate in Big Sur lodging, the **Ventana Inn** *(48123 Calif. 1, Big Sur, tel 831-667-2331, www.ventanainn.com)* has spacious luxury cabins (with kitchens) built on a sun-flecked hillside. The massages and spa treatments are outstanding, and you can enjoy the Japanese baths, stroll among the trees in Ventana's white bathrobes, and enjoy the peace.

At the **Loma Vista Café & Gardens** *(tel 831-238-2110, www.lomavistagardens.com)* you can enjoy a cup of coffee and explore the fabulous garden.

Approaching Carmel (see pp. 180–181), you reach **Point Lobos State Natural Reserve ❻** *(tel 831-624-4909, www.parks.ca.gov),* whose coves are home to sea lions, sea otters, and pelicans. Literary experts believe this was the inspiration for Spyglass Hill in *Treasure Island* (1883), which Robert Louis Stevenson wrote after visiting in 1879. Follow the **Sea Lion Point Trail** past stands of wild red buckwheat to a lookout onto Sea Lion Rocks, or take the **Cypress Grove Trail** around a grove of ancient cypress hung with green-blue moss. The environs support delicate coastal orchids, which grow along the branches of fallen trees.

Return from Carmel by taking County Road G16 up the **Carmel Valley.** After 9 miles (15 km), the charming town of Carmel Valley is dotted with wine-tasting rooms. Stop in at **7 Holman Ranch** (*60 Holman Rd., tel 831-601-8761, www.holmanranch.com*) for a tour of the olive groves, vineyard, and underground winery.

Return to G16 and continue via Arroyo Seco Road to **Greenfield.** A few miles down U.S. 101, turn off on County Road G14 to the small town of **Jolon,** the setting for John Steinbeck's novel *To a God Unknown* (1933), about a

pioneering California family. In a quiet valley to the north is the restored **Mission San Antonio de Padua 8** (*Mission Rd., tel 831-385-4478, www. missionsanantonio.net*), founded in 1771.

Return to the coast road down **Nacimiento Fergusson Road 9.** In the foothills of the Santa Lucia Range, wildflowers surround you, particularly in spring. The great variety of plant life here includes wild fennel, a non-native that is slowly dominating the coastal underbrush; white-plumed our lord's candle; bright green-yellow mustard (said to have been sown by the padres); and coastal agave, its tendril-like biomorph twisting and looking like a beached octopus.

ECOLOGY OF LIGHT, SEA, & STONE

The artwork of Edward Weston, Ansel Adams, & Robinson Jeffers

Of the many reasons artists and writers came to the Central Coast, the most important are its physical elements—light, sea, and stone. The evanescence of the first, the promise of the second, the hard reality of the third—these the artists of Big Sur cannot avoid. Their combined hardness, as Ansel Adams once put it, forces the artist to focus on "really seeing."

Edward Weston

For photographer Edward Weston (1886–1958), the Central Coast represented both escape and maturation. He came here in 1923, after leaving his wife and taking up with an exotic Italian actress. He began an association with Mexican art "radicals" David Alfaro Siquieros (see sidebar p. 93) and Diego Rivera, and his style became increasingly direct, documentary, erotic. Nude portraits of his many lovers were conscientiously unretouched. In the early 1930s, he settled in Carmel and, with Ansel Adams, founded the f/64 Movement, which pronounced that photography must be severed from the confining strictures of formalistic art.

Weston's photo "The Fishing Fleet, Monterey" captures *his* Central Coast. It shows Monterey Marina in the late afternoon. There is a small rock in the foreground, gulls sunning; in the background bob the little workboats, waiting for their masters. This was an exotic, but contained, aesthetic moment.

Ansel Adams

Weston's friend Ansel Adams (1902–1984) was equally passionate about nature and photography: "I believe in stones and water, air and soil, people and their future, and their fate." This directness with his subjects bursts from all Adams's photographs, the most well known of which are of Half Dome in Yosemite (see pp. 304–309). Travel down to the shoreline of Point Lobos State Natural Reserve (see p. 176), as Adams did, to see *his* Central Coast. Here shadow and light seem to hold their own vast territories, a block of light here, of darkness there. There is a Zen quality to Adams's Big Sur photographs. They are momentary yet hard—a visual "belief" in stones and water.

Robinson Jeffers

It was poet Robinson Jeffers (1887–1962) who perhaps better than anyone fused Weston's personal coast with Adams's natural coast. Jeffers went even further than Adams's and Weston's stripped-down coastal images. For him, *only* nature mattered, mankind being but a passing presence. Only

EXPERIENCE:
Enlightenment

To find *your* Central Coast, pay a visit to the Esalen Institute (map p. 173 A4; 55000 Calif. 1, Big Sur, tel 831-667-3000, www.esalen.org), where Ansel Adams was once an instructor.

Founded in 1962 on a cliff top overlooking the ocean at Big Sur, the institute was a nexus for spiritual studies and alternative philosophies during the flower power era. Since then, it has evolved into a highly respected learning center that presents more than 500 seminars and workshops annually. Workshop topics range from yoga meditation to photography and creative writing. Typical workshops ($$$$$) last one week. You can also sign up for a "personal retreat."

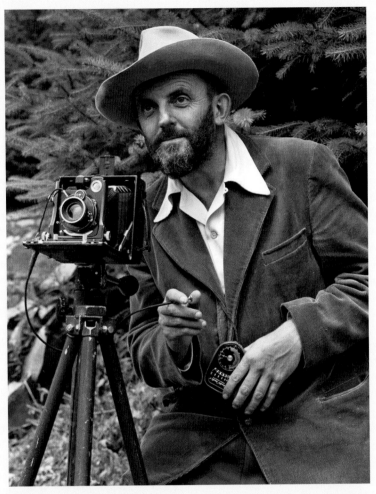

Nature and landscape photographer Ansel Adams advocated "pure" photography favoring sharp focus and use of a full tonal range

those who understood this, he believed, had any chance of finding some peace in an increasingly inhumane world.

The early local population in Big Sur, described in a 1939 guidebook as a folk given to "inbreeding, passion, moroseness, and suspicion," filled Jeffers's prose. Bixby Creek Landing, north of Point Sur, was the setting for his "Thurso's Landing," about a woman who takes up with her husband's only friend, a dynamiter for a roadbuilding crew. In one scene, the wife, Helen, says to her lover: "Do you ever think about death? I've seen you play with it. Strolling away while the fuse fizzled in the rock." "Hell no," the dynamiter replies, "that was all settled when they made the hills."

CARMEL-BY-THE-SEA & AROUND

An artists' colony developed by two nimble real estate developers eager to exploit the post-1906-earthquake residential needs of the rich, Carmel has from its very beginnings epitomized what we have come to call the "lifestyle community." Its cachet lies in its "themed exclusivity" as an arts community. Residents have included poet George Sterling, actor Clint Eastwood, radical Lincoln Steffens, and increasingly conservative Robinson Jeffers (see pp. 178–179).

■ Carmel is known for its easy pace, quintessential English charm, and rich art history.

Carmel-by-the-Sea

🅼 173 A5

Visitor Information

✉ Visitor Center, Carmel Plaza, Ocean Ave. betw. Junipero St. & Mission St.

☎ 831-624-2522, 800-550-4333

www.carmel california.com

In Carmel, business always took a back seat to aesthetics, something even Clint Eastwood had to admit after his failed attempt as mayor to bring the village into the entrepreneurial age. To this day, the recherché tumble of small boutiques on Ocean Avenue epitomizes the word "cute."

Not surprisingly, visitors come to Carmel for peace and quiet. That's good, as there is not a lot to do here except admire the scenery and the wildlife, hike, and wander through art galleries. Stock up on outstanding picnic supplies at the Mediterranean Market (Ocean Ave. & Mission St.) before heading off to **Carmel River State Beach** (off Scenic Rd., S of Carmel Beach, tel 831-649-2836, www.parks.ca.gov). Here, slopes flushed with pine and oak fall to a brilliant white beach, perfect for hiking and bird-watching.

When you tire of the beach, return to town for a little browsing along **Ocean Avenue,** where shops sell everything from proper nautical wear to handmade cardigans and shawls. For some hearty food in a family-style atmosphere, go to **Little Napoli** (Dolores St.

near 7th Ave., tel 831-626-6335, www.pepemag.com), where the food is straightforward and satisfying, the service friendly, and the atmosphere warm and jolly.

Since lounging and sitting by cozy fireplaces are two principal Carmel activities, three inns are worth noting (see also Travelwise p. 363). The first is **Quail Lodge** (8205 Valley Greens Dr., tel 866-675-1101, www.quaillodge.com), which sits in the Carmel Valley. For a more eco-New Age experience, try the **Highlands Inn** (Calif. 1, S of Carmel, tel 831-620-1234, www.hyatt.com). With their balcony views, in-room hot tubs, spas, personal sound systems, and wood-burning fireplaces, the rooms here make for a memorable experience.

Nearer to the center of town, **The Normandy Inn** (Ocean Ave. & Monte Verde St., tel 831-624-3825, www.normandyinncarmel.com) is charming and located near the shops and the beach.

Tor House & Hawk Tower

Perhaps the most original feature in all Carmel is Tor House and its adjoining Hawk Tower, both built by poet Robinson Jeffers between 1914 and 1930 (with later additions). Jeffers and his wife, Una, were attracted to the dramatic site, a tor or craggy hill near the outflow of the Carmel River, and the structures reflect the couple's idiosyncrasies. Almost inseparable from the elements to which it is so exposed, the house is an unforgettable

California monument to creativity, individualism, and strength.

Festivals & Art Venues

As might be expected, Carmel hosts several outstanding cultural events and venues. The **Carmel Bach Festival** (tel 831-624-1521, www.bachfestival.org) takes the spotlight in July and August, when concerts and classes on the composer take center stage. In May, the **Carmel International Arts Festival** (tel 831-626-4000, www.carmelartsfestival.org) offers the works of plein-art painters, who work on-site. The **Pacific Repertory Theater** (tel 831-622-0100, www.pacrep.org) runs year-round.

EXPERIENCE:
Artista Art Vacation

If the creative urge overtakes you before visiting Carmel—and you happen to be a woman—check out the wide range of residential "creative safaris" at Artista (tel 831-625-5748, $$$$$). Classes in abstract painting, encaustic (hot wax) painting, and artistic collage are combined with a two-night/three-day stay at a local boutique inn. The cost includes art supplies, daily yoga session, and two meals each day. Artista's instructors are accomplished artists in their fields.

Tor House & Hawk Tower

✉ 26304 Ocean View Ave. (betw. Stewart Way & Bay View Ave.), Carmel

☎ 831-624-1813

🕐 Foundation open Mon.–Thurs. Hourly tours Sat. No children under 12. Reservations required.

💲 $$$

www.torhouse.org

It is worth checking out the works by locals at the **Carmel Art Association** (Dolores St. between 5th & 6th Aves., tel 831-624-6176, www.carmelart.org). Many visitors end up returning again and again, following and acquiring the works of one artist, year after year.

17-Mile Drive

⚑ 173 A5

Visitor Information

✉ Pebble Beach
Visitor Center
3297 17-Mile Dr.

☎ 831-662-6394

💲 $$

**www.pebblebeach
.com**

17-Mile Drive

A toll road worth every cent, the legendary 17-mile (27 km), coast-hugging drive along the Carmel peninsula encompasses some of Monterey Bay's most spectacular coastal vistas and natural features. The private roadway (closed to motorcycles) snakes through the gated community of Pebble Beach, stippled with luxurious mansions and a mecca for golf enthusiasts. Even on foggy days, it's hard to get lost thanks to red dotted markings along the route.

EXPERIENCE:
Coastal Golfing

Other than winning the Masters with a long 18th-hole putt, playing **Pebble Beach Golf Links** *(tel 800-654-9300, www.pebble-beach.com/golf , $$$$)* is the most enduring dream of golfers nationwide.

The famed seaside course was founded in 1919 and annually hosts the National Pro-Am tournament that pairs the world's best golfers with celebrity show-biz partners. Unlike many exclusive golf clubs, the Pebble Beach links are open to the general public. Pebble Beach's four other courses include the Tiger Woods–designed **Short Course**, new in 2021.

Heading north from the Carmel Gate *(off Calif. 1 at N. San Antonio Rd.)*, the road loops up to **Huckleberry Hill,** smack in the middle of the Del Monte Forest.

The road meets the shore at **Spanish Bay,** where explorer Gaspar de Portola anchored in 1796, believing it to be Monterey Bay. Rising above the southern end of

the beach, the rocky pinnacles of **Point Joe** lured many a mariner to their fate in the false belief that the point marked the entrance to Monterey. The colliding currents here stir up nutrients that feed fishes that in turn bring pelicans, cormorants, and other seabirds in vast numbers. **Bird Rock** is a favored roost; seals and sea lions often snooze at nearby **Seal Rock** and **Fanshell Beach.**

INSIDER TIP:

Be sure to pick up the brochure available at the start of the drive. It spells out all the details of the route.

—JOE YOGERST
National Geographic author

Nearby, various species of native cypress and pine are a highlight of **Crocker Grove,** a 13-acre (5.2 ha) nature reserve. The lone twisted tree at **Cypress Point** must be one of the world's most photographed living things.

To end, stop for a drink or meal at the **Lodge at Pebble Beach** *(tel 831-624-3811)*, a world-class resort renowned as the setting for **Pebble Beach Golf Links** (see sidebar), where crooner Bing Crosby launched the Pebble Beach National Pro-Am, which still draws the world's top golfers. Auto aficionados flock in each August for the **Concours d'Elegance** *(tel 831-622-1700, www.pebblebeachconcours. net)*, a showcase of historic cars.

Mission Carmel

The second mission built in California by Padre Junípero Serra, **Mission San Carlos Borroméo del Río Carmelo**— or Mission Carmel—is historical ground zero for almost all modern discussions of the mission system and its legacy. This was Serra's place of great toil, the center of his attempt to re-create Spanish civilization in a raw new world. Between 1770 and 1836, he and his successors confirmed more than 4,000 neophytes here.

■ **Built in 1770, the Carmel Mission is still an active place of worship today.**

Today the deep interconnectedness of Serra and California's self-identity can be seen in the statue located in the restored **Old Quadrangle.** Entitled the "Serra Cenotaph" and sculpted in 1924 by local artist Jo Mora, the work portrays a triumphant Serra, a California grizzly bear at his feet.

In the ornate **basilica** are the graves of the mission's founders, including Serra, whose living quarters, or **cell,** has also been restored, albeit with some creative revisionist spin: The leather scourges or whips that used to hang here have been removed, likely out of fear that visitors might "misinterpret" their use. (The padres used them on themselves and, occasionally, on their converts.) On a lighter note, the restored **kitchen** gives an idea of the simplicity of mission life. The **garden** possesses a fine collection of native plants and a range of dahlias, some of them as large as eight inches (20.3 cm) in diameter.

Other Missions

Two lesser known missions are within driving distance of the Carmel mission south on U.S. 101. Founded by Padre Lasuén in 1791, **Mission Nuestra Señora de la Soledad** was one of the most remote of the missions. As such, it offered a hiding place to padres and neophytes in 1818 when French pirate Hippolyte de Bouchard was ravaging the other missions. A fine icon is its statue of the Virgin, dressed in the black of a Spanish doña in mourning.

Farther south on U.S. 101 is **Mission San Miguel Arcángel** *(see map p. 173 C3; 775 Mission St., tel 805-467-3256, www.mission sanmiguel.org).* Founded in 1797 as an agricultural outpost, this mission has kept some original interior art. Created by neophytes, it is an original fusion of Old World medievalism and New World fecundity of color. ■

Mission San Carlos Borromeo del Rio Carmelo (Carmel Mission)
✉ 3080 Rio Rd., Carmel
☎ 831-624-1271
www.carmelmission .org

Mission Nuestra Señora de la Soledad
🔺 173 B5
✉ 36641 Ft. Romie Rd., off U.S. 101, 3 miles SW of Soledad
☎ 831-678-2586
www.missions california.com

DRIVING IN STEINBECK COUNTRY

It would take too long to list all the many real-life touchstones found in the stories of John Steinbeck. It is enough to say that his writing is inextricably woven into the vast Salinas Valley and points just beyond. These two drives convey much of the atmosphere of Steinbeck country. The Steinbeck Center in Salinas has a brochure with other tours.

Drive One: Salinas & the "Long Valley"

Orient yourself to Steinbeck country in **Salinas ❶** *(visitor information, 1213 N, Davis Rd., tel 831-757-8687)* at the **National Steinbeck Center** *(1 Main St., tel 831-796-3833, www.steinbeck.org),* a modern facility rising out of the author's cherished **Old Town.** The center has an extensive collection of Steinbeck memorabilia—including Rocinante, the pickup truck in *Travels With Charley* (1962)—and several interactive exhibits. There are also displays of Hollywood's various renditions of his work. The Rabobank Wing celebrates the valley's rich agriculture heritage.

Just down the street is the **Steinbeck House** *(132 Central Rd., tel 831-424-2735, www.steinbeckhouse.com),* where the author was born and raised, and where you can have lunch. Other attractions here include the **Roosevelt School** *(120 Capitol St.),* the West End School in the epic *East of Eden* (1952). The author attended grades 3–8 here. On Main Street in Old Town are several sites mentioned in the same book, among them the San Francisco Chop House *(No. 116),* Krough's Drug Store building *(No. 156),* and Elks Building *(No. 247).* The **Garden of Memories Cemetery** *(850 Abbott St.)* is where the author is buried, along with several of the real-life characters in *East of Eden,* including the Hamilton Family, William J. Nesbitt (Sheriff Quinn), and Mary Jane Reynolds (Jenny).

Leave Salinas on U.S. 101 south. The town of **Soledad ❷** *(visitor information, Visitor Center, 248 Main St., tel 831-204-7208, www.soledadca.org)* was the setting for *Of Mice and Men* (1937); the general store is still here. Continue on U.S.

> ### NOT TO BE MISSED:
>
> **National Steinbeck Center ● Cannery Row ● Fisherman's Wharf ● Fremont Peak ● Pinnacles National Monument**

101, then turn northeast on County Road G13 to **King City ❸** *(visitor information, Visitor Center, 200 Broadway, Ste. 40, tel 831-385-3814, www.kingcity.com, closed Sat.–Sun.),* where Steinbeck set scenes in *The Red Pony* (1937). Return to U.S. 101 and go west to the Jolon Rd./G14 turnoff. Take this to **Jolon ❹,** where the action takes place in *To a God Unknown* (1933).

Return to Salinas on U.S. 101, and take Calif. 68 west to pass the scenic **Salinas River Basin ❺,** where Steinbeck swam and hunted rabbits. Farther along is the mountainscape known as **Corral de Tierra** and **Castle Rock.** The latter was an inspiration for Steinbeck's *The Acts of King Arthur and His Noble Knights* (1976).

Continue on Calif. 68 into **Monterey ❻** (see pp. 186–187). The town's **Cannery Row** was the setting for the 1945 novel of the same name, as well as *Tortilla Flat* (1935) and *Sweet Thursday* (1954). The lab of the real-life Ed Ricketts, Steinbeck's raconteur-marine biologist protagonist, is at 800 Cannery Row; Wing Chong's Market (now Kristonio's Shell Shop) is at No. 835. La Ida's Café (now called Austino) is at No. 851. At 399 Alvarado Street, you can see the second-floor room in which Steinbeck wrote *The Pearl* (1947). It was from **Fisherman's Wharf** that Steinbeck and Ricketts set out for the Gulf of California in 1940, the inspiration for *Sea of Cortez* (1951).

See also area map p. 173
Salinas
Drive 1: 5 hours
Drive 2: 3 hours
Drive 1: 152 miles
Drive 2: 95 miles
(245/153 km)
Drive 1: Monterey
Drive 2: Pinnacles NM

Drive Two: The Badlands

Heading north from Salinas on U.S. 101, go east on Calif. 156 to **San Juan Bautista** ❶ (*www.sanjuanbautistaca.com*). The restored **Mission San Juan Bautista** (*N side of Plaza, tel 831-623-2127, www.missionscalifornia.com*) has an altarpiece painted by Thomas Doak, the first American settler in Alta California. Steinbeck was fond of the mission and its stories.

From Calif. 156, exit on San Juan Canyon Road and head to **Fremont Peak State Park** ❷ (*tel 831-623-4255, www.parks.ca.gov*).

It was on Fremont Peak that Steinbeck, in *Travels With Charley*, chose to go east, never to see his beloved valley again. To the west is the old Steinbeck ranch.

Down from the peak, continue east on Calif. 156, then go south on Calif. 25. In the tiny hamlet of **Paicines** ❸ you can still buy a soda at the store where in 1873 the *bandito* Tiburcio Vásquez shot his last victim. **Pinnacles National Park** ❹ (*tel 831-389-4486, www.nps. gov/pinn*), a mass of volcanic rock formations with hiking trails, looms to the south.

HISTORIC MONTEREY

Claimed for Spain in 1770, Monterey was the political, social, and economic hub of California until the California Gold Rush of 1849, when the Americanos decided to locate their new statehouse elsewhere. As an economic force, Monterey kept surging ahead, its fishing industry fueled by successive waves of immigrants. Today this bayside city teems with new enterprise, museums, art galleries, and an extensive restored historic district. Fisherman's Wharf is a favorite place to grab a bite to eat, shop, and stroll.

Popular with tourists, Cannery Row reminds visitors of the bayside city's long fishing history.

Monterey

🗺 173 A5

Visitor Information

✉ Visitor Center, 401 Camino El Estero

☎ 877-666-8373

www.seemonterey.com

Monterey State Historic Park

✉ 20 Customs House Plaza, Monterey

☎ 831-649-2907

www.parks.ca.gov

Monterey State Historic Park

With headquarters near the Customs House, the park links more than 30 historical places. Peppered with historical adobes, Monterey-style mansions, and public gardens, its "path of history" is well marked, beginning with the restored, waterfront **Customs House,** the oldest government building in California. Here, in 1846, Commodore John Drake Sloat proclaimed California part of the United States. Immediately south, across Customs Plaza, is the **Maritime & History Museum of Monterey,** which explores the city's maritime history. To its west, the **Pacific House Museum** *(tel 831-649-7118),* in a beautifully restored two-story adobe, profiles California history and has a fine collection of Native American artifacts.

The **Larkin House,** a two-story adobe built during the Mexican period, was home to Thomas Oliver Larkin, the first and only U.S. consul to California under Mexican rule.

One of the more remarkable old-time adobes is the **Casa Soberanes Adobe,** also known as the House of the Blue Gate. Built in the 1840s, it has been beautifully restored, complete with original furnishings.

The **Pacific House,** originally used during the 1847 U.S. occupation of California, contains museums on early Monterey and Native American life. Perhaps the best single place to get a sense of early merchant life in Monterey is the **Cooper Molera Adobe,** named for trader John Rogers Cooper, who married into a prestigious Mexican family. The grounds include barns, farm animals, and vegetable and fruit gardens. **Colton Hall,** where the California constitution was signed, is another outstanding example of Monterey architecture. It now contains a museum about early state history.

The **Stevenson House** (*530 Houston St.*) is best known for Scottish writer Robert Louis Stevenson, who stayed here in 1879, recovering from an illness, before marrying and setting off for Napa Valley.

The **Old Whaling Station** on Pacific Street was built in 1847 and later served as headquarters of the Old Monterey Whaling Company. The adobe's front walkway is paved with whale vertebrae.

Immediately northwest, outside the historic park, the **Presidio of Monterey** (*http://home.army.mil/ monterey*) affords access to Sebastián Vizcaíno's 1602 landing site and the location of Padre Junípero Serra's first Mass in 1770. More recent military history is explored at the **Presidio of Monterey Museum** (*Corporal Ewing Rd., Bldg. 113, tel 831-646-3456, closed Sun. a.m., Mon. p.m., & Tues.–Wed.*), which houses materials on local military history from the Spanish period through WWII.

Since its early days, Monterey has attracted more than its share of ambitious young artists. The **Monterey Museum of Art** holds an outstanding collection of their work and that of other Californians in its two locations (on Via Mirada and at the Civic Center).

Maritime & History Museum of Monterey

✉ 5 Customs House Plaza, Monterey

☎ 831-372-2608

🕐 Closed Sun. a.m. & Mon.

💲 $$ (free 1st Tues. p.m. of month)

Monterey Museum of Art

✉ 720 Via Mirada & 559 Pacific St., Monterey

☎ 831-372-3689 (Via Mirada), 831-372-5477 (Civic Center)

🕐 Closed Mon.–Tues.

💲 $$

www.monterey art.org

EXPERIENCE: Hollywood's Wildlife

Perched on a hilltop overlooking the Salinas Valley and just a 30-minute drive from historic Monterey, **Vision Quest Ranch** (*400 River Rd., Salinas, tel 800-228-7382, www.visionquestranch.com*) offers a true California experience. Guests can stay overnight at a "safari style" bed & breakfast: canvas-walled cabins set on wooden platforms around the edge of an elephant sanctuary. The ranch is the home of many of the creatures that appear in Hollywood television and movie productions. From tarantulas and Bengal tigers to bears, birds, and baboons, animals of all types relax on the ranch between gigs. The ranch includes a compound for exotic animals and an equestrian center. Tours (*$–$$$*) range from one-hour guided walks to daylong "full contact" experiences and customized photo safaris. Vision Quest also arranges summer camps and sleepovers for kids, as well as animal training courses and scuba diving in Monterey Bay.

Monterey Bay Aquarium

🗺 173 A5

✉ 886 Cannery Row, Monterey

☎ 831-648-4800

💲 $$$$$

www.montereybay
aquarium.org

Monterey Bay Aquarium

One of the world's preeminent education/research establishments of its kind, the excellent Monterey Bay Aquarium is dedicated to the vast realm of Monterey Bay, the nation's largest marine sanctuary, located just outside its door. Allow about three hours for your visit. If you intend to see one of the various regular specialty shows such as

of the **Ocean's Edge** is the **Kelp Forest.** This huge tri-level (which opens to the rooftop patio) tank perfectly simulates a kelp environment, complete with surging waters and a variety of ichthyological inhabitants, including tightly knit schools of anchovies streaming between the long amber fronds. Try to see the twice-daily feeding show, in which scuba divers descend into the tank to hand-feed

The aquarium's Open Sea exhibit includes not only sharks but also sea turtles and schools of fish.

the feeding of the sea otters, check the website for scheduled times, or at the front information desk as you enter.

The aquarium provides a tour of the world's oceans and Monterey Bay's four principal habitats, displayed in two sections, The Ocean's Edge and The Open Sea, each on two levels. Beyond the **entrance hall**, with life-size mother-and-calf California gray whales plus an orca suspended overhead, the central attraction

the creatures. Leopard sharks, moray eels, and lobsters are among the creatures that swim, slither and crawl around an adjoining tank that recreates **Monterey Bay Habitats,** from harbor wharfs to the rocky reefs. Separate tanks in this gallery exhibit such local denizens as the striking velvet-red and highly intelligent Giant Pacific octopus. In the **Rocky Shores** tank, visitors can watch the tiny creatures that thrive at the water's edge. Eels slither about between bizarre-looking

Elkhorn Slough

Located on a tidal channel teeming with wildlife and fish, Elkhorn Slough National Estuarine Research Reserve encompasses 1,400 acres (566 ha) of marshland and tidal flats and is home to more than 400 species of invertebrates, 80 species of fish, and 200 species of birds. Leopard sharks and bat rays cruise these shallow waters, and this is one of the last known reaches of the clapper rail.

After a morning at Elkhorn, stop at **Moss Landing,** where several stores deal in reasonably priced antique California and Arts and Crafts–era pottery. The cafés offer outstanding oyster dishes. The used bookstore is a reader's dream. If you come in early spring, stop at one of the roadside stands and try a fresh artichoke—or have some shipped back home; nearby **Castro-ville** is the artichoke capital of the world.

nudibranches. The highlight is a walkthrough acrylic tunnel that lets you experience the power of waves that crash overhead.

The **Sand Shore Aviary** harbors birds found along the shoreline of Monterey Bay and adjacent wetlands like Elkhorn Slough (see sidebar above), including the western sandpiper, red phalarope, long-billed curlew, and ruddy turnstone.

On the second floor, the interactive **Splash Zone** grants a more detailed look at kelp forest, rocky shore, and coral reef habitats. The **Tide Pool Life** exhibit uses man-made waves to enliven several tidal habitats, including that of the hermit crab, sculpin, sea stars, and various forms of anemone. This area also displays African penguins, which thrive in the cold-water currents of the South Atlantic. And children can handle bat rays and starfish in several touch pools.

The 50,000-gallon (189,270 L) **Sea Otter** tank gives visitors a close-up look at these playful creatures, which the aquarium obtained as rescued orphans. **Mission to the Deep** combines high-definition video footage with interactive computer animations of underwater robots and other high-tech tools used in underwater research.

The aquarium's wave-swept outdoor **Great Tidepool,** enclosing the wharf, often draws wild sea otters (in 2015, an otter gave birth here) and has a viewing station for spotting harbor seals, California gray whales, and other marine mammals that routinely make their way through the bay.

The separate **Open Sea** section explores a world of light, temperature, and salinity of the deep offshore oceans. It contains the aquarium's largest tank (one million gallons/3,785,410 L), where hammerhead sharks and ocean sunfish leisurely swim, blackfin tuna speed past, and sea turtles lazily float by as you watch mesmerized through the 90-foot (27.4 m) window. Nearby, colorful puffins await their next meal in the **Ocean Travelers** gallery, where in dramatically-lit tanks, jellyfish pulse through the water and glow like diamonds against a vast black velvet robe. The first floor is dedicated to changing special exhibitions, which have included "Secret Lives of Seahorses," "Tentacles," and "¡Viva Baja!". ∎

Elkhorn Slough National Estuarine Research Reserve

🗺 173 A6

✉ 1700 Elkhorn Rd., Elkhorn

☎ 831-728-2822

🕐 Closed Mon.– Tues.

💲 $

www.elkhorn slough.org

Moss Landing

🗺 173 A6

Visitor Information

☎ 831-633-4501

www.mosslanding chamber.com

Castroville

🗺 173 A6

SANTA CRUZ & AROUND

For those with a slightly more bohemian approach to travel, the beach town of Santa Cruz is an outstanding destination. The city and its surrounding areas, now fully recovered from the devastating 1989 Loma Prieta earthquake, offer reasonably priced lodging, excellent seafood, stunning scenery, and sensational surfing.

Santa Cruz
🅰 173 A6

Visitor Information

✉ 303 Water St. #100, Santa Cruz

☎ 831-425-1234, 800-833-3494

www.santacruz.org

Natural Bridges State Beach
🅰 173 A6

✉ 2531 W. Cliff Dr., Santa Cruz

☎ 831-423-4609

www.parks.ca.gov

Big Basin Redwoods State Park
🅰 173 A7

✉ 21600 Big Basin Way, Boulder Creek

☎ 831-338-8860

www.parks.ca.gov

Soquel
🅰 173 A6

The main attraction in town is the **Santa Cruz Beach Boardwalk** *(400 Beach St., tel 831-423-5590, www.beachboardwalk.com)*, an historic amusement park.

A favorite activity is to rent a bicycle and ride the bike path on the bluffs above. The exhilarating 5-mile (8 km) round-trip to the stunning rock formations at **Natural Bridges State Beach** is unforgettable. In late fall, thousands of monarch butterflies arrive and roost in adjoining Monarch Grove. On the way back, stop by the **Santa Cruz Surfing Museum** *(1305 E. Cliff Dr, tel 831-420-6289)* for its vintage surfboards and shark attack photos.

The Santa Cruz Mountains are rich in early pioneer history, with sites such as the 1892 **Felton Covered Bridge** *(Calif. 9, 5 miles/8 km N of Santa Cruz, www.scparks.com)* in the San Lorenzo Valley. Nearby, at **Roaring Camp Railroads** *(tel 831-335-4484, www.roaringcamp.com)*, steam trains puff to the Bear Mountain summit. The camp's several working antique steam trains date back to the 1890s logging boom.

Farther north, off Calif. 9, is **Big Basin Redwoods State Park,** where you can rent tent cabins *(tel 800-444-7275)* set beneath towering coast redwood trees.

The park has more than 80 miles (128 km) of trails. To the east, **Soquel** is now part of a wine-growing region with more than 70 wineries *(tel 831-685-8463, www.winesofthesantacruzmountains.com)*. Try **Bargetto Winery** *(3535 N. Main St., tel 831-475-2258, www.bargetto.com)*.

INSIDER TIP:

With its creekside setting, Shadowbrook restaurant in Capitola *(www.shadowbrook-capitola.com)* promises an evening to long remember.

—BARBARA A. NOE
National Geographic Travel Books senior editor

South of Soquel, the city of **Capitola** *(see map p. 173 A6, www.capitolavillage.com)* is now a romantic's redoubt, complete with quaint beach cafés and several inns with beautiful views of northern Monterey Bay. The **Pacific Migrations Visitor Center** *(see map p. 173 A6, tel 831-464-6329, closed in winter)*, at New Brighton Beach in Capitola, explores the interactions of human and animal migratory patterns in California. ∎

Art museums flush with new acquisitions, Victorian architecture on bold display, and cuisine supremely gourmet, in the city by the Bay

SAN FRANCISCO

An iconic cable car climbs Hyde Street with Alcatraz Island visible across the bay.

SAN FRANCISCO

Affluent yet bohemian, cosmopolitan yet provincial, gay yet buttoned-down, old-worldly yet youthful—San Francisco has something for every contemporary urban traveler. A patchwork of diverse neighborhoods, and an epicenter of artisanal culture and ethnic politics, the city is compact, electric, romantic, exotic, and scenically stunning.

During the gold rush, the population of San Francisco rose from a sleepy 500 in 1847 to a raucous 20,000 in 1849. Then came the Yankee merchants, intent on making the city, as Richard Henry Dana had observed decades before, "the emporium of a new world." They would succeed beyond their wildest dreams.

Devastation came with the great earthquake and consequent fire of 1906. But the success of the Panama-Pacific Exposition in 1915 declared that the city was back. While the Depression certainly burnished the city's liberal democratic reputation, it was the AIDS crisis of the

1980s and beyond that once again invigorated San Francisco's eclectic character.

Travelers in San Francisco today confront a feast of cultural and culinary delights. Fueled in large part by Silicon Valley money, the city has become the site of America's most venturesome high cuisine. Money from "the valley" has also remade venerable cultural institutions, such as the new Civic Center location of the Asian Art Museum. The city's fine-art museums have also benefited from public commitment. And the Golden Gate National Recreation Area, a vast expanse of meadows, windswept beaches, gnarled madrone trees, and misty forest trails, beckons.

NOT TO BE MISSED:

See p.195

FINANCIAL DISTRICT

The Financial District (between Pine, Washington, Montgomery, and Drumm Streets) features several interesting buildings. With its foundations in the era of the gold rush, San Francisco's banking industry has long maintained a high profile. Since the late 1960s, its buildings—literally—have, too.

■ The Transamerica Pyramid covers an entire city block.

Financial District
🅰 193 G3 & 195

The first of the city's skyscrapers were the 1969 Bank of America Building (555 California St.), at 52 stories, now called **555 California Street,** followed by the distinctive 853-foot (260 m) **Transamerica Pyramid** (Clay & Montgomery Sts., www.pyramid center.com) in 1972. Older buildings worthy of a look include the **Pacific Exchange** (301 Pine St.), remodeled in 1930, and the

1903 **Merchant's Exchange** (465 California St.).

The 1875 **Palace Hotel** (2 New Montgomery St., tours tel 415-512-1111, www.sfpalace.com), rebuilt in 1909 and now lavishly refurbished, is known as the place where President Warren Harding drew his last breath in 1923. The **Garden Court** astounds with its incredible architecture, dome stained-glass ceiling, and Austrian crystal chandeliers and in its early 20th-century heyday was the setting for some of the nation's most prestigious events. Today it's a perfect setting for afternoon tea.

At the modern end of the scale are the strikingly trapezoidal **181 Fremont** (181 Fremont St., www.181fremont.com) luxury condominium complex, and the bullet-shaped **Salesforth Tower** (415 Mission St., www.salesforcetower.com), at 1,070 feet (326.1 m) the tallest building in San Francisco.

Montgomery Street
Access to many Financial District buildings is restricted, but looking from the outside is free, as is the lively **Montgomery Street** scene—watch the brokers either looking depressed or ordering caviar for breakfast. A swell place from which to view it all is the Starbuck's café (44 Montgomery St., tel 415-397-4394).

Jackson Square, up the street, offers perhaps the single best congregation of buildings from the gold rush era. Take a look at the 1852 Golden Era Building *(730–752 Montgomery St.)* and the gorgeous Italianate facade of the Hotaling Building *(451 Jackson St.)*. The shop called W. Graham Arader III *(435 Jackson St.)* has a huge selection of antique prints and rare maps.

Back down Montgomery Street, stop at the Wells Fargo History Museum to learn how the West was financed—largely through the efforts of this prestigious bank. The jewels here are the well preserved, mid-19th-century stagecoaches. San Francisco's "other" downtown centers around Union Square *(Geary St. at Stockton St., www.visitunionsquaresf. com)*, the historic center of the downtown retail trade. Nearby, at Powell and Market Streets, is the Powell Street Cable Car Turntable, from where you can begin a scenic journey to Nob Hill (see pp. 202–205), Fisherman's Wharf (see pp. 206–207), or Chinatown (see pp. 196–197). ■

Wells Fargo History Museum

- 🏛 195
- ✉ 420 Montgomery St.,
- ☎ 415-396-2619
- 🕐 Closed Sat.–Sun.
- 🚋 Cable car: California St.; Bus: 1, 12, 15, 42

www.wellsfargo history.com

CHINATOWN

Founded in the mid-19th century, San Francisco's Chinatown has long served as a historical touchstone for the city's now highly assimilated but ethnically proud Chinese-American community. It is, to be sure, somewhat faded by age, and many of its older Chinese families have moved elsewhere. Yet this noisy quarter (bounded by Broadway, Powell, Kearny, and Bush Sts.) remains a vibrant and richly evocative travel destination.

 After roast duck? Head to Stockton Street, the center of commerce—and food—in Chinatown.

Chinatown

193 G3 & 195

Cable car: California St., Powell-Hyde, Powell-Mason; Bus: 1, 9X, 15, 41, 45, 83

www.sanfrancisco chinatown.com

Shopping looms large in Chinatown, from cheap Asian curios and timeless San Francisco souvenirs to jade pieces and gold jewelry. The ornate, green-tiled **Chinatown Gate** *(map p. 195, Bush & Grant Sts.)* marks the start of the quarter. Those with a bent for shopping can visit the many shops along historic **Grant Avenue.**

Specialty shops include Golden Gate Fortune Cookies *(56 Ross Alley, tel 415-781-3956, www.golden gatefortunecookies.com)* and Chinatown Kite Shop *(717 Grant Ave., tel 415-989-5182, www.chinatownkite.*

com), where the stock ranges from traditional Chinese dragon and goldfish kites to modern power foils and sports kites. Foodies should take to **Stockton Street,** where produce sellers hawk their wares next to Chinese herbal medicine stores.

One of Chinatown's best views is from the rooftop **Moongate Lounge** *(28 Waverly Pl., tel 415-857-9688, closed Mon.),* the sophisticated lounge-bar of Michelin-starred **Mister Jiu's** *(www.misterjius.com).* Savor the restaurant's delicious Cantonese classics with a California twist, then pop upstairs to the minimalist bar to sip an Asian-inflection cocktail and enjoy the panoramic view of Chinatown and the Transamerica Pyramid (see p. 194).

The **Chinese Culture Center** exhibits local art, as well as musical instruments and other cultural items. Its real specialty, however, is its historical walking tours, well worth the cost.

Among the traditional historical stops is **Old St. Mary's Cathedral** (map p. 195, Grant Ave. & California St., www.oldsaintmarys. org), the West Coast's first Roman Catholic cathedral and one of the few buildings here to survive the 1906 earthquake and fire. In the park across the street, you'll find mah-jongg players and a rendering of Sun Yat-Sen by local artist Benjamin Bufano.

The relatively new (1977) redbrick **Kong Chow Temple** contains one of the oldest Taoist shrines in America; on its ruby-red walls is a 19th-century statue, from Canton,

of the patron deity Kuan Ti. The statue was rescued from the ashes of the original temple on Pine Street after the 1906 earthquake.

Colorful Waverly Place has restaurants and both churches and temples, including the **Tin How Temple** (map p. 195, 125 Waverly Pl.). Established in 1852 by Day Ju, one of the city's first Chinese immigrants, the temple is dedicated to the "Queen of the heavens and goddess of the Seven Seas." The remarkable "Life of Confucius" altar has been a spiritual and social core ever since.

The **Chinese Historical Society Museum**—occupying architect Julia Morgan's 1932 Chinatown YWCA, with its towers and painted ceiling panels—focuses on early Chinatown. Other sites offering a sense of the early neighborhood include the **Old Chinese Telephone Exchange** (743 Washington St.) and **Chinese Six Companies** (843 Stockton St.)—which once informally "ran" the enclave. ■

Chinese Culture Center
- 🅰 195
- ✉ Hilton Hotel, 3rd Floor, 750 Kearny St.
- ☎ 415-986-1822
- 🕐 Closed Sun.– Mon. Call for tours.
- 🅢 Tour: $$$$$

www.cccsf.us

Kong Chow Temple
- 🅰 193 G3 & 195
- ✉ 855 Stockton St., 4th floor
- ☎ 415-788-1339

Chinese Historical Society Museum
- 🅰 195
- ✉ 965 Clay St.
- ☎ 415-391-1188
- 🕐 Closed Sun.– Mon.

www.chsa.org

EXPERIENCE: Sampling Chinatown

For some guidance on Chinatown food, it is worth turning to a local expert. **Wok Wiz** (tel 415-795-8303, www.wokwiz. com) offers four outstanding culinary tours that also include a good dose of local history.

The **Wok Wiz Classic Tour** ($$$$$) will introduce you to the history and architecture of Chinatown, with visits to an herbalist, tea shop, and local farmers market. The tour begins at 10 a.m. at the Hilton Financial District (750 Kearny St.). For an extra fee, you can finish with an excellent dim sum lunch at one of Chinatown's oldest restaurants.

The three-hour **I Can't Believe I Ate My Way Through Chinatown! Tour** ($$$$$) begins with a traditional Chinese breakfast—congee and dumplings. You'll then sample tea at a local tea shop and visit some of the neighborhood's best food markets. The tour, which is led by food-loving chef Shirley Fong-Torres, ends with a fabulous lunch. Space is limited, so book early.

If you prefer to plan your own food tour, two reliably delicious restaurants are the **House of Nanking** (919 Kearny St., tel 415-421-1429) and **Lucky Creation** (854 Washington St., tel 415-989-0818).

NORTH BEACH

From its mid-19th-century days as a point of disembarkation for Italian and French immigrants to its 1950s flourishing as a Beat literary center, North Beach has long been the city's entertaining and unself-conscious theater of street life. With its bounty of hearty food, camp (if now somewhat tacky) sex shows, historic literary cafés, and outstanding boutique shopping, it has travelers returning to it again and again.

At dusk, the cafés and restaurants of North Beach catch their second wind.

North Beach
🅰 193 G3

The Beat Museum
🅰 201
✉ 540 Broadway
☎ 800-537-6822
💲 $
www.kerouac.com

Bounded by Broadway to the south, Montgomery Street to the east, Lombard Street to the north, and Mason Street to the west, North Beach was defined by the Italians who settled here late in the 19th century and claimed it for their own after the 1906 earthquake and fire. Today the Italian presence is unmistakable in such establishments as Tosca, Caffè Trieste, and Mara's.

The Italian community's place of worship is the 1922 Romanesque **Sts. Peter and Paul**

Church (map p. 201, 666 Filbert St., tel 415-421-0809, www.parish.sspeter paulsf.org). Here, in 1957, baseball hero Joe DiMaggio and his bride, Marilyn Monroe, had their wedding photos taken. The twin spires of the church overlook **Washington Square,** whose daily parade of Chinese tai chi practitioners and old-style *paisanos* evokes a unique American ambience.

For a bigger draft of the past, visit the **Beat Museum,** where an extensive photo collection documents the district's bohemian history. Recent work by local artists

INSIDER TIP:

Picnic in Washington Square Park near Sts. Peter and Paul Church for a vibrant slice of North Beach.

—ERIN STONE
National Geographic contributor

is found at the beautiful **San Francisco Art Institute** (see p. 201), which also houses the **Diego Rivera Gallery.**

A pilgrimage point for bookish types is **City Lights.** Founded by Beat generation poet Lawrence Ferlinghetti (the city's former poet laureate), the bookstore stocks a wide selection of literary fiction and politically charged nonfiction. There is, of course, a deep shelf of Ferlinghetti's fellow poet Allen Ginsberg (who wrote his most famous poem, "Howl," while living at 1010 Montgomery St.) and the official martyr of the Beat movement, Jack Kerouac, whose *On the Road* (1957) fueled the wanderlust

of 1960s youth. Just across **Jack Kerouac Alley** is **Vesuvio** *(map p. 201, 255 Columbus Ave., tel 415-362-8193)*, another Beat-era touchstone, while the alley itself is ablaze with colorful murals.

Clubs and bars line **Broadway;** a walk along the strip is essential, if only to see the **Condor Club** *(map p. 201, 560 Broadway, tel 415-781-8222, www.condorsf. com)*, where, in 1964, Carol Doda stunned America by dancing topless with her "twin 44s." In **Club Fugazi** *(678 Green St.)*, the musical spoof *Beach Blanket Babylon* enjoyed a 45-year run of mad satire and over the top hats until it closed in 2019.

The antique shops of North Beach are worth checking out for their Italo-Americana. Or wander a few blocks up to **Grant Avenue,** where you will discover some highly individualistic shops. Number 1529B was the **workshop of Peter Macchiarini,** a former Works Progress Administration artist whose sculptures and jewelry still evoke the best of that period's folk modernism. ∎

San Francisco Art Institute

- 🅰 193 F4 & 201
- ✉ 800 Chestnut St.
- ☎ 415-771-7020
- 🚋 Cable car: Powell-Hyde, Powell-Mason; Bus: 30

www.sfai.edu

City Lights

- 🅰 Map p. 201
- ✉ 261 Columbus Ave.
- ☎ 415-362-8193
- 🚋 Bus: 8X, 30, 41, 45

www.citylights.com

Riding Through History

The **Cable Car Museum** *(map pp. 193 F3 & 195, Mason St. & Washington St., tel 415-474-1887, www.cablecarmuseum.org)* has a small but exquisite collection of cable car artifacts and history. The city's machine-age (but still digital-era-functioning) cable cars were originally constructed to solve a transportation problem: how to get people up a hill too steep for horses. San Francisco industrialist Andrew Hallidie came up with the idea of using cable traction to power public transport; the system was

inaugurated on August 2, 1873—and hasn't stopped since.

Some of the old cable cars here date from as far back as the 1870s. It is worth going downstairs to see the "brains" of the system. The massive wheels carrying the cable that moves the cars along are beautiful in their early industrial-age simplicity.

Present-day cable cars start at Powell and Market and at Powell and Van Ness and run from 6:30 a.m. to 1 a.m. daily *(tel 311 or 415-701-2311, www.sfmta.com)*.

TELEGRAPH & RUSSIAN HILLS WALK

Notable for stunning views of both the bay and the city, Telegraph Hill and Russian Hill hold a number of delights (particularly the singularly crooked Lombard Street) within reasonable walking distance.

The iconic curves of Lombard Street were added in 1922 so cars could safely descend.

Walk One: Coit Tower to Russian Hill Park

Chief among the sights on this walk is **Coit Tower** ❶ (1 Telegraph Hill Blvd., tel 800-655-6751 tickets, www.sfrecpark.org, $$), a 284-foot (86.5 m) fluted tower designed by architect Arthur Page Brown—architect of City Hall and the Swedenborgian Church (see p. 209), among other buildings—and set at the top of Telegraph Hill. It was built with funds left to the city after the death of eccentric philanthropist Lillian Coit in 1929. The tower is her memorial to the city's firefighters: An obsessive devotion to them was one aspect of Coit's eccentricity. She wore a diamond-studded fireman's badge everywhere she went, even to elegant balls.

The **elevator ride** ($) to the top of Coit Tower promises superb views of the city and

> **NOT TO BE MISSED:**
>
> Coit Tower • Lombard Street • San Francisco Art Institute • Filbert Steps

the bay. The building's other highlights are its **murals,** which line the inside walls. Painted in the early 1930s by a group of artists employed by the Public Works of Art Project (a precursor to the Works Progress Administration, or WPA), the paintings were controversial in their time. Today they are icons of the city's vaunted tolerance for the politically charged. Particularly arresting is the mural titled "Banking and Law," created in 1933–34 by artist George Harris.

A multimillion-dollar renovation has brought new life to the already splendid

See also area map p. 193 G3
► Coit Tower
🕐 2 hours
↔ 1.1 miles (1.7 km) to Russian Hill Park
► Russian Hill Park or Levi's Plaza

Pioneer Park, surrounding the tower, with a series of new terraces and lookout points, making this an even more perfect place for a picnic. Buy the makings for one at **Molinari's Deli** *(373 Columbus Ave., tel 415-421-2337, www.molinaridelisf.com).*

From Telegraph Hill, you have two main paths of discovery. The first is more traditional. Stroll down **Lombard Street ②.** Then cross Columbus Avenue and head uphill, still on Lombard, to Leavenworth Street. From here, Lombard Street—called the "world's crookedest street"—twists and turns its way uphill.

A right turn on Leavenworth and again on Chestnut takes you to the **San Francisco Art Institute ③** (see p. 199). The prize here is Diego Rivera's "Making of a Fresco" (1931), but the 1926 Spanish Colonial building and all its contents are worth a stop. From here, walk along Chestnut to Hyde Street and turn right

to **Russian Hill Park ④,** a wonderful place to rest, recoup, and gaze out on the bay.

Walk Two: Telegraph Hill Toward the Waterfront

An alternative walk from Coit Tower, and a splendid end to an afternoon on Telegraph Hill—or perhaps a good prelude to a day on the waterfront (see pp. 206–207)—is to go down the **Filbert Steps ①,** just to the east of the tower. Beginning by a notable art moderne apartment building, the steps descend amid a series of terraced gardens, all of them flush with basketball-size hydrangeas, lush ivies, loquat trees, and magnolias.

The Filbert Steps end at **Levi's Plaza ②** *(map p. 193 G3, 1155 Battery St.).* Landscaped with water cascades, the plaza, behind the headquarters of the legendary jeans manufacturer whose fame stretches from the gold rush to the global, opens to the waterfront.

"The Irish they live on th' top av it,
And th' Dagoes they live on th' base av it,
And th' goats and th' chicks and th' brickbats and
*   shticks*
Is joombled all over th' face av it."
    —Wallace Irwin, from *Telygraft Hill*

NOB HILL

As the highest point in the city (338 feet—103 m—above sea level), it is hardly surprising that Nob Hill *(California & Taylor Sts.)* has long been San Francisco's most visible indicator of wealth and status. A good way to take in the hill's main attractions is to visit its grand early 20th-century hotels. For an understanding of how the modern city communes with the traditional, older era, visit Nob Hill's architectural gem: Grace Cathedral.

California Street on Nob Hill offers a view of the Bay Bridge.

The Hotels

Nob Hill's three principal hotels—the Mark Hopkins, the Fairmont, and the Huntington—are well worth a visit. The Mark Hopkins and the Huntington, in particular, warrant consideration by the traveler in search of a memorable San Francisco experience. Given the prices at the deluxe chain hotels, these gracious old piles offer sumptuous spas, unbeatable dining, and often good value.

Mark Hopkins: At the Mark Hopkins *(map p. 195, 1 Nob Hill, tel 415-392-3434, www. sfmarkhopkins.com),* built in 1926, take the elevator up to the art deco-ish **Top of the Mark** *(tel 415-616-6916, www.sfmarkhopkins. com/top-of-the-mark),* the hotel's grande dame of a watering spot. It is without peer as a place from which to view the entire cityscape and has an outstanding wine and mixed drinks list. Sunset is the time to be here.

Fairmont: Across California Street is the Fairmont *(map p. 195, 950 Mason St., tel 415-772-5000, www.fairmont.com/ san-francisco),* saved from the earthquake wreckage by architect Stanford White in 1907.

King of the Hills

Its name cribbed from the Hindi *nabob*, roughly meaning "big shot," Nob Hill was the residence of choice for such late 19th-century figures as business and railroad barons Leland Stanford, Charles Crocker, and Mark Hopkins. Men like these led lives of such ostentation as to provoke Irish labor leader Denis Kearny to lead an angry mob of workers up the hill in protest in 1878.

Only the earthquake and fire of 1906 put a (temporary) stop to the bacchanal. The great mansions were replaced—by luxury hotels, city clubs, churches for the wealthy, and parks for the few hoi polloi who made it up the hill for the views. Today the views are still free and still stunning. Most wealthy residences are now in other parts of the city, but Nob Hill stands as glorious as ever.

Take in the ornate lobby, the oldest in the three hotels. An extensive renovation has restored its Florentine mirrors and gold leaf. Its Laurel Court, Venetian Room, and facade have also been restored. The Fairmont sits on the foundations of the mansion built by the daughter of James G. "Bonanza Jim" Fair, an also-ran in the "robber baron" coterie alongside the Big Four: Crocker, Stanford, Hopkins, and Collis P. Huntington (see sidebar above).

INSIDER TIP:

Pop into the Venetian Room at the Fairmont Hotel to see where Tony Bennett first performed "I Left My Heart in San Francisco."

—JUSTIN KAVANAGH
National Geographic International Editions editor

Huntington: To cap a perfectly opulent day in this perfectly opulent terrain, the restaurant at the Huntington *(map p. 195, 1075 California St. at Taylor St., tel 415-474-5400, www. huntingtonhotel.com)* is hard to beat. Named the Big 4 in reference to city plutocrats of old, it successfully conjures the best of the old days. Its crab cakes and rack of lamb, not to mention rabbit, quail, and champagne, are exactly what the Big Four would be eating today.

Clift Royal Sonesta Hotel: The Clift Royal Sonesta Hotel *(map p. 195, 495 Geary St., tel 415-775-4700, www.clifthotel.com)* boasts the **Redwood Room,** a moderne-style 1934 cocktail lounge wrought from the wood of a single redwood tree and overhauled with a mirrored bar, "digital art," and dim lighting—at once chic and decadent.

Grace Cathedral

The nation's third largest Episcopal cathedral measures 329 feet (100 m) long, with a spire rising 247 feet (75 m). It is modeled on Paris's Notre Dame, but unlike a European cathedral, it

Nob Hill

▲ 193 F3 & 195

Grace Cathedral

▲ 193 F3 & 195
✉ 1100 California St. at Taylor St.
☎ 415-749-6300
🚋 Cable car: all lines; Bus: 1

www.grace cathedral.org

was built not of stone but of reinforced concrete—a material perhaps incongruous for a sacred space. (It was used for earthquake safety.) Here, where old-line Episcopalianism meets the globally minded ways of the urban affluent, you will find the focal point of a unique and modern religious culture.

Officially established in 1853, Grace Cathedral had as its first bishop William Ingraham Kip, a Yale-trained historian. Although

A joyful noise rises in Grace Cathedral when the bells ring.

orthodox and East Coast urbane, Kip quickly saw a unique opportunity for Episcopalianism in the West. (He was not without a few initial doubts; the bawdy excesses of the gold rush period, he wrote, were "enough to convince one of the doctrine of total depravity.") Kip quickly took to his role as an evangelizing "frontier bishop," delighting in California's Roman Catholic past and Mediterranean climate. By embracing the state's past, aesthetically, oratorically, and socially, Kip believed that Episcopalianism could plant its rich apostolic traditions in an unfolding new world. His would be a Californian Episcopalianism, orthodox but open, its eye on the past yet, as scholar Kevin Starr has noted, "redeemed in futurity . . . and the aesthetic elaboration of the present." That this doctrine might produce the wide-open, progressive spirit now abundantly in evidence at Grace would likely startle Kip were he alive today. But he would likely come to embrace it. Everywhere here, the modern and the ancient combine in a spirit of mystical openness.

Some highlights of the church bear this out. The classic French Gothic architecture is fronted by bronze **entrance doors,** duplicates cast from the originals of Lorenzo Ghiberti's "Doors of Paradise" in the baptistry of the cathedral in Florence. Just inside the doors, to the right, is the **AIDS Interfaith Memorial Chapel,** with its altarpiece by the late graphic artist Keith Haring. There is also an AIDS quilt panel, the most universal memorial to victims.

Inside the cathedral proper, directly behind the **Meditation Labyrinth** (modeled on that of Chartres), is a beautifully wrought statue of St. Francis by San Francisco artist Benjamin Bufano. An interesting way of linking the

---

INSIDER TIP:

Attend yoga classes with 60 or 80 locals every Tuesday night at Grace Cathedral near Union Square.

—KAY RABIN
*City guide, San Francisco
Public Library*

1930s part of the building with the 1960s section can be seen by standing here and looking up and back, toward the entrance. Here you will see the **East Rose Window,** a copy of the "Canticle of the Sun," by Gabriel Loire of Chartres in France. The canticle was inspired by St. Francis's celebratory poem in praise of the Creator and Creation. Looking down at the floor of the nave, you will discover another iteration of that theme, this time in the form of the Chi Rho, a Greek monogram for Christ.

Perhaps the best expression of the uniquely Californian and progressive religious aesthetic can be found in the sanctuary. The **altar** is made of granite from the High Sierra and a piece of 2,000-year-old coastal redwood. The altar rail cushions are stitched with wildflowers of various Californian Episcopal dioceses.

The many outstanding original works of Renaissance art include the "Madonna and Child" plaque by Antonio Rossellino, just to the right of the choir stall.

The most memorable and moving works are probably the more recent ones in the **Chapel of Grace Baptistry,** to the left of the choir stall. Two icons done in 1990 by painter Robert Lenz seem an appropriate coda to the Grace experience. The first, to your left, is of John Donne, the 17th-century mystic poet and preacher, dean of St. Paul's Cathedral in London. The other is of Mary

---

The Other Cathedral

To the south, between Nob Hill and Pacific Heights (see pp. 209–211), is the **Cathedral of St. Mary of the Assumption** *(map pp. 193 F2 & 211, 1111 Gough St., tel 415-567-2020, www.smcsf.org).* Completed in 1970, the cathedral is one of the most dramatic buildings in California. Covering two city blocks, it has a sweeping modern ceiling and outstanding interior sculptures by Mario Rudelli and Enrico Manfridi. The building's remarkable postmodernist shape—a cruciform cone on a square base—evokes the optimistic era of post–Vatican II American Catholicism.

Magdalene holding in her hand an egg, the instrument by which she is said to have taught Emperor Tiberius the story of the resurrection. This icon was dedicated in 1990 to Bishop Barbara Harris, the first woman bishop in the Episcopal Church.

A brochure map is on sale in the lobby and gift shop, and afternoon tours are available. ■

THE WATERFRONT

Second only to Chinatown in popularity with tourists, Fisherman's Wharf anchors the waterfront, a triptych extending for five miles (8 km) from the foot of Market Street westward to Crissy Field and the Golden Gate Bridge. There was a time when the urban shoreline was synonymous with a stroll-and-spend on the highly themed Pier 39. No more. Today, the city's shore can fill an entire day and fit a wide range of interests.

■ The huge sign in Ghiradelli Square went up in 1915.

Ferry Building
🄰 193 H3
✉ Embarcadero at Market St.
☎ 415-983-8030
**www.ferrybuilding
marketplace.com**

Exploratorium
🄰 193 G3
✉ Piers 15 & 17
☎ 415-528-4444
🕐 Closed Mon. except some holidays
💲 $$$. Free 1st Wed. of month
🚌 Bus: 22, 28, 30, 41, 43, 45
**www.exploratorium
.edu**

A good starting point for exploring is the historic **Ferry Building.** Opened in 1898 to serve the ferries connecting San Francisco to the East Bay, it entered a long period of disuse after the opening of the Bay Bridge in 1937. Recently restored, it is now a magnificent marketplace, and the 240-foot-tall (73 m) clock tower again serves as a welcoming beacon.

Joggers and historic trams run the length of the **Embarcadero** (map p. 193 G4–H3), lined with piers used by cruise ships.

Founded by physicist Frank Oppenheimer in 1969, the popular **Exploratorium** utilizes every piece of technological wizardry imaginable to engage young minds in the sciences. Its 800 interactive exhibits, displays, and original artworks include a computer-simulated flight over the city, a distorting room that makes children look bigger than their parents, and even an antigravity mirror. A giant prism teaches the principles of light refraction, while visitors can learn about water dynamics by creating their own vortex in a 7-foot (2 m) Plexiglas beaker. The Exploratorium has become something of a media darling in recent years. But be warned: This place is *loud.*

Farther west, **Pier 39** (map p. 193 G4, Embarcadero at Beach St., www.pier39.com) delights tourists with its shops, restaurants, and amusements, including a carousel. Sea lions often laze on the boat docks. At **Aquarium of the Bay** (tel 415-623-5300, www.aquarium ofthebay.org, $), a moving walkway goes through a see-through tunnel, while sharks and other sea creatures swim about you. Ferries run from here to Sausalito (see p. 245), Tiburon (see p. 244 and sidebar opposite), and Alcatraz and Angel Islands (see p. 208).

Farther west, **Fisherman's Wharf** (map p. 193 F4, www .fishermanswharf.org) is named for the brightly painted fishing fleet that has berthed here since the late 19th century. The area is now mostly a jumble of kitschy boutiques and tourist traps, but with some splendid restaurants and streetside stalls where you can buy the city's famous Dungeness crab. Attractions include **Ripley's Believe It or Not! Museum** (*175 Jefferson St., tel 415-202-9850, www.ripleys. com/sanfrancisco, $$$$*) and the **Cannery** (*2801 Leavenworth St.*), a former peach cannery now housing shops and eateries.

The **USS *Pampanito*** (*Pier 45, tel 415-775-1943, $$$$*), a World War II submarine open to the public, is part of **San Francisco Maritime National Historical Park.** Located in a streamlined art deco building, the park's mainstay, the **Maritime Museum** (*www. maritime.org*), exhibits model ships and nautical miscellany that document San Francisco's maritime grandeur. The park's historic vessels at Hyde Street Pier include the 1886 *Balclutha* square-rigger (of

Cape Horner style); the 1895 *C. A. Thayer* (a lumber schooner); and the last of the city's paddle-wheel steam-powered ferryboats, the 1890 *Eureka*.

The Maritime Museum abuts **Fort Mason,** a former Army barracks and now a lively cultural center with three outstanding theaters and several small museums.

To the south, **Ghiradelli Square** (*map p. 193 F4, 900 N. Point St., tel 415-775-5500, www .ghirardellisq.com*), a brick-terraced 19th-century chocolate factory, today comprises shops and fine restaurants.

The **Marina Green** (*map p. 193 E3–E4*) is a fun place to stroll, roller-skate, or fly a kite. The esplanade leads to the **Palace of Fine Arts,** a lone but grand reminder of the 1915 Panama-Pacific Exposition. It is well worth a visit, if only to get an idea of how early 20th-century San Franciscans viewed the city's future in the wake of the 1906 earthquake and fire. ∎

San Francisco Maritime National Historical Park

- 🅰 193 F4
- ✉ Jefferson & Hyde Sts.
- ☎ 415-561-7000
- 💲 $$$ to board historic ships
- 🚡 Cable car: Powell-Hyde, Powell-Mason; Bus: 30, 41, 45; Streetcar: F-line

www.nps.gov/safr

Fort Mason

- 🅰 193 E4–F4
- ✉ Marina Blvd. & Buchanan St.
- ☎ 415-345-7500

www.fortmason.org

Palace of Fine Arts

- 🅰 193 E4
- ✉ 3301 Lyon St.
- ☎ 415-563-6504

www.palaceoffine arts.org

EXPERIENCE: Out on the Bay

Those who crave their own sail on the bay have a number of choices. Start by consulting **Sailing San Francisco** (*www .sfsailing.com*), which lists yacht charters, sailing schools, and races. Or try one of the cruises offered by the **Blue & Gold Fleet** (*tel 415-705-8200, www.blueandgold fleet.com, reservations recommended, $$$$*). Boats depart several times a day from Pier 41 on Fisherman's Wharf and Pier 39. One option is a trip to **Tiburon** (see p. 244), a quaint, small former railroad town across the bay, good for food and with an excellent bike path (*rent a bike when you depart from Pier 41*). Or take a

cruise along the waterfront, passing such landmarks as the Palace of Fine Arts and the Golden Gate Bridge (see p. 214).

Captain Kirk's Sailing Adventures (*tel 650-930-0740, www.sfbaysail.com, $$$$$*) offers lessons and several beneath-the-canvas adventures, including a 4-hour sail around the bay, Angel Island barbecue, open ocean sail beyond the Golden Gate, and harbor porpoise excursion. **Adventure Cat Sailing Charters** (*tel 800-498-4228, www.adventurecat .com, $$$$$*) organizes similar sailing trips on two huge catamarans.

ALCATRAZ & ANGEL ISLANDS

A trip to Alcatraz Island has become an essential part of any first-time visit to San Francisco. The thrill in walking in the steps of Al Capone and "Machine Gun" Kelly is tempered by the melancholic nature of the world's most famous prison, but visitors agree that it is a uniquely memorable experience. Nearby Angel Island—the "Jewel of the Bay"—provides the freedom that Alcatraz once denied.

Alcatraz Island

🗺 233 B3
☎ 415-561-4900; Ferry bookings: 415-981-7625
💲 $$$$$

www.nps.gov/alcatraz

Angel Island

🗺 233 B4
☎ 415-435-1915; Ferry bookings: 415-435-2131 from Tiburon; 415-705-8200 from San Francisco

www.parks.ca.gov

Alcatraz Island

On Alcatraz, guides tell of escape attempts (all convicts who tried were either shot, recaptured, or presumed drowned) and the various criminal personalities. Among these are Robert Stroud, the original "birdman of Alcatraz"; Al Capone, whose five-year stint in isolation left him mentally deranged; and the Anglin brothers, who escaped by chipping through the walls of their

---

INSIDER TIP:

Be sure to get tickets for an Alcatraz cruise and tour early as they often sell out. Tickets are available up to 90 days in advance.

—CHARLES KOGOD
National Geographic contributor

---

cells but most likely drowned. The prison also held the Native American rebel Kaetena (a friend of Geronimo), who in 1887 had led a mutiny against the government in Arizona.

Try to leave time during your visit to Alcatraz for a walk along the quarter-mile (0.4 km) **Agave Trail**, which leads through the island's

bird sanctuary. Pelicans, for which Alcatraz was named, dominate, but different seasons bring dozens of other species.

Alcatraz Cruises (*tel 415-981-7625, www.alcatrazcruises.com*) offers various themed interpretive tours, including a night trip.

Angel Island

Unlike Alcatraz, Angel Island remains a relatively untouristy destination. The largest island in the bay, at 1 square mile (2.5 sq km), it is known for the old **Immigration Station at China Cove,** where hundreds of thousands of Asian and Russian immigrants were "processed" around the turn of the 20th century. During World War II, it served as a prisoner of war camp and, later, a missile base. An excellent museum (*www.aiisf. org*) profiles the often traumatic immigrant experience.

Angel Island also offers miles of outstanding hiking trails as well as an interesting Civil War camp and fort. A perimeter trail winds about the entire island; a trail near the marina in Ayala Cove takes you to the highest peak, 771 feet (235 m), for sweeping views.

The Angel Island Company (*tel 415-435-3392, http://angelisland.com*) offers tram and Segway tours, plus bike rentals. ■

AROUND PACIFIC HEIGHTS

Setting for San Francisco's most eclectic and magnificent mansions, Pacific Heights is lofty in more ways than one: Its panoramic views of the bay and Golden Gate Bridge are unrivaled, while it has the distinction of being the most expensive residential neighborhood in the U.S.

Named for its elevated perch atop an east-west ridge, the district resembles Beverly Hills on steroids. High-tech billionaires rub elbows with old money on street after street of grandiose houses spanning an architectural spectrum from Victorian and Beaux Arts to French Châteaux-style (see pp. 210–211).

If one end of the San Francisco architectural aesthetic is historicism—the attempt to recreate a selective European past—the other end is naturalism, rendering architecture as a harmonic natural atmosphere. The **Swedenborgian Church** is a prime example. This little structure was built in 1894 for followers of Emmanuel Swedenborg, an 18th-century Swede who preached "reverence for the divine in nature." Although a tiny commission by the day's gilded-age standards, the project nonetheless attracted the leading craftsmen of the period. The madrone tree ceiling supports heighten the rustic-Zen quality of the church, making a visit here a prized moment for those interested in American architecture. Two circular stained-glass windows lend a calm glow to the Shaker-simple seating below. Outside, the garden is planted with olive trees, cedar of Lebanon, elm, pine, plum, and crabapple.

■ The Swedenborgian Church, with its madrone wood ceiling, has been called the "church of the simple life."

If you walk north from the Swedenborgian, there's a fine photo opportunity of the bay from the **Lyon Street Steps.** For those interested in Victoriana, it is worth visiting the classic 1866 **Haas-Lilienthal House,** a beautifully restored and furnished Queen Anne structure.

To the south, the **Japan Center** *(map pp. 193 F2 & 211, 1730 Geary Blvd., www.sfjapantown.org)* is the historic heart of the area's Japanese-American community. Enjoy Japanese food, art, and, most refreshing after a long day, a dunk in the old-style Japanese baths at the **Kabuki Springs & Spa** *(1750 Geary Blvd., tel 415-922-6001, www.kabukisprings.com).* A shiatsu massage and scrub are available by appointment. ■

Swedenborgian Church

🅰 193 E3
✉ 2107 Lyon St.
☎ 415-346-6468
🚍 Bus: 3, 12, 22, 24

www.sfsweden borgian.org

Haas-Lilienthal House

🅰 193 F3 & 211
✉ 2007 Franklin St.
☎ 415-441-3000
🕐 Tours Wed., Sat., & Sun.
💲 $$
🚍 Bus: 1, 12, 19, 27, 47, 49

www.haas-lilienthalhouse.org

PACIFIC HEIGHTS WALK

During the years following the 1906 earthquake and fire, the epicenter of wealth and power in San Francisco shifted westward to the hills now known as Pacific Heights. Here, as one WPA writer put it, the rich "could dwell surrounded by gardens overlooking the Golden Gate." In grand style, modern San Franciscans carry on that tradition, everywhere evident during a pleasant morning's walk.

The remarkable Spreckels Mansion covers an entire block and has 26 bathrooms.

There are some wonderful surprises on this walk and many highlights. (Please remember that nearly all the buildings are privately owned and not open to the public, so view them only from the sidewalk.)

The French baroque **Spreckels Mansion ❶**, just west of Gough Street at 2080 Washington Street, is a good starting point. The architect of the Palace of the Legion of Honor, George Applegarth, built the house in 1912 for sugar magnate Adolph Spreckels. From here Spreckels's wife, Alma, the doyenne of early 20th-century San Francisco, ruled the social scene. Romance novelist Danielle Steel now owns the "Sugar Castle," although she lives in Paris.

Walk west up Washington, passing the **Phelan House** (three houses up on the right), where Sen. James D. Phelan entertained when the city was run by an oligopoly in the late 19th century. Turn south through **Lafayette Park ❷**, at the top of which are some of the best views in town. On the southern side, pass the

NOT TO BE MISSED:

Spreckels Mansion ● Century Club
● Row house Victorians

Atherton House, at Octavia and California. It is perhaps the most eclectic hodgepodge of Victorian styles anywhere.

Proceeding east on California Street past Gough, you will see two outstanding examples of Victoriana. The **Wormser House ❸**, at 1834 California Street, was built in 1877 by San Francisco merchant Isaac Wormser. It is interesting for its mix of styles: Queen Anne on the left side and the vertically exaggerated Stick style on the right. At 1818 California sits the **Sloss Home.** Built in 1876 by a fur trade millionaire, it is also in the Stick style, with Italianate lines on the side and cornice.

Next to Sloss House at 1701 Franklin (at California) is the **Edward Coleman House ❹**, built in the Queen Anne style in 1895. If you walk south down Franklin, you can see the remarkable stained-glass enclosed stairway in the rear. A true historic gem is the former **Century Club,** located at 1355 Franklin. Its architect was the renowned Julia Morgan, who also designed Hearst Castle (see pp. 174–175). The Spanish consulate now occupies the building.

Go west on Sutter to Gough Street and the **Hotel Majestic ❺** (1500 Sutter St., tel 415-441-1100, www.thehotelmajestic.com). In the 1960s, this 1905 Victorian gem was run as the notorious Brothel, a hotel for gay men. Closed by Mayor Dianne Feinstein (along with the bathhouses) during the early AIDS epidemic, it is now an excellent bed-and-breakfast hotel, known for its elegant Butterfly Lounge.

Walk north on Gough Street and turn west on Bush Street. More examples of the area's architectural heritage warrant note on Bush. Houses called **row house Victorians** ❻ can be seen here—middle-class houses of mixed styles, ranging (often in one house) from Queen Anne to Stick. The house at 1803 Bush is Italianate; next door is an example of a "smothered" Victorian, a description that refers to mid-20th-century "improving" of 19th-century houses with stucco and brick.

An architectural oddity is the **Ohabai Shalome Temple** ❼ ("Loves of Peace") synagogue at 1881 Bush Street Modeled on the Doge's Palace in Venice, it is redwood right down to its "stone carved" exterior.

Continue west on Bush Street and turn north on Pierce. You can enjoy another aspect of Pacific Heights as you walk northward on

Pierce through **Alta Plaza Park** ❽, with its stunning views, and on north to the junction with Broadway, into the wealthier section of town. Several houses on Broadway have famous associations. The **Mary Martin House** at Pierce and Broadway once belonged to the actress. The real pièce de résistance of the neighborhood is the **Casebolt House** ❾ (2727 Pierce St.), built by a hardware magnate in 1915. Appearing to be a kind of inflated Brooklyn brownstone, it is made completely of carved redwood. Its owners came from New York and wanted to feel at home.

Return to Broadway. The Victorian at No. 2311 is where the hit TV show *Party of Five* was filmed, while the house at 2640 Steiner Street (at Broadway) was the location of the 1993 movie *Mrs. Doubtfire*. Go east, and then turn south on Gough Street to your starting point.

🗻	See also area map p. 193
➤	Spreckels Mansion
🕐	2 hours
↔	3.2 miles (5.1 km)
➤	Spreckels Mansion

GOLDEN GATE BRIDGE & AROUND

In San Francisco's northeast corner lies a 1,491-acre (603 ha) haven of forests, grasslands, and sea cliffs—a miracle considering how much the rest of the city is built up. You'll find hiking trails, beaches, and some of the most magnificent views in the United States. Tour some of the 19th-century structures (there are 477 of them) and then head for Golden Gate National Recreation Area, which links the Golden Gate Bridge with the California Palace of the Legion of Honor.

Want some postcard shots? Baker Beach offers superb views of the Golden Gate Bridge.

Golden Gate Bridge

🗺 192 C4

Golden Gate Bridge

A remarkable piece of art, the Golden Gate Bridge—an elegant 8,900 feet (2,712 m) of concrete and steel supported by just two deftly designed piers—symbolizes San Francisco for locals and people the world over. As a feat of engineering, it represents a pure force of will and is a testimony to the engineering skills of Joseph Strauss, the architectural brilliance of Charles Ellis and Leon Moisseiff, and the financial acumen of A. G. Giannini, whose Bank of America floated the bond issue that paid for it. When the bridge was dedicated in 1937, it was the largest single structure in the world.

Today it would be hard to imagine a better place from which to begin a romantic trip to San Francisco. Mornings, misty and cool, are the perfect time for a bracing walk across the bridge to gain an overview of the city and its setting.

Almost 2 miles (3.2 km) long, the bridge is open to walkers (east walkway only) from 5 a.m. to 9 p.m. Daylight Savings Time, and until 6:30 p.m. Standard Time *(access from Lincoln Blvd.).* Wear a jacket as winds are often strong. To the northwest, a silvery stream might light up the Marin Headlands (see p. 244); behind them stands mysterious Mount Tamalpais (Mount Tam to the locals). To the northeast are the lonely shapes of Alcatraz and Angel Islands (see p. 208), flocks of gulls and pelicans floating on the air as if hanging from invisible rope. Across the bay are Berkeley and Oakland. To the southeast is the skyline of the city itself, perhaps the most memorable in all America.

Below you, on the south shore, sits **Fort Point National Historic Site.** This redbrick fortress was built during the Civil War to protect San Francisco from

Confederate attack. Cannon-loading demonstrations are held here, and Civil War reenactments bring the fort to life.

The bridge is a jewel in the crown of the **Golden Gate National Recreation Area.** This stretch of beach, forest, and grasslands runs from **Fort Funston** *(map p. 192 A1, tel 415-561-4700, www.parksconservancy.org)* in the south, eastward to **Fort Mason** (see p. 207), and north as far as **Tomales Bay** (see p. 246). The best place to take photographs of the city skyline is from the aptly named **Vista Point,** on the Marin side of the bridge.

Presidio

First established by the Spanish in 1776, the Presidio served as an army post commanding the Golden Gate straits. In 1994, the U.S. Army pulled out and the vast green swath was incorporated into the Golden Gate

Fort Point National Historic Site
📍 192 C4
☎ 415-561-4959
www.nps.gov/fopo

Golden Gate National Recreation Area
📍 192 B3–D4

Visitor Information
✉ Fort Mason, Bldg. 201
☎ 415-561-4700
www.nps.gov/goga

Presidio
📍 192 C3–D4

Visitor Information
✉ Visitor Center, 50 Moraga Ave.
☎ 415-561-4323
**www.nps.gov/prsf &
www.presidio.gov**

Getting Around San Francisco

Although San Francisco is a fine city to visit on foot, there comes a time when you'll want to avoid climbing yet another hill. Luckily, the city is well supplied with user-friendly and affordable public transportation (see inside the back cover for more information).

The **Bay Area Rapid Transit** (BART; *tel 415-989-2278, www.bart.gov*) is a sleek, well-groomed, 104-mile (167 km) rail system that links San Francisco and the peninsula with cities in the East Bay (via a 3.8-mile-long—6.1 km—transbay tube), making outings to Oakland (see pp. 234–237) and Berkeley (see pp. 238–242) an easy day trip; an extension feeds

San Francisco International Airport. The trains run from dawn to midnight. You can purchase multi-excursion passes at any of five BART stops along Market Street—Van Ness, Civic Center, Powell, Montgomery, and Embarcadero.

For information on the **Muni bus system** and advice on which bus to take, call the Muni information line *(tel 311 within San Francisco or 415-701-2311)* or go to www.sfmta.com.

The historic **cable cars** (see p. 199) start at Powell and Market and Powell and Van Ness and run all day. Passes, which are also accepted on the city's Muni bus system, can be purchased at Muni kiosks.

Legion of Honor

▲ 192 B2

✉ 100 34th Ave.

☎ 415-750-3600

🕐 Closed Mon.

💲 $$ (free 1st Tues. of month)

🚌 Bus: 1, 18, 38

http://legionof honor.famsf.org

National Recreation Area. Thanks to the restoration of several historic gems and an intelligent conversion of former military installations, the park features well-preserved military buildings, a museum, mile upon mile of looping roads, and great stands of eucalyptus trees, plus hiking trails and picnic areas with stupendous views of the Golden Gate Bridge.

The Spanish originally built the Presidio to discourage the Russians; as usual, this was a sad tale for the Ohlone, who had lived here for about 5,000 years. In 1822, the site fell under Mexican rule until the U.S. Army took control in 1846. During the next 148 years, the Army transformed the mostly empty windswept dunes and scrub into a verdant jewel-in-the-crown of military posts. The U.S. Army Corps of Engineers planted thousands of cypress and eucalyptus trees. The result is a splendid urban forest enclosing sweeping lawns where military history topples over itself.

Start at the **Presidio Visitor Center** (map p. 192 D3), in the former barracks, facing onto the original Spanish parade ground. This Spanish mission-style building was erected around the original Spanish adobe fort, which can be seen. Nearby, the U.S. Army's oldest general hospital today houses the **Letterman Digital Arts Center,** a division of LucasFilms. Visit the *Star Wars* exhibit in Building B, which is open to the public.

On the bay shorefront, windsurfers launch from beach-lined **Crissy Field** (map p. 192 D4, Mason St.). Here, the **Farallones**

Marine Sanctuary Visitor Center (map p. 192 D4, tel 415-561-6625, www.farallones.org, closed Mon.–Tues.) features hands-on exhibits about local marine life. On the park's south side, the public **Presidio Golf Course** (map p. 192 D3, 300 Finley Rd., tel 415-561-4661, www.presidiogolf.com) enfolds **Mountain Lake,** popular with waterfowl and picnickers.

INSIDER TIP:

Head to Baker Beach in the morning, when crowds are light and fog hovers around the Golden Gate Bridge.

—ERIN STONE
National Geographic contributor

Lincoln Boulevard (map p. 192 C3) leads past a series of batteries pointing their cannons toward the Pacific and across the Golden Gate. **Baker Beach** (map p. 192 C3) is a popular spot for strolling the sands.

Before leaving, pay your respects at the **World War II Memorial** (map p. 192 C3, Lincoln Blvd. & Kobbe Ave.) and **San Francisco National Cemetery** (map p. 192 D3, Lincoln Blvd. & Crissy Field Ave.), burial place of more than 26,000 American soldiers killed in battle.

Legion of Honor

The westernmost part of San Francisco, known as **Lands End,** lies within the Golden Gate National Recreation Area. Enshrined in **Lincoln Park** (map

Rodin's "The Thinker" graces the entrance of the California Palace of the Legion of Honor.

p. 192 B2–B3), this craggy region boasts one of the city's premier art galleries in the neoclassical Legion of Honor (formerly the California Palace of the Legion of Honor)—the 1924 gift of social doyenne Alma Spreckels.

The stupendous museum exhibits an extensive collection of old masters, including Rembrandt, Rubens, and Watteau; Impressionist paintings by Monet and Cézanne; works by Picasso and Matisse; and a vast collection of works by Auguste Rodin, not least an original cast for "The Thinker."

One particularly spectacular piece is the circa 1500 "Last Judgment Triptych," by an unknown artist. The exquisite collection of antiquities includes Egyptian, Grecian, and Roman pottery, sculpture, and metalwork. Other highlights include an entire 15th-century Spanish ceiling, plus a superb grouping of furniture and decorative items with a vast hoard of English and French 18th-century porcelain. The more eclectic offerings include the Reva and David Logan Collection of Illustrated Books.

The museum also hosts temporary exhibitions, as well as a Sunday brunch with live music in the Legion Café.

Cliff House

To the southwest, at **Point Lobos,** the Cliff House (map p. 192 A2) overlooks the ocean, and you can watch the sea lions and pelicans offshore on **Seal Rocks** (map p. 192 A2). Built in 1863, it served as a hotel, then a restaurant, before closing in 2020. Eastward, the coastal trail takes you to **China Beach** (map p. 192 C3), ideal for picnicking. ■

GOLDEN GATE PARK

Established in 1870 on a thousand acres (404 ha) of sand and windswept dunes, Golden Gate Park remains the single best daytime destination in San Francisco. Among its attractions are several world-class art and science museums, gardens representing flora and fauna from near and far, and a wide variety of picnic and hiking areas.

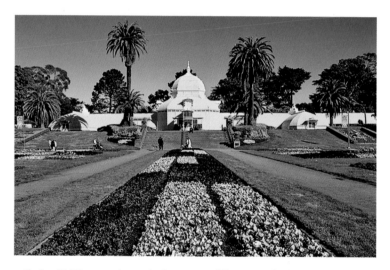

The beautiful blooms on show at the Conservatory of Flowers are a floral inspiration.

Golden Gate Park

▲ 192 B2–D2

Visitor Information

✉ Visitor Center (inside Beach Chalet), 1000 Great Hwy.; park HQ, 501 Stanyan St.

☎ 415-750-5105 visitor center; 415-831-2700 park HQ

www.sfrecpark.org

The park's varied landscapes—hillocks, glens, lakes, knolls, and meadows—are largely the work of a Scotsman, John McLaren, who nurtured it from 1887 to 1943. McLaren succeeded William Hammond Hall, the park's first superintendent, after many in the San Francisco establishment ridiculed the notion of creating a park from wasteland.

Experimenting with various native grasses and trees, McLaren eventually prevailed over the park's apparently self-destructive tendencies. (As well as bureaucratic ones: He once faced down his own Public Works board by directing his staff to remove a parking lot and replant it with oaks.) So popular was "Uncle John" that an attempt to force him into retirement resulted in a minor uprising, causing the city to adopt a special exemption for him.

How to Visit

Walking (or cycling) is the best way of getting around inside the park. Wear comfortable shoes—the park is three miles (5 km) long! Many roads within the park are closed on weekends to enhance the safety of pedestrians and cyclists. Trams serve seniors and disabled travelers.

The Museums

Often bypassed in the rush to take in the entire park in one day, the museums located here are superb, whether it is art that draws you or the excitement of science.

De Young Museum: The de Young is one of those quiet old California institutions that only slowly yields its treasures—at least at first. In fact, it holds one of the most comprehensive collections of art on the West Coast. Anyone who spends more than an hour here will end up spending a day. Don't miss it.

Erected in 1895, the original Egyptian Revival–style buildings of San Francisco's oldest public museum were irreparably damaged by the 1989 earthquake. The museum is now in a brand-new state-of-the-art structure.

Among the treasures of the museum's vast **American collection,** look for "Dinner With Threshers" (1934) by Grant Wood, the pop art classic "Three Machines" (1963) by Wayne Theibaud, and "Rainy Season in the Tropics" (1866) by landscape maestro Frederic Edwin Church.

The collection presents a veritable pantheon of other 19th- and early 20th-century Americans, including Bill Copley, Paul Revere (silverware), Frederic Remington, Winslow Homer, John Singer Sargent, and Mary Cassatt. Many works expand on Western themes, such as Charles Nahl's troubling 1867 "Sacramento Indian with Dogs" and Thomas Cole's 1847

"Prometheus, Bound." Along these lines, it is well worth seeking out George Caleb Bingham's "Boatmen on the Missouri" (1846). "Susanna and the Elders" (1938) by Thomas Hart Benton is a Depression-era retelling of the classic Biblical tale about moral depravity and a prime example of the artist's proclivity for testing America's moral hang-ups.

Many of these works were donated by California's most aggressive late 19th-century capitalists and were supplemented in 1979 by acquisition of the Rockefeller Collection of American Art.

The permanent collection also includes sculpture by Joan Miró, Louise Nevelson, Isamu Noguchi, and Claes Oldenburg in the **Barbro Osher Sculpture Garden.**

De Young Museum

🅼 192 D2

✉ 50 Hagiwara Tea Garden Dr.

☎ 415-750-3600

🕐 Closed Mon.

💲 $$$

http://deyoung .famsf.org

Recreation in Golden Gate Park

The park offers all kinds of outdoor pursuits, from soccer and jogging to fishing and archery. Some popular activities are:

Biking: Bikes can be rented in the park *(tel 415-671-8989, www.parkwide.com).*

Boating: Pedalboats and rowboats are available for rent on Stow Lake *(tel 415-702-1390. www.stowlakeboathouse.com).*

Golf: The park has an eccentric nine-hole course *(47th Ave., tel 415-751-8987, www. goldengateparkgolf.com).*

Lawn Bowling: Free lessons are given on Wednesdays and Saturdays *(near Sharon Meadow and the Carousel, tel 415-487-8787).*

Tennis: There are 17 courts *(John F. Kennedy Dr., opposite Conservatory, tel 415-831-5500, www.spotery.com/site/sfrp).*

For a comprehensive listing of park facilities, consult the park website or the maps throughout the park.

California Academy of Sciences

🅰 192 D1

✉ 55 Music Concourse Dr.

☎ 415-379-8000

💲 $$$$$

www.calacademy.org

Another mission of the de Young is expressed in the **Arts of Africa, Oceania, and the Americas** collection. Far from the catchall that its title might imply, this collection maintains a fine emphasis on the most primary of pieces, from the Central Asian door rugs in the Wiedersperg Collection to the terra-cotta vessels from seventh-century Teotihuacan in Mexico. The textile collection alone includes more than 13,000 items, from European tapestries and oriental silks to fashionable 18th-century dress and fine African costumes.

The **photography collection** includes early daguerreotype portraits, pre-1906-earthquake snaps of San Francisco, and the groundbreaking locomotion photography of Eadweard Muybridge.

California Academy of Sciences: Across the concourse from the de Young is the California Academy of Sciences,

established in 1853. After a complete redesign by Pritzker Prize–winning architect Renzo Piano, the academy reopened in 2008 in a new facility whose shape suggests hills, with a living roof where native plants thrive.

Highlights of the spectacular lower-level **Steinhart Aquarium** include a 212,000-gallon (802,507 L) **Philippines coral reef habitat**—the world's deepest such interior ecosystem; a **replication of a U.S. swamp,** complete with alligators; and the multimedia **Water Planet,** which brings to life an array of ocean and freshwater environments. Plus, jellyfish, giant octopuses, and sharks swim inside the 100,000-gallon (378,541 L) **Northern California Coast** exhibit.

Visitors walk through a glass tube inside the **Amazon Flooded Forest**—a highlight of the **Rainforest** section, teeming

▪ The 2.5-acre (1 ha) Living Roof at the California Academy of Sciences bursts with 1.7 million native plants.

EXPERIENCE: National AIDS Memorial Grove

Take a quiet walk in this grove, which defines itself as "a dedicated space in the national landscape where millions of Americans touched directly or indirectly by AIDS can gather to heal, hope, and remember." Or you can pitch in as a volunteer to maintain the grove by weeding, mulching, and planting.

Begun in 1991, the project rehabilitated the overgrown de Laveaga Dell at the east end of Golden Gate Park. It brought together professional landscape architects and designers with volunteer workers, who have donated more than 10,000 hours in clearing overgrowth and planting new trees and shrubs, as well as creating six gathering spots.

Free 20-minute tours of the grove are offered from March through October on the third Saturday of the month. On the same days, visitors can take part in volunteer workdays (tel 415-765-0497, www.aidsmemorial.org).

Donors of $1,000 or more can engrave a name in the **Circle of Friends** to honor someone they love and/or miss.

INSIDER TIP:

The botanical garden in Golden Gate Park is a treat anytime, but visit at twilight and walk quietly, and you may see families of quail out for a stroll.

—FORREST MCGILL
Chief curator, Asian Art Museum

---

with slithery reptiles, colorful insects, and hundreds of free-flying birds. The **Tusher African Hall,** with zoological dioramas, highlights the **Natural History Museum,** with its giant skeletons of a *T. rex* and an 87-foot-long (26.5 m) blue whale.

The three-story state-of-the-art **Morrison Planetarium** hosts mind-bending presentations.

The Gardens

One of McLaren's legacies is the patchwork of special garden-meadows throughout the park.

Although not as intensively curated as other attractions, they are pleasant places for picnics and walks. They include the **National AIDS Memorial Grove** (see sidebar above), **Shakespeare Garden, Rose Garden,** and McLaren's own **Rhododendron Dell.** The park service visitor center provides a map of the gardens.

San Francisco Botanical Garden at Strybing Arboretum:

Of the three formal botanical sites, the San Francisco Botanical Garden at Strybing Arboretum is the most spectacular. The arboretum was founded in 1937 with a gift from Helen Strybing, widow of a wealthy San Francisco merchant. Strybing was particularly interested in indigenous botany and plants with medicinal purposes.

Many of the early collections focused on plants from Mediterranean climates: coastal California, South Africa, western Australia, the central coast of Chile, and the

San Francisco Botanical Garden at Strybing Arboretum

- 🅰 192 D1
- ✉ 9th Ave. & Lincoln Way
- ☎ 415-661-1316
- 🕐 Call for tours
- 💲 $$$
- 🚌 Bus: 5, 21 26, 42, 47

www.sfbotanical garden.org

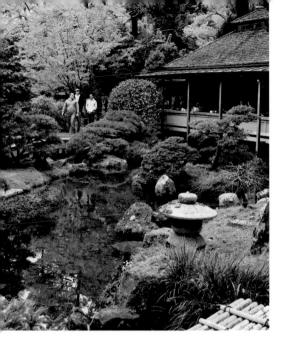

■ Koi ponds add to the serenity of the Japanese Tea Garden.

Japanese Tea Garden
🅰 192 D1
✉ 75 Hagiwara Tea Garden Dr.
☎ 415-752-1171 (tour information)
💲 $$

www.japanesetea gardensf.com

Conservatory of Flowers
🅰 192 D2
✉ 100 John F. Kennedy Dr.
☎ 415-831-2090
🕐 Closed Mon.
💲 $
🚌 Bus: 5, 7, 21, 33, 44, 71; Streetcar: N

www.conservatory offlowers.org

Mediterranean itself.

One of the most striking of these collections is the **Cape Province Garden,** which displays a number of amazingly well adapted plants from this unique botanical region on the southern tip of Africa. The various heaths, for example, can bloom year-round because their small needle-like leaves diffuse heat so well. The Cape Province Garden also showcases several varieties of aloe, kniphofia, and ice plant (the last are showier than their freeway-strip cousins might suggest).

One of the Strybing's three cloud-forest replications is the **MesoAmerican Cloud Forest,** which is a testing ground for tropical plants, many of which are endangered in their native habitats. The garden is using the Bay Area's natural fogginess to approximate conditions in tropical cloud forests such as those in Chiapas, Mexico. Check out the giant lobelias, salvias, and daisies as large as small trees.

Japanese Tea Garden: Built for the 1894 Midwinter Exposition, the Japanese Tea Garden, at the north entrance to the Strybing, is the oldest Japanese-style garden in the United States. Take in the perfectly manicured grounds, and then relax in the open-air pavilion with tea and cookies. Do not miss Nagao Sakurai's 1953 **Zen Garden,** with its astonishing bonsai cypress. In spring, cherry and azalea blossoms explode in a riot of color.

Conservatory of Flowers: The Conservatory of Flowers, which attracts more visitors than any other place in Golden Gate Park, is a huge Victorian greenhouse filled with a riotous profusion of tropical plants. The Western Hemisphere's oldest existing conservatory, it was erected from a "kit" acquired from the estate of business magnate James Lick, who had planned to assemble it on his property in the Santa Clara Valley. Erected in 1879, the greenhouse was badly damaged in the 1990s in a windstorm. After eight years and $25 million worth of restoration, it reopened in 2003. Today, plants from more than four dozen countries—some 1,500 species—are displayed under one vast roof of glass.

Enter the **Lowland Tropics** section and you step into a realm of palm canopies and immense leaves (look for the 100-year-old imperial philodendron). There are "economic plants"—coffee, chocolate, vanilla—that have had worldwide commercial importance for centuries, as well as cycads, a species that dates back before the age of dinosaurs.

Orchids star in the **Highland Tropics** gallery, growing among ferns and creepers. The conservatory boasts the world's best public collection of Dracula orchids.

The **Aquatic Plants** gallery showcases huge lilies (one variety has leaves of up to six feet/two meters in diameter) and flowers that float. Another wing holds seasonal displays and special exhibits.

Historic Buildings

Fittingly, park headquarters is in the **McLaren Lodge.** Uncle John lived in this Moorish-cum-Gothic confection at the eastern end of the park until his death in 1943.

Opposite the Japanese Tea Garden is the ornate Spreckels Temple of Music, now known as the **Bandshell** *(map p. 192 D1).* Built in 1899, it is home to the oldest continuously operating municipal band in the U.S.

Near Stow Lake is the **Pioneer Log Cabin,** a restored 1911 structure made from Humboldt redwoods. For an example of 1930s Works Progress Administration architecture, see the **Angler's Lodge,** opposite the historic **Buffalo Paddock** *(map p. 192 B1),* with its herd of shaggy beasts.

If you are heading east, take a walk through the neighborhood of **Haight-Ashbury** (see sidebar below). If you are going west, see the **Beach Chalet.** The brewery-restaurant, with its Depression-era frescoes, is a great place to eat. ■

McLaren Lodge
- 192 D2
- 501 Stanyan St.
- 415-831-2700
- Closed Sat.–Sun.

Beach Chalet
- 192 A1
- 1000 Great Hwy.
- 415-386-8439

www.beachchalet .com

San Francisco's Sixties Heritage

Just to the east of Golden Gate Park lies the venerable old neighborhood of **Haight-Ashbury** *(map p. 193 E1),* which began life as a Victorian escape from the city center. Growth boomed after the 1906 fire, which left the area untouched. In the 1930s it declined, the Victorian houses split into flats. Drawn by low rents, Beats and African Americans arrived in the 1950s, followed by hippies and the flower-power generation.

In the 1960s, Haight-Ashbury had its 15 minutes of fame, becoming the locus of just about everything that characterized the decade, from peace signs and tie-dyed clothing to black-light posters and head shops. By night, the area's musical denizens took the stage at Fillmore West, the legendary concert hall that lives on as the modern **Fillmore** *(1805 Geary Blvd., tel 415-346-6000, www.thefillmore.com).*

By the 1970s, however, Haight-Ashbury was a trash-littered ghetto with boarded-up shops. Remarkably, it made a comeback. Young professionals and gays moved into restored Victorian houses, and interesting shops opened (look for vintage clothes and records).

Stroll past the Victorians on Masonic Avenue or by the Queen Anne **Richard Spreckels Mansion** *(map p. 193 E1, 737 Buena Vista Ave. W., not open to the public).* Continue up Buena Vista (daytime only) to **Buena Vista Park** *(map p. 193 E1)* and take in the views. South Haight has a fine community of retailers and specialty shops.

VICTORIANS ON THE BAY

Although many American cities flirted with Victorianism, few reveled in it in quite the same way as 19th-century San Francisco. Victorian architecture was, after all, a perfect synthesis of everything the booming city's new rich craved: status (the style had rich European antecedents), conformity, domesticity, and order (each room had a special purpose, unlike the boardinghouses that were the principal domiciles of the gold rush).

Quintessential Victorian row houses—the famed "Painted Ladies"—line Alamo Square.

And yet no city confounded, or continues to confound, Victorian stereotypes as much. Consider, for example, the story of the building now known as the **Queen Anne Hotel** at 1590 Sutter Street. With its domed turret, peaked gables, and gingerbread details, it certainly embodies Victorianism externally. But what happened inside its doors? It was built in 1889 for Sen. James G. Fair, one of the Comstock Lode silver kings and the force behind the Nob Hill landmark now known

as the Fairmont Hotel (see pp. 202–203). At the time, the senator had already been sued by his first wife on grounds of "habitual adultery," according to an account by San Francisco historian Bob Bills.

This was apparently not a happy house. Although the senator kept custody of his two sons, both of them went on to blaze decidedly non-Victorian trails in the annals of family dysfunction. His son James, following a long battle with alcoholism, killed himself in 1892 at the young age of 27. The very next year, the other son, Charles, publicly married one of the era's most prominent prostitutes. In 1890, the building was sold to the Miss Mary Lakes School for Girls, which trained young women in more proper pursuits. It later went through iterations as a men's club and as an Episcopal girls' lodge before being boarded up in the late 1950s.

The most pronounced element of the Victorian style was **ornamentation**—ways to call attention to one's own individual taste while remaining safely inside the framework of Victorian architecture. To do this, the typical San Franciscan could employ several forms of artifice, some interesting, others frilly, and some outlandishly garish. There were the wall textures known as fishscaling and gingerbread, or the window decoration known as puddling, in which one layer of curtain was piled upon another to lend a regal effect. An Italian style could be added to a house by adding a simple eyebrow dormer.

Center of 1960s counterculture, Haight-Ashbury managed to retain its Victorian grandeur.

INSIDER TIP:

For an inside look at a true-blue San Francisco Victorian, don't miss the Hass-Lilienthal House (www.sfheritage.org/haas -lilienthal-house), the only private home open to the public.

—BARBARA A. NOE
National Geographic Travel Books senior editor

Color, too, functioned as a social barometer. Although the average late 19th-century home might not have been as bright as some of today's candy-colored versions, color was often used to set off various exterior elements.

From the 1930s through the postwar years, as these neighborhoods declined, many of the Victorians became run-down housing stock, rented out on a month-to-month basis and seldom appreciated by their owners. The dominant color was battleship gray. Tour guide Jay Gifford *(tel 415-252-9485, www.victorianhomewalk.com)* credits the hippie movement with saving the Victorian row houses. "Painting those drab buildings with bright colors saved them because it renewed interest in all those lost and faded details that no one had noticed for so long."

But what also transformed "those drab buildings" was the combination of two social trends: the remaking of downtown San Francisco as a financial center, and the growing population of gay professionals who worked there and needed housing. Author Richard Rodriguez has noted the irony that "it was thus a coincidence of the market that gay men found themselves living within the architectural metaphor for family."

The late 1990s wrought new changes. Outrageous colors went out of fashion, but an indicator of the boomtime stock market and new Millennium's tech millionaire investors was the use of gold leafing as ornamentation.

CASTRO DISTRICT

Although well past its prime as "gay capital of the world," the Castro, with its many cafés, clubs, and bars, still offers fast-paced entertainment and busy street life.

The pink neon of the Castro Theatre *(reflected in car window)* acts as a beacon in San Francisco's gay center.

Castro District
🗺 193 E1–F1

It was here during the 1970s that gay men first began the often difficult process of leading openly gay lives. Their patron saint was Harvey Milk (see sidebar), a flamboyant and politically astute man who became the city's first openly gay supervisor before being shot, along with San Francisco mayor George Moscone, in 1978.

Two longtime Castro hangouts are the gay **Midnight Sun** *(4067 18th St., betw. Castro & Hartford Sts., tel 415-861-4186, www.midnightsunsf. com)* and revamped **Café du Nord** *(2174 Market St., tel 415-471-2969, www.swedishamericanhall. com)*. For film buffs, the ornate **Castro Theatre** *(429 Castro St., tel 415-621-6120, www.castrotheatre. com)*, a 1922 film palace, features a Wurlitzer organ that rises from the floor and plays before the featured film. ∎

Leader of Gay Community

Elected to the San Francisco County Board of Supervisors in 1977, **Harvey Milk** was the first openly gay person to hold elected office in the U.S. Born on Long Island, Milk moved to San Francisco in 1972 and opened a camera shop in the Castro District, quickly becoming an activist for both his neighborhood and the gay movement. "If a gay man can win," declared Milk on the night of his election victory, "it proves there is hope for all minorities." Little more than a year later, Milk and Mayor George Moscone were assassinated by fellow supervisor Dan White inside City Hall.

MISSION DISTRICT

San Francisco's Mission District, which is situated east of the Castro (see p. 224), has traditionally been the city's most Latino district. Once a rough neighborhood, it was revitalized in recent decades and continues to change. The Hispanic murals, taquerías, and produce marts that brought life to the streets remain, but Indian, Chinese, and Vietnamese eateries have exploded. San Francisco's tech boom is reshaping "The Mission" again, displacing long-term residents and further diluting its once-edgy Latino character.

The main attraction of this district is in fact a mission nicknamed **Mission Dolores,** after a now dried-up creek called Arroyo de Nuestra Señora de los Dolores—*dolores* meaning "sorrow." Its real name is San Francisco de Asís,

vanquisher. The **reredos,** or decorative altar, was made in San Blas, Mexico, in 1796.

The **cemetery** is also worth visiting. In its center is a statue of Junípero Serra by California artist Arthur Putnam. The surrounding **garden** contains many native plants, from huge Mexican sages to Matilija pop-

Mission District
🅰 193 F1

Mission Dolores
🅰 193 F1
✉ 3321 16th St.
☎ 415-621-8203
🚇 Muni: J car, Van Ness Station

www.missiondolores.org

INSIDER TIP:

At Mission Dolores cemetery, fans of Alfred Hitchcock's film *Vertigo* can look for the grave of the fictional Carlotta Valdes.

—KENNY LING
National Geographic contributor

---

for its founder's patron saint. Founded five days before the signing of the Declaration of Independence, Mission Dolores is rather plain and spare by the standards of its own era. It is, however, remarkable for its seamless blending of Old World and New World aesthetics, from its colorful **roof beams** (originally painted by Ohlone Indians) to the **statue of the Archangel Michael,** dressed as an Indian

■ More than 200 murals adorn walls and garage doors in the Mission.

pies. Here lie the remains of some of early San Francisco's most important figures, including Don Luis Antonio Arguello, the first governor of Alta California under Mexican rule. ■

CIVIC CENTER

The hub of San Francisco's government, the Civic Center is an impressive urban landscape dominated by the classical columns and gleaming dome of the 1915 City Hall. But this is also a neighborhood of serious culture, boasting a symphony hall, the War Memorial Opera House, the Asian Art Museum, with its many treasures, and most recently the SF JAZZ center.

The Asian Art Museum displays more than 2,000 objects, including this Chinese seated Buddha.

Civic Center

🏛 193 F2

www.sfciviccenter.org

City Hall

✉ Polk St. betw. Grove & McAllister Sts. For tours, go to Van Ness Ave. entrance

☎ 415-554-6139

🕐 Tours Mon.–Fri. 10 a.m., 12 p.m., & 2 p.m.

🚌 Bus: 5, 19, 21, 47, 49; BART: Civic Center

www.sfgov.org/cityhall

After the 1906 earthquake and the devastating fire that followed it, San Franciscans vigorously debated how they wanted their rebuilt city to look. Their loftiest hopes for a "City Beautiful," contained in the Burnham Plan, were largely abandoned for more practical ideas, with the lone exception of the splendid Civic Center.

Located between Market, McAllister, and Gough, the Civic Center is still one of the nation's most complete collections of beaux arts buildings set in a formal plan. Broad red plazas and buildings with gold domes, Doric columns, and masses of California granite, convey the city's regal sense of itself after the earthquake. After some years of decline, the Civic Center has been revitalized, centering on **City Hall,** whose $300 million refurbishing in 1999 brought back to life an urban temple of granite, marble, and gilded ironwork.

The 1995 **San Francisco Public Library** (map p. 193 F2, 100 Larkin St., tel 415-557-4400, www.sfpl.org, closed Fri. & a.m. Sun.) attracts people of all ages conducting research at computers and in specialized study centers whose scope ranges from Native American and African-American materials to the nation's first library center for gay and lesbian studies.

The Civic Center, the heart of the city's arts district, is replete with world-class and architecturally striking performance venues. Opposite City Hall, the Romanesque twin-building **War Memorial and Performing Arts Center**, completed in 1923, hosted the organizing assembly of the United Nations in April 1945 and includes the **War Memorial Opera House** (301 Van Ness Ave., tel 415-864-3330, www.sfopera.com) and **Herbst Theater** (401 Van Ness Ave.). To its south is the 2,743-seat **Louise M. Davies Symphony Hall** (201 Van Ness Ave., tel 415-864-6000, www.sfsymphony.org), completed in 1980. One block to the southwest, the sleek contemporary **SF JAZZ Center** (201 Franklin St., tel 866-920-5299, www.sfjazz.org) opened in 2013 and hosts jazz concerts year-round.

Asian Art Museum

Asian culture and art come to life in a stunning setting: the Italian Renaissance–style old public library given a new interior by contemporary architect Gae Aulenti, known for the Musée d'Orsay in Paris. The museum is the nation's largest devoted entirely to Asian art.

Religious statuary illuminates India's diverse religions. From Thailand and Southeast Asian islands come ornate daggers (krises), while Cambodian sculptures show the refined temple decorations created by the Khmer people of the

Angkor kingdom. Tibetan arts are represented by monastery scrolls, 15th-century ritual objects of gilded metal, and lacquered wood figures. Works from Nepal include mystical diagrams, or mandalas, that aid meditation.

Neolithic oracle bones show China's first written language. Other objects include the first Chinese Buddha (A.D.

Embracing the Seedy Side

Wedged between the Civic Center and Union Square is the once seedy **Tenderloin** neighborhood (map p. 193 F2). As the city's favorite "underbelly," the Tenderloin hosted gambling dens, burlesque shows, speakeasies, and brothels as far back as the 1890s. The area was also home to many down-and-out artists, including budding jazz greats and a young Dashiell Hammett, who set The Maltese Falcon (1930) in the district. Although the dramatic arts continue to thrive in dozens of local theaters in recent decades, it has once again become the city's seediest district, with high levels of prostitution, street crime, and homelessness.

338), ceramics, fan paintings, Ming calligraphy, and a large collection of jade objects. The finest collection of Korean objects outside Korea includes Bronze Age slate daggers, earthenware vessels, gilded Buddha figures, and paintings on silk. A broad survey of Japanese art takes in painted screens, dry lacquer figures, glazed stoneware and porcelain, bronze bells, carved netsuke, and hanging scrolls. ∎

War Memorial and Performing Arts Center
- ⊠ 401 Van Ness Ave.
- ☎ 415-621-6600
- **www.sfwarmemorial. org**

Asian Art Museum
- 🅰 193 F2
- ⊠ 200 Larkin St.
- ☎ 415-581-3500
- 🕐 Closed Tue.– Wed.
- 💲 $$$ (free 1st Sun. of month)
- 🚌 Bus: 5, 19, 21, 26, 47; BART: Civic Center

www.asianart.org

SOMA & YERBA BUENA

SoMa is the universally recognized abbreviation for the area of San Francisco that lies south of Market Street. Yerba Buena, named for the landing cove on its seaward side, was the city's business epicenter well into the 20th century. In recent decades, both areas have been reborn. With museums, playhouses, galleries, and the San Francisco Giants' AT&T Stadium, SoMa and Yerba Buena easily compete with Golden Gate Park and the waterfront as lively destinations.

The San Francisco Museum of Modern Art is housed in an outstanding contemporary building.

**SoMa &
Yerba Buena**

🅰 193 G2 & 195

Visitor Information

**www.visityerba
buena.com**

**San Francisco
Museum of
Modern Art**

🅰 193 G2 & 195
✉ 151 3rd St.
☎ 415-357-4000
🕐 Closed Tue.-
Wed., and a.m.
Thur.
💲 $$$ (free 1st
Tues. of month)
🚍 Bus: 5, 9, 12, 14,
15, 30, 38, 45

www.sfmoma.org

Once an industrial district, SoMa's renaissance as a hip center of culture owes much to warehouse space rehabbed as live-work loft condos and as incubators for the dot-com revolution. A more recent building boom has been led, in part, by such tech heavyweights as **Twitter** (1355 Market St.), headquartered here in a restored 1920s art deco building.

San Francisco Museum of Modern Art

The main draw in the area is the San Francisco Museum of Modern Art (SFMOMA), partly housed in a red-orange structure designed by Swiss architect Mario Botta and opened in 1995. It was vastly expanded in 2016 with an addition featuring seven levels of new galleries to become one of the largest museums in the U.S. With its wide, open galleries and airy interior, it is the perfect place to view this outstanding collection of modern and contemporary art.

Given its location in the city that helped invent the 1960s counterculture, it comes as no surprise that SFMOMA boasts works by iconic pop art figures like Andy Warhol, plus compelling abstract works by Jackson Pollack. Pablo Picasso is amply represented by "Women of Algiers" (1955), one of SFMOMA's 14 works by the Spanish master. Cranking back the clock to cubism, the collection includes a quintessential George Braque entitled "Violin and Candlestick" (1910). Another SFMOMA favorite is Henri Matisse, whose range of paintings here show his artistic progression from "Woman With a hat" (1905) to "The Conversation" (1938).

The museum has a fine representation of Mexican modernists. A triumph is Diego Rivera's 1935 "The Flower Carrier," which fuses the abstract concern for primal shape with the realist's attraction to biomorphism (how the body works).

The collection spans Hockneys and Lichtensteins to Francis Bacon

---

INSIDER TIP:

A favorite brewery is 21st Amendment (563 2nd St.). Try the Hell or High Watermelon Wheat beer.

—RYAN GADDUANG
Supervisor, Sir Francis Drake Hotel

---

and Robert Rauschenberg. The biggest coup came in 2009, when Gap founders Doris and Donald Fisher inked an agreement with the museum to show pieces from their private collection—more than 1,100 works by 185 artists.

With exhibits now spread over seven stories, SFMOMA can be a maze for first-time visitors. After admiring Richard Serra's behemoth sculpture "Sequence" (2006) in the **entrance hall,** look for the following highlight works, beginning with pieces by Robert Rauschenberg and Mark Rothko, plus Matisse's "Femme au Chapeau" (1905) and Frida Kahlo's "Frida and Diego

Rivera" (1931) on the **Second Floor.** Photography informs the **Third Floor,** with its outside vertical terrace garden.

Above, look for Ellsworth Kelly's "Cité" (1951) and Canadian abstract expressionist Agnes Martin's sparse untitled artworks. The **Fifth Floor** offers plenty of pop art and minimalist works, such as Andy Warhol's "Triple Elvis" (1953), plus photorealist pieces by Chuck Close. Many works of the Fisher Collection are here and also on the **Sixth Floor,** with galleries dedicated to postwar German art, while the **Seventh Floor** includes contemporary pieces by Cindy Sherman plus Jeff Koons' explosively chromatic "Large Vase of Flowers" (1991).

Other Attractions

Across the street is **Yerba Buena Gardens.** Ten acres of child-size gardens, labyrinths, play spaces, and a glass-enclosed antique carousel are atop the **Moscone Center,** offering some of the liveliest daytime entertainments in town. Also on the Rooftop is the interactive **Zeum (Children's Creativity Museum),** which explores the visual and performing arts. The Rooftop also runs the **Yerba Buena Ice Skating & Bowling Center.**

Nearby is the **Yerba Buena Center for the Arts,** which features changing exhibitions of local art and includes the **YBCA Theater,** whose works reflect the cultural diversity of San Francisco. Relax in the adjoining **Esplanade Gardens** *(map p. 195),* and see the **Martin Luther King Memorial** while you are here.

Yerba Buena Gardens

🅰 193 G2 & 195

✉ Betw. 3rd., 4th, Mission, & Howard Sts.

☎ 415-351-3684

www.yerbabuena gardens.com

Zeum (Children's Creativity Museum)

✉ 221 4th St.

☎ 415-820-3320

💲 $

www.creativity.org

Yerba Buena Ice Skating & Bowling Center

✉ 750 Folsom St.

☎ 415-820-3532

💲 $

www.skatebowl.com

Yerba Buena Center for the Arts

🅰 195

✉ 701 Mission St.

☎ 415-978-2787

💲 $$ for galleries (free 1st Tues. of the month)

🚌 Bus: 9, 12, 14, 15, 30, 45, 76

www.ybca.org

EXPERIENCE:
Baseball by the Bay

The Giants of Major League Baseball moved from New York to San Francisco in 1958. But the biggest move the franchise has made in recent years was the long-awaited migration in 2000 from windy Candlestick Park to a new stadium, **Oracle Park** *(map p. 193 H2, www.mlb.com/giants).* Set in the revitalized South Beach neighborhood, the 41,000-seat stadium—named America's Sports Facility of the Year in 2008—is considered one of the nation's best places to watch baseball. Tickets are available online for a season that runs April to October. For a unique San Francisco experience, join a guided tour with **City Kayak** *(South Beach Harbor, tel 888-966-0953, www.citykayak. com, $$$$$)* to McCovey Cove, where floating fans await home-run balls smacked over the right field wall.

Cartoon Art Museum

- 193 G3 & 195
- ✉ 781 Beach St.
- ☎ 415-227-8666
- 🕐 Closed Mon.
- 💲 $$

www.cartoonart.org

California Historical Society

- Map p. 195
- ✉ 678 Mission St.
- ☎ 415-357-1848
- 🕐 Closed a.m. and Sun.–Tues.
- 💲 $$

www.california historicalsociety.org

The newest addition to SoMa's burgeoning culture is **Salesforth Park**—an elevated landscaped park extending four blocks atop the new state-of-the-art, four-level **Transit Center** *(www.salesforcetransitcenter. com).*

To the north of Yerba Buena Gardens, the Gothic Revival, **St. Patrick Church** *(map pp. 193 G2 & 195, 756 Mission St., tel 415-421-3730, www.stpatricksf.org)* dates from 1851. Pedestrian-only **Mint Plaza** *(map pp. 193 G2 & 195)* hums with cafés, public art, cultural programs, street fairs, and a farmers market.

The **Cartoon Art Museum** showcases selections from its collection of 6,000 pieces of original art—ranging from *Li'l Abner* and *Peanuts* drawings to cels from Walt Disney cartoon features. Highlights include animation drawing from

Gertie the Dinosaur (1914) by the "father of the animated cartoon," Winsor McCay; underground comix (R. Crumb, *Zippy the Pinhead*); and an early character sheet from Disney's *Snow White and the Seven Dwarfs* (1937) showing some dwarfs who didn't make it to the film, among them Jumpy and Baldy.

The **Contemporary Jewish Museum** *(736 Mission St., tel 415-655-7800, www.thecjm.org, closed Wed., $)* stands on the site of the former power station. The **California Historical Society** puts on some of the best historical shows anywhere. It has 500 works by such artists as Albert Bierstadt and Thomas Hill, not to mention photos by Carleton Watkins, Eadweard Muybridge, and Arnold Genthe.

The **Museum of the African Diaspora** *(map p. 195, 685 Mission St., tel 415-358-7200, www.moadsf .org, closed Mon.–Tues. & a.m. Sun., $$)* looks at the journeys and achievements of Africa-descended people around the world. Permanent exhibitions include the highly moving "Slavery Passages."

While you are in the SoMa area, stroll up Market Street to the **Rincon Center** *(map p. 193 H3, 121 Spear St.).* This complex of stores and offices incorporates the 1930s **Rincon Annex Post Office.** The draw here is the post office's murals, painted in 1941–1948 by Russian artist Anton Refregier. The works were so critical of the city establishment that the artist had to make 92 changes to placate various interest groups. The murals also withstood a McCarthy-era attempt to destroy them for being "communistic" in tone. ∎

Offering Muir Woods in Marin, the coast at Point Reyes, Berkeley's funky street scene, a great museum in Oakland, and Silicon Valley

BAY AREA

■ The San Jose Museum of Art, Silicon Valley's leading art institution

BAY AREA

If the charms of San Francisco seem to radiate outward, its surrounding territories (though substantial in size and at some distance from it) at times seem wholly directed toward the city, as if it were the very reason for their being. That is far from true, but each area's principal attributes do figure heavily in the city's character.

From the east comes much of the region's political, artistic, and literary history. Oakland gave the world Jack London (whose Yukon cabin stands on the bayfront mall) as well as many of the great plein air painters (whose works hang in the Oakland Museum of California). The much lampooned neighboring city of Berkeley (columnist Herb Caen dubbed it "Berserkeley") still exports the revolutionary impulse, but today it is more likely to be culinary, as at Alice Waters's Chez Panisse restaurant, than political. Still, the university named for the 18th-century Irish philosopher Bishop Berkeley ("Westward lies the course of empire . . .") remains a great excursion in tolerance, learning, and intellectual inquiry.

NOT TO BE MISSED:

Browsing the eclectic collection at the Oakland Museum **236–237**

Expanding your intellect (and your college sweatshirt collection) in Berkeley **238–239**

Munching California cuisine at the place it was invented **240–241**

The spectacular coastal trails of the Marin Headlands **244–245**

Point Reyes's secluded beaches and rich wetlands **246–247**

The lively farmers market of San Rafael **249**

Egyptian mummies and the Winchester Mystery House in San Jose **250–251**

From the rugged north—the Muir Woods and the Marin Headlands—comes much of the region's avid environmental ethos. There, between the mystical sea fogs and mists, visible from many points in the city, is nature preserved for all . . . and harvested for all. Travelers here find some of the best produce in the country: the famed oysters of Tomales Bay, found in luxury restaurants around the nation; the cheeses of Point Reyes Station; and the produce of the Marin Farmers' Market. Today's visitors to this whole remarkable area also find an outstanding travel infrastructure, and many small inns and bed-and-breakfasts featuring world-class cuisine, historical ambience, and comforts galore.

And the south? The land south of the city—best seen on the way to the Central Coast (see pp. 171–190) or on a day trip—is still very much the great experiment. San Jose and its environs are the land of technology entrepreneurs, their fortunes, like their mini-mansions, quickly made. Here technology is king.

San Jose's Technology Interactive, and the Intel Museum of the giant Intel Corporation, world leader in the production of semiconductors, are two of the immensely popular venues on the theme. By contrast, nearby Palo Alto has one of the world's greatest private colleges, Stanford University. Built with a 19th-century railroad fortune, its little university area is a more genteel version of Berkeley. ■

Area of map detail

WINE COUNTRY
p.253
Santa Rosa

GOLD COUNTRY
p.289

CENTRAL VALLEY
p.317

Novato
Black Point
Vallejo
Grizzly Bay
680

37

San Pablo Bay
Rodeo
Benicia
Benicia Capitol S.H.P.
Suisun Bay
Pittsburg

San Anselmo
San Rafael
San Pablo
Hercules
Martinez
John Muir N.H.P.
Concord
4

Richmond
Pleasant Hill
Clayton

101

2571ft
Larkspur
Stinson Beach
Muir Woods National Monument
El Cerrito
Albany
Berkeley
Lafayette
Walnut Creek
Mount Diablo 3849ft
MT. DIABLO S.P.

580

Tiburon
Angel Island S.P.
University of California
24

Mount Tamalpais S.P.
Sausalito
Treasure Is.
Alcatraz Is.

Oakland
Lake Merritt
Oakland Museum of California
Danville

SAN FRANCISCO
Alameda
580
Castro Valley
Dublin
San Ramon

3▷
Daly City
101
San Leandro
580
Livermore

South San Francisco
Hayward
Pleasanton

1
San Bruno
SAN MATEO BRIDGE
92
Union City
880
680
84

Pacifica

San Mateo
Foster City
Fremont
Arroyo Valle

Moss Beach
280
San Carlos
Newark
84
Mission San José de Guadalupe

Redwood City
Black Mountain ▲ 3951ft

Half Moon Bay
Menlo Park
Palo Alto
NASA Ames Research Center
Calaveras Reservoir
Milpitas

2▷
Woodside
101
Arroyo Hondo

PACIFIC OCEAN
Stanford University
280
Sunnyvale
Santa Clara
SAN JOSE
Lick Observatory
4213ft Mount Hamilton

Sky Londa
Paramount Great America
Tech Interactive

San Gregorio
La Honda
Mission Santa Clara de Asís
Cupertino
Rosicrucian Egyptian Museum & Planetarium

Winchester Mystery House
85

35
Saratoga

B
Los Gatos
17
101
E

CENTRAL COAST
p.171

1▷
C
D

0   20 kilometers
0   10 miles

OAKLAND

Oakland has long labored under Gertrude Stein's memorable, if misquoted, comment—that "there is no *there* there." However, it possesses more than its share of classic American qualities. Oakland's character derives from its history: In 1869, the city fathers accepted an offer from the Central Pacific to become the railroad's western terminus—something its snootier neighbor to the west had fought against with all the money and political might it could muster.

Shedding its long-held reputation as a gritty port city, Oakland now attracts young professionals.

Oakland

🅰 233 C3

Visitor Information

✉ Oakland Convention and Visitors Bureau, 481 Water St., Oakland

☎ 510-839-9000

www.visitoakland .org

In one sense, Oakland's genius was to turn San Francisco's throwaways into one of the West Coast's most dynamic industrial cities, a distinction it held until well after World War II. If a steel mill, a chemical plant, or a new shipyard was too dirty for the swells across the bay, Oakland would have it. Even today, the city's broad harbors and numerous light industrial areas thrum with commerce, though these zones have witnessed an astounding

renaissance as forward-thinking investors and progressive mayors have metamorphosed them into loft-condos, warehouse workspace, and parks.

A good notion of the new Oakland can be found inside the old one, particularly on Friday mornings at the **Old Oakland Farmers Market** *(9th St. betw. Broadway & Clay, tel 510-745-7100, 8 a.m.–2 p.m.).* This is an electric scene, vibrant with entrepreneurship of Latinos, Asians, and African Americans.

A typical lineup might include an Armenian olive-oil maker from Modesto, a seller of sweet-potato pies and other African-American pastries, a Hmong tribeswoman in bright red selling fresh ginger and lemongrass, and a Vietnamese youngster hawking slippery shrimps and gleaming snapper.

A more historical slice of Oakland can be seen at **Jack London Square** (tel 510-645-9292, www. jacklondonsquare.com), located on the waterfront Embarcadero south of Broadway. Few modern literary figures have been quite so intertwined with a city as was London (see p. 44 & sidebar

---

INSIDER TIP:

Gertrude Stein's oft-misquoted "There's no *there* there!" referred to her demolished child-hood home in Oakland. To discover the city's charming *there*, walk the Rockridge district.

–CHRISTOPHER BAKER
National Geographic author

---

p. 237). Born in 1876 and raised in Oakland, he found fame as a working-class adventure novelist (*The Call of the Wild* and *White Fang*). London's **Yukon cabin,** from his days in the Klondike gold rush, has been relocated to the square. You can also visit the **Heinold's First and Last Chance Saloon** (48 Webster St., tel 510-839-6761, www.heinolds

firstandlastchance.com), still a bar, with its unnervingly slanted floor. The square hosts free concerts, and a weekend farmers market. Nearby, the **U.S.S. Potomac,** President Franklin D. Roosevelt's "floating White House," welcomes visitors at **FDR Pier.**

Lake Merritt, in the city's heart, is a relaxed weekend destination. Its pathways frame **Lakeside Park,** on its north shore, where a wildlife sanctuary draws wild geese and other waterfowl. You can rent boats, or Gondola Servizio (tel 510-663-6603, www .gondolaservizio.com) will punt you around the lake. On its north side is the venerable **Grand Lake Theater** (3200 Grand Ave., tel 510-452-3556, www.renaissancerialto. com), with its Wurlitzer organ. The thickly forested Oakland Hills are studded with giant redwoods, including those within the 500-acre (202 ha) **Joaquin Miller Park.** Here you'll find hiking trails, equestrian areas, and an amphitheater hosting summertime musicals.

EXPERIENCE:
Black Panthers

Hotbed of the civil rights and free speech movements during the turbulent 1960s, Oakland keeps its revolutionary heritage alive with "The Spirit of '66" from **Black Panther Tours** (tel 505-884-4860, www .blackpanthertours.com, $). You will see Bobby Seale's home, the first Black Panther party office, and the place where Huey P. Newton was murdered. Tours begin at the West Oakland Branch Library (1801 Adeline St.).

U.S.S. Potomac

- ✉ FDR Pier, 540 Water St.
- ☎ 510-627-1215
- 💲 $$

www.usspotomac .org

Lakeside Park

- ✉ 1520 Lakeside Dr.
- ☎ 510-238-7275

www.oaklandca.gov/ topics/lakeside-park

Joaquin Miller Park

- ✉ 3450 Joaquin Miller Rd.
- ☎ 510-238-7275

www.oaklandca. gov/topics/joaquin-miller-park

Oakland Museum of California

🅰 233 C3

✉ 1000 Oak St.

☎ 510-318-8400

🕐 Closed Mon.–Tues.

💲 $$$$. Free 1st Sun. of month

www.museumca.org

Oakland Museum of California

In 1969, the citizens of Oakland combined the collections of three older institutions to form the Oakland Museum of California, one of the finest regional museums in the country. Lodged in a sprawling but spare modern complex, dotted with verdant gardens and placid ponds, the museum brilliantly grounds its patrons in the ecology, history, and art of the state. Its atmo-

■ An exhibit at the Oakland Museum of California retraces the journey of settlers during the Dust Bowl.

sphere is relaxed, and the staff is helpful and knowledgeable.

The museum features many interactive and multimedia experiences and an offbeat blend of history, art, and science.

Gallery of Art: Perched on the third floor, the new Gallery of Art features selected works from the museum's 70,000-strong collection, including painting, sculpture, photography, decorative arts, and new media, as well

as documentary materials like sketchbooks and artists' tools. The space is divided into separate areas for works that represent California land, people, and creativity.

The collection hints at the scale and achievement of California's artistic community, which in a little more than 200 years has confronted colonialism, industrialization, the enclosure of the wild, and the emergence of the world's first "permanent" frontier.

Many of these themes are readily identifiable in such works as Thomas Hill's "El Capitan," an 1866 piece with strong leanings toward the impressionist style of later years; the brilliant early tonalism of George Inness's "California, 1894"; and the early plein air works of J. H. E. Partington and his 1890 "Lake Temescal."

One particularly memorable section is dedicated to the Society of Six (see p. 40), a 1920s group of Oakland-based painters who used a style of bold, simple brushstrokes. Aiming to communicate a "joy of vision" via the arrangement of abstract elements, such artists as William H. Clapp ("Bird-Nesting") and Maurice Logan ("Point Richmond") reveled in the state's sky and soil colors. The great Millard Sheets explored the more human dimensions of this aesthetic in paintings such as "California Dock Scene" (1929).

One of the museum's great joys is its inclusion of less celebrated artists from the state's past, many of whom are only now growing in stature. One of these is Rinaldo Cuneo, whose transfixing

"Earth Patterns" (1932) will forever change the way you look at the furrowed landscape of California agriculture. Other delights lie in the museum's collection of decorative and ceramic arts.

Of particular interest to photography enthusiasts is the museum's extensive holding of photos by Dorothea Lange; her 1936 "Migrant Mother" holds a special fascination for those interested in the artistic response to the Great Depression.

The gallery is topped off with a significant collection of California moderns, from Richard Diebenkorn and Joan Brown to some lesser known work of David Park and M. Louise Stanley.

Gallery of California History: Down one level, this gallery uses an abundance of artifacts to present a detailed chronology of the state, including actual covered wagons, gold-mining equipment, and some of the earliest correspondence between pioneers and their "folks back home." Some of the daguerreotypes are particularly entertaining, as in Gabriel Harrison's 1848 "California News," depicting the enthusiastic response of Eastern newspaper readers to the discovery of gold at Sutter's Creek. Early examples of mythmaking shine in the museum's collection of souvenir lettersheets used by illiterate miners to send home the "good news"—even when it was bad.

Gallery of California Natural Sciences: Down one more level is an extensive (38,000 square feet/3,530 sq m) display of elemental California, from flora and fauna to lava beds and the Great Basin. The gallery simulates a walk across the state's many habitats.

Try to make time to visit the **California Library of Natural Sounds**—a unique "sound walk" across California that includes audio recordings of the state's indigenous animals as well as ambient soundscapes. ∎

Jack London: Call of the Wild

Not only did Jack London master the adventure novel—his style carried over into other genres, too. His later reporting of sporting events is also characterized by his trademark inclinations toward the working class, as demonstrated in this excerpt from *The Night Born* (1913):

"To his ears came a great roar, as of the sea, and he saw Danny Ward, leading his retinue of trainers and seconds, coming down the center aisle. Everybody proclaimed him. Everybody was for him. Even Rivera's own seconds warmed to something akin to cheerfulness when Danny ducked jauntily through the ropes and entered the ring. His face continually spread to an unending succession of smiles, and when Danny smiled he smiled in every feature, even to the laughter wrinkles of the corner of the eyes and into the depths of the eyes themselves. Never was there so genial a fighter. His face was a running advertisement of good feeling, of good fellowship. He joked, and laughed, and greeted his friends through the ropes. Those farther away cried 'Oh, you Danny!' It was a joyous ovation of affection that lasted a full five minutes."

BERKELEY

Although it traces its roots to the creation of the College of California in 1866 on the site of an early rancho, Berkeley's slow growth was accelerated overnight when the 1906 earthquake sent many San Francisco folk in search of new homes and Phoebe Apperson Hearst, mother of William Randolph Hearst, transformed the small Christian college of Berkeley into one of the nation's preeminent educational institutions. Berkeley has ever since been a liberal and politically radical bastion.

University of California at Berkeley

Hearst money also made the University of California at Berkeley such a fine architectural gem, with such masters as John Galen Howard, Julia Morgan, and Bernard Maybeck brought in to design its key buildings.

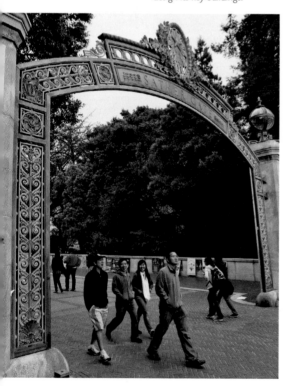

■ The restored Sather Gate

A walk through the campus, starting perhaps at the Telegraph Avenue entrance, takes one past **Sproul Hall** and the **Sather Gate,** site of many 1960s free-speech demonstrations. To the north is the principal landmark, **Sather Tower,** also known as the **Campanile.** Built by Howard in 1914, it is said to have been modeled on the tower of the Piazza San Marco in Venice. Farther north sits the regal **Hearst Mining Building,** built by Howard in 1907. To the east of it is the **Hearst Greek Theater** where, in 1903, Theodore Roosevelt delivered the commencement address. To the west is the **Life Sciences Building,** a huge concrete edifice with lovely external ornamentation in the shape of fishes, reptiles, and mammals. For a relaxing coda, stroll to the **Faculty Glade,** between **Stephen's Union** and the **Men's Faculty Club;** the glade is full of oaks, cedars, and restful green spaces.

The **Berkeley Art Museum and Pacific Film Archive** *(2155 Center St., tel 501-642-0808, www. bampfa.org, closed Mon.–Tues., $$$)* was established in 1963 by abstract expressionist painter Hans Hofmann and has been housed since 2016 in a dramatic, metal-sheathed new building. There are the requisite Cézannes and Monets expected of any modern museum, but the Berkeley's unique strength lies in the core collection of Hofmann's own works.

The **University Botanical Garden** showcases another of the university's areas of expertise, with more than 13,000 botanical specimens. The 34-acre site contains a huge variety of exotic species, acquired since the uni-

---

INSIDER TIP:

Berkeley's "gourmet ghetto" is a gourmand's paradise. Chez Panisse (see pp. 240–241)—the birthplace of California nouvelle cuisine—is at the ghetto's crux, at Shattuck Ave. and Cedar St.

—CHRISTOPHER BAKER
National Geographic author

---

versity first began collecting them in 1890. If you plan to visit the Mendocino Coast later, be sure to see the **pygmy forest** to get a scholarly view of the phenomenon so prevalent at Van Damme State Park (see pp. 272–273).

For a shot of astronomy, visit the **Lawrence Hall of Science** *(1 Centennial Dr., off Stadium Rimway, tel 510-642-5132, www. lawrencehallofscience.org, $$$)*, where the brains behind some of today's top research put together planetarium shows. The museum and its workshops make science accessible and fun. Its hilltop perch offers spectacular vistas across the bay.

The **Hearst Museum of Anthropology** holds the keys to one of the great anthropological puzzles of modern times: How did a lone man named Ishi, the last known representative of the Stone Age Yahi people, come to be discovered in the Central Valley town of Oroville in 1911? A permanent exhibition of his work with UC scholars is on view, along with artifacts from ancient Egypt and Peru. Do not miss this gem.

For those not inclined to meander among the bookstores and cafés of Telegraph Avenue, **Tilden Regional Park** *(N of the university, tel 888-327-2757, www. ebparks.org/parks/tilden)* is a tonic. The park's gardens emphasize California's native plants. Romantics (and their kids) will love the old carousel and steam trains *(Closed Mon.–Fri. in winter).*

Around Berkeley

Not surprisingly, the hills and glens of Berkeley hold several one-of-a-kind architectural gems. This is partly due to the freethinking, creative atmosphere that has long characterized the town's academic community. Another factor is money: This was a wealthy community with the resources to commission some of the top architects of the day.

For example, when Phoebe Apperson Hearst underwrote Berkeley's early 20th-century expansion, she also made Berkeley into a stage for the era's leading architects. Competition, ego, and inspiration fueled their architectural brilliance.

(continued on p. 242)

Berkeley

🗺 233 C4

Visitor Information

✉ Convention & Visitors Bureau, 2030 Addison St. #102, Berkeley

☎ 510-549-7040

🕐 Closed Sat.–Sun.

www.visitberkeley. com

University of California at Berkeley

🗺 233 C4

Visitor Information

✉ Visitor Center, California Memorial Stadium, 2227 Piedmont Ave.

☎ 510-642-5215

https://visit. berkeley.edu

University Botanical Garden

✉ 200 Centennial Dr., off Stadium Rimway

☎ 510-643-2755

💲 $$$

http://botanical garden.berkeley.edu

Hearst Museum of Anthropology

✉ 103 Kroeber Hall, Bancroft Way & College Ave.

☎ 510-642-3682

🕐 Closed Mon.– Tues. Tours by appt.

💲 $$

🚌 Bus 7, 40, 51, 52, 64

http://hearst museum.berkeley .edu

CALIFORNIA CUISINE

"All I cared about was a place to sit down with my friends and enjoy good food while discussing the politics of the day. And I believed that in order to experience food as good as I'd had in France, I had to cook it myself." So explains Alice Waters, founder of Berkeley's famed Chez Panisse restaurant, of the inspiration that launched her now famous culinary career.

The Farmers Market Hall inside San Francisco's Ferry Building is known for its farm-fresh produce.

Anyone who follows food knows that Waters has far exceeded her own modest goals. More than 50 years after the creation of Chez Panisse, she is widely credited for the popularity of California cuisine.

The hallmarks of Waters's cuisine are classic French technique (albeit with a lighter hand with fats) combined with the freshest local, seasonal ingredients obtainable. A sample spring menu might include wild mushrooms on croutons, thin pasta with spring vegetables, charcoal-grilled salmon with grilled red onions, and buckwheat crêpes with tangerines, glacé fruit butter, and eau-de-vie. A summer menu could offer yellow squash and blossom soup, grilled whole filet of beef with deep-fried onion rings, and honey ice cream with lavender. Fall brings smoked trout mousse with chervil butter and champagne sauerkraut. Winter? Try oysters on the half shell with champagne sausages and mignonette sauce.

Waters has also deeply influenced the way we think about food, particularly restaurant food. To this day, she has kept the European

EXPERIENCE: Marin County Cooking Classes

If you are among the many foodies who flock to California panning for culinary gold in a state with a long tradition of top-notch cuisine, you'll discover a wide choice of cooking classes in Marin County.

Pine Point Cooking School (tel 415-332-4352, www.pinepointcooking.com, $$$$$) in Sausalito offers year-round adult culinary workshops as well as summer camps and holiday season classes for kids. You'll find an emphasis on fresh Mediterranean cuisine made with organic produce, dairy, poultry, and sustainable seafood. Your training will include blind tastings to differentiate between organic and industrial fruit and vegetables.

The posh **Cavallo Point Lodge** (tel 415-339-4799, www.cavallopoint.com, $$$$$), at the southern tip of Marin, organizes monthly cooking classes and tastings with its own chefs and visiting experts. Themes run a broad gamut from artisan cheesemaking and Malaysian cuisine to winter comfort food and soufflés.

Just over the Marin county line, the **Ramekins Culinary School** (tel 707-933-0450, www.ramekins.com, $–$$$) in Sonoma offers a selection of classes in two kitchens. The mouthwatering courses include Tuscan cuisine, Asian noodles, Basque tapas, custards, curry workshops, and French Quarter cuisine. And nearby, the **Culinary Institute of America** (2555 Main St., tel 707-967-1100, www.ciachef.edu/cia-california), in St. Helena, offers intensive training to wannabe professionals. **The CIA at Copia** (500 1st St., tel 707-967-2500) offshoot, in downtown Napa, has cooking and beverage classes taught by top chefs, restaurateurs, master sommeliers, and other faculty members of the main institute.

---

tradition of a single, five-course, prix-fixe menu (a preference shared now by many California chefs, including Thomas Keller at Napa's French Laundry). "When people come to the restaurant, I want to insist that they eat in a certain way, try new things, and take time with the food," she writes. "For me food is a totally painless way of awakening people and sharpening their senses. I opened a restaurant so that everybody could come and eat."

You will need to make a reservation if you want to eat at **Chez Panisse.** Choose between the restaurant (1517 Shattuck Ave., Berkeley, tel 510-548-5525, www.chezpanisse.com) and the less pricey café (tel 510-548-5049) upstairs.

Other Berkeley Restaurants

Two other brilliant eateries in Berkeley are worth the time and the often inevitable wait. **Zachary's Chicago Pizza** (1853 Solano Ave., tel 510-525-5950, www.zacharys.com) is legendary for its "stuffed" deep-dish pizzas

INSIDER TIP:

The Ferry Building in San Francisco is one of the great "foodie" destinations in the world. Amid culinary-related stores, you'll find the Slanted Door, considered the best Vietnamese restaurant in the U.S.

—STEPHEN C. FERNALD
*Culinary arts program director,
Lake Tahoe Community College*

smothered with zesty tomato sauce. At **Bette's Oceanview Diner** (1807 4th St., tel 510-644-3230, www.bettesdiner.com, closed dinner) locals line up for outstanding down-home breakfasts.

Afterward, stroll the outstanding Fourth Street Shopping District for some of the city's best gardening, cooking, and design boutiques.

Two examples can be found at the corner of Dwight and Bowditch Ways. If some modern-day architects regard San Francisco's Swedenborgian Church (see p. 209) as the primal altar of the native Arts and Crafts movement, many others revere Berkeley's **First Church of Christ, Scientist** (2619 Dwight Way, www.friendsoffirstchurch.org). Designed by Bernard Maybeck, who also had a hand in the Swedenborgian, this 1910 structure shows the style in full experimental swing. With its great gilded cruciform truss and Romanesque columns of exposed concrete, the church illustrates two of Maybeck's aesthetic concerns, according to historian Jeffery W. Limerick: the "love of grandeur, mood and atmosphere" and the "concern for craftsmanship and the rustic."

Opposite is the **Berkeley School of Theology** (2606 Dwight Way, www.gtu.edu/schools/bst), originally the Berkeley Baptist Divinity School, designed in 1918–19 by Julia Morgan of Hearst Castle (see pp. 174–175) fame. With its slate roof, bay,

and turret, the school represents one of the earliest American attempts at an English institutional style.

Another example of Morgan's work can be found at the **Berkeley City Club** (2315 Durant Ave., www.berkeleycityclub.com), originally the Berkeley Women's City Club. Built in 1929 in what she called the "late medieval style," the club included a 25-by-75-foot (7.6 by 22.8 m) pool. As historian Sara Holmes Boutelle writes, "Every aspect of pool life was considered and planned for: changing, swimming, watching, sunning. Morgan's dressing rooms shine in comparison with most of the mildewed dungeons set aside for this purpose."

Of lesser caliber, but still monumental, is the **Claremont Club & Spa** (Ashby & Domingo Aves., tel 510-843-3000, www.fairmont.com/claremont-berkeley). A white castle set against verdant hills, the hotel offers bay views, a spa, and tennis courts. Its restaurant, Limewood, is a fine eatery, and has a martini bar that combines contemporary chic with live jazz and a to-die-for view of the bay. ∎

John Muir National Historic Site

Although John Muir, grandfather of the environmental movement, is most often linked with Yosemite and the Sierra Nevada, he kept his permanent address in Martinez, a laid-back town in Contra Costa County. His rambling Victorian home is now part of the John Muir National Historic Site (4202 Alhambra Ave., Martinez, tel 925-228-8860, www.nps.gov/jomu). The site's visitor center offers exhibits on Muir

and a 20-minute film about his life. Guided tours of his 17-room mansion are offered daily. Much of the ranch is also open for exploration, including the orchards and Mount Wanda, where Muir often took his daughters for nature walks. An exhibit housed in the Martinez Adobe on the ranch grounds traces the route of Spanish explorer Juan Bautista de Anza from Mexico to the Bay Area in 1775–76.

BENICIA

Situated northeast of San Francisco, east of the entry to the scenic Carquinez Strait, is Benicia—with crisp sea air, a significant history as a former state capital, and abundant small-town delights.

Benicia is home to the **Benicia Capitol State Historic Park,** a perfectly preserved piece of California history. Originally built to be City Hall, it housed the state legislature from February 1853 through February 1854, when Sacramento took over. The first Women's Suffrage Act, permitting women to own property under their own names, was passed here. One of the legislators was Mariano Vallejo, who had originally sold the land to the town founders on the condition that it be named for his wife, Francesca; the city fathers later settled on her middle name, Benicia, to avoid conflicts with their growing neighbor, San Francisco.

For military buffs, the **Benicia Historical Museum** *(2060 Camel Rd., tel 707-745-5435, www.beniciahistoricalmuseum.org, closed a.m. & Mon.–Tues., $, free 1st Wed. of month)* displays artifacts from the history of Benicia and the U.S. Army arsenal. The road name derives from the camels originally brought west to transport troops over desert terrain.

Others will enjoy the **First Street Antiques District** *(C St. to F St.),* whose shops offer a wide variety of Americana.

Visitors seeking something a bit more romantic should head to **St. Dominic's Cemetery.** There you'll find a gravestone to

Of California's early capitol buildings, Benicia's is the only one still surviving.

Sister Mary Dominica Arguello. Born Maria Concepción Arguello, the daughter of the military commandante in San Francisco, she had fallen in love with a visiting Russian, Count Nicolai de Rezanov. Her father opposed the union, but Maria won a compromise: If the count went to Rome and received the permission of the Holy Father, then they could wed. The count hurried off, but died while crossing Siberia. For ten years, Maria pined, unsure of Rezanov's fate. Finally, in 1816, his death was confirmed. Maria became a nun and died in 1857, "the first native daughter," as her headstone reads, "to receive the Dominican habit in California." ■

Benicia
🅰 233 C4
Visitor Information
✉ 250 E. L St., Benicia
☎ 707-746-4202
www.visitbenicia.org

Benicia Capitol State Historic Park
🅰 233 C4
✉ 115 W. G St.
☎ 707-745-3385
www.parks.ca.gov

St. Dominic's Cemetery
✉ 585 Hillcrest Ave.
☎ 707-747-7220
www.stdombenicia.org

DRIVE: MARIN HEADLANDS TO MOUNT TAMALPAIS

Mysterious fogs, lush redwood forests, and dramatic rocky shorelines make the Marin Headlands a popular yet unspoiled destination. That rare combination—the result of a century of environmental activism by Bay Area citizens—yields a seemingly endless parade of spectacular and accessible treats.

Arriving on the Marin Headlands via the Golden Gate Bridge on U.S. 101, go west on scenic Conzelman Road—offering stupendous views of the Golden Gate Bridge and San Francisco—via **Point Bonita** to the **Marin Headlands Visitor Center** ❶ *(Fort Barry Chapel, Field Rd. & Bunker Rd., 415-331-1540, www.nps.gov/goga/marin-headlands.htm)*. Nearby are the **Marine Mammal Center** *(tel 415-289-7325, www.marinemammalcenter.org)* and starting points for hikes along the **Miwok Trail.**

Driving north on U.S. 101, consider a detour to sleepy **Tiburon** *(visitor information, Chamber of Commerce, 96B Main St., tel 415-435-2298, www.destinationtiburon.org)*, an attractive little town noted for houseboats pulled onto land and used as shops and restaurants. The **Richardson Bay Audubon Center & Sanctuary** *(376 Greenwood Beach Rd., Tiburon, tel 415-388-2524, www.richardsonbay.audubon.org)* has self-guided trails and wetlands full of waterfowl.

Head north on U.S. 101. Take Calif. 1, the dramatic **Shoreline Highway,** west past **Green Gulch Farm Zen Center** *(1601 Shoreline Hwy., tel 415-383-3134, www.sfzc.org/ggf)*, which offers courses, lectures, retreats, and overnight stays.

Farther along Calif. 1, at the **Muir Beach Overlook** ❷ get your first view of the shore and, in late January to March, possibly of migrating California gray whales. Then drive north to **Stinson Beach** ❸ *(www.nps.gov/goga/stbe.htm)*, popular with surfers and swimmers.

Bird-watchers should visit the **Audubon Canyon Ranch** *(4900 Calif. 1, Stinson Beach, tel 415-868-9244, www.egret.org)*, a breeding site for Great Egrets and Great Blue Herons, and the **Point Reyes Bird Observatory** ❹ *(Mesa Rd., Bolinas, tel 415-868-0655, www.pointblue.org)*.

NOT TO BE MISSED:

Muir Beach Overlook • Mount Tamalpais • Muir Woods NM

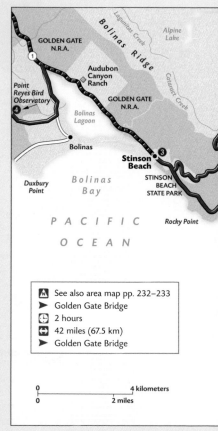

See also area map pp. 232–233
► Golden Gate Bridge
🕐 2 hours
↔ 42 miles (67.5 km)
► Golden Gate Bridge

0   4 kilometers
0   2 miles

Inland from Stinson Beach stretches **Mount Tamalpais State Park** ❺ *(801 Panoramic Hwy., tel 415-388-2070, www.parks.ca.gov)*. You can drive to the 2,571-foot (783 m) East Peak of Mount Tam's double peak via the Panoramic Highway, which goes east from Calif. 1 a mile (1.6 km) south of Stinson Beach and Ridgecrest Boulevard. The 2-mile (3.2 km) **Pantoll Easy Grade Trail** is perfect for an afternoon hike. Or take to the trails on a mountain bike.

Farther south on the Panoramic Highway is **Muir Woods National Monument** ❻ *(Muir Woods Rd., Mill Valley, tel 415-561-2850, www. nps.gov/muwo)*, where a nature trail guides you through every element of the soaring redwood forest—from salmon and steelhead trout of the Redwood Creek to the ferns, huckleberries, and violets of the forest floor.

Take the Panoramic Highway to U.S. 101 and back toward San Francisco. Stop in the quaint waterside town of **Sausalito** ❼ *(Visitor information, Visitor Center, 1913 Bridgeway Ave., tel 415-331-7262, www.visitsausalito.org)*. A unique attraction here is the **Bay Model Visitor Center** *(2100 Bridgeway Ave., Sausalito, tel 415-332-3871, www.spn. usace.army.mil/Missions/Recreation)*, a detailed 1.5-acre (.6 ha) hydraulic model of San Francisco Bay complete with tides and currents.

POINT REYES

Point Reyes, at the core of the 75,000-acre (30,350 ha) Point Reyes National Seashore, lies on the eastern edge of the Pacific plate, which creeps northwestward past the North American plate at about two inches (5 cm) a year. At the Bear Valley Visitor Center, you can stand on the spot where, during the 1906 San Francisco earthquake, the peninsula leaped 20 feet (6 m) to the northwest. It is perhaps the most dramatic place in California to view the San Andreas Fault.

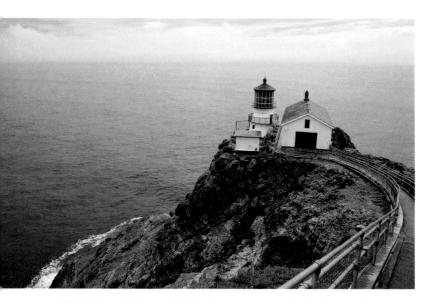

The Point Reyes Lighthouse guided ships through dangerous wind and fog for more than a century.

Point Reyes National Seashore

🏕 232 A4–A5

Visitor Information

✉ Bear Valley Visitor Center, 1 Bear Valley Rd. (off Calif. 1 at Olema)

☎ 415-464-5100

www.nps.gov/pore

Ruler-straight Tomales Bay runs along the fault line; **Tomales Bay State Park** (*1208 Pierce Point Rd., Inverness, tel 415-669-1140, www.parks.ca.gov*) protects wetlands and surf-free beaches good for picnics. Full of natural and historic wonders, the point was discovered in 1579 by English explorer Sir Francis Drake. It was later claimed for the English crown, unbeknown to the Miwok Indians who had helped Drake resupply his ship, the *Golden Hind.*

At the northern end of Point Reyes is the historic **Pierce Point Ranch.** Founded in 1858, it is perhaps the oldest dairy farm in California; the state now manages the original structures and maintains a self-guided trail. Not far away is the **Tule Elk Preserve,** where, after a century of near-extinction, this magnificent mammal has staged a comeback. To the south lies **Abbotts Lagoon,** where bird-watchers may paddle canoes to see the annual waterfowl migration.

INSIDER TIP:

Point Reyes Lighthouse is often shrouded in cold, dense fog in summer. Arrive in a T-shirt and shorts, and you'll be in for a chilly surprise!

—CHRISTOPHER BAKER
National Geographic author

To catch the grand sweep of Drakes Bay itself, make the pilgrimage to the recently restored **Point Reyes Lighthouse** (*Sir Francis Drake Blvd., tel 415-669-1534, closed Tues.–Wed.*). The original tower, with a 3-ton lens ground in France, was constructed in 1870 to prevent ships from running aground in the area's notorious fogs. Despite its 24-mile (38 km) visibility, the lighthouse has not prevented several crashes, including at least one involving an airplane. The estuary called **Drakes Estero,** where the explorer is said to have repaired his ship, is woven with hiking trails; some pass by oyster beds. Bring binoculars in the winter months to scan the horizon for migrating gray whales.

The town of **Point Reyes Station** on the eastern edge of the park has emerged as a hub for both adventure sports and the "farm-fresh food" movement. **Blue Waters Kayaking** (*80 4th St., tel 415-669-2600, www.bluewaters kayaking.com*) offers guided trips and canoe/kayak rentals for exploring the peninsula and its many inlets on your own. In 1994, **Tomales Bay Foods** (*www. tomalesbayfoods.com*) started to market locally produced vegetables and cheeses. A key to its success is access to one of the state's oldest organic dairies, the **Straus Family Creamery** (*www.strausfamily creamery.com*). At **Bovine Bakery** (*11315 Hwy. 1, tel 415-663-9420, www.bovinebakeryptreyes.com*), you can buy great desserts and breads. Ask local retailers for the best places to buy the noted Hog Island oysters. ■

Point Reyes Station

🗺 232 A4

Visitor Information

☎ 415-663-9232

www.pointreyes.org

POINT REYES PICNICS
Michael Bauer, food editor of the *San Francisco Chronicle,* has recommended four picnic spots less than 30 minutes' drive from Point Reyes Station: **Chimney Rock,** on the road to Point Reyes Lighthouse; **Heart's Desire Beach,** located in Tomales Bay State Park; **Drakes Beach,** southwest of Inverness along Sir Francis Drake Boulevard; and **Samuel P. Taylor State Park,** near Olema, with picnic tables under a redwood canopy.

EXPERIENCE: Mountain Biking in Point Reyes

The Bay Area boasts some of the nation's best mountain biking trails, routes that are both scenic and technically demanding. Although mountain biking is prohibited in much of Point Reyes National Seashore (*www.nps.gov/pore*), the park has several challenging trails. Perfect for summer, the shady **Bear Valley Trail** follows the valley for a relatively easy 4 miles (6.4 km) to the coast. The trail starts at the visitor center parking lot in Olema. After a stiff climb, the 5.2-mile (8.3 km) **Olema Valley Trail**—which begins at the Five Brooks Trailhead in Olema—follows the eastern edge of Inverness Ridge in a gradual descent to the sea. Despite its bumpy climbs and descents, the 4.4-mile (7 km) **Estero Trail** rewards the brave with views across the coastal grasslands. You can pick up the trail along the western shore of Tomales Bay. Consult the park website for more mountain biking trails. Top trails are also found at **Annadel State Park** (*www.parks.ca.gov*) in Santa Rosa, **Henry W. Coe State Park** (*www. parks.ca.gov*) in the mountains south of San Jose, and at **Skeggs Point** on the peninsula.

URBAN MARIN COUNTY & AROUND

The hippie-turned-yuppie townsfolk of Marin have, over the past few decades, earned for themselves a reputation for being trendy, health conscious, self-involved, and politically correct. The resulting farmers markets, boutiques, New Age galleries, and healing centers all make for pleasant and stimulating outings (whether or not you share the philosophy behind them). Many of the region's towns have outstanding historical and architectural sites, too.

The views from atop Mount Tamalpais span the San Francisco Bay and Pacific shoreline.

San Rafael

San Rafael

🏛 233 B4

Visitor Information

✉ Marin
Convention &
Visitors Bureau,
1 Mitchell Blvd.

☎ 415-925-2060

www.visitmarin.org

Mission San Rafael Arcángel
(5th & A Sts., tel 415-454-8141, www.saintraphael.com), the 20th mission established in California, was founded in 1817, when Lt. Gabriel Moraga convinced the padres at Mission San Francisco to allow their more sickly neophytes to move to San Rafael's warmer and drier climate. The neophytes recuperated, and San Franciscans have ever since sought relief from their winters (and summers) in this gem of a town.

The pristine, small-town atmosphere was not lost on local resident George Lucas, who used it as a backdrop to his classic movie *American Graffiti* (1973). The surrounding geology also fueled one of the last great projects of architect Frank Lloyd Wright, who called it "one of the most beautiful landscapes I have ever seen." Wright's **Marin County Civic Center** *(3501 Civic Center Dr., tel 415-473-6400, www.marincounty. org/depts/cu/tours),* finished after his death, was conceived as a "bridge between hills," illustrating the harmony Wright sought to bring between his medium and, as he would have put it, "Nature with a capital N."

Modern Cuisine in a 19th-Century Setting

Founded in the late 19th century, the town of **Larkspur** *(Chamber of Commerce, 1013 Larkspur Landing Circle, tel 800-596-0747, www.visitmarin.org)* has a pleasant mix of architecture, ranging from Victorian to log cabin to mission, and brick-lined **Magnolia Avenue,** a colorful shopping district, is listed on the National Register of Historic Places.

However, most folk come here for another reason: **Perry's** *(234 Magnolia Ave., tel 415-927-1877, www.perryssf. com/location/larkspur)*, a world-class restaurant formerly the Tavern at Lark Creek. After a hearty American meal of, say, grilled salmon with quinoa, cherry tomatoes, and spring peas take a stroll to the north end of town to see the remains of the historic **Escalle Winery.** Notice the wildflowers, for which the town is said to have been misnamed (they are actually lupins!).

Located just 3 miles (4.8 km) south of the city of San Rafael near Mount Tamalpais, Larkspur has a busy ferry terminal, conveniently connecting the town with San Francisco.

The **Marin Veterans' Memorial Auditorium** at the Civic Center hosts a wide range of world-class performing arts, including music, dance, comedy, and the prestigious Marin Speaker Series.

The summer Thursday evening **farmers market** *(tel 415-492-8007, www.sanrafaelmarket.org)* along Fourth Street in downtown San Rafael mixes fresh food with local wines, live music, vintage clothing, handcrafted jewelry, and other local fortes. The civic center also hosts two weekly farmers markets *(415-472-6100)*, on Sundays and Thursdays.

San Anselmo

Founded in 1875 as the result of a legendary feud between the wives of two railroad men, San Anselmo is now known as the capital of the antiques trade in northern California. Buyers be warned: Prices are high. The town also has its share of cafés and restaurants, with an especially lively and rather upscale Sunday brunch scene.

Novato

The north Marin competitor of San Rafael, Novato offers many of the lures of its southern sister, from an **Old Town** district to a summer Tuesday evening **farmers market.**

Above all, it is the town's deep identification with the area's Native American days that distinguishes it for the traveler. An **adobe wall** just outside the Old Town, a former part of Rancho Burdell, once belonged to the home of Camillo Ynitia, last chief of the Olompali. Ynitia is believed to have been killed by his brother for not sharing the proceeds of the sale of the land to a pioneer family.

The **Marin Museum of the American Indian** *(Miwok Park, 2200 Novato Blvd., tel 415-897-4064, www.marinindian.com, closed Mon., $ donation)* is a must for anyone interested in the region's history before the arrival of Europeans. ∎

San Anselmo
🅰 233 B4
Visitor Information
☎ 415-233-7464
www.destinationsan anselmo.com

Novato
🅰 233 B4
Visitor Information
✉ Chamber of Commerce, 807 DeLong Ave., Novato
☎ 800-897-1164
www.visitnovato.com

SAN JOSE & AROUND

Although its history dates back to 1777, when the Spanish attempted to found a mission and agricultural outpost at the southern end of San Francisco Bay, San Jose clearly takes its cues from a more modern moment. The Hewlett-Packard Company began in nearby Palo Alto in 1939, fueling the growth of the top technopolis in the U.S. Apple, Google, Facebook, and IBM are all headquartered here, in a one-time piece of farmland now known as Silicon Valley.

The Tech Interactive appeals to the "inner techno geek" in every visitor.

San Jose

🗺 233 D2

Visitor Information

✉ Convention &
Visitors Bureau,
408 Almaden
Blvd., San Jose

☎ 408-792-4511

www.sanjose.org

**The Tech
Interactive**

🗺 233 D2

✉ 201 S. Market
St., San Jose

☎ 408-294-8324

💲 $$$

www.thetech.org

For a long time, much of the new wealth tended to travel to San Francisco and other cities. That pattern has changed in recent years with the formation of several new museums and cultural institutions in San Jose. The most glamorous of these is **The Tech Interactive** with more than 250 exhibits and interactive displays, an interactive media lab, and an IMAX theater. Eight permanent galleries demonstrate every techie aspect of modern life.

Three other museums are worth your time. By far the best is the **San Jose Museum of Art** (*110 S. Market St., tel 408-271-6840, www.sjmusart.org, closed Mon., $$*). The museum focuses on works by West Coast artists since 1980. Particularly engaging are the many artists who fuse the area's rich agricultural history with its present fixation on technology.

The **Rosicrucian Egyptian Museum & Planetarium** (*1600 Park Ave., tel 408-947-3635, www.egyptianmuseum.org, closed Mon.–Tue., $$*) houses the largest collection of Egyptian artifacts in the western U.S. It includes a large collection of human and animal mummies, a full-scale reconstruction of an Egyptian noble's tomb, walls of hieroglyphs, a collection of

Coptic textiles, extensive gardens, and free hieroglyphic workshops on weekends.

The **San Jose Museum of Quilts & Textiles** *(520 S. First St., tel 408-971-0323, www.sjquilt museum.org, closed Mon.–Tue.)* prides itself on an international mix, with changing exhibitions.

San Jose is perhaps best known for the **Winchester Mystery House,** a Victorian mansion famous for its weirdness: 160 rooms (many too tiny to be useful) and staircases, corridors, and doorways that lead nowhere. The owner, rifle heiress Sarah Winchester, was convinced that she would die if the building was completed, so work continued for nearly 40 years. Guided tour options include spooky nighttime tours.

Santa Clara

In Santa Clara, just 4 miles (6.4 km) west of San Jose, thrill-seekers are drawn to **California's Great America** *(tel 408-988-1776, www.cagreat america.com)*, a 100-acre theme park. Or visit the **Intel Museum**

to journey through decades of innovation, and see chips being made in one of the industry's "clean rooms."

While in the Santa Clara area, visit the **Mission Santa Clara de Asís,** on the campus of Santa Clara University. Nothing remains of the 1777 mission, but later buildings can be seen, as well as a beautiful facsimile of the original church; many of the old garden's roses—including an 1822 Castilian rose bush—are now classified as antiques by experts. **Mission San José de Guadalupe** *(map p.233 D2, 43300 Mission Blvd., Fremont, tel 510-657-1797, www.missionsan jose.org)* lies northeast of the city.

Farther Afield

Aerospace buffs might like to visit the famed **Lick Observatory,** on 4,213-foot (1,284 m) Mount Hamilton, and the **NASA Ames Research Center** *(Moffett Field, tel 650-604-5000, www.nasa.gov/ ames).* Here, the NASA Ames Exploration Center lets visitors experience NASA technology and missions firsthand and includes an IMAX theater. ∎

Winchester Mystery House
- 233 D2
- ✉ 525 S. Winchester Blvd., San Jose
- ☎ 408-247-2000
- 🕐 Closed Mon.–Tues.
- 💲 $$$$$
- **www.winchester mysteryhouse.com**

Intel Museum
- ✉ 2200 Mission College Blvd., Santa Clara
- ☎ 408-765-5050
- 🕐 Closed Sun.
- **www.intel.com/ museum**

Mission Santa Clara de Asís
- 233 D2
- ✉ 500 El Camino Real, Santa Clara
- ☎ 408-554-4000
- **www.scu.edu/mission**

Lick Observatory
- 233 D2
- ☎ 408-274-5061
- 🕐 Closed Mon.– Wed., & a.m. Thur.–Sun.
- **www.ucobservatories. org**

San Jose's "Urban Village"

One of California's most creative urban renewal projects in recent years is the bold, brash **Santana Row** *(tel 408-551-4611, www.santanarow.com)* in San Jose. Packed into 42 acres (17 ha or roughly ten city blocks), the development opened in 2003 to rave reviews and several national design and engineering awards. A blend of residences, restaurants, and upscale shops, this "urban village" draws its architectural inspiration from several sources,

including Mediterranean and art deco. Extra-wide sidewalks, grassy plazas, benches, open-air cafés, and courtyards make Santana Row pedestrian friendly. Among the tenants are almost 100 shops and restaurants, plus the CinéArts 6 movie house and the boutique Hotel Valencia Santana Row *(tel 866-842-0100, www.hotelvalencia-santanarow.com).* Park Valencia hosts live music and a popular hot dog stand.

STANFORD UNIVERSITY

Stanford, one of the world's most prestigious academic institutions, was founded in 1887 in Palo Alto by railroad baron Leland Stanford and his wife to honor their son, who had died at age 16 from typhoid fever. From the beginning, it set high-minded goals. With the grand Romanesque architecture, red-tiled roofs, and wide brick plazas, form certainly followed ambition. The university visitor service offers free one-hour walking tours daily from Memorial Hall.

Stanford Memorial Church holds regular multifaith services.

Stanford University

🅰 233 C2

Visitor Information

✉ Memorial Hall, 295 Galvez St., Stanford

☎ 650-723-2560

www.stanford.edu

Hoover Institution

✉ 434 Galvez Mall

☎ 650-723-1754

🕐 Closed Sat.–Sun.

www.hoover.org

http://museum.stanford.edu, closed Tues.), which combines many of the university's older collections—including works by Goya, Piranesi, and Delacroix—with more recent acquisitions. The centerpiece is the Cantor collection of sculptures by Auguste Rodin, the largest in the world. There is also an extensive collection of Asian and American art.

INSIDER TIP:

When visiting Stanford University, don't miss nearby Filoli (86 Cañada Rd., Woodside, tel 650-364-8300, www.filoli.org), a breathtaking English-style estate with spectacular gardens.

—GREG CRITSER
National Geographic author

Although there are many interesting historical sites to see, the **Stanford Memorial Church** *(Central Quad)* warrants special note. The church was the special project of Jane Stanford, who commissioned Maurizio Camerino, a great 19th-century Italian mosaicist, to render a reproduction of Cosimo Roselli's fresco of the Last Supper in the Vatican's Sistine Chapel. At the time of its completion in 1903, it was the largest mosaic in the United States. Like the church, it had to be rebuilt after the 1906 earthquake.

A more recent addition (1999) is the beautifully realized **Cantor Arts Center** *(Lomita Dr. at Museum Way, tel 650-732-4177,*

The influential **Hoover Institution,** named for its founding alumnus President, was one of the first "think tanks" in the U.S. The library holds Herbert Hoover's 150,000-piece collection of manuscripts and documents on international relations. ■

Emerald green valleys, where wine is a way of life and simple outdoor pleasures reign

WINE COUNTRY

◼ Sonoma Valley's Sebastiani Winery, one of the largest wineries in the U.S.

WINE COUNTRY

Although many have written about the grandeur of California's wine country, few have captured it as well as author Robert Louis Stevenson, who, in the summer of 1880, visited pioneer winemaker Jacob Schram. "In this wild spot, I did not feel the sacredness of ancient cultivation," Stevenson wrote. "Here . . . earth's cream was being skimmed and garnered, and customers can taste, such as it is, the tang of the earth in this green valley."

Today, as California wine country increasingly becomes an oenophile theme park, it is easy to forget the primal pleasures of the land itself. True, the crush of summer traffic, the jockeying for dinner reservations, and the collecting of the newest vintages make traveling in this region exciting. But the joy is in the land—seeing it, smelling it, feeling it connect in your belly with that first drop of a simple cabernet or syrah.

Some planning before you arrive is certainly worthwhile. First, when to come? California's wine country is at its best in late fall or early winter, when the crowds thin and the foliage puts on a spectacular show. Second, where to go? Consider staying away from the main action, perhaps in Calistoga, where the food is outstanding and the room rates more reasonable (albeit not cheap). Make reservations if you want to eat at any of the top restaurants. Lastly, bone up on your wine basics. It is hard even for the uninitiated to buy a bad bottle of wine here, but a little background knowledge always helps. ■

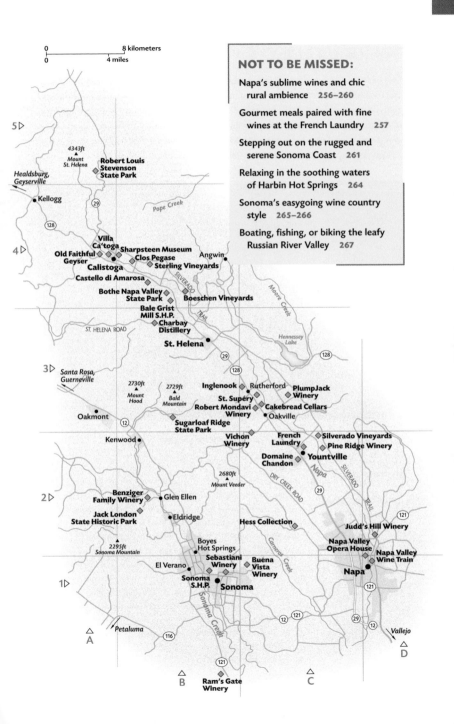

0 | 8 kilometers
0 | 4 miles

NOT TO BE MISSED:

Napa's sublime wines and chic
rural ambience 256–260

Gourmet meals paired with fine
wines at the French Laundry 257

Stepping out on the rugged and
serene Sonoma Coast 261

Relaxing in the soothing waters
of Harbin Hot Springs 264

Sonoma's easygoing wine country
style 265–266

Boating, fishing, or biking the leafy
Russian River Valley 267

4343ft
Mount
St. Helena

Robert Louis
Stevenson
State Park

Healdsburg,
Geyserville

Kellogg

29

Pope Creek

128

Villa
Ca'toga

Old Faithful
Geyser

Sharpsteen Museum

Clos Pegase

Angwin

Calistoga

Sterling Vineyards

Castello di Amarosa

SILVERADO

Bothe Napa Valley
State Park

Boeschen Vineyards

Moore Creek

Bale Grist
Mill S.H.P.

ST. HELENA ROAD

Charbay
Distillery

TRAIL

Hennessey
Lake

St. Helena

29

128

128

Santa Rosa,
Guerneville

2730ft
Mount
Hood

2729ft
Bald
Mountain

Inglenook

Rutherford

PlumpJack
Winery

St. Supéry

Robert Mondavi
Winery

Cakebread Cellars

Oakville

Oakmont

12

Sugarloaf Ridge
State Park

Kenwood

Vichon
Winery

French
Laundry

Silverado Vineyards

Pine Ridge Winery

Domaine
Chandon

Yountville

SILVERADO

Napa

2680ft
Mount Veeder

DRY CREEK ROAD

29

Benziger
Family Winery

Glen Ellen

Jack London
State Historic Park

Eldridge

Hess Collection

Judd's Hill Winery

121

2295ft
Sonoma Mountain

Boyes
Hot Springs

Napa Valley
Opera House

Napa Valley
Wine Train

El Verano

Sebastiani
Winery

Buena
Vista
Winery

Carneros Creek

Napa

Sonoma
S.H.P.

Sonoma

121

Sonoma Creek

12

121

29

12

Vallejo

Petaluma

116

A

121

Ram's Gate
Winery

B

C

D

NAPA VALLEY

The heart of California's wine country begins at Napa, about an hour's drive north of San Francisco (see pp. 191–230). Volcanic soils and a favorable climate first attracted vintners to the region in the mid-19th century. Today, the valley stretching from Napa to the old spa of Calistoga, some 30 miles (48 km) northwest, has more than 200 wineries, some of them world famous and very much geared to visitors. They need to be. Annually, as many as five million people make the pilgrimage up Calif. 29, the backbone of Napa Valley.

Passengers on the deluxe Napa Valley Wine Train have good reason to smile!

Napa

 254 C1 & 255 D1

Visitor Information

✉ Welcome Center, 1290 First St., Napa

☎ 707-257-0322

www.donapa.com

Napa

The southern gateway to the valley, Napa has evolved in recent years as a destination in its own right thanks to the new **Napa River Promenade** (700 Main St., www.napasriverfront.com), offering a rewarding riverside walk past old warehouses converted to fine-dining restaurants, wine bars, and boutique hotels. The **Napa Valley Opera House** (1030 Main St., tel 707-226-7372, www.nvoh. org) hosts dramatic performances by the American Conservatory Theater.

St. Helena

At the heart of the oasis, St. Helena, with its downtown lined with charming Victorian buildings, is the perfect spot for the **Culinary Institute of America** (2555 Main St., tel 707-967-1100, www.ciachef. edu). With its fragrant herb gardens and food-is-all atmosphere, it would be engaging enough as a travel destination. The addition of a restaurant makes it a foodie theme park, where you can spend half a day eating. The seasonal menu is influenced by new Mediterranean cuisine, and

Best Meal in the U.S.

A food lover's dream, the **French Laundry** *(map p. 255 C2, 6640 Washington St., Yountville, tel 707-944-2380, www.frenchlaundry.com)* serves food that many believe is the nation's best. Some samples from a recent prix-fixe tasting menu: Sabayon of pearl tapioca with poached Malpeque oysters and Osetra caviar; new potatoes and French winter truffles; butter-poached Maine lobster with wilted arrowleaf spinach and saffron-vanilla sauce. These chef Thomas Keller serves in, as critic Ruth Reichl put it,

"small, intense bites that add up to the valley's most incredible dining experience."

Although the courses are small, there are so many of them that, as one diner remarked, "It was like that movie *Groundhog Day*. Just when we thought we had finished, here came the waiter with another round!"

Reservations can be made between 10 a.m. and 7 p.m., two months to the day before you plan to dine. In other words, make this reservation before you buy your plane ticket. It is worth it.

INSIDER TIP:

Cycling is a great way to see wine country. Napa Valley Bike Tours *(www.napavalleybiketours.com)* also offers bicycle rental.

—BOB HOLMES
Author, A Traveller's Wine Guide to California

the emphasis is on local foods and wines.

The good life continues at the luxury resort of **Meadowood** *(900 Meadowood Ln., tel 877-963-3646, www.meadowood.com),* where gabled hillside cabins are set in a 250-acre (101 ha) valley of oaks, pines, azaleas, and rhododendrons. Many come for the food, the golf course, and summer opera.

St. Helena also has associations with Robert Louis Stevenson, who spent his honeymoon near here in 1880. The **Robert Louis Stevenson Museum** *(1490 Library Ln., tel 707-963-3757, www.stevensonmuseum.org, closed Mon., donation)* recalls his stay.

Calistoga

Reposing, in Stevenson's words, "on a mere film above a boiling, subterranean lake," is the spa town of Calistoga. **Old Faithful Geyser** *(1299 Tubbs Ln., tel 707-942-6463, www.oldfaithfulgeyser.com)* erupts every 15 to 30 minutes, proving Stevenson's point.

Founded by pioneer Sam Brannan as a health resort in 1859, Calistoga offers good bed-and-breakfasts, cafés, boutiques, and restaurants.

For the past 50 years, Calistoga has also provided balm to the weary by means of **Dr. Wilkinson's Backyard Resort & Mineral Springs** *(map p. 255 A4, 1507 Lincoln Ave., tel 707-942-4102, www.drwilkinson.com),* which offers reasonably priced spa services: massages, salt glow rubs, and "the mud," a complete immersion in warm volcanic ash and natural hot spring water.

The **Sharpsteen Museum** *(map p. 255 B4, 1311 Washington St., tel 707-942-5911, www.sharpsteenmuseum.org, $ donation)* displays artifacts dating back 200 years. Nearby, the sumptuously decorated **Villa Ca'toga** re-creates the feel of ancient Rome. ■

St. Helena
- 254 C2 & 255 B3

Visitor Information
- Chamber of Commerce, 1320 Main St., St. Helena
- 800-799-6456

www.sthelena.com

Calistoga
- 254 C2 & 255 A4

Visitor Information
- Visitor Center, 1133 Washington St., Calistoga
- 707-942-6333, 866-306-5588

www.visitcalistoga.com

Villa Ca'toga
- 255 A4
- 3061 Myrtledale Rd., Calistoga
- 707-942-0212
- Closed Nov.–April. Tours 11 a.m. Sat.
- $$$$$

www.catoga.com

NAPA VALLEY WINERIES

Sitting in one of Napa's glamorous but rustic tasting rooms or restaurants, it's hard to believe that just a few decades ago the idea that California wineries would ever be anything more than a footnote in the annals of wine would have been a joke. But now the footnote is a tome.

■ Extravagant Domaine Carneros sits atop a vine-lined knoll.

Inglenook

In 1975, director Francis Ford Coppola bought part of the Niebaum estate, which had been involved in winemaking since 1872. Three years later, he made his first vintage of Rubicon. Now Inglenook, formerly Niebaum-Coppola, is known as an outstanding producer of wines, from its trademark Rubicons (labeled by *Wine & Spirits* as "dense, rich, sumptuous—even when young") to its newer Rosso and Bianco line of family-style blends.

Robert Mondavi
- 🅰 255 C3
- ✉ 7801 St. Helena Hwy. (Calif. 29), Oakville
- ☎ 888-766-6328
- 💲 Tastings: $$$$$
- **www.robertmondavi winery.com**

Inglenook
- 🅰 255 C3
- ✉ 1991 St. Helena Hwy., Rutherford
- ☎ 707-968-1100 (tours by appt. only)
- 💲 Tastings: $$$$$
- **www.inglenook.com**

Robert Mondavi Winery

Set in a stylish country villa headquarters, this winery was the brainchild of Robert Mondavi, who departed the family's old Charles Krug Winery to experiment with realizing the world-class potential of Napa's rich soils and outstanding climate. He studied French winemaking techniques with the masters, bringing home new ideas, experimenting, adapting, failing, succeeding. In 1976, Napa entries in the Paris Wine Tasting won top honors, proving Mondavi right and launching Napa and California onto the world stage. Today, Mondavi's legacy winery offers some of the more (deservedly) popular tours in the valley.

St. Supéry

St. Supéry's Sauvignon Blanc and Chardonnay are considered outstanding among wines made to be drunk fresh. The tour includes a visit to the Victorian **Atkinson House,** built in 1881. Among the other delights here are a display vineyard, and, for the technophile, an exhibit dubbed "Smell-aVision," a hands-on display to help one understand the language of aroma, appearance, and taste.

The Silverado Trail

Founded in the 1970s, **Silverado Vineyards** is situated along the scenic Silverado Trail, a 19th-century Napa Valley mining road that runs along the eastern side of the Napa River. Grown under the retreating cool air from San Pablo Bay, its merlots and cabernets are especially known for their "rounded" flavors and silky textures. A tour takes in the dining room, with original works by such California painters as Thomas Hill and William Keith. From the back terrace of the house, there is a stunning view of Mount St. Helena, to the northwest, and of the surrounding countryside.

Not far away on the Silverado Trail, the acclaimed daily tours of the **Pine Ridge Vineyards** (5901 Silverado Trail, tel 800-575-9777, www.pineridgevineyards.com, tastings $$$$) concentrate on various aspects of the growing process. A visit to the winery's hillside caves is followed by a tasting of Pine Ridge's fine cabernets, merlots, and chardonnays.

Calistoga (see p. 257) marks the northern end of the Silverado Trail. Here, **Clos Pegase** (1060 Dunaweal Ln., tel 707-942-4981 or 866-474-3021, www.clospegase.com), founded by Jan and Mitsuko Shrem in 1987, manages to pull off a triple treat—art, wine, and architecture—with grace and aplomb. True, the award-winning

headquarters at first shocked the valley's more traditionally minded vintners. But the Shrems have integrated much tradition at their winery, the most engaging being their aging caves, 20,000 square feet (1,858 sq m) of wooden barrels buried below a nearby rocky knoll. Sculptures by Henry Moore, Richard Serra, and Anthony Caro dot the property. The winery offers free "Grand Tours" every day, plus the Harvest Bacchanal and Grape Stomp in October.

Vintners & Gardeners

Several Napa Valley wineries take great pride in their gardens. Don't miss the innovative vegetable gardens at Cakebread Cellars (map p. 255 C3, 8300 St. Helena Hwy., Rutherford, tel 800-588-0298, www.cakebread .com); the choreographed landscaping at **Boeschen Vineyards** (map p. 255 B4, 3242 Silverado Trail, Calistoga, tel 707-963-3674, www.boeschenvineyards.com), or the tomato extravaganza at the **Robert Mondavi Winery** (see p. 258). One of the valley's finest gardens flourishes at **Peju Province Winery** (8466 St. Helena Hwy., Rutherford, tel 707-963-3600, http://peju.com). As professional landscape gardeners and floral nursery owners, Tony and Herta Peju were well equipped to design and nourish a garden when they started the winery in 1983.

Nearby, **Sterling Vineyards** (1111 W. Dunaweal Ln., tel 800-726-6136, www.sterlingvineyards.com, tastings $$$$$) perches atop a hill and is accessed via an aerial tram. Modeled on the architecture of the Greek island of Mykonos, it offers the best panoramic vistas in the entire valley.

St. Supéry

- ▲ 255 C3
- ✉ 8440 St. Helena Hwy., Rutherford
- ☎ 707-963-4507
- $ Tastings: $$$$$. Tours: $$$$$ (by appt. only)

www.stsupery.com

Silverado Vineyards

- ▲ 255 C2
- ✉ 6121 Silverado Trail, Napa
- ☎ 707-257-1770
- $ Tastings: $$$$$, Thur.-Sun.

www.silverado vineyards.com

Castello di Amorosa

🅰 255 B4

✉ 4045 N.
St. Helena Hwy.,
Calistoga

☎ 707-967-6272

💲 Tastings: $$$$$

www.castellodi
amorosa.com

Hess Collection

🅰 255 C2

✉ 4411 Redwood
Rd., Napa

☎ 707-255-1144

💲 Tastings & Tours:
$$$$$

www.hesscollection
.com

Charbay Distillery

🅰 255 B3

✉ 4001 Spring
Mtn. Rd.,
St. Helena

☎ 707-963-9327

💲 $$$$. Visits by
appt. only.

www.charbay.com

Castello di Amorosa

The most visually astonishing is Castello di Amorosa. Thirteen years in the making, this 121,000-square-foot (11,240 sq m) Tuscan-style castle perched on a hill south of Calistoga features a frescoed great hall, secret passageways, and even a torture chamber. Other castle activities include horse-drawn carriage rides and hiking vineyard tours.

Hess Collection

The most outstanding art collection belongs to the Hess Collection, in the hills west of Napa. Established in 1896, the winery occupies a centenarian, three-story stone structure built into the side of Mount Veeder. The self-guided tour begins in the theater, where visitors are introduced to Hess's traditional Burgundian winemaking practice, resulting in quality wines of richly satisfying complexity. The second- and third-floor galleries meld a contemporary redesign into the historic sandstone shell, with 13,000 square feet (1,207 m) of art space displaying 115 contemporary pieces, including works by such masters as Francis Bacon and Franz Gertsch.

Charbay Distillery

In recent years, many wineries have begun producing grappa, port, and various trendy spirits. The family-run Charbay Distillery, a mountaintop aerie outside St. Helena, leads the spirited pack with its apple brandy, black walnut liqueur, and award-winning trademark fruit-flavored vodkas. It also produces the world's only dessert chardonnay, as well as California's first pastis, a California vermouth, and even a sunroot spirit—the first original, purely American spirit—made from sunflower tubers. ■

Meals on the Move

As you might expect, picnics in the Napa Valley are an art form. To get just the right cold chicken, salads, cheeses, and, of course, wine, try the **V. Sattui Winery** (*1111 White Ln., St. Helena, tel 707-963-7774, www.vsattui. com*), which offers an extensive deli and a fine picnic area. Among prime picnic spots on the wine circuit for locals in the know are the **Vichon Winery** (*map p. 255 C2*), which has its own bocce ball court, and the picnic tables at **PlumpJack Winery** (*map p. 255 C3*).

As you also might expect, there is no shortage of places to buy picnic supplies. The famed **Oakville Grocery** (*7856 St. Helena Hwy., Oakville, 707-944-8802,* *www.oakvillegrocery.com*) offers outstanding specialties, from fig-olive tapenade to local fruits and salads.

If you don't want to picnic but are tired of the restaurant scene, try a jaunt on the **Napa Valley Wine Train** (*1275 McKinstry St., Napa, tel 707-253-2111, www.winetrain .com*). A restored diesel locomotive car trundles you through wine country at a leisurely clip as you eat a gourmet brunch, lunch, or dinner in a 1917 Pullman dining car or Vista Dome observation car. Your half- or full-day tour includes stops at two wineries as you journey between Napa and Calistoga, plus you get to watch chefs at work in the kitchen car.

SONOMA VALLEY

If Napa Valley is the Florence of American viticulture, full of talent, pomp, and wealth, then Sonoma Valley is its Siena, a place just as deeply committed to the art of wine but with a quieter air about it. In sheer number of wineries, Sonoma is outdone by its neighbor; in landscapes and ambition, it is its equal. And as the site of California's most northerly mission and the Bear Flag Revolt, the town of Sonoma has a historical importance that Napa can never match.

Hot-air ballooning at sunrise offers an unforgettable panoramic view of Sonoma Valley.

Sonoma

The heart of town comprises **Sonoma State Historic Park,** centered on the **Central Plaza.** Here, the **Bear Flag Monument** marks the place where, on June 14, 1846, a ragtag group of fur trappers and mountain men charged the quarters of Mexican commandante Mariano Vallejo, took him into custody, and raised a crude flag bearing a star, a grizzly bear, and the words "California Republic." The republicans were independent for less than a month. On July 9, U.S. Army captain John C. Frémont declared them part of the territorial United States.

The **Sonoma Barracks** (20 E. Spain St., tel 707-939-9420), built for the Mexican army, is also in the plaza, as is **Lachryma Montis** (Spain & 3rd Sts., tel 707-938-9559), the Gothic Revival mansion built in 1852 near a mineral water spring–hence the name, meaning "tears of the mountain."

Just off the plaza is **Mission Solano** (tel 707-938-9560), the last of California's missions to be built. Founded in 1819, it represented the ambitions of its founder, Padre José Altamira. He hoped to use it to usurp the leadership of Mission Dolores and Mission San Rafael to the

(continued on p. 264)

Sonoma

🗺 254 C1 & 255 B1

Visitor Information

✉ Visitors Bureau, 453 1st St. E., Sonoma

☎ 707-996-1090

www.sonoma valley.com

Sonoma State Historic Park

✉ 363 Third St. W.

☎ 707-938-9560

www.parks.ca.gov

ANATOMY OF A SPARKLING WINE

First associated with the kings of France, champagne—or sparkling wine as it is more properly called in general—came to be linked across Europe, in the 17th to 19th centuries, with power and royalty. Later, upwardly mobile middle classes adopted the drink for festivals and rites of passage, a potent symbol of the levels of luxury and wealth to which they aspired.

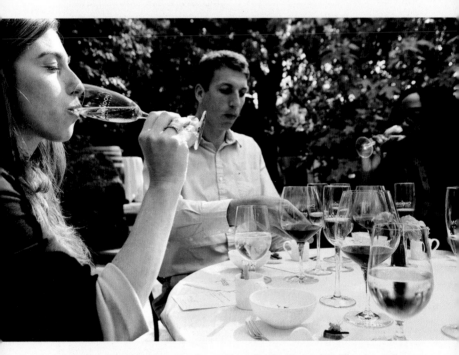

Established in 1973, Domaine Chandon was Napa's first French-owned sparkling wine producer.

Although it is fairly easy to learn about the making of wine in the U.S. these days, the same cannot be said of sparkling wine. Its production continues to mostly be a European affair, even to the extent that, in recent years, there has been bitter controversy over the use of the name "champagne" to refer to wines produced anywhere except in the Champagne region of France.

In wine country, however, there are several places where you can get an idea of what goes into a bottle of the drink that, as Woody Allen said, "tingles the tongue as it mangles the brain." One such place is **Domaine Chandon** (*map p. 255 C2, 1 St. Helena Hwy., Yountville, tel 707-204-7461, www.chandon.com*). Here they still use the ancient and revered *méthode champenoise,* as worked out by a 17th-century monk named Dom Pérignon, to create a sparkling wine.

The first step in the method is the crush— or, rather, **the press.** Sparkling wine requires a lighter hand than still wine in order to minimize the presence of tannin, a bitter chemical compound that comes from grape skins. The juice then goes into its first fermentation in giant stainless steel tanks.

Next comes the **blending** process, a careful addition and mixing of various grape juices that will produce the desired flavors. To this *cuvée* the winemaker adds a *liqueur de tirage*, a mixture of yeast and sugar that activates another round of **fermentation** as the liquid is poured into bottles and sealed. This causes the wine to produce more carbon dioxide, infusing itself with champagne's characteristic bubbles. Now the bottles are put in storage for two to five years, depending upon the cuvée.

During this period of **autolysis,** the wine takes on its unique characteristics—its smell, texture, and color. To collect the yeast sediment, the bottles are riddled, or turned, several times a day. At Domaine Chandon, the process is done by a machine called a gyropallette, or by hand. Winemakers have devised an ingenious method to disgorge the sediment by first freezing the neck of the bottle, then unplugging it and letting the built-up carbon dioxide jettison it. The bottle is then corked, wired shut, and labeled.

EXPERIENCE:
Making Your Own Wine in Wine Country

Always wanted to try your hand at making wine? You're in luck because there are a few locals in wine country who will help you experience winemaking firsthand. One option is **Judd's Hill Winery** *(2332 Silverado Trail, Napa, tel 707-255-2332, www.juddshill.com)*, which offers a "Bottle Blending Day Camp" combining a class in viticulture and wine-tasting with a session in which you make your own wine by blending several varietals straight from the barrel. Although footstomping the grapes is passé, **Ram's Gate Winery** *(28700 Arnold Dr., Sonoma, tel 707-721-8700, www.ramsgatewinery. com)* lets you roll up your sleeves for its "Day in the Life" experience. After a Viticulture 101 amble through the estate with the winemaker, you may help thin or leaf the vines, help sort grapes or perform other tasks in the barrel hall, before enjoying a five-course flight.

Sparkling wine is stored in tanks at Domaine Chandon, which also produces still wines.

Glen Ellen

🗺 254 C1 & 255 B2

Jack London State Historic Park

🗺 255 B2

Visitor Information

✉ 2400 London Ranch Rd., Glen Ellen

☎ 707-938-5216

www.parks.ca.gov

Santa Rosa

🗺 254 C2

Visitor Information

✉ Convention & Visitors Bureau, 9 4th St.

☎ 707-577-8674

www.visitsantarosa.com

Charles M. Schulz Museum

✉ 2301 Hardies Ln., Santa Rosa

☎ 707-579-4452

🕐 Closed Tues. Sept.–May

💲 $$$

www.schulz museum.org

south, but his plans were found out. Altamira nonetheless built a substantial plantation, though his abused Native American laborers rebelled in 1826 and sacked the mission. The chapel on display today was built in 1841.

Facing the mission, the restored adobe **Blue Wing Inn** was originally built to house soldiers assigned to the mission; U.S. Army officer (and future President) Ulysses S. Grant was a guest.

The elegantly restored gold rush–era **El Dorado Hotel** (405 1st St. W, tel 707-996-3030, www .eldoradosonoma.com) features a good restaurant offering contemporary California cuisine.

The **California Missions Museum** (24737 Arnold Dr., tel 707-939-8051, www.californiamis sionsmuseum.com), at Cline Cellars winery, displays scale models of all 21 California missions.

Glen Ellen

For an introduction to California's olive oil industry, drive up the valley to Glen Ellen. Near the center of town is the **B.R. Cohn**

Winery & Olive Oil Company (15000 Sonoma Hwy., tel 707-938-5064, www.brcohn.com. $$$$$, by reservation), featuring a tasting bar and pressing mill.

To the northwest of town is **Jack London State Historic Park,** where the author is buried. His legacy to the valley was a nickname: the title of his book *Valley of the Moon,* by which this area is still known.

Santa Rosa

At the northern end of the Sonoma Valley, **Santa Rosa** warrants a visit to see its historic downtown; the **Charles M. Schulz Museum,** celebrating the life and art of the eponymous cartoonist who created *Peanuts;* and the **Luther Burbank Home & Gardens** (204 Santa Rosa Ave., tel 707-524-5445, www.luther burbank.org), where the famed horticulturist experimented with everything under the California sun. Some of Burbank's great triumphs are on display, including the Burbank russet potato and the Shasta daisy. ■

EXPERIENCE: Ancient Valley Retreat

Tucked into oak-strewn foothills about 50 miles (80 km) north of Sonoma Valley, you'll find the 1,600-acre (647 ha) **Harbin Hot Springs** (18424 Harbin Springs Rd., Middletown, tel 707-987-2477, www. harbin.org). Visit this nonprofit retreat and workshop center to explore its New Age benefits such as holistic healing and universal spirituality. Water is the main event here, with manmade pools of various temperatures fed by seven different springs. But you can also experience

plenty of other activities, including yoga lessons, massage and meditation sessions, shamanic circles and Kirtan chanting, Native American sweat lodges, and Tantric sex workshops.

You'll sleep well, too: Harbin offers a wide range of crash pads, from dorms and motel rooms to cottages and geodesic domes. You can also visit the complex without reservations with a six-hour or 24-hour pass ($$$$$). Camping is available nearby. No one under 18 is admitted.

SONOMA VALLEY WINERIES

In recent years, Sonoma wineries have attracted increasing attention for their diversity of flavor and mood—probably due to the weather, influenced by to the largely volcanic soils, and to microclimates owed to the Mayacmas Mountains and, in the southern Carneros AVA, the cool air of San Francisco Bay. Sonoma's wineries today offer vinos equal to any in neighboring Napa.

■ Visitors taste wine at Buena Vista Winery, said to be the oldest winery in the region.

Benziger Family Winery

A great place to start a Sonoma journey is at the Benziger Family Winery, near Jack London State Historic Park (see p. 264). To quote the prestigious *Wine Spectator* magazine, this is "one of the top ten winery visits in California." The winery was founded in 1980 by Mike Benziger, a native New Yorker. Later joined by his father and siblings, Benziger is focused on building a world-class *terroir*, or soil.

The tour, winding through unmatched wine country scenery complete with a redwood grove, brilliantly explicates the Benziger mission. Innovative trellising techniques, visible near the Viticulture Discovery Center, allow for maximum regulation of light, which in turn enables the vineyard to produce 25 different wines and 350 different flavors. Visitors also see how vines are grafted, trained, and maintained. There is a fine exhibit on cooperage—the art of barrelmaking—and a working bug farm, where natural methods of fighting pests are developed. Finally, there is the wine tasting room. The wine seems even better after a few hours spent wandering around in this blissful landscape of flavor.

Benziger Family Winery

🏔 255 B2

✉ 1883 London Ranch Rd., Glen Ellen

☎ 707-935-3000

🕐 By appointment only; closed Tue.–Wed.

💲 Tastings: $$. Tours: $$$$

www.benziger.com

EXPERIENCE: Fishing & Boating Clear Lake

The largest natural freshwater lake entirely in California, Clear Lake basks in the uplands 80 miles (129 km) north of Sonoma Valley. Its hundred miles (160 km) of shoreline support boating, fishing, waterskiing, and windsurfing. As the self-proclaimed "Bass Capital of the West," the lake hosts several national fishing competitions and is renowned for the immense size of its largemouth bass.

Travelers who have their own watercraft can launch from 11 free public ramps around the lakeshore. A number of outfitters rent boats and equipment, including **Disney's** (401 S. Main St., Lockport, tel 707-263-0969, www.disneysboatrentals.com). Alternatively, let someone else do the "driving" and sign up for a 1.5-hour cruise on the lake aboard the **Lady of the Lake** (Seawall, Clear Lake, tel 641-357-2243, www.cruiseclearlake.com, $$$).

For a list of local fishing guides, log onto the Lake County tourism website (www.lakecounty.com).

Buena Vista Winery

🏔 255 C1
✉ 18000 Old Winery Rd., Sonoma
☎ 800-926-1266
💲 Tastings: $$$$$

www.buenavista winery.com

Kendall-Jackson Winery

🏔 254 B2
✉ 5007 Fulton Rd., Fulton
☎ 866-287-9818
💲 Tour & Tastings: $$$$$

www.kj.com

Sebastiani Winery

🏔 255 B1
✉ 389 4th St. E., Sonoma
☎ 707-933-3201
💲 Tastings: $$$$$

www.sebastiani.com

The Benziger family's **Imagery Estate Winery & Art Gallery** (14335 Hwy. 12, Glen Ellen, tel 707-935-3000 or 877-550-4278, www.imagerywinery.com, tastings: $$) produces rare wines. Its "Artists Collection," numbering almost 200 uncommon varietals, features labels specially commissioned from leading contemporary artists.

Buena Vista Winery

Historic Buena Vista Winery, in the Carneros region south of Sonoma, certainly lives up to the regal aspirations of its founder, Agostin Haraszthy. This Hungarian noble-turned-émigré-farmer came to Sonoma seeking a rustic empire. By 1860, after a tumultuous stint as an official at the U.S. Mint in San Francisco, Haraszthy had amassed some 6,000 acres of pristine valley floor. Not content with the local vines, he returned to Europe in 1861 and sent back more than 200,000 cuttings from 1,400 grape varieties. Among them were some of a pest-resistant strain that would save the nascent industry time and time again in subsequent decades. The result of his labors, much of it in evidence today, has earned him the uncontested title of father of California viticulture.

Kendall-Jackson Winery

Buena Vista may be Sonoma's most historic winery, but, with 3,700 acres (1,497 ha), the largest vineyard owner in the valley is the Jackson Family, whose Kendall-Jackson Winery is their flagship estate. The tour here includes a wine-tasting, and you can splurge for wine-and-food pairings, or even chocolate or cheese pairings. Also explore its four acres (1.6 ha) of gardens, including fruit, herb, and vegetable gardens; try the one-hour guided tour ($$$), offered twice daily.

Sebastiani Winery

Just a few blocks from the plaza in Sonoma lies the Sebastiani Winery. Its tour has been highly praised by Wine Spectator. ■

RUSSIAN RIVER

The area most favored by Bay Area weekenders for nearly a century, this lush and scenic river valley offers outdoor pursuits—canoeing, fishing, swimming, and bicycling, to name just a few—and is dotted with a number of outstanding wineries.

The tiny resort town of **Guerneville,** in the heart of the valley, offers one of the most interesting wineries: **Korbel Champagne Cellars.** Founded about 130 years ago on the site of a lumber mill, the winery retains an old blacksmith shop and general store for viewing. A rose garden, with more than 250 varieties of antique roses, is the subject of a half-hour tour. Two miles (3 km) north of town, **Armstrong Redwoods State Natural Reserve** *(17000 Armstrong Woods Rd., tel 707-869-2015, www.parks.ca.gov)* beckons with trails through a Coast redwood grove.

Charming Healdsburg *(visitor information, 217 Healdsburg Ave., tel 707-433-6935, www.healdsburg.com)* has many wine tasting rooms. North of town, the **Francis Ford Coppola Winery** is outstanding for its bocce courts and movie gallery, including memorabilia from the eponymous director's movies, most notably a Tucker car from the namesake movie.

For a good sandwich, stop at the Dry Creek General Store on Dry Creek Road just outside of Healdsburg. Then go on to the splendid **Ferrari-Carano Winery.** The wine is outstanding, but so are the 5-acre (2 ha) gardens, with 18,000 tulips in spring.

Northeast of Santa Rosa is lush Alexander Valley, famous for its orchards. In summer, **Foley Sonoma** offers food and wine events, as well as a series of evening concerts. The setting alone is worth the drive. Beautiful **Trentadue Winery** *(19170 Geyserville Ave., Geyserville, tel 707-433-3104 or 888-332-3032, www.trentadue.com)* is known for its outstanding sangiovese. ■

Guerneville

🏞 254 B2

Visitor Information

✉ Visitor Center, 16209 1st St., Guerneville

☎ 707-869-9000

www.russianriver.com

Korbel Champagne Cellars

✉ 13250 River Rd., Guerneville

☎ 707-824-7000

www.korbel.com

Francis Ford Coppola Winery

✉ 300 Via Archimedes, Geyserville

☎ 707-857-1471

💲 Tastings & Tours: $$$$$

www.thefamilycoppola.com

Ferrari-Carano Winery

✉ 8761 Dry Creek Rd., Healdsburg

☎ 707-433-6700, 800-831-0381

www.ferrari-carano.com

Foley Sonoma

✉ 5110 Calif. 128, Geyserville

☎ 707-433-1944

www.foleysonoma.com

▪ The heat of summer recedes with a float down the Russian River.

THE SONOMA COAST

Due west of wine country is the gorgeous Sonoma Coast, a 50-mile (80 km) stretch of seaside hamlets, tranquil farmland, and rugged seascapes that rivals Big Sur in terms of sheer beauty.

■ Pacific sunset at Bodega Bay

Bodega Bay

Start your exploration of the Sonoma coast at its southernmost point, **Bodega Bay** (map p. 254 B1; visitor information, Chamber of Commerce, tel 707-347-9645, www.visitbo degabayca.com), named for Spanish mariner, Juan Francisco de la Bodega y Quadra, who charted this coast in 1775. This is also the place where Alfred Hitchcock filmed The Birds (1963), and visitors still flock to the town in search of movie locations like the old Potter Schoolhouse in inland Bodega village.

Get out on the water during a 3-hour voyage with **Bodega Bay Sailing Adventures** (tel 707-318-2251, www.bodegabaysailing.com, $$$$), or with **Bodega Bay Kayak** (tel 707-875-8899, www.bodegabaykayak.com), which also has paddleboards. Afterward, dine along the waterfront at **Spud Point Crab Company** (1860 Westshore Rd., Bodega Bay, tel 707-875-9472, www.spudpointcrabco.com), or buy your own picnic fixings at **Diekmann's Bay Store** (1275 Calif. 1, Bodega Bay, tel 707-875-3517).

Sonoma Coast State Park (park headquarters, 3095 Hwy. 1, Bodega Bay, tel 707-875-3483, www.parks.ca.gov) begins on the northern outskirts of Bodega Bay, a sprawling reserve broken into several sections that embrace some of the most dramatic scenery along the Sonoma shore. Among its many natural landmarks are the **Bodega Dunes** and a rocky headland called **Bodega Head; Goat Rock,** near the mouth of the Russian River (see p. 267) and its resident harbor seals; and **Salmon Creek Beach,** with its tranquil lagoon, sandy spit, and turbulent surf. The circular drive around **Duncan's Landing** provides a great vista up and down the coast. The visitor center in Jenner is open only on weekends during the summer months.

Fort Ross

A dozen miles (19 km) north of Jenner is **Fort Ross** (map p. 254 B2, tel 707-847-3286, www.parks.ca.gov), one of California's more remarkable historic sites. Established in 1812 as Russia's southernmost point in the New World, the fort was abandoned in 1841 when the Russians left California. The reconstructed stockade and its redwood buildings reflect what life must have been like in this far-flung outpost.

Just beyond Fort Ross, enjoy a gourmet meal at Alexander's at **Timber Cove Resort** (21780 Calif. 1, Jenner, tel 707-847-3231, www.timbercoveresort.com), on a cliff-top perch above the waves.

Gualala

The Gualala River marks the northernmost extent of the Sonoma coast. Wedged between the river and the ocean is **Sea Ranch,** a sprawling resort community that includes the **Sea Ranch Golf Links** (42000 Calif. 1, tel 707-785-2468, www.searanchgolf.com) and **Gualala Point Regional Park** (42401 Calif. 1, tel 707-785-2377). ■

Cooler, greener, and full of natural wonders—home to coast redwoods and a paradise for outdoors folk

THE NORTH

One-room schoolhouse at Stone Lagoon, Orick, north of Eureka

THE NORTH

If much of California imagines itself as Mediterranean, its northern reaches identify with lands of higher latitudes. This is, after all, a land that Russian settlers tried (and failed) to claim in the early 19th century; it is a coast where Finns and Swedes dominated the fishing and shipping industries. Central to it is a storm system known as the Aleutian Low, which sends icy winds down from the Gulf of Alaska.

This is the California of great natural resources, its rugged terrain sprouting fine woods for the lumber industry, its waters giving bounty to generations of fishermen. Fortunately for travelers, much still remains. In and around Mendocino, great conifers still dominate the coastal rain forests. Farther north, coast redwoods tower over the junglelike vegetation of Redwood National Park. Here giant ferns and wild orchids create a dream world of filtered sun and foliage. Inland, at Mount Shasta, the manzanitas appear, their red stems hoisting aloft great low clouds of foliage.

In the Trinity Alps, you can drive all day through towering pines blanketed with fresh snowfall. Farther east, in remote Lassen Volcanic National Park, you can explore bubbling volcanic fumaroles, take a horseback ride

NOT TO BE MISSED:

through wildflower meadows, and stay at an old-fashioned summer lodge where hot springs run through the outdoor swimming pool.

Close to the Oregon border is Lava Beds National Monument, where battles once raged between Native Americans and settlers. Today,

amateur cavers can climb through the lava tubes that have been preserved here.

Alturas, in the northeastern corner of the state, is the capital of California bird-watching. Stay the night, and wake to the sounds of migrating wildfowl. ■

VAN DAMME STATE PARK

Its floor carpeted with lush ferns and redwood sorrel, its paths dotted with little log benches, Van Damme State Park makes for a perfect stopover on the long, winding, and windy road between San Francisco and Mendocino. Here, in a small area beside Calif. 1, is a classic northern rain forest with streams containing coho salmon, masses of wild rhododendrons, and one of the world's greatest stands of pygmy pine trees.

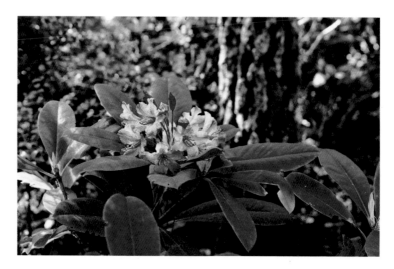

The cheery pink blooms of the Pacific rhododendron pepper the forest floor beneath tall redwoods.

**Van Damme
State Park**

🏕 270 B1

✉ E side of Calif. 1, 2 miles (3.2 km) S of Mendocino

☎ 707-937-5804 or 707-937-4016 (visitor center, open summer only)

www.parks.ca.gov

For the best views of the park, follow the **Fern Canyon Trail** from the end of the entrance road. Flat and well-marked with a series of numbered salmon sculptures, the trail originated as a logging road in the late 1800s. In 1936, the Civilian Conservation Corps built nine stream crossings and a series of rock embankments along the side of the streams. An idea of the difficulties encountered by the workers comes across in a staff report from the era: "This project is without a doubt the most disagreeable project we

are working on . . . the walls of the canyon are steep and heavily timbered and at this season, the sun seldom reaches that portion of the canyon where the men are working."

An opportunity to view the silvery coho salmon can be had nearby along the **Little River.** They were once so numerous that it was possible to catch them with bare hands, but the coho has in recent years suffered from increasing salinity and dwindling spawning habitats. A few moments spent by the stream will reveal the fish in one of three states. In winter, large adult fish begin to spawn, lodging themselves in pebbly basins and laying eggs before drifting down to the sea to die. In spring, the eggs hatch, producing dense schools of young. For the rest of the year, these young salmon feed, growing to a length of four to six inches (10–15 cm). By spring, they're ready for their journey to the sea; having memorized the scent of their home stream, they develop the silvery color required for survival in salt water. After two years in the ocean, they return to the Little River to repeat the cycle.

Visit during May and June and you'll witness another remarkable sight: the blooming of the Pacific rhododendron. Long studied for its adaptive abilities, this member of the heath family has leaves that roll under during the summer heat and pink, bell-shaped flowers in six-inch (15 cm) clusters.

The Pygmy Forest

The park's main attraction is the **pygmy forest,** reached by the old logging road. A self-guided trail leads through this wonderland of cypresses, Bolander pines, and bishop pines that stand only a couple of feet tall. The unique geology, heavy rainfall, and poor soil combine to produce the dwarf effect: Nutrients leached from the topsoil form a hard, impenetrable pan beneath the surface. With reduced nourishment, the trees' growth is stunted.

Various shrubs also grow here, particularly the (edible) huckleberry and the (inedible) manzanita. Walk the entire circumference for some outstanding photo opportunities. You can rent mountain bikes in Mendocino (see p. 274) and ride the trail, but bring a bike rack to avoid having to ride along the perilous Coast Highway. ■

Plant Life of the North

Just about everyone knows about northern California's coast redwoods (see pp. 278–283), but the plant life of the upper reaches of the state offers many other discoveries, too.

Closed-cone pines and cypresses: Four species of pine and ten of cypress dominate this group. All can thrive in infertile soils. Although they grow throughout the state, several species form concentrations in the north, from Van Damme State Park to Humboldt County. The most common are bishop pine, Douglas fir, Mendocino cypress, and Bolander pine. Their cones open only when exposed to intense sun or fire.

Manzanita (Arctostaphylos): A dramatic, low-growing brush with red trunk and lustrous leaves, the manzanita comes in several forms. Inland, at such places as McArthur-Burney Falls Memorial State Park (see p. 287), look for the stunning greenleaf manzanita, often found growing near magnificent incense cedars. On the coast, look for the low-growing Fort Bragg manzanita or the aptly named hairy manzanita.

Sagebrush (Artemisia): Although widely distributed throughout the state, sagebrush dominates much of the northeastern high desert. The plains are sometimes covered with shrubby sagebrush, while the big sagebrush grows on the eastern edge of the Sierra. Both are highly aromatic, the stuff of Native American and New Age apothecary alike.

MENDOCINO & AROUND

Inhabited by the valley-dwelling Pomo tribe from approximately 9500 B.C., the area was named by 16th-century Spanish settlers for Antonio de Mendoza, viceroy of New Spain. At the mouth of the Big River's outflow into the ocean, Mendocino's first Yankee pioneers quickly set up a lumber mill, and a town sprang to life. Its New England cast and stunning coastal setting attracted lumber barons and artists, lending Mendocino a uniquely photogenic charm.

■ Point Cabrillo Light Station

Mendocino & Fort Bragg

🗺 270 B2

Visitor Information

✉ Visitor Center, 45035 Main St., Fort Bragg

☎ 707-961-6300

www.visitmendocino.com

Today, the buffed-up village of Mendocino offers several good bed-and-breakfasts and lovely restaurants located in restored Victorians. Galleries on and around Main Street offer local art, some of it by nationally known landscape painters. Artists here are known for their creative use of natural materials such as wood and stone.

An excellent way to explore Mendocino's hinterland is by canoe, rentable at **Catch a Canoe** (*1 S. Big River Rd.707-937-0273, www.catchacanoe.com*). The canoes are fitted with special outrigger-style stabilizing devices, allowing even novices to explore the lush reaches of the **Big River.** Along the way to the **Mendocino Woodlands,** a wooded upland

area, lies a series of breathtaking scenic canyons, salt marshes, and streambeds populated with great blue herons, ospreys, and even harbor seals.

If you are here in winter, go to **Mendocino Headlands State Park** (*map p. 270 B1, off Calif. 1 just S of town, tel 707-937-5804, www.parks. ca.gov*) for gray whale-watching. To the north, **Russian Gulch State Park** (*map p. 270 B2, tel 707-937-5804, www.parks.ca.gov*) offers 36 miles (58 km) of coastal trail and the unique Devil's Punch Bowl—a collapsed sea cave through which waves churn dramatically. Just up the coast, the restored 1909 **Point Cabrillo Light Station** (*map p. 270 B2, tel 707-937-6122, www.parks. ca.gov*) is open for public tours.

In midsummer do not miss the **Mendocino Music Festival** (*tel 707-937-2044, www.mendocino music.com*), held on the bluffs above the sea!

Redwood Wine Country

Situated southeast of Mendocino along Calif. 128, the wine country of the redwood region is known for its diverse microclimates, producing leading labels of chardonnay, pinot noir, and sauvignon blanc. Many of the 300 vineyards center on the scenic Navarro River in the Anderson Valley (*www.*

avwines.com), the coolest wine-growing region in California.; in recent years, **Navarro Vineyards** *(5601 Calif. 128, Philo, tel 707-895-3686, www.navarrowine. com)* has received high praise for its pinot gris and cool-climate Alsace Varietals, notably Rieslings and Gewürztraminers.

A nice intermezzo to a day of winery touring is a picnic at the nearby **Navarro River Redwoods State Park** *(map p. 270 B1, just off Calif. 128, 2 miles/3.2 km E of Calif. 1, tel 707-937-5804, www. parks.ca.gov),* an 11-mile-long (18 km) "redwood tunnel to the sea," as local literature puts it.

Fort Bragg

The working lumber town of Fort Bragg was founded in 1857 as a military outpost and named for Gen. Braxton Bragg, hero of the Mexican War. On the edge of a redwood forest, it sits between two bodies of running water, the Noyo River to the south and Pudding Creek to the north. A charming way to see much of the hinterland is via the old **Skunk Train Railroad,** which takes passengers on rides hauled by a 1924 Baldwin steam locomotive. Constructed by lumber barons in the 1880s, the 40-mile (64 km) line snakes through dense stands of redwoods to **Willits,** where the notorious Black Bart robbed 27 coaches between 1875 and 1883, when he was "retired" to San Quentin prison in Marin County.

On the coast to the south are the **Mendocino Coast Botanical Gardens.** Founded in 1961, the gardens specialize in colorful rhododendrons, including hybrids, with collections of heathers, dahlias, camellias, and ivies. There are picnic areas, winding grass paths, and an ocean overlook. ∎

Skunk Train Railroad
- ✉ 100 W. 100 W. St., Fort Bragg
- ☎ 707-964-6371
- 💲 $$$$$
www.skunktrain.com

Willits
- 🅰 270 B2
Visitor Information
- ✉ Chamber of Commerce, 299 E. Commercial St., Willits
- ☎ 707-459-7910
www.willits.org

Mendocino Coast Botanical Gardens
- 🅰 270 B2
- ✉ 18220 N. Calif. 1, Fort Bragg
- ☎ 707-964-4352
- 💲 $$$
www.gardenby thesea.org

EXPERIENCE: Hiking the Lost Coast

North of Fort Bragg, California's Pacific Coast Highway (Calif. 1) suddenly jogs inland around shoreline too wild and rugged for even the most ambitious road engineers. Beyond this point, the 80-mile (128 km) stretch of redwoods and amber-colored sea cliffs, pristine beaches, and secluded hamlets is known as the Lost Coast. This region—the most remote stretch of coast between Canada and Mexico—is preserved within the **King Range National Conservation Area** *(U.S. 101 N to Garberville, follow signs, tel 707-986-5400, www.blm. gov/visit/king-range-national-conservation-area)* and the **Sinkyone Wilderness State Park** *(1 hr. N of Fort Bragg, tel 707-986-7711,* *www.parks.ca.gov),* both of which offer top-notch coastal hiking. The easiest access to the Lost Coast is via Shelter Cove *(map p. 270 B3),* 23 miles (37 km) west of Redway off U.S. 101 (exit 639B) along narrow Briceland Road. Shelter Cove offers the area's only noncamping accommodation. The 60-mile (96 km) **Lost Coast Trail** *(www.blm. gov/visit/lost-coast-trail)* starts at Black Sand Beach, in Shelter Cove, and ends in Mattole, where the campground *(tel 707-986-5400, www.blm.gov/visit/mattole-campground, $)* sits right on the beach at the north end of King Range. Allow about a week for the trip, which requires hikers to pack in all equipment and supplies.

EUREKA & AROUND

The center of California's massive lumber industry since the late 1800s, Eureka is like many midsize towns in the state—blessed with a charming historic core surrounded by ugly industrial zones. Yet Eureka holds several delights, both within its city limits and just beyond. Anyone planning to trek through some of the number of memorable national and state parks in this part of northern California will likely end up staying—or at least dining—here.

The William Carson Mansion is made mainly of redwood.

Eureka

🗺 270 A4

Visitor Information

✉ Convention & Visitors Bureau, 201 E. St., Eureka

☎ 707-798-6411

www.visiteureka. com

Eureka

Eureka's **Old Town** includes three fully restored Victorians. The extraordinary **William Carson Mansion** (143 M St., closed to the public), built in 1884 and now a private club, is a combination of Queen Anne, Italianate, and Stick-Eastlake styles. Also look for the 1889 **J. Milton Carson House** (202 M St., closed to the public) and the **Clarke Historical Museum** (240 E St., tel 707-443-1947, www.clarke museum.org), built in 1888.

At the **Blue Ox Millworks Historic Park** (1 X St., tel 707-444-3437, www.blueoxmill.com, closed Sun., $$) you can watch craftspeople use vintage machinery to make the gingerbread so evident in regional Victoriana. Finally, look in on the **Fort Humboldt Museum & State Historic Park** (3431 Fort Ave., tel 707-445-6564, www.parks.ca.gov) and find out about Ulysses S. Grant, who was stationed in Eureka in 1854.

The **Humboldt Bay Maritime Museum** (foot of C St., next to Samoa Cookhouse, tel 707-445-1910, www.humboldtbaymaritime museum.com, closed Sun.–Mon. & Thurs.) features a number of exhibits about local shipwrecks.

Before looking outside the city limits for travel destinations, try the 75-minute **Humboldt Bay Harbor Cruise** (tel 707-445-1910, operates summer only, $$$) on the old Madaket, a 1910 passenger ferry operated by the museum.

South of Eureka

Several places of interest lie south of Eureka on or around U.S. 101. The first is **Fortuna**, where an 1893 railroad depot is home to the **Fortuna Depot Museum** (3 Park St., tel 707-725-7645, closed p.m. Mon.–Wed. Sept.–May), specializing in antique train, fishing, and logging memorabilia.

Off U.S. 101 to the west is the delightful town of **Ferndale,** where one can ride in a horse-drawn carriage through a largely untouched 1890s town. Farther south on U.S. 101, at the riverside town of **Scotia** (map p. 270 B3), visitors can tour the **Scotia Museum** (tel 707-764-4252, 122 Main St., open summer only), which spins the story of the local logging industry.

South again, lies the little town of **Garberville** (map p. 270 B3, visitor information, Chamber of Commerce, 782 Redwood Dr., tel 707-923-2613, www.garberville.org), blessed with turn-of-the-twentieth-century architecture. One not to be missed is the Tudor-style **Benbow Inn** (see Travelwise p. 380). Between Ferndale and Garberville, the magnificent **"Avenue of the Giants"** (SR-254) snakes 32 miles (51 km) between soaring redwoods edging tight to the road in **Humboldt Redwoods State Park.**

Around Humboldt Bay

Across Humboldt Bay from Eureka is the historic **Samoa Cookhouse** (79 Cookhouse Ln., Samoa, tel 707-442-1659, www.samoacookhouse.net), the last logging-camp cookhouse in the western U.S. Enjoy a very hearty meal here and see the intriguing logging museum adjacent.

On the north side of the bay is the town of **Arcata.** Here the restored Gold Rush-era **Jacoby Storehouse** (791 8th St., tel

707-822-4500) is an architectural gem containing restaurants and historic displays and artifacts, and the **Arcata Marsh & Wildlife Sanctuary** (569 S. G St., tel 707-826-2359, www.arcatamarshfriends. org) is a perfect place for watching northern shorebirds. Just a bit farther north, the beach town of **Trinidad** (map p. 270 B4) stands on a dramatic seaside point.

Local Specialties

Regional specialties abound. Visit the **Loleta Cheese Factory** (252 Loleta Dr., tel 707-733-5470, www.artisancheesefactory. com), in nearby Loleta, where you can watch the company's award-winning cheese being made and try some free samples. Thin out your blood at Eureka's **Lost Coast Brewery** (1600 Sunset Blvd, tel 707-267-9651, www. lostcoast.com), which makes no fewer than eight award-winning brews. The Nectar ales and "beer cuisine" are served in a brewpub full of football memorabilia.

Nearby is **Sumeg Village** (map p. 270 B4, 4150 Patrick Point Dr., Patrick Point State Park, tel 707-677-3570, www.parks.ca.gov, $$). This 1990 re-creation of an ancient village has a working reconstruction of a traditional sweathouse. Today, the large Hoopa Indian reservation (map p. 270 B4), about 60 miles (96 km) inland from Eureka, is home to some 2,000 of the tribe. The **Hoopa Tribal Museum** (Hoopa Shopping Center, Calif. 96, tel 530-625-4110, www.hoopa-nsn.gov, closed Sat.–Sun. in winter) includes examples of dugout canoes and ceremonial regalia and offers tours of local villages and ceremonial sites. ∎

Fortuna
🗺 270 A3
Visitor Information
✉ Chamber of Commerce, 735 14th St., Fortuna
☎ 707-725-3959
www.friendly fortuna.com

Ferndale
🗺 270 A3
Visitor Information
✉ Visitor Center, 580 Main St., Ferndale
☎ 707-796-4477
www.visitferndale. com

Arcata
🗺 270 B4
Visitor Information
✉ Chamber of Commerce, 1635 Heindon Rd.
☎ 707-822-3619
www.arcata chamber.com

REDWOOD NATIONAL PARK

Coast redwoods have existed since the time of the dinosaurs. Awesomely large, like the dinosaurs, these Brobdingnagian trees towering up to 380 feet (116 m) appear on a scale not of a human-size world. They're ancient too: Some individual trees are more than 2,000 years old! Containing the largest concentration of living biomass in the world, these forests suffered immensely from logging in the late 19th-century: Today only about five percent remain. No wonder millions of visitors come every year to marvel at the few remaining stands of old-growth redwood forest.

Hikers appear Lilliputian beneath a fallen Brobdingnagian coast redwood.

Redwood National Park

⚐ 270 B4

Visitor Information

✉ Information Centers: 1111 2nd St., Crescent City; U.S. 199 at Hiouchi; & U.S. 101, S of Orick

☎ 707-464-7335

www.nps.gov/redw

Today, thanks to the renewed interest in the outdoors, California's redwoods are again the subject of human scrutiny. In fact, so many backpackers head into the wilderness that it has become necessary to control their numbers and activities more closely. Yet so far-reaching and awe-inspiring are these parks that, on a hike or even stopping for a picnic, it is still easy to feel you are the only person for miles around.

Four major redwoods parks in northern California lie close to the coast north of Orick, on coastal U.S. 101 north of Eureka, stretching almost to the state border with Oregon. Redwood National Park (1968) is by far the largest and the youngest. Together with three redwood-filled state parks (see pp. 280–283), it forms the heart of both a World

Redwood Flora & Fauna

First, a few redwood facts: The coast red-wood (Sequoia sempervirens) is the world's tallest tree, but not the thickest or the oldest. Those distinctions belong, respectively, to the giant sequoia (Sequoiadendron giganteum) or Wellingtonia of the Sierra and the bristlecone pine (Pinus longaeva), also an inland mountain species.

Although some specimens have been known to reach more than 2,000 years old, California's coast redwoods average between 500 and 700 years in age. Suffering from no known pestilence or fatal disease, the tree thrives on a vast system of ancillary roots that supports its main taproot. It can reproduce via sprouts as well as seeds, and new stems and roots can shoot from burned or cut-down trunks.

Redwoods are denizens of fog. They grow only in a narrow coastal strip some 450 miles long (725 km), from southern Oregon to southern Monterey county, subject to mild wet winters and to summer fog that swaddles the crowns and drips down to water the roots during dry summer months.

With a natural rain forest ecosystem feeding it moisture and nutrients, the floor of redwood forests teems with many smaller but equally fascinating and rare plants. Look for deer and sword ferns, redwood sorrel, redwood violet, and western trillium. Chanterelle mushrooms and many other fungi also thrive in this habitat.

The most common animals include Roosevelt elk, chinook salmon, and the huge banana slug, which flourishes in the damp conditions. Among birds to look for in the redwood parks are small seabirds called murrelets, and Steller's jay, a dark blue woodland bird with a black crest.

Heritage site and an International Biosphere Reserve.

At the **Kuchel Visitor Center** in Orick, you will find maps, books, displays, and helpful park rangers. (Requests for campground reservations should be made several months beforehand, particularly if you are planning a summer visit.)

To see the **Tall Trees Grove,** home of the world's second largest tree (360 feet/112 m; a 378-foot/115 m tree, Hyperion, was discovered in 2007 but is inaccessible by trail), you must first obtain one of a limited number of permits that allow you to drive to the trailhead. To get a permit, arrive at the visitor center early. The round-trip takes about four hours.

Lady Bird Johnson Grove can be reached by a self-guiding

INSIDER TIP:

If your time is limited, take in a 45-minute ranger-led forest walk at Stout Grove in Jedediah Smith Redwoods State Park (see p. 282).

—MICHAEL GLORE
Park ranger,
Redwood National & State Parks

loop trail that goes through mature forest and, finally, into the majestic grove dedicated by the former first lady in 1968. A flatter trail to the north, just south of the Prairie Creek park, is **Lost Man Creek.** This fern and moss forest has some fine rain forest flora. ∎

REDWOODS STATE PARKS

Together with Redwood National Park (see pp. 278–279), this region's three redwoods state parks—Prairie Creek, the farthest south; Del Norte Coast; and Jedediah Smith, in the north—are, with Humboldt Redwood State Park south of Eureka, the crown jewels of California's 48 coast redwood state parks. The parks, and the redwood forests they protect, spread along the northern coast of California and are the high points of any tour to the north.

■ A hiker looks up to a giant tree at Redwoods National & State Park.

Keep in mind that the entire coast redwood area is likely to be damp, misty, and often rainy—these are the climatic conditions in which redwoods flourish. But do not let the weather deter you from a thorough exploration of this area.

Prairie Creek Redwoods State Park

The 70 miles (112 km) of hiking trails in Prairie Creek Redwoods State Park range in difficulty from easy to very strenuous. There is also a scenic, 3-mile (4.8 km) drive, **Cal-Barrel Road,** to which any ranger can direct you, as well as the **Revelation Trail,** specially created for blind and partially sighted visitors.

At center stage of the Prairie Creek experience are the Roosevelt elk, which graze placidly on the **Elk Prairie** and on **Gold Bluffs Beach.** A member of the deer family, the elk or, as the Shawnee knew them, wapiti, have a tawny brown coat and a thatch of white on their rump. The animal is native to the Pacific Northwest, with a population numbering approximately 2,000. Do not approach them. Rather, use the well-marked **Elk Prairie Trail,** a 1.3-mile (2 km) loop skirting the eastern edge of the Elk Prairie. Black bear also roam

The Klamath River Overlook is a must-see. On a clear day, you can often spot Pacific gray whales, sea lions, harbor seals, osprey, and bald eagles as the river empties into the Pacific Ocean.

—MICHAEL GLORE
Park ranger,
Redwood National & State Parks

the forest, and mountain lions are active by night.

From here begin a number of hiking trails *(maps from the visitor center at park entrance).* If time is limited, try the **Five-Minute Trail,** which begins just behind the visitor center. Along this trail are several trees that have been hollowed out by fires; a close look may reveal traces—carved initials,

gougings, seat-worn spots—of the families who lived here during the Great Depression.

The **Fern Canyon Loop,** about half a mile in length, takes in a spectacular natural feature where 50-foot (15 m) canyon walls tower above a mossy floor. Among the species of fern that grow luxuriantly in this sheltered, moist spot are the five-fingered, deer, lady, and sword varieties.

A favorite trail is the beautiful **South Fork–Rhododendron– Brown Creek Loop.** A walk of just over 3 miles (4.8 km), it takes in ghostly stands of moss-covered redwoods, ancient tree trunks covered with red, green, orange, and yellow mushrooms, and placid ponds, their surfaces mirrorlike in stillness. For mountain bikers, who are discouraged from most state and national parks, there is a designated 19-mile (30 km) **Bicycle Trail.** It begins where the Elk Prairie campground road links with the jogging trail.

Prairie Creek Redwoods State Park

🏕 270 B4
✉ Turn off U.S. 101 at Newton B. Drury Scenic Parkway
☎ 707-488-2039 or 707-465-7335

www.parks.ca.gov

Klamath River Overlook

🏕 270 B5
✉ Turn off U.S. 101 at Requa Rd.

CAMPING: Prairie Creek Redwoods State Park, Elk Prairie Campground, 127011 Newton B. Drury Pkwy., tel 707-488-2171

The Indian Jerusalem

North of Prairie Creek, near Klamath at the **Klamath River Overlook,** you can visit a place that is the source of an enchanting Native American myth. Walk down the hillside path, past fragrant wild fennel. At the top of an old wooden stairway, as you gaze out onto the mouth of the Klamath River, contemplate the following story.

Once upon a time, according to Klamath oral tradition, the river's outlet was located 6 miles (9.6 km) to the north, retained in its path by two sharp parallel bluffs. Then came the Klamath version of Jesus Christ, a man named

Po-Lick-O-Quare-Ick. The Wise One, as he was known, had a long and fruitful mission among his people and was greatly loved. When his mission ended, his subjects grieved as he paddled down the river, out to sea. Then, as the Wise One wound his way downriver, he issued a command, obeyed immediately by the twin bluffs, which separated, allowing the river to run a more natural course. Po-Lick-O-Quare-Ick then disappeared into the gold rays of the Pacific sun. Ever since, the Klamath has followed his course, and the Wise One's people have had something by which to remember him.

EXPERIENCE: Mountain Biking in the Redwoods

Encompassing more than 9,600 acres (3,884 ha), Jedediah Smith Redwoods State Park (see below, and www.redwood hikes.com) is home to many of the world's oldest redwood trees. In the early 1900s, the park's **Howland Hill Road** was a thoroughfare for logging operations. Today, the hard-packed dirt road that ascends gently through these silent giants is great for mountain biking.

Begin the ride (5 miles/8 km each way) at the point where the park's paved road becomes gravel and dirt. As you begin pedaling, the hill slopes gently down on your right into Mill Creek. The old-growth trees are dense here, and the towering canopy filters most of the sunlight. The mostly shaded forest floor is smothered with all kinds of green understory, including ferns, redwood sorrel, and wild rhododendron. Continue past several hiking trails and through an intersection with a paved road to the left. When the path levels, park your bike and hike the **Stout Grove Trail** to see some of the park's oldest trees. The Howland Hill Road is an easy, nontechnical trail that is suitable for most riders, even children.

**Del Norte
Coast Redwoods
State Park**

🄰 270 B5

✉ U.S. 101,
13 miles (21 km)
N of Klamath

☎ 707-464-6101,
or 707-465-7335

www.parks.ca.gov

Crescent City

🄰 270 B5

Visitor Information

✉ Chamber of
Commerce,
1001 Front St.

☎ 800-343-8300

www.crescentcity.
org

**Jedediah Smith
Redwoods
State Park**

🄰 270 B5

✉ U.S. 199
(off U.S. 101)

☎ 707-464-6101,
or 707-465-7335

🕐 Closed Oct.–
mid-May

www.parks.ca.gov

Del Norte Coast Redwoods State Park

This 6,400-acre (2,590 ha) park stretches along the Pacific shore for some 8 miles (12.8 km) south of **Crescent City,** the most northerly town on the California coast. Del Norte's shoreline is spectacularly wild, and much of it is fairly inaccessible—not to mention foggy. Almost half of Del Norte consists of old-growth trees, from coast redwood to tan oak, madrone, red alder, and bigleaf maple. The dense understory vegetation supports a wide range of wildlife, from bobcat and coyote to bear and deer. Maps and guides for Del Norte, and other parks in the area, are available either from the visitor center in Orick (see p. 278), to the south, or from the main information center for the redwoods state parks in Crescent City, to the north.

A tsunami triggered by an Alaskan earthquake swept through much of Crescent City in 1964, causing several fatalities and wiping out most traces of the town's history as a focus for the surrounding gold mines.

From Crescent City, you can reach the ocean by car, driving south for 2 miles (3.2 km) to **Crescent Beach** and **Enderts Beach** (map p. 270 B5). A map of the coastal Damnation Trail is available at the visitor center. During the summer, guided tidepool walks take place at Enderts Beach, which is known for its teeming marine life.

Jedediah Smith Redwoods State Park

Named for the 19th-century pioneer-explorer who opened a trail to Oregon, Jedediah Smith Redwoods (east of Crescent City) is the northernmost of California's redwoods parks. Because of its situation a few miles inland, this park is sometimes sunny when the nearby coast is blanketed in the fog that is such a feature of the Pacific

Northwest seaboard. However, the weather is often wet and cold. The **Hiouchi Information Center** *(tel 707-458-3294, closed mid-Nov–mid-May)* is situated on U.S. 199.

Jedediah Smith has a range of hiking trails. A popular short hike, just half a mile (.8 km), is the **Simpson-Reed Discovery Trail,** which passes through a stand of western hemlock, Douglas fir, and tan oak. Another begins at the trailhead and goes to the 44-acre (17.8 ha) **Stout Grove** (see sidebar p. 282), where some coast redwoods are 1,500 to 2,000 years old.

You can also enjoy the park from the **Smith River** on a guided kayak tour. Fishing enthusiasts know the Smith for its runs of chinook and steelhead trout, but it is also popular for swimming and other water-based activities. Go rafting or kayaking, or rent bicycles, with Redwood Rides *(tel 707-951-6559, www.redwoodrides.*

com) in little **Hiouchi** *(map p. 270 B5),* where the Jed Smith Redwood Burl Company *(tel 707-458-3112, www.jedsmithredwood. com)* sells wooden tabletops and intriguing carvings. ∎

In Search of Sasquatch

Bigfoot legends have been around for centuries, but the hairy creature didn't become a household name until 1967, when Roger Patterson and Robert Gimlin filmed a creature walking casually along Bluff Creek in the Six Rivers National Forest of northern California. Although derided as a hoax by scientists, the film kicked off a bigfoot craze that endures to this day. Those interested in undertaking their own Sasquatch search can hike the **Bluff Creek Trail,** near the town of Orleans *(map p. 270 B4),* off Calif. 96. The **Willow Creek–China Flat Museum** *(tel 530-629-2653, www.bigfootcountry.net),* in nearby Willow Creek *(map p. 270 B4),* boasts plaster cast footprints and other alleged proof of the creature's existence.

Well-manicured trails lace the forests of Jedediah Smith Redwoods State Park.

DRIVE: MOUNT SHASTA

This driving tour, lasting up to a leisurely week, will take you to the major attractions of the remote and beautiful north, which is blessed with some of the state's most stunning scenery and least crowded parks. Depending on your schedule, you can treat it as a series of separate drives or opt for a shorter circular route by omitting the section north of Mount Shasta. Each major stopping point has accommodations and places to eat.

Start in the small town of **Red Bluff** ❶ (visitor information, Chamber of Commerce, 100 Main St., tel 530-527-6220, www.redbluffchamber.com), reached from the south on I-5 or from the west on Calif. 36, which cuts across the scenic South Fork Trinity River. (If you are coming from the coast, the latter entails a full day's drive. Be sure to check your brakes before departing.) Red Bluff, set on the Sacramento River at the junction of several routes, has a long tradition of hosting travelers.

Take I-5 north and make a brief stop, about a mile north of Red Bluff, at the **William B. Ide Adobe State Historic Park** (21659 Adobe Rd., tel 530-529-8599, www.parks.ca.gov). Ide was an early settler, an entrepreneur, and a leader of the 1846 Bear Flag revolt in Sonoma (see p. 261). In early Red Bluff, he literally served as judge, clerk, prosecutor, and defense attorney in trials of horse thieves. After a jury found them guilty, he would invariably sentence them to be hanged. His home has been preserved here, along with some fascinating relics of mid-19th-century ranch culture.

Arriving in **Redding** (visitor center, 1448 Pine St., tel 530-225-4100, www.visitredding.com), the region's largest city, the **Turtle Bay Exploration Park** (840 Sundial Bridge Dr., tel 530-243-8850, www.turtlebay.org, closed Mon.–Tues.) is worth a stop. This sprawling campus includes an arboretum and garden, an underground aquarium focused on the salmon's life-cycle, plus educational exhibits tracing the relationship between humans and nature. Walk the park's 710-foot-wide (216 m) Sundial Bridge—the world's largest sundial—spanning the Sacramento River; on the far side, a river trail offers a lovely stroll.

> **NOT TO BE MISSED:**
>
> Shasta Lake • Mount Shasta area • Lava Beds National Monument • Modoc National Wildlife Refuge • McArthur-Burney Falls Memorial State Park • Lassen Volcanic National Park

I-5 now cuts through increasingly dramatic terrain, crossing an arm of scenic **Shasta Lake** ❷, California's largest reservoir (29,740 acres/12,035 ha). If you have time for a detour, visit **Shasta Dam** (tel 530-247-8555, www.usbr.gov/mp/ncao), where tours of the powerhouse are given, and/or **Lake Shasta Caverns** (tel 800-795-2283, www.lakeshastacaverns.com, $$$$ including ferry from Lakeview Marina, E of O'Brien exit off I-5 on Shasta Caverns Rd.), on the lake's eastern shore. Here, you'll find illuminated stalagmites and stalactites.

Farther north, as you approach Dunsmuir, **Castle Crags State Park** (I-5, exit 724, tel 530-235-2684, www.parks.ca.gov) looms dramatically. Its 6,000-foot (1,828 m) spires mark the site of a war in 1855 between settlers (and their Shasta allies) and the Modoc. The Modoc fled, their numbers greatly reduced.

At 14,162 feet (4,316 m), **Mount Shasta** ❸ is almost permanently snow covered. A volcanic peak that last erupted more than 200 years ago, it is still an active volcano. The mountain left John Muir with a less than pleasant memory—so bad was the frostbite he suffered there one winter that the great man walked with a limp for the rest of his life. Today, with some planning, the area is at least as comfortable—and every bit as scenic—as

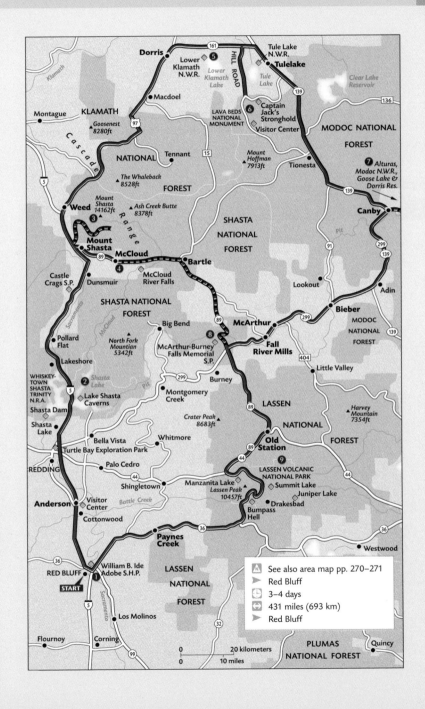

Dorris
161
Tule Lake N.W.R.
5
Tulelake
Lower Klamath N.W.R.
Lower Klamath Lake
Tule Lake
Clear Lake Reservoir
136
HILL ROAD
Montague
KLAMATH
Macdoel
Goosenest 8280ft
97
139
LAVA BEDS NATIONAL MONUMENT
6
Captain Jack's Stronghold
Visitor Center
MODOC NATIONAL FOREST
Klamath
Cascade
NATIONAL
Tennant
15
Mount Hoffman 7913ft
Tionesta
7
Alturas, Modoc N.W.R., Goose Lake & Dorris Res.
5
FOREST
The Whaleback 8528ft
139
Canby
Weed
Mount Shasta 14162ft
3
Ash Creek Butte 8378ft
SHASTA
NATIONAL
91
299
139
Range
Mount Shasta
McCloud
Bartle
FOREST
Lookout
Adin
89
4
Castle Crags S.P.
Dunsmuir
McCloud River Falls
McCloud
89
McArthur
299
Bieber
MODOC NATIONAL FOREST
139
Sacramento
SHASTA NATIONAL FOREST
Big Bend
8
Fall River Mills
Pollard Flat
North Fork Mountain 5342ft
McArthur-Burney Falls Memorial S.P.
404
Little Valley
Lakeshore
Pit
299
Burney
5
WHISKEY-TOWN SHASTA TRINITY N.R.A.
Shasta Lake
2
Lake Shasta Caverns
Montgomery Creek
Harvey Mountain 7354ft
Shasta Dam
Crater Peak 8683ft
LASSEN
Shasta Lake
Bella Vista
Whitmore
89
NATIONAL
Turtle Bay Exploration Park
Old Station
44
FOREST
REDDING
Palo Cedro
89
LASSEN VOLCANIC NATIONAL PARK
9
44
44
Shingletown
Manzanita Lake
Summit Lake
Anderson
Visitor Center
Lassen Peak 10457ft
Juniper Lake
Cottonwood
Bumpass Hell
Drakesbad
Battle Creek
36
Westwood
36
Paynes Creek
William B. Ide Adobe S.H.P.
36
LASSEN
RED BLUFF
1
START
NATIONAL
5
FOREST
Los Molinos
32
Quincy
Flournoy
Corning
PLUMAS
99
NATIONAL FOREST

See also area map pp. 270–271
Red Bluff
3–4 days
431 miles (693 km)
Red Bluff

20 kilometers
10 miles

The snow-covered cone of volcanic Mount Shasta last erupted in 1786.

other ski country. Mount Shasta may also be of interest for its mystical legends. A good place to stay, particularly when you are traveling in the summer, is the old lumber town of **McCloud** ④ *(visitor information, 303 Main St., tel 530-964-3113, www.mccloudchamber.com)*, a few miles east of I-5 on Calif. 89. The restored McCloud Hotel (see Travelwise p. 380) offers fine bed-and-breakfast service with beautiful rooms. During the day, visit one of the three local natural waterfalls in the area, where you can swim, picnic, and hike along easy trails *(maps available at the hotel)*.

At this point, you can opt for an abbreviated version of this drive: Rather than heading into the northern section, proceed southeast from McCloud on Calif. 89 and rejoin the drive at McArthur-Burney Falls.

The main drive continues north on I-5 to the old lumber town of **Weed** *(visitor information, Chamber of Commerce, 34 Main St., tel 530-938-4624, www.weedchamber.com)*. Bear northeast on U.S. 97 to cross the **Cascade Range.** The Great Basin region is represented here by the **Modoc Plateau**—high, dry, and flat. The **Klamath Basin National Wildlife Refuges Complex** *(visitor center, 4009 Hill Rd., Tulelake, tel 530-667-2231)*, encompassing six refuges, extends across the Oregon-California border and is home to spectacular bird populations.

Just before the state border, don't miss the turnoff on Calif. 161. Head east, cutting across California's northernmost reaches. A worthwhile first stop is at the **Lower Klamath National Wildlife Refuge** *(www.fws.gov/refuge/lower_klamath)* ⑤. This refuge and the nearby **Tule Lake National Wildlife Refuge** *(turn off Calif. 151 on Hill Rd. S,, www.fws.gov/refuge/Tule_Lake)* are a dream come true. The vast basin of marshes and shallow lakes is a winter haven for bald eagles and for more than a million migrant ducks, geese, and swans. During the breeding season, it is common to see herons and egrets, double-crested cormorants, and cinnamon teal.

Just to the south of Tule Lake is **Lava Beds National Monument** ⑥ *(tel 530-667-8113, www.nps.gov/labe)*. Be prepared here for extremes: of heat during the day, of cold in the evening. Begin by visiting a battleground most Americans do not even know about—that of the Modoc War. **Captain Jack's Stronghold,** at its center, is named for the ingenious Modoc warrior who in 1872 startled the U.S. Army by beating them in a series of skirmishes over land policy. Two short walking trails take visitors around Captain Jack's fortifications. Clustered near the park's visitor center are the famous lava tubes. These 30,000-year-old signs of volcanic activity were formed when the exterior of long lava flows cooled and hardened before their centers. When the flow stopped and the remaining molten lava ran out of the other end, a tube resulted. Many of these tubes contain brightly colored lichens. Some are open for visitors to explore. To do so, you will need warm clothes, hard-soled shoes, a helmet, a flashlight (the visitor center provides these), and a lot of common sense—for example, do not go alone. Park rangers conduct regular walking tours. They can also direct you to a number of petroglyphs, ancient Native American rock carvings before leaving the park on Calif. 139.

A detour for wildlife enthusiasts is to take Calif. 299 east from Canby to the little town of **Alturas** ⑦ *(visitor information, Chamber of Commerce, 600 S. Main St., tel 530-233-2512, www*

.cityofalturas.us), the focal point of an area that is outstanding for bird- and animal-watching. For a hearty meal, drive over to the Brass Rail (see Travelwise p. 379), which serves up giant portions of Basque-style cuisine in a family setting.

The big attraction in the Alturas area is the **Modoc National Wildlife Refuge** (5364 Cty. Rd. 115, Alturas, tel 530-233-3572, www.fws.gov/ refuge/modoc), a 7,000-acre (2,832 ha) park dedicated to the management and protection of migratory waterfowl. Don't underestimate its popularity; it may be remote, but professional ornithologists flock here every year. The reason: The refuge is an important resting and feeding area for migratory birds on the Pacific flyway. A total of 246 bird species have been spotted on the refuge, including 40 accidentals. In spring and fall, Canada geese and teal, mallard and widgeon, are everywhere. In summer come wading birds such as willets and avocets, plus several species of gulls and herons. In winter, you might spot a bald eagle. On your way, you may see a herd of pronghorn gathered on the edge of a local wild-rice farm. The best birding is April to May and September to October, when the greatest diversity of species is present. **Dorris Reservoir** permits boating and fishing April to September.

Anyone interested in pioneer history should make a further side trip north from Alturas on U.S. 395 to **Goose Lake.** Here, close to the point where California, Oregon, and Nevada meet, two important migrant trails converged. One, the **Applegate Trail,** was made in 1846 by a party of 15 men following cartographic information developed by the Hudson's Bay Company's trappers in the 1820s. The second, the **Lassen Trail,** was first trekked in September 1848; after a winter of few supplies and rough weather, the party was rescued, 40 miles (64 km) north of Sacramento, by Peter Burnett, who later became the first governor of California. Staff of the Modoc National Wildlife Refuge information center will give you information on these trails. Continuing the drive from Canby, follow Calif. 299 southwest, then head north on Calif. 89 for the entrance to **McArthur-Burney Falls Memorial State Park** ❽ (tel 530-335-2777, www.parks.ca.gov). Its 129-foot (39 m) waterfall—Theodore Roosevelt proclaimed it the "eighth wonder of the world"—is reached by a well-maintained footpath. Teeming with wildlife (the rare black swift nests here) and stands of fantastic incense cedar and ponderosa pine, the park is yet another of this region's undervisited gems. Several campsites are available, as are cabins, and small motels and inns just outside the park offer a restful natural getaway.

On the road once more, drive south on Calif. 89 to reach **Lassen Volcanic National Park** ❾ (see p. 288). The spectacular drive across the park on Calif. 89 is closed to travelers in winter, and occasionally even in summer in bad weather. Check current conditions with the park. Continue on Calif. 89 to Calif. 36, and go west to return to Red Bluff. In winter, take Calif. 44 to Redding, and then drive down I-5.

Scaling & Skiing Mount Shasta

Towering more than 14,000 snowcapped feet (4,267 m), Mount Shasta is a magnet for year-round outdoor activities. The most popular climbing route is **Avalanche Gulch,** on the southwest flank, an 11-mile (17.7 km) round-trip with 7,200 feet (2,195 m) of vertical gain that experienced hikers can knock off in a single day. Even during the peak of summer, crampons, helmets, and ice axes are highly recommended. During winter, Avalanche Gulch morphs into a gnarly backcountry ski piste that sometimes lives up to its deadly name.

More sedate slopes can be found at nearby **Mount Shasta Ski Park** (104 Siskiyou Ave., Mount Shasta, tel 530-926-8610, www.skipark.com), where the terrain ranges from beginner to black diamond.

LASSEN VOLCANIC NATIONAL PARK

One of the best kept secrets of the northwest is this 100,000-acre (40,468 ha) wilderness. Anyone wishing to impress friends with their summer vacation photos and have a great time in truly stunning scenery, away from the crowds of Yosemite, will find this place pure magic.

Lassen Volcanic National Park

🗺 271 D3 & 285

Visitor Information

✉ Calif. 36 E., Mineral

☎ 530-595-4480

💲 $$$-$$$$$

www.nps.gov/lavo

The park centers on 10,457-foot (3,187 m) **Lassen Peak,** a volcano that last erupted in 1915, producing an immense cloud of dust and covering the land around it with deep mud. The effects are still visible where Calif. 89, or Lassen Park Road, crosses the **Devastated Area** to the north of the peak.

The park's extraordinary volcanic landscape includes hot springs, bubbling mud pots, and gas seeping from holes called fumaroles at **Bumpass Hell** in the southwest. Elsewhere there are blue-green volcanic ponds, crystal-clear lakes, forests, and, in spring, wonderful verdant wildflower meadows.

Trails have been laid out by the National Park Service to enable visitors to explore the park's wonders. Keep to them—it goes without saying that hot springs, steam, and unstable ground can be hazardous and that care and common sense are necessary as you follow the trails.

The free "Lassen Park Guide" includes a list of accommodations. Choose from six campsites, most close to dramatic natural features, among them **Manzanita Lake** in the northwest, **Butte** in the east, and **Summit Lake** in the center. For a more comfortable stay, make reservations at Drakesbad Guest Ranch (see Travelwise p. 379). ∎

California's Lake District

Perched in the Cascade Range just north of Redding are three large reservoirs—Shasta, Trinity, and Whiskeytown—that make up the sprawling **Whiskeytown National Recreation Area** (map p. 271 C3–C4; visitor information, Visitor Center, Calif. 299 & John F. Kennedy Dr., tel 530-242-3400, www.nps.gov/whis). The watery wilderness lends itself to numerous outdoor pursuits, among them fishing, swimming, boating, waterskiing, and waterfront camping.

Jointly managed by the National Park Service and U.S. Forest Service, the three enormous lakes are best explored by houseboat over several days or even weeks. Larger than San Francisco Bay,

Lake Shasta is the largest of the trio, with 370 miles (595 km) of shoreline and seven marinas. **Shasta Marina Resort** (tel 800-959-3359, www.shastalake.net, $$$$$) rents luxury houseboats with full kitchen, multiple bathrooms, and satellite TV that sleep as many as 16 people. **Trinity Lake Marina** (tel 530-286-2225, www.trinitylakemarina.com, $$$$$) operates two marinas with similar houseboat rentals on secluded Trinity Lake. Those wishing to boat Whiskeytown, smallest of the lakes, can dock or rent boats at **Oak Bottom Marina** (tel 530-359-2671, www.whiskeytownmarinas.com), but note that "water craft" (Jet Skis) and water-skiing are not permitted.

The historic—and dramatic—core of California, now mined for great wines and stunning scenery

GOLD COUNTRY

Old-fashioned sign advertising gold prospecting for modern tourists

GOLD COUNTRY

Based on a chain of picturesque towns along Calif. 49, from Mariposa to Nevada City, Gold Country is a traveler's delight. Drive through it in a day, or probe, ponder, and explore it for a week. Unlike the far north, Gold Country—setting of the 1849 Gold Rush—has a strong tourist infrastructure, relatively short distances between major points, and (in season) a pleasant, warm climate. No wonder that its beautiful landscapes inspired the plein air painters of the early 20th century.

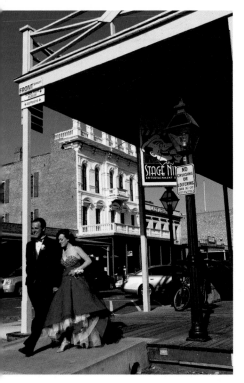

■ Old Sacramento, commercial hub of the gold rush

It is a region of grand, epic history. On January 24, 1848, a New Jersey émigré named James Marshall, working at a wood mill on the American River, spotted a lentil-size speck of yellow ore. He picked it up and then smashed it between stones. It was soft. It was gold. Word spread—to the bay, then

back east, then around the world. California was transformed. By 1850, its population had soared from 15,000 to nearly 100,000. As historian J. S. Hallidie wrote, "The world had rushed in."

The refined version of the story adds nuance, tragedy, and color. The gold rush was a triumph for some, but a disaster for the Native Americans routinely stripped of land and made ill with white man's diseases. It was also, in a sense, the end of Latin Catholic California, bringing as it did many Anglo Protestants and Yankee reformers. It was also a multicultural world, where Chinese mixed with Peruvians and blacks and Swedes and mountain men.

NOT TO BE MISSED:

Sacramento's splendid
    State Capitol building   292

Contrasting contemporary and
    Victorian architecture at the
    Crocker Art Museum   292

Bustling Old Sacramento   292–293

Historic trains at the California State
    Railroad Museum   292–293

Panning for gold   295

Sutter's Mill, where the story of the
    gold rush began   296

Getting cold and muddy in the
    region's celebrated caverns   298

Historic gold rush towns of Murphys
    and Jamestown   298–300

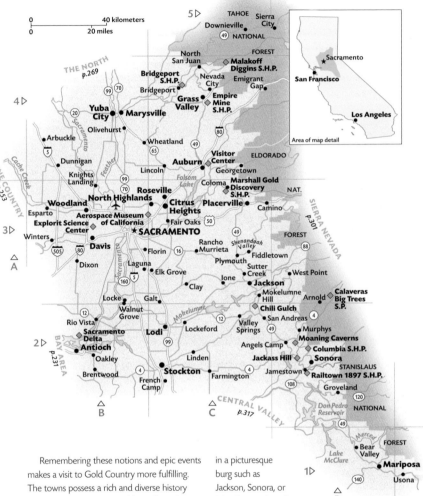

Remembering these notions and epic events makes a visit to Gold Country more fulfilling. The towns possess a rich and diverse history that can best be appreciated by walking along their streets. Each town offers mini-excursions and secret histories to visitors.

The Gold Country is a fine lead-in to Yosemite (see pp. 304–309). You could spend the first night in Grass Valley, with its fine restaurants and inns. Next day, explore the famous Empire Mine before heading south to Marshall Gold Discovery State Historic Park. Then stay

in a picturesque burg such as Jackson, Sonora, or Murphys—an introduction to the local wine and arts scene, both on an upward trend. Spend the next day seeing southern Gold Country, eventually putting up in Mariposa, a morning's drive away from Yosemite.

As with all historical destinations, it is a good idea to bone up before departing (for some suggestions, see Travelwise p. 347). ■

SACRAMENTO

Founded in 1839 by Swiss-born entrepreneur John Augustus Sutter, what is now the capital of California began its postcolonial life as one man's attempt to build his own feudal agricultural colony at the confluence of the American and Sacramento Rivers. When the gold rush came, the site was thrust into overnight prominence as gateway to the Mother Lode. Today, Sacramento is a sophisticated center of culture, history, and governance.

Find the center of California politics at the State Capitol in Sacramento.

Sacramento
🔲 291 B3
Visitor Information
✉ Convention &
Visitors Bureau,
1608 I St St.,
Sacramento
📞 916-808-7777
**www.
visitsacramento.com**

**Sutter's Fort
State Historic
Park**
🔲 2701 L St.
📞 916-445-4422
💲 $

www.parks.ca.gov

You can view what remains of Sutter's Fort, including copper and blacksmith's shops, a bakery, and a prison, on a self-guided audio walking tour of **Sutter's Fort State Historic Park.**

Sacramento's most distinctive building is the elegant 19th-century neoclassic **State Capitol** (10th St. & Capitol Mall, tel 916-324-0333, www.capitolmuseum.ca.gov). Guided tours include its superb museum.

Although politics dominates Sacramento's social landscape, the art scene thrives. Located in a 19th-century mansion and the futuristic new Teel Family Pavilion, the **Crocker Art Museum** (216 O St., tel 916-808-7000, www.crockerart.org, closed Mon.–Wed., $$$) has works by many European painters, from Albrecht Dürer to Hendrick Goltzius, as well as contemporary works by California artists.

In revitalized **Old Sacramento** (www.oldsacramento.com), a 28-acre (11.3 ha) site on the Sacramento River and onetime mercantile epicenter of the gold rush days, wooden sidewalks in front of historic buildings give the town a Wild West flavor. Don't miss the **California State Railroad**

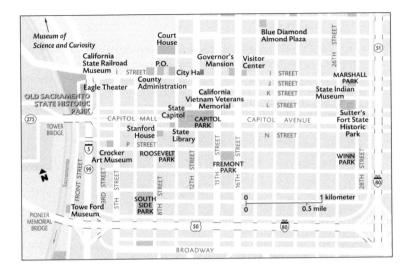

Museum (125 I St., tel 916-445-5995, www.californiarailroad.museum), the largest interpretive railroad museum in North America. From April to September, you can take a 40-minute steam train ride. Its 19 meticulously restored locomotives include many dating from the Gold Rush era, and a highlight is an impressive toy train collection and working layout.

The interactive **Museum of Science and Curiosity** (400 Jibboom St., tel 916-674-5000, www.visitmosac.org, $$), new in 2021, examines topics like science, space, natural history, archaeology, and robotics. The **State Indian Museum** (2818 K St., tel 916-324-0971, www.parks.ca.gov, closed Mon.–Tues., $) presents a different perspective on regional history. The **Explorit Science Center** (3141 5th St., tel 530-756-0191, www.explorit.org), in the nearby university town of Davis, is a hands-on science museum,

while the **Aerospace Museum of California,** on the former McClellan Air Force Base, showcases 34 aircraft, from early prop planes to supersonic jets.

For a novel and relaxing view of Sacramento, hop aboard the *Delta King* stern-wheel riverboat (1000 Front St., tel 916-444-5464, www.deltaking.com). ∎

Aerospace Museum of California

🖼 291 B3
✉ 3200 Freedom Park Dr., McClellan
☎ 916-643-3192
🕐 Closed Mon.
💲 $$

www.aerospaceca.org

Sacramento Delta

Many of the towns of the Sacramento Delta were founded by Asian immigrants. The "Potato King," George Shima, a 19th-century Japanese immigrant, created a potato empire on delta soil regarded as wasteland by his Anglo contemporaries.

The tiny town of **Locke** (map p. 291 B3), on Calif. 160, was the first community in the U.S. built entirely by Chinese for Chinese. Once a rowdy Wild West town full of booze, prostitutes, and opium, it now stands, picturesque and weathered, as a piece of working history. A museum traces its past.

NORTHERN GOLD COUNTRY

The towns of California's northern Gold Country are characterized by a cooler climate than those to the south, a strong community spirit, and a local pride in historical continuity–a history that stretches back to the first mid-19th century gold strike.

Old mining equipment and a prospector statue greet visitors in historic Auburn.

Downieville

291 C5

Nevada City

291 C4

Visitor Information

Chamber of Commerce, 132 Main St., Nevada City

530-265-2692

www.nevadacity chamber.com

Downieville

Established in 1851 by Maj. William Downie, Downieville, on Calif. 49, sat on so much gold that, as legend has it, a man boiling a locally caught fish found gold dust at the bottom of the pot. In the town center, on Main Street, is the 1855 **Sierra County Courthouse,** where several men were sentenced to swing from the gallows on Piety Hill, just behind. The **Downieville Museum** *(330 Main St., tel 530-289-3423, closed in winter)* displays a wide range of gold-rush artifacts. Amateur gold seekers can buy equipment at Sierra Hardware *(305 Main St., tel 530-289-3582, www.sierrahardware store.com).*

Nevada City

To the southwest on Calif. 49 is Nevada City, established in 1849 by miners seeking the rich gravel beds of the Lost Hill section, which yielded $8 million in gold dust in two years. The **National Exchange Hotel** *(211 Broad St., tel 530-265-4551, www.thenation alexchangehotel.com),* totally renovated in 2020, claims to be the "oldest continuously operating hostelry west of the Rockies."

Nevada City is still a welcoming tourist town, and also a base for gold-panning tours (see sidebar p. 295) and for visiting **Malakoff Diggins State Historic Park,** to the northeast. The broken landscape there still demonstrates the rapacious nature of the early (and fortunately short-lived) practice of hydraulic (or "placer") gold mining.

For a change of scene, admire the beautiful wildflowers along the **Buttermilk Bend Trail** near the South Yuba River State Park visitor center. Nearby is the 1862 **Bridgeport Covered Bridge,** at 229 feet (69 m) thought to be the longest single-span wooden covered bridge in the world.

Grass Valley

Grass Valley is acknowledged as the richest of California's mining towns, with production of more than $400 million over the course of a century following its founding in 1849. At 258 Mill Street is the 1852 home of sultry and bawdy-minded

dance-hall performer Lola Montez, known for her Spider Dance and the fact that she divorced her husband because he killed her pet bear when it attacked him.

The historic **Holbrooke Hotel** (212 W. Main St., tel 530-460-4078, www.holbrooke.com) was home away from home for Mark Twain, Bret Harte, and several U.S. presidents; the bustling hotel now offers fine cuisine in the restaurant, including local mushrooms and wild lettuce in the fall. Outside town is **Empire Mine State Historic Park** (10791 E. Empire St., tel 530-273-8522, www.parks.ca.gov), the oldest, richest mine in California. Guided tours are given, and the visitor center has a scale-model of the mine's 367 miles (591 km) of underground tunnels.

Malakoff Diggins State Historic Park

⬛ 291 C4

✉ 23579 N. Bloomfield Rd., Nevada City

☎ 530-265-2740

$ $

www.parks.ca.gov

Grass Valley

⬛ 291 C4

Visitor Information

✉ 248 Mill St., Grass Valley

☎ 530-273-4667

www.grassvalley chamber.com

EXPERIENCE: Panning for Gold

Although the Mother Lode is long gone, searching for gold remains a popular pastime and is generally allowed on public lands, including state and national parks. Many of the region's state parks also offer panning lessons. Among these are Bekeart's Gun shop (tel 530-295-1850) at **Marshall Gold Discovery State Historic Park** (see p. 296) in Coloma; **South Yuba River State Park** (tel 530-432-2546, www.parks.ca.gov) near Nevada City (see pp. 294–295); and **Matelot Gulch Mining Company** (22675 Main St., tel 209-532-9693, www.matelotgulchminingco.com) in Columbia State Historic Park.

Check with local chambers of commerce about conditions and the best places to pan. Or join an expedition with **Gold Prospecting Adventures** (18170 Main St., tel 209-984-4653, www.gold

prospecting.com, $$$), in Jamestown, which offers panning experiences and multiday prospecting courses in placer mining and mineral claims. **Roaring Camp Mining Company** (Calif. 88, Pine Grove, tel 209-296-4100, www.roaringcampgold.com, $$$$$), on the Mokelumne River, blends its gold-panning experience with a pioneer-style barbecue dinner on Saturdays.

You only need a few simple tools to try your hand at prospecting: a small trowel, a shovel, a gold pan to swirl the water and gravel to separate gold flecks, and an optional pair of waders.

Buy pans, shovels, and sluice box kits at **Matelot Gulch Mining Company** (see above) in historic Columbia or **Big Valley Metal Detectors** (8153 Juli Ct., Citrus Heights, tel 916-225-9150, www.bigvalley metaldetectors.com), near Sacramento.

Auburn

🏔 291 C4

Visitor Information

✉ Visitors Bureau,
1103 High St.
Auburn

☎ 530-887-2111

www.visitplacer.com

Coloma

🏔 291 C3

Visitor Information

www.coloma.com

**Marshall Gold
Discovery State
Historic Park**

🏔 291 C3

✉ 30 Back St.,
off Calif. 49,
Coloma

☎ 530-622-3470

💲 $

www.parks.ca.gov

Sutter Creek

🏔 291 C3

Visitor Information

✉ Visitor Center,
71A Main St.,
Sutter Creek

☎ 209-267-5647

www.suttercreek.org

Avio Vineyards

✉ 14520 Ridge
Rd., Sutter Ridge

☎ 209-267-1515

www.aviowine.com

Auburn

Established in 1848, the town of Auburn, at the junction of Calif. 49 and I-80, sits on a streamlet named Auburn Ravine, once the site of the richest placer gold mines in the state. The handsome 19th-century **Placer County Courthouse** (101 Maple St.) presides over the Old Town, and its museum (tel 530-889-6500) has several interesting historical exhibits.

Coloma

Coloma, farther south on Calif. 49, was the site of James Marshall's gold discovery. Spend an afternoon picnicking, hiking, and investigating the historical sites at the **Marshall Gold Discovery State Historic Park.** Trails lead from the Gold Discovery Museum & Visitor Center uphill to the Marshall Monument and Gravesite, to the riverside site of **Sutter's Mill,** to the Gold Discovery Site, to **Bekeart's Gun Shop** and a blacksmith's shop.

Shenandoah Valley

The rolling, oak-dotted hills around the **Shenandoah Valley** (map p. 291 C3) are well suited to farms and fruit orchards. This is also the center of Amador wine country, which is focused along Shenandoah and Fiddletown Roads. A beautiful back-roads drive can be made northward from Fiddletown to the Apple Hill farm collective, off U.S. 50 near the little town of **Camino** (map p. 291 C3); a more direct route runs east from **Placerville** (map p. 291 C3) on U.S. 50. Back south,

on Shenandoah School Road near the town of Plymouth (map p. 291 C3), the **Amador Flower Farm** (tel 209-245-6660, www.amadorflower farm.com) specializes in daylilies. It is surrounded by more than two dozen wineries open to visitors.

Sutter Creek

Sutter Creek played a key role in gold-rush history, attracting a number of investors to mine the Widman, Lincoln, and Central Eureka sites. The last, once almost abandoned by Leland Stanford, eventually produced the funds for him to invest in the Central Pacific Railroad. Sutter Creek is now the center of its own thriving mini wine country, typified by **Avio Vineyards.**

INSIDER TIP:

In Sutter Creek, stop into Knight Foundry (81 Eureka St., www.knightfoundry.com) to view America's last water-powered foundry, with functioning pulley-driven antique machinery.

—CHRISTOPHER P. BAKER
National Geographic author

The town, formerly a key goldfoundry center, has a fine historic district. Many old mercantile buildings built by Italian immigrants can be toured with the help of a map from the visitor center. On weekends from March to October, you can also explore the productive **Kennedy Gold Mine** (tel 209-223-9542, www.kennedygoldmine.com). ∎

SOUTHERN GOLD COUNTRY

It was in southern Gold Country that, with the stakes so palpably high, the gold rush turned violent. Here the "Mexican Robin Hood," Joaquín Murieta, is said to have begun his bloody pillaging. Here the first Chinese Tong wars were fought, and here slaves were allegedly sold and race riots fought over mining rights. Today the quiet, picturesque streets of southern Gold Country— from "Moke Hill" (Mokelumne Hill) to Mariposa—betray none of that churning, fugitive, and violent history. Instead, there is a placid ambience of a wine country in the Sierra.

Costumed guides at Columbia State Historic Park show visitors how to pan for gold.

Jackson to Angels Camp

Once a prominent stop on the old Carson Emigrant Trail and now the crossroads of north–south Calif. 49 and east–west Calif. 88, **Jackson** came into its own as a town in 1850. Its early name, Bottileas, was a reference to the many broken whiskey bottles found on its hell-raising streets. The Argonaut Mine, still visible south of Calif. 88, sunk its shafts more than one mile below the surface. The town briefly became the seat of Calaveras County after ambitious Jacksonians literally pilfered government archives from nearby Double Springs, only to be out-politicked the next year by neighboring "Moke Hill," which then assumed the title. Today Jackson is a bustling town, full of cafés, Italian restaurants, and bookstores (see sidebar p. 300).

Established as a Mexican mining camp in 1849, **Mokelumne Hill,** farther south on Calif. 49, was once one of the most boisterous gold towns, where shootings were a weekly affair. A walking tour map can be obtained from the Hotel

Jackson

291 C3

Visitor Information

Visitor Center,
125 Peek St.,
Jackson

209-223-1646

www.ci.jackson.ca.us

Mokelumne Hill

291 C3

Calaveras County Museum

✉ 30 N. Main St., San Andreas

☎ 209-754-1058

$ $

www.calaverasco historical.com

Angels Camp

◭ 291 D2

Visitor Information

✉ Visitor Center, 1192 S. Main St., Angels Camp

☎ 209-736-0049

www.angelscamp .gov & www. gocalaveras.gov

Murphys

◭ 291 D2

Leger (830 Main St., tel 209-286-1401, www.hotelleger.com), but it hardly does justice to the region's eventful past. For example, French Hill, just to the south, is where the so-called French War was fought in 1851, when American miners literally took up their picks to drive off overly aggressive French upstarts. South of there on Calif. 49 is **Chili Gulch** (map p. 291 C2), site of the Chilean War of 1849. This time, the Americans were driven out by Chileans angered by attempts to expropriate their mining claims.

Another Mexican camp, established in 1848, **San Andreas** (map p. 291 C2) may be the site of the tavern portrayed in Mark Twain's story "The Celebrated Jumping Frog of Calaveras County" (see p. 42). Ask at the **Calaveras**

County Museum if you can see the reputedly genuine red sash of the local bandito Joaquín Murieta (see Murphys, below). The museum also has relics of the Miwok, who once dominated the region.

Then again, **Angels Camp,** say locals, is where Twain got the inspiration for the bar scene in "Jumping Frog." Today the historic main street is lined with several boutiques, a few cafés, and **Angels Camp Museum & Carriage House** (753 S. Main St., tel 209-736-2963, $$, closed Tue.–Wed.), displaying a large collection of wagons, stagecoaches, and Gold Rush memorabilia.

Murphys & Around

Established in 1848, Murphys, off Calif. 49 on Calif. 4, is said to be where Joaquín Murieta got his ire. A three-card monte dealer in 1851, Joaquín had watched as his brother was hanged on a bogus charge of horse thievery. After Joaquín himself was flogged, he embarked on two years of his own brand of bloody thieving. Murieta was eventually killed near Fresno. The Yankees hated him so much they cut his head off and displayed it in a jar.

Today Murphys is one of the best preserved gold rush towns. **Murphys Historic Hotel** (457 Main St., tel 209-728-3444, www.murphyshotel.com) is worth a look—after all, Mark Twain and President Ulysses S. Grant both slept there. The **Murphys Creek Theatre** (tel 209-728-8422, www .murphyscreektheatre.org) produces

---

EXPERIENCE:

Spelunking

Caves of all shapes and sizes riddle the ground beneath Gold Country. **Moaning Caverns** (map p. 291 D2; 5350 Moaning Cave Rd., Vallecito, tel 209-736-2708, www. moaningcaverns.com), south of Murphys, began attracting the curious during pioneer days. Choose a short descent by spiral staircase or a more adventurous 3-hour tour that involves crawling through narrow passages. **Gold Country Adventures** (tel 888-488-1960, www.cavetouring.com) offers descents into **Black Chasm Cavern,** near the town of Volcano in Amador County, and **California Cavern,** 12 miles (18 km) east of San Andreas. The Yokut once used the **Mercer Caverns** (1665 Sheep Ranch Rd., Murphys, tel 209-728-2101, www.mercercav-erns.net) in Calaveras County as a place to bury their dead, but nowadays the living limestone wonder is open to visitors.

For a taste of the Old West, take a walk down Main Street in Angels Camp.

excellent year-round drama, ranging from Shakespeare and Moliére to Henry James and Stephen Sondheim.

To see giant sequoias close up, travel northeast from Murphys on Calif. 4 to **Calaveras Big Trees State Park,** near the little town of Arnold. The biggest trees are in the more popular North Grove; the more remote, and therefore less-visited, South Grove offers solitude in which to commune with nature.

Murphys is a good place from which to explore Calaveras wine country, particularly the beautiful **Ironstone Vineyards** *(1894 Six Mile Rd., tel 209-728-1251, www .ironstonevineyards.com).* The winery occupies a stunning building modeled on a 19th-century gold stamp mill. Pick up a picnic lunch in Ironstone's deli and drive south on Parrotts Ferry Road to **Columbia State Historic Park,** a preserved gold rush town with a difference: Here it is not only the buildings that recall the 1850s. A stagecoach, costumed guides, gold panning, live theater, and music in historic saloons all help Columbia to re-create the days when its

importance made it a rival of Sacramento (see pp. 292–293) in the race to be state capital.

While there may be disputes over aspects of Twain's "Jumping Frog," no one contests its provenance—now a tiny, dilapidated wooden shack perched in a quiet grove of black and live oaks on **Jackass Hill** *(map p. 291 D2, turn left up Jackass Hill Rd. from Calif. 49, S of Carson Hill, N of Turtletown).* Here Twain, puffing his pipe and worrying over his San Francisco debts, crafted his tale. Anyone with a literary soul should make this pilgrimage. Yet few do, making this a lonely and beautiful site.

Established in 1848 by Mexican miners, **Sonora** teemed with political intrigue during its early years. A riot almost occurred in 1850, when the new U.S. government imposed a $20 tax on foreign-born miners. Eventually the Mexicans fled, but not before a group of Anglo settlers had marched in a display of bellicosity. Today Sonora is an exciting little town, replete with cafés, restaurants, shops, and cultural events such as the Twaine Hart Summer Art & Wine Festival held

Calaveras Big Trees State Park

🔺 291 D3

✉ 1170 Calif. 4, Northeast of Murphys

☎ 209-795-2334

www.parks.ca.gov

Columbia State Historic Park

🔺 291 D2

✉ 22708 Broadway St., Columbia

☎ 209-588-9128

www.parks.ca.gov

Sonora

🔺 291 D2

Visitor Information

🔲 Visitors Bureau, 193 S. Washington St, Sonora

☎ 209-533-4420, 800-446-1333

www.visittuolumne. com

Railtown 1897 State Historic Park

✉ 5th Ave., Jamestown

☎ 209-984-3953

🕐 No trains Nov.–March

💲 $$$

www.railtown 1897.org

Mariposa

🗺 291 D1

Visitor Information

✉ Tourism Bureau, 5065 Calif. 140

☎ 209-966-7081, 866-425-3366

www.yosemite.com

here in July (tel 209-533-3473, www.fireonthemountain.com). See gold rush memorabilia at the **Tuolumne County Museum & History Center** (158 Bradford Ave., off Washington St., tel 209-532-1317, www.tchistory.org).

Jamestown (map p. 291 D2), established in 1849 by Col. George James, is now a tiny burg with many cute shops. The main attraction here is the **Railtown 1897 State Historic Park,** an extension of the California State Railroad Museum in Sacramento (see pp. 292–293). A 40-minute, 6-mile (9.6 km) ride in an old steam-powered train is a fine way to end a day of exploring, and there is a collection of locomotives, carriages, and mementoes.

Mariposa

A gateway to Yosemite (see pp. 304–309), Mariposa has an interesting old courthouse and jail. Details of its days as a 19th-century mining and railroad center are preserved at the **Mariposa Museum & History Center** (5119 Jessie St., tel 209-966-2924, www.mariposa museum.com, $) and the **California State Mining & Mineral Museum** (off Calif. 49, S of Mariposa, tel 209-742-7625, www .parks.ca.gov, closed Mon.–Wed., $). After his run for the Presidency failed in 1856, John C. Frémont lived in a house on Calif. 140 with his wife, whose Mother Lode Narratives gives insight into her remarkable life. ■

Gold Country Shopping

Although Gold Country shopping has its requisite share of cute, it also has a great variety of refreshingly down-to-earth establishments. **Antiques:** An outstanding antique collective is **Creekside Shops** (22 Main St., Sutter Creek, tel 209-267-5520), where you might pick up anything from a McCoy vase to a first edition of an 1896 Bret Harte biography. Two popular items are turn-of-the-20th-century stereographs and period postcards. **Antiques Etcetera** (18 Washington St., Sonora, tel 209-532-9544) specializes in early 20th-century dinnerware. **Art:** Gold Country is alive with talented artists, many of whom established their reputations in San Francisco before heading upriver. The **Holbrooke Hotel** (see p. 295) in Grass Valley has prints by Peggy Swan, a brilliant printmaker. A sampling of the region's talent can be seen at the **Calaveras County Arts Council Gallery** (22 Main St., tel 209-754-1774, www.calaverasarts.org) in San Andreas. A coterie of young painters has

grown up in and around Sonora. **Aloft Art Gallery** (105 S. Washington St., Sonora, tel 209-588-8604, www.aloftartgallery.com) represents many of them. **Books:** Several outstanding secondhand bookstores include **Hein & Company** (204 N. Main St., Jackson, tel 209-223-9076), where you might find a 1930s Maxfield Parrish album or a rare hardcover edition of Gertrude Atherton's Rezanov. **Produce:** Local produce and many things made from it are available through the **Apple Hill Growers Association** (www.applehill.com) in Camino, east of Placerville. In the fall, try **Abel's Apple Acres** (2345 Carson Rd., Placerville, tel 530-626-0138, www.abelsappleacres. com) for homemade apple pies and jams; the **North Canyon Cider Company** (3451 N. Canyon Rd., Camino, tel 650-520-4349, www.northcanyoncider.com, open weekends Sep.–Nov.) for cider; or **Boa Vista Orchards** (2952 Carson Rd., Placerville, tel 530-622-5522, www.boavista.com) for fruit, wine, pies, and pastries.

Wildest California, from the wonders of Yosemite, Sequoia, and Kings Canyon National Parks to Lake Tahoe's ski slopes

SIERRA NEVADA

"Powder hounds" enjoy all the adventure the Sierra Nevada has to offer.

SIERRA NEVADA

The Sierra Nevada mountain range runs from south of Mount Lassen to beyond Sequoia National Park. This 400-mile (644 km) chain is the result of massive volcanic activity some 130 million years ago. Today it is a paradise of deep forests, ice-blue lakes, glacier-carved valleys, and snowy mountain peaks.

■ **Camping in the High Sierra, Kings Canyon**

Travelers interested in the flora and fauna (not to mention weather) of this region will need to know the basics of Sierra topography before setting out. Ascending the range compares to a trip into Arctic tundra, with every 1,000 feet (305 m) of elevation equivalent to traveling 300 miles (482 km) northward.

The Sierra Nevada can be broken down into four ecological zones. The first, the mixed conifer zone (3,500–6,000 feet/1,065–1,830 m), is a zone of frequent precipitation and dense vegetation. Here giant sequoias, Jeffrey pines, and Douglas firs provide cover for deer, bears, and other forest mammals. The lodgepole pine–red fir zone (6,000–8,500 feet/1,830–2,590 m) is a region of deeply shaded forests, increasing snowfall, and wet mountain

meadows—perfect for western and lodgepole pine and Sierra juniper. In the third zone, the subalpine (8,500–10,500 feet/2,590–3,200 m), the effects of wind and snow begin to contort the natural landscape; vegetation is low growing, often gnarled and twisted. The alpine zone (from 10,500 feet/3,200 m) marks the timberline; here precipitation falls off dramatically and vegetation grows sparsely.

The centerpiece of the "Sierra experience" is Yosemite National Park. But in recent years, the area's two other national parks—Kings Canyon and Sequoia—have also become first-choice destinations. The great expanse of Lake Tahoe to the north has always been a draw, particularly for those seeking the added distractions found across the Nevada border. The eastern flank of the Sierras fall sharply to the Owens Valley, a volcanically active tectonic depression offering the best views of the snow-capped mountains from scenic Cal. 365. Here ancient bristlecone

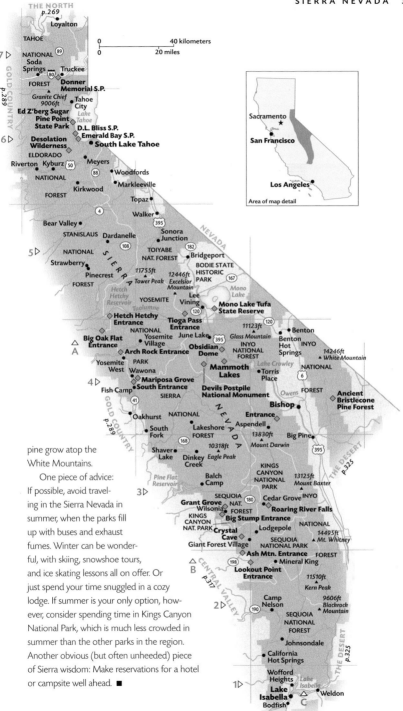

THE NORTH
p.269

Loyalton

TAHOE

0   40 kilometers
0   20 miles

7▷ NATIONAL   89
Soda
Springs   80   Truckee

FOREST   Donner
Memorial S.P.

Granite Chief
9006ft   Tahoe
City
Ed Z'berg Sugar   *Tahoe*
Pine Point
State Park   D.L. Bliss S.P.
Emerald Bay S.P.
6▷ Desolation   South Lake Tahoe
Wilderness
ELDORADO   Meyers
Riverton   Kyburz   50

NATIONAL   Woodfords
Kirkwood   Markleeville
FOREST
Topaz

4

Walker
395

Bear Valley
STANISLAUS   Dardanelle
108
NATIONAL   Sonora
Junction
5▷
Strawberry   TOIYABE
NAT. FOREST   Bridgeport

Pinecrest   *11755ft*   BODIE STATE
182
FOREST   *Tower Peak*   *Excelsior*
12446ft   HISTORIC
Mountain   PARK   167
Hetch
Hetchy   *Mono*
Reservoir   YOSEMITE   Lee   *Lake*
Tuolumne   Vining
120
Hetch Hetchy   Mono Lake Tufa
Entrance   Tioga Pass   State Reserve
Entrance
NATIONAL   *11123ft*
120
Big Oak Flat   Yosemite   June Lake   *Glass Mountain*   Benton
Entrance   Village   395
A   Arch Rock Entrance   Obsidian   INYO   Hot
Dome   NATIONAL   Springs   *14246ft*
Yosemite   PARK   FOREST   *White Mountain*
West   Wawona   Mammoth   *Lake Crowley*
4▷   Mariposa Grove   Lakes   Torris   NATIONAL
Fish Camp   South Entrance   Devils Postpile   Place
41   SIERRA   National Monument   *Owens*   FOREST   Ancient
Oakhurst   NATIONAL   Entrance   Bishop   Bristlecone
South   Lakeshore   Aspendell   Pine Forest
Fork   168   FOREST   *13830ft*
Shaver   Dinkey   *Eagle Peak*   Big Pine
Lake   Creek   *10318ft*   *Mount Darwin*   395

Pine Flat   KINGS
Reservoir   Balch   CANYON   *13125ft*
Camp   NATIONAL   *Mount Baxter*
3▷   PARK   INYO
SEQUOIA
180   Cedar Grove
Grant Grove   NAT.
Wilsonia   FOREST   Roaring River Falls
KINGS   Big Stump Entrance
CANYON   NATIONAL
NAT. PARK   Crystal   Lodgepole
Cave   SEQUOIA   *14495ft*
Giant Forest Village   NATIONAL PARK   *Mt. Whitney*
Ash Mtn. Entrance   FOREST
B   198   Mineral King
Lookout Point   *11510ft*
Entrance   *Kern Peak*

2▷   Camp   *9606ft*
Nelson   *Blackrock*
190   SEQUOIA   *Mountain*
NATIONAL
FOREST
Johnsondale

California
Hot Springs

Wofford
Heights   *Lake*
1▷   *Isabella*
Lake   Weldon
Isabella
Bodfish   C

S I E R R A
N E V A D A

NEVADA

GOLD COUNTRY
p.289

THE DESERT
p.325

GOLD COUNTRY
p.317

CENTRAL
VALLEY

Sacramento
★

San Francisco

Los Angeles

Area of map detail

pine grow atop the
White Mountains.

One piece of advice:
If possible, avoid traveling in the Sierra Nevada in
summer, when the parks fill
up with buses and exhaust
fumes. Winter can be wonderful, with skiing, snowshoe tours,
and ice skating lessons all on offer. Or
just spend your time snuggled in a cozy
lodge. If summer is your only option, however, consider spending time in Kings Canyon
National Park, which is much less crowded in
summer than the other parks in the region.
Another obvious (but often unheeded) piece
of Sierra wisdom: Make reservations for a hotel
or campsite well ahead. ■

YOSEMITE NATIONAL PARK

For more than 9,000 years, Indian communities inhabited the Yosemite Valley. For the last thousand years, it was the home of the Miwok, a subgroup of the Ahwahneechee. *Ahwahnee* means "valley that looks like a gaping mouth," a vivid description of this glacier-carved slash across the Sierra, considered by many to be California's physical crown jewel.

 El Capitan *(left),* Bridalveil Fall *(right),* and Half Dome in the distance distinguish Yosemite Valley.

Yosemite National Park

🏕 303 A4–B4, 305

☎ 209-372-0200 (24-hour updates on weather and trail conditions, plus campground info.); 602-278-888 or 888-413-8869 (campground & lodging reservations)

www.nps.gov/yose
www.travelyosemite.com

In 1851, the governor of California asked the Mariposa Brigade of the U.S. Army to put an end to the conflicts between Native Americans and miners. Following a group of Native Americans into the mountains, the troops came upon this magical valley, the first non-Native Americans to see it. The great naturalist John Muir (1838–1914) was seduced by Yosemite's spell and spent much of his life defending it. In 1890, the spell conjured a miracle—Congress created Yosemite

National Park. Today, with more than four million visitors each year, Yosemite, a World Heritage site, is one of the world's most famous wilderness areas.

Yosemite Valley at the heart of the park, formed by glaciers and further cut by the Merced River, is surrounded by awesome peaks: the 8,842-foot (2,695 m) **Half Dome,** its other half carved off by glaciers; the massive bulk of the 7,569-foot (2,307 m) **El Capitan** at the western end of the valley, the world's tallest exposed granite monolith; **Glacier Point,**

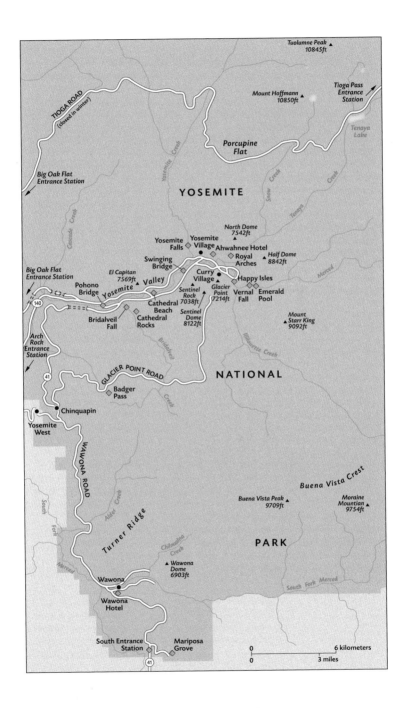

Tuolumne Peak
10845ft

Mount Hoffmann
10850ft

Tioga Pass
Entrance
Station

TIOGA ROAD
(closed in winter)

Tenaya
Lake

Porcupine
Flat

Yosemite Creek

Snow Creek

Tenaya Creek

Big Oak Flat
Entrance Station

YOSEMITE

Cascade Creek

North Dome
7542ft

Yosemite
Falls

Yosemite
Village

Ahwahnee Hotel

Royal
Arches

Half Dome
8842ft

Swinging
Bridge

El Capitan
7569ft

Curry
Village

Happy Isles

Merced

Big Oak Flat
Entrance Station

Pohono
Bridge

Yosemite Valley

Glacier
Point
7214ft

Vernal
Fall

Emerald
Pool

140

Cathedral
Beach

Sentinel
Rock
7038ft

Mount
Starr King
9092ft

Bridalveil
Fall

Cathedral
Rocks

Sentinel
Dome
8122ft

Bridalveil Creek

Illilouette Creek

Arch
Rock
Entrance
Station

GLACIER POINT ROAD

NATIONAL

41

Badger
Pass

Bridalveil Creek

Chinquapin

Yosemite
West

WAWONA ROAD

Buena Vista Crest

Alder Creek

Buena Vista Peak
9709ft

Moraine
Mountian
9754ft

South Fork

Turner Ridge

Chilnualna Creek

PARK

Wawona
Dome
6903ft

South Fork Merced

Merced

Wawona

Wawona
Hotel

South Entrance
Station

Mariposa
Grove

0   6 kilometers
0   3 miles

41

EXPERIENCE: Rafting the Sierra Nevada

The Tuolumne is one tough river, an untamed torrent of melting snow and spring rain that starts high in the Sierra Nevada of Yosemite National Park and churns its way through deep Tuolumne Canyon on its long journey to the Central Valley and eventually the Pacific Ocean. Given its isolation and fluvial dangers, the only way to explore the watercourse is on a guided whitewater rafting trip.

Based in Angels Camp (see p. 298), **O.A.R.S.** *(tel 800-346-6277, www.oars.com)* —one of the oldest whitewater rafting outfits in the world—offers guided trips *($$$$$)* on the Tuolumne lasting one, two, or three days. The trips begin and end in Groveland, just outside Yosemite. Along the way are abandoned mines and pioneer towns,

relics of the day when even this remote corner of California was part of the gold rush, as well as sandy beaches, swimming holes, and small waterfalls that provide cool respite from the blazing summer sun. Camp beneath the stars, and fall asleep to the sound of the rushing river.

Other Sierra rivers ripe for adventurous rafting include the gnarly Kern River in Sequoia National Forest *(map p. 303 C2)*, the Stanislaus River near Calaveras Big Trees State Park (see p. 299), and the American River near Sacramento (see pp. 292–293). **Kern River Outfitters** *(tel 760-376-3370, www.kernrafting.com)* and **Whitewater Voyages** *(tel 800-400-7238, www.whitewatervoyages.com)* run trips on these rivers.

at the top of a 3,200-foot-high (975 m) rock wall. These are among the most photographed natural wonders of Yosemite. Visitors flock to the valley to see them, resulting in traffic jams, pollution, and all the accompanying problems. However, at 7 miles long by 1 mile wide (11 km x 1.6 km), the valley represents only a tiny fraction of the park's total area of more than 1,000 square miles (2,590 sq km). In much of the rest of Yosemite, the park's spell is unbroken—especially for those who can leave their cars and walk its trails.

Tioga Pass Road *(closed spring & winter)* crosses the park from Crane Flat, near the Big Oak Flat entrance. The road climbs to the high country of the Sierra and crosses **Tuolumne Meadows** to Tenaya Lake and on to the 9,945-foot (3,031 m) **Tioga Pass** and

INSIDER TIP:

From Glacier Point, you can see Yosemite Valley, the Clark Range, Vernal and Nevada Falls, and a great profile of Half Dome.

—SCOTT GEDIMAN
Assistant superintendent, Yosemite National Park

the eastern entrance of the park.

This is serious hiking country, and the park offers some 800 miles (1,287 km) of marked trails, many of which are fine for inexperienced hikers. Discovering Yosemite's colors and smells can be as easy as the stroll to **Mirror Lake** or as taxing as the steep haul to the top of North America's highest waterfall, 2,425-foot

(739 m) **Yosemite Falls.**

The park is remarkably user friendly, with major information stations at Yosemite Village, Wawona, and Tuolumne Meadows. The park information service provides excellent trail maps and weather information.

Valley Floor Trek

This flat, 5-mile (8 km) trail loops through the most popular part of the park. Set out early and plan on spending most of a morning. Pick up a map at the Valley Visitor Center and take the free bus to the Yosemite Falls stop.

After walking the gentle slope up to the foot of the falls, go downhill to the lovely **Cooks Meadow.** From here, the entire pantheon of Yosemite icons looms upward like great granite sentries—as well as Half Dome and Glacier Point, look out for **Sentinel Rock** and the **Cathedral Rocks.**

Cast your eyes lower and the meadow's flora and fauna come into view. Spring is the best time for the wildflowers here. The meadow lands are often alive with red-wing blackbirds, robins, and Steller's jays; predators such as owls, peregrines and other falcons, and even golden eagles are sometimes spotted hunting over the valley.

Keeping the burbling Merced River to your left, you will come to **Leidig Meadow,** named for Charles Leidig, the first non-Native American male born in Yosemite. This is one of the largest remaining meadows in the valley. Follow the bike path to its edge and to the river, where you may see stunning reflections of **Sentinel Falls.** Follow the trail along the north side of the meadow to **Rocky Point,** easily recognizable by the rubble at its base, then continue to the river and a large wooded area. Now stick to the trail along the river to an area known as **Indian Swamp.** In spring, the meadow here floods, giving amazing reflections of Cathedral Rocks and Spires.

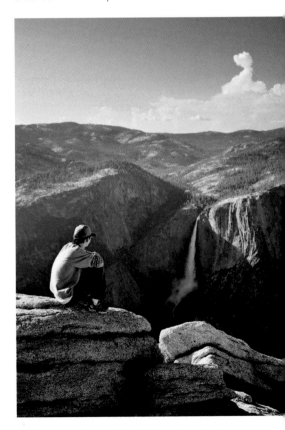

■ **The view from the top of Sentinel Dome is spectacular.**

Yosemite Essentials

There are several entrance stations to the park. The south entry *(Calif. 41)* is the most popular. During peak season, you will save time and frustration by using one of the three western gates: Arch Rock *(off Calif. 140)*, Big Oak Flat *(off Calif. 120)*, or Hetch Hetchy *(N of Mather on Hetch Hetchy Rd.)*. To the east is the Tioga Pass entrance *(off Calif. 120)*, closed winter through spring.

The main sources of information for the park are the entrance stations and the visitor centers, where one can obtain up-to-date weather and trail condition reports and the "Yosemite Guide."

Camping is allowed only in designated campgrounds. You may need to make a reservation up to three months in advance to be sure of your preferred site at popular times. There are also a number of first-come, first-served sites, for which you register at an entrance.

The three hotels within the park itself (see Travelwise pp. 382–383) are the Ahwahnee, beyond Yosemite Village; the Wawona, near the southern entrance; and Yosemite Lodge, near Yosemite Falls. All suggest advance booking; for the Ahwahnee, make reservations several months in advance.

The trail then takes you to **El Capitan Meadow,** where you can view the towering sheer slab of granite, the subject of so many Yosemite photos. Across the valley is **Bridalveil Fall,** a spectacular 620-foot (189 m) vertical torrent in spring. Continue along the riverside to **Gates of the Valley,** one of the best spots from which to view the entire valley.

At **Pohono Bridge,** cross the river to **Fern Spring.** From here, you can either follow the trail to the base of the fall or return along the Merced River going through a gate to **Cathedral Beach.** The view of the **Three Brothers** is outstanding. Continue to the **Swinging Bridge** for a final sweeping view.

Happy Isles to Vernal Fall

To begin this two-hour out-and-back trek, take the bus to Happy Isles, then go along the trail beneath Glacier Point to the popular **Mist Trail.** After about 50 minutes of steady climbing, a bridge appears. From here, you have your first clear view of 317-foot (96 m) **Vernal Fall.** Return to the Happy Isles bus or go farther up the switchback trail to the brilliant view near **Emerald Pool.** Return on the **John Muir Trail** (see sidebar p. 312).

Mariposa Grove Trail

If you are going south out of Yosemite, this 5-mile (8 km) hike to see the giant sequoias is a perfect farewell. Take the trail just before Calif. 41 leaves Yosemite to the south. Walk through the lower grove until you reach the **Fallen Monarch.** At the 1-mile point, you will come upon the **Grizzly Giant,** thought to be more than 2,700 years old. The trail winds past the **Faithful Couple** and **Clothespin** trees. A loop at the top passes a log-cabin museum *(open in summer),* then returns to the trail. ■

EXPERIENCE: Yosemite in Winter

Yosemite is a far different park in winter than the one that most people know or imagine. When the cold weather comes, the crowds vanish, making even normally crowded Yosemite Valley feel like it must have a hundred years ago when John Muir wandered the landscape. Storms bring a shroud of fresh snow to the granite domes, alpine meadows, and towering trees. And the park throws on its winter sports coat.

Outdoor Activities

Developed for Yosemite's bid to host the 1932 Winter Olympics (it lost out to Lake Placid), **Badger Pass Ski Area** (tel 209-372-1000, www.travelyosemite.com/winter/badger-pass-ski-area) is now considered one of the best places in California for kids to learn how to ski or snowboard. It also has gentle kid-friendly slopes for snowtubing. Lifts operate from 9 a.m. to 4 p.m. Equipment rentals and lift tickets are available from 8:30 a.m. to 4 p.m. (tel 209-372-1000 for current snow conditions).

Guided snowshoe tours, another way to explore the white wilderness, range from relatively easy, rangerled, 2-hour jaunts around Badger Pass to a 6.5-hour "adventure hike" to Dewey Point run by the **Yosemite Mountaineering School** (tel 209-372-8444. www.travelyosemite.com). YMS also gives cross-country skiing lessons and leads guided trips along Old Glacier Point Road. One of the holy grails of American cross-country skiing, the 21-mile (33.7 km) round-trip normally includes an overnight at the Glacier Point Ski Hut overlooking Half Dome and Yosemite Valley.

Down in Yosemite Valley is another vestige of the '32 Olympics bid: the **Curry Village Ice Rink** (tel 209-372-8333), with two to four skating sessions per day between November and early March. After dark, big band music fills the air and skaters can curl up around a fire pit blazing at one end.

In mid- to late February, grab your camera and photograph El Capitan's **Horsetail Falls;** when given the correct conditions the setting sun creates the illusion of a firefall.

Last but not least, the giant sequoias of the Tuolumne Grove are magical to trek or snowshoe with snow all around.

Indoor Activities

Gourmet events in Yosemite during the winter months include the celebrated **Bracebridge Dinners** (tel 888-413-8869, www.bracebridgedinners.com) at the Ahwahnee Hotel in December and other special events like the **Vintners' Holidays** in November and December and **Chefs' Holidays** in January and February (tel 888-413-8869 to book either culinary experience).

Hiking and driving options may be limited in Yosemite in winter, but there is no shortage of natural beauty to be experienced.

SEQUOIA & KINGS CANYON NATIONAL PARKS

Along the wet, western side of the Sierra Nevada crest east of Fresno lie two breathtakingly beautiful national parks, almost as dramatic as Yosemite (see pp. 304–309) to the northwest but not as well known. One reason is elevation. Much of Sequoia and Kings Canyon is perched above 11,000 feet (3,352 m)—about 4,000 feet (1,219 m) above the highest road. Fortunately, several roads wind through the parks, with viewing points all along the way. But, as in Yosemite, the best way to see these 862,000 acres (348,840 ha) is to get out there and sweat a little.

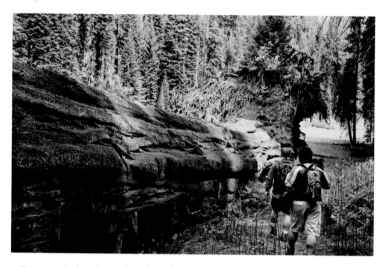

■ Giant sequoias here die not from disease but from toppling over—they simply grow too big.

Sequoia & Kings Canyon National Parks

🏔 303 C2–C3

Visitor Information

✉ Visitor Center, 47050 Generals Hwy., Three Rivers

☎ 559-565-3341

www.nps.gov/seki

If Sequoia and Kings Canyon were a movie, its stars would be the giant sequoias. Of the 75 groves of these trees in the world, only eight grow north of the Kings River, and those are scattered over more than 200 miles (321 km); the rest are close together in a 60-mile-long (96.5 km) area south of the river. The ecology of Sequoia and Kings Canyon—their precipitation, elevation, and soil—is perfect for these trees.

Sequoia National Park

Sequoia National Park has been organized with a variety of fitness levels in mind. The campgrounds (first come, first served), many of which sit along cool, clear streams, are close to interesting hike destinations, and none are too far from ranger outposts. The popular **Lodgepole Campground** and **Dorst Campground** (tel 877-444-6777, www.recreation.gov) require you to book in advance; each offers

INSIDER TIP:

Wake early and go for a sunrise hike. You're more likely to catch sight of a grazing mother deer and her fawn.

—ERIN STONE
National Geographic contributor

educational services and fireside entertainment in summer. Built of cedar and stone, the 102-room **Wuksachi Lodge** *(tel 888-252-5757, www.visitsequoia.com/lodging.aspx)* offers overnight and dining options in the Giant Forest area.

Entering Sequoia National Park on Calif. 198 (Generals Highway) from Three Rivers brings you to **Amphitheater Point;** stop for a stunning view of the San Joaquin Valley before driving on to see the astonishing sequoias of the **Giant Forest,** one of the great altars of the American environmental movement and an area explored and named by John Muir.

Starting at the **General Sherman Tree**—at 52,500 cubic feet (1,486 m³) the world's largest living thing (though not the tallest)—visitors can take the 2-mile (3.2 km) **Congress Trail** past all of the major giant sequoias here, including the **House** and **Senate** groups, as well as the **President** and **McKinley** trees.

Giant Forest Village marks the start of a 3-mile (4.8 km) road that will take you, either on foot or by shuttle (in summer), to two outstanding sights. About

2 miles (3.2 km) down is the steep, quarter-mile staircase up to **Moro Rock.** From the top of this granite dome is a spectacular view, particularly at sunset. Below stretches the blue-green Kaweah River, while to the west one can see beyond the San Joaquin Valley and over into the Coast Range.

At the road's end is **Crescent Meadow,** perhaps the finest of all midaltitude meadows. It was here, in 1875, at the lodge of pioneer Hale Tharp, that Muir spent several nights, later crowning this meadow the "gem of the Sierras." If you get ambitious, you can start the **High Sierra Trail** here; it finishes at **Mount Whitney,** the highest point in the coterminus United States, 14,495 feet (4,418 m) tall and 71 miles (114 km) away.

HOW TO GET THERE
If you are arriving from the south on Calif. 99, take Calif. 198 northeast to Sequoia; from Fresno, follow Calif. 180 east to Kings Canyon. As in almost all national parks, entrance stations provide maps and more detailed trail and climate information.

The Yokut

Reflect for a moment on the original inhabitants of the Kings Canyon area, the Yokut. Although at first these Native Americans welcomed their mid-19th-century pioneer acquaintances, by 1862 the same Anglo newcomers were already forcing the Yokut into the meager backcountry. Simultaneously the Yokut began to perish from the first infection by the white man's diseases—smallpox, measles, and scarlet fever. A particularly poignant moment came in 1864, when the chief of the remaining Yokut directly asked a leading pioneer, Hale Tharp, to leave. According to the contemporary accounts, when Tharp refused, "the chief and his brave sat down and cried." By the following year, all of the Yokut had retreated to the remote back canyons, where they would scratch out only a shell of their former existence.

Crystal Cave

⛰ 303 B3

✉ 12 miles W
of Lodgepole
Visitor Center

☎ 559-565-3759

🕐 Closed winter

💲 $$$ (45-minute
tour; tickets
at www.
sequoiaparks
conservancy.
org/crystalcave.
html or
Lodgepole or
Foothills Visitor
Centers)

Four-and-a-half miles (78.2 km) north of the Giant Forest is Lodgepole Camp. The **Tokopah Falls Trail** starts here. The walk ascends steadily (but manageably), leading along the magnificent Marble Fork Kaweah River and on into a series of cliffs and the waterfall of Tokopah Canyon, 2 miles (3.2 km) from the start.

A short drive west of Lodgepole is **Crystal Cave,** a series of underground caverns with superb specimens of stalactites, stalagmites, and other geological formations. The tour is worthwhile. In summer, when temperatures can reach the 90s (32° C and higher), the cave's cool interior is welcome.

Kings Canyon National Park

North and west, Generals Highway goes to Kings Canyon National Park and reaches **Grant Grove.** The giant sequoia called **General Grant** is the world's third largest living tree, at more than 42,000 cubic feet (1,189 m³). It is also, in the words of the Park Service, a "designated national shrine"

and "the only living memorial to those who gave their lives for freedom."

The 1.5-mile (2.4 km) **North Grove Loop** gives a closer look at the trees. The **Redwood Canyon Trail,** beginning at Redwood Saddle, is the start of two easy, 6-mile (9.6 km) loops through sequoia groves; the **Sugarloaf Trail,** at Sunset Meadow, is a moderate effort for 2 miles (3.2 km) along a spectacular glaciated canyon.

North and then east along Calif. 180 (this part is only open in summer) brings hikers into **Sequoia National Forest** and then on to a remote corner of Kings Canyon and **Cedar Grove.** The grove is pleasantly quiet, even during peak season. To get an idea of the glacial history of Kings Canyon, take the **Canyon View** turn a mile (1.6 km) past Cedar Grove Village. Another mile east is the entrance to **Roaring River Falls,** where a five-minute walk leads to a waterfall pulsing through a narrow ravine. A farther 1.5 miles (2.4 km) east is the scenic **Zumwalt Meadow.** ■

EXPERIENCE: Hiking From Yosemite to Sequoia

The shortest path between Yosemite National Park (see pp. 304–309) and Sequoia National Park is the 215-mile (346 km) **John Muir Trail** (www.john muirtrail.org), but you'll have to hike it. The route follows the crest of the High Sierra between Yosemite Valley and Mount Whitney, threading a landscape mottled with alpine tarns and snow-capped peaks, rocky cirques, and

sun-splashed meadows that only ardent hikers ever see. Thirty days is the recommended time for walking the entire trail, but shorter sections can be navigated in a week or even less. Hikers must pack in all of their supplies and pack out all of their garbage; bear canisters are a must. A backcountry permit is required from the national park or forest where you commence your hike.

MONO LAKE & MAMMOTH LAKES

Despite its location at the base of the Sierra Nevada, Mono Lake's ecology is distinctly that of the Mojave Desert. Since 1941, Los Angeles' water agency has diverted the freshwater streams that feed this ancient lake, causing the water level to drop some 45 feet (13.7 m) and raising salinity to extreme levels. It wreaked havoc on many indigenous birds, fish, and flora, and the millions of transient waterbirds that flock year-round. Since 1994, restrictions on water diversion have raised the lake level by 17 feet (5 m), although habitat restoration is ongoing.

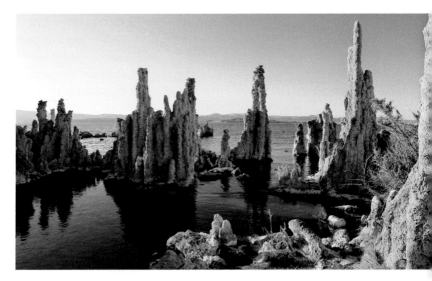

Dramatic towers rise at South Tufa in Mono Lake Tufa State Natural Reserve.

As Mono Lake's water level dropped, spectacular geological formations called tufa towers have been exposed. Resembling stalagmites, these towers—formed when freshwater underground springs mix their calcium with the carbonate-rich lake water—conjure the effect of a city skyline against the background of snowy mountain peaks. They are one of the most peculiar and beautiful sights in the state. Some of the best are preserved at **Mono Lake Tufa State Natural Reserve.**

Some species of wader and waterfowl have successfully adapted to the unusual environment here, and it is a popular destination for bird-watchers. Between August and April, the lake is home to one of the largest populations of eared grebes in the Northern Hemisphere; the Audubon Society estimates their numbers at up to 800,000. Snowy plovers, avocets, and phalaropes also overwinter

Mono Lake Tufa State Natural Reserve

🗺 303 B5

Visitor Information

✉ Park Office, 395 & Visitor Center Dr. Lee Vining

☎ 760-647-6331

www.parks.ca.gov

Ancient Bristlecone Pine Forest

🏔 303 C4

Visitor Information

✉ Visitor Center, White Mtn. Rd. off Calif. 168, NE of Big Pine

☎ 760-873-2500

🕐 Closed winter

www.fs.usda.gov

Inyo National Forest

🏔 303 B4–C4

Visitor Information

✉ Visitor Center, 351 Pacu Ln., Bishop

☎ 760-873-2400

www.fs.usda. gov/inyo

Mammoth Lakes

🏔 303 B4

Visitor Information

✉ Visitor Center, 2520 Main St., Mammoth Lakes

☎ 760-934-2712, 888-466-2666

www.visitmammoth .com

Mammoth Mountain Ski Area

✉ 10001 Minaret Rd., Mammoth Lakes

☎ 760-934-0745

www.mammoth mountain.com

here, while in spring and summer the lake hosts a large breeding population of California gulls.

Ancient Bristlecone Pine Forest

South of Mono Lake, lush **Owens Valley** is framed to the west by the Sierra Nevada and to the east by the **White Mountains**—home of the world's oldest living trees, deep inside **Inyo National Forest.** From the tiny town of Big Pine, Calif. 168 snakes into the mountains; turn left onto White Mountain Rd. for the forest. From on high, the views of the glistening snow-capped Sierra Nevada are unmatched.

There are two principal groves worth visiting. The first is the 4,000-year-old **Schulman Grove,** named for naturalist Julius Schulman, who was the first to announce the grove's antiquity in 1958. The Forest Service maintains a **Discovery Trail** off White Mountain Road that takes you past dozens of the trees. One of the grove's most stunning features is its brilliant palette of primary colors, heightened by the crystal-clear mountain air: cinnamon red trunks against deep blue skies, beige trunks with striking black grain, rich red-orange wood, and purple-black tips to the branches.

The second grove, of even older bristlecones, is the **Patriarch Grove.** It is a few miles farther along White Mountain Road and several hundred feet higher, just south of the White Mountain Natural Area. In it is the venerable **Methuselah,** a tree estimated to be more than 4,700 years old.

The bristlecone pine *(Pinus longaeva)* acquired its twisted, stunted form in response to its extremely cold and windy environment.

INSIDER TIP:

Head to Bodie State Historic Park (tel 760-616-5040, *www.parks. ca.gov*) to explore California's largest and best-preserved gold-mining ghost town, northeast of Mono Lake.

—CHRISTOPHER P. BAKER
National Geographic author

Mammoth Lakes

One of North America's most volcanically active regions, Mammoth, 20 miles (32 km) south of Mono Lake, is named for the crystal-clear lakes filled with fish in summer. In winter, Mammoth favors skiing, snowmobiling, and dog-sled adventures at the **Mammoth Mountain Ski Area,** which has 150 downhill runs plus the **Tamarack Cross-Country Ski Center** *(163 Twin Lakes Rd., tel 760-934-2442)* with 19 miles (30.5 km) of trails. Calif. 203 snakes west from US 395 past Mammoth Mountain to **Devils Postpile National Monument** *(map p. 303 B4),* featuring huge columns of ancient basalt lava. North of Mammoth Lakes rises **Obsidian Dome** *(map p. 303 B4),* a great dome of solid volcanic glass. ∎

LAKE TAHOE

German skiers have their own fond name for Lake Tahoe: *der Blaue*—the blue one. It is often also called one of the most beautiful lakes in the world. Even Mark Twain lost his characteristic bluster when first seeing "the mountains brilliantly photographed upon its surface . . . surely it must be the fairest picture the whole earth affords."

Tahoe is 1,640 feet (500 m) deep, making it the world's tenth deepest inland body of water. Created when the Tahoe Basin sank between parallel faults two million years ago and lava blocked the water's outflow, the alpine lake (elevation 6,224 feet/1,897 m) is now 22 miles (35.4 km) long and 12 miles (19 km) wide. Golf, fishing, waterskiing, boating, biking, and swimming are among summer activities here; skiing, snowmobile riding, and snowboarding are the main winter pastimes. (For skiing information, see Travelwise, p. 390.) The lake's 72-mile (115 km) shoreline, straddling the California-Nevada border, is home to everything from quiet forests to glamorous casinos. There is something here for everyone. The summer peaks with 100,000 visitors, so if you're looking for peace and quiet, come in spring or fall.

The lakefront on Tahoe's California side includes a number of state parks, historic sites, and ski resorts. **South Lake Tahoe,** the biggest city in the region, is a good place for an overview. Here one can board the authentic *M.S. Dixie II* **paddle wheeler** (*900 Ski Run Blvd., South Lake Tahoe, tel 775-589-4906 or 800-238-2463, www.*

■ The lake's sublime color is owed to its clarity.

laketahoecruises.com, $$$) and sail to Emerald Bay and back, taking in the vast shore and the mountain skyline.

Many prefer to spend their first day here doing the 72-mile (115 km) **Shoreline Drive,** which takes you around the lake's entire circumference. A fun way to do this is to buy the two-hour audio tour "Drive Around Lake Tahoe," available from the South Lake Tahoe Chamber of Commerce. The commentary provides a series of colorful facts, tales, and legends about the area as you drive.

Another popular outing is to take the **Heavenly Valley Gondola** (*tel 775-586-7000*) at Heavenly Ski Resort (*3860 Saddle Rd., South Lake Tahoe, tel 530-541-4418, www.skiheavenly.com*), which

Lake Tahoe
🗺 303 A6
Visitor Information
✉ Visitors
   Authority,
   4114 Lake Tahoe
   Blvd., South
   Lake Tahoe
☎ 530-542-4637
✉ N. Lake Tahoe
   Visitor Center
   100 N. Lake
   Blvd., Tahoe City
☎ 530-581-6900

**www.visitinglake
tahoe.com**

**www.tahoesouth
.com**

**www.gotahoenorth.
com**

Emerald Bay State Park

🗺 303 A6

✉ 22 miles S of Tahoe City

☎ 530-541-3030 (summer only)

www.parks.ca.gov

D. L. Bliss State Park

🗺 303 A6

✉ 17 miles S of Tahoe City on Calif. 89

☎ 530-525-7277

www.parks.ca.gov

Ed Z'berg Sugar Pine Point State Park

🗺 303 A6

✉ Follow signs from Sugar Pine Point

☎ 530-525-7982 (summer), 530-525-9528 (winter)

www.parks.ca.gov

will whisk you up 3,000 feet (914 m) to the peak restaurant.

There are plenty of places to visit around the lake. **Tallac Historic Site** (*Calif. 89, tel 530-543-2600 or 530-543-0956, www.tahoeheritage.org, closed Oct.–May*), northwest of South Lake Tahoe, boasts a resort of late 19th-century houses built as vacation homes by rich San Franciscans.

On the lakeshore 10 miles (16 km) north of South Lake Tahoe is **Emerald Bay State Park,** where you can visit **Vikingsholm** (*www.vikingsholm.com*), in the style of a medieval Norse fortress. The site can be reached via a short hiking trail or by boat. Vikingsholm was the dream home of Lora J. Knight, a wealthy Chicago widow who, in 1928, asked Swedish architect Lennart Palme to build it "without moving a single tree." He did. Emerald Bay also offers hiking trails and picnic areas.

Farther along the shoreline are

two other state parks. The first, 3 miles (4.8 km) north of Emerald Bay, is **D. L. Bliss State Park,** laced with scenic hiking trails, outlooks, and the outstanding **Lester Beach.** Farther north still is **Ed Z'berg Sugar Pine Point State Park,** with the 1903 **Hellman-Ehrman Mansion** (*closed Oct.–May, $$*), a lighthouse, and a log cabin. A bike trail to Tahoe City starts here.

Desolation Wilderness (*map p. 303 A6*) consists of 63,000 acres (25,495 ha) of alpine and subalpine lakes, and can only be traversed by foot, bike, or horse (*www.recreation.gov/permits/233261 for permits and regulations*). A driveable part of the **Tahoe National Forest** (*map p. 303 A7, tel 530-265-4531*) can be found in the old **Foresthill Road District.** This stretch of road was once trod by Native Americans, then later by covered wagons and gold seekers. ∎

Truckee & Donner Memorial State Park

The quaint little town of **Truckee** (*map p. 303 A7, Calif. 267, off I-80*) has emerged in recent years as a thriving place to visit, complete with a tolerably cute historic shopping district and several decent eateries. The town was founded in the mid-19th century, first as a stagecoach stop, then as a home to railroad workers maintaining the transcontinental railroad. Later decades saw the town become a center for the flourishing lumber and ice-harvesting industries.

In the early 20th century, the historic **Truckee Hotel** (*10007 Bridge St., tel 530-587-4444, www.truckeehotel.com*) briefly hosted actor Charlie Chaplin, who made

his movie *The Gold Rush* (1925) here. A number of structures survive, including a **Chinese herb shop,** a reminder of the international workforce that built the railroads, and the **Old Truckee Jail** (*10142 Jibboom St., tel 530-582-0893*), now a museum of the town's history.

Two miles (3.2 km) to the west is **Donner Memorial State Park** (*map p. 303 A7, off I-80, tel 530-582-7892, www.parks.ca.gov*) on beautiful Donner Lake. Here you will find the **Emigrant Trail Museum** and **Donner Party Memorial.** The museum profiles the doomed 91-person Donner Party, trapped by bad weather in 1846 and whose 45 survivors had resorted to cannibalism.

The world's single richest agricultural region, worth the heat to visit a rural culture intertwined with farming

CENTRAL VALLEY

Merced County Courthouse, built in 1875, is one of the region's oldest historical buildings.

CENTRAL VALLEY

Many visitors experience the great Central Valley of California in much the same way as the Spaniards, who were fearful of its "great heat and desolation"—they simply don't stop there. And not simply because Interstate 5 freeway cuts through it, providing a fast track from north to south. Flat as a billiard table, the valley has none of the scenic grandeur of California's other regions. Plus, in summer it's as hot as Hades, and its air quality the worst in the nation.

■ Workers handpick cherries at family-run Simonian Farm in Clovis, north of Fresno.

NOT TO BE MISSED:

But in winter and spring, the valley can be an intoxicating, uniquely Californian place to visit. Then, as the heat slackens and the tule fogs rise up, earth and sky, as the native poet William Everson says, become "one mingle of color." The harvest in, another on its way (the land never rests here), the valley thrums with enterprise and optimism.

You will find here in the countryside a wild admixture of cultures, of Mexican Americans, Hmong tribesmen, fourth-generation Portuguese, and fifth-generation Japanese. One gets a feeling for the culture, in the words of writer Gerald Haslem, the dean of valley authors, who writes of "biscuits and gravy for breakfast, or *chorizo con huevos para desayuno.*" The ethnic potpourri is kaleidoscopic, as each generation brings a new influx.

Regardless of culture, California's Central Valley comprises a huge chunk of the state—15 million acres (6,070,284 ha) in all, stretching 430 miles (692 km) in length and, at its midriff, 75 miles (120 km) in width. Enormous economic power rests in the Central Valley. In fact, the valley is the centerpiece of California's $50 billion agriculture industry. Today, more money is made here from raisins, strawberries, almonds, and the like in one year than has been made since 1848 in all of the state's gold mines put together. ■

Manteca ●
7 ▷
Tracy ●
580
Escalon ●
Ripon ●
5
Salida ●
580
132
Modesto ●

BAY AREA
p.231

6 ▷
3347ft
▲
Mount Oso
Patterson ●

Delta-Mendota Canal

San Joaquin

3804ft
▲ Mount Stakes 5
Newman ●

Gustine ●

San Luis
N.W.R.
152

CENTRAL COAST
p.171

San Luis
Reservoir

5 ▷

△
A

FRESNO

The story of Fresno, the raisin capital and the Central Valley's biggest city, goes a long way toward explaining the serendipitous *and* intentional nature of the valley's agricultural success. Founded as a station along the Southern Pacific line in 1872, the town held little allure for its original settlers. They named it Fresno—Spanish for "dry ash." Today, however, Fresno reigns as the nation's most prolific producer of high-value farm products, the Tuscany of the western United States.

■ Designed by Arthur Erickson, Fresno's angular City Hall echoes the Sierra Nevada to the east.

Fresno

🗺 319 C5

Visitor Information

✉ Fresno Convention & Visitors Bureau, 1180 E. Shaw Ave., Fresno

☎ 559-981-5500, 800-788-0836

www.visitfresno county.org

Reedley

🗺 319 D4

At the turn of the 20th century, fruit growing was successful, but the marketing of Fresno's biggest cash crop, raisins, was so pitiable that many growers sold them under dubious Spanish labels. Then, in 1915, a head of the California Raisin Exchange "happened upon a young woman drying her curly jet-black hair under a red bonnet in the front yard of her Fresno home," writes Kevin Starr in *Inventing the Dream*. "[The executive] glimpsed what would eventually be one of the most famous trademarks in history . . . the Sun Maid, a marketing image

so successful in its suggestions of health, abundance, and rural charm that in 1920 the Cooperative took Sun Maid as its formal name." The rest, as a glance along the shelf at any grocery store will tell you, is history.

As a travel destination, Fresno has improved over the past decade. One attraction is the **Blossom Trail,** a 62-mile (100 km) self-guided tour *(maps at www.visitfresnocounty.org)* through orchards, vineyards, and wildflower meadows. March is the best time to view the blossoms. Along the way are growers such as **Simonian Farms** *(S. Clovis St., off Calif. 99, tel 559-237-2294, www.simonianfarms. com),* growing more than a hundred kinds of fruit and vegetables.

Also along the drive is the quaint town of **Reedley,** named for wheat baron Thomas Law Reed, and it's worth a stop at the **Mennonite Quilt Center** *(1012 G St., Reedley, tel 559-638-3560, www .mennonitequiltcenter.org, closed Mon.),* where you can see patient craftsfolk at work on their beautiful—and rare—quilts (buy one, it would make a wonderful family heirloom).

Fresno itself has some (sometimes eccentric) historical sites. The best is the **Forestiere**

INSIDER TIP:

Spring is a great time to visit the Forestiere Underground Gardens, as orange blossom fragrance fills the subterranean courtyards.

—KENNY LING
National Geographic contributor

Underground Gardens, part of the underground retreat of Baldasare Forestiere. Between 1906 and 1950, Forestiere sculpted a subterranean home with bedrooms, kitchen, library, and even a walk-under aquarium. More extraordinary still are the huge, productive skylit gardens and orchards from which he not only fed himself but also sold surplus crops.

More conventional is the **Kearney Mansion** *(Kearney Blvd., 7 miles/11 km W of downtown Fresno, tel 559-441-0862, www.valleyhistory .org, closed a.m. & Mon.–Thurs., $$).* Built by the raisin king, Theodore Kearney, between 1900 and 1903, the house, constructed in French Renaissance style and furnished in keeping, is on the National Register of Historic Places. It is now a museum of local history.

For a different impression of early Fresno life, see the restored **Meux Home Museum** *(1007 R St., Fresno, tel 559-233-8007, www.meuxhomemuseum.org, closed Mon.–Thurs., $$).* Its 19th-century owner, T. R. Meux, was a Confederate surgeon.

The **William Saroyan House Museum** *(2729 W. Griffith Way, tel 559-360-5058, www.saroyanhouse. com)* honors the eponymous author (1908–1981) who lived here and captured Fresno's immigrant tongues, oddball characters, and unique small-town drama in his plays and novels, many of which were produced on Broadway and rendered in films.

The **Fresno Art Museum** is worth a visit for its Mexican and Impressionist collections, as well as American sculpture, native California art, and works on paper.

The **Fresno Chaffee Zoo** *(894 W. Belmont Ave., Fresno, tel 559-498-5910, www.fresnochaffeezoo.org, $$$),* located in **Roeding Park,** is home to more than 700 birds, mammals, and reptiles. Visit the Tropical Rain Forest and catch a "Winged Wonders" show, a free-flight performance of eagles, hawks, vultures, and parrots. ∎

Forestiere Underground Gardens

✉ 5021 W. Shaw Ave., 2 blocks E of Calif. 99, Fresno

☎ 559-271-0734

🕒 Closed Mon.–Tues. & mid-Dec.–mid-Mar.

💲 $$

www.underground gardens.com

Fresno Art Museum

✉ 2233 N. 1st St., Fresno

☎ 559-441-4221

🕒 Closed Mon.–Wed.

💲 $$

www.fresnoart museum.org

EXPERIENCE:
Basque Celebrations

Basques began immigrating to California during Spanish colonial times, and in the late 1800s they began to form distinct enclaves in the Central Valley. In Fresno, you can tuck in at half a dozen Basque restaurants scattered around town, but to really immerse yourself, visit during the annual **Fresno Basque Club Festival** *(www. facebook.com/FresnoBasqueClub).* Held the first Saturday in May, the festival features a huge outdoor picnic, complete with hearty lamb stew, pork loin, and spicy sausages. Eventgoers eat at a long communal table and then celebrate with traditional dancing. For other Basque festivals in the area, consult the Kern County Basque Club *(tel 559-833-9420, www.kcbasqueclub.com).*

NORTH OF FRESNO

Classic Californian small towns and some excellent wildlife refuges, offering many superb opportunities for bird-watchers, characterize the Central Valley country north of Fresno.

Modesto

 318 A6

Visitor Information

✉ Modesto Convention & Visitors Bureau, 1008 12th St., Modesto

☎ 209-526-5588

www.visitmodesto .com

Merced

 319 B6

Visitor Information

✉ California Welcome Center, 710 W. 16th St., Merced

☎ 209-724-8104

www.visitcentral valley.com

Modesto

Modesto, established in 1870 by the Central Pacific Railroad, was the inspiration for the classic film *American Graffiti* (1973)—filmmaker George Lucas, who grew up here, modeled the memorable cruising scenes in his film after Modesto's own teen scene. Another mark of true Californiana is the **Modesto Arch,** one of the few early 20th-century icons of civic pride still extant.

Modesto is also a foodie paradise—not so much for its restaurants as for its orchards, vineyards, and food producers. **Sciabica Familys** (2150 Yosemite St., Modesto, tel 800-551-9612, www. sunshineinabottle.com) has been

growing olives and pressing fine oil for four generations. At the **Hilmar Cheese Company** (9001 N. Lander St., Hilmar, tel 209-656-1196, www. hilmarcheese.com) you can take a free factory tour and munch on a wide selection of cheeses produced on the premises. Shop for locally grown almonds at the **Blue Diamond Growers Store** (4800 Sisk Rd., Modesto, tel 209-545-3222, www.bluediamond.com).

Merced & Around

South of Modesto is the town of Merced, known as the gateway to Yosemite. Just west of town you'll find the **San Luis National Wildlife Refuge Complex** (7376 S. Wolfsen Rd., Los Banos, S of Calif. 140 between Merced and Gustine, tel 209-826-3508, www.fws.gov/ refuge/san_luis), which consists of three separate refuges totaling some 27,000 acres (10,926 ha) around the San Joaquin River. **Merced National Wildlife Refuge** is a haven for flocks of snow geese and sandhill cranes. Similar birdlife, as well as tule elk, flourish farther west at the **San Luis National Wildlife Refuge** and the **San Joaquin River National Wildlife Refuge.** The latter has spectacular spring wildflowers. For herons and migrating geese, visit **Los Banos Wildlife Area** (18110 W. Henry Miller Ave., Los Banos, tel 209-826-0463, www.wildlife.ca.gov). ∎

EXPERIENCE:

The Madera Wine Trail

Visit the boutique wineries of Madera County, between Fresno and Yosemite, to enjoy some of the Central Valley's best wines (www.maderawinetrail.com). Your visit should include the old-timers like **Ficklin Vineyards** (30246 Ave. 7½, Madera, tel 559-661-0075, www.ficklin.com) plus **San Joaquin Winery** (21821 Ave. 16, Madera, tel 559-673-0066, www.sjwineco.com) and **Idle Hour Winery** (41139 Calif. 41, Oakhurst, tel 559-760-9090, www.idlehourwinery.com, closed Mon.–Tue.), near Yosemite's south entrance. Download a map of the wineries at www.maderawinetrail.com and create your own itinerary.

SOUTH OF FRESNO

More wildlife refuges feature south of Fresno, but it is history that draws visitors to this area. Agriculture rules in this region, and the towns have grown up around packing stations and food-processing companies. Nonetheless, there's plenty of culture and natural draws.

Hanford

With its pleasant atmosphere, quiet ways, and railroad-era buildings, you would never guess that little **Hanford** *(W from Calif. 99 on Calif. 198)* was the scene of a bloody and historically important feud. In May 1880, settlers and the Southern Pacific Railroad got in a dispute over land titles, resulting in a bloody gun battle: The Mussel Slough feud left seven men dead. Today Hanford bakes lazily in the California sun. It is best known for the remains of its once thriving Chinatown. You can still tour **China Alley** and the historic 1893 **Taoist Temple** by contacting the visitor center.

Visalia

A few miles to the east of Hanford on Calif. 198, Visalia was founded in 1852 by a bear hunter named Nathaniel Vise. It has since grown in classic Central Valley fashion, dominated by packinghouses, food-processing companies, and growers.

Two places in Visalia are worth a stop. Pay a visit to the **Tulare County Museum** *(27000 S. Mooney Blvd., tel 559-733-6616, www.tularecounty museum.org, closed Tues.–Wed.)* to see a copy of the famed "End of the Trail Monument" and many artifacts detailing ancient Yokut

Indian culture. Distinguished by its two 12-ton marble Shih Tzu lions, the **Central California Chinese Cultural Center** *(500 S. Akers St., tel 559-625-4545, by appt. only)* contains several fine holdings of ancient Chinese art and culture.

Lake Kaweah

A popular outing (and a good way to beat the heat) is to head east on Calif. 198 to Lake Kaweah, in the foothills west of Sequoia National Park. Boats can be rented at **Kaweah Marina** *(tel 559-597-2526, www.kaweahmarina.com)*, and the lake is a good place for swimming and fishing. Here, during the

---

The "Bakersfield Sound"

To music buffs, Bakersfield (see p. 324) is the Nashville of the West. Local hero Buck Owens (1929–2006) had 21 number one hits on the *Billboard* country charts, including "Tiger by the Tail" and "Act Naturally." Hard-edged Merle Haggard (1937–2016) was born and raised in Oildale, on the outskirts of Bakersfield. His classic "Okie From Muskogee" is one of the great country music anthems of the last 50 years. Together, Owens and Haggard helped craft the "Bakersfield Sound," a rough-hewn West Coast version of the Nashville sound. Today you can catch live country music up and down the valley, including at **Buck Owens' Crystal Palace** *(map p. 319 D2, 2800 Buck Owens Blvd., Bakersfield, tel 661-328-7560, www.buckowens.com)*.

Hanford
🗺 319 D4
Visitor Information
✉ Hanford Chamber of Commerce, 113 Court St. #104, Hanford
☎ 559-582-0483
www.hanford chamber.com

Visalia
🗺 319 D4
Visitor Information
✉ Visalia Convention & Visitors Bureau, 112 E. Main St., Visalia
☎ 559-334-0141
www.visitvisalia.com

Lake Kaweah

319 E4

Allensworth
319 D3

1880s, a socialistic experiment called the Kaweah Colony briefly flourished.

Allensworth

A utopia of a different kind can be found farther south, west of Calif. 99 near Delano. Founded in 1908 by Col. Allen Allensworth, the highest ranking African-American military officer of his day, Allensworth was a "self-governing" town where

Tricolored blackbirds may be hardest to spot in summer.

Bakersfield
319 E2

Visitor Information

✉ Bakersfield Convention & Visitors Bureau, 515 Truxtun Ave., Bakersfield

☎ 661-852-7282, 866-425-7353

www.visitbakers field.com

liberated blacks could live free of discrimination. From 1909 to 1919, Allensworth thrived, but in the 1920s, the town's water supplies ran low, and a slow exodus began. By the late 1950s, it was a ghost town. In the 1970s, preservationists began restoring the town, which is now **Colonel Allensworth State Historic Park** (*Cty. Rd. J22, off Calif. 43 N of Wasco, tel 661-849-3433, www.parks.ca.gov, closed to vehicles Mon.–Thurs.*).

Bird-watchers should visit the

Kern National Wildlife Refuge (*19 miles/30.5 km W of Delano, off Calif. 155, tel 661-725-2767, www. fws.gov/kern*), southwest of Allensworth. This managed wetland in the San Joaquin Valley supports a breeding colony of the endangered tricolored blackbird. If it is too hot to hike, there is a 6-mile (9.6 km) self-guided driving tour.

Bakersfield

At the southern end of the valley, Bakersfield, with a population of 350,000, has been one of California's fastest-growing cities in recent decades. The fine **Kern County Museum/Lori Brock Children's Discovery Center** (*3801 Chester Ave., tel 661-437-3330, www.kerncounty museum.org, closed Mon.–Tues., $$*) in Bakersfield showcases Native American artifacts and local history. The **Buena Vista Museum of Natural History** (*2018 Chester Ave., tel 661-324-6350, www.buenavistamuseum.org*) is renowned for its fossils of dinosaurs, and even ancient sharks, found in the Sierra foothills.

South from Bakersfield, I-5 snakes up "The Grapevine" to Tejon Pass, northern gateway to Los Angeles. **Fort Tejon State Park** (*5201 Ft. Tejon Rd., tel 661-248-6692, www.parks.ca.gov*), near Grapevine Canyon summit, preserves the historic U.S. Army fort. Docents in period costume lead tours.

East from Bakersfield, Calif. 58 climbs through the wildly scenic Tehachapi Mountains to **Tehachapi,** a gateway to the Mojave Desert (see p. 328). ■

One of the trendiest places to visit, attracting spiritual and ecological adventurers alike to a region of compelling beauty

THE DESERT

Cactus at the Living Desert wildlife and botanical park

THE DESERT

The vast area known to Californians as "the desert" is actually two deserts. The northern one, Death Valley and the Mojave "High Desert," is kept dry by the rain shadow cast by the Sierra to the west. The southern "Low Desert" of Palm Springs and Anza-Borrego is a small part of the Colorado Desert, itself part of the Sonoran Desert, and occupies a mountain-girt tectonic depression.

■ Death Valley dunes rise near Stovepipe Wells.

NOT TO BE MISSED:

This is a land of extremes. In summer, temperatures soar by day to 110 or 120°F (43 or 48°C), plunging by 50° (10°C) at night. Winds shape entire dune canyons in a single season. Water is a rumor for most of the year; in winter and summer storms, flash floods can carve new landscapes overnight. These extremes, paradoxically, have made the desert even more enticing to Californians. Since the 1920s, the Hollywood elite have been transfixed by the oasis of Palm Springs. In recent years, it has again become fashionable, attracting not only the rich and famous but also festival-goers and a growing contingent who come to see its modernist architecture.

Desert extremes have wrought a highly diverse ecology. In the far north is the Owens Valley, its beautiful green meadows a sharp contrast to the snowy Sierras and dun desert to each side. More superlatives are to be found in Death Valley National Park, while Joshua Tree National Park is the show-stopper of the desert experience.

The basics of desert travel bear repeating. If you will be camping in the desert overnight, register at one of the sign-up boards, usually found at visitor centers and trailheads. Take at least one gallon (4 L) of water per person per day just for drinking; for a strenuous trip, take two gallons (8 L) each. If you are going *anywhere* except along well-known trails, take a map and

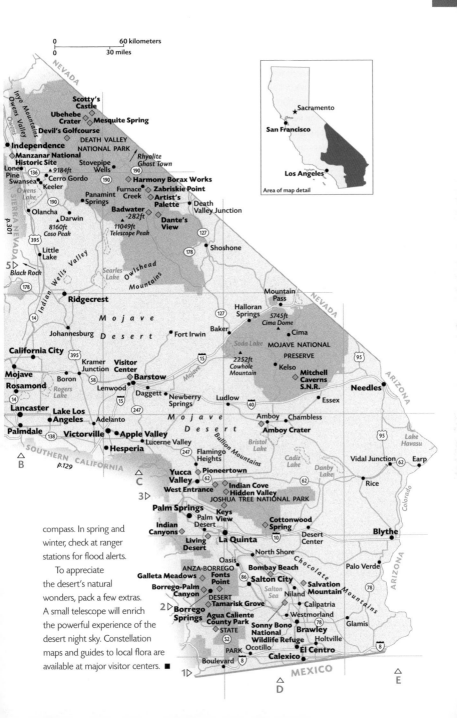

0   60 kilometers
0   30 miles

NEVADA

Inyo Mountains
Owens Valley
Owens

Scotty's Castle
Ubehebe Crater
Mesquite Spring
Devil's Golfcourse
DEATH VALLEY NATIONAL PARK
Independence
Manzanar National Historic Site
Lone Pine
136
▲9184ft
Stovepipe Wells
Rhyolite Ghost Town
190
Swansea
Cerro Gordo
Keeler
190
Harmony Borax Works
Furnace Creek
Zabriskie Point
Panamint Springs
Artist's Palette
Olancha
Darwin
Badwater -282ft
Dante's View
Death Valley Junction
8160ft Coso Peak
11049ft Telescope Peak
395
127
Little Lake
178
Shoshone
5▷
Black Rock
178
Searles Lake
Owlshead Mountains
14
Ridgecrest
Mountain Pass
NEVADA
Mojave
Halloran Springs
127
5745ft Cima Dome
Johannesburg
Desert
Fort Irwin
Baker
Cima
Soda Lake
MOJAVE NATIONAL PRESERVE
95
California City
395
Kramer Junction
Visitor Center
15
2252ft Cowhole Mountain
Kelso
Mojave
Boron
58
Barstow
Mitchell Caverns S.N.R.
Needles
Rosamond
Rogers Lake
Lenwood
Daggett
Newberry Springs
Ludlow
40
Essex
ARIZONA
14
Lancaster
Lake Los Angeles
Adelanto
247
Mojave
Desert
Amboy
Chambless
Palmdale
138
Victorville
Apple Valley
Lucerne Valley
247
Amboy Crater
Bristol Lake
95
Lake Havasu
Hesperia
Flamingo Heights
Bullion Mountains
Cadiz Lake
Danby Lake
Vidal Junction
62
Earp
B
SOUTHERN CALIFORNIA
P.129
C
Yucca Valley
Pioneertown
62
Rice
Colorado
3▷
West Entrance
Indian Cove
Hidden Valley
JOSHUA TREE NATIONAL PARK
Palm Springs
Keys View
Indian Canyons
Palm Desert
Cottonwood Spring
Desert Center
Blythe
Living Desert
La Quinta
10
North Shore
Chocolate
Palo Verde
Oasis
ANZA-BORREGO
Fonts Point
Bombay Beach
86
Salton City
Salvation Mountain
Mountains
ARIZONA
Galleta Meadows
Borrego-Palm Canyon
DESERT
Salton Sea
Niland
78
2▷
Tamarisk Grove
Calipatria
Borrego Springs
Agua Caliente County Park
Sonny Bono National
Westmorland
78
Glamis
52
STATE
PARK
Wildlife Refuge
Brawley
Holtville
Boulevard
8
Ocotillo
El Centro
8
Calexico
1▷
MEXICO
D
E

compass. In spring and winter, check at ranger stations for flood alerts.

To appreciate the desert's natural wonders, pack a few extras. A small telescope will enrich the powerful experience of the desert night sky. Constellation maps and guides to local flora are available at major visitor centers. ∎

THE DESERT
Sacramento
San Francisco
Los Angeles
Area of map detail

TOWARD DEATH VALLEY

The sites and towns that dot the Mojave Desert are a study in stubbornness, hinting at the tenacious if somewhat wistful pioneering mind-set of those who struggled to arrive here, and settled the area, in the 1800s. Here, as Ambrose Bierce once said, the "horrible is allied with the beautiful." The inhospitable terrain permits few roads, but the intrepid with time to explore will find opportunities for many memorable hikes. Even from your car, there are many natural wonders and historic sites to see as you go to Death Valley.

Drivers ascending to Whitney Portal have an awesome view of Mount Whitney and the Pinnacles.

Edwards Air Force Base

✉ 1 S. Rosamond Blvd., Edwards AFB

☎ 661-277-3510 (tours)

🕐 Tours by appt. twice monthly on Fridays 9 a.m.–1 p.m.; book 2 weeks in advance

www.edwards.af.mil

The town of **Mojave** (map p. 327 B4), gateway to the eponymous desert, is surrounded by intriguing sites, including **Edwards Air Force Base,** birthplace of supersonic flight and many other aviation firsts. The base's Air Force Flight Test Center Museum includes a Lockheed SR-71 Blackbird, Bell X-1, and other seminal aircraft. Public tours include a visit to the **NASA Armstrong Flight Research Center** (www.visitnasa. com), the primary landing site for the Space Shuttle and NASA's foremost testing ground for atmospheric flight research and

operations. In springtime, the 1,745-acre (706 ha) **Antelope Valley California Poppy Reserve** (1501 Lancaster Rd., tel 661-724-1180, www.parks.ca.gov), 25 miles (40 km) west of Palmdale, bursts into audacious color with its bloom of native wildflowers.

Calif. 14 leads north to Death Valley National Park (see pp. 330–331) via **Red Rock Canyon State Park** (Ridgecrest, 25 miles N of Mojave on Calif. 14, tel 661-946-6092, www.parks .ca.gov), geological wonder and setting for the opening scenes in Jurassic Park (1993).

INSIDER TIP:

If you are driving to Mammoth Lakes (see p. 314) via U.S. 395, stop at Manzanar National Historic Site, where Japanese Americans were incarcerated during World War II.

—ERIN STONE
National Geographic contributor

The town of **Independence** stands not far from the ruins of old Fort Independence, where, in the 1860s, there occurred a number of often violent uprisings by the Paiute. The fort closed in 1872, after the Paiute were violently suppressed. Today the main attraction is the **Eastern California Museum,** which houses a detailed collection of pioneer and Native American history and a re-created village.

South of Independence is the site of the Manzanar Relocation Camp, where 10,000 Japanese Americans were interned during 1942–45, after the bombing of Pearl Harbor. This relic of a dark period in the nation's history is now **Manzanar National Historic Site,** with a superb museum.

To reach Death Valley National Park, you turn east off U.S. 395 onto Calif. 136 just south of **Lone Pine** (see sidebar). Near the junction is dry **Owens Lake,** named after Richard Owen, a member of Frémont's 1845 expedition. The lake was a viable waterway for steamers into the early 1900s, but since the arrival of the Los Angeles Aqueduct in 1913, which sapped most of the feeder streams, it has shrunk away to nothing. It contains some of the world's largest sodium silicate deposits.

Along Calif. 136 are several ghost towns, including **Keeler** *(map p. 327 B5),* a former mining town with a museum and ghost mines to explore. **Cerro Gordo** *(map p. 327 B5, tel 760-876-5030, www.cerrogordomines.com)* was once known as California's Comstock, producing more than 4.5 million ounces (127,570 kg) of silver, lead, and zinc during the 19th century. ■

Lone Pine

The little town of Lone Pine is a base for climbers and skiers on **Mount Whitney,** whose peak soars to 14,495 feet (4,418 m) 25 miles (40 km) to the west. **Whitney Portal,** 11 miles (17 km) west of Lone Pine, is the start of several hiking trails, including the one that leads to the summit. Movie enthusiasts know Lone Pine for its October film festival *(tel 760-876-9909)* featuring old cowboy movies. The visitor information center has a map to movie sites. Among the classics filmed in the nearby **Alabama Hills** were *Gunga Din* (1939) and *The Lone Ranger* (1956).

Independence
🅰 327 B6
Visitor Information
✉ Indepdence Chamber of Commerce, 139 N. Edwards St.
☎ 760-878-0084

Eastern California Museum
✉ 155 N. Grant St., Independence
☎ 760-878-0258
💲 Donation
www.inyocounty.us/ecmsite

Manzanar National Historic Site
🅰 327 B6
✉ US 395, 9 miles N of Lone Pine
☎ 760-878-2194
www.nps.gov/manz

Lone Pine
🅰 327 B6
Visitor Information
✉ Chamber of Commerce, 120 S. Main St., Lone Pine
☎ 760-876-4444
www.lonepine chamber.org

DEATH VALLEY NATIONAL PARK

Perhaps more than any one of its singular geological wonders, it is the ride down into Death Valley on Calif. 190, through the dusty Panamint Mountains, that lingers in the memory. It is a descent of grandeur into the hottest, driest, lowest place in the U.S. There is no better way to appreciate the entire sweep of Death Valley National Park. Take it slowly.

■ Sunrise at Zabriskie Point reveals some of Death Valley's mesmerizing geological grandeur.

Death Valley National Park

⛰ 327 B6–C5

Visitor Information

✉ Visitor Center, Calif. 190, Furnace Creek

☎ 760-786-3200

www.nps.gov/deva

Scotty's Castle

⛰ 327 B6

☎ 877-444-6777

💲 $$$

www.recreation.gov

The best time to visit is February through mid-April, when the desert wildflowers bloom and temperatures remain tolerable. Winter is the most crowded season. Visitors coming in summer will need an air-conditioned car, a supply of water, and a carefully timed plan: Walking is bearable very early or very late in the day. You will find accommodations, restaurants, and a store in **Furnace Creek** *(map p. 327 C5)*.

In the far north of Death Valley, at **Mesquite Spring** *(map p. 327 B6)*, on a sharp turn in Calif. 267, is one of the stranger manifestations of émigré architectural fever in the state. It is **Scotty's Castle,** a Moorish-style mansion built in the 1920s. In 2015, it was badly damaged by a flash flood; it closed for eight years of repairs. The **Death Valley Natural History Association** *(tel 800-478-8564, www.dvnha. org)* offers walking tours of the grounds. A few miles to the west is the **Ubehebe Crater** *(map p. 327 B6),* caused by volcanic activity.

Several popular natural wonders within a few miles of Furnace Creek (all well marked) include the **Devil's Golf Course,** a huge salt pan where winds push boulders across the slick surface during rare rains; a 4WD vehicle is required. Farther east is the **Artist's Palette** *(map p. 327 C5)*, a series of hills colored with a rainbow of various mineral hues. The colors are especially stunning around dawn and dusk. The same is true of nearby **Golden Canyon.**

If you have time and the heat is not too intense, explore the 4-mile (6.4 km) **Gower Gulch Loop,** a trail that winds through colorful badlands, multi-hued canyons, and old borax mines.

Though it lacks the romance of silver and gold, borax—a chemical deposited when alkaline lakes evaporate—was one of few valuable resources found in Death Valley. It was mined here from the 1880s. The **Borax Museum** at Furnace Creek tells the story of the mines through its collection of wagons and machinery. The **Harmony Borax Works Interpretive Trail**—at a quarter mile (.4 km) long, manageable in all but

the worst heat—starts at the Borax Works parking area two miles (3 km) north of Furnace Creek.

Don't leave Death Valley without visiting one of its spectacular viewpoints—ideally at sunrise or sunset. **Zabriskie Point** *(map p. 327 C5)* is the site of the 1970 Antonioni movie of the same name. One of the valley's most memorable sights, it has inspired dozens of well-known plein air painters from around the world.

About 20 miles (32 km) south of Furnace Creek is **Dante's View** *(map p. 327 C5)*, which overlooks the valley from the Black Mountains. From here, you can see the 14,495-foot (4,418 m) peak of Mount Whitney and **Badwater Basin** *(map p. 327 C5)*, site of the lowest point in the U.S. (282 feet/86 m below sea level). West of Badwater, the land rises impressively, reaching 11,049 feet (3,367 m) at the top of **Telescope Peak,** only a few miles away. ■

Borax Museum

✉ The Ranch at Furnace Creek, Date Grove Rd. & Calif. 190

☎ 760-786-3215

Singing Sands

Overshadowed by its more famous northerly neighbor, **Mojave National Preserve** *(map p. 327 D4, tel 760-252-6100, www. nps.gov/moja)*, more than three million desolate acres (1.2 million ha), lies south of I-15, southeast of Death Valley.

If you travel here, be sure to see the unique sand formation of **Kelso Dunes,** near Kelso. This sea of delicate, wind-created sand sculpture spreads out at the base of Providence Mountain. Golden-rose quartz grains, blown down from Afton Canyon over the course of 25,000 years, create a richly colored palette. Even more engaging is the unmistakable loud thrumming noise caused by loose sand

sliding down the steep 600-foot (183 m) dunes. Study of such dunes has led some anthropologists to link their subaural wavelengths to religious experiences by native peoples.

This part of the Mojave contains a number of other unusual geological sites. North from Kelso on Kelso-Cima Road are extensive ancient lava flows traced by fossilized tube worms. This road takes you to **Cima Dome** *(map p. 327 D4)*, a high rounded hunk of rock thrust some 1,500 feet (457 m) above the desert floor. Turning back south from Kelso on Kelbecker Road, visit the **Amboy Crater** *(map p. 327 D3)*, a 250-foot (76 m) cinder cone.

WATER, WATER

There is, indisputably, a lot of it: Every year, some 200 million acre-feet (each enough to flood an acre of land under a foot of water) fall on California, two-thirds of it in the northern half of the state. And therein lies the rub. The water falls in the wrong place. It tends to evaporate or go where no one wants it to go. And most population growth has occurred in the south, a land of few rivers and even fewer lakes and streams.

It takes a lot of water to support California's suburbs, like this one in San Bernadino.

The story of the first aqueduct is a familiar one to most Californians. A turn-of-the-20th-century Los Angeles business cabal, worried about the impact of drought on land prices, convinced a panicked citizenry to underwrite a 230-mile (370 km) water canal from Owens Lake. Visionary engineer William Mulholland built the aqueduct, the water from which was promptly used to "green up" San Fernando Valley real estate. The fat cats profited, but the public still needed water. A new study was commissioned, and a new aqueduct was built, this one from Sacramento. More water. More suburban growth. The story was repeated again and again.

The pattern persists to this day. Yet as suburban growth continues, many in California have come to question the belief that water needs can be filled by importing more and more water from far reaches of the state. Take the case of metropolitan Los Angeles. Today the region has 45 percent of the population on 6 percent of the state's habitable land—but only .06 percent of the state's total stream flow. With the population predicted to grow from 16 to 24 million over the next few decades, the region would seem ripe for yet another large-scale public works project.

Recent experience, however, suggests otherwise, says UCLA's Martha Davis, who

What Water Does in California

Left undirected and unrestrained, water has had a profound impact on the topography of California. Four interesting manifestations of this impact are:

Underground rivers (Mojave Desert): Created 15,000 years ago when sedimentation on aboveground rivers hardened to form a sandy "lid."

Alluvial fans (Death Valley): Formed when periodic downpours loosen hillside rubble and carry it to the bottom, creating fan-shaped mounds. *Bajadas,* also in deserts, are essentially spread-out, large-scale alluvial fans.

Badlands (statewide): Thin spires, thick columns, and undulating folds carved into soft sandstone hills by surface runoff.

Underground caves (throughout Sierra parks): Made by groundwater percolating through soluble limestone rock.

---

studies water-use issues and the environment. In 1990, a drought that had begun in 1987 unexpectedly intensified. For the first time, the Metropolitan Water District mandated water rationing. "The response was dramatic," says Davis. "In 1990, water sales peaked at an all-time high of 2.6 million acre-feet; by 1993, these sales had plummeted to 1.5 million acre-feet . . . We have fundamentally changed the water demand curve for the southland. We are supporting more people with less (not more) water."

But can such policies really meet the water needs of L.A.'s future population? Ultimately such questions are resolved not by public policy planners but by politicians, who must balance the short-term needs of their constituents with the longer-term needs of the state as a whole. The former usually prevail.

Yet an enlightened public is beginning to alter water politics as well. A good example is the emergence of the Los Angeles River as an important political touchstone. For decades treated as little more than a giant drainage ditch, the river in recent years has become the focus of an intense debate over urban water use. A group named Friends of the Los Angeles River (*www.folar.org*) has successfully fought to restore parts of the stream to a more natural state. The result is striking. Yet whether that kind of sustained civic activism can alter the larger patterns of water use is still unclear. The hand of *Homo sapiens,* after all, has made southern California what it is today.

Sand dune formations are no match for the hot sun in Death Valley National Park.

JOSHUA TREE NATIONAL PARK

Although there is much to see within this 800,000-acre (324,000 ha) park, no one element has attracted as much comment, speculation, and even poetry as the Joshua tree, a plant so biomorphically abstract that it might have been designed by a demented artist—its branches set at right angles to its trunk and then bent upward, as in prayerful supplication.

A characteristic sight: The afternoon sun warms a Joshua tree and rock formation near Split Rock.

**Joshua Tree
National Park**

🗺 327 C3–D3

Visitor Information

✉ Oasis Visitor
Center, Calif. 62
& Utah Trail,
Twentynine
Palms; Joshua
Tree Visitor
Center, 6554
Park Blvd.,
Joshua Tree

☎ 760-367-
5500 (Twenty
Nine Palms),
760-366-1855
(Joshua Tree)

💲 $$$ individual,
$$$$ per vehicle
& occupants per
vehicle

www.nps.gov/jotr

Not all have fallen in love with the Joshua tree. Capt. John C. Frémont, the first English-speaking traveler to record the trees, spoke of "their stiff and ungraceful forms . . . the most repulsive tree in the vegetable kingdom." To California Mormons, migrating back to Utah in the 1850s, the tree's branches seemed like prophetic guideposts. They promptly named the tree for the prophet Joshua. To many contemporary hikers, however, the Joshua tree's spareness, silhouetted against the evening sky, embodies the natural solitude they seek in the park.

The area was long the home of the Chemehuevi before becoming a popular stop for miners in the late 1800s. Later, cattle ranchers arrived.

In the 1920s came homesteaders and the onslaught of cactus poaching—poaching that became so severe as to cause one prominent Pasadena matron, M. H. Hoyt, to lead a drive to win government

INSIDER TIP:

Combine the park with a visit to nearby Pioneertown (*www.visitpio neertown.com*), a former Hollywood Western movie set that is a lived-in museum with mock gunfights.

—CHRISTOPHER P. BAKER
National Geographic author

protection, achieved in 1936 when the Roosevelt administration created Joshua Tree National Monument; in 1994 it was declared a national park.

Perhaps the most important natural aspect of the park is its merging of two distinct deserts: the hot, dry Colorado at its lower eastern end with the slightly wetter, cooler, higher Mojave in the west. In the former grow the ground-hugging creosote bush and the spread-eagled ocotillo. In the latter, Joshua trees proliferate, as well as several distinctive groves of fan palms. The park represents a wide diversity of geological activity, its stones and alluvial fans and varnished rock producing a kind of desert mosaic. Most visitors spend their time in the west, with the highest concentration of sites of interest.

Camping and Activities

If you plan on camping—and during the spring many do—the campground at nearby **Indian Cove** (tel 877-444-6777) is hard to beat. This is also a center of activity for the growing number of rock-climbing enthusiasts (Joshua Tree Rock Climbing School, tel 760-366-4745, www.joshua treerockclimbing.com). Not far away, off Canyon Road, is the **Fortynine Palms Oasis.** Here a 1.5-mile (2.4 km) trail takes you to a desert oasis, replete with fan palms and animals slaking their thirst amid rare desert shade.

The most scenic drive begins at the west entrance on Park Boulevard. Go south from the entrance station to **Hidden Valley,** with some of the most astounding rock formations in the park. To its west is

the trailhead for **Lost Horse Mine,** about 2 miles (3.2 km) away. (Do not enter this, or any other, mine.) Farther south still is **Keys View,** an overlook at 5,815 feet (1,772 m). A number of the more ambitious trails also originate around here (maps from the visitor center). Though walking is the best way to experience the park, there is also the well-marked **Geology Motor Tour,** an 18-mile (29 km) unpaved road through

Hidden Oasis

South from the Cholla Cactus Garden is **Cottonwood Spring** (map p. 327 D3, also accessible from I-10), one of the best kept secrets in Joshua Tree National Park and a welcome oasis. The spring, formed eons ago by an earthquake, was long used by Native Americans; their mortars, clay pots, and various other reminders of habitation can be seen throughout the spring area. Bighorn sheep can often be spotted in the Cottonwood Wash. For the hardy, the **Lost Palms Oasis Trail** rewards the 8-mile (12.8 km) effort with great views and the largest grove of fan palms in the park.

dramatic rockscapes. Farther east, **Skull Rock** is one of the park's most popular sites; here a giant bolder is eroded to resemble a skull.

With more time, explore the central and eastern parts of the park. The former affords a rare glimpse at a desert-to-desert transition zone. Stop at the **Cholla Cactus Garden.** Here grows the teddybear cholla, a.k.a. the jumping cholla, named for the tendency of its spiny needles to "jump" onto the clothes of passing hikers. The garden is best seen in early morning or late afternoon, when the cactus seem to glow. ∎

PALM SPRINGS

The ultimate American oasis had its beginnings in 1885, when a health resort was built around hot springs in the traditional home of the Cahuilla Native Americans. Revivified as a celebrity hideaway in the 1920s by the likes of Rudolph Valentino and Marlene Dietrich, remade in the 1950s as home to such Hollywood stars as Bob Hope and Frank Sinatra, Palm Springs owes its irresistible charms to its stunning setting and winter weather.

■ A journey on Palm Springs Aerial Tramway is equivalent to traveling from Mexico to Alaska as it traverses five ecosystems.

Palm Springs

◭ 327 C3

Visitor Information

✉ Visitor Center, 2901 N. Palm Canyon Dr., Palm Springs

☎ 760-778-8418, 800-347-7746

www.visitpalm springs.com

Today, after an interregnum of benign neglect, Palm Springs has been revitalized with youthful vigor. The draw for the traveler can be summed up in five attractions: sun, pool, spa, golf, and more golf—more than 110 courses carpet Palm Springs and the seven adjoining communities that make up the Coachella Valley, rimmed by dramatically sculpted mauve mountains. A sixth might be shopping: **Palm Canyon Drive** and **El Paseo**, in nearby **Palm Desert** (*map p. 327 C3, visitor information,*

Visitor Center, 73-470 El Paseo, Ste. F-7, tel 760-568-1441 or 800-873-2428, www.discover palmdesert.com), are both upscale shopping areas where people-watching during the high season (*Oct.–May*) is a draw in itself.

One experience not to miss is the **Palm Springs Aerial Tramway** (*1 Tramway Rd., tel 760-325-1449 or 800-515-TRAM, www.pstramway. com, $$$$$*). Spanning the 2.5 miles (4 km) between the desert floor and the top of Mount San Jacinto, the tramway, which has the longest single span of cable in the world, was completed in 1963. The tram, which revolves through 360 degrees, offers fantastic views of desert and mountains. At the top, 8,516 feet (2,595 m) up, an upscale restaurant offers amazing views, while **Mount San Jacinto State Park** *(tel 951-659-2607, www.parks. ca.gov)* offers more than 54 miles (87 km) of trails.

Palm Springs Culture

Another magnificent aspect of the Palm Springs scene is the popular **Palm Springs Air Museum,** which has one of the world's largest collections of flying World War II planes, along with rare and an extensive collection of World War II artifacts, uniforms, and memorabilia.

The **Palm Springs Art Museum** has an outstanding collection (see p. 339) and a well-curated series of changing exhibitions. It also holds a number of Native American artifacts and offers concerts and lectures. In front, since April 2021, stands Seward Johnson's provocative 26-foot-tall (7.9 m) "Forever Marilyn" statue of Marilyn Monroe *(Museum Way)*. Nearby, the new **Agua Caliente Cultural Museum** combines a stunning museum dedicated to the history and culture of the Cahuilla peoples with a spa that taps the natural hot spring on the site of the city's founding.

A small but engaging historical stop is **Village Green Heritage Center** *(221 S. Palm Canyon Rd.)*, featuring the **McCallum Adobe** *(tel 760-323-8297, closed Mon.–Tues., a.m. Wed.–Sun., and June–Sept., $)*, displaying artifacts of Palm Springs's original settler, John Guthrie McCallum.

Also named for McCallum is the **McCallum Theatre for the Performing Arts** *(7300 Fred Waring Dr., Palm Desert, tel 760-340-2787, www. mccallumtheatre.com)*, on the campus of College of the Desert. The McCallum presents a full program including theater and music.

Palm Desert's streets are enlivened by more than 150 public sculptures, notably along the ritzy El Paseo boulevard and in the 72-acre (29 ha) Civic Center Park *(San Pablo Ave.)*; not to be missed in the park are David Phelps's "The Dreamer" and Dee Clements's 88-foot (27 m) "Holocaust Memorial." Pick up a map and booklet at the visitor center.

Scenic Calif. 111 links Palm Springs with Palm Desert and the other neighboring desert communities, including **Indian Wells**, with its world-class **Indian Wells Tennis Garden** *(www.indianwellstennisgarden. com)*, and **La Quinta,** known for its premier golf courses. ∎

Palm Springs Air Museum

- ✉ 745 N. Gene Autry Trail, Palm Springs
- ☎ 760-778-6262
- 💲 $$$$

www.palmspringsair museum.org

Palm Springs Art Museum

- ✉ 101 Museum Dr. Palm Springs
- ☎ 760--322-4800
- 🕐 Closed Mon.
- 💲 $$ (free 1st Thurs. of month)

www.psmuseum.org

Agua Caliente Cultural Museum

- ✉ Tahquitz Canyon Way & N. Indian Canyon Dr. Palm Springs
- ☎ 760-778-1079
- 🕐 Closed Mon.– Tues. & a.m. Sun.

www.accmuseum.org

EXPERIENCE: Tracing the San Andreas Fault

The San Andreas—California's notorious earthquake fault—in the Coachella Valley, runs ruler-straight along the depression's eastern edge, along the base of the Indio hills. For those who know what to look for (like linear oases of native fan palms), the fault and its fractured off-shoots can be spotted from the air or from atop the **Palm Springs Aerial Tramway.** One of the smaller faults is responsible for the string of hot springs (for which Palm Springs is named) along the base of Mt. San Jacinto. Visitors can cycle the fault with **Big Wheel Bike Tours** *(tel 760-779-1837, www.bwbtours.com, $$$$$)* or drive it on a **Red Jeep Tours** *(tel 760-477-4217, www.red-jeep. com, $$$$$)* adventure.

GLAMOUR IN THE DESERT

Except for the late 1970s to the early '90s, when Palm Springs was considered outdated and déclassé, the city has been synonymous with wealth and glamour. The mountains, palm oases, and winter weather attracted not just Hollywood stars and starlets, but architects whose mid-century "desert modernist" designs helped define the glamorous lifestyle of the rich and famous and Palm Springs' vernacular style of "indoor-outdoor" living.

■ The Elvis Presley "Honeymoon House" is one of many Palm Springs homes associated with the rich and famous.

In recent decades, Palm Springs has staged an impressive comeback as a trendy desert destination du jour. One reason is that a new generation of urbanites has discovered the blessings of its natural surrounds and elegantly informal "desert zen" style. Add to this the upsurge of interest in postwar modernist architecture of which Palm Springs (with its more than two thousand modernist homes and public buildings) can be considered ground zero.

Much of the renewed interest has been generated by younger bicoastal types who have snapped up and restored such architectural gems as the seven 1960s experimental steel houses (*Sunnyview Dr.*) by renowned architect Donald Wexler. This urban revival is epitomized by famed Kaufman House (*470 W. Vista Chino*), built in 1946 by the great Richard Neutra and once owned by singer and Palm Springs' resident Barry Manilow. Following restoration in 2008 it was auctioned by Christie's as a work of art for $15 million (and listed for sale in October 2020 for $25 million). The work of the late Albert Frey is also attracting attention. Next to the Kaufman House stands one of his most engaging pieces of work, the Loewy House (*500 W. Panorama Rd.*), which was commissioned in 1946 for Raymond Loewy, designer of the Coca-Cola bottle.

Celebrity, of course, fuels much of the scene (Palm Springs still hosts a number of celebrities, such as Manilow, actress Suzanne Somers, and novelist Anne Rice). Bob and Dolores

Hope were the king and queen of the desert; their 1979, 23,600-square-foot (2,190 m²) hilltop mansion was designed by architect John Lautner, a largely unsung genius of California modernism. The Hopes' first home *(1014 Buena Vista Dr.)* was just two blocks north of that of his inseparable sidekick Bing Crosby *(1011 E. El Alameda)*. Frank Sinatra's first Palm Springs house is nearby at 1148 Alejo Road.

Old-time celebrity homes abound. Local experts (see below) will guide the truly curious to several of them. De rigeur stops on the celebrity circuit include Liberace's Neoclassical style home *(1441 N. Kaweanah Rd.)* and Elvis Presley's "Honeymoon House", known as "House of Tomorrow" *(1350 Ladera Circle)*, a dramatic structure originally built for Donald Alexander, the midcentury developer responsible for building many of Palm Springs's modernist homes.

■ **Duane Hanson's lifelike "Old Couple on a Bench" is an icon of the Palm Springs Art Museum.**

INSIDER TIP:

Frank Sinatra's first Palm Springs house, on Alejo Road, can be rented for a cool $2,500 a night *(tel 877-318-2090, www.sinatra house.com)*.

—ANN MARIE HOUPPERT
Librarian, National Geographic Socitey

Many period motels have metamorphosed into chic boutique hotels furnished with classic retro kitsch pieces by Saarinen, Noguchi, and other famous modernist designers. The younger crowd flocks to such places as the Korakia Pensione *(www.korakia.com)*, a 1920s Hollywood getaway in Moroccan style, and the recently renovated modernist Monkey Tree Hotel *(www.themonkeytreehotel.com)*, designed in 1960 by Albert Frey as a reclusive escape for celebrities. Another place for the younger set is Arrive *(www.arrivehotels.com)*, a chic contemporary hotel built in 2015 and inspired by the sun-worshiping lifestyle and such distinctive "desert modernist" elements as classic butterfly rooflines. In Palm Springs, culture abounds, although much of it is the preserve of the locals, who have elevated fundraising parties to an art form and their own homes into architectural shrines. Fortunately, the E. Stewart Williams-designed Palm Springs Art Museum (see p. 337) offers a look into the collecting habits of this megaclass. Much of the museum's Western and Native American art was donated by Palm Springs residents, film star Kirk Douglas (1916–2020) and author Sidney Sheldon (1917–2007). It includes some fine examples of work by British sculptors Henry Moore and Barbara Hepworth, American Old West master Frederic Remington, and California pop art maestro Edward Ruscha. A treat awaits in the work of actor and Palm Springs resident George Montgomery (1916–2000), who created a notable collection of sculpture and furniture. The museum's Architecture and Design Center *(300 S. Palm Canyon Dr.)* occupies the former Santa Fe Federal Savings and Loan building, designed by E. Stewart Williams in 1961.

Before setting out to see Palm Springs's celebrity homes, pick up a map of celebrity home locations at the Palm Springs Visitors Center (see p. 336). Palm Springs Celebrity Tours *(tel 760-895-8005, www.palmspringscelebrity tours.com)* offers guided "talk and gawk" trips.

INDIAN CANYONS

Four spectacular desert canyons scythe the base of Mt. San Jacinto in Palm Springs (see pp. 336–337). Although today traversed by hikers and equestrians, the area was once the domain of a single hardy people, the Agua Caliente band of the Cahuilla. Their imprint on the area remains in the form of pictographs, used to mark holy places, and bedrock mortars, which the Cahuilla used to grind the nuts, seeds, and berries that sustained them for centuries. Their descendants administer the canyons—which are considered sacred—and are major sponsors of the new, 50-acre (20 ha) Agua Caliente Cultural Museum complex in downtown Palm Springs.

Indian Canyons

 327 C3

✉ South Palm
  Canyon Dr.,
  Palm Springs

☎ 760-323-6018

🕐 Closed late Apr.–
  early May

$ $$

www.indian-canyons.
com

Tahquitz Canyon

✉ 500 W.
  Mesquite,
  Palm Springs

☎ 760-323-6018

$ $$$

www.tahquitz
canyon.com

Circled by barren hills, the four canyons each have a stream surrounded by steep rocky sides. The 15-mile-long (24 km) **Palm Canyon,** accessed via South Palm Canyon Drive, is the biggest of the four. The vast grove of *Washingtonia* palms that stretches for several miles along Palm Canyon is one of the biggest in the world.

After visiting the **Trading Post,** where you can buy hiking maps and Native American crafts, take the moderately graded trail into the canyon, which follows a beautiful palm-shaded stream before climbing up into the cactus-studded mountains. Nearby **Murray Canyon** has herds of wild horses running through it. Bighorn sheep and deer are also numerous in the vicinity. An easy hike leads to **Andreas Canyon,** the site of another enormous grove of *Washingtonia* palms.

Closer to the city center, **Tahquitz Canyon** is the setting for a huge natural amphitheater beneath Tahquitz Peak. Snowmelt from the peak feeds a spectacular waterfall. Ranger-led tours that depart the visitor center show ancient pictographs and irrigation systems. ■

EXPERIENCE: Floating the Colorado

A hundred miles (160 km) east of the Coachella Valley, the Colorado River is still largely wild and unfettered, a watery divide between California and Arizona protected within the confines of several national wildlife refuges and state parks. Float trips start from the tiny hamlet of Walter's Camp, 38 miles (61 km) south of Blythe *(map p. 327 E2)*. Whether in canoe, kayak, or homemade raft, the float trip is normally done over two days with an overnight at **Picacho State Recreation Area** *(tel 760-996-2963, www.parks.ca.gov)*, on the California side. The Colorado is strong and wide in these lower reaches, but lack of rapids makes for an easy passage. Wildlife along the banks includes coyotes and desert bighorn sheep, rattlesnakes, and myriad migratory waterbirds. Abandoned 19th-century mines and homesteads add a touch of human history. The 35-mile (56 km) downriver journey ends at Lake Martinez on the Arizona side. For those who don't have their own boats, **Lake Martinez Resort** *(tel 928-783-9589)* will deliver rented canoes to Walter's Camp and for a small fee drive your vehicle to the take-out point downriver.

THE LIVING DESERT

Deserts and their denizens have long captured the minds of curious travelers and mystics, but seldom seem to have inspired those charged with putting together parks and zoos. Established in 1970, the Living Desert wildlife and botanical park is a rare exception.

Rattlesnakes are among the deadliest inhabitants of the Living Desert.

The Living Desert offers a complete introduction to desert ecologies worldwide. Spread over 1,200 acres (485 ha) of desert wash in **Palm Desert,** the park contains nearly 400 species of animals (from aardvark to zebra) and a wide array of desert flora.

Although the **Discovery Room** near the entrance is ostensibly set up for children, it provides all ages with a tutorial on desert basics. Animal exhibits are interspersed throughout specialized ecosystems, among them the shady Palm Oasis (with its walk-through aviary), the Mojave Garden, and the Sonoran Pond with its desert fishes.

To the east is a section dedicated to African deserts and savannas, with animals ranging from gazelles and warthogs to giraffes and cheetah.

The big attraction is **Eagle Canyon,** with hiking trails, streams, and native fauna like mountain lions, bobcats, Mexican wolves, and golden eagles. Another exhibit explains the San Andreas Fault (see sidebar p. 337). Visitors can also watch animals being treated in the **Tennity Wildlife Hospital.** ∎

INSIDER TIP:

The Living Desert allows your family to adopt a desert animal, or species, for one year (www.livingdesert.org).

—JENNIFER ALLARD
National Geographic contributor

Living Desert

🅰 327 C2

✉ 47900 Portola Ave., Palm Desert

☎ 760-346-5694

🕐 Closed p.m. June–Sept.

💲 $$$$$

www.livingdesert.org

FRAGRANT TREES OF THE DESERT

Although the spring bloom of the desert wildflowers gets all the press, much of the glorious fragrance that accompanies it is provided by the spring and early summer flourish of the desert trees. The most numerous species are all represented at the Living Desert zoo and gardens (see p. 341).

This crowning bloom of paloverde illustrates the Living Desert's surprising flora.

Blue paloverde *(Cercidium floridum)* has a pale green trunk, spiny olive-green twigs, and sparse (if not entirely absent) foliage. Short and willowy, it is often found along stream and wash banks, performing a vital service in preventing erosion. Once a year, it bursts into bright yellow bloom. Desert burros can be seen champing on its soft wood in stupid delight.

Desert smoketree *(Dalea spinosa)* is one of the great landscape treasures of the Palm Springs area. It owes its mystical image—a fog-shrouded tangle of wooden antlers—to its evanescent foliage. Until its third year, its twigs are thickly coated with gray hairs, which explains the tree's ghostly appearance under the summer moon. It

flowers purple precisely in the dead heat of summer, when tourists have departed.

Desert catalpa *(Chilopsis linearis)* was once used to make hunting bows. Fittingly known as the bow willow, it has long, thin, light green leaves and is willowlike in appearance. It often stands—hunches, rather—over washed-out culverts and ditches throughout the Colorado Desert. Its remarkable hibiscus-like flowers are showy pink with white and yellow spots in the throat. Later in the summer, the heat draws out their subtle fragrance, which resembles that of sweet violets.

Desert ironwood *(Olneya tesota)* more than lives up to its name. With a specific gravity of 1.14, a piece of it will sink in water. Its notable red-brown bark peels in long downward strips, and it has gray leaves. If you are in the desert in early summer, you will witness its remarkable flowering, a flourish of thousands of indigo and rose-purple blooms with a subtle perfume.

True mesquite *(Prosopis juliflora)* is among the Colorado Desert's dominant flora. It has dark, reddish-brown bark and slim, smooth twigs like tendrils waving at the bottom of the sea. Its usefulness to a range of inhabitants is legendary. Native American peoples of the Southwest used its strong wood to erect their homes; their children used it to make a wooden kickball; the elders made of its sugary fruit a nasty liquor. Spaniards fed their cattle on it; confectioners used it to make gum; the U.S. Cavalry fed it to their horses. Nevertheless, mesquite has rarely received its due praise, probably because it is one of the desert's most invasive plants. Its scent—piney and smoky—is the desert's own.

ANZA-BORREGO DESERT STATE PARK

The fact that this 600,000-acre (242,811 ha) park is tucked into one of the most remote no-man's-lands in the state doesn't stop thousands of wildflower lovers from making their spring pilgrimage. And little wonder: Anza-Borrego is a capital of desert botanica. These blooms begin in February, with the blue sand verbena. Then come the agave, the mallow, the ocotillo, and the brittlebush. By April, the desert has become a vast—albeit temporary—wonderland of color.

Memorable places to go include the **Borrego-Palm Canyon Trail** *(trailhead on Borrego-Palm Canyon, W of Borrego Springs).* The path first winds through a bamboo-filled grove before ending at a waterfall and a grove of 800 fan palms. The **Tamarisk Grove** *(Calif. 78 and Yaqui Pass Rd.)* has a number of palm canyons and spectacular gorges. **Agua Caliente County Park** *(Cty. Rd. S2, S of Calif. 78)* is a site of the ancient Kumeyaay culture and a habitat for bighorn sheep and other desert wildlife. Ask for guides to archaeological sites at the visitor center.

For those staying in Borrego Springs, the one-hour round-trip east to see the views from **Fonts Point,** in the Borrego Badlands, is a must at sunset. A major draw is the two **Galleta Meadows** outside Borrego Springs, featuring more than 130 life-size dinosaurs and other welded-metal creatures, including a massive dragon, by artist Ricardo Breceda. ∎

INSIDER TIP:

The night sky above Anza-Borrego offers stargazers a glorious view of the universe unavailable from most of southern California.

—DENNIS MAMMANA
Professional astronomer & sky guide

Anza-Borrego Desert State Park

🗺 327 C2–D2

Visitor Information

✉ Visitor Center, 200 Palm Canyon, Borrego Springs

☎ 760-767-5311 (Park HQ), 760-767-4205 (Visitor Center)

www.parks.ca.gov

NOTE:
For up-to-date information on the spring bloom, contact the Anza-Borrego Desert State Park visitor center (see above) or the Payne Foundation *(tel 818-768-1802, www.theodorepayne .org, closed June–Feb.).*

EXPERIENCE: Borrego Desert Stargazing

Clear arid skies and far distances from California's big coastal cities give Anza-Borrego Desert State Park the distinction of being one of the best places in the U.S. to watch the heavens at night. The small desert town of Borrego Springs is the state's first and only designated International Dark Sky Community. In addition to the more common stars and constellations, dim objects like the Andromeda Galaxy and even rarities like the aurora borealis can sometimes be seen from Borrego.
Borrego Night Sky Tours *(tel 760-767-3656, www.borregonightskytours.com)* offers stargazing and photography workshops under the guidance of veteran astronomer Dennis Mammana. The **Springs at Borrego** *(tel 760-767-0004, www.springsat borrego.com)* RV resort has created its own small observatory with an 11-inch (38 cm) telescope, focus of the stargazing events that it organizes every year.

SALTON SEA

About 30 miles (48 km) south of Palm Springs, the Salton Sea was formed in 1905, when the Colorado River burst out of irrigation canals in nearby Yuma, Arizona, and ran, unchecked for almost two years, into a 35-by-15-mile (56 by 24 km) desert basin with no natural outlet. The river water picked up salts, which were left behind when the desert heat evaporated the water. Salts from surrounding farmlands also drain into the sea, increasing its salinity one percent yearly. Despite which, it is a mecca for bird-watching and fishing.

■ Seabirds flock to the shores of the Salton Sea.

Salton Sea

🗺 327 D2

Visitor Information

✉ 100-225 State Park Rd., North Shore (Mecca)

☎ 760-393-3052

www.parks.ca.gov

Sonny Bono Salton Sea National Wildlife Refuge

✉ Sinclair Rd. & Gentry Rd., Niland

☎ 760-348-5278

🕐 Visitor center closed Sat. & Sun.

www.fws.gov/ refuge/sonny_bono_ salton_sea

The Salton Sea's unique biology has had remarkable consequences. On the one hand, it has become one of the West Coast's great bird-watching areas, with a huge population of pelicans and egrets, among others. The birds come to feed on the equally huge fish population. On the other hand, the sea is also a quagmire of ecological problems, including occasional massive die-offs of fish. Authorities are shaping a plan to rehabilitate the sea, which is surrounded by the intensely irrigated Imperial Valley—a lush Eden where avocados, dates, grapes, tomatoes, and other vegetables are grown in astounding abundance. Nevertheless, the sea remains a popular destination for fisherfolk and campers. The **Mecca Beach** campground, about 1 mile (1.6 km) south of park headquarters, is a perfect base camp for fishing. For bird-watchers, the months from October through May are a delight. At that time, up to four million migrating birds flock about the sea. The **Sonny Bono Salton Sea National Wildlife Refuge** is the preferred destination for ornithologists.

The sea (elevation 236 feet/72 m below sea level) was in the 1950s and '60s a popular resort and water-skiing and powerboat racing destination, drawing celebrities such as Frank Sinatra and The Beach Boys. Most motels and yacht clubs are now derelict, but the community of **Bombay Beach** has been revived as a bohemian enclave of artists, drawing visitors to marvel at the surreal street art. Nearby, outside Niland, is **Salvation Mountain,** a massive Christian homage made of discarded tires, bricks, and other miscellany painted over with murals and Bible verses. ■

TRAVELWISE

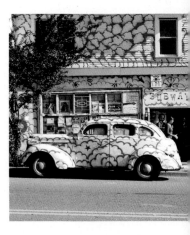

Traffic coordination, California style

TRAVELWISE

PLANNING YOUR TRIP
When to Go
Is there really a bad time to visit California? It depends upon which California you mean. If northern California, then the late winter and early spring months are a chilly proposition. If southern California, late August and September can be too hot for some. The basic climatic signposts are: In summer, go north; in winter, go south. Of course, this means you will encounter heavy tourist traffic. One alternative worth the effort is to explore the various tourist "cusp seasons" (very early spring in Wine Country, for example, or very early summer in L.A.).

Events & Festivals
California is full of cultural events: colorful agricultural festivals, seasonal music fests, sporting and ethnic venues. Check out each city's website and/or visitor information bureau for an up-to-date listing. Some favorites are:

January On Jan. 1, the Tournament of Roses Parade and Football Game (www.tournamentofroses.com) makes Pasadena one big party.

February San Francisco's Chinese New Year Parade (www.chinese-parade.com) still outclasses L.A.'s by far.

March The Mendocino Whale Watch Festival (www.mendowhale.com) commences with great gusto, and a lot of beer.

April The Antelope Valley's blooming of native poppies is a good excuse for music, art, food, and fun at the California Poppy Festival, in Lancaster (www.poppy festival.com).

May Mark Twain buffs will love the Jumping Frog Jubilee in Angels Camp, Gold Country (www.frogtown.org).

June For pure Wine Country atmosphere, you must experience the Napa Valley Wine Auction (www.auctionnapavalley.org).

July Right on the Central Coast are two great entertainment choices, the esteemed Carmel Bach Festival (www.bachfestival.org) and the Gilroy Garlic Festival (www.gilroygarlicfestival.com).

August At the Old Spanish Days Fiesta in old Santa Barbara (www.sbfiesta.org), you can get all dressed up and play hidalgo and hidalga for a day.

September The Monterey Jazz Festival (www.montereyjazz festival.org) competes with the Delta Blues Festival (www.deltablues festival.net)–and everybody wins!

October An air show by the Blue Angels at San Francisco's Fleet Week (www.fleetweeksf.org) highlights a week of events.

November This is a good time to attend Death Valley 49ers Encampment (www.deathvalley 49ers.org) at Furnace Creek. The Western heritage is revived with music, dance, and family-friendly activities.

December Multimillion-dollar yachts, small boats, and even kayaks bedecked in Christmas lights emblazon Newport Beach harbor during the Christmas Boat Parade (www.christmasboatparade.com).

GETTING AROUND
Airports
Californians pioneered the use of multi-passenger vans for to-and-from airport trips, and a number of companies ply their services (for example Shuttle Vans, Freeway Flyers, etc.) at all airports. Most are reliable, reasonable, and friendly. If you are staying at a major airport hotel, it will probably provide a free van ride to and from the airport; additionally, all the major car rental outfits provide a shuttle service to their outlets. Super Shuttle (tel 800-258-3826, www.supershuttle.com) offers door-to-door service in many cities.

John Wayne Orange County (tel 949-252-5200, www.ocair.com) This growing regional airport is a reasonable alternative to flying into L.A.

Los Angeles International (tel 855-463-5252, www.flylax.com) A taxi ride to downtown or Beverly Hills will cost approximately $50.

Oakland International (tel 510-563-3300, www.oaklandairport.com) A taxi ride to Oakland city center will cost about $40. A shuttle connects to the BART system.

Palm Springs (tel 760-318-3800, www.palmspringsairport.com) Taxi to center about $15.

Sacramento (tel 916-929-5411, www.sacramento.aero/smf) Taxi to center about $50.

San Francisco International (tel 650-821-8205, www.flysfo.com) For a taxi ride downtown, expect to pay $50. There is a BART station at the airport.

San Jose (tel 408-392-3600, www.flysanjose.com) Taxi to center approximately $20.

By Car

Unless you plan on landing in San Francisco and staying within the metropolitan area, get a car. The most helpful motorists' organization is the California State Automobile Association *(Northern California, tel 800-222-4357, www. calstate.aaa.com; Southern California, tel 800-400-4222, www.ace.aaa.com).*

California has a huge array of car rental agencies. If you respond to a "bargain" ad, only to find there are no longer any cars of the "bargain" line left to rent, ask for a free upgrade.

Avis: tel 800-325-7900, www.avis.com
Budget: tel 800-527-0700, www.budget.com
Dollar: tel 800-800-5252, www.dollar.com
Hertz: tel 800-654-4173, www.hertz.com

Public Transportation

Amtrak *(tel 800-872-7245, www .amtrak.com),* the nationwide rail network, has been enjoying good press and a revival among travelers who want to see the state more slowly. **Greyhound Lines** *(tel 800-231-2222, www.greyhound.com)* is the bus system, with services to most cities.

In San Francisco, the **Muni bus system** *(tel 311 or 415-701-2311, www.sfmta.com)* is quite well regarded. **BART** *(tel 510-464-6000, www.bart.gov),* the famous rapid transit train system, will whisk you comfortably from downtown to the East, North, and South Bays. Call the visitor bureau for details on passes.

In Los Angeles, the **Dash bus system** covers much of the city *(tel 213-808-2273, www.ladottransit .com).* The Metro system, currently fairly limited, is being extended *(tel 323-466-3876, www.metro.net).*

PRACTICAL ADVICE

- California is still paradise, but even paradise has a few rotten apples. Behave appropriately; do not walk alone in unknown districts; do not display expensive equipment or jewelry.
- Do not call it "Frisco."
- Do not call it "The Big Orange," "La La Land," "Tinseltown," or "El-Lay."
- Use common sense. Do not use an ATM machine if you are alone late at night.
- Do not expect everyone to speak English, particularly in some of the more "ethnic" parts of L.A. and San Francisco.
- Do not "flip the bird" to any other drivers, regardless of how badly they may be driving.
- Do not pick up hitchhikers and, save for extreme emergencies, do not stop to help anyone along the freeway unless there is another person in the car with you and you can telephone for help *(911)* immediately.
- Buy some good maps.
- Carry bottled water and a cell phone with you in the car.

Emergencies

In any part of the state, the 911 number is set aside for reporting all emergencies. If you are a victim of a crime, you may want to avail yourself of the counseling services at the Crime Victims' Hotline *(tel 800-394-2255).*

Visitors With Disabilities

The California legislature has enacted a number of laws requiring restaurants, universities, municipal facilities, and all transport systems to provide wheelchair access. To find out about your rights, call 510-644-2555. The hearing impaired can get information by calling 800-622-3277.

Visitor Information

The first resource is the **California Division of Tourism** *(555 Capital Mall, Ste. 1100, Sacramento, CA 95814, tel 916-444-4429, www. visitcalifornia.com),* which publishes a variety of helpful guides. Its website contains a list of regional convention and visitor bureaus and is linked to hundreds of region-specific sites, leading in turn to hotel, food, and attractions listings. The division has visitor information centers in 17 locations throughout the state.

An outstanding resource for outdoor folks is the **National Park Service** *(www.nps.gov).*

The principal city visitor information bureaus are in Los Angeles *(6801 Hollywood Blvd., Hollywood, tel 323-467-6412, www.discover losangeles.com),* San Diego *(1549 El Prado, Balboa Park, tel 619-239-0512, www.sandiego.org),* and San Francisco *(749 Howard St., tel 415-391-2000, www.sanfrancisco.travel).*

BACKGROUND READING

To really get up on California culture and history, there is no better single volume in print than Carey McWilliams's classic *California: The Great Exception.* Unfortunately, McWilliams's narrative ends in 1949, leaving the rest of the tale to countless imitators and others. One generally reliable commentator is the omni-intellectual state librarian, Kevin Starr. See any title under his name, particularly *Inventing the Dream* and *Material Dreams.* The novels of John Steinbeck profile life of Central California in the early 1900s; *The Grapes of Wrath* and *Cannery Row* are classics. Jack London's *San Francisco Stories* give a good sense of the city a century ago. John Muir's *The Mountains of California* is a must for all outdoor folk.

HOTELS & RESTAURANTS

California has an abundance of outstanding restaurants, with its principal cities at the top of the national culinary tree. Wealthy areas, such as Hollywood in the south and Silicon Valley in the north, have helped to attract some of the world's great chefs to the region. But the real deals—and some of the best food—are to be found in the ethnic restaurants run by first-generation immigrants from Asia and the Middle East. There the ingredients are fresh, the food is prepared with familial vigor, and the prices are modest.

The state's hotels, inns, and bed-and-breakfast establishments span a wide range of styles and amenities, from the super-chic Peninsula in Beverly Hills and the traditional Mark Hopkins in San Francisco to the indulgently quiet and restful Madrone Manor in Healdsburg. Save yourself some money—sometimes up to 50 percent—by looking in the Sunday edition of the *L.A. Times (www.latimes.com)*, where many weekday and weekend bargains are advertised.

What to Expect

Most California hotels operate what has become known as the "American plan," which simply means breakfast is not included in the price. What *should* be included is attentive, pleasant service, knowledgeable and proactive staff, and a database of local and regional information about everything from local eateries to cultural and arts venues or sports teams. All of the hotels and inns listed below should be able to provide these, although the degree to which their staff will do so varies enormously. Service, even in the priciest hotels, is a spotty commodity these days.

The listings that follow attempt to strike a balance between chain hotels and regionally unique hotels. The major chains listed all do a good job of the basics. The better bed-and-breakfasts are a worthwhile alternative; you may have to do a bit more homework before traveling, but, in general, you will get cheerier staff—and also breakfast.

Bed-and-Breakfast Association

California Association of Boutique & Breakfast Inns: tel 800-373-9251, www.cabbi.com

Credit Cards

AE American Express, DC Diners Club, MC Mastercard, V Visa

Hotel Chains & Groups

Doubletree: tel 800-610-8733, www.hilton.com/en/doubletree
Hilton: tel 800-445-8667, www.hilton.com
Holiday Inn: tel 888-465-4329, www.holidayinn.com
Hyatt: tel 800-233-1234, www.hyatt.com
Marriott: tel 800-627-7468, www.marriott.com
Ramada: tel 800-854-9517, www.ramada.com
Sheraton: tel 800-325-3535, www.sheraton.com
Westin: tel 800-937-8461, www.westin.com
Wyndham: tel 877-999-3223, www.wyndham.com

Hotel Restaurants

Outstanding restaurants in hotels are listed separately and a cross-reference is made in the hotel entry. Where a hotel restaurant is above the standard one would expect for a hotel of that quality, the restaurant symbol is given as well as the hotel one, and the restaurant is described in the entry. No indication is given where the hotel has a restaurant of no particular merit.

Parking

Where a hotel or restaurant has its own parking, the symbol **P** is included in the entry. Some hotels and restaurants offer valet parking, shown as **P** Valet.

Restaurants

Holiday closings may vary from year to year. It is advisable to check and to reserve a table.
L = lunch
D = dinner

Smoking

Smoking is not allowed in restaurants in California. By law, hotels must have 80 percent nonsmoking rooms and nonsmoking areas in the lobby. A few hotels do not allow smoking at all, and this is indicated in the entry.

Tipping

Except in rare situations (or when large groups are involved), tipping in California restaurants is, in theory, entirely voluntary. In reality, you are expected to leave around 15 percent of the subtotal (before tax, although some restaurants now suggest an outrageous 25 percent!). Still, if you have a bad experience, do not hesitate to leave less, or even nothing.

Organization

In the following section, hotels are listed under each location by price, then in alphabetical order, followed by restaurants also by price and alphabetical order.

PRICES

HOTELS

An indication of the cost of a double room in the high season is given by **$** signs.

$$$$$	Over $280
$$$$	$200–$280
$$$	$120–$200
$$	$80–$120
$	Under $80

RESTAURANTS

An indication of the cost of a three-course meal without drinks is given by **$** signs.

$$$$$	Over $80
$$$$	$50–$80
$$$	$35–$50
$$	$20–$35
$	Under $20

► LOS ANGELES

AIRPORT

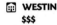 WESTIN
$$$

5400 W. CENTURY BLVD.

TEL 310-216-5858

www.marriott.com

One of the closest hotels to LAX, L.A.'s airport, has features that will endear it to anyone who must stay near the airport; these include deluxe soundproofing, spacious public areas, and contemporary styling.

🛈 747 🅿 🚭 🌀 🏊 🐚 🌀 All major cards

BEVERLY HILLS

BEVERLY HILLS HOTEL & 🍴 BUNGALOWS
$$$$$

9641 SUNSET BLVD.

TEL 310-276-2251

www.beverlyhillshotel.com

More than a hundred years old, this hotel has never seen better days than now, and remains a favorite of the Hollywood A-list. The gardens are lush, the service is excellent, and the rooms are elegantly appointed with just about every amenity known to Hollywoodkind. The **Polo Lounge** is still a fine place to eat, particularly at the ideal hour (1–2 p.m.), when you can observe the local wildlife devouring fresh shrimp salad and cool tomato soup.

🛈 208 rooms, 23 bungalows 🅿 Valet 🚭 🌀 🏊 🌀 🐚 All major cards

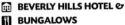 BEVERLY WILSHIRE
$$$$$

9500 WILSHIRE BLVD.

TEL 310-275-5200

www.fourseasons.com/bever lywilshire

This grandiose history-rich hotel, which sits at the base of Rodeo Drive, defines luxury with its Italian Renaissance architecture and sumptuous decor. Guests can choose bedrooms with contemporary chic styling or more sedate, traditional furnishings. Its Wolfgang Puck's Cut restaurant, plus the pool bar and spa are trendy spots for Hollywood celebs. It has been featured in many movies, notably *Pretty Woman*, starring Julia Roberts and Richard Gere, and swinging bachelor Warren Beatty once lived here for 15 years.

🛈 132 🅿 🚭 🌀 🏊 🌀 🐚 All major cards

PENINSULA BEVERLY HILLS
$$$$$

9882 S. SANTA MONICA BLVD.

TEL 310-551-2888

www.peninsula.com/en/ beverly-hills

Without a doubt, the most elegant hotel in L.A. Rooms are the height of luxe–amazingly soft linens, deep soaking tub, tasteful period furniture. Outside are I. M. Pei's famous CAA headquarters and a whole lot of shopping. Here a splurge is a splurge–in the splurge capital of the Western world. The Belvedere restaurant (see this page) is the gilding on the lily.

🛈 196 🅿 Valet 🚭 🌀 🏊 🌀 🐚 All major cards

SLS LOS ANGELES
$$$$$

465 S. LA CIENEGA BLVD.

TEL 310-247-0400

www.marriott.com

Although recently renovated, this deluxe hotel stays true to the sophisticated vision of Philippe Starck. If you like avant garde, this is the place. The hotel combines Japanese practicality and coolness with Western luxury and Starck's signature colorful textures. There's even a meditation garden in the lobby, and the hotel's chic bar and restaurants are considered places to see and be seen.

🛈 297 🅿 🚭 🌀 🏊 🌀 🐚 All major cards

🍴 STK
$$$$$

930 HILGARD AVE.

TEL 310-659-3535

www.stksteakhouse.com

Swanky and deliciously hip, this steakhouse serves quality meat, cooked to perfection with sides like truffle fries, asparagus, and creamed corned pudding. As an added bonus, just about anything on the menu can be topped with truffles and/or lobster. Located in the trendy W Los Angeles hotel in West Beverly Hills, it's a celebrity hotspot.

🍴 200 🅿 Valet 🕐 Closed L 🌀 🐚 All major cards

🍴 CRUSTACEAN
$$$$–$$$$$

468 N. BEDFORD DR.

TEL 310-205-8990

www.crustaceanbh.com

You'd expect something special after a recent eight-month-long, $10 million revamp, and this iconic Beverly Hills restaurant delivers with sensational walk-on-water floors and an open kitchen.

The celebrity-filled Asian hotspot is renowned for its beloved garlic noodles and dungeness crab and other deliciously inventive dishes, such as caviar-topped tuna egg rolls.

🛏 50 🅿 🕐 Closed Mon. 🄯 🄯 All major cards

🍴 LE PETIT BELVEDERE
$$$$

PENINSULA BEVERLY HILLS,
9882 S. SANTA MONICA BLVD.
TEL 310-975-2736

The Belvedere does not only fine modern American cuisine (sesame roasted prawns, New York steak with truffled hollandaise and fries) but also an outstanding brunch. A scene, but a quiet scene.

🛏 85 🅿 Valet 🄯 🄯 All major cards

🍴 MATSUHISA
$$$$

129 N. LA CIENEGA BLVD.
TEL 310-659-9639
www.matsuhisabeverlyhills.com

The place to eat sushi in haute Los Angeles, Matsuhisa is not a sushi bar, it's a sushi monument. Chef Nobu specializes in the most delicate of tastes, from sea urchin and shiso leaf to truffled sea scallops with caviar.

🛏 76 🅿 Valet 🄯 🄯 All major cards

🍴 SPAGO BEVERLY HILLS
$$$$

176 N. CANON DR.
TEL 310-385-0880
www.wolfgangpuck.com

This is still one of the top five restaurants in the city (in the country, some would argue). Wolfgang Puck is at the top of his form here, with the kitchen dishing out amazing works such as ragout of shrimp with chicken oysters (the morsels close to the backbone) and black truffles; osso buco and Knödel stuffed with pork crackling.

🛏 300 🅿 Valet 🕐 Closed Sun. L 🄯 🄯 DC, MC, V

🍴 CULINA
$$$–$$$$$

FOUR SEASONS HOTEL,
300 S. DOHENY DR.
TEL 310-860-4000
www.culinarestaurant.com

It may be located in the Four Seasons, but Culina feels and acts more like a modern Italian, neighborhood restaurant. The menu ranges from gourmet pizzas and panini sandwiches to *pesce spada* (Californian swordfish) served with eggplant caponata and a grape-tomato vinaigrette and *lombatina capricciosa* (veal chop) with aciabatta crust and arugula. For dessert try the delicious panna cotta (basil seed tapioca with strawberry sorbet).

🛏 231 🅿 Valet 🄯 All major cards

🍴 CUT
$$$–$$$$$

BEVERLY WILSHIRE,
9500 WILSHIRE BLVD.
TEL 310-276-8500
www.wolfgangpuck.com

Another chicly contemporary offering from Wolfgang Puck, CUT—a contemporary twist on the classic steakhouse—has proved itself a cut above since opening in 2006, garnering a Michelin star in 2019, and drawing Hollywood's finest. Try the lobster and crab Louis cocktail with spicy tomato horseradish, followed by the signature Kobe beef short ribs with Indian spices.

🛏 140 🅿 Valet 🕐 Closed L 🄯 🄯 All major cards

CENTURY CITY

🏨 FAIRMONT CENTURY PLAZA
$$$$–$$$$$

2025 AVE. OF THE STARS
TEL 310-228-1234
www.fairmontcenturyplaza.com

A city within a city, the swank, chicly contemporary Plaza, President Reagan's favorite campaign stopover, is perfectly situated between Beverly Hills and nearby shopping, live theaters across the street and in Westwood, and cultural happenings at UCLA and the Getty.

🛈 726 🅿 🖇 🄯 🛗 🄯 🄯 All major cards

CHINATOWN

🍴 LAO TAO
$–$$

727 N. BROADWAY #207
TEL 213-372-5318
www.laotaostreetfood.com

Hidden upstairs in Far East Plaza, this order-at-the-counter restaurant specializes in inexpensive Taiwanese street snacks, from delicious crispy popcorn chicken to beef ban mian (flat noodles in a bone marrow broth).

🛏 24 🅿 🕐 Closed Tue. 🄯 🄯 MC, V

🍴 LASITA
$–$$

727 N. BROADWAY
TEL 213-443-6163
www.lasita-la.com

A popular Filipino rotisserie in Far East Plaza, this family-run restaurant specializes in the lechon (slow-cooked pork) dishes of the homeland. Another winning dish is the chicken inasal, with garlic fried rice.

🛏 40 🅿 🄯 🄯 AE, MC, V

DOWNTOWN/LITTLE TOKYO

🏨 RITZ-CARLTON
🍴 $$$$$

900 W. OLYMPIC BLVD.
TEL 213-743-8800
www.ritzcarlton.com

From the California-chic rooms to the 3,400-square-foot (316 sq m) Ritz-Carlton Club Lounge and the exclusive, rooftop pool and bar, this new high-rise hotel has become the hallmark for luxury in downtown L.A. Rounding out the offerings are a full-service spa and the nouvelle Chinese cuisine of Wolfgang Puck's **WP24** restaurant. Perched between the 22nd and 26th floors of a sleek 54-story tower, the Ritz-Carlton overlooks Staples Center, Microsoft Theater, and the rest of the new L.A. Live complex.

🛈 123 🅿 Valet 🅢 ❄ 🐟 🎽
🅢 All major cards

🏨 DOUBLETREE BY HILTON
$$$–$$$$

120 S. LOS ANGELES ST.

TEL 213-629-1200

www.hilton.com

Located in the heart of historic Little Tokyo, this hotel features a lovely oriental garden. Recently revamped by the Hilton chain, it has stylishly contemporary rooms in chocolate, strawberry, and vanilla ice cream tones. Dining options include a gastropub.

🛈 434 🅿 🅢 ❄ 🎽 🅢 All major cards

🍴 MARUGAME MONZO
$$$

329 E. FIRST ST.

TEL 213-346-9762

www.marugamemonzola.com

Locals consider this modern venue a mecca for delicious, thick udon noodles, served in such signature dishes as Mentai squid butter udon and sea urchin cream udon. Sit at the bar to watch the chefs cut the fresh-made noodles behind a glass screen.

🍴 32 🅿 🕐 Closed AM
❄ 🅢 All major cards

SOMETHING SPECIAL

🍴 FUGETSU-DO CONFECTIONERY
$

315 E. 1ST ST.

TEL 213-625-8595

www.fugetsu-do.com

Step back in time, to an era when immigrant mom-and-pop candy shops made traditional Japanese sweet *manju* in hand-carved wooden forms, then wrapped them in maple leaves and ferns. The Fugetsu-do make their pastel-colored rice goodies exactly the way they did 100 years ago. A unique souvenir, a tasty treat.

🕐 Closed D 🅢 No credit cards

FAIRFAX DISTRICT

🍴 CANTER'S DELI
$

419 N. FAIRFAX AVE.

TEL 323-651-2030

www.cantersdeli.com

The original L.A. deli comes complete with wisecracking waitstaff, garish lighting, and characters out of a Bernard Malamud novel. The food is acceptable, predictable deli food. You won't leave any on your plate. Open 24 hours a day.

🍴 450 🅿 ❄ 🅢 MC, V

HANCOCK PARK & KOREATOWN

🍴 HOUSE OF CHAN DARA
$$–$$$

310 N. LARCHMONT BLVD.

TEL 323-467-1052

www.chandararestaurants.com

A Thai hangout, where the waitstaff is at least as nice as the food, Chan Dara nevertheless is the best place to eat in Hancock Park. The mee krob is an old standard—and very good. Ditto the appetizers, particularly the shrimp in lemongrass.

🍴 115 🅿 ❄ 🅢 All major cards

HOLLYWOOD/ WEST HOLLYWOOD

🏨 CHATEAU MARMONT
$$$$$

8221 SUNSET BLVD.

TEL 323-656-1010

www.chateaumarmont.com

If you want to experience a slice of true Hollywood, you can do no better than the Chateau. Over the years, this 1929 castlelike mansion-hotel, with only 63 rooms, has hosted some of the great Hollywood eccentrics, from Christopher Walken (who once lived here) to John Belushi (who died here). The place has loads of charm and elegance, and the rooms are comfortable and well appointed, if a bit old. The Bar Marmont is a stylish hangout.

🛈 63 🅿 🅢 ❄ 🐟 🎽 🅢 All major cards

🏨 MONDRIAN
$$$$$

8440 SUNSET BLVD.

TEL 323-650-8999

www.mondrianhotel.com

Quintessential California chic draws the glamour set and hip executives to this sexy, showy, slightly surreal Ian Schrager hotel. The stunning lobby, with its diaphonous curtains and objets d'art, sets the urbane tone, as do full entertainment centers and well-chosen literature in suave guest rooms. The open-air SkyBar restaurant and lounge is quite the scene.

🛈 237 🅿 Valet 🅢 ❄ 🐟 🎽
🅢 All major cards

🏨 HOLLYWOOD ROOSEVELT
$$$$–$$$$$

7000 HOLLYWOOD BLVD.

TEL 323-466-7000

www.thompsonhotels.com

Another onetime stronghold of the famous and rich, the Roosevelt is a more modestly priced alternative to the Chateau Marmont. Now part of the Hyatt chain, it has recently been restored to its original 1920s grandeur, with painted ceilings, ornate tilework, and a balconied mezzanine. Some rooms are a little on the small side, but all have been revamped with luxury

🅢 Nonsmoking 🅢 Air-conditioning 🅢 Indoor Pool 🐟 Outdoor Pool 🎽 Health Club 🅢 Credit Cards

contemporary furnishings. Gable and Lombard once romped here.
ⓘ 333 **P** Valet 🔲 💳 ♨ 📺 🏦 All major cards

🍴 PROVIDENCE
$$$$–$$$$$
5955 MELROSE AVE.
TEL 323-460-4170
www.providencela.com
Michelin-starred Chef Michael Cimarusti's seminal restaurant is a bastion of formal fine dining, and well worth a detour and splurge. The menu is driven by sustainability, with only wild-caught seafood from American waters used in Cimarusti's eclectic California dishes infused with Asian and Mediterranean flavors. The three tasting menus begin with pickled sardine crostini, or a selection of canapés. Follow, perhaps, with sashimi with bergamot, rosemary, and sea-grapes; or black cod with black truffle and Zuckerman asparagus.
🍴 50 **P** 🕐 Closed Sun.–Mon, L Tue.–Sat 💳 All major cards

🍴 MEROIS
$$$$
8430 SUNSET BLVD.
TEL 323-918-3410
www.wolfgangpuck.com
The rooftop of the Pendry West Hollywood Building is a perfect venue for Wolfgang Puck's penthouse jewel in the crown, which opened in April 2021. A wall of glass offers stunning and unfettered views over Los Angeles, while the menu reflects a classic Puck combo of Californian and French techniques wed to Japanese and Southeast Asian influences. Executive Chef Mark Andelbradt oversees such mouth-watering creations as squid noodles with ginger-garlic clam sauce; whole crisp-fried sea bass with vegetable fried rice; and Kona kampachi with lemon ponzu.
🍴 100 **P** Valet 🕐 Closed L 💳 All major cards

🍴 PIZZERIA MOZZA
$$
641 N. HIGHLAND AVE.
TEL 323-297-0101
www.la.pizzeriamozza.com
When you crave nothing more than a wholesome deep-dish Cal-Italian pizza, this place can't be beaten. How about the goat cheese, leeks, scallions, and garlic? Chicken-liver crostini makes a fine starter. Close with a nectar-smooth butterscotch budino.
🍴 40 💳 All major cards

🍴 THE EVELEIGH
$$$
8752 W. SUNSET BLVD.
TEL 424-239-1630
www.theeveleigh.com
Featuring a seasonal, largely local menu, the Eveleigh offers up a splendid gourmet take on country cooking. From rib-eye and braised beef cheeks to pork belly, there's plenty for carnivores to sink their teeth into. Equally delicious seafood includes roasted barramundi and crispy seasoned squid. The shady back patio is especially popular for weekend brunch.
🍴 150 **P** Valet 🕐 Closed L Mon.–Fri. 💳 All major cards

🍴 MAROUCH
$$–$$$
4905 SANTA MONICA BLVD.
TEL 323-662-9325
www.hollywoodmarouch.com
This highly popular Middle Eastern restaurant does a little bit of Armenian, a little bit of Lebanese, a little bit of Arabic—very well. The portions are huge, the pita bread freshly baked, and the attitude totally upbeat. Enjoy—this is a part of L.A. cuisine that is not much publicized, but well worth twice the modest price, not least for the belly dancing.
🍴 70–80 **P** 🕐 Closed Mon. 💳 All major cards

🍴 MUSSO & FRANK GRILL
See Hollywood, p. 83.

LOS FELIZ/GRIFFITH PARK

🍴 IZAKA-YA BY KATSU-YA
$$–$$$
8240 W. 3RD ST.
TEL 323-782-9536
www.katsu-yagroup.com
Here you'll find the freshest sushi together with Okinawa specialties like yakisoba and pork rib stew, with many different types of sake.
🍴 48 **P** Valet 🕐 Closed L Sun. 💳 All major cards

🍴 TRATTORIA FARFALLA
$$–$$$
1978 HILLHURST AVE.
TEL 323-661-7365
www.farfallatrattoria.com
Small and cozy, Farfalla cooks up consistently good southern Italian fare. The roasted chicken, the pasta in tomato-onion sauce, and the tiramisu are all delicious. No reservations—you may have to wait for a seat.
🍴 50 **P** Valet 🕐 Closed L Sat.–Sun. 💳 All major cards

🍴 PINE & CRANE

$

1521 GRIFFITH PARK RD.

TEL 323-668-1128

This modern, fast-casual restaurant offers authentic, artfully presented Taiwanese dishes such as spicy shrimp wontons, three cup jidori chicken, pork mapo tofu, and beef noodle soup. It has a large selection of craft beers and sakes.

🛏 50 🅿 🕐 Closed Tue. 🔆 🔅 MV, V

MALIBU/SANTA MONICA MOUNTAINS

🍴 GEOFFREY'S

$$$$$

27400 PACIFIC COAST HWY.

(4 MILES N OF MALIBU CANYON RD.)

TEL 310-457-1519

www.geoffreysmalibu.com

International cuisine dished up in the ultimate beachside location; some believe this is the only place where the food truly matches the quality of the view, best enjoyed from the clifftop patio. Enjoy a mid-day brunch of crab Benedict, or watch the sunset as you savor jumbo coconut shrimp, a seafood paella, and maple blueberry cheescake.

🛏 150 🅿 🔆 🔅 All major cards

🍴 INN OF THE SEVENTH RAY

$$$$

128 OLD TOPANGA CANYON RD.

TEL 310-455-1311

www.innoftheseventhray.com

The ultimate New Age dining experience, this venerable inn, its open-air seating perched on the side of a babbling brook, offers fine vegetarian and other specialties. The baked salmon and pecan pie are outstanding.

🛏 200 🅿 🔅 All major cards

🍴 SADDLE PEAK LODGE

$$$$

419 COLD CANYON RD.

(E OF MALIBU CANYON)

TEL 818-222-3888

www.saddlepeaklodge.com

The ne plus ultra of rustic California cuisine, this very woodsy and elegant canyon cottage offers adventurous game dishes, such as wild game trio with the chef's choice of three meats. For the tamer at heart, brunch on Sunday morning features delicious applewood-smoked bacon and waffles.

🛏 180 🅿 Valet 🕐 Closed L & Mon.–Tues. 🔆 🔅 AE, MC, V

MARINA DEL REY

🏨 RITZ-CARLTON
🍴 MARINA DEL REY

$$$$$

4375 ADMIRALTY WAY

TEL 310-823-1700

www.ritzcarlton.com

A luxury hotel with outstanding concierge service, tastefully decorated rooms, and quiet, impeccable service. The hotel's Cast & Plow restaurant offers indoor and outdoor dining with views over the marina.

🛏 304 🅿 🔄 🔆 🏊 📺 🔅 All major cards

MELROSE AVENUE & AROUND

🍴 OSTERIA LA BUCA

$$$

5210 MELROSE AVE.

TEL 323-462-1900

www.osterialabuca.com

With a down-to-earth setting and casual, no-frills, old-school Italian style, Osteria La Buca dedicates itself to hearty pastas and pizzas. Inspired by traditional Italian country fare, the dishes are uncomplicated yet delicious. With bare red-brick walls, chic contemporary styling, and old motorcycle paraphernalia, its cool vibe is

enlivened by spot-on music. It's perfectly located if you're planning on visiting nearby Paramount Studios.

🛏 68 🔆 🔅 All major cards

🍴 GRACIAS MADRE

$$

8905 MELROSE AVE.

TEL 323-978-2170

www.graciasmadre.co

A vegan's dream, trendy, upscale Gracias Madre serves plant-based traditional meatless Mexican cuisine using all-organic ingredients. Even carnivores will become converts to its satisfying dishes intended to honor Pachamama—Mother Earth. It serves delicious agave-based cocktails, to be enjoyed on the airy patio.

🛏 70 🔆 🔅 All major cards

🍴 BLU JAM CAFÉ

$–$$

7371 MELROSE AVE.

TEL 323-951-9191

www.blujamcafe.com

For those getting a late start, breakfast (their specialty) is served until 5 p.m., while Sunday brunch is the way to refuel between bouts of shopping. The eclectic dinner menu, designed by chef/co-owner Kamil Majer, is built around medium-size California cuisine dishes that are meant to share. It has five other locations around Los Angeles.

🛏 49 🅿 Valet 🕐 Closed D Sun.–Tues. 🔆 🔅 All major cards

MOCA & AROUND

🏨 HILTON CHECKERS
🍴 $$$$

535 S. GRAND AVE.

TEL 213-624-0000

www.hilton.com

A small, luxurious antidote to downtown's megahotels, Checkers has panache and quietude. Guest rooms are smallish but nicely appointed, with service—something rare these days at any price—among the best in town. The Checkers Restaurant is well known for its artful and satisfying California cuisine; the crab cakes are a favorite.

🛈 188 🅿 Valet 🔄 📶 📧 🎦 🗝 All major cards

🏨 MILLENNIUM
🍽 BILTMORE
$$$–$$$$
506 S. GRAND AVE.
TEL 213-624-1011
www.millenniumhotels.com
If it's history and elegance you want, this is the place. Built in 1923, the Biltmore was one of the grandest hotels of its day. Now completely restored and recently refurbished, it offers fine dining at **Smeraldi's,** a top-rated Italian eatery, well appointed guest rooms, and a sense of luxury, from old tiled fountains to a rococo-revival exterior and interior.

🛈 683 🅿 Valet 🔄 📶 📧 🎦 🗝 All major cards

🏨 KAWADA HOTEL
$$
200 S. HILL ST.
TEL 213-621-4455
www.kawadahotel.com
A budget alternative for downtown, close to Chinatown, MOCA, and various cultural venues, the Kawada provides serviceable rooms with TV, and two phones. The hotel shuttle is helpful for those who don't like driving.

🛈 116 🅿 Valet 🔄 📶 🗝 All major cards

🍽 WATER GRILL
$$$
544 S. GRAND AVE.
(E SIDE OF LIBRARY)
TEL 213-891-0900
www.watergrill.com
This is the place to eat fish—bluefin tuna tartare, grilled rock bass, black sea bass with eel pot stickers. The sea bass in braised fennel is popular with the bankers and attorneys who keep coming back again and again.

🍽 140 🅿 🕐 Closed L Sat.–Sun. 📶 🗝 All major cards

🍽 SHIBUMI
$$
815 S. HILL ST.
TEL 323-484-8915
www.shibumidtla.com
At this intimate heart-of-downtown Japanese restaurant, Chef David Schlosser uses organic, sustainable ingredients to fill his to-go bento boxes with delicious treats such as grilled unagi, chicken katsu, and black cod.

🍽 40 🅿 🕐 Closed Mon., L Tue.–Sun. 📶 🗝 All major cards

🍽 UPSTAGE BURGER
$$
WALT DISNEY CONCERT HALL,
135 S. GRAND AVE.
TEL 213-972-8000
www.musiccenter.org/visit/
Dining-On-Site
This gourmet burger joint in the Music Center is one of two recently added low-cost eateries (the other is the outdoor Cocina Roja Latin restaurant) in the adjoining Ahmanson Theatre and Walt Disney Concert Hall. The delicious burgers use premium grass-fed beef. It also offers free-range chicken, plus veggie burgers, as well as made-to-order sandwiches.

🍽 80 🅿 🕐 Closed D 📶 🗝 All major cards

🍽 WOODSPOON
$$
107 W. 9TH ST.
TEL 213-629-1765
www.woodspoonla.com
Brazilian-born Natalia Pereira's exquisite little Fashion District restaurant is a visually uplifting delight. She conjures divine croquettes, traditional fish soup, and other Brazilian dishes, including a signature chicken pot pie with potatoes, hearts of palm, roasted corn, and olives.

🍽 30 🅿 🕐 Closed Sun.–Mon. 📶 🗝 All major cards

🍽 SHIKU
$–$$
317 S. BROADWAY
TEL 213-265-7211
Tucked inside Grand Central Market, Kwang Uh and Mina Park's Korean take-out restaurant serves classic *doshirak*—lunch-box—meals to go, including such delights as shiitake mushrooms, fried chicken, and soy-marinated short-rib galbi, served over rice.

🍽 30 🅿 🕐 Closed Mon.–Tue. 🗝 MC, V

🍽 ORIGINAL PANTRY CAFÉ
$
877 S. FIGUEROA ST.
TEL 213-972-9279
www.pantrycafe.restaurant
An original downtown eatery, in continuous operation since 1924, the Pantry is now owned by Richard Riordan, the former L.A. mayor, who often eats here with constituents and staff. The menu is pure diner fare: huge pancakes, omelettes, steaks, and a daily blue plate special. Bring a hefty appetite.

🍽 64 🅿 🕐 Closed Mon.–Tue. 📶 🗝 No credit cards

MONTEREY PARK/ ALHAMBRA

See the feature on Monterey Park, pp. 124–125.

PASADENA

🏨 LANGHAM HUNTINGTON HOTEL & SPA
$$$$$
1401 S. OAK KNOLL
TEL 626-568-3900
www.pasadena.langham
hotels.com
Pasadena has a long tradition as a winter haven for East Coast millionaires, so the luxury standards of this venerable hotel (the former Ritz-Carlton) are, in keeping with the tradition, quite high: The rooms are ample, with marble bathrooms and cozy robes; the services are impeccable; and the ancillaries make the stay as engag-

ing as it is restful. The brunch is the best offering.

① 392 **P** Valet ⬚ ⬚ ⬚ ⬚
⬚ All major cards

🏨 WESTIN PASADENA
🍴 $$$

191 N. LOS ROBLES AVE.
TEL 626-792-2727
www.westin.marriott.com
This solid business hotel is perfectly located right in the middle of the Plaza Los Flores. Stylish rooms are airy, the food at the **Ventanas Restaurant** is quite good, and the overall feeling is one of glowing ease.

① 350 **P** ⬚ ⬚ ⬚ ⬚
⬚ All major cards

🏨 PASADENA HILTON
$$–$$$

168 S. LOS ROBLES AVE.
TEL 626-577-1000
www.hilton.com
This is Rose Bowl central come New Year's Day; during the rest of the year, the Hilton is the old standby, relied upon by business-folk, visiting Caltech types, and many smaller conventions.

① 296 **P** ⬚ ⬚ ⬚ ⬚
⬚ All major cards

🍴 CAFÉ SANTORINI
$$$

64 W. UNION ST.
TEL 626-564-4200
www.cafesantorini.com
With its warmly intimate Mediterranean ambiance, this restaurant is a local favorite. The menu of mouthwatering dishes from around that sea spans mezes, moussaka, and creamy risottos to Moroccan lamb shank and wood-fired pizzas. The outdoor rooftop patio is the place to be.

🍽 160 **P** 🕐 L Mon.–Fri.
🕐 ⬚ All major cards

🍴 SHIRO
$$$

1505 MISSION ST.
TEL 626-799-4774
www.restaurantshiro.com

Shiro pulls off a tricky blend of French-Japanese cuisine and is rated one of L.A.'s best restaurants. The sizzling catfish in ponzu and the shrimp-salmon mousse in smoked salmon sauce are the reason so many go here for the most special of occasions. A decent (and reasonably priced) wine list, too.

🍽 75 **P** 🕐 Closed L & Mon.–Tue. 🕐 ⬚ AE, MC, V

SOMETHING SPECIAL

🍴 EURO PANE BAKERY
$–$$$

950 E. COLORADO BLVD.
TEL 626-577-1828
www.europanebakerycafe.com
Former Spago pastry chef Sumi Chang brings a penchant for fine ingredients, fresh fruits, and traditional baking methods to this unassuming but wildly popular bakery. Try some brioche bread or a slice of the famous pear spice cake.

🍽 20 **P** 🕐 Closed D 🕐
⬚ MC, V

🍴 ALL INDIA CAFÉ
$–$$

39 S. FAIR OAKS AVE.
(JUST S OF COLORADO BLVD.)
TEL 626-440-0309
www.allindiacafe.com
Intensely flavored Indian street fare done with a light use of traditional oils. The bargains, and some of the best cooking, are found in the lunch specials. These consist of a half dozen filling meals—curries, tandooris, thalis—made of smaller dishes.

🍽 45 **P** 🕐 ⬚ All major cards

🍴 SALADANG
$–$$

363 S. FAIR OAKS AVE. (BETW. CALIFORNIA BLVD. & DEL MAR AVE.)
TEL 626-793-8123
www.saladang-pasadena.com
Artsy and moderne, this thriving Thai eatery serves up all the basics with style. Try the green

curry, the apple and chicken salad, the salad rolls, and the sweet rice dessert.

🍽 94 **P** 🕐 ⬚ All major cards

SAN FERNANDO VALLEY

🏨 SHERATON UNIVERSAL
$$$$

333 UNIVERSAL
HOLLYWOOD DR. PKWY.
TEL 818-980-1212
www.marriott.com
The best place to stay in the valley, this hotel is located on the Universal lot. A good business hotel, it has spacious rooms and a giant lobby in which to meet friends before setting off for sightseeing.

① 436 **P** Valet ⬚ ⬚ ⬚ ⬚
⬚ All major cards

🏨 THE GARLAND
$$–$$$

4222 VINELAND AVE.
TEL 800-238-3759
www.thegarland.com
This former Holiday was once considered a homey place to stay, but has recently been jazzed up in appealingly sophisticated retro-chic style. It sits on seven landscaped acres (2.8 ha) and has the usual Holiday Inn amenities, plus tennis courts. Free shuttle to Universal.

① 255 **P** ⬚ ⬚ ⬚ ⬚ All major cards

🏨 SPORTSMEN'S LODGE
$$–$$$

12825 VENTURA BLVD.
TEL 818-769-4700
www.sportsmenslodge.com
Steeped in film history and within easy driving distance of Universal Studios, the lodge has likewise traded in its "home on the range" theme for chic styling more suited to mod Studio City. The hotel's tiny but tasty restaurant pays homage to celluloid heroes—like John Wayne, Roy Rogers, and Gene Autry—who used to hang out here.

① 190 **P** 🕐 ⬚ ⬚ All major cards

⬚ Nonsmoking 🕐 Air-conditioning ⬚ Indoor Pool ⬚ Outdoor Pool ⬚ Health Club ⬚ Credit Cards

🍴 SUGARFISH BY SUSHI NOZAWA
$$$$–$$$$$
11288 VENTURA BLVD.
(NEAR VINELAND ST.)
TEL 818-762-2322
www.sugarfishsushi.com
Cool slices of flavorful seafood, from salmon to mussels to shrimp, done with a skillful hand. The chef is known for his delicate flavor combinations, such as seaweed noodle on salmon or mussels in rice vinegar broth.
🔲 30. No reservations
🕐 Closed Sat.–Sun. 🔳 💳 MC, V

🍴 CHIBA SUSHI
$$$$
7515 LANKERSHIM BLVD., N. HOLLYWOOD
TEL 818-765-9119
www.chibasushinoho.com
This large, multi-roomed sushi restaurant with maroon leather booths and two sushi booths is always packed for good reason. Serving only the freshest seafood, its biggest draw is the a la carte sushi menu. It also offers non-fishy treats, such as pork ginger yaki and chicken karaage.
🔲 200 🅿 Valet 🕐 Closed L Sat.–Sun. 🔳 💳 All major cards

🍴 MISTRAL
$$–$$$
13422 VENTURA BLVD.
TEL 818-981-6650
www.mistralrestaurant.com
Outstanding Provençal cuisine with all the standards, from grilled entrecôte to the oniony French version of pizza, pissaladière. A good deal in an elegant place.
🔲 55 🅿 Valet 🕐 Closed Mon., L Tue., & Sat.–Sun. 🔳 💳 All major cards

🍴 LE PETIT RESTAURANT
$$
13360 VENTURA BLVD.
TEL 818-501-7999
www.lepetitrestaurant.net

Simple, authentic French food with the added benefit of charming surroundings. Try the eggplant and tomato tart.
🔲 80 🅿 Valet 🕐 Closed L Fri.–Sun. 🔳 💳 AE, MC, V

🍴 BRENT'S DELI
$–$$
19565 PARTHENIA ST., NORTHRIDGE
TEL 818-886-5679
www.brentsdeli.com.
A Los Angeles institution for four decades, Brent's is known for its signature black pastrami Reuben sandwich—reason enough to make a beeline. Blintzes, latkes, stuffed kishkas, and an assortment of triple-deckers, wraps, and specialty sandwiches are other temptations.
🔲 80 🅿 🔳 💳 All major cards

🍴 CILANTRO MEXICAN GRILL
$–$$
7214 WHITSETT AVE., N. HOLLYWOOD
TEL 818-765-7998
www.cilantromexican.com
Sure, it's a counter-style fast food restaurant attached to a gas station, but it packs in hungry diners for good reason. The big, budget-friendly burritos are as good as you'll find in Los Angeles, thanks to Le Cordon Bleu graduate chef Adolfo Pérez. Options range to Angus beef steak and seared shrimp surf 'n' turf.
🔲 40 🅿 Valet 🔳 💳 All major cards

SANTA MONICA

🏨 LOEWS
🍴 $$$$$
1700 OCEAN AVE.
TEL 310-458-6700, 866-991-1698
www.santamonicaloews hotel.com
Another fine beachside hotel, the Loews features sun-filled atria, tasteful guest rooms, and

up-to-date business services for those who must tear themselves away from the beach to send something back to the office. The Loews restaurant, **Ocean and Vine**, serves notable California cuisine.
ℹ️ 359 🅿 🔳 🔲 🏊 📺 💳 All major cards

🏨 OCEANA
$$$$$
849 OCEAN AVE.
TEL 800-777-0758
www.hoteloceanasanta monica.com
In a great location just steps from the beach and Santa Monica Pier, and one block from upscale Montana Avenue, the designer-savvy Oceana is a boutique hotel reincarnation of a classic southern California oceanfront apartment building. Many of the large rooms have expansive ocean views, while the place to hang out is the center courtyard with the heart-shaped swimming pool.
ℹ️ 70 🅿 Valet 🏊 📺 💳 All major cards

🏨🍴 SHUTTERS ON THE BEACH
$$$$$
1 PICO BLVD.
TEL 310-458-0030, 866-527-6612
www.shuttersonthebeach.com
Intimate and sun-filled, this luxury hotel on the coast features spacious, bright rooms evocative of 1930s beachside cottages. The **One Pico** restaurant is a regular for local celebrities like Mel Brooks.
ℹ️ 198 🅿️ Valet 🔲🛏️🏊🔲 🔲 All major cards

🍴 CHINOIS ON MAIN
$$$$
2709 MAIN ST.
TEL 310-392-9025
www.wolfgangpuck.com
Slick, breezy, and always crowded, Wolfgang Puck's family-style fusion cuisine (like Cantonese duck with plum sauce) is hard to beat. The charred tuna exemplifies Puck's puckishness with sauces.
🔲 100 🅿️ Valet 🕐 Closed Mon.–Tue., L Wed.–Sun. 🔲🔲 All major cards

🍴 BIRDIE G'S
$$$
2421 MICHIGAN AVE.
TEL 310-310-3616
www.birdiegsla.com
Chef Jeremy Fox's laid-back, in-the-groove restaurant within the historic Bergamot Station art complex delivers globally inspired comfort food, from beet-and-beef borscht and spicy Italian ravioli to its signature "Hangtown Brei" (soft-scrambled egg topped with matzo, pork belly, fried oysers, and spicy hollandaise).
🔲 40 🅿️ 🕐 Mon.–Tue., L Wed.–Sun. 🔲🔲 All major cards

🍴 YE OLDE KINGS HEAD
$$$
116 SANTA MONICA BLVD.
TEL 310-451-1402
www.yeoldekingshead.com
A Santa Monica institution, this quintessential British pub-restaurant serves the to-be-expected faves, such as a classic English breakfast, fish 'n' chips, and traditional Sunday roast. The decor unashamedly plays up the theme with "all things British," although disappointingly its beers are mostly from across the Channel.
🔲 80 🅿️ 🔲 All major cards

🍴 CASSIA
$$$
1314 7TH ST.
TEL 310-393-6699
www.cassiala.com
Big and boisterous, Bryant and Kim Ng's Cassia combines a chic spacious ambiance with spot-on French-Vietnamese fare, from spicy wontons and noodle soup to grilled lamb with sichuan peppers, cumin, sambal, and creamy sesame sauce.
🔲 60 🅿️ 🕐 Closed L 🔲 All major cards

🍴 PENTHOUSE
$$–$$$$
HUNTLEY HOTEL, 1111 2ND ST.
TEL 310-393-8080
www.thehuntleyhotel.com
Wrapped in glass, the Penthouse perches 18 stories above the California coast. Executive chef Seth Greenburg offers novel takes on traditional American dishes like an open-faced grilled cheese starter and a crispy-skin salmon main. In the lounge bar, resident mixologist Ryan Magarian conjures up creative cocktails (coconut espresso martini, spicy-hot margarita).
🔲 319 🅿️ Valet 🔲🔲 All major cards

🍴 TUMBI
$$–$$$$
115 SANTA MONICE BLVD.
TEL 310-892-7200
www.tumbibar.com
Tumbi brings a whole new level of appreciation to the concept of an Indian restaurant with its sophisticated ambiance and an innovative menu that raises regional Indian dishes to the level of haute cuisine. Executive Chef Ram Krishna Naidu focuses on street fare and keeps things simple, while drawing on local ingredients from the nearby farmers market for his *pani puri* puff pastry, charbroiled *paneer tikka*, and Goan prawn marsala.
🔲 68 🅿️ 🔲 🔲 All major cards

VENICE

SOMETHING SPECIAL

🍴 DUDLEY MARKET
$$$–$$$$
9 DUDLEY AVE.
TEL 310-392-0825
www.dudleymarketvenice.com
This boat-to-table restaurant just steps from the beach culls its own fish, line-caught, from the sea. It shows in the perfectly fresh and inventive seafood on the daily menu, such as its whole-fried fish with nuoc cham. Wine plays a big part of the experience here, and the servers are trained to help in selecting an appropriate champagne pairing for your fresh oysters or the best Riesling, perhaps, for your fried chicken with chili cornbread. The industrial warehouse-style interior is suffused with sunlight through a wide wall of glass.
🔲 38 🅿️ 🕐 Closed L 🔲 MC, V

🍴 THE PIER HOUSE
$$$
7 WASHINGTON BLVD.
TEL 310-439-1770
www.pierhousevenice.com
A casually stylish option next to the pier, this seafood-centric beachfront restaurant offers a wonderfully inviting whitewashed space for enjoying innovative, globally-inspired cuisine. Chef Terry Kim's menu sings with such irresistible

dishes as crunchy wax bean Thai salad, shellfish spaghetti pomodoro, blue crab cakes with panko crust, and kanpachi-strawberry aguachile. Artisanal draft beers and some killer signature cocktails are a bonus.

🛏 50 🅿 🔲 🔲 All major cards

🍴 ROSE CAFÉ
$$
220 ROSE AVE. (AT MAIN ST.)
TEL 310-399-0711
www.therosevenice.la
A big, airy cafeteria where the cappuccino is good, the breakfasts are satisfying, and the various cold salads are a favorite of the very trendy locals who hang out here.

🛏 150 🅿 🕐 Closed Mon.
🔲 AE, MC, V

WESTWOOD/WEST L.A.

🏨 HOTEL BEL AIR
🍴 $$$$$
701 STONE CANYON RD.
TEL 310-472-1211
www.dorchestercollection.com
For more than half a century, the Hotel Bel Air has charmed guests with its blend of mission architecture, lush gardens, and fine food (Wolfgang Puck at Hotel Bel Air is among the top California-Mediterranean eateries in the city). A good idea is simply to drop in for a drink at the Lobby Lounge, perhaps in the early evening when the gardens turn to pure magic.
ⓘ 58 rooms & 45 suites 🅿 🔲
🔲 🔲 🔲 🔲 All major cards

🏨 W LOS ANGELES
$$$–$$$$$
930 HILGARD AVE.
TEL 310-208-8123
www.marriott.com
This moderne California hotel is perfect for those who want to play on L.A.'s Westside at night while exploring inland during the day. Situated across the street from UCLA, the W offers a luxurious spa, spacious suites, and a fine

lobby bar where the people-watching just goes on and on.
ⓘ 297 rooms & suites 🅿 🔲
🔲 🔲 🔲 🔲 All major cards

🍴 VINCENTI
$$$$$
11930 SAN VICENTE BLVD.
TEL 310-207-0121
www.vincentiristorante.com
Chef Nicola Mastronarti is noted as one of the best Italian chefs in LA. The fresh whole fish cooked over glowing embers is the main attraction, with such innovations as penne with rapini and pressed tuna roe done in a surprisingly light, fresh manner. For fans of the trendy guanciale (pig's jowl), this is the place.

🛏 90 🅿 Valet 🕐 Closed Sun. & L Sat.–Thurs. 🔲 🔲 All major cards

🍴 FATHER'S OFFICE
$$
3229 HELMS AVE., CULVER CITY
TEL 310-736-2224
www.fathersoffice.com
Close to the historic Sony MGM Studio, this edgy gastropub has 40 microbrews on tap, plus organic salads, steak, ribs, sweet potato fries, and what many consider the best burger in LA. There is also a variety of tasty tapas.

🛏 150 🅿 🕐 Closed Mon.–Tue, L Wed.–Fri. 🔲 🔲 All major cards

🍴 LA BRUSCHETTA
$$
1621 WESTWOOD BLVD.
TEL 424-273-4892
www.labruschetta
restaurant.com
Northern Italian fare–osso buco, risotto Milanese, and veal scaloppini–combines with an impressive wine list to make this local favorite a reliable, festive affair.

🛏 78 🅿 Valet 🕐 Closed Mon.–Tue. 🔲 🔲 AE, MC, V

🍴 PASTINA
$$
2260 WESTWOOD BLVD.
TEL 310-441-4655
www.pastina.net
Tasty neighborhood Italian food that won't wreak havoc on a diet, despite the large portions of pasta, pizza, and gnocchi.

🛏 86 🅿 Valet 🕐 Closed Mon., L Sat.–Sun. 🔲 🔲 AE, MC, V

🍴 MOGUMOGU
$–$$
11555 W. OLYMPIC BLVD.
TEL 424-371-5085
www.mogumoguus.com
There are no pretensions at this simple ramen shop specializing in steaming hot mazemen (brothless ramen), served in mix-it-yourself bowls with sliced pork chashu, soft-boiled egg, seaweed, chives, savory Umami vinegar, and your choice of toppings.

🛏 24 🕐 Closed Mon. 🔲 MC, V

🍴 APPLE PAN
$
10801 PICO BLVD.
TEL 310-475-3585
www.theapplepan.com
The old-fashioned U-shaped counter is always packed with locals waiting for their hit of hamburgers, fries, and apple pie. Great if you've been shopping and need sustenance.

🛏 23 🅿 🕐 Closed Mon. 🔲 No credit cards

🍴 JOHN O'GROATS
$
10516 PICO BLVD.
(NEAR BEVERLY GLEN)
TEL 310-204-0692
www.johnogroats.us
Just the greatest little down-home breakfast spot on the Westside, O'Groats is legendary among UCLA grad students, who succor themselves on the café's homemade biscuits and fries, only to return with their families years later–just to order the same thing!

🛏 65 🅿 🕐 Closed D 🔲
🔲 All major cards

🏨 Hotel 🍴 Restaurant ⓘ No. of Guest Rooms 🛏 No. of Seats 🅿 Parking 🕐 Closed 🔲 Elevator

▶ **SOUTHERN CALIFORNIA**

ANAHEIM

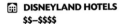 **DISNEYLAND HOTELS**
$$–$$$$
www.disneyland.disney.
go.com/hotels
To extend the Disney experi-
ence, try one of the Walt
Disney Company hotels. The
newly renovated **Disneyland
Hotel** *(1150 Magic Way, tel 714-
778-6600)* is located just off the
Monorail. **Disney's Paradise
Pier** *(1717 S. Disneyland Dr., tel
714-999-0990)* has a spa, shop-
ping, and a grill where Disney
characters appear regularly.
The **Grand Californian Hotel**
*(1600 S. Disneyland Dr., tel 714-
635-2300)* is done in an Arts
and Crafts style. The park/hotel
packages offer good deals.
[P] [⊖] [❄] [≋] [♼] [⬤] All major
cards

CATALINA

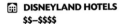 **BELLANCA HOTEL**
$$–$$$$
111 CRESCENT AVE.
TEL 310-510-0555
www.bellancahotel.com
Reliable and relaxed, the Porto-
fino offers all modern amenities
in a comfortable setting. Behind
its classic Mediterranean exterior, rooms boast understated
European elegance. It has a
fine-dining **restaurant** and
splendid waterfront views.
[🛈] 34 [P] [⊖] [❄] [⬤] All major
cards

COSTA MESA

**LEATHERBY'S CAFÉ
ROUGE**
$$$$$
SEGERSTROM CENTER FOR THE
ARTS, 615 TOWN CENTER DR.
TEL 714-429-7640
www.patinagroup.com

Sophisticates with deep pockets
and an eye for aesthetics
appreciate the sexy contemporary surrounds, including
a curvaceous glass wall and
orange mohair booths. This
stylish restaurant also delivers
in the culinary arena, with an
Asian-inspired fusion menu that
offers such innovative items as
sea urchin *brulé* over tilefish.
The limited wine list is pricey.
[📶] 120 [P] Valet [❄] [⬤] Closed
L Mon.–Fri. & nonperformance
weekends, D Mon., & D nonperformance Sun. [⬤] All major cards

DANA POINT

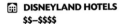 **RITZ-CARLTON
LAGUNA NIGUEL**
$$$$$
1 RITZ-CARLTON DR.
TEL 949-240-2000
www.ritzcarlton.com
Watch the wealthy old-timers
take on body-crunching waves
below, then retire to the wood-
paneled elegance of the Ritz,
where tea awaits. The Ritz's
pan-Latin restaurant, **Raya,** has
a knockout ahi tuna.
[🛈] 393 [P] Valet [⊖] [❄] [≋] [♼]
[⬤] All major cards

LAGUNA BEACH

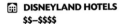 **INN AT LAGUNA BEACH**
$$$$
211 N. COAST HWY.
TEL 949-497-9722, 800-544-4479
www.innatlagunabeach.com
The true beach romantic's
favorite, the inn, low slung and
unassuming, offers some of the
best views in southern California. From a roomy guest suite,
one can watch morning sea
mists, blue afternoon skies, and
spectacular boiling sunsets.
[🛈] 70 [P] [⊖] [❄] [≋] [⬤] All
major cards

DIZZ'S AS IS
$$$
2794 S. COAST HWY.

(AT NYES PLACE)
TEL 949-494-5250
www.dizzsasis.com
The aptly named Dizz serves
up solid, honest fare. A great
atmosphere in which to eat
perfectly grilled fish, pink lamb
chops, and steak au poivre. No
reservations.
[📶] 50 [P] [🕐] Closed Mon., L
Tue.–Sun. [❄] [⬤] All major cards

LONG BEACH

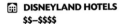 **QUEEN MARY**
$$$
1126 QUEEN'S HWY.
TEL 877-342-0742
www.queenmary.com
Launched in 1936, the *Queen
Mary* set the standard for art
deco luxury, and it remains
much the same today. Guest
rooms have ship-style bathrooms, wood paneling, and
period furniture. Ask for an outside room with a view—and one
of those swell round porthole
windows! **Sir Winston's Restaurant** serves a double dose of
elegance and nostalgia.
[🛈] 347 [P] [⊖] [❄] [♼] [⬤] All major
cards

**ALEGRIA COCINA
LATINA**
$$
115 PINE ST.
TEL 562-436-3388
www.alegriacocinalatina.com
A festive atmosphere (live
flamenco music and dancing
on stage) and good tapas add
charm here. If you have a big
appetite, choose the paella.
[📶] 175 [P] Valet [❄] [🕐] Closed
Mon.–Wed. [⬤] All major cards

NEWPORT BEACH

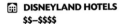 **RESORT AT PELICAN
HILL**
$$$$$
22701 PELICAN HILL RD. S.
TEL 888-507-6427
www.pelicanhill.com

This deluxe resort boasts a spectacular and serene seaside setting. Spacious and sumptuous rooms in bungalows and villas offer ocean views and lavish amenities. Other draws include a circular "Coliseum" pool, state-of-the-art spa, five restaurants, and a 37-hole Tom Fazio–designed golf course.

🛈 204 🅿 🛗 🏊 📺 ♿ All major cards

🏨 THE FASHION ISLAND 🍴 HOTEL

$$$$

690 NEWPORT CENTER DR.

TEL 877-591-9145

www.fashionislandhotel.com

Jumbo rooms with rich appointments combine with top-of-the-line service at this former Four Seasons. The indoor/outdoor **Palm Terrace** offers one of the better dining experiences on this coast.

🛈 295 🅿 🛗 🏊 📺 ♿ All major cards

🍴 PASCAL

$$$

2647 E. COAST HWY., CORONA DEL MAR

TEL 949-673-0033

www.pascalrestaurants.com

Considered, at least by regulars, perhaps the best French cooking in Orange County. Sea bass is done with a deft hand.

🍴 100 🅿 🕐 Closed Mon.-Tue. 🌴 ♿ All major cards

OJAI

🏨 OJAI VALLEY INN 🍴 $$$$

905 COUNTRY CLUB RD.

TEL 855-697-8780

www.ojaivalleyinn.com

This 1930s establishment in mission revival architecture was restored in the 1980s and again in 2005. Guest rooms and villas were refurbished in 2013 and are cozy and well appointed,

many with antiques. The rolling grounds, spa, and fine dining at **Maravilla** enhance the charm.

🛈 308 🅿 🛗 🏊 📺 ♿ All major cards

🍴 THE RANCH HOUSE

$$$

S. LOMITA AVE.

TEL 805-646-2360

www.theranchhouse.com

Many credit the founders of this rustic eatery with the creation of modern California cuisine. The influence persists, with brasserie staples like lamb chops and artichoke salad. Stunning gardens.

🍴 140 🅿 🕐 Closed L & all Mon. 🌴 ♿ All major cards

SAN DIEGO/LA JOLLA

🏨 THE GRAND DEL MAR

$$$$$

5300 GRAND DEL MAR CT.

TEL 858-314-2000, 888-590-1113

www.fairmont.com/san-diego

Tucked into a lush coastal valley behind Torrey Pines and the Del Mar coast, this eclectic resort is truly grand, starting with the super-wide hallways, capacious lounges, and full-scale, mission-style wedding chapel. Golf, tennis, fitness classes, spa treatments, horseback trail rides, mountain biking, hiking, and trips to the beach are among the many recreation options.

🛈 249 🅿 Valet 🛗 🌴 🏊 📺 ♿ All major cards

SOMETHING SPECIAL

🏨 LA VALENCIA $$$$–$$$$$

1132 PROSPECT ST.

TEL 855-476-6870

www.lavalencia.com

Perched above the waters of La Jolla Cove, the historic Spanish-style La Valencia, onetime summer home to Charlie Chaplin and others, is still a great place to stay. Rooms and villas are old fashioned but comfortable, the lounge and bar

PRICES

HOTELS

An indication of the cost of a double room in the high season is given by $ signs.

$$$$$	Over $280
$$$$	$200–$280
$$$	$120–$200
$$	$80–$120
$	Under $80

RESTAURANTS

An indication of the cost of a three-course meal without drinks is given by $ signs.

$$$$$	Over $80
$$$$	$50–$80
$$$	$35–$50
$$	$20–$35
$	Under $20

have loads of hidalgo charm, and the views are unsurpassed.

🛈 112 rooms, suites, & villas 🅿 🌴 🏊 ♿ All major cards

🏨 LOEWS CORONADO 🍴 BAY RESORT

$$$$

4000 CORONADO BAY RD.

TEL 619-424-4000, 855-946-5966

www.loewshotels.com

Blessed with a spectacular location on the southern end of San Diego Bay, Loews, unlike the brassier Hotel Del across the way, specializes in elegant informality, as reflected in its **Crown Landing** restaurant and three other casual dining spots.

🛈 439 🅿 Valet 🛗 🌴 🏊 📺 ♿ All major cards

🏨 ANDAZ $$$–$$$$

600 F ST.

TEL 619-849-1234

www.hyatt.com

Andaz is a serene oasis in the midst of San Diego's hectic

Gaslamp Quarter. The cool rooftop pool area is a place to relax during the day, but turns into a popular open-air nightclub on weekends. Sexy guest rooms have glass-enclosed bathtubs that come complete with mood lighting. The rooftop pool and open-air lounge bar draw chic locals.

🛏 159 🅿 Valet 🚻 🟢 ♨
🌀 All major cards

🍴 ISLAND PRIME & LEVEL C
$$$$
880 HARBOR ISLAND DR.
TEL 619-298-6802
www.islandprime.com
Another creation by executive chef Deborah Scott, Island Prime & Level C combines incredible food with amazing waterfront views across the bay. The surf-and-turf menu features pan-roasted day-boat scallops and an array of artisan steaks finished off with a trio of rotating flavors of crème brulée.

🍴 180 dining room, 230 outdoor deck (Level C) 🅿
🕐 Closed Mon.–Tue. & L Wed.–Sun (Island Prime)
🟢 🌀 All major cards

🍴 MILLE FLEURS
$$$$
6009 PASEO DELICIAS
TEL 858-756-3085
www.millefleurs.com
Mille Fleurs is a delight for those who appreciate a chef's dedication to fresh ingredients and impeccable preparation. Fish—grilled, poached, or baked—is outstanding; so are game meats and (seasonal) suckling pig. Extensive wine list.

🍴 120 🅿 🕐 Closed L Sat.–Mon. 🟢 🌀 All major cards

🍴 CUCINA URBANA
$$–$$$
505 LAUREL AVE.
TEL 619-239-2222
www.cucinaurbana.com

The cuisine of Italy is the star here, with California inspirations. Try the delicious braised black cod or ricotta gnudi. Great wine list; simple but decadent desserts.

🍴 130 🅿 Valet 🕐 Closed L & all Sun.–Mon. 🟢 🌀 All major cards

🍴 BO-BEAU
$$
4996 W. POINT LOMA BLVD.
TEL 619-224-2884
www.bobeaukitchen.com
This neighborhood bistro aims to transport diners to another place and time with a French farm chic atmosphere. Main courses range from the burger royale (pork belly with Gruyère cheese, green peppercorn aioli) to boeuf bourguignon.

🍴 78 🅿 🕐 Closed L & all Mon.–Tue. 🟢 🌀 All major cards

SANTA BARBARA & AROUND

🏨 ALISAL GUEST RANCH RESORT
$$$$$
1054 ALISAL RD.
TEL 805-693-4208, 800-425-4725
www.alisal.com
This 10,000-acre (4,047 ha) working cattle ranch with charming studios, suites, and bungalows welcomes guests with a range of resort-like activities, including golf, tennis, fishing, and spa services. But horseback riding is its claim to fame. Every Wednesday during the summer season, the ranch also puts on a full-scale rodeo. At the end of a day on the range, soothe your weary muscles with a deep-tissue massage and a glass of superb Santa Ynez Valley wine.

🛏 73 🅿 🟡 🌀 AE, MC, V

🏨 FOUR SEASONS
🍴 BILTMORE
$$$$$
1260 CHANNEL DR.
TEL 805-969-2261
www.fourseasons.com
Spanish-Mediterranean elegance, California amiability, and historic grandeur make this 21-acre (8.5 ha) resort a prime destination for Angelenos seeking respite from the city. The gardens, the mariachis in the sunset lounge, and the ever-pounding Pacific will lure you out of your impeccably appointed room. If you can't stay here, at least have lunch on the patio of the restaurant, **Bella Vista.**

🛏 207 rooms, 12 cottages 🅿 🚻
🟢 ♨ 🟡 🌀 All major cards

🏨 TEMECULA CREEK INN
🍴 $$$$$
44501 RAINBOW CANYON RD.
TEL 888-976-3404
www.temeculacreekinn.com
Enjoying a lush golf-course setting in the heart of southern California wine country, this lodge offers spacious guest rooms with rich Southwestern decor combining cozy comforts and modern amenities. In a town better known for fast food than gourmet fare, **Cork Fire Kitchen** stands out as an oasis of fine dining.

🛏 130 🅿 🟢 ♨ 🟡 🌀 AE, MC, V

🏨 SAN YSIDRO RANCH
🍴 $$$$–$$$$$
900 SAN YSIDRO LN.
TEL 805-565-1700
www.sanysidroranch.com
Nestled among the foothills of Montecito, this ranch is a perfect place for living out the fantasy of the good Santa Barbara life. The cottages are beautifully appointed, with soft gauzy linens, fireplaces, and little gardens outside. Call for an in-room massage, then eat at the **Stonehouse Restaurant,** where lobster and a

saffron-potato soufflé await your discerning taste buds.

(i) 41 **P** 🔄 🅢 🌊 ▨
🌐 All major cards

🏨 EL ENCANTO HOTEL
🍴 $$$-$$$$

800 ALVARADO PLACE
TEL 805-845-5800
www.elencantohotel.com
Overlooking the city from verdant hills, El Encanto is all charm, from its nine Craftsmen and 11 Spanish Revival cottages to its breezy, sun-filled dining room, where you can sample classic California cuisine. The salads and soups in summer are simple, zesty, and beautifully presented.

(i) 92 **P** 🔄 🅢 🌊 🌐 All major cards

🏨 SANTA BARBARA INN
$$-$$$

901 E. CABRILLO BLVD.
TEL 800-231-0431
www.santabarbarainn.com
This hotel offers solid value, consistently good service, big rooms—and it's just across the street from the beach!

(i) 71 **P** Valet 🔄 🅢 🌊
🌐 All major cards

🍴 HITCHING POST
$$$$

406 E. CALIF. 246 (OFF US 101)
TEL 805-688-0676
www.hitchingpost2.com
Eat here when visiting the Santa Ynez backcountry, where wineries spring from land that once belonged to old California dons. Think cowboy steak house, then add a moderne penchant for fresh ingredients. The steaks are huge, the french fries award winning.

🪑 125 **P** 🕐 Closed L 🅢
🌐 AE, MC, V

🍴 ARIGATO SUSHI
$$-$$$

1225 STATE ST.
TEL 805-965-6074
www.arigatosb.com

This small, unpretentious eatery has the feel of a sushi bar in the older sections of the Ginza in Tokyo. The fish, particularly the various sushi rolls, keep the locals and out-of-town weekenders coming back.

🪑 40 **P** 🕐 Closed L 🅢
🌐 AE, MC, V

🍴 BROPHY BROTHERS
$$-$$$

119 HARBOR WAY
TEL 805-996-4418
www.brophybros.com
A local institution, this popular harborside restaurant with views over the marina is known for its fresh-off-the-boat seafood dishes, including its signature clam chowder. It even has a raw oyster and clam bar.

🪑 80 **P** 🌐 AE, MC, V

🍴 MOTHER'S KITCHEN
$-$$

33120 CANFIELD RD.
TEL 760-742-4233
www.motherskitchenpalomar.com
The only restaurant on Mount Palomar serves excellent vegetarian dishes in a rustic setting. Sit inside around a stone hearth or outdoors on the front balcony or beneath the towering pines out back. Among its specials are pancakes and French toast, breakfast burritos, club sandwiches, homemade mac & cheese and lasagna, and veggie chili.

🪑 48 **P** 🕐 Closed L Sat.–Sun.
🌐 All major cards

🍴 LA SUPER-RICA TAQUERIA
$

622 N. MILPAS ST.
TEL 805-963-4940
An endorsement by the late Julia Child has made this modest taco stand a foodie icon. It also ensures long lines as locals line up for green chile and cheese corn tortilla soft

tacos, *adobado* (marinated pork), *gorditas* (thick corn masa pockets filled with spicy beans), and the "Super-Rica Especial" (a combo of roasted pasilla peppers, cheese, and pork).

🪑 50 **P** 🕐 Closed Wed. 🌐 No credit cards

▶ CENTRAL COAST

APTOS

🍴 BITTERSWEET BISTRO
$$$

787 RIO DEL MAR BLVD.
TEL 831-662-9799
www.bittersweetbistro.com
Coastal bistro meets Mediterranean ristorante in a relaxed atmosphere. The rack of lamb is a feast for all senses.

🪑 100 **P** 🕐 Closed Mon.–Tue.
🌐 AE, MC, V

AVILA BEACH

🏨 AVILA LA FONDA
$$$-$$$$

101 SAN MIGUEL ST.
TEL 805-595-1700
www.avilalafonda.com
Located just a block from Avila's pleasure pier and the long white-sand strand, Avila La Fonda is an artsy boutique hotel with an early 19th-century California-Mexico design theme, as well as Wi-Fi, wide-screen TVs, and Jacuzzi tubs.

🪑 28 **P** 🔄 🅢 🌐 All major cards

BIG SUR

🏨 POST RANCH INN
🍴 $$$$$

HWY. 1, ACROSS FROM VENTANA
TEL 831-667-2200
www.postranchinn.com
The inn is the exact opposite of Deetjen's (see below), from its Zen-ranch architecture to the spare California cuisine in the acclaimed **Sierra Mar** restaurant. Every known comfort is here: deep soaking tubs, thick terry

robes, bedside massages, Indian slate bathrooms, stunning views of the ocean.

🚪 41 P 🔄 ❄ 🏊 💚
🅂 AE, MC, V

🏨 VENTANA INN & SPA
🍴 $$$$–$$$$$
48123 CALIF. 1
TEL 800-628-6500
www.ventanabigsur.com
Many people still consider the Ventana the ultimate in Big Sur luxury, with giant guest suites, fully equipped kitchens, open-air decks and hot tubs, and a decent **restaurant.** Don't count on much in the way of room service, but do make your way to the breakfast and the afternoon wine and cheese spread.

🚪 60 P 🔄 ❄ 🏊 💚 🅂 All major cards

🏨 GLEN OAKS BIG SUR
$$$–$$$$$
47081 CALIF. 1
TEL 831-667-2105
www.glenoaksbigsur.com
This classic 1950s adobe motor lodge has been updated with modern amenities and decor, but retains its rustic hipster ambience and the rates that make it a reasonable alternative to the super-high-priced lodges that spangle this coast. Rooms in the main lodge feature fireplaces, recycled peroba wood furnishings, modern bathrooms with walk-in showers and heated stone floors, and Wi-Fi. Many of them have private patios or outdoor seating areas.

🚪 20 plus two cottages
P 🅂 MC, V

🏨 BIG SUR LODGE
$$–$$$
CALIF. 1, PFEIFFER BIG SUR STATE PARK
TEL 831-667-3100, 855-238-6950
www.bigsurlodge.com
Old-fashioned, basic family accommodations set in a scenic meadow surrounded by

redwoods and pines make this an affordable and joyful destination. No TVs!

🚪 61 P 🔄 🏊 🅂 AE, MC, V

SOMETHING SPECIAL

🏨 DEETJEN'S
🍴 BIG SUR INN
$$–$$$
48865 CALIF. 1, S OF BIG SUR
TEL 831-667-2378
www.deetjens.com
The ultimate in coastal rusticity, Deetjen's is a collection of woodstove-heated cabins planted deep in the redwoods. For romantics, old Deetjen's is a must, if only for a night of listening to the wind rustle the trees and reading old books left for nature lovers. Breakfasts are particularly good.

🚪 20 P 🅂 All major cards

🍴 NEPENTHE
$$$$
48510 CALIF. 1
TEL 831-667-2345
www.nepenthe.com
A local institution since 1949, Nepenthe was one of the first eateries along the Big Sur stretch of Calif. 1 and continues to offer a quintessential California coastal experience. Perched 800 feet (244 m) above the Pacific, the restaurant serves up Lolly's roast chicken, Ambrosia burgers, and filet mignon with a cabernet demi-glace, as well as local artisanal cheeses and celebrated triple berry pie, all served indoors or on long, outdoor tables with spectacular views.

🪑 36 P 🅂 All major cards

CAPITOLA

🏨 INN AT DEPOT HILL
$$$–$$$$
250 MONTEREY AVE.
TEL 831-462-3376
www.innatdepothill.com
Depot Hill has 12 tastefully

decorated rooms, each inspired by a different region, from the Mediterranean to England. No children.

🚪 12 P 🅂 All major cards

🍴 SHADOWBROOK
$$$–$$$$
1750 WHARF ROAD
TEL 831-475-1511
www.shadowbrook-capitola.com
Reached via a funicular or zigzagging hillside path, this old-world-style restaurant, full of nooks and crannies, is set amid lush gardens on the banks of Soquel Creek. The vegan-friendly menu includes a vegan main course, plus such coastal staples as fried calamari and grilled wild salmon.

🪑 175 ⏰ Closed L 🅂 All major cards

CARMEL/PEBBLE BEACH

See more hotel listings p. 181.

🏨 CASA PALERMO
$$$$$
1518 CYPRESS DR.
TEL 831-624-3811, 800-877-0597
www.pebblebeach.com
Evocative of a lush Mediterranean village, this elegant enclave features sun-drenched patios and lush landscaped grounds overlooking the Pebble Beach Golf Links. Lavish guest rooms feature wood-burning fireplaces, oversize soaking tubs, and plush robes. Tennis and billiards are among the refined activities to enjoy.

🚪 24 P ❄ 🏊 💚 🅂 All major cards

🏨 HYATT CARMEL
🍴 HIGHLANDS
$$$$–$$$$$
120 HIGHLANDS DR.
TEL 831-620-1234
www.hyatt.com
More coastal luxury, this time perched above the rocks of Point Lobos, where seals frolic on jagged rock islands and mists float to and fro. Big guest suites all have great views; in-room Jacuzzis are perfect

for after-hiking aches. Room service could be better, but the restaurant, **Pacific's Edge,** has few coastal peers. Steer for the caramelized sea scallops and potato and basil salad.

ⓘ 142 🅿 ⬛ ⬛ ⬛ ⬛ 🅰 All major cards

🏨 LODGE AT
🍴 PEBBLE BEACH
$$$$–$$$$$
17 MILE DR.

TEL 831-647-7500, 800-877-0597
www.pebblebeach.com
This luxurious lodge has been setting the standard for the haute golf world since 1919. The rooms are impeccably appointed with crisp linens and richly burnished decor. The **Stillwater Bar & Grill** is the place for contemporary seafood, while the low-key **Gallery Café** offers homestyle meals.

ⓘ 161 🅿 ⬛ ⬛ ⬛ ⬛ 🅰 All major cards

🏨 LA PLAYA HOTEL
$$$$
8TH AVE. & CAMINO REAL

TEL 831-293-6100, 800-582-8900
www.laplayahotel.com
Cool and serene, with beautifully tended central gardens and views of the Carmel coastline, this decades-old favorite has plenty of charm. White throughout, with swatches of blue here and there, the sunlit mood in guest rooms is soothingly Mediterranean. A sweet retreat still.

ⓘ 75 rooms, 5 cottages 🅿 ⬛ ⬛ ⬛ 🅰 All major cards

🏨 QUAIL LODGE RESORT
🍴 & GOLF CLUB
$$$$
8205 VALLEY GREENS DR.

TEL 831-620-0802, 866-675-1101
www.quaillodge.com
A luxury deal on the coast, the Quail has great service, outstanding dining at **Edgar's,** and everything the golf fanatic could ever want, set in a serene

and dreamy spot with rugged peaks and green valleys.

ⓘ 100 🅿 ⬛ ⬛ ⬛ ⬛ 🅰 All major cards

🍴 PÈPPOLI
$$$$
THE INN AT SPANISH BAY,
2700 17 MILE DR.

TEL 831-647-7433, 800-877-0597
www.pebblebeach.com
Exuding cozy Tuscan ambience, Pèppoli also offers flavorful, rustic Italian dishes paired to classic Italian wines. Consider these favorites: mussels and clams steamed in a spicy shallot saffron broth, and slow-braised veal shank with Pèppoli wine and gremolata. The sweeping views over the Links at Spanish Bay and the Pacific Ocean are dessert enough.

➕ 120 🅿 🕐 Closed L ⬛ 🅰 All major cards

🍴 ANTON & MICHEL
$$$
MISSION & 7TH STS.

TEL 831-624-2406
www.antonandmichel.com
Classic, elegant Continental cuisine with an emphasis on fresh ingredients makes Anton & Michel one of the first dining stops for many coastal regulars. The wine list, featuring several area vineyards, has grown substantially in recent years.

➕ 90 🅿 🅰 All major cards

🍴 LITTLE NAPOLI
$$$
DOLORES & 7TH STS.

TEL 831-626-6335
Serving southern Italian country cooking from Pèpe family recipes since 1990. Here you can get all the favorites: antipasti, pizza, pasta, risotto, and traditional Italian desserts served in a friendly, inviting atmosphere. Being so close to the sea, there's also plenty of seafood on offer, and the garlic bread is outstanding.

➕ 60 🅿 🕐 Closed Tue, L Wed.–Sun, D Sat. & Mon. 🅰 All major cards

---

PRICES

HOTELS
An indication of the cost of a double room in the high season is given by **$** signs.

$$$$$	Over $280
$$$$	$200–$280
$$$	$120–$200
$$	$80–$120
$	Under $80

RESTAURANTS
An indication of the cost of a three-course meal without drinks is given by **$** signs.

$$$$$	Over $80
$$$$	$50–$80
$$$	$35–$50
$$	$20–$35
$	Under $20

MONTEREY

🏨 HYATT REGENCY MON-
🍴 TEREY HOTEL & SPA
$$$$–$$$$$
1 OLD GOLF COURSE RD.

TEL 831-372-1234
www.hyatt.com
The Hyatt Monterey perches on the edge of Del Monte Golf Course. Guest rooms feature private patios, wide-screen TVs, and bathrooms with walk-in rain showers. The resort offers direct access to the golf links, several swimming pools, 24-hour gym, and racquet club, as well as hiking, biking, and jogging trails. **Sea Root** serves up gourmet Mediterranean-inspired cuisine.

ⓘ 550 🅿 Valet ⬛ ⬛ ⬛ 🅰 All major cards

🏨 MONTEREY PLAZA
🍴 HOTEL & SPA
$$$–$$$$
400 CANNERY ROW

TEL 831-920-6710
www.montereyplazahotel.com

Occupying a former cannery just steps from Monterey Bay Aquarium, this delightful hotel hangs dramatically over the Pacific Ocean, with bay views and the sound of lapping waves as a lullaby. Guest rooms exude contemporary elegance and comfort, while **Schooners Coastal Kitchen** specializes in fresh seafood dishes and contemporary American cuisine.

🛈 290 **P** Valet 🎽 🕲 All major cards

🍴 MONTRIO
$$–$$$
414 CALLE PRINCIPAL
TEL 831-648-8880
www.montrio.com
For anyone who has grown impatient with the New American fad of recent years, this is where the form finds redemption in tasty, ingredient-savvy cooking by chef Tony Baker. Try the crab cakes or the rotisserie-cooked rib-eye steak.

🛏 200 **P** 🕒 Closed L Sun. 🕲 All major cards

🍴 TARPY'S ROADHOUSE
$
2999 MONTEREY-SALINAS HWY.
TEL 831-647-1444
www.tarpys.com
More American fare, but that would be to sell Tarpy's short. Inside the lovely ivy-shrouded stone house is some fine cooking, with the "American" menu including roast rabbit and a pecan-barbecued duck that will drive you quackers for more.

🛏 120 **P** 🕲 All major cards

MORRO BAY

🏨 INN AT MORRO BAY
🍴 $$–$$$
60 STATE PARK RD.
TEL 805-772-5651
www.innatmorrobay.com
Simple and quiet, the inn sits above Morro Bay's rocky shore, where the famous Morro Rock

juts from the ocean floor. Guest rooms are equipped with state-of-the-art amenities. The restaurant, **60 State Park,** offers fine seafood at decent prices.

🛈 98 **P** 🔙 🕲 All major cards

PACIFIC GROVE

🏨 GREEN GABLES INN
$$$–$$$$
301 OCEAN VIEWS BLVD.
TEL 831-375-2095
www.greengablesinnpg.com
A cross between an inn and a bed-and-breakfast, the Gables offers spacious rooms in its carriage house out back and more intimate, historic *chambres* in the main house, which was built, legend holds, by an enterprising sea captain for his mistress.

🛈 11 **P** 🕲 AE, MC, V

🏨 SEVEN GABLES INN
$$$–$$$$
555 OCEAN VIEW BLVD.
TEL 831-372-4341
www.thesevengablesinn.com
The ocean view, the European antiques, and the gilded-age decor combine to make this clutch of yellow-gabled wood buildings a fine period hideaway.

🛈 25 **P** 🕲 MC, V

SOMETHING SPECIAL

🍴 PASSIONFISH
$$$$
701 LIGHTHOUSE AVE.,
PACIFIC GROVE
TEL 831-655-3311
www.passionfish.net
This renowned pioneer of sustainable seafood offers an elegantly contemporary setting for enjoying Chef Ted Walter's remarkable California cuisine inspired by conscientious fishing. The menu changes daily, but might include basil-stuffed rainbow trout, fresh-caught sea scallops drizzled with tomato-truffle butter, or farmed

sturgeon with a spicy red curry vinaigrette.

🛏 80 **P** 🕒 Closed L 🕲 🕲 All major cards

🍴 FANDANGO
$$–$$$
223 17TH ST.
TEL 831-372-3456
www.fandangorestaurant.com
A fine midrange alternative to the French fever that possesses the peninsula these days, Fandango's zesty Mediterranean fare (from Spanish paellas to Moroccan couscous) has locals lining up. The osso buco is heady with wine and veal stock, simmered just right.

🛏 140 **P** 🕲 All major cards

PASO ROBLES

🍴 BL BRASSERIE
$$$
1202 PINE ST.
TEL 805-226-8191
www.bistrolaurent.com
If you're deep into cowboy wine country, you can't do better than this purveyor of rustic French cuisine, made with the freshest of local ingredients. The roasted squab is great, as is the roast chicken with garlic and rosemary.

🛏 50 **P** 🕒 Closed Mon. & D Sun. 🕲 🕲 MC, V

SAN LUIS OBISPO

🏨 APPLE FARM INN
🍴 $$–$$$
2015 MONTEREY ST.
TEL 805-544-2040
www.applefarm.com
Down-home coziness, in the form of fireplaces, canopy beds, and flowers, greets visitors to this happy abode. Located along sycamore- and live oak–dotted San Luis Obispo Creek, this Victorian also offers affordable, satisfying dining at its **Apple Farm Restaurant.** Don't miss the homemade ice cream.

🛈 106 **P** 🔙 🕲 AE, MC, V

🏨 SYCAMORE MINERAL
🍴 SPRINGS RESORT
$$–$$$
1215 AVILA BEACH DR.
TEL 805-595-7302
www.sycamoresprings.com
A classic inland spa, complete
with Mediterranean architecture,
outdoor mineral spas (for soaking
under crystal-clear summer
skies), and luxury suites with
fireplaces. The **Gardens of Avila
Restaurant** is cozy and romantic.
🛏 55 🅿 🛗 🟥 AE, MC, V

SANTA CRUZ

🏨 INN AT PASATIEMPO
🍴 $$–$$$
555 CALIF. 17
TEL 831-423-5000
www.innatpasatiempo.com
Set alongside Pasatiempo Golf
Course, this fine country inn
offers serene gardens, solid
service, and rooms with fireplaces and Jacuzzis. **Back 9 Grill
& Bar** (at the golf course), with
panoramic views of Monterey
Bay, features no-nonsense (and
very tasty) regional American
cuisine.
🛏 54 🅿 🛗 🟥 All major cards

PISMO BEACH

🏨 THE CLIFFS
$$$
2757 SHELL BEACH RD.
TEL 805-773-5000
www.cliffshotelandspa.com
Pacific elegance in a tranquil
clifftop setting characterizes this
favorite weekend haunt. Many
rooms come with wonderful
ocean views.
🛏 160 🅿 🔄 🟥 🛗 🛁 🟥
🟥 All major cards

TEMPLETON

🍴 MCPHEE'S GRILL
$$
416 S. MAIN ST.
TEL 805-434-3204
www.mcpheesgrill.com

If all the walking at Mr. Hearst's
little getaway has left you han-
kering for a bit of pampering,
try McPhee's, a modernish grill
room with inspired contemporary California cuisine. Locally
raised meats make the steak
offerings a good bet.
🛏 100 🅿 🟦 🟥 Closed Mon.–
Tue. 🟥 MC, V

▶ SAN FRANCISCO
San Francisco is a grand city—
and hard to beat for its wide
range of hotels, inns, bed-
and-breakfasts, and, of course,
restaurants. Travelers also
can consult the San Francisco
Convention & Visitors Bureau
*(749 Howard, tel 415-391-2000,
www.sanfrancisco.travel)*. One of
the best-run such organizations in the country, it offers
a variety of free lodging and
food guides that are constantly
updated by an ambitious,
discerning staff.

CHINATOWN &
TELEGRAPH HILL

🍴 MISTER JIU'S
$$$–$$$$
28 WAVERLY PLACE
TEL 415-857-9688
www.misterjius.com
Rated as one of the top new
restaurants in the U.S. when it
launched in 2017, this Michelin-
starred restaurant sets the
standard for suave decor and
traditional Chinese cuisine with
inventive contemporary flair.
Plus, the cocktails have earned
just renown for their creativity,
making this one of San Fran-
cisco's hippest bar scenes.
🛏 40 🟦 Closed Mon.
🟥 All major cards

🍴 HOUSE OF NANKING
$$
919 KEARNY ST.
TEL 415-421-1429
www.houseofnankingsf.com
Not much to look at, and the
service can be surly and abrupt,

but aficionados of true Szechuan
cuisine—fiery soups, even hotter
sizzled eggplant—still come.
Locals bring their out-of-town
friends to show them that San
Francisco Chinatown still has a
few great eateries.
🛏 45 🟥 MC, V

🍴 LUCKY CREATION
$
854 WASHINGTON ST.
TEL 415-989-0818
Lucky is the vegetarian who dines
at Chef Kwok Lom's eatery. Try
the various meatless meats—
goose, pork, chicken—they're all
good. Purists might stick with the
mushroom-and-greens-stuffed
dumplings or smoky oyster-sauce
broccoli.
🛏 40 🅿 🟦 Closed Wed.
🟥 MC, V

🍴 SAM WO
$
713 CLAY ST.
TEL 415-989-8898
Open for more than a century
(although its location changed
in 2015), this casual, no-frills restaurant is old-school Chinatown,
serving such staples as BBQ pork
rice noodle rolls. Service has
improved since the days when it
drew masochistic patrons for the
most abusive treatment in town.
🛏 32 🟦 Closed Tue. 🟥 MC, V

CIVIC CENTER

🍴 ABSINTHE BRASSERIE &
BAR
$$$
398 HAYES ST.
TEL 415-552-1590
www.absinthe.com
Exuding a distinctly French feel,
this dim-lit, Michelin-starred
brasserie plays on the theme with
its absinthe cocktails. The menu,
however, weds French classics such
as coq au vin and oxtail terrine with
Caesar salad, burgers, and such Cali-
fornia fusions as risotto with fava
beans and parmesan. Weekend
brunch is particularly popular.

🏨 Hotel   🍴 Restaurant   🛏 No. of Guest Rooms   🪑 No. of Seats   🅿 Parking   🟦 Closed   🛗 Elevator

🔲 40 🕐 Closed Mon.–Tue.
💳 All major cards

🍴 LERS ROS THAI

$$

307 HAYES ST.

TEL 415-874-9661

www.lersros.com

Dedicated to serving authentic Thai dishes in stylish surrounds, this upscale chain restaurant—other locations are on Larkin St. and 17th St.—delivers the goods. In addition to faves such as pad thai, look for some experimental dishes, such as garlic quail appetizer, and frog with basil leaves, young peppercorn, and galingale.

🔲 44 🈳 💳 All major cards

FINANCIAL DISTRICT/ UNION SQUARE

🏨 JW MARRIOTT

🍴 $$$$$

500 POST ST.

TEL 415-398--8900

www.marriott.com

A wonderful place to stay in the city's theater district, the JW Marriott fuses the comfort and amenities demanded by today's luxe travelers with the services required by business travelers (complimentary limousines, etc.). The rooms are soothing (pastels dominate), and the lunch menu at the **The Restaurant** is tasty and diverse. Check for weekday deals.

ℹ️ 329 🅿️ 🈳 🈳 🎽 💳 All major cards

🏨 PALACE

🍴 $$$$$

2 NEW MONTGOMERY ST.

TEL 415-512-1111

www.marriott.com

Another classic San Francisco hotel, with grand mahogany furniture, old-style ambience, and large, well-lit rooms, combined with many modern comforts. The Palace even has an indoor lap pool for chilly summer days. Diners in the

Garden Court restaurant eat under a high domed glass roof hung with chandeliers.

ℹ️ 552 🅿️ 🈳 🈳 🈳 🎽 💳 All major cards

🏨 TAJ CAMPTON PLACE

🍴 $$$$$

340 STOCKTON ST.

TEL 415-781-5555

www.tajcamptonplace.com

Set between Union Square and Chinatown, this chic boutique hotel lures guests with uncluttered, sophisticated rooms and discreet but friendly service. The rooms are cozy but cleverly designed, with large beds, soak tubs, writing desks, and handcrafted hardwood furniture. The outdoor fitness center offers great city views. The menu in the hotel's namesake **restaurant** revolves around California organic and free-range produce. The multi course tasting menus—paired with splendid California wines—are especially decadent.

ℹ️ 100 🈳 🈳 🎽 💳 All major cards

🏨 THE MARKER

🍴 $$$$-$$$$$

501 GEARY ST.

TEL 415-292-0100,800-237-2508

www.themarkersf.com

Super-chic decor is the name of the game at this fun-loving hotel near Union Square. The suites are especially playful, blending old-world glamour with modern amenities. The spa includes sauna, steam room, and Jacuzzi. The hotel goes out of its way to welcome pets. The elegant **Tratto** restaurant serves well-executed Italian classics.

ℹ️ 100 🈳 🈳 🎽 💳 All major cards

🏨 CLIFT ROYAL SONESTA HOTEL

$$$$

495 GEARY ST.

TEL 415-775-4700

www.clifthotel.com

Longtime tradition meets trendy style in this classic hotel given a makeover by Ian Schrager and his designer, Philippe Starck, but dialled back a notch under new Sonesta management. Enjoy a cocktail in the Redwood Room (made from a single redwood tree, before such acts were considered abominations).

ℹ️ 372 🅿️ Valet 🈳 🈳 🎽 💳 All major cards

🏨 HOTEL NIKKO

🍴 $$$$

222 MASON ST.

TEL 415-394-1111

www.hotelnikkosf.com

Solid, upscale service, roomy guest suites, a great location, and the award-winning **Anzu** restaurant make this a favorite. The spa services are worth checking out.

ℹ️ 533 🅿️ 🈳 🈳 🈳 🎽 💳 All major cards

🏨 WESTIN ST. FRANCIS

🍴 $$$$ (TOWER $$$$$)

335 POWELL ST.

TEL 415-397-7000

www.westinstfrancis.com

A fine old downtown standby, the St. Francis is a hotel for people who love to stroll the city, like the grand boulevardiers of old. Its lobby is sumptuous, its rooms warm and recently upgraded in stylish vogue, and its wood-paneled **Oak Room** restaurant is a local landmark favorite for steaks.

ℹ️ 1,254 🅿️ 🈳 🈳 🈳 🎽 💳 All major cards

🏨 HOTEL TRITON

$$$-$$$$

342 GRANT AVE.

TEL 415-394-0555

www.hoteltriton.com

Another boutique hotel—one with outstanding decor (a kind of neo art deco), impeccable (but smallish) rooms, good service, and a great location: just steps from the old Chinatown Gate.

ℹ️ 140 🅿️ Valet 🈳 🈳 🎽 💳 All major cards

🈳 Nonsmoking   🈳 Air-conditioning   🈳 Indoor Pool   🈳 Outdoor Pool   🎽 Health Club   💳 Credit Cards

🏨 **PETITE AUBERGE**
$$$–$$$$
863 BUSH ST.
TEL 415-928-6000
www.petiteaubergesf.com
Another "personal suite" setup, this one with a tasteful French accent. Although the rooms are small, they are very comfortable. No concierge service to speak of, but the breakfast (included) and afternoon wine and cheese (free) are outstanding.
ⓘ 26 🅿 Valet ⊟ ▦
� All major cards

SOMETHING SPECIAL

🍴 **SONS & DAUGHTERS**
$$$$$
708 BUSH ST.
TEL 415-994-7933
www.sonsanddaughterssf.com
Chef-owner Teague Moriarty created a classic when he opened this small and cozy black-and-cream restaurant resembling a cross between a stylish home and an art gallery with chandeliers. His sophisticated California-inspired, prix-fixe tasting menu features playfully inventive dishes that change monthly. Typical and irresistible oddities might include chilled melon soup with a horseradish cracker and sea urchin, and coal-roasted leeks with charred fennel cream and boiled peanuts. Signature desserts are no less sublime.
🍴 28 🄲 Closed L & Mon.–Tue. 🄲 All major cards

🍴 **AKIKO'S**
$$$$
HOTEL VINTAGE COURT,
431 BUSH ST.
TEL 415.397.3218
http://akikosrestaurant.com
Not to be confused with Akiko's Sushi on Market St., this tiny upscale Japanese restaurant serves some of the freshest and most heavenly sushi and top-shelf sake in the city. The menu includes some rarely seen items,

such as seared baby barracuda and monkfish liver.
🍴 28 🄲 Closed Sun. & D Sun.
🄲 All major cards

🍴 **MOURAD**
$$$$
140 NEW MONTGOMERY ST.
TEL 415-660-2500
www.mouradsf.com
Named for Michelin-starred owner-chef Mourad Lahlou, this eponymous restaurant brings a high level of sophistication to Moroccan cuisine. The setting at the base of the PacBell Building offers a boldly contemporary North African design, and the kitchen showcases vibrant dishes cross-pollinated with California ingredients and infused with mouth-pleasing flavors.
🍴 60 🄲 Closed L Sat.–Sun.
🄲 🄲 All major cards

🍴 **LE COLONIAL**
$$$
20 COSMO PL.
TEL 415-931-3600
www.lecolonialsf.com
With an atmosphere out of 1920s Vietnam, this stylish spot serves French-Vietnamese cuisine that might include scallop-ginger pot stickers or pomegranate-glazed Peking duck. For a lively scene and good appetizers, head for the upstairs cocktail lounge.
🍴 320 🅿 Valet 🄲 Closed L
🄲 🄲 All major cards

🍴 **HOGWASH**
$$–$$$
582 SUTTER ST.
TEL 415-361-5500
www.hogwashsf.com
A sudsters' dream, this classy pub has a dozen beers on tap, plus excellent pub fare, from beet salad, curry fries, and cheeseburgers with jalapeños and spicy brown mustard, to lamb merguez sausage with blue cheese sauce, pickled cabbage, and beet relish.

PRICES

HOTELS
An indication of the cost of a double room in the high season is given by $ signs.

$$$$$	Over $280
$$$$	$200–$280
$$$	$120–$200
$$	$80–$120
$	Under $80

RESTAURANTS
An indication of the cost of a three-course meal without drinks is given by $ signs.

$$$$$	Over $80
$$$$	$50–$80
$$$	$35–$50
$$	$20–$35
$	Under $20

🍴 80 🄲 Closed Mon.-Tue. 🄲
🄲 MC, V

GOLDEN GATE & AROUND

🍴 **KABUTO SUSHI**
$$$
5121 GEARY BLVD.
TEL 415-752-5652
www.kabutosf.com
Though his restaurant is plain plain plain, Kabuto's chef is considered one of the city's best sushi masters, carving up some of the finest fatty toro and briny uni found anywhere.
🍴 31 🄲 Closed Mon. & L Sun.
🄲 AE, MC, V

🍴 **DELAROSA**
$$
2175 CHESNUT ST.
TEL 415-673-7100
www.delarosasf.com
A "happening" institution in the Marina District, Delarosa is a chain Italian restaurant and pizzeria with attitude. The vibe is uber-chic, youthful, and fun, although long waits to get in are a norm.
🍴 70 🄲 🄲 All major cards

🍴 TAQUERIA LOS MAYOS
$$

331 CLEMENT ST.
TEL 415-548-2800
www.taquerialosmayassf.com
This no-frills Mexican restaurant in Inner Richmond specializes in Yucatán dishes, such as ceviche, plantain burriots, *panuchos* (crispy tacos filled with citrus-marinated meats), and *pozole*—pork or chicken hominy with chile in a spicy broth.

🪑 28 🅰 MC, V

HAIGHT-ASHBURY

🍴 CHA CHA CHA
$$

1801 HAIGHT ST.
TEL 415-386-7670
www.chachachasf.com
This longtime Haight hangout is renowned for its Cajun shrimp and steamed black mussels dishes, but the eclectic menu also features a *plato vegetariano* (seasonal vegetables with black beans, fried sweet plantains, *yuca con mojo*) and Jamaican jerk chicken. It's often jam-packed, so make reservations.

🪑 60 🅿 🅢 🅰 All major cards

MISSION DISTRICT

🍴 LA TRAVIATA
$$

2854 MISSION ST.
(BETW. 24TH & 25TH STS.)
TEL 415-282-0500
www.latraviatasf.com
A closely held secret of the younger, groovier folk now gentrifying the district, La Traviata offers affordable, classic Italian cuisine (tortellini, prosciutto, zuppa di pesce) in a delightful atmosphere.

🪑 60 🅿 🕑 Closed L 🅢 🅰 AE, DC

🍴 LA TAQUERIA
$

2889 MISSION ST. (AT 25TH ST.)
TEL 415-285-7117
Truly an amazing deal: down-

right seductive Mexican food with zesty fresh salsas, tacos so yummy you'll want to take some back to your hotel room, and fast service. Stop here after touring the Mission.

🪑 70 🕑 Closed Mon.–Tue.
🅢 🅰 No credit cards

🍴 PANCHO VILLA TAQUERIA
$

3071 16TH ST. (BETW. VALENCIA & MISSION STS.)
TEL 415-864-8840
www.sfpanchovilla.com
A friendly purveyor of such specialties as barbecued pork burritos, prawn tacos, and an array of Tex-Mex as well.

🪑 90 🅰 AE, MC, V

NOB HILL

SOMETHING SPECIAL

🏨 THE HUNTINGTON
🍴 $$$$$

1075 CALIFORNIA ST.
TEL 415-474-5400
www.huntingtonhotel.com
For the money, the best San Francisco experience around. The staff is excellent, rooms large, opulent, and quiet, and the extras don't stop, from limo service to personal modems to unbelievable room service; the spa has an indoor infinity pool and elegant treatment rooms. The **Big 4** restaurant is soothing and rich.

🛏 136 🅿 🔗 🅢 🅰 🐦 🅰 All major cards

🏨 RITZ-CARLTON
🍴 SAN FRANCISCO
$$$$$

600 STOCKTON ST.
TEL 415-296-7465
www.ritzcarlton.com
Pricey but, by most standards, one of the best hotels in the world. There is so much splendor: chandeliers, museum-quality oil paintings, flowers,

chocolates, and personal maids. Staff is helpful and stylish. The brilliant, top-ranked **The Lounge** restaurant celebrates the city's many cultural influences, from sashimi to fettucine. The variety makes it one of the best places on the West Coast, if not the country, in which to dine.

🛏 336 🅿 Valet 🔗 🅢 🅰 🐦
🅰 All major cards

🏨 STANFORD COURT
🍴 $$$$$

905 CALIFORNIA ST.
TEL 415-989-3500
stanfordcourt.com
Situated on the site of Leland Stanford's Nob Hill mansion, the Court was recently revamped with a more contemporary, yet still elegant, style to appeal to a sophisticated hip clientele. Its classy **SC Bar & Lounge** offers a broad dinner menu plus artisanal beers and cocktails.

🛏 393 🅿 Valet 🔗 🅢 🐦
🅰 All major cards

🏨 FAIRMONT
$$$$–$$$$$

950 MASON ST.
TEL 415-772-5000, 866-540-4491
www.fairmont.com
The Fairmont, with its gilded-era lobby and soaring staircases, perhaps best evokes the city's golden age. Rooms are bigger in the new addition. The Tonga Room tiki lounge bar features live music.

🛏 606 🅿 Valet 🔗 🅢 🐦
🅰 All major cards

🏨 INTERCONTINENTAL MARK HOPKINS
$$$$–$$$$$

1 NOB HILL
TEL 415-392-3434, 800-424-6835
www.sfmarkhopkins.com
Built by another of the Big Four railroad barons, the Mark, with an infusion of investment from the InterContinental Group, maintains much of the elegance, service, and atmosphere of old San Francisco. The lobby is grand and lively, the service polished.

🅢 Nonsmoking 🅢 Air-conditioning 🅰 Indoor Pool 🅰 Outdoor Pool 🐦 Health Club 🅰 Credit Cards

The views from the Top of the Mark cocktail bar are hard to beat.

① 380 **P** Valet **⬆** **☎** **📺** **🅂** All major cards

🍴 ACQUERELLO

$$$$

1722 SACRAMENTO ST.

TEL 415-567-5432

www.acquerellosf.com

Acquerello serves up grand and very modern Italian cuisine, in the style of the edgiest Roman ristorante, with such zesty chemistry as salmon with lemon oregano oil and black olive and parsley salad Siciliana. If the house gelato is on the menu, don't miss it. It has a dress code.

🍴 55 **P** **🕑** Closed L & Sun.–Mon. **☎** **🅂** All major cards

NORTH BEACH

🏨 HOTEL BOHEME

$$$–$$$$

444 COLUMBUS AVE.

TEL 415-433-9111

www.hotelboheme.com

Some fine Beat-generation atmospherics in a well-run old hotel right in the center of historic North Beach. What you save on the room, you can spend on food.

① 15 **P** **⬆** **🅂** All major cards

SOMETHING SPECIAL

🍴 SOTTO MARE

$$–$$$

552 GREEN ST.

TEL 415-398-3181

www.sottomaresf.com

The update editor's favorite Italian restaurant in San Francisco, intimate and homey Sotto Mare is a virtual museum of nautical memorabilia and provides an authentic North Beach experience. Renowned—and beloved—for its fresh seafood dishes, it excels at crab cioppino and seafood risotto. You'll also find Boston clam chowder,

plus oysters and clams on the half shell.

🍴 70 **🅂** All major cards

🍴 MARIO'S BOHEMIAN CIGAR STORE CAFÉ

$

566 COLUMBUS AVE.

TEL 415-362-0536

Just across from Washington Square, Mario's is the classic Italian coffeehouse. The focaccia sandwiches are as good as the wonderful cappuccino.

🍴 65 **🅂** MC, V

🍴 MO'S GOURMET BURGERS

$

1322 GRANT AVE.

TEL 415-788-3779

www.mosgrill.com

The namesake burgers rank among San Francisco's best; also good chicken and steaks.

🍴 40 **🅂** MC, V

PACIFIC HEIGHTS/ JAPANTOWN

🏨 HOTEL DRISCO

$$$$

2901 PACIFIC AVE.

TEL 415-346-2880

www.hoteldrisco.com

A 1903 hotel located in the heart of Pacific Heights; views of the city, bay, and Golden Gate Bridge. Plush rooms and suites. No parking available.

① 48 **⬆** **📺** **🅂** All major cards

🏨 HOTEL KABUKI

$$$

1625 POST ST.

TEL 415-922-3200

www.jdvhotels.com/kabuki

A perfect compromise between bed-and-breakfast and the megahotel scene, this midsize hotel was recently refurbished and features an exquisite decor blending Japanese and Western themes.

Some rooms have their own Japanese-style soaking tubs.

① 218 **P** Valet **⬆** **☎** **📺** **🅂** All major cards

🏨 LAUREL INN

$$$

444 PRESIDIO AVE.

TEL 415-346-7431

www.jdvhotels.com

Units with kitchenettes, free covered parking, and stylish spare decor create a place well suited to an extended stay, located on the margin of Pacific Heights. A chic cocktail lounge and coffee club, Laureate, is on the property.

① 49 **P** **🅂** All major cards

🍴 SASA

$$$–$$$$

22 PEACE PLAZA, STE. 530

TEL 415-683-9673

www.sasasf.com

Owner-chef Weidi Chen launched this sleek, modern Japanese restaurant in late 2018, focusing on sushi and modern Japanese kaiseki-style cuisine. Opt for a "mystery box" containing six or nine pieces of Chen's choosing, or a prix-fixe eight-piece sushi flight. Dinner includes an optional tasting menu ($$$$) that includes a hassun, five-item kaiseki platter, plus eight pieces of sushi.

🍴 40 **P** **🕑** Closed Mon. **🅂** All major cards

🍴 MARUFUKU RAMEN

$$$

JAPAN CENTER, 1581 WEBSTER ST., STE. 235

TEL 415-872-9786

www.marufukuramen.com/sanfrancisco

Contemporary Japanese minimalism meets traditional Hakata-style tonkotsu ramen, comprising creamy rich pork and chicken broth served with thick noodles and slices of simmered pork, wood ear mushrooms, bean sprouts, and soft-boiled egg. The menu also features rice bowls and Takoyaki small plates.

⊞ 60 🅿 🔅 ⊗ All major cards

🍴 JACKSON & FILLMORE
$$–$$$
2506 FILLMORE ST.
TEL 415-346-5288
www.jacksonfillmoresf.com
A simple, cozy, and popular family-run trattoria amid the glamour of Pacific Heights, this restaurant delivers straightforward yet tasty Italian staples.

⊞ 50 🕐 Closed Mon.–Wed. ⊗ MC, V

🍴 ON THE BRIDGE
$$–$$$
JAPAN CENTER, 1581 WEBSTER ST., STE. 205
TEL 415-922-7765
www.onthebridgesf.com
Named for its position on the span connecting the two halves of Japan Center Mall, Chef Nakamura's colorful and cozy restaurant is a paean to manga: It even has an anime library and film collection. Its culinary specialty is *yoshoku*, or Western-style Japanese, dishes, such as Japanese spaghetti, *okonomiyaki* pizza, and fish roe-topped Japanese-style pasta dishes.

⊞ 36 🅿 🕐 Closed Thur. ⊗ MC, V

🍴 CHOUQUETS
$$
2500 WASHINGTON ST.
TEL 415-359-0075
www.chouquets.com
Dedicated to hearty French-California fare, this casually-elegant European bistro draws a loyal local clientele for such no-frills dishes as boeuf bourguignon, roasted chicken breast with black truffles, and classic veal stew in white cream sauce. Of course, crème brûlée is there too. Its impressive wine list includes 15 wines by the glass.

⊞ 50 ⊗ All major cards

RUSSIAN HILL

🍴 LA FOLIE
$$$$$
2316 POLK ST.
TEL 415-776-5577
www.lafolie.com
Another top choice, La Folie has garnered acclaim in several surveys as the city's preferred purveyor of New French cuisine; that the room is simply breathtaking and the service perfect makes it a "can't miss" for a night out. Chef Roland Passot never misses with such dishes as roasted Scottish salmon with braised escarole, gnocchi, smoked ham hock, and sweet onion sauce.

⊞ 62 🅿 Valet 🕐 Closed L & Sun.–Mon. 🔅 ⊗ All major cards

WATERFRONT

🏨 FOUR SEASONS
$$$$$
222 SANSOME ST.
TEL 415-633-3000, 800-819-5053
www.fourseasons.com
Perched on top of the First Interstate Bank, one of the city's tallest buildings, the Four Seasons has views of the entire cityscape. Much acclaimed for comfort and attention, it offers some of the suavest guest rooms in town.

ⓘ 158 🅿 ⬍ 🔅 🎽 ⊗ All major cards

🏨 ARGONAUT HOTEL
$$$$
495 JEFFERSON ST.
TEL 415-563-0800, 800-790-1415
www.argonauthotel.com
Occupying the old brick Del Monte warehouse, the hotel has a seagoing theme, right down to porthole-shaped windows and star-emblazoned blue carpeting in the guest rooms. A quiet retreat on Fisherman's Wharf.

ⓘ 252 🅿 Valet ⬍ 🎽

🏨 FAIRMONT HERITAGE PLACE
$$$$
900 N. POINT ST.
TEL 415-268-9900
www.fairmont.com
A large portion of Ghirardelli's renowned chocolate factory has been reinvented as a residential-style hotel near Fisherman's Wharf. The one-, two-, and three-bedroom units include gourmet kitchens and fireplaces. Prearrival grocery shopping, in-residence spa treatments, view terraces with fire pits, and chauffeured house cars are all available. For those who don't want to cook, the Fairmont can arrange a personal chef or help with reservations at the many nearby restaurants. Minimum three-night stay.

ⓘ 131 🅿 ⬍ 🔅 ⛱ 🎽 ⊗ All major cards

🏨 HARBOR COURT
$$$$
165 STEUART ST.
TEL 415-882-1300
www.harborcourthotel.com
A moderately priced business-tourist hotel with several outstanding amenities, including free area limousine service, a health club, and a pool with sauna. Rooms are comfortable.

ⓘ 131 🅿 ⬍ 🔅 ⛱ 🎽 ⊗ All major cards

🏨 LE MÉRIDIEN
🍴 $$$$
333 BATTERY ST.
TEL 415-296-2900
www.marriott.com
Freshly invigorated, stylishly modern hotel combines the Marriott chain's competence with class, plus plenty of business services. The **Park Grill** offers splendid fine dining.

ⓘ 360 🅿 Valet ⬍ 🔅 🎽 ⊗ All major cards

🏨 HOTEL GRIFFON
$$$–$$$$
155 STEUART ST.
TEL 415-495-2100
www.hotelgriffon.com
One of the better small hotels in the city, the Griffon is perfect if you don't need concierge services or the doting of a bed-and-breakfast. Rooms here are elegant yet conservative.

🛈 62 🅿 ⬆ 🕓 ⚓ 🎮 🖥 All major cards

SOMETHING SPECIAL

🍴 RESTAURANT GARY DANKO
$$$$$
800 NORTH POINT ST.
TEL 415-749-2060
www.garydanko.com
Flawless California-French cooking and beautiful fresh ingredients add up to the city's hottest dinner ticket, where the menu may include horseradish-crusted salmon with dilled cucumbers, or lemon-herb duck breast with duck hash and rhubarb compote. The Michelin-starred restaurant offers striking decor, including wood-paneled dining rooms adorned with fabulous flower arrangements and stunning artwork.

🍽 65 🅿 Valet 🕓 Closed L Sat.–Sun. 🖥 All major cards

🍴 BOULEVARD
$$$$
1 MISSION ST., EMBARCADERO
TEL 415-543-6084
www.boulevardrestaurant.com
Boulevard, with its beautiful lush interior and memorable bay views, delivers some of the best brasserie cooking in town. At lunch, try the fish du jour, particularly if it happens to be roasted sea bass. The appetizers alone are worth coming for: The potato cake napoleon is not only satisfying but also artfully pretty.

🍽 180 🅿 🕓 Closed L Sat.–Sun. 🖥 All major cards

🍴 WATERFRONT
$$$–$$$$
PIER 7, THE EMBARCADERO
TEL 415-391-2696
www.waterfrontsf.com
An A-list menu of patrons from Hunter S. Thompson to Lady Gaga and Barack Obama have dined at this over-the-wharf restaurant with a killer bay view. Seafood is the name of the game, including cioppino, lobster risotto, and whole wood-oven-roasted Dungeness crab. Leave room for its signature sticky toffee pudding.

🍽 110 🅿 🕓 🖥 All major cards

SOMETHING SPECIAL

🍴 GREENS
$$$
BLDG. A, FORT MASON,
OFF MARINA BLVD.
TEL 415-771-6222
www.greensrestaurant.com
The mecca for the modern vegetarian, Greens shines as one of the best restaurants in the Bay Area. Its chef, Annie Somerville, has shepherded along the new vegetarian cooking with such dishes as griddle cakes with corn served with tomatoes, crème fraîche, and tomatillo sauce; melon and figs paired with goat cheese and peppery vinaigrette; and desserts like cherry pie with honey ice cream. Marvelous waterfront views. Find a selection of bread and Italian sandwiches at Greens to Go up front.

🍽 200 🅿 🕓 Closed Mon. 🖥 D, MC, V

🍴 PIPERADE
$$$
1015 BATTERY ST.
TEL 415-391-2555
www.piperade.com
Gerald Hirigoyen's Basque food is served among wine barrels and bright fabrics. Try the seafood and shellfish stew in red pepper sauce, or braised veal sweetbreads with madeira.

🍽 60 🕓 Closed Sun.–Mon., L 🖥 All major cards

🍴 SLANTED DOOR
$$$
1 FERRY BLDG. #3, MARKET ST.
AT EMBARCADERO
TEL 415-861-8329
www.slanteddoor.com
Chef Charles Phan does a spicy, bold Vietnamese cuisine featuring items like "shaking beef" (stir-fried filet mignon with garlic), peppery Chinese squid with mustard greens, and chicken simmered in a clay pot with caramel sauce.

🍽 150 🅿 Valet 🕓 🖥 AE, MC, V

🍴 BEACH CHALET
$$
1000 GREAT HWY.
TEL 415-386-8439
www.beachchalet.com
If you've been hiking on scenic Ocean Beach, or exploring Golden Gate Park this renovated historic 1930s WPA building is the place for a great designer beer and your basic minibrewery food. It's noisy but pretty—and the view is unforgettable; behind, the adjacent park chalet has indoor/outdoor dining by a fire.

🍽 140 🅿 🖥 MC, V

▶ BAY AREA

BENICIA

⊞ UNION HOTEL
$$$

401 FIRST ST.
TEL 707-746-0110
www.unionhotelbenicia.com

Charmingly furnished with antiques and reproductions, this comfy option dates back to the Gold Rush, and there are fantasies about it being haunted by ghosts. Some rooms have kitchenettes.

🚪 12 P 🔊 🔲 🌐 All major cards

BERKELEY

⊞ CLAREMONT CLUB
🍴 & SPA
$$$$

41 TUNNEL RD.
TEL 510-843-3000, 888-560-4455
www.fairmont.com/claremont-berkeley

This elegant and luxurious hotel in a giant white hillside manse offers remarkable views of the bay. Built in the early 1900s, restoration has made it one of the Bay Area's top hotels. Its restaurant, **Limewood,** adds the finishing flourish.

🚪 279 P ⊜ 🛁 🌐 🌐 All major cards

⊞ BANCROFT HOTEL
$$

2680 BANCROFT WAY
TEL 510-549-1000
www.bancrofthotel.com

There are only 22 rooms in this historic arts and crafts hotel, originally built in the 1920s as a women's club, a fact that gives the Bancroft its unique sense of elegant intimacy—for a great price, too.

🚪 22 P ⊜ 🔲 🌐 All major cards

SOMETHING SPECIAL

🍴 CHEZ PANISSE
$$$$

1517 SHATTUCK AVE.
TEL 510-548-5525

www.chezpanisse.com

The temple, mecca, cathedral, and, just for fun, the Taj Mahal of modern California cooking, Chez Panisse has been turning out amazing food for more than 30 years. Legendary for its perfectionism and insistence on only the freshest ingredients—from Sonoma-raised duck to Meyer lemons from Ventura or San Joaquin Valley lamb and olive oils. Reserve as far in advance as possible.

🍴 50 🕐 Closed Sun.–Tue. 🌐 All major cards

🍴 IPPUKU
$$$–$$$$

2130 CENTER ST.
TEL 510-665-7969
www.ippukuberkeley.com

Called the next best thing to actually dining in Japan, this low-profile restaurant is as close to an authentic *izakaya* as possible, from its low Japanese-style *seiza*-pit tables to what is claimed to be the biggest selection of *shochu* hard-liquor outside the homeland. The specialty is yakitori, such as *tori tataki*—lightly seared chicken sashimi served raw in ponzu sauce.

🍴 40 P 🕐 Closed L & Mon.–Tue. 🌐 All major cards

🍴 SAUL'S RESTAURANT & DELI
$$

1475 SHATTUCK AVE.
TEL 510-848-3354
www.saulsdeli.com

This longstanding Gourmet Ghetto staple is a delightfully casual haven for enjoying traditional Jewish deli dishes, such as crispy latkes, and chicken soup with matzo balls or noodles. Diner-style seating is in cozy booths.

🍴 58 🔲 🌐 AE, MC, V

🍴 BETTE'S OCEANVIEW DINER
$

1807 4TH ST.

TEL 510-548-9494
www.bettesdiner.com

The classic 1950s atmosphere complete with jukebox add to this diner's popularity. For breakfast, wait in line for a down-home feast of beef hash and poached eggs, soufflé pancakes, or even a cheesy herb omelet. If you can't wait, go next door to the bakery and dig into superb muffins.

🍴 50 P 🕐 Closed D 🌐 MC, V

HALF MOON BAY

⊞ RITZ-CARLTON HALF
🍴 MOON BAY
$$$$$

1 MIRAMONTES POINT RD.
TEL 650-712-7000
www.ritzcarlton.com

Dramatically perched atop a bluff with the ocean on three sides, the Ritz-Carlton exudes luxury in its sumptuously-appointed guest rooms and public lounges. It has a spa, and golf course, and the oceanfront **Navio** restaurant offers fine-dining.

🚪 261 P ⊜ 🛁 🌐 🌐 All major cards

⊞ SEAL COVE INN
$$$$$

221 CYPRESS AVE.
TEL 650-728-4144, 800-884-4331
www.sealcoveinn.com

A gracious shorefront property, this luxurious country manor-style manse set in landscaped gardens is elegantly furnished. Guest rooms have fireplaces.

🚪 10 P 🌐 AE, MC, V

🍴 BARBARA'S FISH TRAP
$

281 CAPISTRANO RD.
TEL 650-728-7049
www.barbarasfishtrap.com

On the pier, this is the perfect place for a quick—but expertly executed—meal of fish and chips (or its local variant, calamari and chips).

🍴 38 P 🌐 No credit cards

🌐 Nonsmoking 🔊 Air-conditioning 🔲 Indoor Pool 🛁 Outdoor Pool 🌐 Health Club 🌐 Credit Cards

MILL VALLEY

🏨 MILL VALLEY INN
$$$
165 THROCKMORTON AVE.
TEL 415-389-6608
This lovely boutique hotel exudes Victorian charm in its seven-room Creek House, more modern main building, and cozy cottages, all surrounded by redwood and pine forest at the edge of town.
🛏 25 **P** 🅰 All major cards

🍴 BUCKEYE ROADHOUSE
$$$
15 SHORELINE HWY.
TEL 415-331-2600
www.buckeyeroadhouse.com
Where foodies from the city come to PARTY! The Roadhouse's hearty, zesty, and impeccably prepared New American cuisine is the reason; the bar, where you can eat a dish called Oysters Bingo, is packed most nights.
🪑 40 **P** 🅰 MC, V

OAKLAND

🏨 WATERFRONT PLAZA
$$$
10 WASHINGTON ST.
TEL 510-836-3800, 888-842-5333
www.jdvhotels.com
Well-equipped modern hotel with spacious, light-filled guest suites, some with fireplaces, many with wonderful views across the bay.
🛏 154 **P** Valet 🔀 🅂 🏊 🛗 🅰 All major cards

SOMETHING SPECIAL

🍴 COMMIS
$$$$–$$$$$
3859 PIEDMONT AVE.
TEL 510-653-3902
www.commisrestaurant.com
On culinary-rich Piedmont Avenue, Laotian Chef James Syhabout's Commis sets the standard for well-conceived, sublimely executed, and subtly Southeast Asia–infused fine dining. His texture-rich artistry has earned him two Michelin stars. The nightly tasting menu might reveal delicately glutinous tapioca dumplings, long bean salad with crab, shrimp paste, and tamarind, white sturgeon caviar with lushly creamed potato and beer-marinated onion, and silky scallops with tangy crème fraiche. The chic and sophisticated, yet sparse minimalist ambiance includes suave, mood-filled music plus a counter overlooking the detail-oriented kitchen.
🪑 48 **P** 🕐 Closed L & Sun.–Mon. 🅂 🅰 All major cards

🍴 KINGSTON 11
$$
2270 TELEGRAPH AVE., OAKLAND
TEL 510-282-8266
www.kingston11eats.com
Recreating the perfect Jamaican mood with infectiously upbeat reggae music and zesty flavors, owner-chef Nigel Jones' ethnic crowd-pleaser serves genuine island fare. Oxtail stew, jerk chicken, curry goat, and even ackee and salt fish, all with rice 'n' peas. Brilliant!
🪑 34 **P** 🕐 Closed Mon.–Tue. 🅰 All major cards

🍴 LE CHEVAL
$$
1007 CLAY ST.
TEL 510-763-8495
www.lecheval.co
What a deal: beautifully prepared Vietnamese-French food in a lively, unpretentious setting. Try the outrageously good Singapore noodles or the prawns in Vietnamese curry. Wash it down with decadent iced Vietnamese coffee.
🪑 385 **P** Valet 🕐 Closed L Sun. 🅂 🅰 All major cards

🍴 YOSHI'S
$$
510 EMBARCADERO W.
TEL 510-238-9200
www.yoshis.com
The Bay Area's top jazz venue also boasts a top-notch restaurant with classy contemporary decor. Take off your shoes in the traditional tatami seating and enjoy fresh sushi and classic Japanese dishes before taking in a show.
🪑 330 **P** 🕐 Closed L 🅂 🅰 All major cards

🍴 ZACHARY'S CHICAGO PIZZA
$$
5801 COLLEGE AVE., OAKLAND
TEL 510-655-6385
www.zacharys.com
Serving pizza since 1983, Zachary's is a beloved local institution and has added four other East Bay outlets. Its signature deep-dish pizzas with flaky, golden-brown crust come stuffed with zesty, diced tomato sauce and whatever combo of fresh ingredients you choose.
🪑 34 **P** 🅰 All major cards

PALO ALTO

SOMETHING SPECIAL

🏨 🍴 NOBU EPIPHANY
$$$$$
180 HAMILTON AVE.
TEL 650-798-8300
www.paloalto.nobuhotels.com
Chicly minimalist Japanese design meets West Coast luxury in this sensational newcomer in the heart of Silicon Valley. It even includes two floors dedicated to ryokan-style suites for guests seeking an indulgently purist experience, and the celebrated **Nobu** restaurant serves the very best of sushi and other Japanese fare.
🛏 73 **P** 🔀 🅂 🏊 🛗 🅰 All major cards

🍴 TAMARINE
$$$
546 UNIVERSITY AVE.
TEL 650-325-8500
www.tamarinerestaurant.com
Vietnamese food, including many vegan and vegetarian dishes, is the forte at this Silicon

🏨 Hotel 🍴 Restaurant 🛏 No. of Guest Rooms 🪑 No. of Seats 🅿 Parking 🕐 Closed 🔀 Elevator

Valley favorite. The extensive menu includes dishes such as sugarcane prawns, wok pho noodles (rice noodles tossed with Chinese broccoli beef and eggs), tofu with basil leaves, clay pot cod (black cod caramelized in garlic, fish sauce, and black pepper), and *bun cha* (grilled pork served in fish sauce with rice vermicelli noodles). Tamarine also boasts a good wine selection and a happening bar with happy hour specials.

🛏 150 🅿 🍽 All major cards

POINT REYES

🏨 FERRANDO'S HIDE-AWAY
$$$$
31 CYPRESS RD.,
POINT REYES STATION
TEL 415-663-1966
www.ferrando.com
Set amid towering pines along the coast, Ferrando's, with cozy cottages and flowering gardens, is a home away from home for many vacationing San Franciscans, who love the interesting and friendly owners' dedication to detail and comfort.

🚪2 🅿 🍽 MC, V

SAN JOSE

🏨 FAIRMONT
$$$$
170 S. MARKET ST.
TEL 408-998-1900, 866-540-4493
www.fairmont.com
If you like the luxe treatment, you'll love this comfortable—and modern—San Jose variant of the San Francisco hotel.

🚪 551 🅿 Valet 🔄 🄰
🏊 🍽 🍽 All major cards

🍽 HENRY'S HI-LIFE
$$
301 W. ST. JOHN ST.
TEL 408-295-5414
www.henryshilife.com
The house specialty here is barbecued ribs, chicken, or steak liberally slathered in exquisite barbecue sauce. But there are also hot dogs and burgers, as well as prime rib on Friday and Saturday nights. Henry's has been serving up the good food for more than 50 years.

🛏 74 🅿 ⏰ Closed L Mon.–Tue. 🍽 🍽 All major cards

🍽 FALAFEL'S DRIVE-IN
$–$$
2301 STEVENS CREEK BLVD.
TEL 408-294-7886
www.falafelsdrivein.com
A beloved favorite of locals for five decades, Falafal's Drive-In is a San Jose institution. Israeli immigrants Zahie and Anton Nijmeh continue to serve delicious, made-to-order, bargain-priced falafels and other Middle Eastern dishes, to be enjoyed alfresco at classic drive-in bench seating. It also serves burgers, burritos, and hot dogs, but the item of choice is the huge daily special pita stuffed with fresh chopped vegetables, falafel balls, and creamy tahini sauce, and served with a banana shake.

🛏 36 🅿 🍽 MC, V

SAUSALITO

🏨🍽 CAVALLO POINT LODGE
$$$$$
601 MURRAY CIRCLE
TEL 415-339-4700, 888-651-2003
www.cavallopoint.com
When old Fort Baker was transferred from the U.S. Army to the National Park Service in 2002, somebody got the bright idea that the bayside military outpost would make an incredible luxury hotel. The prize guest rooms are located in former officers' quarters overlooking a parade ground that tumbles down to the bay. Rooms feature gas fireplaces, elegant modern furnishings, and breathtaking views of San Francisco, Alcatraz, and the bridges. In **Murray Circle** the resort also boasts one of the best hotel restaurants in the Bay Area.

🚪 142 🅿 🍽 🍽 All major cards

🏨 INN ABOVE THE TIDE
$$$–$$$$
30 EL PORTAL
TEL 415-332-9535, 800-893-8433
www.innabovetide.com
Sausalito is relaxing and quiet—especially at this stylishly modern waterfront hotel, which blends the charm of a bed-and-breakfast (the breakfast is elaborate and tasty) and the professional services of a hotel (massage, concierge, turn-down, and morning paper).

🚪 33 🅿 🔄 🄰 🍽 All major cards

🍽 POGGIO
$$$$
777 BRIDGEWAY BLVD.
TEL 415-332-7771
www.poggiotrattoria.com
One of the broadest panoramic views of the bay can be caught from the portals of this classic Italian trattoria, where chef Chris Fernandez's soulful dishes include wood-roasted mussels with saffron tomato broth, and local Petrale sole with buttered spinach and poached potatoes with lemon caper sauce.

🛏 120 🅿 Valet 🍽 All major cards

🍽 THE TRIDENT
$$$–$$$$
558 BRIDGEWAY
TEL 415-331-3232
www.thetrident.net
One-upping Poggio with its fabulous over-the-water location, the historic Trident has been a landmark bar-restaurant-music venue for decades. Retaining some of its 1960s decor, such as rich woodwork and curved booths, the elegant restaurant still has live jazz. Seafood is the name of the game, from fried calamari, fish 'n' chips, and seafood linguini to the signature

cioppino and Dungeness crab kimchi "martini."

🔧 140 🅿 Valet 🅰 All major cards

WALNUT CREEK

🍴 HAVANA
$$$
1516 BONANZA ST.
TEL 925-939-4555
www.havanarestaurant.net
A lively Cuban restaurant serving hearty, delectable dishes, including mango gazpacho, Havana crab cakes with pineapple aioli, and garlic-studded pork with mojo sauce, mashed yuccas, and black beans. The Latin rhythms create just the right mood for enjoying killer mojitos and Cuban cocktails.

🔧 100 🕐 Closed L Mon.–Fri.
🅰 All major cards

🍴 KACHA THAI BISTRO
$$–$$$
1665 MT. DIABLO BLVD.
TEL 925-988-9877
www.kachathai.com
This colorful and sleek award-winning restaurant offers every Thai dish under the sun, with a huge menu spanning pad thai, mango shrimp salad, and pumpkin curry served in a scooped-out squash shell stuffed with baby corn and other veggies, to mystery dishes such as "The Lover."

🔧 140 🅿 🅰 All major cards

▶ WINE COUNTRY

Wine country has so many inns, hotels, and bed-and-breakfasts that many visitors rely on booking services to make reservations for them. This is particularly helpful during the high season (late spring through fall), when local wisdom (and a fee) will help you navigate the maze of available choices. Among the top services are: **Napa Valley Reservations Unlimited** (tel 707-252-1985, www.napavalleyreservations.com)

and **Wine Country Concierge** (tel 707-225-2781, www.winetrip. com).

CALISTOGA

🏨 MOUNT VIEW HOTEL
🍴 $$$
1457 LINCOLN AVE.
TEL 707-942-6877
www.mountviewhotel.com
The Mount View is one of the area's most pampering getaways. Located in a historic setting, its guest rooms are big, cozy, stylish—just like the "Southern Calistoga American" cuisine served at the popular **Johnny's**, where Cajun meets California, and the fine-dining **Amaro Italian Kitchen**.

🛏 32 🅿 🅢 🏊 🅰 AE, MC, V

🏨 DR. WILKINSON'S HOT SPRINGS RESORT
$$–$$$
1507 LINCOLN AVE.
TEL 707-942-4102
www.drwilkinson.com
A wonderful, recently updated and upgraded, 1950s-style motel that can now be considered colorfully elegant, particularly when taken with the on-site hot springs, volcanic ash mud baths, and extensive spa services. Midweek specials offer "the works" (mud, aromatic whirlpool, mineral steam, and massage).

ℹ 50 rooms, 17 cottages
🅿 🅢 🏊 🅰 AE, MC, V

🍴 EVANGELINE
$$–$$$
1226 WASHINGTON ST.
TEL 707-341-3131
www.evangelinenapa.com
A casually-elegant European bistro dedicated to hearty French-California fare, this restaurant has plenty of old-world charm. The menu features such staples as steak frites, shrimp étouffée, and Tuesday-night duck cassou-

let. The outdoor patio, heated in winter, is the venue of choice.

🔧 80 🅿 🕐 Closed L Mon.–Fri.
🅰 All major cards

GLEN ELLEN

🏨 GAIGE HOUSE INN
$$$$$
13540 ARNOLD DR.
TEL 707-935-0237
www.thegaigehouse.com
A high-end country inn that prides itself on service and attention to detail. Ryokan Zen suites are particularly appealing. A great place from which to visit some wineries or to see Jack London State Historic Park.

ℹ 14 rooms, 4 cottages
🅿 🅢 🏊 🅰 AE, MC, V

🏨 BELTANE RANCH
$$$$–$$$$$
11775 SONOMA HWY.
TEL 707-833-4233
www.beltaneranch.com
For anyone who really wants to get back to the land, this is the place. Beltane is a working ranch,

full of cattle and grapevines, set amid miles of oak-bordered trails. The charming ranch is family run, which brings a warm feeling, particularly evident during long siestas on the old wraparound porch.

🛈 5 rooms, 1 cottage 🅿 🚭 🚭 All major cards

HEALDSBURG

🏨 THE MADRONA
$$$$$
1001 WESTSIDE RD. (NEAR MILL ST.)
TEL 707-433-4231
www.themadronahotel.com

This late 19th-century house is more than the usual redone Victorian—it's a three-story mansion, set on eight acres (3.2 ha) of wooded splendor (and some gardened splendor as well). Most guests prefer the regally-appointed rooms in the main house, where the food action is. The **restaurant** is one of Healdsburg's finest and serves nouvelle California dishes using ingredients fresh from the hotel's own garden.

🛈 23 🅿 🕐 Closed L & Mon.–Tue. 🚭 🏊 🚭 AE, MC, V

🍴 BARNDIVA
$$$
231 CENTER ST.
TEL 707-431-0100
www.barndiva.com

With its soaring barn-like ceiling and spacious patio dripping with fairy-lights at night, Chef Ryan Fancher's restaurant is justly acclaimed for its creative and divine dishes, from Alaskan halibut served with spring pea risotto to herb-roasted Pacific sole. For post-prandial pleasure, check out the restaurant's adjoining art gallery.

🍽 100 🅿 🕐 Closed Mon.–Tue. 🚭 🚭 All major cards

KENWOOD

🍴 SALT & STONE
$$–$$$
9900 CALIF. 12 (SONOMA HWY.)

TEL 707-833-6326
www.saltstonekenwood.com

The setting, right in the middle of Kenwood, draws locals from all around the valley to this bistro, where ingredients are just out of the ground and views are out of this world. The menu offers well-executed seafood, steak, and, California-classic dishes, plus there's an oyster bar.

🍽 150 🅿 🕐 Closed L Tue.–Wed. 🚭 🚭 MC, V

NAPA

🏨 CARNEROS RESORT & 🍴 SPA
$$$$$
4048 SONOMA HWY.
TEL 707-299-4880
www.farmatcarneros.com

Surrounded by rolling vineyards, stylishly luxurious Carneros Resort and Spa appeals for its irresistible secluded cottages and modern full-service spa. The **Farm at Carneros** restaurant draws produce from its own organic garden for its nouvelle cuisine, including a popular Sunday brunch.

🛈 86 suites and cottages 🅿 🕐 Closed Mon.–Thur., L Wed.–Sat. 🚭 🏊 🚭

🏨 SILVERADO RESORT
🍴 **$$$**
1600 ATLAS PEAK RD.
TEL 707-257-0200, 844-421-6474
www.silveradoresort.com

An upscale 1,200-acre (486 ha) retreat centered on a white-pillared mansion exuding yesteryear elegance and sophistication. Modestly furnished cottage clusters encircle swimming pools and line the fairways of this acclaimed golf resort. The **Grill** restaurant serves grilled prime steaks and fresh seafood over mesquite.

🛈 280 🅿 🚭 🏊 🚭 🚭 All major cards

RUTHERFORD

🏨 AUBERGE DU SOLEIL
🍴 **$$$$$**
180 RUTHERFORD HILL RD.
TEL 707-963-1211, 800-348-5406
www.aubergedusoleil.com

Hotel meets country estate in this elegant getaway, where you can take in stunning views of olive groves while feasting on the Provençal cuisine.

🛈 52 🅿 🚭 🚭 🏊 🚭 🚭 All major cards

ST. HELENA

SOMETHING SPECIAL

🏨 MEADOWOOD
🍴 **$$$$$**
900 MEADOWOOD LN.
TEL 707-963-3646, 844-774-6462
www.meadowood.com

Perhaps the region's best luxury destination, set amid groves of redwoods and firs, Meadowood is the kind of place you will tell your grandchildren about. Besides its huge guest cottages, it offers a spa, tennis courts, a golf course, and even a professional croquet court. Three Michelin-star **The Restaurant at Meadowood**, rated among the state's top ten, has a menu with such delights as roasted rabbit with bay leaf gnocchi, crab and papaya confit appetizers, and seafood—steamed, fried, grilled—that will make you want to take up fishing. It was destroyed by a 2020 wildfire, but rebuilding was almost complete at press time.

🛈 85 🅿 🚭 🏊 🚭 🚭 All major cards

🏨 WINE COUNTRY INN
$$$$–$$$$$
1152 LODI LN.
TEL 707-963-7077, 888-465-4608
www.winecountryinn.com

This inn sits on a delightful hilltop, its old stone tower conjuring the feeling of being in one of Robert Louis Stevenson's idylls about the place.

🛈 24 rooms, 5 cottages 🅿 🚭 🏊 🚭 MC, V

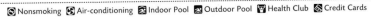
🚭 Nonsmoking 🄰 Air-conditioning 🄸 Indoor Pool 🏊 Outdoor Pool 🚩 Health Club 🚭 Credit Cards

🏨 EL BONITA MOTEL
$–$$$

195 MAIN ST.
TEL 707-963-3216
www.elbonita.com

The budget alternative for those who want to spend their money on wine rather than luxurious suites, El Bonita is a pleasant, well-tended old motel within walking distance of a number of wineries.

🛈 41 P ⛁ 🌊 🏧 All major cards

🍴 GATEHOUSE RESTAURANT
$$$

2555 MAIN ST.
TEL 707-967-2300
www.ciarestaurants.com

The restaurant of the Culinary Institute of America is in the old Christian Brothers Winery, a cavernous stone mansion. The creative cuisine reflects the two-year training of the student chefs, using produce from CIA's own gardens. A fine collection of cigars and aperitifs, many of the latter made in the valley, complete a wonderful experience.

🪑 90 P Valet ⛁ 🏧 All major cards

🍴 TRA VIGNE PIZZERIA
$$$

1016 MAIN ST.
TEL 707-967-9999
www.pizzeriatravigne.com

This is the kind of Italian food— and surroundings—one would get in the very best Tuscan eateries: lots of fresh beans, fish, broths, and cracker-thin breads, although pizzas rule the roost.

🪑 60 P ⛁ 🏧 DC, MC, V

SONOMA

🏨 FAIRMONT SONOMA MISSION INN & SPA
$$$$–$$$$$

100 BOYES BLVD.
TEL 707-938-9000, 866-540-4499
www.fairmont.com/sonoma

A sprawling, modern, mission-style inn with outstanding spa facilities and wonderfully cozy and well-appointed rooms. A fine base for a visit to Sonoma Valley.

🛈 198 P ⛁ 🌊 🏧 🍴 All major cards

🏨 EL DORADO
🍴 $$$

405 1ST ST. W.
TEL 707-996-3030
www.eldoradosonoma.com

This impeccable hotel over-looks the Sonoma Plaza. With sumptuous rooms and equally sumptuous breakfasts, it is a true find. The **El Dorado Kitchen** serves excellent California-inspired cuisine.

🛈 26 P ⛁ 🏧 🍴 🏧 AE, MC, V

🍴 LA CASA
$$

121 E. SPAIN ST.
TEL 707-996-3406
www.lacasarestaurants.com

An old-fashioned Mexican food hangout not far from Sonoma Plaza. Where better to celebrate General Vallejo's wise decision, 150 years ago, to "help out" the American insurrectionists?

🪑 180 P ⛁ 🏧 All major cards

SONOMA COAST

🏨 TIMBER COVE INN
🍴 $$$$

21780 CALIF. 1, TIMBER COVE
TEL 707-847-3231
www.timbercoveinn.com

Perched dramatically atop a bluff, this recently modernized iconic hotel offers soul-satisfying sophistication and heaps of comfort. The romantic **Alexander's** restaurant has magical ocean views and great food using local, sustainable, and organic ingredients.

🛈 46 P 🏧 All major cards

🍴 SPUD POINT CRAB COMPANY
$

1860 WESTSHORE RD., BODEGA BAY
TEL 707-875-9472
www.spudpointcrab.com

Picnic tables provide a simple but scenic spot to enjoy steamed crab and other seafood selections like clam chowder, shrimp cocktail, and shrimp sandwiches. Crab cakes are reserved for weekends.

P ⛁ Closed Wed. & 2 wks. Oct. 🏧 All major cards

YOUNTVILLE

🏨 BARDESSONO
$$$$$

6526 YOUNT ST.
TEL 707-204-6000, 855-232-0450
www.bardessono.com

On the sumptuous side, this gorgeous, environmentally-friendly hotel flaunts stylish, comfortable rooms, cozy fireplaces, and intimate private nooks.

🛈 51 P ⛁ 🌊 🏧 All major cards

🏨 YOUNTVILLE INN
$$$–$$$$

6462 WASHINGTON ST.
TEL 707-967-7900, 855-232-0452
www.hotelyountville.com

A rustic community just minutes away from some of the valley's finest dining, the inn offers luxurious amenities and your own patio.

🛈 51 P ⛁ 🌊 🏧 All major cards

SOMETHING SPECIAL

🍴 FRENCH LAUNDRY
$$$$

6640 WASHINGTON ST.
TEL 707-944-2380
www.frenchlaundry.com

A few years ago, a picky *New York Times* critic dubbed the French Laundry the best restaurant in America. So many people now agree that the only way you can get in is to call, between 10 a.m. and 7 p.m., exactly two months before the day you want to dine here. If you are a foodie, it's worth it. The astronomically-priced nine-course lunch and dinner menus are prix fixe. The cuisine, dubbed California-French, offers entrées such as roasted rabbit saddles in pumpkin risotto and white truffle custard for an appetizer. Jackets are required for both lunch and dinner. If you can't make a two-month commitment but want to try chef Thomas Keller's fine food, go down the street to his equally raved-about **Bouchon** *(tel 707-414-6200, www.thomaskeller.com)* for a scaled-down version.

🛏 62 🅿 Valet 🕐 Closed L Mon.–Thurs. 🌀 🌀 AE, MC, V

🍽 MUSTARDS GRILL
$$$–$$$$
7399 ST. HELENA HWY.
TEL 707-944-2424
www.mustardsgrill.com
The cradle of Napa California cuisine, Mustards has for more than 18 years served up a hearty menu including its famous smoked Peking duck, baby back ribs with corn pudding, and tempting hamburgers.

🛏 60 🅿 🌀 🌀 DC, MC, V

🍽 BISTRO JEANTY
$$$
6510 WASHINGTON ST.
TEL 707-944-0103
www.bistrojeanty.com
Phillippe Jeanty, the chef who put Domaine Chandon on the culinary map, has garnered outstanding reviews for his fine bistro fare here; the rabbit and cassoulet are huge favorites with the foodie class.

🛏 50 🅿 🕐 Closed Tue.–Wed.. 🌀 🌀 MC, V

▶ THE NORTH

ALBION

🏨 ALBION RIVER INN
🍽 $$$–$$$$
3790 HWY. 1
TEL 707-937-1919
www.albionriverinn.com
A Mendocino Coast wonder, this one with fantastic coastal views, deluxe amenities, and a **restaurant** that has won raves from locals and out-of-towners.

🕐 22 🅿 🌀 All major cards

ALTURAS

🍽 BRASS RAIL
$
395 LAKEVIEW HWY.
TEL 530-233-2906
It may not be much to look at, but the Basque food just keeps on coming. And it's good: big rib-eye steaks, lamb chops, fried chicken, red beans, Spanish rice, garbanzo beans, ravioli. For an amazingly low all-in price, you also get wine, homemade bread, soup, salad, coffee or tea, and ice cream.

🛏 200 🅿 🕐 Closed Mon. 🌀 🌀 MC, V

BOONVILLE

🏨 BOONVILLE
🍽 HOTEL
$$–$$$$
**14050 CALIF. 128
(AT LAMBERT LN.)**
TEL 707-895-2210
www.boonvillehotel.com
If you're out cruising the backwoods area, this is a good place to stay or to stop for a meal at **Table 128**, which serves constantly changing prix fixe fare.

🕐 15 🅿 🕐 Closed Dec. 24 & 25 🌀 MC, V

CHESTER

🏨 DRAKESBAD GUEST RANCH
$$$$–$$$$$
14423 CHESTER WARNER VALLEY RD.
TEL 877-622-0221
www.lassenlodging.com
Set on natural hot mineral springs in the midst of Lassen Volcanic National Park (see p. 288), Drakesbad is the last of the 19th-century country lodges. The owner-hosts make a stay here absolutely delightful, with an informal atmosphere and satisfying, unfancy cooking (three meals a day are included in the price). Horseback riding, volleyball, and trail hiking are among the offered activities.

🕐 20 🅿 🕐 Closed Oct.–Jan. 🌊 🌀 MC,V

EUREKA

🏨 CARTER HOUSE
🍽 $$$$
301 L ST.
TEL 707-444-8062
www.carterhouse.com
Actually three properties—a hotel, a bed-and-breakfast, and a separate cottage, itself with three rooms—the award-winning Carter is the place on the north coast. The decor is tasteful, with either period-perfect heirloom furniture or pleasing Southwesternalia. Big suites have all the right amenities, from whirlpool baths to jumbo beds. Its elegant candlelit **Restaurant 301** serves up impeccably prepared dishes—fish, usually local, sautéed just right with chanterelle mushrooms brought in by a ranger from the nearby national forest.

🕐 33 🅿 🌀 🌀 🌀 All major cards

🍴 CAFÉ NOONER TOO
$$
2910 E ST.
TEL TEL 707-407-3664
This hole-in-the-wall may not look like much from outside, but its intriguing menu spans burgers to Greek mezes and even Creole food, all of which the kitchen conjures with aplomb.
🪑 40 🕐 Closed Mon.–Tue., D Sun. 🏧 MC, V

GARBERVILLE

🏨 BENBOW INN
🍴 $$$$–$$$$$
445 LAKE BENBOW DR.
TEL 707-923-2124, 800-355-3301
www.benbowinn.com
Host to Hollywood stars from Charles Laughton to Joan Fontaine, the Benbow, with its grand Tudor architecture and up-country setting, has been completely restored. Guest rooms are cozy and full of period decor, the **restaurant** serves fine regional cuisine, and there's boating, tennis, golf, swimming, and hiking.
🚪 55 🅿 🈂 🏊 🏧 All major cards

GUALALA

🏨 WHALE WATCH INN
$$$–$$$$
35100 CALIF. 1
TEL 800-942-5342
www.whalewatchinn.com
Large, airy modern rooms in a contemporary architectural complex perched high on a cliff overlooking the Pacific. A footpath takes you to a deserted beach. In the winter, watch whales through the telescope in the cozy lodge.
🚪 18 🅿 🏧 AE, MC, V

MCCLOUD

🏨 MCCLOUD HOTEL
$$–$$$$
408 MAIN ST.

TEL 530-964-2822
www.mccloudhotel.com
Big, light-filled rooms with Victorian-era decor, heirloom furniture, in-room Jacuzzis, and an atmospheric lobby make the McCloud a unique place from which to explore Shasta country and beyond.
🚪 17 🅿 🈂 🏧 All major cards

MENDOCINO

SOMETHING SPECIAL

🏨 STANFORD INN
🍴 $$$$$
CALIF. 1 & COMPTCHE-UKIAH RD.
TEL 707-937-5615, 800-331-8884
www.stanfordinn.com
This is the kind of place we would all build if we were as single-minded, as energetic, and as creative as the Stanford family. The Stanford Inn is wonderful, from its modern but woodsy guest rooms to its vegetarian **restaurant.** The Stanford sits at the mouth of the Big River, an unspoiled estuary, home to great blue herons, ospreys, and harbor seals.
🚪 41 🅿 🈂 🈂 🈂 🈂 🈂 🏧 All major cards

🍴 CAFÉ BEAUJOLAIS
$$$$
961 UKIAH ST. (BETW. EVERGREEN & SCHOOL STS.)
TEL 707-937-5614
www.cafebeaujolais.com
For many years, this rustic cottage set amid the wood and clapboard jumble of quaint Mendocino has attracted pickier diners from all over the country. The California country cuisine—with local wines, herbs, vegetables, and game—is a delight. The surroundings are intimate and memorable.
🪑 60 🅿 🕐 Closed Mon.–Tues. 🏧 All major cards

PRICES

HOTELS
An indication of the cost of a double room in the high season is given by $ signs.

$$$$$	Over $280
$$$$	$200–$280
$$$	$120–$200
$$	$80–$120
$	Under $80

RESTAURANTS
An indication of the cost of a three-course meal without drinks is given by $ signs.

$$$$$	Over $80
$$$$	$50–$80
$$$	$35–$50
$$	$20–$35
$	Under $20

▶ **GOLD COUNTRY**
Although not as organized as San Francisco or Wine Country, Gold Country has its own unique brand of help for travelers. Friendly, informal "tourist bureaus" are found in almost every small city and town. As well as the larger places like Sacramento, even tiny Angels Camp, Sutter Creek, and Sonora have their own helpful offices, staffed through the week. Just follow the "Gold Country" signs.

AUBURN

🏨 PARK VICTORIAN
$$$
195 PARK ST.
TEL 530-330-4411
www.parkvictorian.com
This hilltop inn is a beautifully restored 1874 Victorian, with period decor and antiques yet given a magnificent contemporary edge by a recent remake. Its biking and rafting packages are a deal.
🚪 6 🅿 🏧 AE, MC, V

🏨 Hotel   🍴 Restaurant   🚪 No. of Guest Rooms   🪑 No. of Seats   🅿 Parking   🕐 Closed   🈂 Elevator

GRASS VALLEY

🏨 HOLBROOKE
🍽 $$$$–$$$$$
212 W. MAIN ST.
TEL 530-460-4075
www.holbrooke.com
The refurbished rooms are now gorgeous-chic, the atmosphere is artsy Gold Country fun, and the food is the **Holbrooke Restaurant** is earthy, flavorful, and bountiful—New American with a sprinkling of local wild game and fruits (huckleberries, miners' lettuce, elderberries).

🚪 28 🅿 😊 🆒
🧳 All major cards

MURPHYS

🏨 DUNBAR HOUSE 1880
$$$$
271 JONES ST.
TEL 209-728-2897
www.dunbarhouse.com
This historic house is overflowing with Victoriana, the service is impeccable, and the breakfast gourmet. The place exudes yesteryear charm.

🚪 6 🅿 🆒 🧳 AE, MC, V

NEVADA CITY

🏨 THE MADISON HOUSE
$$$–$$$$
427 BROAD ST.
TEL 530-470-6127
www.themadisonhouse.net
A Victorian house built in the 1860s, the Madison House Inn has been restored to its gold rush grandeur and lovingly upgraded by new owners. Breakfasts are hearty affairs.

🚪 6 🅿 🕙 Closed Jan.
🆒 🧳 MC, V

PLYMOUTH

🏨 AMADOR HARVEST INN
$$$
12455 STEINER RD.

TEL 209-245-5512
www.amadorharvestinn.com
Situated in one of the most lovely spots in Gold Country (or for that matter, the state), the inn is just next door to Deaver Vineyards and a deep blue lake. A full breakfast comes with the room price.

🚪 4 🅿 🧳 AE, MC, V

SACRAMENTO

🏨 THE CITIZEN
$$$$
926 J ST.
TEL 916-447-2700
www.thecitizenhotel.com
Fitting to its grandiose 1900s classic exterior and proximity to the State Capitol, The Citizen's sophisticated interior styling celebrates California's history and Sacramento's political power. Luxurious guest rooms, plus award-winning dining, and a superb location within walking distance of the main sites add up to a first-rate choice.

🚪 196 🅿 😊 🆒 🔽 🧳 All major cards

🏨 DELTA KING
$$–$$$$
1000 FRONT ST.
TEL 916-444-5464
www.deltaking.com
Of the staterooms on this old riverboat, those toward the stern are the best, with views and elegant furniture. Breakfast is included.

🚪 44 🅿 Valet 😊 🆒 🧳 All major cards

🍽 LEMON GRASS
$$$–$$$$
601 MONROE ST.
TEL 916-486-4891
www.lemongrassrestaurant.com
A beloved local institution for three decades, Chef-owner Mai Pham's awarding-winning Vietnamese/Thai restaurant will have your taste buds singing. The pad thai is memorable,

the crispy vegetable rolls to die for, while curries feature pink prawns swimming in fragrant and zesty coconut milk sauce.

🍴 56 🅿 🕙 Closed L & Sun.–Mon. 🆒 🧳 All major cards

SUTTER CREEK

🏨 THE FOXIE
$$$$
77 MAIN ST.
TEL 209-267-5882
www.thefoxie.com
With its elegant breakfast service, ornate period beds, clawfoot bathtubs, and high ceilings, Foxes is a place where one can imagine what it was like to be a big-spending city slicker in gold-rush times.

🚪 7 🅿 🆒 🧳 MC, V

▶ SIERRA NEVADA

LAKE TAHOE

🏨 RITZ-CARLTON
$$$$$
13031 RITZ-CARLTON
HIGHLANDS CT., TRUCKEE
TEL 530-562-3000
www.ritzcarlton.com
This top-of-the-line, ski-in, ski-out property brings a whole new level of panache to Lake Tahoe with its deluxe suites themed with logs and granite.

🚪 170 🅿 😊 🔽 🧳 All major cards

🏨 HOTEL AZURE TAHOE
$$$–$$$$
3300 LAKE TAHOE BLVD.,
SOUTH LAKE TAHOE
TEL 530-542-0330, 800-877-1466
www.hotelazuretahoe.com
This upscale motel recently given a suave facelift, is conveniently located just across the way from the swimming beach, close to Heavenly ski resort, accessed by free shuttle. Stay here and you can get a free ride to the casinos just east on the lake.

🚪 100 🅿 😊 🆒 🏊 🧳 All major cards

🍴 SIX PEAKS GRILL
$$$$
**RESORT AT SQUAW CREEK,
400 SQUAW CREEK RD.,
OLYMPIC VALLEY**
TEL 530-581-6621
www.squawcreek.com
Though the view of the Sierra Nevada is what may attract people here, it is the food at Six Peaks Grill that brings them back again and again. The Grill has also received accolades from serious foodies for its California fusion cuisine and comfort foods, such as roasted corn chowder and grilled rib-eye steak. Leave room for the beehive-baked Alaska with meringue and raspberry sauce. The wine list is award winning.
🪑 75 🅿 🅂 🕸 All major cards

🍴 GRAHAM'S
$$$
**1650 SQUAW VALLEY RD.,
OLYMPIC VALLEY**
TEL 530-581-0454
www.dinewine.com
Glowing with cozy intimacy, Graham's intimate pine-paneled dining room is warmed by log fires in river-rock hearths. The California-Mediterranean menu is typified by the seared ahi with noodles appetizer, and three-peppercorn-crusted elk loin with lingonberry demi-glace. A vast wine list spans the globe.
🪑 125 🕒 Closed L & Mon. 🕸 AE, MC, V

MAMMOTH LAKES

🏨 WESTIN MONACHE
$$$$$
50 HILLSIDE DR.
TEL 760-934-0400
www.marriott.com
Catering to outdoorsy folks with deep pockets, the all-suite, full-service Westin Monache brings a high level of luxe to Mammoth. Open-plan rooms

here have gas fireplaces and flat-panel TVs.
ⓘ 230 🅿 🅂 🕸 🕸 All major cards

🏨 MAMMOTH MOUNTAIN INN
$$$–$$$$$
10400 MINARET RD.
TEL 760-934-2581, 800-626-6684
**www.themammoth
mountaininn.com**
At 9,000 feet (2,743 m), this modern alpine lodge offers cozy contemporary decor, blending comfort, convenience, and heaps of amenities, just steps away from the ski lifts. The Dry Creek Bar is the perfect spot for après ski.
ⓘ 216 🅿 🅂 🕸 🕸 AE, MC, V

OAKHURST

🏨 CHATEAU DU
🍴 SUREAU & ERNA'S ELDERBERRY HOUSE
$$$$$
48688 VICTORIA LN.
TEL 559-683-6860
www.chateausureau.com
After the French Laundry, perhaps the closest thing there is to "destination dining." **Erna's** (tel 559-683-6800) serves California-French with hints of the owner Erna Kubin. Impeccable food. Chateau de Sureau, run by the same owners, is fabulously luxurious: goosedown pillows, stone fireplaces, and staff who just won't let you do a thing! No wonder it's a member of Relais & Chateaux!
ⓘ 12 🅿 🕒 Restaurant closed L Mon.–Tues. 🅂 🕸 🕸 🕸 AE, MC, V

SEQUOIA NATIONAL PARK

🏨 WUKSACHI LODGE
$$–$$$
P.O. BOX 89, SEQUOIA NP
TEL 866-807-3598

www.visitsequoia.com
Beautifully blending into the big trees of Sequoia National Park, the lodge features roaring fireplaces, the park's best restaurant, and the likelihood of wildlife outside your window in the early morning light. Rooms have mission-style furnishings, en suite baths, ski racks, and everything else you would expect from an upscale mountain resort.
ⓘ 18 🅿 🕒 Closed mid-Nov.–Apr. 🅂 🕸 MC, V

🏨 CEDAR GROVE LODGE
$–$$$
P.O. BOX 909, CEDAR GROVE
TEL 866-807-3598
www.visitsequoia.com
Modest, functional, and right in the middle of some of the park's most spectacular scenery, this little lodge is perfect if you just want a burger and a bed. You can also picnic here, right on the river's edge.
ⓘ 18 🅿 🕒 Closed mid-Nov.–Apr. 🅂 🕸 MC, V

YOSEMITE NATIONAL PARK

🏨 AHWAHNEE
🍴 $$$$
1 AHWAHNEE DR.
TEL 209-372-1407, 866-413-8869
www.yosemitepark.com
Make reservations several months ahead if you want to stay in this grandiose 1920s mountain lodge, replete with Native American decor, stone-and-sugar-pine construction, and cozy rooms with magnificent views of the valley's meadows and Half Dome. Also book ahead if you plan to luxuriate in the grandest dining room in the state—the Ahwahnee's breathtaking light-filled **restaurant,** where the superb American cuisine comes with great service and memories to last a lifetime. A dress code applies.
ⓘ 123 🅿 🅂 🕸 🕸 All major cards

🏨 TENAYA LODGE
🍴 $$$

1122 CALIF. 41 (S OF YOSEMITE
S ENTRANCE), FISH CAMP
TEL 559-683-6555, 888-514-2167
www.tenayalodge.com
Big, very professionally run, and
with cozy rooms, the Tenaya
offers what people who stay here
want: a comfortable, amenities-
filled getaway offering rest,
relaxation, and food for those
long evenings after a day's hiking.
Its **Jackalopes Bar & Grill** is well
regarded for its straightforward
American cuisine.
🛈 244 P 🖻 🔇 🌊 🏊 🛡
🔇 All major cards

🏨 WAWONA HOTEL
🍴 $$–$$$

8308 WAWONA RD.
TEL 888-413-8869
www.yosemitepark.com
More modest than the
Ahwahnee, the Wawona
nevertheless holds its own on the
Yosemite charm scale. The hotel
consists of a sprawl of low-slung,
whitewashed wooden cottages,
with wraparound porches and
views into a central meadow.
Spend the day hiking, then come
back to the **restaurant's** grilled
trout and steaks—satisfying and
tasty. Rooms are plain but comfortable. Includes breakfast.
🛈 104 P 🕒 Can be closed
Feb.–Mar. 🏊 🔇 All major cards

🏨 YOSEMITE VALLEY LODGE
$$–$$$

YOSEMITE VALLEY
TEL 888-413-8869
www.yosemitepark.com
Right in the heart of the valley,
close to Yosemite Falls, the lodge
offers motel rooms with Southwestern decor, as well as more
rustic cabins.
🛈 249 🏊 🔇 All major cards

🏨 EVERGREEN LODGE
$–$$$$$

33160 EVERGREEN RD., GROVELAND
TEL 209-379-2606
www.evergreenlodge.com

Evergreen offers a homey,
hands-on alternative to the
corporate hotels of Yosemite
Valley. Guests can choose
from a variety of different cabins, from furnished tents and
vintage cabins to the roomy
John Muir House, which can
sleep as many as ten people.
While the "unplugged" cabins
have no televisions or phones,
they do have comfy beds,
satellite radios, minifridges,
and an assortment of board
games to entertain after dark.
Internet and Wi-Fi are available in the lodge recreation
building.
🛈 66 cabins P 🏊 🔇 All
major cards

▶ CENTRAL VALLEY

BAKERSFIELD

🏨 THE PADRE HOTEL
$$$–$$$$

1702 18TH ST.
TEL 661-427-4900
www.thepadrehotel.com
Chic, contemporary, endearing,
this thoroughly modern boutique hotel occupies a Spanish
Colonial Revival building and
is a posh break from the usual
motel-style hotels in town. Its
Brimstone Bar & Grill, with its
stamped tin ceiling and teak
paneling, offers fine-dining
dishes.
🛈 112 P 🖻 🔇 🛡 🔇 All
major cards

🍴 CHALET BASQUE
$–$$

200 OAK ST.
TEL 661-327-2915
www.basquerestaurantbakers
field.com
People make a special trip just
for the Chalet's wonderful roast
lamb and pink beans special.
Memorable Basque fare in a
family atmosphere.
🍴 100 P 🔇 🔇 AE, MC, V

FRESNO

🏨 HOTEL PICCADILLY
$$–$$$

2305 W. SHAW AVE.
TEL 559-348-5520
www. hotel-piccadilly.com
The jumbo swimming pool
will come in handy during
the sweltering valley days; the
amply sized guest rooms have
recently been refurbished with
graceful decor.
🛈 194 P 🔇 🔇 🏊 🛡 🔇 All
major cards

HANFORD

🏨 IRWIN STREET INN
🍴 $–$$

522 N. IRWIN ST.
TEL 559-583-8000
www.facebook.com/irwin
streetinn
A nicely restored, tree-shaded
Victorian, the inn is a pleasant
place to stop on the way
north or south. Rooms feature
antiques and period reproduc-
tions.
🛈 30 P 🕒 Closed Mon. &
L Sat. 🔇 🔇 All major cards

VISALIA

🏨 THE DARLING
🍴 $$$

210 N. COURT ST.
TEL 559-713-2113
www.thedarlingvisalia.com
Occupying the restored art
deco former courthouse, this
boutique hotel has been fitted
with graceful 1930s-inspired
furnishings. The contemporary rooftop **Eldwerwood
Restaurant** has a lounge and
panoramic views over town.
🛈 32 P 🖻 🔇 🔇 🔇 All major
cards

▶ THE DESERT

Accommodations and eateries
of note are thin in the desert,
except for the Palm Springs
region, known for its bounty

of spa resorts, trendy boutique hotels, and private rentals—from golf course condos to deluxe villas. Visitors seeking rental lodgings should consult specialist online booking services, such as **McLean Company Rentals** (tel 760-322-2500 or 8044-322-2500, www.mclean.company). The **Palm Springs Desert Resorts Convention & Visitors Authority** (tel 760-770-9000, www.visitgreaterpalmsprings.com) is a helpful resource.

DEATH VALLEY

🏨 THE OASIS AT DEATH VALLEY
$$$$$
CALIF. 190
TEL 760-786-2345, 800-236-7916
www.oasisatdeathvalley.com
Cool off at this historic inn, where the pool is supplemented by a natural mineral spring, the food is climate adjusted, and the golf course is equipped with plenty of refreshing sprinklers, beer, and umbrella drinks.
🛏 66 🅿 🔄 🗲 🗾 🗾
🗾 All major card

DESERT HOT SPRINGS

🏨 TWO BUNCH PALMS
🍴 RESORT & SPA
$$–$$$
67425 TWO BUNCH PALMS TRAIL
TEL 760-329-8791
www.twobunchpalms.com
It was here that director Robert Altman located the spa scene in his film *The Player*, about the Hollywood elite. Trendy and luxurious, Two Bunch is a wonderful, serene place, where the massages and mud baths are first-rate, the guest rooms stylish and calming, and the California cuisine in the intimate **Casino Restaurant** is exquisite.
🛏 52 🅿 🔄 🗲 🗾 🗾 AE, MC, V

LA QUINTA

🏨 LA QUINTA RESORT
🍴 & CLUB
$$$$$
49499 EISENHOWER DR.
TEL 760-564-4111, 800-598-3828
www.laquintaresort.com
The quintessential desert escape, this legendary hacienda resort features 41 swimming pools, 53 hot spas, and 23 tennis courts, and guests can dine in a different restaurant each night of the week.
🛏 796 🅿 🔄 🗲 🗾 All major cards

PALM DESERT

🍴 CUISTOT
$$$$
72595 EL PASEO DR.
TEL 760-340-1000
www.cuistotrestaurant.com
The menu has been officially dubbed California-French, but that's really a bit tame and buttoned-up for the savvy, freestyle cooking here. Try the quail stuffed with sweetbreads in white wine sauce to get a notion of the chef's deftness with essential flavors. The desserts are equally complex and, ultimately, satisfying.
🪑 290 🅿 🕔 Closed Aug. & L 🔄 🗾 All major cards

PALM SPRINGS

🏨 AVALON HOTEL
🍴 $$$$$
415 S. BELARDO
TEL 760-318-3012
www.avalon-hotel.com/palm-springs
This luxurious boutique hotel is a perfect refuge, and Hollywood's finest are often seen lounging beside the three pools, sipping mojitos at the stylish bar, or relaxing in the spa. The airy **Chi Chi** restaurant focuses on a healthy, California-style fusion cuisine, such as

pumpkin-seed-crusted Chilean sea bass, and baby kale with butternut squash and quinoa.
🛏 68 🅿 🔄 🗲 🗾 🗾 All major cards

SOMETHING SPECIAL

🏨 THE PARKER PALM
🍴 SPRINGS
$$$$$
4200 E. PALM CANYON DR.
TEL 760-770-5000
www.theparkerpalmsprings.com
Topping the crop of deluxe, retro-themed desert spa hotels, the Parker has won accolades for its cutting-edge chic and fine dining. The fun yet glamorous atmosphere is enhanced by the swank Palm Springs Yacht Club spa.
🛏 144 🅿 🔄 🗲 🗾 🗾 🗾
🗾 All major cards

🏨 MOVIE COLONY HOTEL
$$$$–$$$$$
726 N. INDIAN CANYON DR.
TEL 760-320-6340, 888-953-5700
www.moviecolonyhotel.com
With its minimalist furnishings and fabrics from the modernist heyday, this chic compact hotel draws Hollywood mavens. Contemporary rooms and two-story townhouses set a 21st-century tone, and the open-air bar is a popular spot for martinis by the fire pit.
🛏 17 🅿 🔄 🗾 🗲 🗾 All major cards

🏨 THE ROWAN
$$$$–$$$$$
100 W. TAHQUITZ CANYON WAY
TEL 760-904-5015, 800-532-7320
www.rowanpalmsprings.com
Anchoring the city's downtown renaissance, this seven-story "high-rise" combines irresistible retro-chic modernist decor and a groovy vibe, best experienced in the rooftop poolside lounge-bar and adjacent gourmet **4 Saints** restaurant.
🛏 153 🅿 🔄 🗲 🗾 🗾
🗾 All major cards

🏨 Hotel 🍴 Restaurant 🛏 No. of Guest Rooms 🪑 No. of Seats 🅿 Parking 🕔 Closed 🔄 Elevator

COLONY CLUB
$$$–$$$$

572 N. INDIAN CANYON DR.
TEL 760-969-1800
www.colonypalmshotel.com
Overlooking and open to the garden and pool of the Colony Palms Hotel, the Colony Club reimagined American and California classics, like New York prime steak with duck-fat fries, garlic aioli, and peppercorn sauce; and herbed polenta with pomegranate, beluga lentils, and pea tendrils.

🛏 100 🅿 Valet 🅢 🅢 All major cards

JOHANNES
$$$–$$$$

196 S. INDIAN CANYON DR.
TEL 760-778-0017
www.johannespalmsprings.com
At chef Johannes Bacher's hip, high-end shrine to cosmopolitan dining, the minimalist decor is matched by precise service and attention to detail in the imaginative California-Asian-Austrian fusion cuisine.

🛏 🕒 Closed L & Mon.
🅢 🅢 All major cards

PEAKS
$$$

ONE TRAMWAY RD.
TEL 760-325-1391, 888-515-8726
www.pstramway.com
At this elegant mountaintop aerie (accessed by the Palm Springs Aerial Tramway), chef David Le Pow delivers delicious California fusion dishes such as rack of lamb with fresh peach compote and truffled mashed potatoes. Go not least for the peerless vistas from 8,560 feet (2,609 m).

🛏 125 🅢 All major cards

FISHERMAN'S MARKET & GRILL
$–$$$

235 S. INDIAN CANYON DR.
TEL 760-327-1766
www.fishermans.com
You're guaranteed only the freshest seafood at this homey local favorite. The oyster shooters are a hit at adjoining Shanghai Red's, where live R&B music can be heard on Friday and Saturday nights.

🛏 140 🅿 🅢 🅢 All major cards

RICK'S
$–$$$

1973 N. PALM CANYON DR.
TEL 760-416-0090
www.ricksrestaurant.biz
A friendly Cuban-American 1950s-style diner that packs in the locals for hearty American favorites, Cuban *ropa vieja*, and eclectic treats such as seared ahi tuna salad.

🛏 104 🅿 🕒 Closed D
🅢 🅢 AE, MC, V

RANCHO MIRAGE

RITZ-CARLTON RANCHO MIRAGE
$$$$$

68900 FRANK SINATRA DR.
TEL 760-321-8282
www.ritzcarlton.com
Set on a plateau in the mountains, this sumptuous modern resort hotel emerged in 2008 from a $500 million remake and is now perhaps the desert's most luxurious hotel.

🛏 260 🅿 ⬌ 🅢 🏊 🎽 🅢 All major cards

DESERT SPRINGS JW MARRIOTT RESORT & SPA
$$$–$$$$$

74855 COUNTRY CLUB DR.
TEL 760-341-2211
www.marriott.com
This large hotel combines style with all the amenities you could wish for, not least a massive state-of-the-art spa, the hottest nightclub in the valley, and excellent dining options.

🛏 884 🅿 🏊 🎽 🅢 All major cards

WALLY'S DESERT TURTLE
$$$$$

71775 CALIF. 111
TEL 760-568-9321
www.wallys-desert-turtle.com
To some minds, this lavish restaurant serves the best cuisine in the desert. Try the pan-broiled Lake Superior whitefish, with mussels, leek fondue, and lemon beurre blanc apricot soufflé.

🛏 180 🅿 🕒 Closed L & Mon.
🅢 🅢 All major cards

LAS CASUELAS NUEVAS
$$

70050 CALIF. 111
TEL 760-328-8844
www.lascasuelasnuevas.com
An upbeat California-Mexican restaurant with free-flowing Mexican beer, hearty Mexican-American classics (burritos, tacos, quesadillas), and some actual Mexican food as well (soups, *carne asadas*).

🛏 450 🅿 🕒 Closed Tue.
🅢 🅢 All major cards

TWENTYNINE PALMS

29 PALMS INN
$$$–$$$$

73950 INN AVE.
TEL 760-367-3505
www.29palmsinn.com
Each quaint adobe and quirky cabin has a patio, hot tub, and fireplace, and the **restaurant** means you don't have to leave the place for a good meal. Located on the famed Oasis of Mara.

🛏 19 🅿 🅢 🏊
🅢 All major card

SHOPPING

Even the locals regard shopping as recreation in California. This section suggests some places where you can find the unusual, the special, or the bargain.

■ LOS ANGELES

Antiques

Rose Bowl Flea Market
Rose Bowl, Pasadena, www.rgc shows.com. 2nd Sun. of month.
Second Time Around Watch Co.
160 S. Beverly Blvd., Beverly Hills, tel 310-271-6615, www.second timearoundwatchco.com

Art

Gagosian Gallery 456 N. Camden Dr., Beverly Hills, tel 310-271-9400, www.gagosian.com
L.A. Louver Galleries 45 N. Venice Blvd., Venice Beach, tel 310-822-4955, www.lalouver.com
Latin American Masters
2525 Michigan Ave., Santa Monica, tel 310-829-4455, www.latin americanmasters.com

Arts & Crafts/ Mission-Period Pieces

Gamble House Bookstore
4 Westmoreland Pl., Pasadena, tel 626-449-4178, http://gamble house.org
Voorhees Craftsman 1419 N. Lake St., Pasadena, tel 626-298-0142, www.voorheescraftsman.com

Books & Music

Amoeba Music 6200 Sunset Blvd., West Hollywood, tel 323-245-6400, www.amoeba.com
Book Soup 8818 Sunset Blvd., West Hollywood, tel 310-659-3110, www.booksoup.com

Fashion & Boutiques

American Rag Company 150 S. La Brea Ave., Melrose District, tel 323-935-3154, www.americanrag.com
Fred Segal 8500 Sunset Blvd., West, Hollywood, tel 310-432-0560 www.fredsegal.com
Grove 189 The Grove Dr., Los Angeles, tel 323-900-8080, www.thegrovela.com
Y-Que 1770 N. Vermont Ave., tel 323-664-0021, www.yque.com. T-shirts and kitsch.

Food

Grand Central Market 317 S. Broadway, tel 213-624-2378, www.grandcentralmarket.com
Pasadena Farmers Market Various locations, tel 626-449-0179, www.pasadenafarmersmarket.org
Santa Monica Farmers Market Various locations, 310-458-8712, www.santamonica.gov

Furniture & Design

Pacific Design Center 8687 Melrose Ave., tel 310-657-0800, www.pacificdesigncenter.com
Rehab Vintage
511A S. Raymond Ave., Alhambra, tel 626-872-0771, www.rehabvin tage.net

Hollywoodalia

Hollywood Toys & Costume
6600 Hollywood Blvd., Hollywood, tel 866-232-1829, www.holly woodtoysandcostumes.com
Western Costume 11041 Vanowen Blvd., North Hollywood, tel 818-760-0900, www.western costume.com. Studios' choice.

Pampering

Beverly Hot Springs
308 N. Oxford Ave., tel 323-734-7000, www.beverlyhotsprings.com
Burke Williams Spas
tel 866-239-6635, www.burke williamsspa.com. Check website for locations.
Ciel Spa 465 S. La Cienega Blvd, Beverly Hills, tel 310-246-5560, www.cielspabeverlyhills.com

■ SOUTHERN CALIFORNIA

Antiques

My Granny's Attic 28450 Felix Valdez Ave., Temecula, tel 951-699-9449, www.mygrannysattic.net

Art

Artist Eye Gallery 1294 S. Coast Hwy., Laguna Beach, tel 949-947-5898, www.artisteyegallerylaguna.com
National Geographic Fine Art Gallery 218 Forest Ave., Laguna Beach, tel 949-627-8230
Santa Barbara Contemporary Arts Forum 653 Paseo Nuevo, tel 805-966-5373, www.sbcaf.org
Sparks Gallery 530 6th Ave., San Diego, tel 619-696-1416, www.sparksgallery.com

Books

The Book Den 15 E. Anapamu St., Santa Barbara, tel 805-962-3321, www.bookden.com
Chaucer's Books 3321 State St., Santa Barbara, tel 805-682-6787, www.chaucersbooks.com

Fashion

Las Americas Premium Outlets
4211 Camino de la Plaza, San Diego, tel 619-934-8400, www.premiumoutlets.com/outlet/las-americas

Food

Julian Pie Company
2225 Main St., Julian, tel 760-765-2449, www.julianpie.com. In fall, the apple of everyone's eye.

■ CENTRAL COAST

Art

Classic Art Gallery 6th & Carlo St., Carmel-by-the-Sea, tel

831-625-0464, www.classicartgallery.com

Food

Casa de Fruta 10021 Pacheco Pass Hwy., Hollister, tel 408-842-7282 or 800-543-1702, www.casade fruta.com. Fresh produce.
Pezzini Farms 460 Nashua Rd., Castroville, tel 831-757-7434, www.pezzinifarms.com. Artichokes and all things artichoke.

Funk

Nipomo Swap Meet 263 N. Frontage Rd., Nipomo, tel 805-929-7000

Outlet Stores

American Tin Cannery Factory Outlets 125 Ocean View Blvd., Monterey, tel 831-372-1442, www.americantincannery.com

Wines & Olives

Folktale Winery 8940 Carmel Valley Rd., Carmel, tel 831-293-7500, www.folktalewinery.com
The Quail & Olive 14 Del Fino Pl., Carmel Valley, tel 831-659-4288, www.quailandolive.com

■ SAN FRANCISCO
Art & Antiques
Gagosian 657 Howard St., tel 415-546-3990, www.gagosian.com
Gump's 250 Post St., Union Square, tel 866-612-2226, www.gumps.com
Hang Gallery 567 Sutter Square., tel 415-434-4264, www.hangart.com
Isak Lindenauer Antiques 4143 19th St., tel 415-552-6436, www.isaklindenauer.com
Jack Fischer Gallery 311 Portrero Ave., tel 415-522-1178, www.jackfischergallery.com
Montgomery Gallery 545 Sansome St., tel 415-788-8300, www.montgomerygallery.com. Art of California.

Beauty
Kabuki Springs & Spa 1750 Geary Blvd., tel 415-922-6005, www.kabukisprings.com

Books
City Lights 261 Columbus Ave., North Beach, tel 415-362-8193, www.citylights.com. Landmark literary bookstore.
Green Apple Books 506 Clement St., tel 415-387-2272, www.greenapplebooks.com. New and used books.
Museum Books SFMOMA, 151 3rd St., tel 415-357-4035, https://museumstore.sfmoma.org

Fashion
Diesel 800 Market St., tel 415-398-4055, www.diesel.com
Union Square www.unionsquare shop.com. Serious shopping, with Hermès, Gucci, Cartier, Macy's, Nieman Marcus, Victoria's Secret, etc.
Wasteland 1660 Haight St., Haight-Ashbury, tel 415-863-3150, www.shopwasteland.com. Vintage and trendy secondhand clothes.

Food
Ferry Plaza Farmers Market 1 Ferry Bldg., Embarcadero, tel 415-291-3276, www.ferrybuild ingmarketplace.com. Tues., Thurs., & Sat.
Ghirardelli Chocolate 900 N. Point St., Ghirardelli Square, tel 415-474-3938, www.ghirardelli.com
Super Mira Market 1790 Sutter St., tel 415-921-6529. Japanese favorites.
Swan Oyster Depot 1517 Polk St., Polk Gulch, tel 415-673-1101. Fresh mussels, oysters, and more.

Funk
Alemany Flea Market 1100 Alemany Blvd., Bernal Heights, tel 415-647-9423.

■ BAY AREA
Art & Antiques
Alameda Point Antiques Faire Alameda Point, Alameda, tel 510-522-7500, www.alamedapoint antiquesfaire.com, 1st Sun. of month. Antiques/collectibles.
Dove Place Antiques & Consignments 160 Sir Francis Drake Blvd., San Anselmo, tel 415-453-1490, www.doveplaceantiques.com
Imari Gallery 40 Filbert Ave., Sausalito, tel 415-332-0245, www.imarigallery.com. Japanese screens.
Telegraph Avenue, Berkeley. This street is lined with off-beat stores and street vendors selling antiques, artwork, jewelry, and clothing.
Traywick Gallery 895 Colusa Ave., Berkeley, tel 510-527-1214, www.traywick.com. By appt. only.

Books
Book Passage Marin 51 Tamal Vista Blvd., Corte Madera, tel 415-927-0960 & 1 Ferry Building, San Francisco, tel 415-835-1020, www.bookpassage.com

Food
Downtown Farmers Market Festival 4th St., San Rafael, tel 415-492-8007, www.sanrafael market.org. Thurs. (May–Sep.).
Marin Farmers Market 3501 Civic Center Dr., San Rafael, tel 415-472-6100. Thurs. & Sun. 8 a.m.–1 p.m.
Oakland Farmers Market 9th St. betw. Broadway & Clay, tel 510-745-7100, https://uvfm.org. Fri. 8 a.m.–2 p.m.
Tomales Bay Foods & Cowgirl Creamery 80 4th St., Point Reyes Station, tel 415-663-9335, www.cowgirlcreamery.com. Fresh cheeses, organic everything.
Tomales Bay Oyster Company 15479 Hwy. 1, Marshall, tel 415-663-1243, www.tomalesbayoyster company.com

Funk

Berkeley Flea Market 1837 Ashby Ave., tel 510-644-0744, www.berkeleyfleamarket.com
San Jose Flea Market 1590 Berryessa Rd., San Jose, tel 408-453-1110, www.sjfm.com

Music

Amoeba Music 2455 Telegraph Ave., Berkeley, tel 510-549-1125, www.amoeba.com. Thousands of titles from classical to hip-hop.

■ WINE COUNTRY
Food

Oakville Grocery 7856 St. Helena Hwy., Oakville, tel 707-944-8802, www.oakvillegrocery.com. Local cheeses, oils, etc.
Oxbow Public Market 610 1st St., Napa, tel 707-226-6529, www.oxbowpublicmarket.com. Almost two dozen food purveyors.
Sonoma Country Farm Trails tel 707-837-8896, www.farmtrails.org. Chart course for local farms; downloadable map & guide.
Vella Cheese Company 315 2nd St. E., Sonoma, tel 707-938-3232, www.vellacheese.com

Outlet Stores

Napa Premium Outlets 629 Factory Stores Dr., Napa, tel 707-226-9876, www.premiumoutlets.com

Wines

Napa Valley Vintners 1475 Library Ln., St. Helena, tel 707-963-3388, www.napavintners.com
Sonoma Valley Vintners' Association P.O. Box 1698, Sonoma, tel 707-935-0803, www.sonomavalleywine.com
Vintners Collective 1245 Main St., Napa, tel 707-255-7150, www.vintnerscollective.com.
V Wine Cellar 6525 Washington St., Yountville, tel 707-531-7053, www.vwinecellar.com

■ THE NORTH
Art

Arcata Artisans 883 On the Plaza, Arcata, tel 707-825-9133, www.arcataartisans.com.
Redwood Burl 5151 Hwy. 101, Arcata, tel 707-826-9663, www.redwoodburl.com.

Food

Apple Farm 18501 Greenwood Rd., Philo, tel 707-621-0336, www.philoapplefarm.com

Wines

Mendocino Winegrowers Alliance 390 W. Standley St., Ukiah, tel 707901-7629, www.mendowine.com

■ GOLD COUNTRY
Art

Gold Country Artist's Gallery 379 Main St., Placerville, tel 530-642-2944, www.goldcountryartistsgallery.com. Paintings, photography, pottery, sculpture, glass, and jewelry.

Flowers

Amador Flower Farm 22001 Shenandoah School Rd., Plymouth, tel 209-245-6660, www.amadorflowerfarm.com. Specializes in daylilies.

Fruit

Boa Vista Orchards 2952 Carson Rd., Placerville, tel 530-622-5522, www.boavista.com. Fruit, wine, pies, and pastries.
Ikeda's 13500 Lincoln Way, Auburn, tel 520-885-4243, www.ikedas.com. Fruit, pies, pastries, and sauces.

■ CENTRAL VALLEY
Food

Sciabica and Sons 2150 Yosemite Blvd., Modesto, tel 209-577-5067, www.sunshineinabottle.com. Olives/olive oils & oil products.

Simonian Farms 2629 S. Clovis Ave., Fresno, tel 559-237-2294, www.simonianfarms.com. More than 100 kinds of fruits and vegetables.

■ THE DESERT
Fashion

Trina Turk's 891 N. Palm Canyon Dr., Palm Springs, tel 760-416-2856, www.trinaturk.com. Bold designs for fashionistas.

Food

Hadley's Fruit Orchards 48980 Seminole Rd., Cabazon, tel 951-849-5255, www.hadleyfruitorchards.com. Dried fruit.
Villagefest Palm Canyon Dr., Palm Springs, tel 760-320-3781, www.villagefest.org. Food items, art, jewelry, miscellany.

Outlet Stores

Desert Hills Premium Outlets 48400 Seminole Rd., Cabazon, tel 909-849-6641, www.premiumoutlets.com. With 130 stores.

Retro Décor & Kitsch

Iconic Atomic 1103 N. Palm Canyon Dr., Palm Springs, tel 760-320-0777, www.iconicatomic.com
Revivals 611 S. Palm Canyon Dr., Palm Springs, tel 760-318-6491, www.revivalsstores.com

ACTIVITIES

With a hospitable climate year-round, California has become the nation's unofficial sports capital. The tourism bureaus, accessible through the California Division of Tourism (see p. 347), publishes guides and lists on all outdoor activities. Also useful are the Sierra Club *(2101 Webster St., Ste. 1300, Oakland, tel 415-977-5500, www.sierraclub.org)*, the National Park Service *(333 Bush St. #114, San Francisco, tel 415-623-2100, www.nps.gov)*, and the California Department of Parks and Recreation *(1416 9th St., Sacramento, tel 800-777-0369, www.parks.ca.gov)*.

Bicycling
Backroads 801 Cedar St., Berkeley, tel 800-462-2848, www.backroads.com
Getaway Adventures 61 Front St., Healdsburg, tel 800-499-2453, BIKE, www.getawayadventures.com

Bird-watching
Point Reyes Bird Observatory 999 Mesa Rd., Bolinas, tel 415-868-0655, www.pointblue.org
San Francisco Bay National Wildlife Refuge 1 Marshlands Rd., Fremont, tel 510-792-0222, www.fws.gov
Sonny Bono Salton Sea National Wildlife Refuge 906 W. Sinclair Rd., Calipatria, tel 760-348-5278. www.fws.gov

Deep Sea Fishing
Full Throttle Sportfishing 6001 Startare Dr., Eureka, tel 707-498-7473, www.fullthrottlesportfishing.com
H & M Landing 2803 Emerson St., San Diego, tel 619-222-1144, www.hmlanding.com
Wild Wave Sportfishing 250 Jefferson St., San Francisco, tel 415-535-2533, www.wildwavesportfishing.com

Golf
LOS ANGELES AREA
Brookside Men's Golf Course 1133 N. Rosemount Ave., Pasadena, tel 626-585-3594, www.brooksidegc.com
Rancho Park Golf Course 10460 W. Pico Blvd., Beverly Hills, tel 310-838-7373, www.golf.lacity.org

SOUTHERN CALIFORNIA
Alisal Golf Course 1054 Alisal Rd., Solvang, tel 800-425-4725, www.alisal.com
Sandpiper Golf Course 7925 Hollister Ave., Santa Barbara, tel 805-968-1541, www.sandpipergolf.com
Torrey Pines Golf Club 11480 N. Torrey Pines Rd., La Jolla, tel 858-452-3226, www.torreypinesgolfcourse.com

CENTRAL COAST
Del Monte Golf Course 1300 Sylvan Rd., Pebble Beach, tel 831-373-2700, www.pebblebeach.com
Links at Spanish Bay 2700 17-Mile Dr., at Pebble Beach Resort, Spanish Bay, tel 800-977-0597, www.pebblebeach.com
Pebble Beach Golf Links At the Lodge at Pebble Beach, 17-Mile Dr., Pebble Beach, tel 800-977-0597, www.pebblebeach.com

SAN FRANCISCO & BAY AREA
Half Moon Bay Golf Links 2 Miramontes Point Rd., Half Moon Bay, tel 650-726-1800, www.halfmoonbaygolf.com
Presidio Golf Course 300 Finley Rd., Presidio National Park, San Francisco, tel 415-561-4661, www.presidiogolf.com

THE DESERT
Escena Golf Course, 1100 Clubhouse View Dr., Palm Springs, tel 760-778-2737, www.escenagolf.com
La Quinta Resort & Spa 49499 Eisenhower Dr., La Quinta, tel 760-564-4111, www.laquintaresort.com
PGA West 56150 PGA Blvd., La Quinta, tel 800-742-9378, www.pgawest.com

Tahquitz Creek 1885 Golf Club Dr., Palm Springs, tel 760-328-1005, www.tahquitzgolfresort.com

Hang Gliding
Rhodes Hang Gliding 5500 Ben Canyon Rd., San Bernardino, tel 909-771-1991, www.rhodeshanggliding.com
Torrey Pines Glider Port 2800 Torrey Pines Scenic Dr., La Jolla, tel 858-452-9858, www.flytorrey.com

Hiking
Outdoor Adventure Club 1819 Polk St., Ste. 222, San Francisco, tel 415-377-1195, www.outdooradventureclub.com
Sierra Club tel 415-977-5500, or 510-848-0800 www.sierraclub.org
Yosemite Mountaineering School & Guide Service Curry Village, Yosemite Valley, tel 209-372-8344, www.travelyosemite.com

Horseback Riding
Coffee Creek Ranch 4310 Coffee Creek Rd., Trinity Creek, tel 800-624-4480, www.coffeecreekranch.com
Los Angeles Equestrian Center 480 W.Riverside Dr., Burbank, tel 818-840-9063, www.thelaec.com
Smoke Tree Ranch Stables 1850 Smoke Tree Ln., Palm Springs, tel 800-787-3922, www.smoketreeranch.com

Hot Air Ballooning
California Dreamin' 33133 Vista Del Monte Rd., Temecula, tel 951-699-0601, www.californiadreamin.com

Fantasy Balloon Flights
74181 Parosella St., Palm Desert, tel 760-568-0997, www.fantasy
balloonflight.com
Lake Tahoe Balloons 2435 Venice Dr. E., South Lake Tahoe, tel 530-544-1221 or 800-872-9294, www.laketahoeballoons.com
Napa Valley Balloons
4286 Byway E., Napa, tel 707-944-0228 or 800-253-2224, www.napavalleyballoons.com

Hot Springs
The following natural wilderness hot springs require hiking to reach:
Deep Creek Hot Springs, Lake Arrowhead.
Saline Valley Warm Springs, Death Valley National Park.
Skyes Hot Springs, Big Sur.
Travertine Hot Springs, Bridgeport.
Wild Willy's Hot Springs, Mammoth Lakes.
A good resource is www.california.com.

Houseboat Rentals
New Melones Lake Marina
6503 Glory Hole Rd., Angels Camp, tel 209-785-3300, www.newmeloneslakemarina.com
Shasta Marina Resort
18390 O'Brien Inlet Rd., Lakehead, tel 800-959-3359, www.shastalake.net

Kayaking & Paddleboarding
Mission Bay Sportcenter
1010 Santa Clara Pl., San Diego, tel 858-488-1004, www.mission
baysportcenter.com
Monterey Bay Kayaks 693 Del Monte Ave., Monterey, tel 831-373-5357, www.montereybay
kayaks.com
Santa Barbara Adventure Company 32 E. Haley St., Santa Barbara, tel 805-884-9283, www.sbadventureco.com

Mountain Biking
Another Side of San Diego Tours 300 G St., San Diego, tel 619-239-2111, www.another
sideofsandiegotours.com
Bicycle Trails Council tel 510-544-2553, www.bicycletrailscouncil.org

Mountaineering & Rock Climbing
Joshua Tree Rock Climbing School 63439 Doggie Tr., Joshua Tree tel 760-366-4745, www.joshuatreerockclimbing.com
Yosemite Mountaineering School & Guide Service
Curry Village, Yosemite Valley, tel 209-372-8344, www.travel
yosemite.com

Sailing
Fine Day for Sailing Charters
300 Napa St., Sausalito, tel 415-730-0849, www.finedayforsailing.com
Marina Sailing 13763 Fiji Way, Marina del Rey, tel 310-822-6617; 4980 N. Harbor Dr., San Diego, tel 619-221-8286; http://marinasail
ing.com
Santa Barbara Sailing Center
302 W. Cabrillo Blvd., Santa Barbara, tel 805-962-2826, www.sbsail.com

Scuba Diving
Aquarius Dive Shop
2040 Del Monte Ave., Monterey, tel 831-375-1933, http://aquarius
divers.com
San Diego Scuba Dives 1160 Coast Blvd., La Jolla, tel 858-397-8213, www.sandiegoscubaguide.com
Sonoma Coast Divers 5702 Commerce Rd., Rohnert Park, tel 707-586-0272, www.sonoma
coastdivers.com

Skiing
Alpine Meadows/Squaw Valley
1960 Squaw Valley Rd., tel 800-403-0206, www.squawalpine.com

Badger Pass Glacier Point Rd., Yosemite National Park, tel 209-372-8430, www.travelyosemite.com
Bear Mountain Ski Resort
43101 Goldmine Drive, E of Big Bear Lake City, tel 844-462-2327, www.bigbearmountainresort.com
Mammoth Mountain Ski Area
1001 Minaret Rd, Mammoth Lakes, tel 800-626-6684, www.mammothmountain.com.
Mount Shasta Ski Park 4500 Ski Park Hwy., McCloud, tel 530-926-8610, www.skipark.com

Skydiving
Perris Valley Skydiving Center
2091 Goetz Rd., Perris, tel 800-832-8818, www.skydiveperris.com
Skydive Elsinore 20701 Cereal St., Lake Elsinore, tel 951-245-9939, www.skydiveelsinore.com

Surfing
Malibu Surf Coach 29130 Cliffside Dr., Malibu, tel 424-781-7174, www.malibusurfcoach.com
San Diego Surfing Academy
Tower 10, Harbor Dr. S., Oceanside, tel 760-230-1474, www.sandiegosurfingacademy.com
Surf School Santa Cruz 3548 Portola Dr, Santa Cruz, tel 831-428-3647, www.surfschoolsantacruz

Whale-watching
Monterey Whale Watching
96 Fisherman's Wharf #1, Monterey, tel 831-372-2203, www.montereywhalewatching.com
Oceanic Society Expeditions
30 Sir Francis Drake Blvd., Ross, tel 415-256-9604 or 800-326-7491, www.oceanic-society.org

Whitewater Rafting
American River Touring Assoc.
2400 Casa Loma Rd., Groveland, tel 209-962-7873, www.arta.org
O.A.R.S. 2863 CA-49, Angels Camp, tel 800-346-6227, www.oars.com

ENTERTAINMENT

San Francisco has some of the most way-out bars and clubs in the country and a theater scene that is in constant turmoil. L.A. is not far behind, and San Diego seriously enjoys its theater, too. Taking in a game is part of California life whatever your passion. And music happens everywhere.

■ LOS ANGELES

Comedy Clubs

Comedy Store 8433 Sunset Blvd., tel 323-650-6268, www.the comedystore.com

Groundlings Theater 7307 Melrose Ave., tel 323-934-4747, www.groundlings.com

Music

Hollywood Bowl 2301 N. Highland Ave., tel 323-850-2000, www.hollywoodbowl.com.

L.A. Opera Dorothy Chandler Pavilion, 135 N. Grand Ave., tel 213-972-8001, www.laopera.org

L.A. Philharmonic Walt Disney Concert Hall, 111 S. Grand Ave., tel 323-850-2000, www.laphil.com

Microsoft Theater 777 Chick Hearn Ct., tel 213-763-6020, www.microsofttheater.com

Roxy 9009 W. Sunset Blvd., tel 310-278-9457, www.theroxy.com

Whiskey a Go Go 8901 W. Sunset Blvd., tel 310-652-4202, www.whiskyagogo.com

World Stage 4321 Degnan Ave., tel 323-293-2451, www.theworld stage.org

Nightclubs

Avalon Hollywood 1735 Vine St., tel 323-462-8900, www.avalon hollywood.com

Viper Room 8852 W. Sunset Blvd., tel 310-538-1881, www .viperroom.com

Public Arts Events

John Anson Ford Ampitheatre 2580 Cahuenga Blvd., tel 323-850-2000, www.theford.com

Spectator Sports

Angel Stadium 2000 Gene Autry Way, Anaheim, tel 714-940-2000.

L.A. Angels *(www.mlb.com/angels. com)* baseball.

Dodger Stadium 1000 Elysian Park Ave., tel 866-363-4377. L.A. Dodgers *(www.mlb.com/dodgers. com)* baseball.

Dignity Health Sports Park 18400 Avalon Blvd., Carson, tel 310-630-2000. L.A. Galaxy *(www.lagalaxy.com)* soccer.

Santa Anita Racetrack 285 W. Huntington Dr., Arcadia, tel 626-574-7223, www.santaanita .com. Horse racing.

SoFi Stadium 1001 S. Stadium Dr., Inglewood, tel 818-338-0111 (Rams) or 877-242-7437 (Chargers), www. sofistadium.com. Home of the Los Angeles Chargers *(www.chargers. com)* and Los Angeles Rams *(www. therams.com)*.

Staples Center 1111 S. Figueroa St., tel 888-929-7849. L.A. Clippers *(www.nba.com/clippers)* & L.A. Lakers *(www.nba.com/lakers)* basketball. L.A. Kings *(www.nhl.com/ kings)* hockey.

Theater

Ahmanson Theatre 135 N. Grand Ave., tel 213-628-2772, www.centertheatregroup.org

Geffen Playhouse 10886 Le Conte Ave., Westwood, tel 310-208-5454, www.geffenplay house.com

Pasadena Playhouse 39 S. El Molino Ave., Pasadena, tel 626-356-7529, www.pasadena playhouse.org

■ SAN DIEGO

Music

AMSD Concerts 5305 Sweetwater Rd., tel 619-201-0520, www.amsdconcerts.com. Various genres.

Belly Up Tavern 143 S. Cedros Ave., Solana Beach, tel 858-481-8140, www.bellyup.com. Rock.

Brick by Brick 1130 Buenos Ave., tel 619-276-3990, www.brickby brick.com. Alternative.

Dizzy's 1717 Morena Blvd., tel 858-270-7467, www.dizzysjazz. com. Jazz.

House of Blues 1055 Fifth Ave., tel 619-299-2583, www.houseof blues.com/sandiego

Humphrey's 2241 Shelter Island Dr., Shelter Island, tel 619-244-3577, www.humphreysconcerts .com. Outdoor venue. Popular.

La Jolla Music Society 7946 Ivanhoe Ave., Ste. 103, La Jolla, tel 858-459-3728, www.ljms.com. Classical.

Nightclubs

Fluxx 500 4th Ave., tel 619-467-6653, www.fluxxsd.com

Onyx Room 852 Fifth Ave., tel 619-876-8044, www.onyxroom. com

Spectator Sports

San Diego's Qualcomm Stadium was demolished in 2021 and will be replaced by the new Aztec Stadium.

Del Mar Thoroughbred Club 2260 Jimmy Durante Blvd., Del Mar, tel 858-792-4242, www.dmtc .com. Horse racing.

Petco Park 100 Park Blvd., tel 619-795-5555. San Diego Padres *(www.mlb.com/padres)* baseball.

Theater

La Jolla Playhouse 2910 La Jolla Village Dr., UC San Diego, tel 858-550-1010, www.lajollaplayhouse.org.

Old Globe Theater 1363 Old Globe Way, Balboa Park, tel 619-234 5623, www.theoldglobe.org. Contemporary and classic.

San Diego Opera Civic Center Plaza, 1200 3rd Ave., tel 619-533-7000, www.sdopera.org. Classical.

San Diego Repertory Lyceum Theatre, 79 Horton Plaza, tel 619-544-1000, www.sdrep.org. Classic dramas to musicals.

Viejas Arena San Diego State University, tel 619-594-0429, www.as.sdsu.edu/viejas_arena. Popular.

■ SAN FRANCISCO / BAY AREA

In San Francisco unless indicated.

Comedy

Cobb's Comedy Club 915 Columbus Ave., tel 415-928-4320, www.cobbscomedy.com

Punch Line 444 Battery St., tel 415-397-7573, www.punchline comedyclub.com.

Dance

San Francisco Ballet War Memorial Opera House, 301 Van Ness Ave., tel 415-865-2000, www.sfballet.org.

Music

Boom Boom Room 1601 Fillmore St., tel 415-673-8000, www.boomboomroom.com. Venerable jazz and blues joint.

Bottom of the Hill 1233 17th St., tel 415-621-4455, www.bottom ofthehill.com. Alternative.

Cal Performances 101 Zellerbach Hall #4800, UC Berkeley, Bancroft Way & Telegraph Ave., tel 510-642-9988, http://calperformances.org. Eclectic.

Fillmore 1805 Geary St., tel 415- 346-6000, www.thefillmore.com. Rock.

Freight & Salvage Coffeehouse 2020 Addison St., Berkeley, tel 510-644-2020, www.thefreight.org. Folk.

Greek Theatre 2001 Gayley Rd., Berkeley, tel 510-871-9225, www.thegreekberkeley.com. Eclectic.

Levi's Stadium 4900 Marie P. DeBartolo Way, Santa Clara, tel 415-464-9377, www.levisstadium.com. Eclectic.

San Francisco Opera War Memorial Opera House, 301 Van Ness Ave., tel 415-864-3330, www.sfopera.com

San Francisco Symphony Davies Symphony Hall, 210 Van Ness Ave., tel 415-864-6000, www.sfsymphony.org

SF Jazz Center 201 Franklin St., tel 866-920-5299, www.sfjazz.org

Yoshi's 510 Embarcadero, Oakland, tel 510-238-9200, www.yoshis.com. Jazz.

Nightclubs

Café du Nord 2174 Market St., tel 415-471-2169, www.swedish americanhall.com. Everything from swing to salsa.

El Rio 3158 Mission St., tel 415-282-3325, www.elriosf.com. Salsa.

Lizzie's Starlight Sir Francis Drake Hotel, 21st Floor, 450 Powell St., tel 415-395-8595, www.lizziesstar lightsf.com. Stylish live-music lounge.

Tonga Room Fairmont Hotel, 950 Mason St., tel 415-772-5278, www.tongaroom.com. '40s hits.

Public Arts Events

San Francisco Shakespeare Festival Tel 415-558-0888, www.sfshakes.org. Various Bay Area venues. Summer weekends only. Free.

Stern Grove Summer Music Festival Sloat Blvd. & 19th Ave., tel 415-252-6252, www.stern grove.org.

Spectator Sports

Golden Gate Fields 1100 Eastshore Hwy., Albany, tel 510-559-7300, www.goldengatefields.com. Horse racing.

Levi's Stadium 4900 Marie P. DeBartolo Way, Santa Clara, tel 415-464-9377, www.levisstadium.com. San Francisco 49ers (www.49ers.com) football.

Oakland Coliseum 7000 Coliseum Way, Oakland, tel 510-762-2255 (tickets). Oakland A's (www.mlb.com/athletics) baseball.

Oracle Park 24 Willie Mays Plaza, tel 415-972-2000. San Francisco Giants (www.mlb.com/giants) baseball.

PayPal Stadium 451 El Camino Real, Santa Clara, tel 408-556-7700. San Jose Earthquakes (www.sjearthquakes.com) soccer.

Theater

American Conservatory Theater Geary Theater, 405 Geary St., tel 415-749-2228, www.act-sf.org. Repertory.

Berkeley Repertory Theater 2025 Addison St., Berkeley, tel 510-647-2949, www.berkeleyrep.org. Eclectic productions.

Curran Theater 445 Geary St., tel 415-358-1220, www.sfcurran.com. Large productions and musicals.

Exit Theater 156 Eddy St., tel 415-931-1094, www.theexit.org. Experimental to classical offerings.

Golden Gate Theater 1 Taylor St. at Market & 6th Sts., tel 415-551-2000 or 888-746-1799, www.broadwaysf.com. Host to nationally renowned productions.

Magic Theater Fort Mason Bldg. D, Fort Mason Center, Marina Blvd. at Buchanan St., tel 415-441-8822, www.magictheatre.org. New plays.

Theater Rhinoceros 215 Jackson St., tel 415-552-4100 or 800-838-3006, www.therhino.org. Gay and lesbian productions.

INDEX

Bold page numbers indicate illustrations.
CAPS indicates thematic categories.

ILLUSTRATIONS CREDITS

All photographs by Gilles Mingasson unless otherwise noted:

National Geographic

TRAVELER
California
FIFTH EDITION

Since 1888, the National Geographic Society has funded more than 14,000 research, exploration, and preservation projects around the world. National Geographic Partners distributes a portion of the funds it receives from your purchase to National Geographic Society to support programs including the conservation of animals and their habitats.

National Geographic Partners, LLC
1145 17th Street NW
Washington, DC 20036-4688 USA

Get closer to National Geographic explorers and photographers, and connect with our global community. Join us today at nationalgeographic.org/joinus

For rights or permissions inquiries, please contact National Geographic Books Subsidiary Rights: bookrights@natgeo.com

Fifth edition edited by White Star s.r.l.
Licensee of National Geographic Partners, LLC.
Update by Christopher P. Baker

Map illustrations drawn by Chris Orr Associates, Southampton, England.
Cutaway illustrations drawn by Maltings Partnership, Derby, England.

The information in this book has been carefully checked and to the best of our knowledge is accurate. However, details are subject to change, and the publisher cannot be responsible for such changes, or for errors or omissions. Assessments of sites, hotels, and restaurants are based on the author's subjective opinions, which do not necessarily reflect the publisher's opinion.

ISBN: 978-88-544-1799-1

Printed in Poland

MIX
Paper from responsible sources
FSC® C019238
www.fsc.org

NATIONAL GEOGRAPHIC TRAVELER
THE BEST GUIDES BY YOUR SIDE

More than 80 destinations around the globe